MW01644823

The Chinese Origin of the Age of Discovery

Platinum Edition

By

Chao C. Chien

ISBN: 9798389175341

Table of Contents

Brief Table of Contents

Preface

From the title of this work, you should already know what the contents are all about.[1] Emphatically, what this book is not, is another one of those out-of-the-left-field speculations camouflaged as legitimate research. It is not sensationalism. All the events described herein are real, backed up by confirmed, verifiable evidence. It is not an unfounded hypothesis or hearsay. Neither is it muckraking. The book is a sincere report of a serious research. Indeed, one of the missions of this present opus is to crush those wild rumors that have, by some twist of history and fate, attained the status of historical facts through popularism.

Surprisingly, this work is not dry and bland like most such pedantic works. The process of reaching the truth is in fact quite twisted and convoluted. It turned out to be quite entertaining; as a matter of fact, more than entertaining. The evidence was veritably fantastic; so fantastic that I had to stop and assure you that a piece of relic was in fact real.

When you grasp how ridiculous historians had become to come up with explanations for these otherwise untenable facts, you will likely break out and have yourself a good belly laugh. I guarantee that.

Just to make things doubly clear, this book is not about the exploits of the early 15th century navigator Zheng He. There are plenty of wonderful opuses out there that fill that bill. This book, specifically, is proving that the book title is so; that China ushered in the Age of Discovery, not European explorers. It is about the evidence that will take us to that end. In other words, the upending of long held "historical truths" is factual, and this book is about the

---

[1] Incidentally, the title is a true statement, as this book shall prove.

evidence that leads us toward that conclusion. You should, therefore, be in a frame of mind for reading a carefully developed whodunit, for it is akin to a well-crafted prosecutor's case. It is fascinating because the process is like peeling an onion, one layer at a time. Those that appreciate detailed legal cases will be in for a treat.

In the meantime, do anticipate that many of these evidence-supported "facts" may appear bizarre, especially when measured against the "norms" of today's social standards. Hence, keep your mind open, and your reasoning self fully in action.

Enjoy.

January, 2023
Chao C. Chien

PS. I am of age. For that, this likely will be the last update of an noble historical research project, and I am proud to be the torch bearer of the work. If you own this book, do keep it and hold on to it, as it is the one and only of its kind. I assure you there will be no academic attack on it because the evidence and deductions included are factual.

Historical Background

Figure 1

The Eurasian Landmass

Because the present work is an investigation into the past, we shall begin by having a good sense about the historical background against which the events we are probing occurred.

During the Age of Discovery (also known as the Age of Exploration), starting from the 15th century, European seafarers explored previously unknown lands outside Europe. These activities eventually led to the rise of European nations as world powers, ushering in the Ages of Colonialism and Imperialism, during which much of the world's people were subjugated by white Europeans.

Allegedly, it all started with the Portuguese's effort to discover a sea route to the Asian Spice Islands beginning in 1420, which culminated in Vasco da Gama discovering a waterway around the southern tip of Africa to sail to India. Da Gama reached India in 1498. It took Portugal almost a hundred years to accomplish the task. Then, Christopher Columbus, in 1492—note that it was six years before Da Gama— crossed the Atlantic Ocean to discover new lands which we now call the Caribbean and the Americas.

That is the narrative enshrining this high point of European history, which is well-known worldwide, except for one minor issue…

The accounts are hardly informative. They are overly simplified, and also, incorrect.

To begin with, history hardly ever discusses why the Europeans went to sea at that time. What inspired them to do what they did? If the issue is ever confronted, the answer is almost always because of the explorers' "inspirations," sometimes even divine, or the explorers' "acumen." Christopher Columbus hit upon the idea of crossing the Atlantic Ocean by staring into the water at Porto Santo, it was written. Do you know how many people worldwide through the ages had looked at the vast oceans and never came up with the thought that there were lands beyond the horizon? Columbus' enlightenment was therefore immortal. Then there was Prince Henry the Navigator.

Prince Henry the Navigator was the original Portuguese seafaring patron. Why was he interested in the oceans? It is reported that his impetus to go to sea was in fact written in the horoscopes, according to his official biography, no less. In other words, he was fated by Heaven to fulfill his achievements. Now, there is a divine attribute when there was none! (The real reason will be revealed below.)

This is the 21st century, my friend, and we still believe in such fantasies? C'mon!

Sure, thoughtful historians have now mostly abandoned the route to Spice Islands excuse, but no one has seriously investigated this aspect of the Age of Discovery; the real reason behind why European explorers went to sea.

The fact is, Europeans did not discover much of the land they purportedly explored.

Is this an outrageous statement made deliberately for shock value just to cause trouble; to "stir things up?" or, worse yet, to entice you to read on? Not at all. *Au contraire,* the statement is the result arrived at based on historical evidence that still exists. Indeed, this work presents that very research and accompanying evidence.

The research is multifaceted. It does not merely touch on the "cause" issue, but delves into all the other aspects of the history, from the inspirations of the European explorers to their accomplishments—yes, they did accomplish, big time, you have to give them that.

In brief, the research alleges that the European explorers went to sea because they had come into information about the places that they explored. Yet, although they did eventually go to those places, they did not "discover" them. The research in fact concludes that the information that served to instigate them to go to sea came from China, and we shall address in detail how that came to be.

The assertion is a mouthful. So, to facilitate reading, I have broken the presentation of the research into three components, or three parts or phases of discussion, each one to be thrashed out independently of the other; each to be argued as a self-contained unit. They are:

1. Were Europeans in fact the initiators of the Age of Discovery; did they independently chance upon the notion that there were new lands in the world unknown to be explored?
2. Did the Chinese precede the Europeans in having surveyed the world?
3. Did the Chinese visit the Americas before Christopher Columbus?

In other words, even if we demonstrate that the Chinese had knowledge of the world geography before the 15th century; before the Portuguese pioneering sailors and Christopher Columbus, we cannot conclude that they benefited from China's efforts, for they could have come to their own conclusions through other means. Therefore, that they directly ingerits their world geography knowledge from the Chinese must be independently verified and proven as a separate research effort.

The stories of the European Age of Discovery have enjoyed the status of accepted history for a long time. It is assumed that any challenge to such an accepted view will be regarded as being absurd or heretical, at least initially, or in polite company, incredible. It thus follows that should the claim of a Chinese survey of the world before the Age of Discovery fail to pan out, it would be taken as proof that the conventional view stands.

However, the case is not that simple. In such a case, even if it can be shown that the Chinese did no such world surveying, it still must be independently determined that Europeans did not inherit its geographical knowledge from an outside source, any source, regardless of the orthodox historical positions. Such is the nature of proper research; any research. Hence there are two issues at hand. First, did the Europeans "discover" the world? Second, were European explorers in fact inspired by the Chinese who had gained the world geography knowledge before the Europeans?

Between the years 1405 and 1433, the Ming Dynasty Chinese government launched a series of naval expeditions of unprecedented scale led by the legendary "Admiral" Zheng He.[2] Their exact motives as well as destinations, however, were vague. They were not officially documented fully and properly because the Ming court kept the enterprise's true purpose a secret. As a result, despite traditionalists' insistence that the Ming fleets sailed mainly in the Indian Ocean, various writers over time have speculated about where the Ming fleets in fact had gone, with some conjecturing that they might have reached as far as the Americas, and perhaps even circumnavigated the world. Thus, it has been suggested that European explorers of the 15th century had benefited from Zheng He's experiences.

---

[2] 鄭和, Zheng He, sometimes Cheng Ho, is pronounced "Jeng (or Jung) Huh." Zheng rhymes with the English words "hung," "lung," and "sung."

The present researcher/author is keenly aware of the controversy surrounding such claims or assertions, as they infer that Columbus might have had sailing information to his discoveries tied to the Ming Chinese voyages. In recent years, these contentions have precipitated heated debates which were astoundingly contentious; almost acrimonious in character, and in the process tainting an otherwise legitimate dialog.

One of the purposes of the present work is to restore a sense of propriety to the discussions. For one, the quarrel is not simply over who discovered America, because, if that were the issue, we would have to include Eirik the Red and others in the discussion, not to mention the natives who had migrated to the continents tens of thousands of years ago.

The discussion is indeed multifaceted, for, at the end, should one fail to prove that the Chinese had reached America, it still does not infer as a matter of course that the Columbian legend is indeed historical fact. That still must be assessed on its own merits, even though the Columbus allegory has been generally accepted as fact for a long time; a couple of hundred years, as a matter of fact. Also, even if the "Chinese First" claim turns out to be a bust, it does not directly follow that Columbus had not benefited from someone who had preceded him in his quests. Should such be the case, we should certainly like to find out who these predecessors were.

This research will maintain a focused eye on these separate perspectives of the subject matter and attempt to deal with them individually and in a logical fashion.

To give meaning to our work, let us begin with a brief account of the events that framed the present inquiry.

The Place and the Time

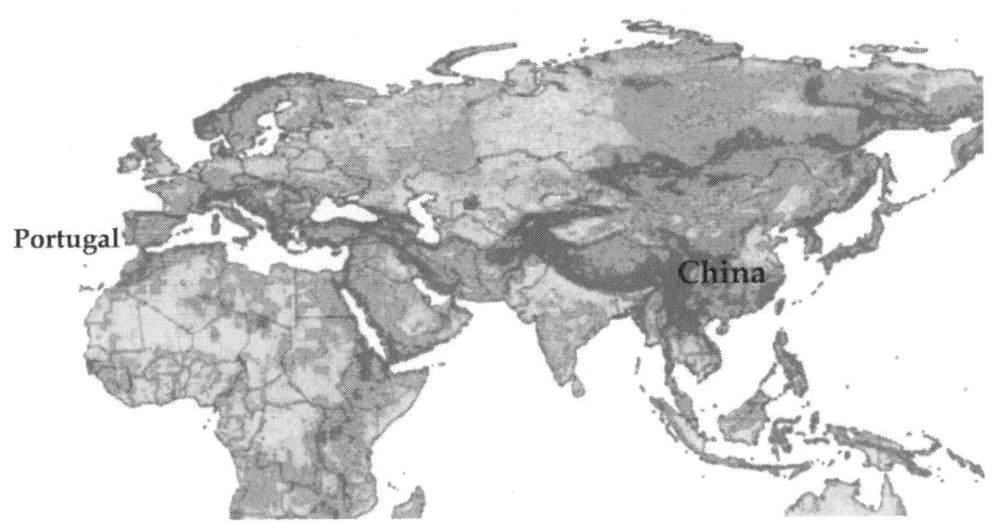

Figure 2

The Geographical Location of Portugal

The Ural Mountains divide the Eurasian landmass into two "continents:" Europe to the west, and Asia to the east (Figure 2). Asia is much larger than Europe, but only a small southerly part of it is truly hospitable. There, the temperatures are moderate and the river-irrigated soil is fecund. From time immemorial, the people living there, known today to the world as the Chinese, practiced agriculture; their mainstay being rice, a crop that grows in waterlogged mud fields.

The people who lived by the coast, called Yue today in the Chinese Mandarin pronunciation (and Yuet in the local dialects or "Viet" as in "Vietnam"), derived their living from the sea. According to ancient Chinese text, these people cut their hair and tattooed their bodies in order to mingle with the fishes in the ocean. Today this tradition is carried on in Taiwan (seldom-seen natives) and in the Pacific islands by natives such as the Hawaiians, the Samoans, the Maori from New Zealand, and others.

It is said that in olden days these Chinese's mode of transportation was by water because the hilly country made road-building difficult, while naturally there were many rivers and streams. These people developed advanced skills in canal and ship building.

In northern Asia, delimited by the Altai and Tianshan Mountains to the west and the Pacific Ocean to the east, the Himalayan Mountains and the Tibetan Plateau on its southwest and the Arctic to the north, the weather is bleak and cold the greater part of the year. The land there mostly consists of deserts and sandy plateaus. The grasslands and oases that exist allow a mobile lifestyle that is primarily limited to life stock breeding and herding. There live the nomads. During bleak times, these roving tribes would be forced to migrate in search of sustenance, which often spelled trouble for their more sedentary and more developed neighbors.

For thousands of years, China, situated in southeastern Asia, had withstood the worst of the northern nomad-warriors who were fierce and strong with their swift horses and fast arrows. Great battles waged between these peoples had been forever memorialized in oral and written traditions. For example, during the second century BCE, the Huns, after being defeated by the Han Chinese, took leave for Western Asia, and in the 4th CE century (half a millennium later) invaded and settled in Eastern Europe via the great steppes of Eurasia. They were in turn followed by the Avars, the Bulgars, the Magyars, and the Mongols in the 13th century.

The Yuan Empire

In the early 13th century, the Mongol chieftain Temujin, conferred the title Genghis Khan[3] by his Siberian tribesmen after having unified them into the greatest fighting force on horseback the world had known, took out Xixia,[4] a Tangut kingdom situated to the northwest of China, and the Jin,[5] the other nomadic nation that occupied the northern half of Song[6] China. He and his warrior sons then advanced against the West, subjugating every nation of Central Asia on their way, and threatened to overrun Europe.

The disaster was averted fortuitously upon the timely death of Ogotai Khan, son and successor of Genghis Khan, in 1241. By 1258, the western Mongol army under Hulegu, grandson of Genghis Khan, had taken Baghdad, while his brother Kublai Khan conquered Southern Song China in 1280. So, for the first time, China fell to a foreign overlord and became a part of the vast Mongol Empire, which consisted of four khanates, each bequeathed to one of Genghis Khan's sons.

The eldest son, Juchi, headed the Golden Horde (Kipchak) Khanate, which controlled today's Russia and a large part of Persia. Chagatai was given the Chagatai Khanate, which occupied the present-day Chinese Turkestan (Xinjiang) and eastern Central Asia. Ogotai inherited the Mongolian homeland in Siberia, and Tului's son Kublai founded the Chinese Yuan Dynasty.

Growing up thoroughly steeped in the Chinese culture by choice, Kublai Khan, the Great Khan of all the Mongols, abandoned the

---

3 "Genghis Khan" roughly means "The Supreme Ruler" or in Western parlance, "The Great" or "King of Kings."

4 西夏.

5 金, a forerunner of the later Manchu.

6 宋. "Song" rhymes with "cone," "hone," "lone," and "tone," not "gong," "Hong," "Kong." And "long."

A Caravel

Mongol capital at Karakorum and established his throne at Yanjing (Beijing today), which he had renamed Dadu, meaning "The Great Capital." He set up his summer capital at Shangdu, which means "The Upper Capital." European writers such as Samuel Taylor Coleridge, who wrote *Kubla Khan,* would later refer to it as *Xanadu*.

At that time (late 13th century and 14th century) the Mongol Empire stretched from Hungary to the Pacific Ocean and from Siberia to the Indian Ocean, although internally the empire was not exactly in unity. The branching of the Khan's family had splintered the empire due to the great distances between their assigned fiefdoms and thus their ever-diverging cultures. The Golden Hordes in the west had adopted the Islam faith while Kublai Khan's Yuan leaned toward the Chinese culture. In a few years, the Il Khanate, founded by Kublai Khan's brother Hulegu, which also had embraced Islam, would fall into Turkish hands and turn on the Mongols themselves.

In any case, because of the network of roads established under Genghis Khan and Kublai Khan's relatively enlightened rules, open trade between Europe and Asia flourished and intercontinental travel was encouraged. As a result, European historians dubbed the Mongol period of 13th century *Pax Mongolica,* or The Period of Mongolian Peace, just as the period of the Roman Empire at its peak was called *Pax Romana*.

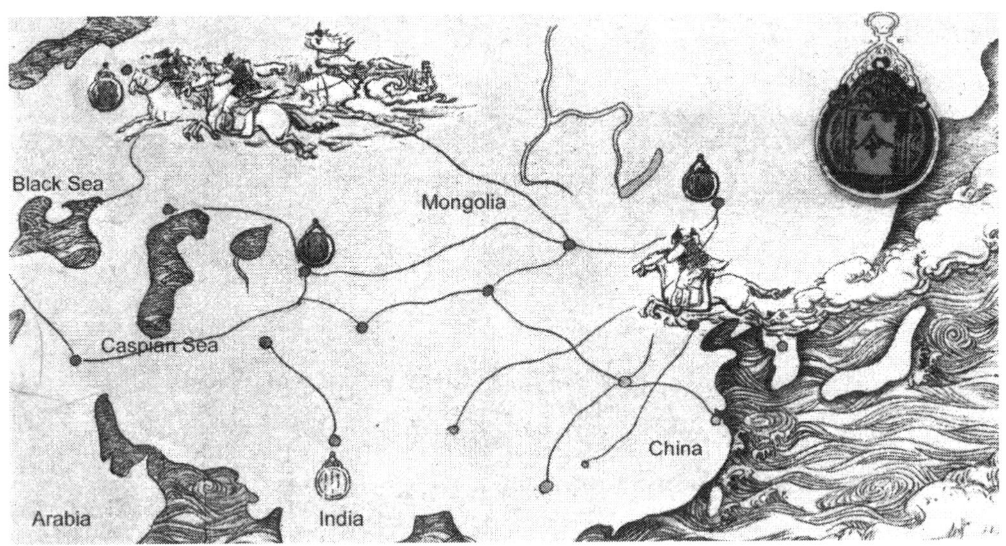

Figure 3

An Ancient Chart of Yuan Dynasty Pony Express System

Figure 3 shows a modern rendition of an ancient chart identifying Yuan Dynasty post stations (pony express) stretching from China on the right to the Middle East on the left. The medallion at the upper right corner shows a Mongolian brass pass that would accord its owner free and safe passage throughout the empire.

Despite Kublai Khan's sincere attempt at an administration, the Mongol occupation of China was doomed to failure. Because of the steadfast Chinese resistance against the conquest, the Mongol invasion of China was exceptionally protracted in comparison to the relatively easy conquest of the rest of the world. For that, the Mongol conquerors held an exceptionally deep resentment toward the defeated Chinese, with the southern Song Chinese even more despised than the northern Chinese who had subsisted under the Jin, who were considered Chinese by the Mongols.

To rule China, the Mongols introduced people from the West; that is, mostly Central Asia, to serve in the government. Indeed, the Mongol rulers instituted a sort of caste system in China, with Mongols ranking supreme, followed immediately by people of "colored eyes;"[7] that is, Persians, Turks, and Europeans.[8] They were followed by the northern Chinese; that is, the Jin and their Chinese subjects. At the bottom were the southern Song Chinese. For this last group the Mongols even adopted the Chinese derogatory label that the Chinese had applied to the alien people of their own south, *Man Zi*,[9] loosely translated as "the savages" or "the uncivilized."

After Kublai Khan, the succeeding Mongol monarchs were given to debauchery and paid little attention to the affairs of state, which they relinquished to their ministers, who almost as a rule were non-ethnic Chinese. Indeed, it has been said that the refusal to be Sinicized—except for Kublai Khan—as did the later Manchu, contributed to the destined and early failure of the Mongols in China.

The upstart nomadic rulers were fascinated by paper money. They could not believe the riches these pieces of paper could fetch. As a result, they abused the system thoroughly by printing money at will. Finally, this irresponsible use of paper money, invented by the Song Chinese to the great success of their economy, eventually plunged the country into financial chaos. That the Yellow River changed its course and devastated the irrigation canals bringing on massive famine in the 1340's did not help Yuan's cause. By 1355, China was in turmoil, ultimately degenerating into a state of warlordom.

---

[7] Semu, Colored-Eyes, 色目.

[8] It is interesting to note that there is no Chinese historical record on Marco Polo.

[9] 蠻子

The Ming Dynasty

When the dust finally settled, Zhu Yuanzhang,[10] a commoner of humble station, alone remained standing, having distinguished himself in battle vanquishing all rival contenders. He took Dadu (Beijing) in 1368 and founded the celebrated Ming Dynasty, driving the Mongols out of China the following year. He dubbed himself the Hongwu Emperor; "hong wu" meaning "immeasurable military might," or, in Western equivalence, "The Great," "The Magnificent," or "The Invincible." Upon his death, he was honored with the temple title of Taizu, which means "Supreme Progenitor;" that is, "Dynasty Founder." Under his reign, China's place in history as a mighty empire was restored.

Taizu Zhu Yuanzhang rose from modest beginnings. In his youth he had been a monk, a vagabond, a soldier of fortune, and members of various religious sects, secretive organizations, and others, just to survive. When rebellion broke out, Taizu joined in the fray, gradually rising up in military ranks, and ultimately founded a new Chinese dynasty after centuries of foreign incursion and subjugation.

By all accounts, Taizu was an able ruler—he is universally hailed as one of China's preeminent emperors. He brought groundbreaking initiatives to Chinese government that served the country well. He recognized that eunuchs and imperial females—empresses, concubines, and court ladies—could do immeasurable harm to the state and the security of the throne, and introduced measures to preclude the members of such groups from holding power. They were denied education so they could not meddle with government affairs.

As with all founders of empires, Ming Taizu was concerned with the stability and longevity of his dynasty. He was also keenly aware

---

[10] Pronounced "yuen-jahng." "Zhu" is the family name, which according to Chinese custom is placed first.

that although the Mongols had been expelled from China proper, they remained a real threat in the north. To safeguard the northern and western frontiers, he dispatched his more capable princely sons to key military posts in command of legions.

Taizu had twenty-six sons. The first and fourth born were his favorites. He designated the eldest, who was well-schooled and showed a penchant for politics, the crown prince.

The fourth prince, Zhu Di, whom he posted to the erstwhile Yuan Dynasty capital Dadu, now named Beiping (Northern Peace)[11] to foster a notion of a peaceful north, excelled in affairs military. Taizu made him the Prince of Yan.[12] As the Prince of Yan, he held perhaps the most important defense post, the frontline facing the Mongols.

As it happened, the crown prince died young due to illness. For a time Taizu considered anointing the Prince of Yan the new heir. However, the ministers made a case for the crown prince's son, the royal grandchild and nephew of the Prince of Yan, on the ground that by going back on the emperor's own device he would surely precipitate the kind of future family bloodletting that he had sought to preclude in the first place.

The royal grandchild had displayed no trace of brilliance that would have impressed the great dynasty founder, and Taizu had expressed misgivings about a possible threat from the visibly more capable and powerful, and perhaps more deserving uncle, the Prince of Yan. Despite the reservations, reluctantly Taizu paid heed to his ministers' input and abided by his earlier decision.

Upon the death of Taizu in 1398, the royal grandson ascended the throne as willed. He was known in history as the *Jianwen*[13] Emperor, "Emperor of the Reign of the Jianwen Period." Because of his youthful age of twenty-one, his royal mentors took up the actual duties of government administration, as the positions of Prime Minister had been abolished by the very capable Taizu earlier.

---

[11] 北平. Today's Beijing.

[12] Yan, 燕, being the ancient name for the area around Beijing.

[13] 建文

Approximately fifteen hundred years prior, the great Chinese Han Dynasty had suffered a debilitating blow by the *Rebellion of the Seven Princes*.[14] Somehow these Ming royal mentors had gotten into their heads that the same drama would play out again if the princely powers were left uncurbed. It is clear that they were merely using history to urge the young emperor on to act against his powerful uncles. For this, they advised the young emperor to take steps toward curtailing their influences. Within a year of the new regime, five princely uncles were removed from office and jailed or driven to suicide on pretexts.

Perhaps it was epiphany that the Prince of Yan had been spared from this initial purge. Perhaps the new emperor thought that the demise of the five fallen princes would serve as some kind of signal to the remaining princes. Historians reasoned that the Prince of Yan might have been too powerful to be provoked at that early stage. Instead, his power was to be gradually curtailed or shaved away. For this, as a first step, the court removed the best of his three legions (numbering about fifteen thousand troops) for special assignments, and redeployed his military allies for remote duties. Then government action was taken directly against him. As a first stroke, Emperor Jianwen placed Beiping under siege on the pretext of extraditing criminals.

To allay suspicion, the Prince of Yan feigned madness, wandering in tattered clothing around the streets of Beiping like a tramp, all the while paying keen attention to the goings-on at the royal court. When the occasion presented itself, he broke out of the siege and marched on the capital, ostensibly to "champion the emperor;" to "cleanse the court of evil counsel."

The Ming Civil War lasted four years. The final breakthrough came from a group of eunuchs seeking refuge from the young emperor on criminal charges. They sought asylum with the Prince of Yan and presented him with secret information on the layout of the capital and royal palace compound. With this intelligence, the Prince

[14] 七國之亂

of Yan breached the imperial defense and captured the capital city of Nanjing (Nanking). The prince declared himself victorious and took the throne, changing the official calendar to the Period of *Yongle* (pronounced "Yung Luh"), which means "Eternal Bliss." The clans of the royal mentors and all those who had connived with the "pretender" were summarily executed. Emperor Jianwen, however, disappeared, never to be found. To date, Emperor Jianwen's disappearance remains a mystery of Chinese History.[15]

Prince of Yan's throne or temple title was Chengzu,[16] which means "The Achiever" or "The Accomplisher." The year of his ascension was 1402. Historians, virtually to a voice, regard Emperor Chengzu (r. 1402 - 1424) as one of China's most illustrious emperors. Under his stewardship, Chinese imperial prestige in the international community reached a new height. Chinese military prowess rose to its most potent in centuries. Some scholars would even go as far as comparing him with the near legendary Emperor Taizong[17] of the 7th century Tang Dynasty, or the mighty Han Dynasty Wudi[18] of the 1st century BCE. However, amid the general exaltations, often little is discussed about the specifics of his reign but for one event.[19]

---

[15] Refer to *The Hunt for the Dragon, 2nd Edition* for possible solutions to the mystery.

[16] 成祖

[17] 唐太宗

[18] 漢武帝

[19] Emperor Chengzu built the Forbidden City and the Wudang Temple Complex. An encyclopedia was compiled under his aegis. Yet nobody remembers these.

Seven Voyages to the Western Ocean

Figure 4

Treasure Fleet at Sea. Ancient Woodcut Copy.

Emperor Ming Chengzu was a man of grand visions and extraordinary abilities. His accomplishments were larger than life in all regards of the attribute. The first thing he did upon ascending the throne was to initiate a project to relocate the capital to Beiping and rename the city Beijing.

"Beiping,"[20] City of "Northern Peace," was so named to give meaning to the hope that the north, perpetually ravaged by nomadic invaders from Siberia, would be finally peaceful. "Beijing"[21] simply means "Northern Capital," thus distinguishing it from Nanjing, "Southern Capital."

Beiping was Chengzu's home district when he was the Prince of Yan, the location of his core support; his base. "Yan" was the name of the ancient state which territories included that of Beijing.

Nanjing, in contrast, was the home of the official Ming court and Confucian ministers, who would have had Chengzu flailed and quartered had they been successful in their conspiracy, because they regarded the prince a usurper. Now that Chengzu had gained the upper hand, it was these ministers and their families that were at the wrong end of the gambit.

With the capital relocated to Beijing, Emperor Chengzu found himself closer to "home" and to the Mongolian and Turkic enemies that dwelt in the northern desert—the Gobi. From the new capital, the emperor could strike out at his foes with greater efficiency to ensure the security of the nation.

For his new capital at Beijing, Chengzu would also build a brand-new palace, which was to become today's Forbidden City, one that would befit his stature, and tower over all such edifices of the past. The project would take years to finish, and cost the treasury a pretty penny, but it would appropriately reflect his special status as one of China's preeminent leaders.

Yet, despite such accomplishments, Emperor Chengzu is best remembered in posterity for the legendary maritime adventures initiated under his administration, known as "the Seven Voyages of Zheng He to the Western Ocean."

---

[20] 北平

[21] 北京, at one time spelled Peking.

Upon inaugurating his administration, Chengzu immediately put in motion a series of naval initiatives in the form of overseas expeditions, which were to last his entire reign, not to say his life time. These maritime expeditions were conducted on an unprecedented scale, with ships that were the mightiest the world had ever seen. Beginning in 1405, the fleets were reported to have made seven trips—some counted eight—around the "Western Ocean"—*Xi Yang*[22] in Chinese. Figure 4 shows a tableau of the Ming fleets at sea copied from an ancient artist's woodcut impression.

Thus, in early 15th century, hundreds of magnificent tall ships swooped across the high seas and made calls at foreign ports. It proved to be quite a sight to the southeast Asian natives. Out of these surreally towering vessels would emerge ornately garbed emissaries from the *Heavenly Realm* bearing luxurious gifts. Such a sight would most certainly have made indelible impressions on any onlooker. Some natives must have even thought that the sailors—soldiers garbed in brilliantly colored uniforms—were gods descending on their humble soils. For this, they erected temples to commemorate the visiting leader Zheng He, a eunuch of the Ming court. Today there are still Zheng He temples scattered around towns and villages in the Indian Ocean. Sailors go there to pray for safe passage, while mothers and wives pray for their safe return.

After Emperor Chengzu's death, the expeditions were abruptly and inexplicably canceled by his successor, and, with a singular exception, Ming China permanently abandoned its foreign maritime enterprise, and forever laid waste to its innovative marine technology.

Having sustained a few hundred years of cultural weather battering, the accounts of the Ming maritime adventures in due course devolved into the stuff of legends. While little known in the West, the naval exploits of Zheng He had become folklore, well told throughout China and the lands of Southeast Asia. As is the way of mythology, from the Greeks' sacking of Troy to King Arthur and his

[22] 西洋

Knights of the Round Table, the plotlines have become complacent through repeated telling. Embellishment and fiction have seeped in, integrating with the few facts that have been retained, serving to shore up the heroism of the protagonists, and at the same time vilifying the evils of the scoundrels. Soon even gods began participating in the action, and no one could tell the real story apart from the invented any more. As a result of this, much of this history has become piquing; many questions yearn to be answered.

Prince Henry the Navigator

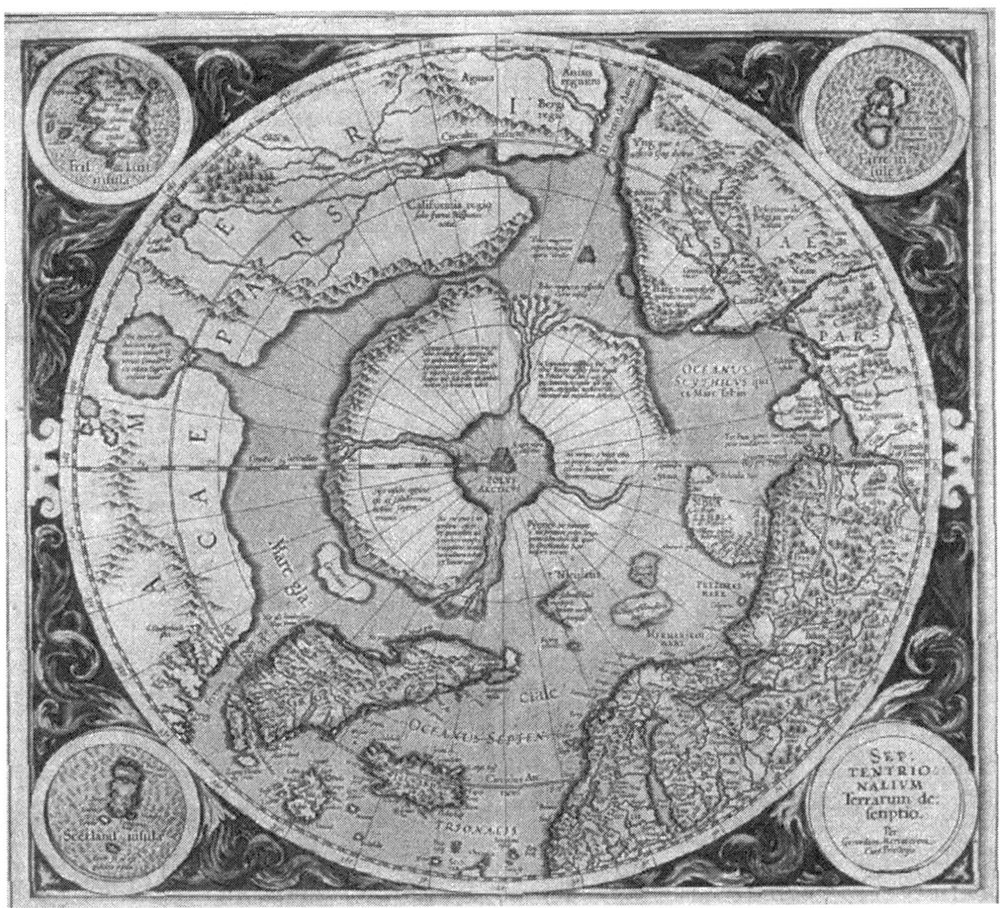

Figure 5

1595 Mercator Map of North Pole

As the Ming navy was blazing the oceans, Portugal, seemingly at the same time, was battling her way down the western African seacoast. Because of the chronological proximity of the two events taking place on the two opposite ends of the Eurasian landmass,[23] we need to review the Portuguese history of the period as well.

Portugal is a country situated at the far western edge of Europe, which Europeans used to consider the end of the world (Figure 2). At one time it was believed that if one were to sail past the Pillars of Heracles (Gibraltar) into the Western Ocean outside Portugal, one would fall off the edge of the world and never to return. Compared with the other European nations, Portugal was a little country, with no naval activity to speak of. Throughout the greater part of history, up to the 15th century, the rest of Europe probably was never truly conscious of it being there. Yet, tiny Portugal was the very nation that was to thrust Europe into world dominance.

When Ming Taizu Zhu Yuanzhang was establishing the Ming Dynasty in China, King John I The Good (João I), founder of the House of Aviz, was on the throne in Portugal. In 1394, four years before the death of Taizu and eleven years before Zheng He's treasure fleets first put to sea, a third son, after princes Duarte and Pedro, was born into the royal household. His name was Henry. In history he is known as Prince Henry (Infante Dom Henrique) or Prince Henry the Navigator, as he is credited with having virtually single-handedly ushered in the European Age of Discovery.

Using today's psychology jargon, Prince Henry would be an overachiever. When he was twenty-one years of age, he led a military force and captured the North African Muslim stronghold of Ceuta on the opposite side of the Strait of Gibraltar.

His most acclaimed triumph, however, was the founding in 1418, while Zheng He was at sea, of a royal naval research center at Cape Saint Vincent in southwestern Portugal, the Institute at Sagres.[24]

---

[23] Portugal beginning with Prince Henry's initiatives in 1420, while Zheng He was entering his "unknown" secret mission just fifteen years before its termination.

[24] Recently some scholars have expressed doubt on the existence of an actual institute.

Figure 6

A Barca

Figure 7

Woodcut Image of a Chinese Junk

The institute was the first all-encompassing European facility of its kind—a sort of 15th century naval high-tech center. It supposedly housed libraries, an astronomical observatory, a shipyard, staff quarters, and even a chapel, for the prince was a devout Catholic. It was designed as a research and training facility for Portuguese seafarers, to collect and preserve geographical knowledge of the world, to develop naval gears and equipment, and to launch naval expeditions.[25]

Hence, under a single sponsorship, one could find would-be sailors learning from some of the most prominent geographers, cartographers, cosmographers, and mathematicians of the day.

One notable product of the institute was the development in 1440 (The Ming voyages were terminated in 1433) of a new kind of ship—a caravel, one that was to be used later by Christopher Columbus in the discovery of the Americas.

---

[25] Portugal was a relatively poor country at the time. It has been written that in 1420 Prince Henry was made the governor of the Order of Christ, the Portuguese branch of the Knights Templar, a wealthy and powerful Christian paramilitary organization, which could easily have funded the projects.

Up to that time, the principal Portuguese sea vessel was the barca Figure 6). The barca (English word *bark*) was in essence a single-sailed boat or barge. It possessed little maneuverability, and was ill suited for open-sea navigation. What Prince Henry's designers came up with was an advanced contraption that could support multiple sails, with a prominent bulkhead, and hind living quarters. Most important, for the first time in European maritime history, it was equipped with a sternpost rudder, the very device that had allowed the Chinese to sail the high seas for over a thousand years. That was quite a coincidence. The Portuguese called the carvel, or caravel, the *nau*; "nau" or "nav" being the etymological root of the word "navigate," thus the name *nau* simply meant "ship."

If you look at a typical caravel Figure 6, you can see that above water it is a dead ringer for a medieval Chinese junk (Figure 7).[26]

For the rest of his life, Prince Henry dedicated himself to the development of Portugal's overseas naval expansion; specifically, the systematic exploration of the West African sea coast and, allegedly, the discovery of a sea route from Portugal to India.

Starting from 1424, for ten years Prince Henry's sailors attempted to negotiate down the western African coast. At first they could not steer their barcas past Cape Bojador (Figure 8). In 1434, Captain Gil Eannes maneuvered his boats westward out to sea to go around the cape, and the Portuguese were able to move further south, reaching Rio de Oro in Western Sahara in 1436. Since then, it had become a Portuguese procedure to first sail west into the Atlantic for hundreds of miles and then sail south, thus avoiding the West African Atlantic counter currents.

In 1441, they learned from the West African natives about territories to the south, and succeeded in reaching Cape Blanco in Mauritania.

---

[26] When all marveling words are brushed aside, the Portuguese *nau* was basically a copy of the Chinese *jhong*.

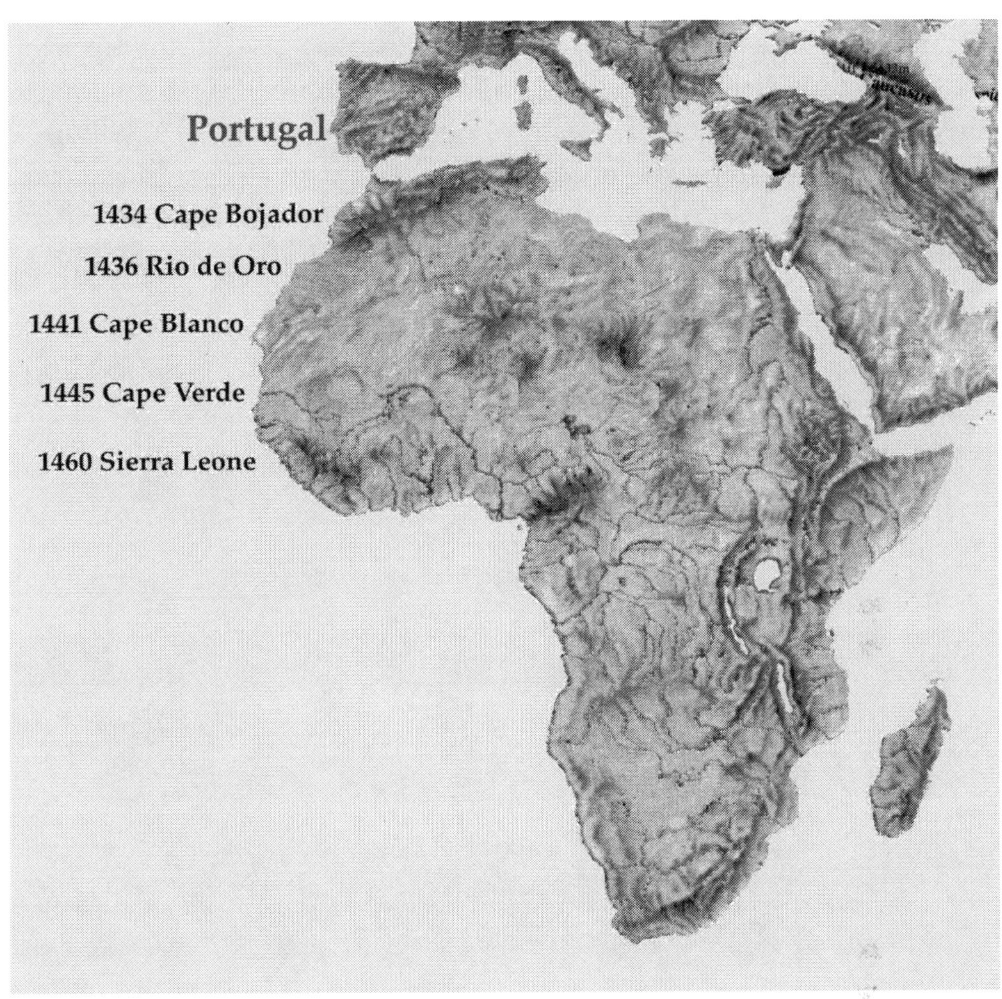

Figure 8

West African Geography

By 1445, they reached Cape Verde, and they made it to Sierra Leone by 1460, the year Prince Henry died. After half a century of tenacious hard work, the Portuguese sailors finally made it round the bulge of Africa.

Incidentally, in 1444, the Portuguese sailors brought back a group of Africans they had captured or purchased, marking the beginning of the European African slave trade.

Why did Prince Henry the Navigator suddenly develop an interest in deep-sea exploration? Was it really because of divine instigation, as claimed in his biography? Europeans did not have the drive nor knowledge to go to sea before. The timing being so close to Zheng He's expeditions was simply eerily tantalizing. Was there a causal relationship between the two events? At this point, that is just a thought. However, that is what all thinking people would suspect. Nonetheless, suspicion is not conclusion. Research is the answer.

Heroes of Exploration

There is no doubt that Europeans' seafaring activities took off after Prince Henry the Navigator, but it took them almost a hundred years to catch on to the caper. Part of the reasons was that Portugal treated its ocean-going and world geography knowledge as national secret. That attitude was followed by the other nations as time went on.

After his death, Prince Henry's nephew King John II took over the Portuguese naval program and carried on his predecessor's maritime initiatives. Soon the Portuguese acquired the Canaries (which later went to Spain) and the Azores. By 1481, the Portuguese had reached the Gold Coast, present day Ghana. So, by the last two decades of the fifteenth century, Portugal enjoyed a monopoly in African gold and slave trades, greatly enriching the royal coffer.

One of the Portuguese ships in the 1481 expedition to the African gold coast was commanded by a captain named Bartolomeu Dias. Under order from King John II, in 1487, Dias sailed toward the southern tip of Africa. Dias' squadron for this outing consisted of three ships, and the trip proved treacherous, as they were sailing against ocean currents. Nonetheless, with the help of an opportune storm they rounded the southern tip of the continent. Dias then pushed up the southeastern African shore until the enterprise was cut short due to exhausting supply and a spent crew. It was during the return trip that the Portuguese discovered the Cape of Good Hope that Dias originally named the Cape of Storms. King John later changed the name to the Cape of Good Hope. The rounding of the Cape of Good Hope allowed the Portuguese to sail into the Indian Ocean and reach the Orient for the first time.

By the end of the century, King John II was dead, and he was succeeded by King Manuel I, who in 1497 organized another expedition bound for India. This time, the fleet consisting of four ships and a crew of about 170 men was commanded by a captain named Vasco da Gama.

By this time, new astronomy-based navigational techniques and modern nautical instruments such as the astrolabe had become available. da Gama set sail from Lisbon in July 1497 and, as almost a hundred years of sailing down the West African coast had taught the Portuguese,[27] the fleet first swung in the southwesterly direction to pick up a favorable current and wind. In November, the fleet reached Santa Helena Bay, where the explorers stopped to make repairs and take on fresh provision. They also got into a skirmish with the natives. By late November, they had rounded the Cape of Good Hope.

At Mossel Bay, the Portuguese again got into a fight with the natives over a cross they tried to erect there. In January the next year, the Portuguese ran into two Bantu chiefs who wore silk and satin. They told da Gama of large sailing ships that had visited them before, so he knew India was within reach. (There is no record on where the Bantu chiefs obtained their silk and satin.) From there, the Portuguese sailors made stops at East African trading posts that included Mozambique, Mombasa, Malindi, and Kenya, battling the natives at every turn.

In May 1498, the Portuguese finally reached Calicut, India, where they failed to establish friendly trading relationship with the Indians—Indians of India, that is. In August, da Gama returned home, arriving in Lisbon in September 1499.

Commercially, the trip could not be regarded as a success because of cultural differences between visitors and hosts. Historians often cited the curious fact that the Portuguese brought gifts of poor quality that unimpressed the local dignitaries. Why poor quality? Poor means in contrast to better. If something is described as poor, it implies there is something of higher quality, but that was not discussed.

---

[27] The African locals told the Portuguese sailors so.

In hindsight, it would be unreasonable to hold the Europeans responsible for not knowing about the precious gifts that the Chinese officials had lavished on the local leaders less than a century earlier.

In addition, due to lack of experience in long distance sailing at sea, most of the crew died of disease.[28] Despite all this, the voyages did technically initiate a sea trade route between Europe and Asia.

To impose trade with the Indians, King Manuel arranged for another expedition in 1500. In 1502, da Gama made a follow-up voyage to officially set up trade with India. It was during this trip that true colonial brutality showed its colors, and established Portugal as the naval power in the Indian Ocean. Later da Gama was named Viceroy of India and made many more trips to that country where he died.

The maritime efforts ultimately led to a vast Portuguese overseas empire, and in less than one hundred years, the Portuguese sailors had gone from essentially unknown saltwater fishermen to pioneering open-sea navigators. During this short adventure, many sailors had become legendary, such as Dias, da Gama, discussed above, and Magellan.

Ferdinand Magellan (Fernao de Magalhaes in Portuguese), who was credited with being the first person to circumnavigate the world, was not a part of the Sagres School that developed the sea route to India. Born in 1480, he was aristocratic. Orphaned at ten, he became a page at Queen Leonor's court, where he was given a good education. By the time he took to sea, Christopher Columbus had already "discovered" the Caribbean and Vasco da Gama had reached India.

His first turn at sea was in 1505 when he went with Viceroy Francisco de Almeida to India. Subsequently, he helped fortify the Portuguese outposts in East Africa, fought the Turks in naval battles in the Indian Ocean, the Malays in Malacca (Melaka today), and was

---

[28] Employing lime to provide vitamin C to counter scurvy on the high sea was yet to be introduced by the British, the limeys. The Chinese sailors, in contrast, supplied themselves with fresh fruits and vegetables from their stops.

wounded in military campaigns in Morocco, giving him a permanent limp.

In the early 16th century, Magellan approached King Manuel I for an expedition to the Spice Islands by sailing west, perhaps to establish a name for himself, for he knew he could do it by sailing eastward. Otherwise, how he got the idea for the project we are not told. Perhaps Columbus, who sailed west, had inspired him, Columbus not having reached India notwithstanding.

It was rumored that Magellan had come into a map or geographical information that convinced him Asia could be reached by sailing west past the southern tip of South America. It was an odd hypothesis because, supposedly, the Spaniards and Portuguese had yet to chart that part of the newly discovered continents.

In any case, King Manuel I turned him down on the proposal. Some commentators suggested that it was due to personality conflict—King Manuel simply disliked the would-be explorer. As a result, Magellan turned to the monarch of Spain for support, pointing out that the Spice Islands actually lay within her overseas territories.[29] Charles I agreed to a contract with Magellan and, in 1519, a fleet of 5 ships and about 240 men was launched for the South China Sea.

After crossing the Atlantic Ocean to what is today the Brazilian coast, Magellan's fleet went south shadowing the South American coastline. It is uncertain if there was a problem with the sailing charts, but Magellan failed to locate the passage to the west side of the continent, and the fleet stalled in what is now southern Argentina. It was not until October, 1520 that he finally located the passage to the Pacific—the Strait of Magellan would eventually be named in his honor. The Pacific Ocean was so-called because it appeared to Magellan to be calm compared to the Atlantic, so we are told by history.

---

[29] In 1494, Pope Alexander VI had divided the world into two, awarding half to Spain and the other half to Portugal. The treaty of Tordesillas will be discussed below.

The crossing of the Pacific took 98 days. Finally, in March, 1521, the fleet of three remaining ships hobbled into the harbor of Guam, where the Europeans battled the natives. Afterward, Magellan sailed on to the South China Sea islands that are now known as the Philippines where the party was welcomed. As bad luck would have it, Magellan was killed when he intervened in a local conflict.

When the expedition realized that they only had enough crewmembers to operate two ships they abandoned the caravel Concepcion. The two surviving ships then went on to the Spice Islands where they loaded up with spice goods and then sailed in opposite directions to return home, one heading east and the other west, perhaps to enhance the chances of success.

It is also possible that some of the crewmen did not believe they could go home heading westward, and opted to retrace their voyage instead. In any case, why did the men believe they could reach home by circumnavigating the globe? What evidence did they have that convinced them that the world could be circumnavigated? Was the geography of south America already known at that time? Did they know that it was a huge continent? How did Magellan sail, ostensibly without any sea chart? It was all baffling, but no explanations were offered.

Ironically, the eastbound ship could not make it and had to return to the Spice Islands, where it was captured by the Portuguese.

The westbound ship, Victoria, captained by Juan Sebastian del Cano, made it back to Spain in September 1522, circumnavigating the globe.

Today, we attribute the first European circumnavigation of the world to Magellan, who did not complete the trip—he died—and accord him the glory of a conquering hero. Back in the 16th century he was considered a traitor by the Portuguese and loathed by the Spanish for his cruelty toward his crew and various navigational errors.

By the time all this happened, Zheng He had been long gone. By 1522, the Ming already had arrested its overseas naval program for almost a hundred years. The two great seafaring nations of China and Portugal never met each other on the high seas; at least that is the impression one gets from established history. It is as if they had passed each other in the dark of night, not knowing the other ever existed. One obliterated its own achievements while the other went on to lead the Renaissance European imperial nations to world dominance.

Christopher Columbus conquered and colonized the West Indies by the end of the 15th century. Soon Italian Amerigo Vespucci and his fellow Spanish explorers were charting out the South American east coast and the area of the Brazilian seacoast specifically. Balboa was checking out Central America, while the Portuguese were establishing strongholds in the Indian Ocean and the South China Sea. A few years later, the British, the Dutch, and the French were penetrating the northeastern seaboard of North America.

By the middle of the 16th century, the Spanish had superficially surveyed a large part of the American Continents and conquered Mexico (the Aztecs) and Peru (the Incas). By the end of the 16th century, Sir Francis Drake circumnavigated the world a second time. At the same time, Henry Hudson was exploring the North American east coast for the Dutch.

Is this true history? The monumental events that occurred at the two ends of the Eurasian landmass, one set by the Europeans and the other series by the Chinese led by Zheng He, being so close in time, was there really no connection whatsoever between the two? This research finds that not only were they connected; one was in fact the cause of the other. This book is the report on the investigations.

Europeans Did Not Do It

Against such unfaltering, long established European tradition, an assertion that the Chinese had instigated the Age of Discovery is a serious one. One must have ample evidentiary support to make such a bold claim. As it is, the argument for the case is necessarily complex, therefore I shall simplify the process by breaking the analysis into two distinct parts.

First, if we were to assert that the Age of Discovery was brought on by the Chinese, we must show that the Europeans did not do it as history has proclaimed it. It turns out this task is rather simple and straight forward.

The fact is, there is clear evidence showing that European cartographers and writers had access to information about the geography of the world outside Europe way before the Age of Discovery; that they were describing and drawing maps of places in the world that they had yet to visit, explore, and survey. Now, then, one cannot very well be a pioneering explorer if one already possesses information about the places one is to explore, can he? We shall look at such evidence next.

Critics may object to this assertion at this point (as they often have done so without having read the theses they attacked) on the ground that one or two old relics do not a case make, but then, that is precisely the point. In historical investigation, one old relic is as good as one million old relics, provided that the specimens are authentic.

The antiquity of the human lineage is determined by one single; indeed, partial, skeletal sample, famously named Lucy, from Africa. If even just one old map drawn before the Age of Discovery shows the geography of the world pre-existed, it demonstrates that at least one European cartographer was drawing a map of places in the world before European explorers had explored them, and therefore he had to have access to that knowledge, which had to have been provided by people who had explored those places.

Yet there is not just one such historic relic in existence. There are literally hundreds, if not thousands, of such unlikely records, carefully preserved in the World's literary institutions. Scholars have even studied them, and then abandoned their efforts, or provided untenable explanations for them, innocently or otherwise.

The sample catalog of such unlikely records, mostly European maps and charts, presented staring below is not meant to be exhaustive, but the numerous entries are included to demonstrate that European cartographers in fact drew their maps based on external sources.

The difficulty is, these places are familiar to us. To understand their significance, one needs to keep in mind that they were not always so. At the time of their creation, did the creators know their existence? How did they know about the, and where did they obtain their information, and how did their audiences understand them?

I shall present them by geographical regions.

The Poles

Figure 9

1506 Giovanni Matteo Contarini Map

Two of the last places on Earth surveyed by humankind are the poles. John Ross reached the magnetic North Pole in 1831, but the geographical North Pole was only reached by Robert Peary and Matthew Henson in 1909. These historic events are well documented.

When Christopher Columbus "discovered" the *New World*; that is, the Caribbean, there was no talk of places such as the poles. Indeed, modern literature continues to argue that many Europeans at the time still thought the Earth was flat. A flat Earth had no poles.

The fact is, the poles were the last places Europeans explored in the long history of the Age of Discovery.

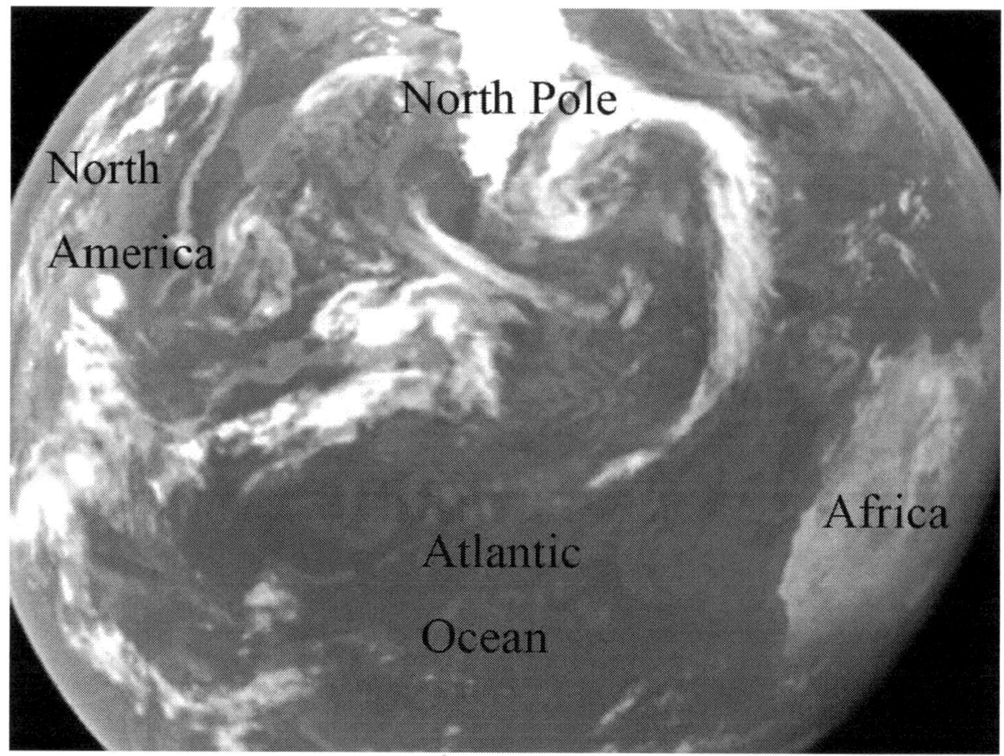

Figure 10

Modern Rendition of 1506 Giovanni Matteo Contarini Map

Indeed, that highlights Columbus' genius in thinking that he could reach Asia by traveling West, a feat that could only have been accomplished if the Earth was round (or, like a cylinder). He was a genius because it was deemed extraordinary to think so. Therefore, nobody could have been thinking that there were lands at the two tips of a spherical world. Yet European cartographers were drawing maps of the North Pole as early as the beginning of the 16th century, virtually coeval with Columbus' activities in the Caribbean. The following are a few such masterpieces that are still in existence.

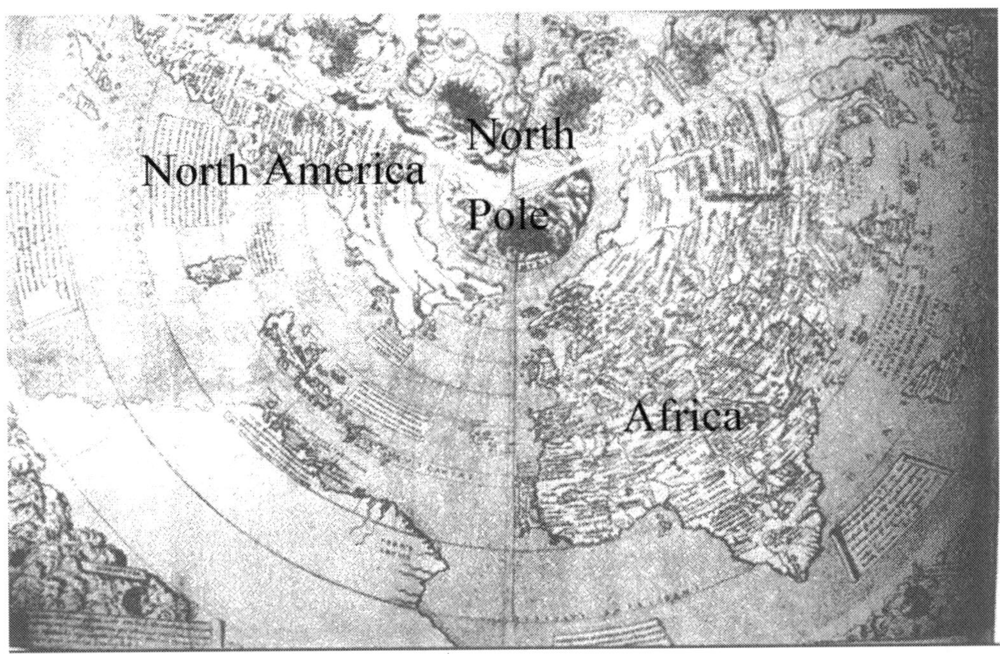

Figure 11

1506 Giovanni Matteo Contarini Map Annotated

The Giovanni Matteo Contarini map (Figure 9 to Figure 11), reportedly published by Italian artist/cartographer Francesco Rosselli in 1506, attempted to show the geography of the North Pole region.[30] What is troublesome is, in 1506 Europeans had not visited the North Pole, let alone drawing its map.

Once more, most Europeans had not suspected that the world had a pole; they had not learned that the world was round! Hence, how did Contarini and colleagues come up with the idea of drawing a North Pole map?

A similar intent can also be found in the 1508 Francesco Rosselli map (Figure 65) in which the pole areas were shown in a world projection.

---

30 Drawn was also North America, in 1506, which had yet to be explored. That will be addressed in detail below

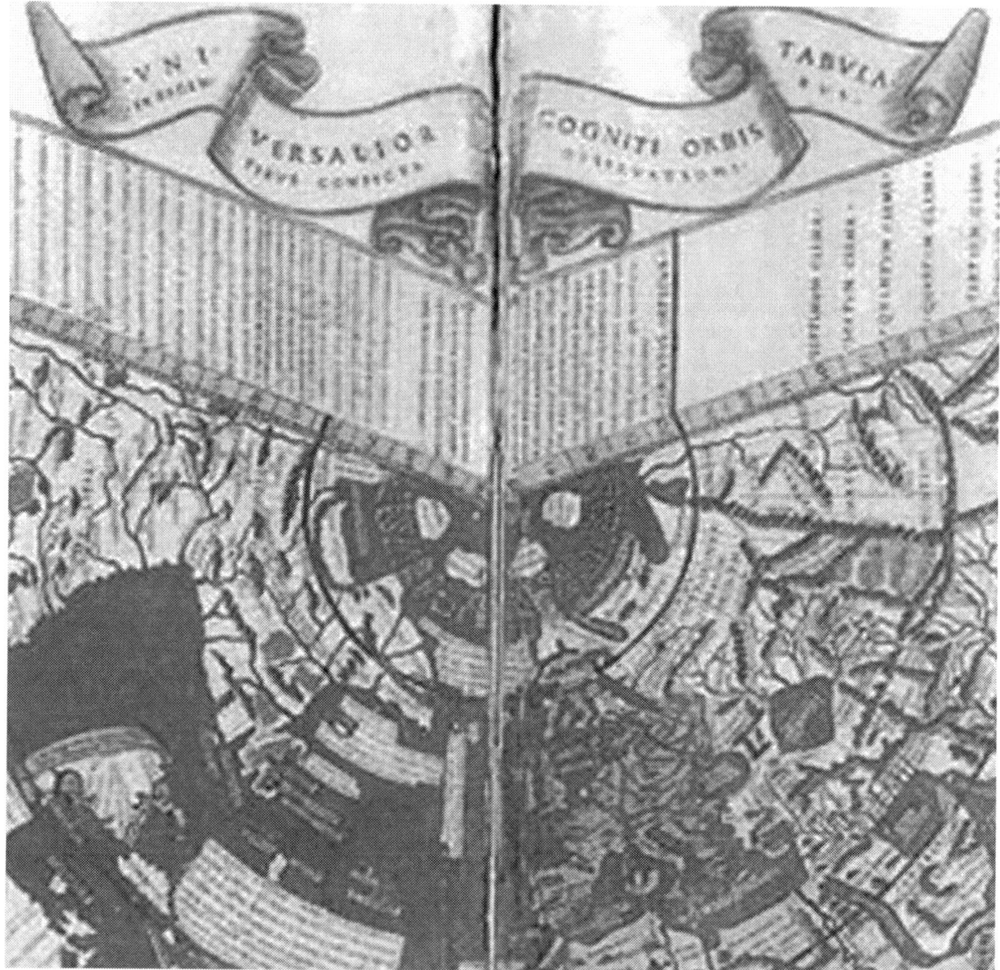

Figure 12

1507 Ruysch World Map

Remember that not five years before this map was drawn, Columbus was still bumbling around the Caribbean wondering where he was.[31] Based on what data were these early 16th century Rosselli maps of the North Pole drawn?

---

[31] Columbus' interest was the Caribbean islands. He never explored the American continental landmasses except for a small patch in northeast South America.

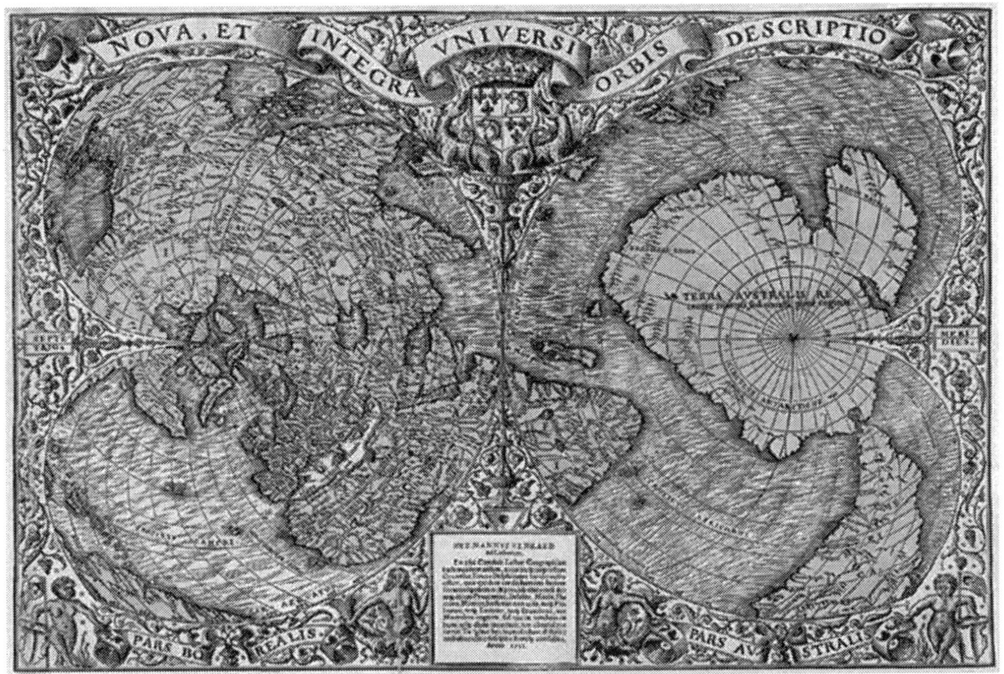

Figure 13

1521 Oronce Finé World Map

No European explorer had been to the North Pole at the time, nor knew of its existence, let alone having surveyed the area. How did the cartographer manage to draw his maps of the North Pole? What did people think when they saw them?

In the early 16th century world map by the Dutch cartographer Johannes Ruysch, four pieces of landmasses are shown to make up the North Pole (Figure 12). The map also features the northeastern part of North America, which was unknown to Europeans.

The same North Pole is shown in the 1521 map (Figure 13 on the left) by French mathematician/cartographer Oronce Finé.

In 1595, the mapmaker updated his map (Figure 14), reaffirming that he knew about the North Pole, that his earlier drawing of it was not a fluke.

Figure 15 shows a 1538 map of the North Pole region by the famed German cartographer Gerard (Gerardus) Mercator.

Figure 14

1569 Mercator Map North Pole Region

Then he did it again in 1569 (Figure 14), and the map was no more accurate than its predecessor. In the lower right quadrant of the map, you can see "unfinished" features indicating that either the mapmaker had difficulty tracing the landmasses or precise information about the sketchy areas was lacking.

Regardless, where the mapmaker obtained his information on the area is undocumented.

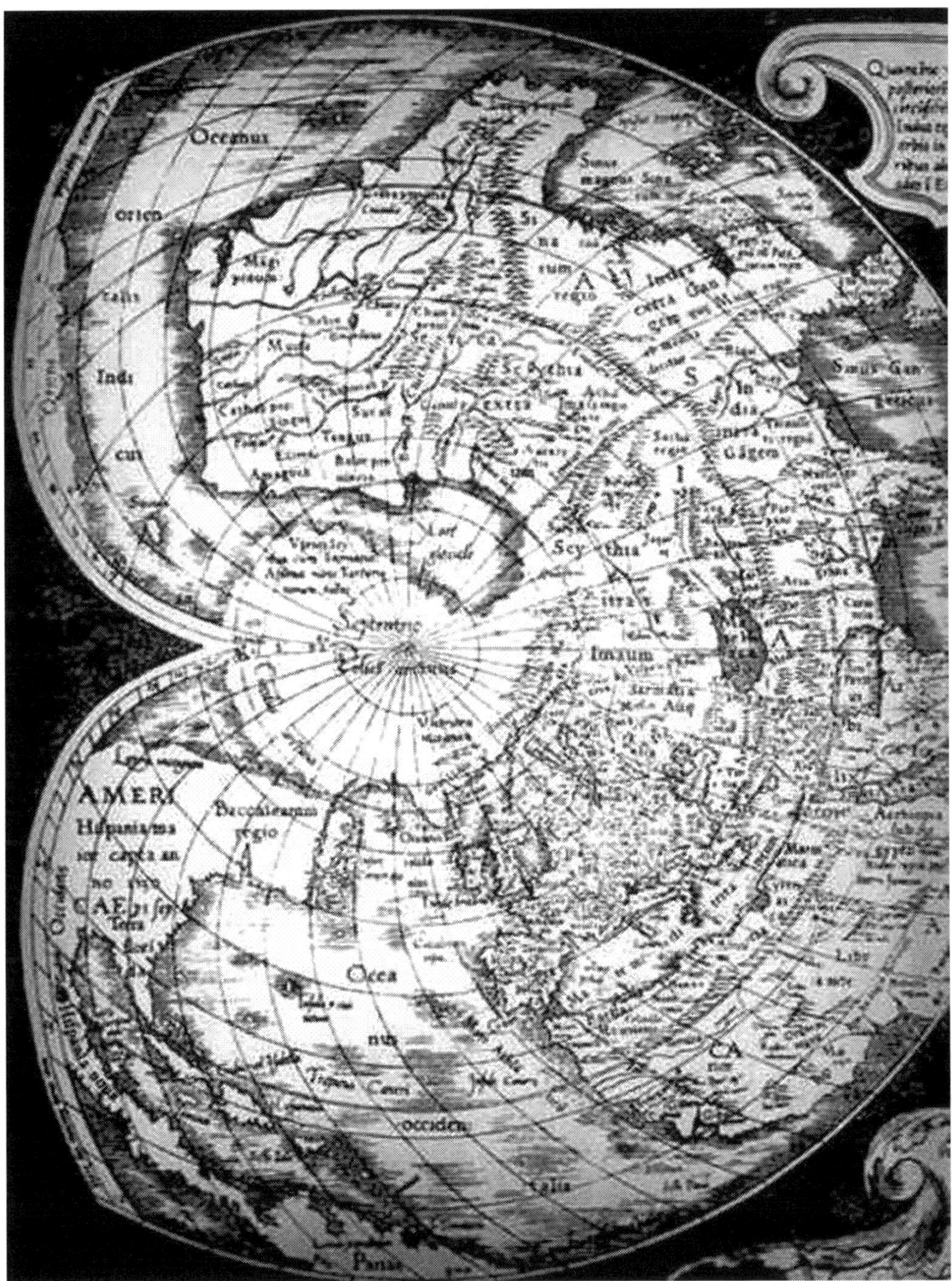

Figure 15

A 1538 Gerard Mercator Map showing the North Pole Region

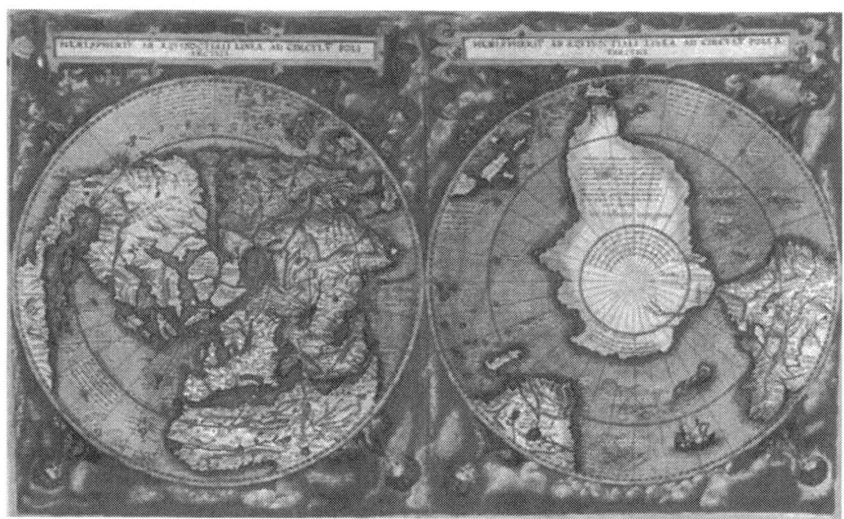

Figure 16

1593 Gerard de Jode Map

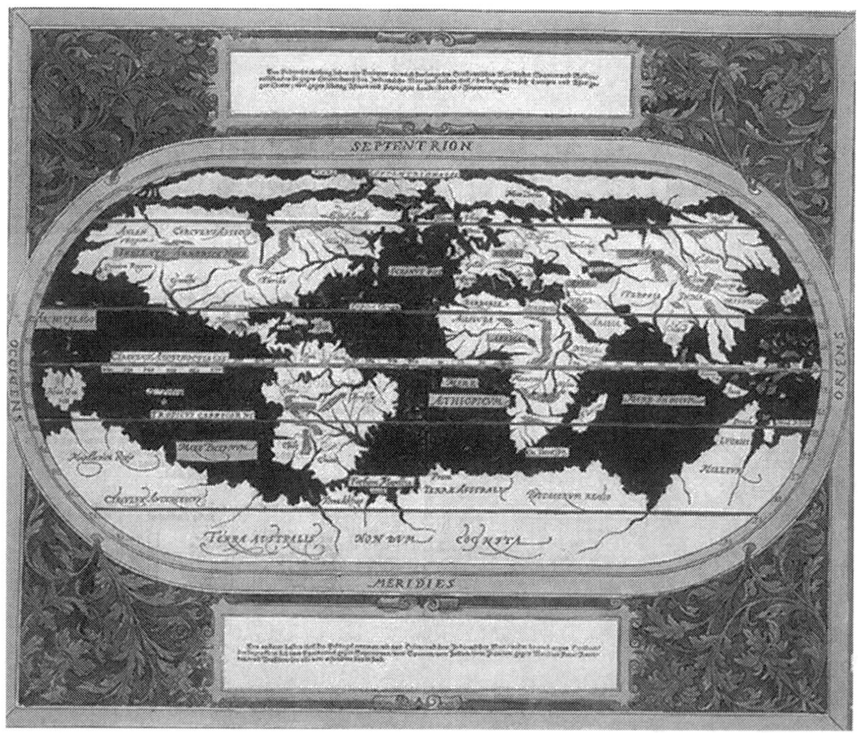

Figure 17

1544 Sebastian Munster Map

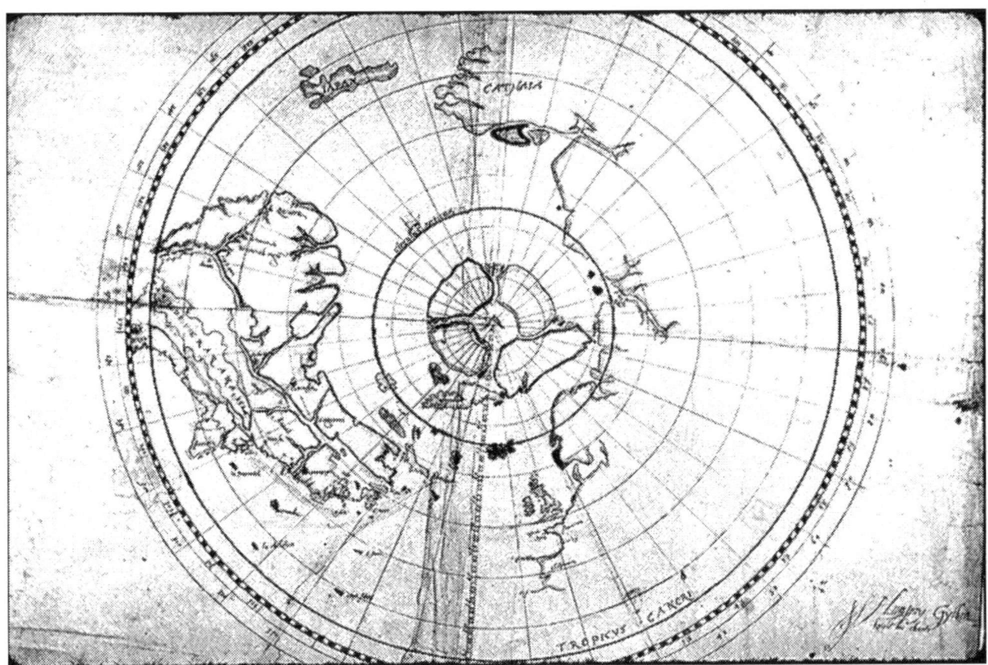

Figure 18

1582 John Dee North Pole

Figure 19

A 1587 Mercator Map

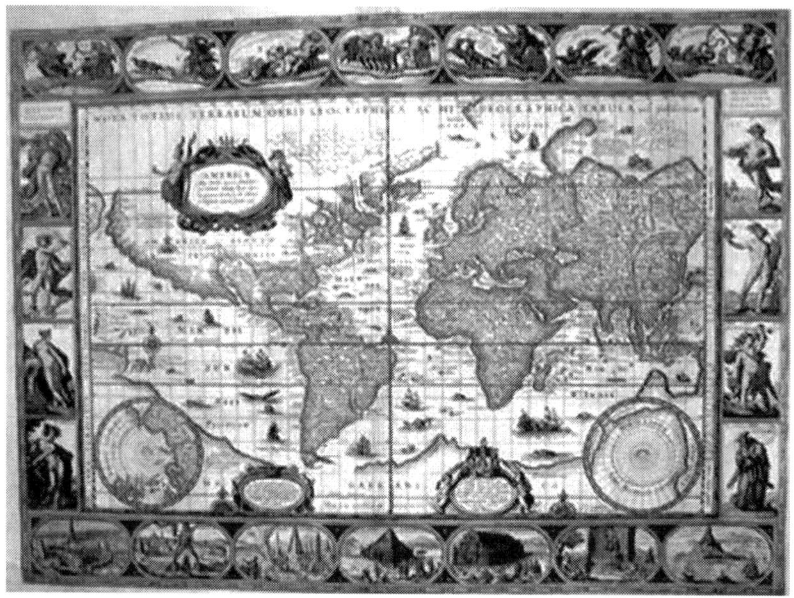

Figure 20

1606 Blaeu Map

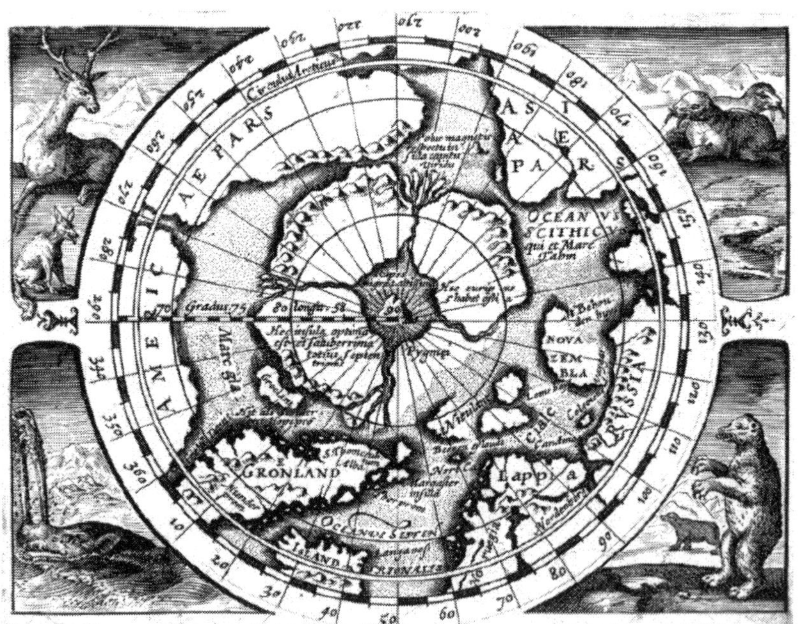

Figure 21

1618 Bertius North Pole

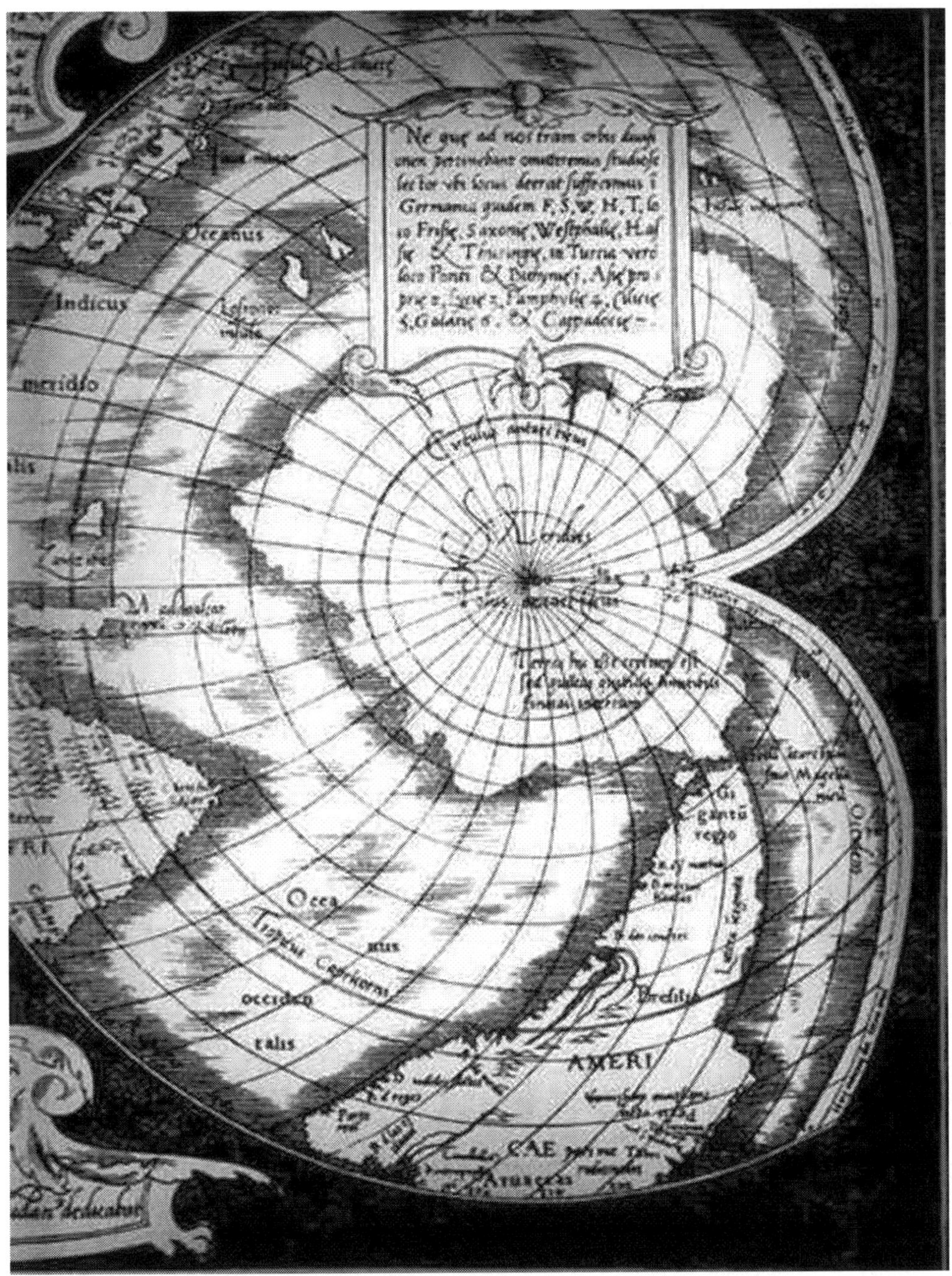

Figure 22

1538 Gerardo Mercator Map of Antarctica

Incidentally, at the center of North Pole (Figure 14) is an island called *Rupes Nigra*. It is told that a 14th century monk had described it in a work titled "Inventio Fortunata." Clearly it was meant to say that the magnetic North Pole was a rock, perhaps of iron—Nigra means black. How a 14th century monk came to know about such things, history does not elaborate.

In 1593, Antwerp, Belgium cartographer Gerard de Jode produced his entry for the polar catalogues with the map depicted in Figure 16.

The 1544 map (Figure 17) of Sebastian Munster, one of the earliest Germans to map the world, shows the Polar Regions with great confidence, even though he was off in his interpretation.

In 1582 English cosmologist John Dee also tried his hands at North Pole, again struggling to mesh the now familiar four gigantic ice blocks (Figure 18).

Figure 19 shows a 1587 Mercator world map, now at the British Museum in London. This map is trying to show the two polar areas. The interest in these "unexplored" areas is manifest.

In the 1606 Blaeu map of the world (Figure 20), the mapmaker noticeably attempted to show that he had the latest on the two poles, as shown in the two circular insets at the two lower corners of the layout.

The chase for the phantom North Pole lasted well into the 17th century. In 1618, the famous ice masses made an encore appearance in the Bertius map (Figure 21), with reindeer, sea lions, polar bears, and monsters in the supporting cast.

There will be more on these monsters below.

The Antarctica was reportedly first sighted by Americans in early 19th century, and the newly discovered continent was immediately surveyed and circumnavigated. However, Norwegian Roald Amundsen only finally reached South Pole in 1911.

Although Amundsen was credited as the first human to reach the South Pole in 1911 (Robert F Scott arrived slightly later in 1912), James Cook was supposed to have circumnavigated the Antarctic continent in 1820, even though he found the shorelines difficult to pin down because of ice.

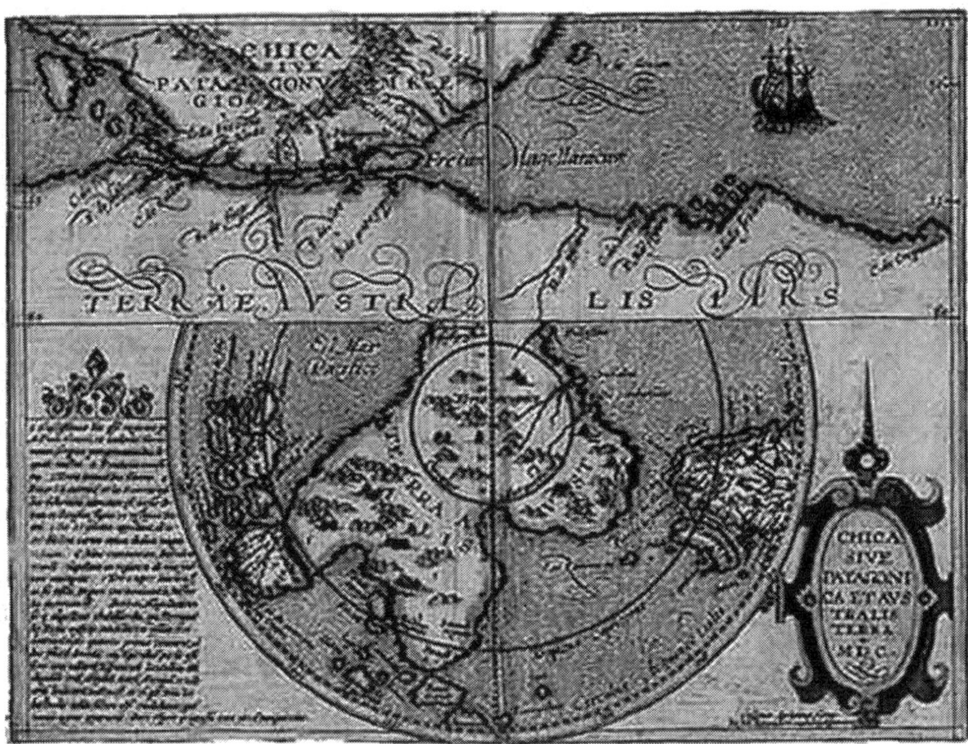

Figure 23

1600 Quad Matthias Map

In 1840, James Clark Ross broke through the ice blocks and reached land. In any case, real surveying of Antarctica by Europeans did not begin until the Sixth International Geographic Congress in 1895.

So, the South Pole was officially unexplored before the 20th century.

Yet. despite all, that fact clearly did not deter our very determined medieval cartographers from trying their hands at charting the region; a phantom region, because at the time no European was supposed to have known of these places.

Notwithstanding, in 1538, almost four hundred years earlier, Gerard Mercator produced a map of Antarctica (Figure 22).

Figure 24

1739 Philippe Buache South Pole

In 1600, the German cartographer Matthias Quad produced his Antarctica, *Terra Australis,* as shown in Figure 23, and the French geographer Philippe Buache his in Figure 24.

What these maps tell us is that long before European explorers attempted to reach the poles; long before they even began suspecting that such places existed; when they did not even have the vehicles and equipment to survey them, European cartographers somehow knew of these places, and even possessed the data with which they used to draw their maps.

These mapmakers should have no business with the poles in the 16th, 17th, and 18th centuries. No European had surveyed those regions at that time. Obviously, the cartographers had obtained their information for the maps from some external source or sources, and those were not European explorers.

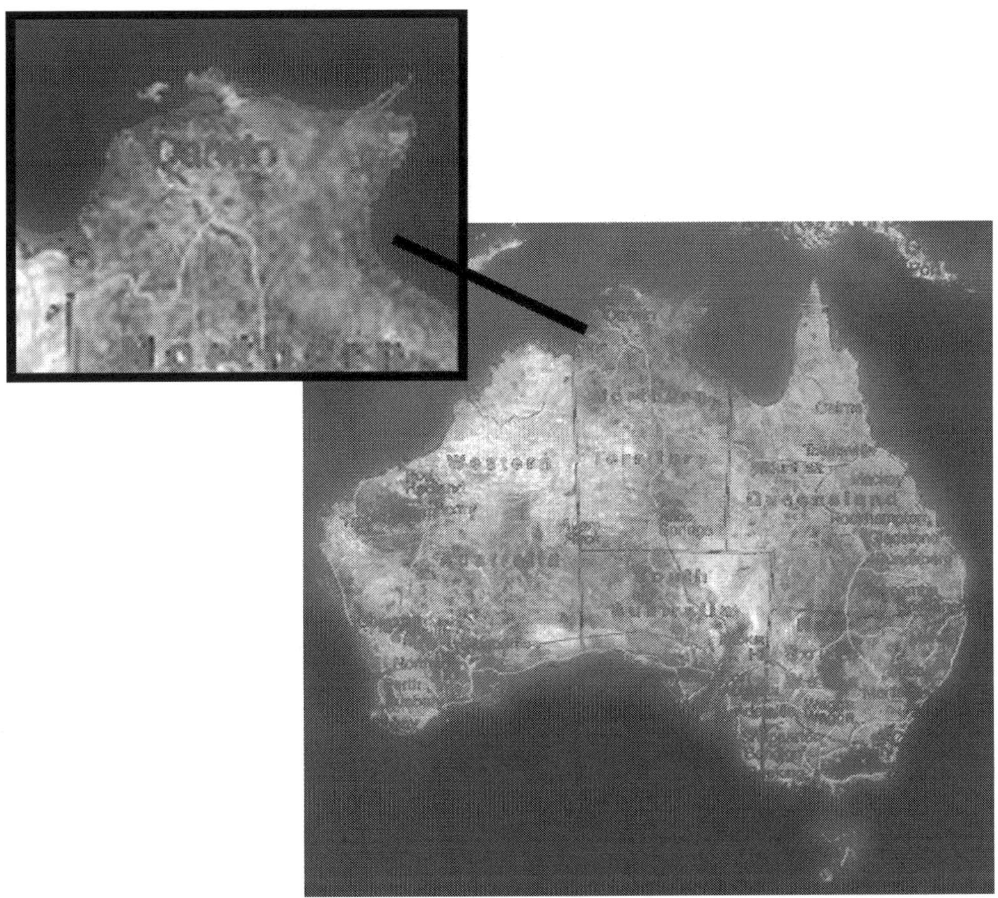

Figure 25

Northwest Australia Today

Putting it another way, as early as the beginning of the 16th century, European cartographers somehow got their hands on the survey data—or maps—of some places at the two ends of the globe and began drawing their maps. Clearly they had no idea what they were drawing, for, as pointed out, no European had been to those places, had known them, or had seen them. The mapmakers were drawing these maps blind, or did they?

Startlingly, these maps were realistic. No. They had survey data; that is, maps and descriptions by others that had been there.

Again, the poles were discovered in the 19th or 20th century. Yet, Europeans were drawing their maps centuries before they were explored. That proves they had the data to the poles from outsiders. We have made our case.

Yet, more intriguing data, not to say more entertaining ones, are ahead. Hence we shall not stop. We shall soldier on.

Australia

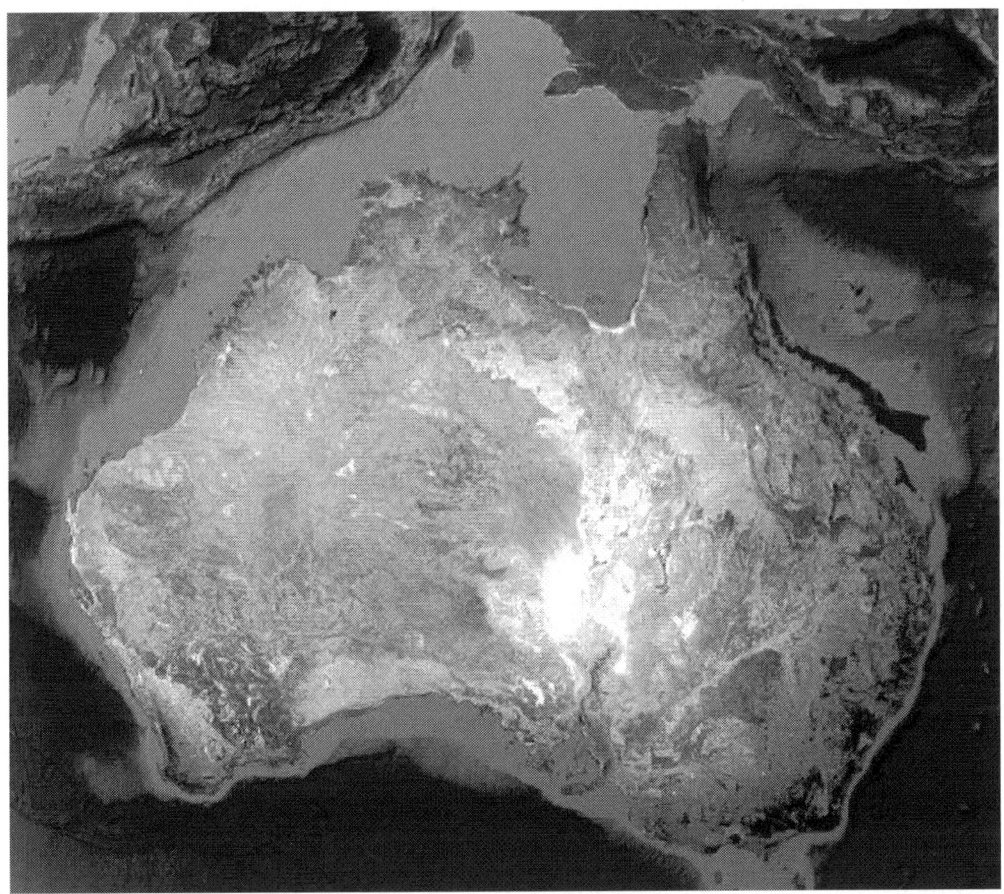

Figure 26

A Modern Rendition of Australia

All students of exploration know, Captain Cook studied Australia (Figure 26) in 1770, and a few years later he surveyed the Hawaii islands. Yet, European cartographers were attempting to render Australia on their maps way before then. Let us look at a few maps of Australia published before Cook's historic "discovery."

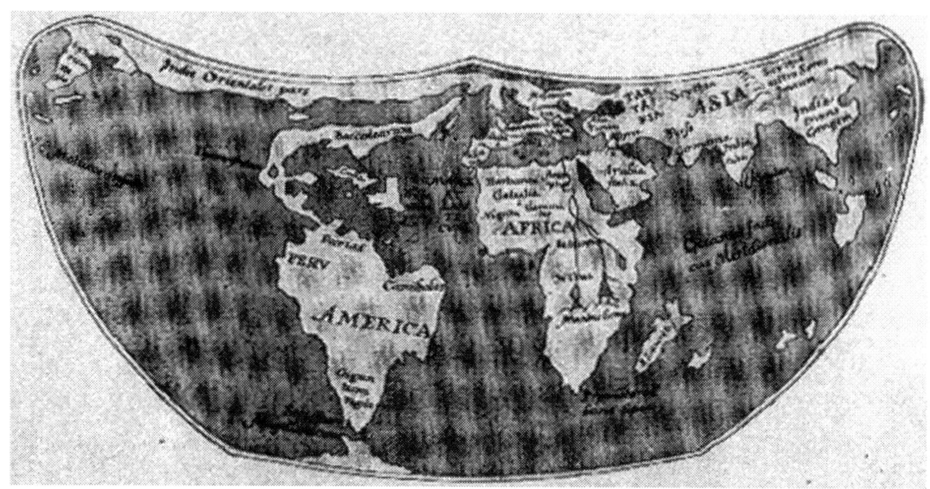

Figure 27

The 1520 Apian World Map

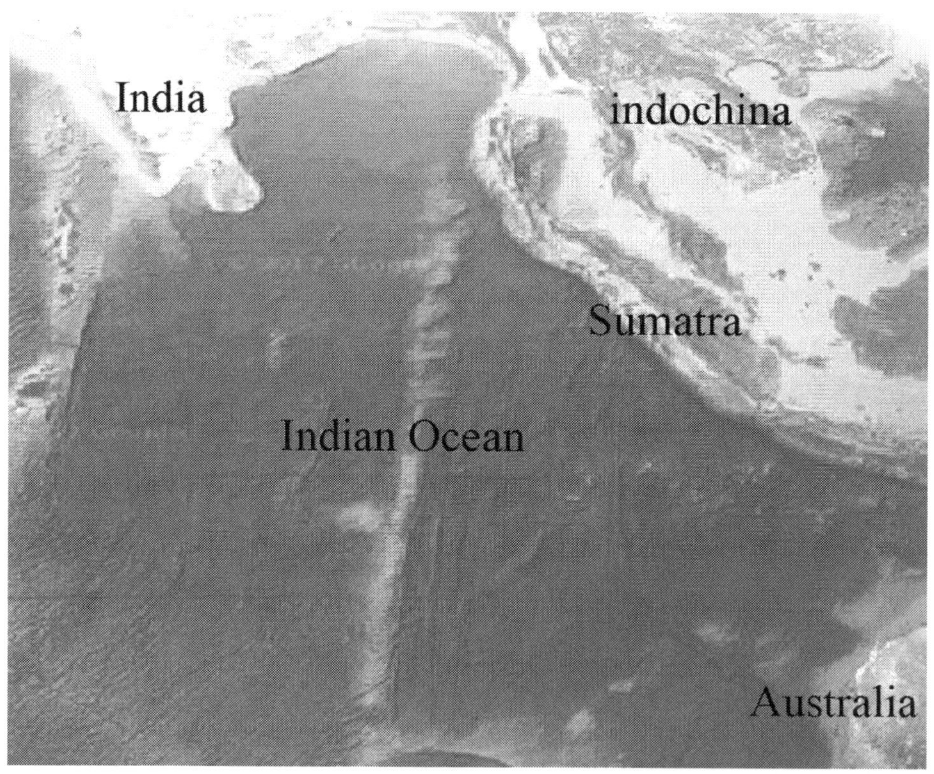

Figure 28

Australia at the Lower-Right, World Map

Figure 29

1547 Harleyan Dauphin Map

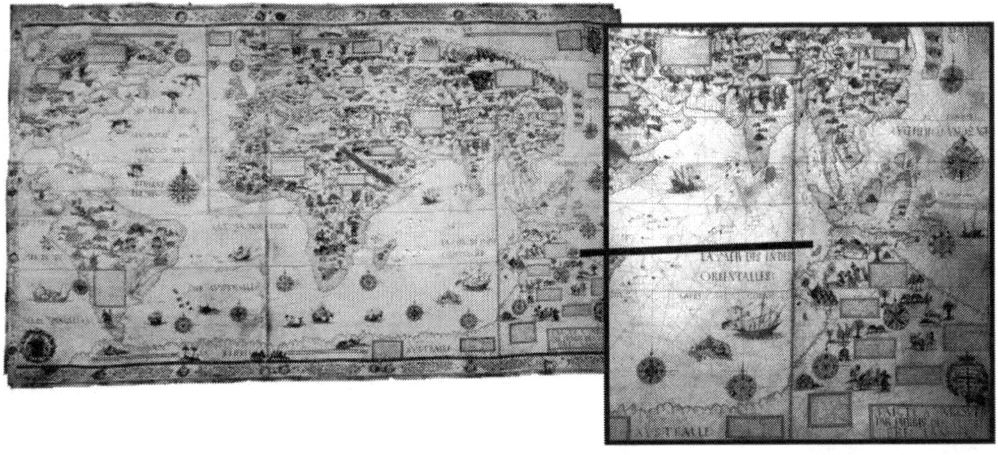

Figure 30

1550 Desceliers World Map

The northwest corner of Australia shows up in the 1520 Peter Apian (Petrus Apianus, prominent German scientist and cartographer) world map (Figure 27, right hand side, center vertically) just 20 years after Columbus began colonizing the Caribbean.

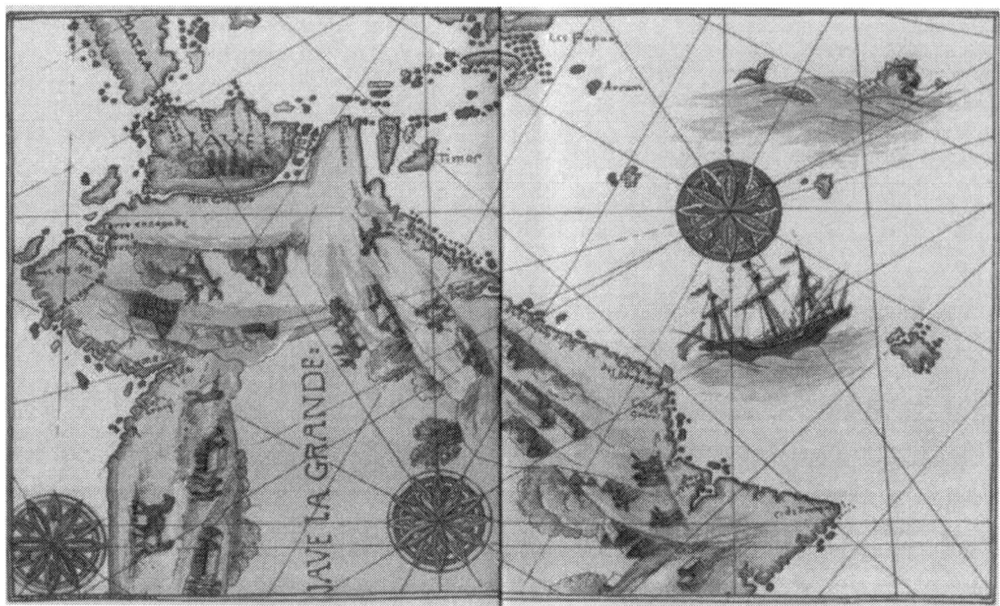

Figure 31

The Dauphin Chart of 1530 or 1536

Figure 32

1566 Desliens World Map

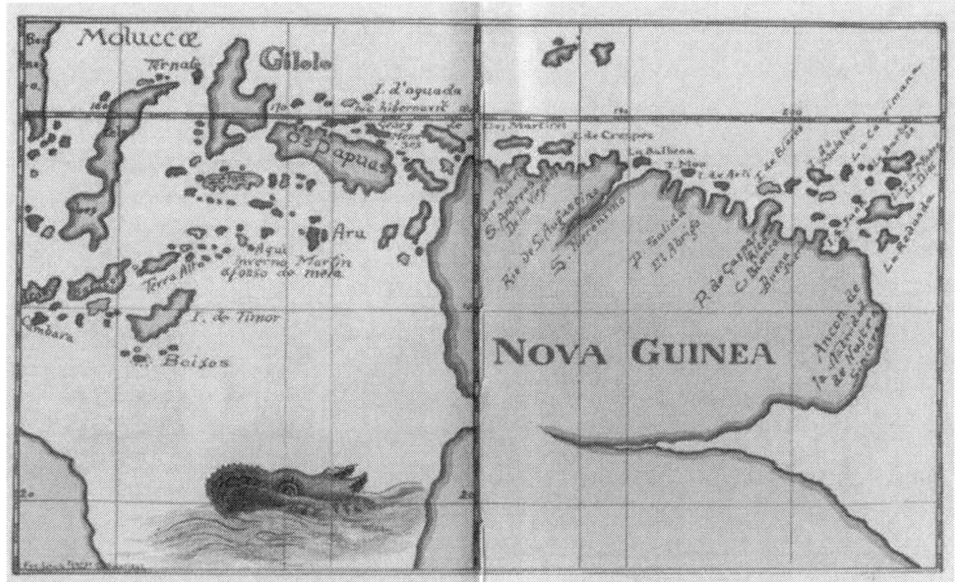

Figure 33

1600 Ribero New Guinea

Figure 34

1570 Ortelius South China Sea

On the map it was just a lump of landmass. No, that's not Australia, you say. Maybe it is Indonesia. It is right smack below a hugely rendered Vietnam! (It will be revisited below.) The island of Indonesia runs in the east-west direction. The landmass on the map runs north-south. Compare this map with a modern map with a similar perspective (Figure 28) and note the partial piece of landmass at the lower-right corner of the map section.

In the Dauphin Chart of 1530s (Figure 31), Australia is identified as Grand Java, *Jave la Grande,* or Greater Java, positioned just southeast of Java. The shape of the northwestern Australian "horn" is clear. A later version is shown in Figure 29. Likewise in the 1550 Desceliers World Map, currently at the British Library (Figure 30), the left horn of the huge landmass of Australia south of Java is officially identified. It should be clear by now what that landmass below Asia in Figure 29 is. If you disagree with this, please tell us what you think that landmass is.

Abraham Ortelius (1527 – 28) is generally hailed as the inventor of modern atlases. He was a Brabantian (Dutch) geographer, cosmographer, and cartographer. In his 1570 map (Figure 34, allegedly by Gastaldi), Australia is hinted at. The same material also found its way into the 1595 Mercator map. Gerardus Mercator was a Flemish geographer and cartographer who created the famous Mercator projection, a cylindrical map projection.

Desliens had a 1566 version shown in Figure 32, with south pointing up. Australia is also visible in the 1598 Ruscelli world map (Figure 33 right hand side). The 1600 Ribero map of New Guinea (Figure 33) shows the island attached to the northwestern tip of Australia.

Even as late as early 18th century, European cartographers were drawing Australia without having surveyed it—Captain Cook had not set sail for the mysterious land yet.

This is demonstrated in the 1667 Joan Blaeu Australia (Figure 36), the 1682 van Keulen map featuring Australia (Figure 36), the 1701 Mortier map (Figure 37), and the 1715 Louis Renard version (Figure 39).

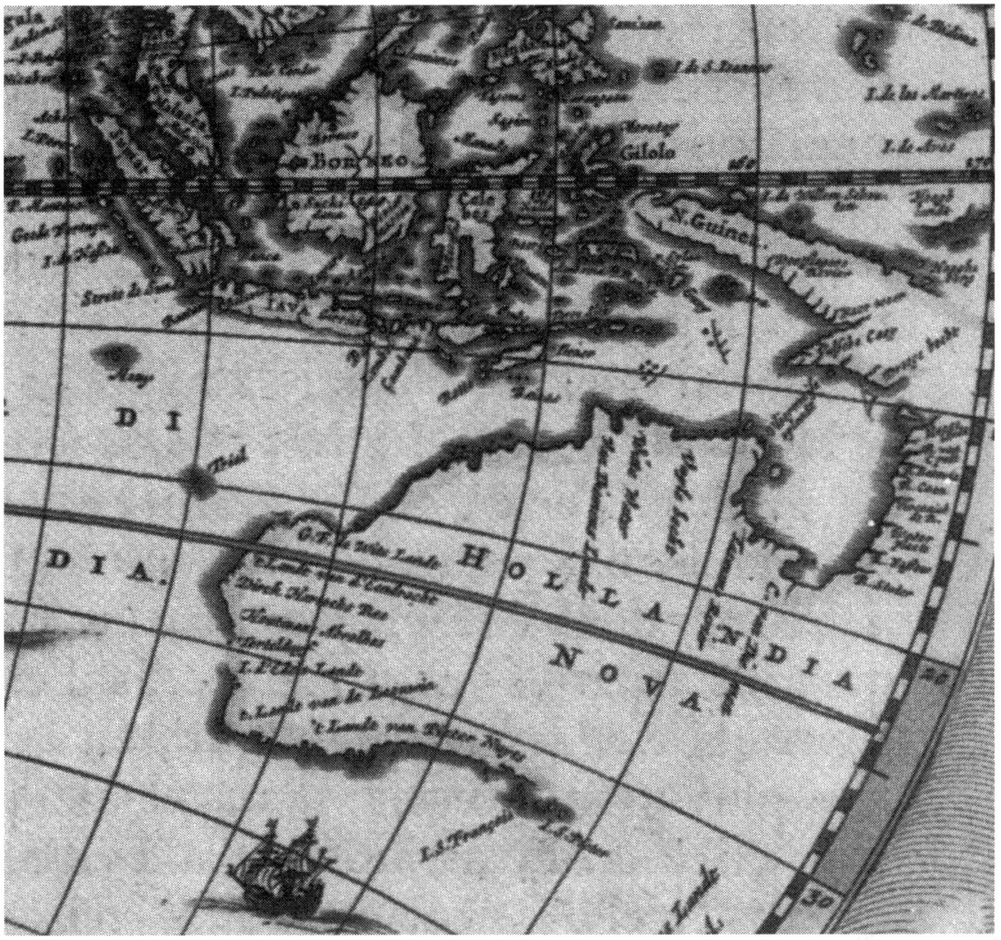

Figure 35

1667 Joan Blaeu Australia

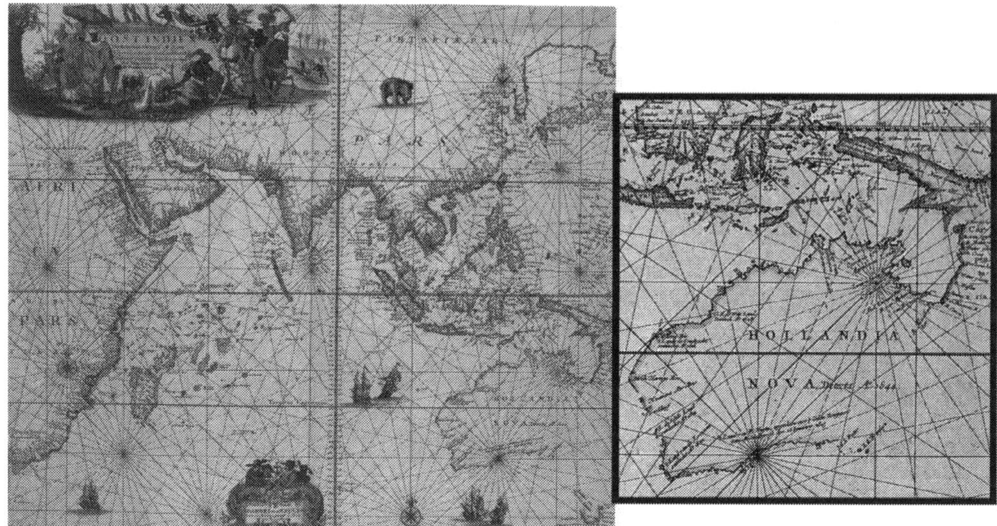

Figure 36

1682 Van Keulen Australia

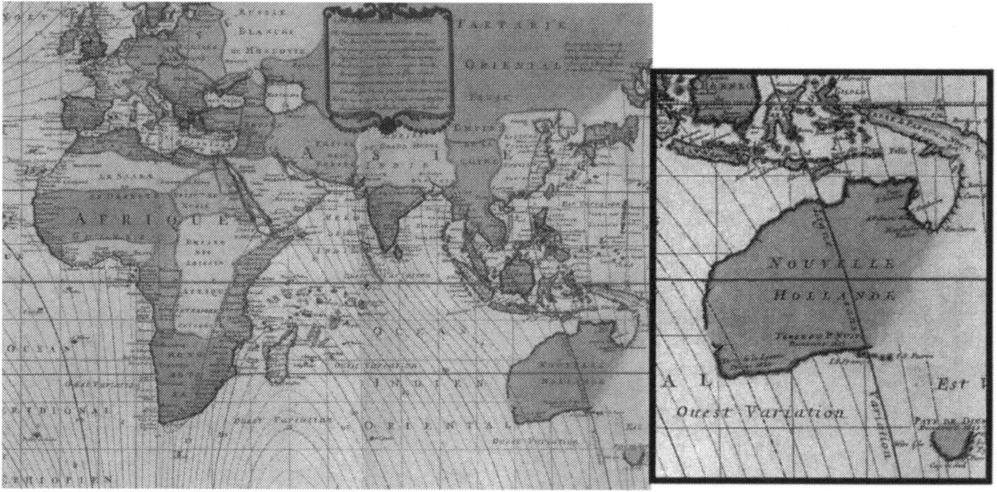

Figure 37

1701 Mortier Australia

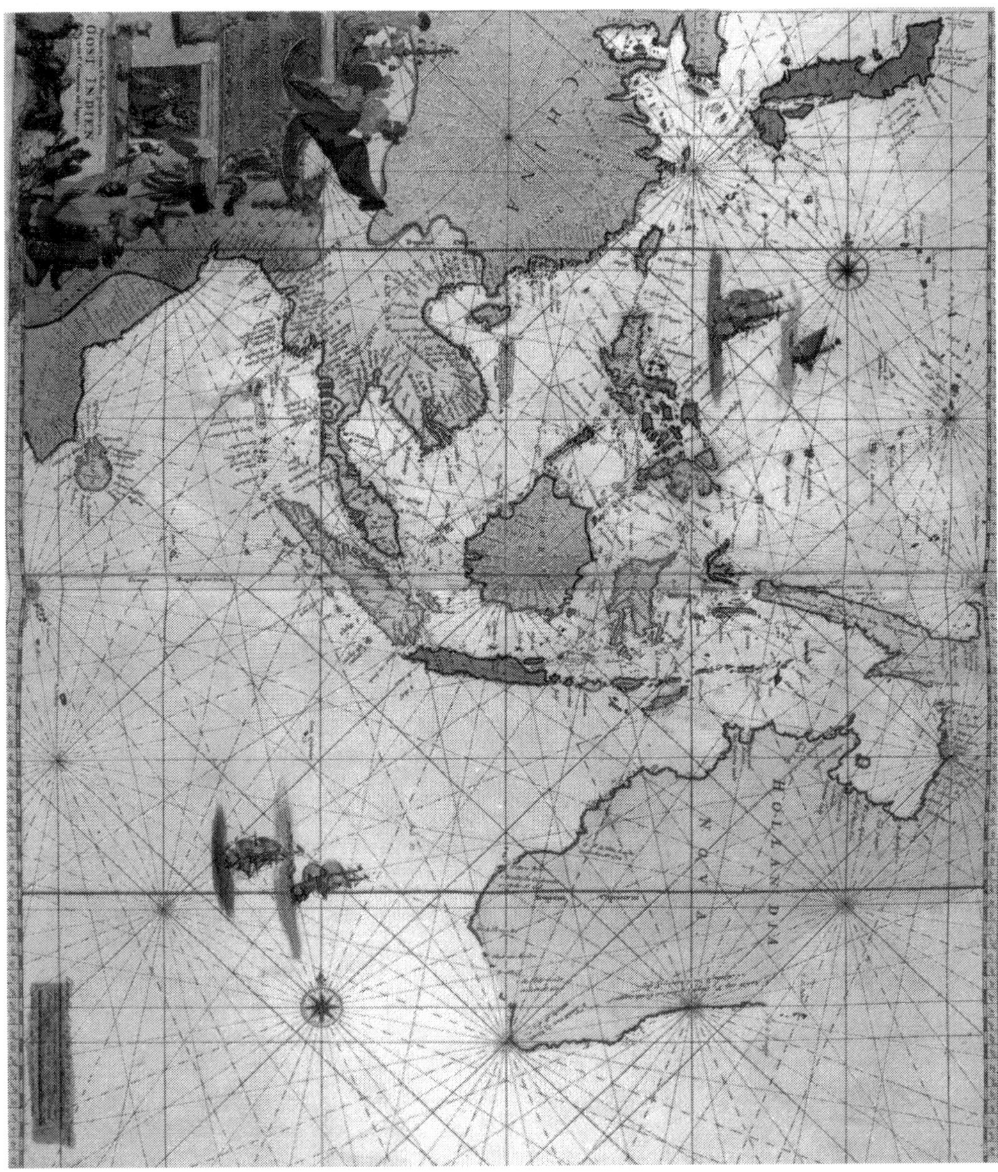

Figure 38

1715 Louis Renard Australia

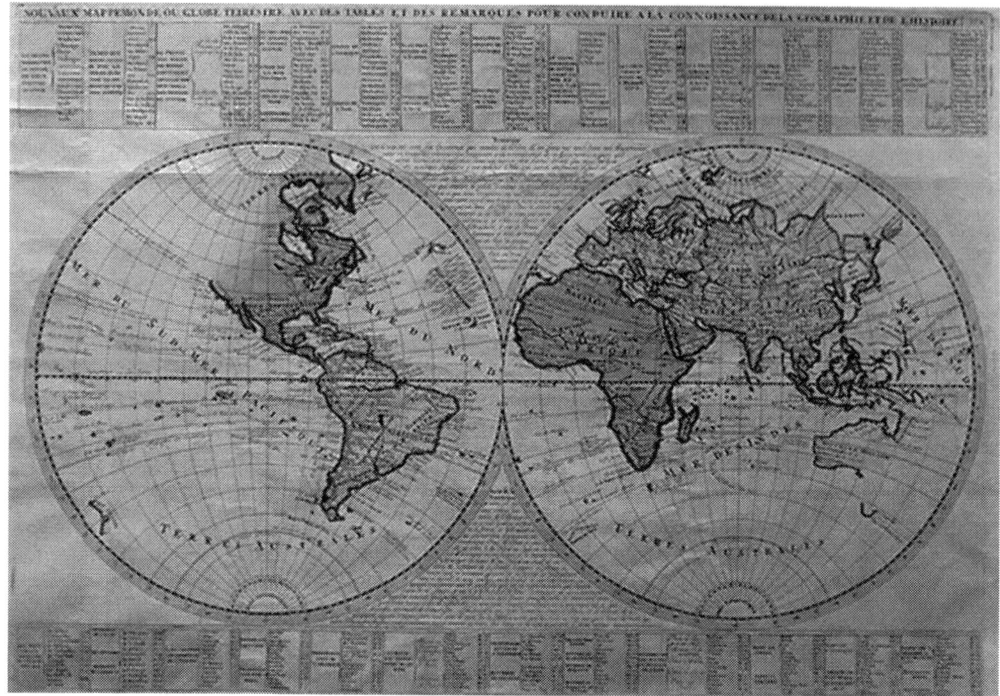

Figure 39

1719 Chatelain Australia

The 1719 Henri Chatelain map shows a partial Australia (Figure 39), but also a southern land block that is detached from the rest of the continent. If European sailors had surveyed this land, it was a unique piece of survey work; one in which an explorer could selectively survey a portion of a continent by blinding oneself to a portion of the coastline. How did the sailors do it, did they blindfold their eyes, sail past the portion of the coastline that they did not want to chart, then opened their eyes again to chart the rest?

Or, is it the plain truth that they got some prototype mapping of Australia, could not interpret a portion of it, or that they got different pieces of the same landmass, but could not quite make out how they pieced together?

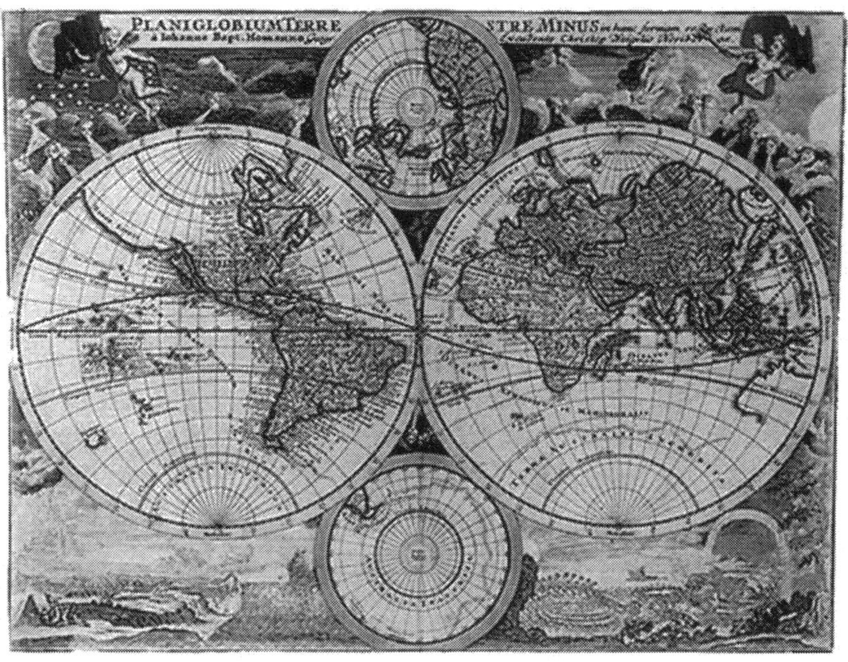

Figure 40

1720 Weigel Australia

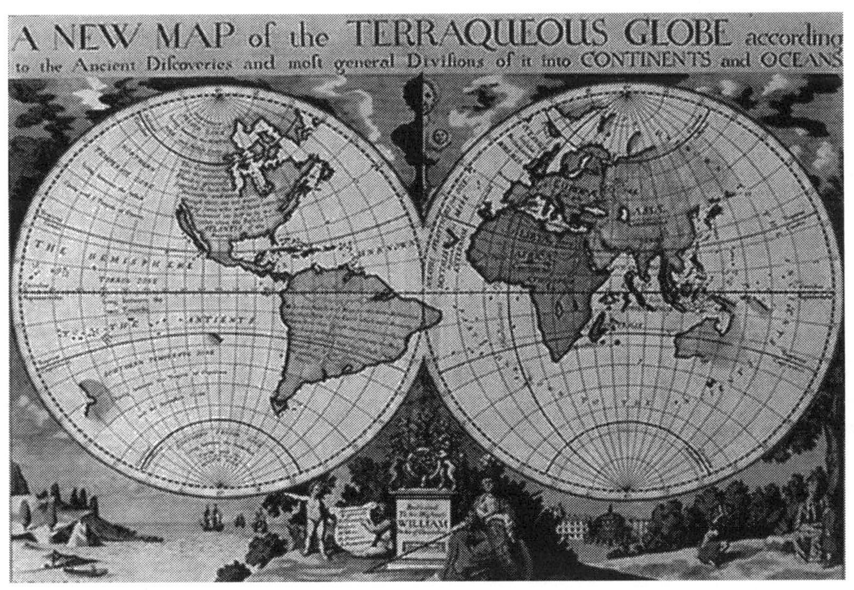

Figure 41

1726 Wells Australia

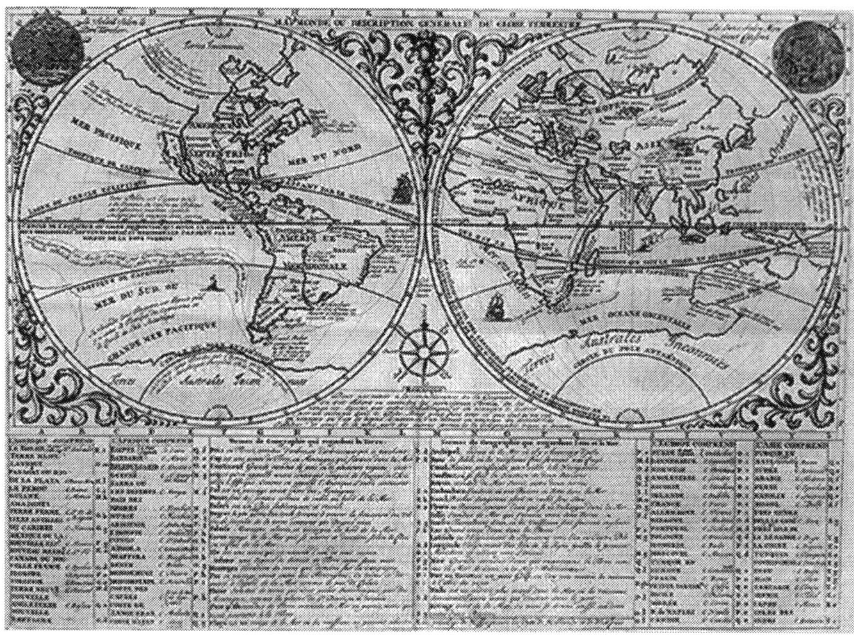

Figure 42

1735 Chatelain Australia

Figure 43

1750 Bellin Australia

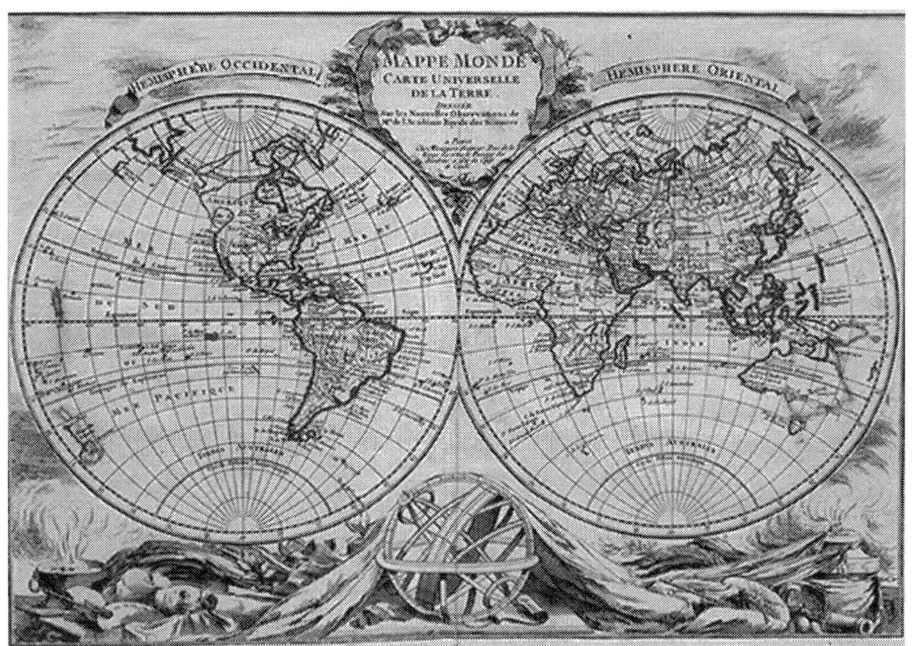

Figure 44

1750 Pierre Bourgoin Australia

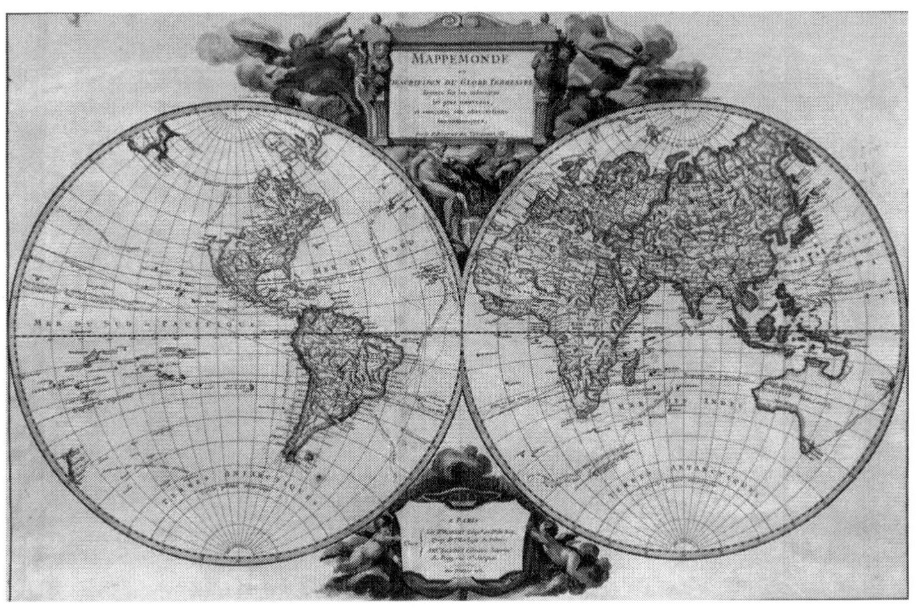

Figure 45

1757 de Vaugondy Australia

Figure 46

1766 Bowen Australia

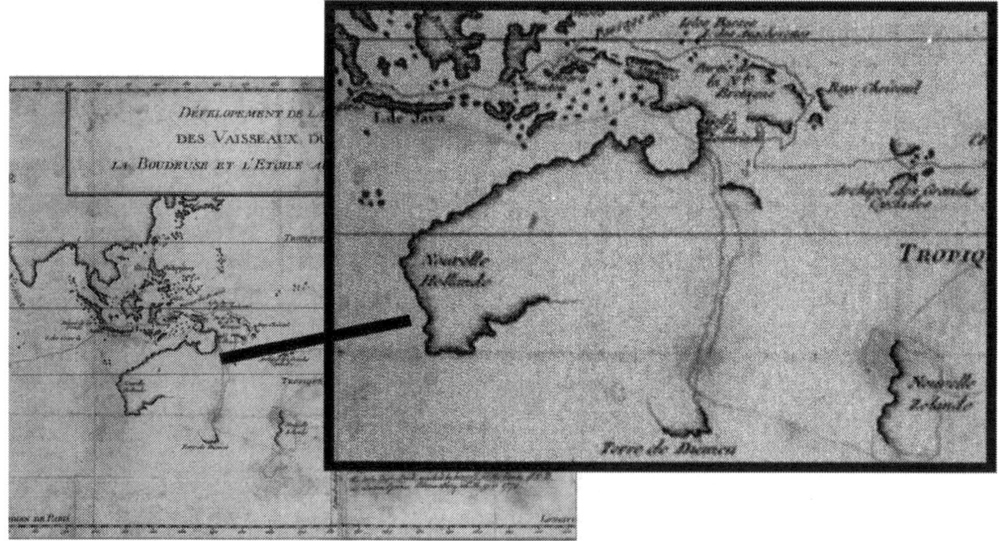

Figure 47

1768 Bougainville Australia

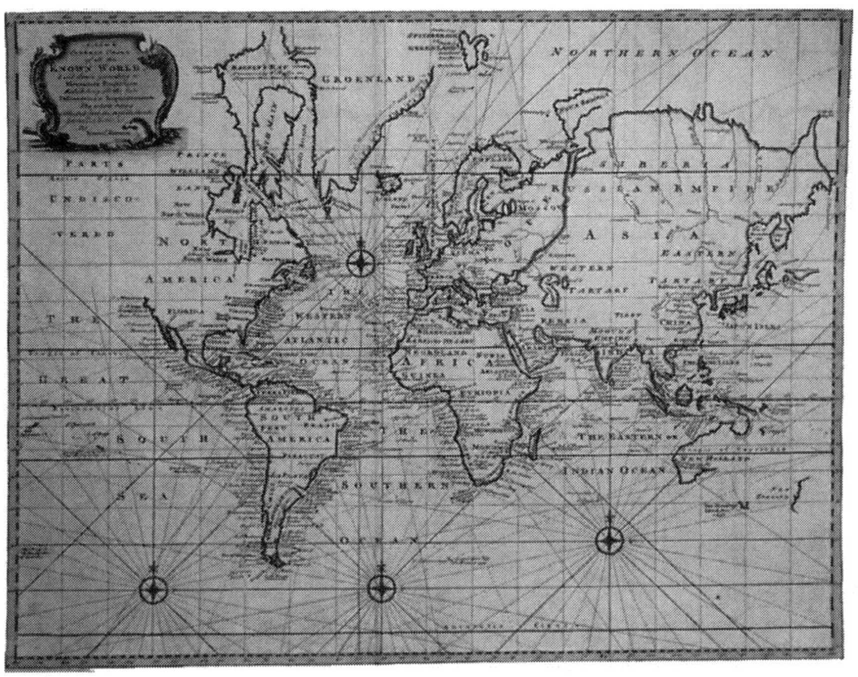

Figure 48

1760 Emanuel Bowen Australia

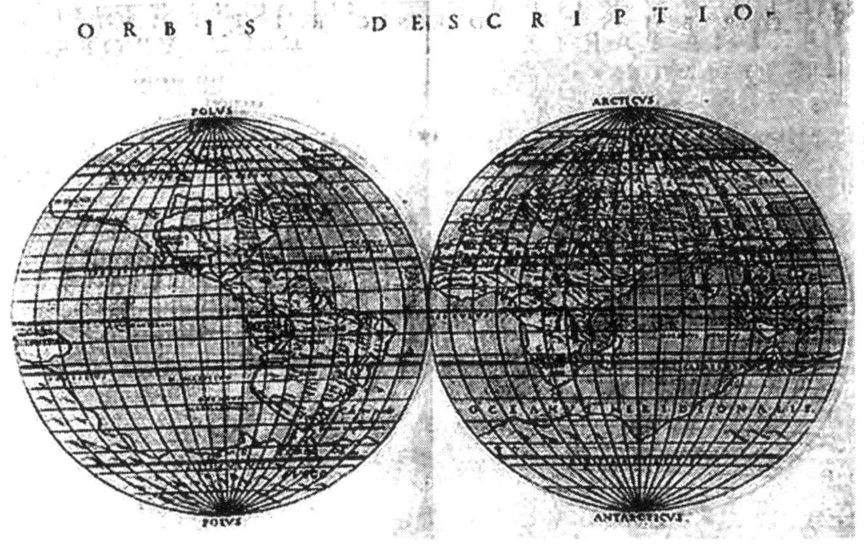

Figure 49

1598 Ruscelli Australia

The 1720 Weigel world map also features a partial Australia (Figure 40).

In 1726, Wells was still drawing a partial Australia (Figure 41 right hand side).

In 1735, Henri Chatelain renewed his effort and produced the map version shown in Figure 42. This time he had Australia attached to Antarctica, which did not exist in his earlier version (compare with Figure 39). What happened? Did some European explorer just go to Antarctica and came back with the new geographical data for the new map, and the explorer saw with is own eyes that the two landmasses were joined together?

All the way until the eve of Captain Cook's historical voyage, European mapmakers continued to turn out various interpretations of Australia (Figure 43 to Figure 48).

In 1766, Bowen decided to simply amputate Australia (Figure 46). It appears that would be the best approach to solving the problem of eastern Australia. This method is apparently favored in the 1776 Gentlemen's Magazine edition as well (Figure 50).

Figure 47 shows the 1768 Bougainville version of Australia. Remember that the first person allegedly to chart Australia, Captain Cook, only surveyed Australia two years later. He obviously had seen or possessed this map, and, in fact, he did. On this map Cook penciled in his own route.

Note that in all these "pre-Cook" maps Australia and New Guinea were linked together, as if there was an isthmus between them. This tells us that the cartographers were creating maps by interpreting a source, not drawing directly from survey data. The reasoning is elementary. If you have been there, you would know that there was no isthmus there, and you would not have drawn it.

These maps cannot all be completely baseless. Evidently someone had surveyed Australia, at least a portion of it, and the data became available at about the time Columbus visited the Caribbean. "At least a portion of it" because all the "Australia"s on the maps were incomplete.

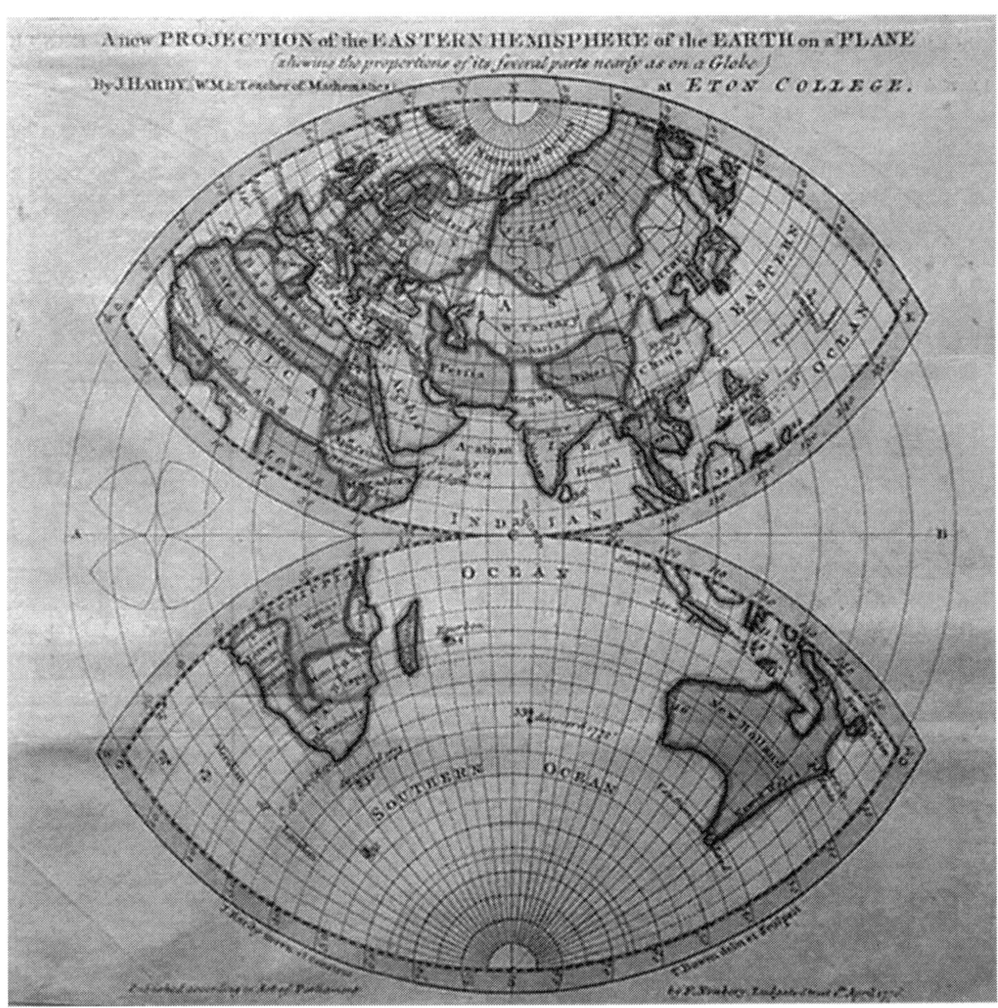

Figure 50

1776 Gentlemen's Magazine Australia

Therefore, it is also possible that the mapmakers only had their hands on fragments of a map of Australia from this mysterious source.

Clearly, European mapmakers had a tradition of drawing partial "Australia"s before Europeans had reached the place.

It is clear that the mapmakers were unsure of what they were drawing. Some solved the problem by linking obviously what is Australia to Antarctica, but they were drawing Australia, nonetheless. Just review the "world" maps above, Figure 17, Figure

20, Figure 24 (showing the southwestern portion of Australia), Figure 29, and so on.

From these old maps, it is clear that European cartographers knew of the Australian landmass way before Captain Cook's historic claim of discovery in 1770. This is not to say that he or European historians lied. For all we know, the landmass was still to be named, and the cartographers had no idea that Captain Cook "discovered" the landmass that they had been drawing for a couple of centuries. Nevertheless, their products; the maps that were seen above, provided indisputable proof that they had prototypes of the landmass in their hands, which were drawn by people who had visited it, surveyed it, and mapped it. We now these were not Europeans. So, we must ask, who were these people?

The Americas

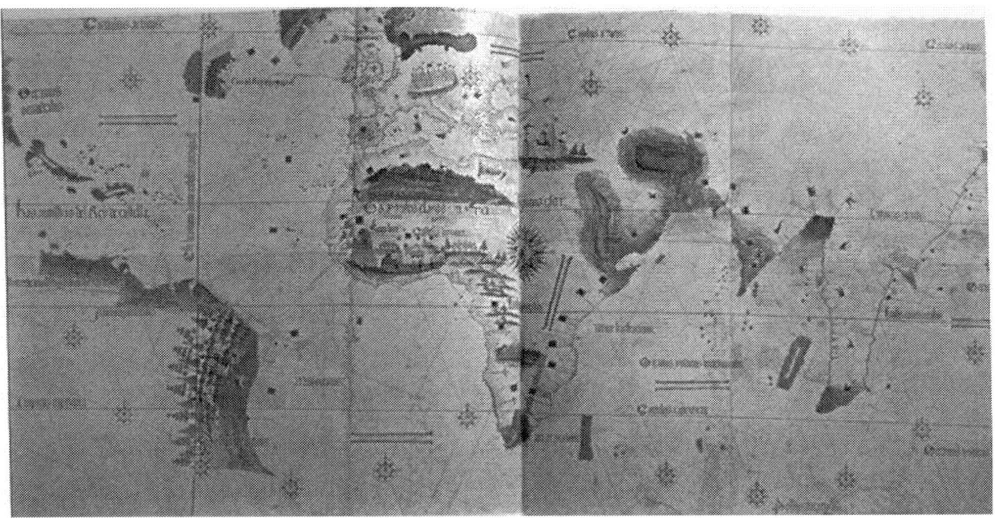

Figure 51

The 1502 Cantino Map

I am sure that you are wise to the gig by now. Nonetheless, for the integrity of science, let us carry on.

Preserved in the Biblioteca Estense of Modena, Italy is a famous Portuguese world portolan map called the 1502 Cantino map (Figure 51), and the history of this map reads like a "whodunit."

In those days of European rivalry on the high seas (ten years after Columbus set sail), maps were hot commodities. Competing nations went to great lengths to safeguard their cartographical possessions while exercising all means to acquire new information in order to enrich their collections. Because of this, countries held on to their navigational charts as we do today with national classified documents; that is, top secrets. The Portuguese protected their charts so tightly that outsiders could not manage to peek at, let alone make copies of them. The Portuguese sailed down the west coast of Africa for 80 years without the rest of Europe knowing what they had.

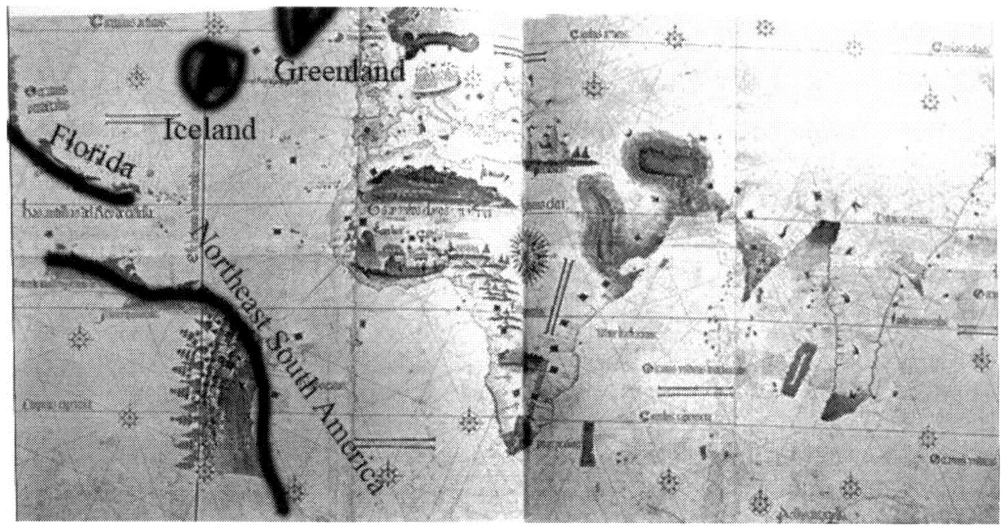

Figure 52

The 1502 Cantino Map Annotated

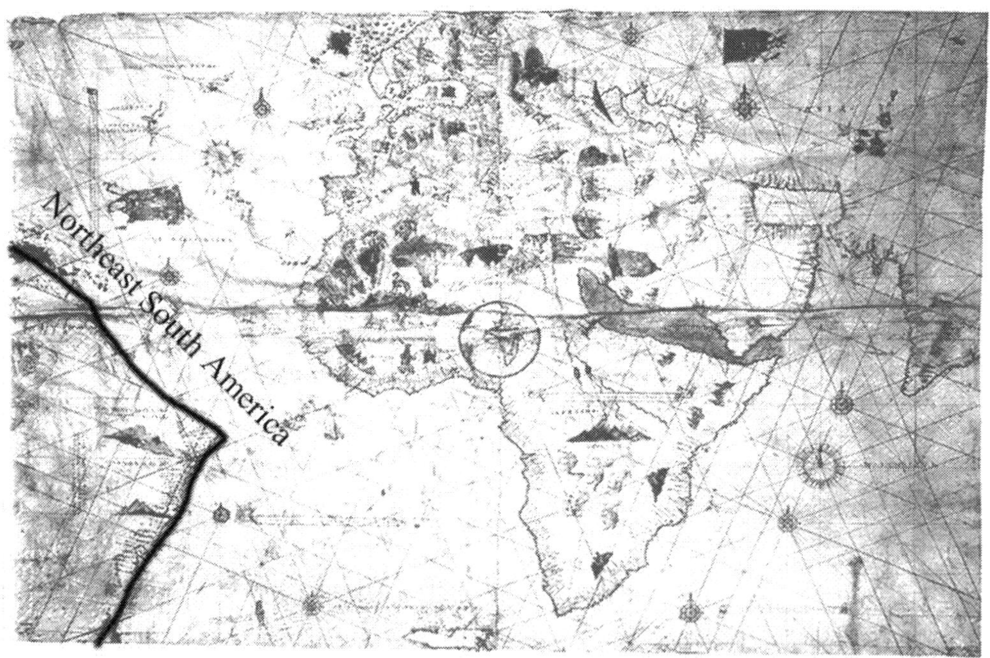

Figure 53

The 1504 Visconte Maggiolo World Map Annotated

Figure 54

The 1504 Visconte Maggiolo World Map

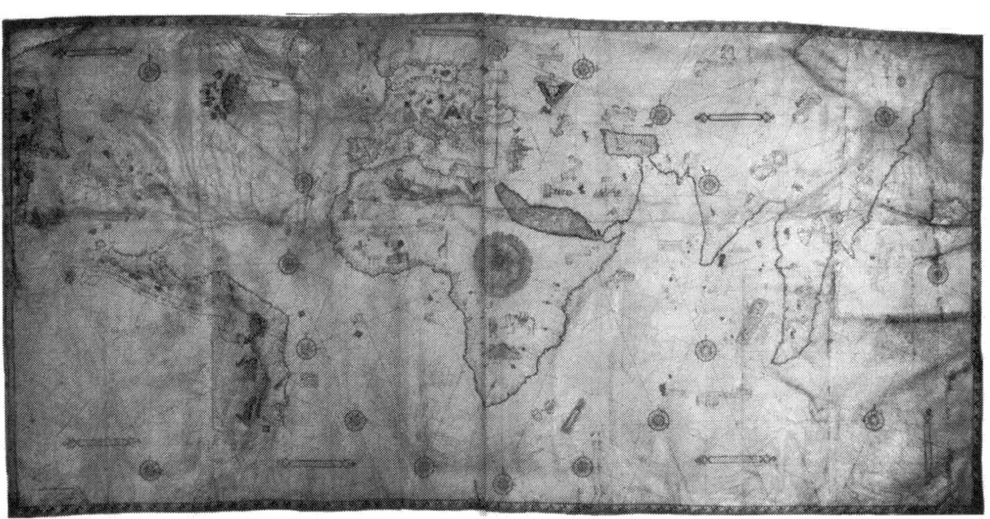

Figure 55

The 1505 Canerio World Map

The creator of the "Cantino" map is unknown, but the date attributed to its creation is year 1502 (Figure 52). It is told that one day in late 19th century, Signor Boni, the librarian of the Biblioteca Estense, passed by a butcher shop owned by a certain Giusti in the Via Farini. He noticed that an ancient map was being used as a lampshade and purchased it. On the backside of the map was a Latin inscription that said: "This navigation chart of the islands recently discovered in the parts of the Indies is presented to the Duke of Ferrara, Ercole d'Este, by Alberto Cantino."[32]

Alberto Cantino was a Lisbon-based agent of Hercules d'Este, Duke of Ferrara of the powerful Italian Este family. In response to the duke's yearning to acquire a map illustrating the latest Portuguese and Spanish maritime exploits, Cantino had one made secretly by a Portuguese cartographer. Who this hired hand was is still being debated, but his or her identity is of no bearing to the present research. In any case, the job took ten months to complete and cost Cantino twelve gold ducats. Cantino took the finished map back to Italy and presented it to his master, who saved it in his archive.

Unfortunately, in 1592, the duke suffered the most unpleasant fate. His entire family and estate were plundered by Pope Clement VIII, who transferred the duke's holdings to his palace in Modena. In 1859, the palace was ransacked by mobs during an uprising and the map disappeared. How it eventually became a lampshade in a butcher shop probably will never be known.

Several features of the map make it unique. The map showed a long, startlingly accurate, but inexplicably broken South American coastline that had yet to be explored. (Christopher Columbus never ventured southward along the South American seacoast toward Brazil.) A long stretch of land to the northwest of Cuba running north and south should be Florida by implication, a land that had not even been discovered by Europeans, let alone explored and surveyed. (Florida was not formally discovered until 1513.)

[32] Carta de navigar per le Isole nouam trovate in le parte de India: dono Alberto Cantino al S. Duca Hercole).

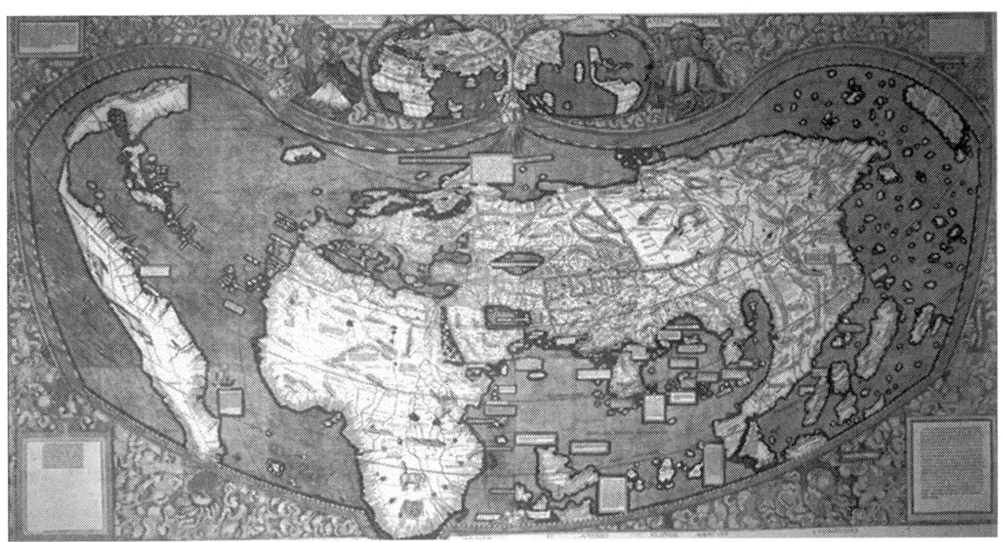

Figure 56

The 1507 Martin Waldseemüller World Map

Then, Greenland and Iceland can be seen by the upper left corner of the map, again drawn before European explorers knew such places existed.

The Cantino map is not the only early 16th century map that includes a highly accurate, albeit incomplete, South America. In the 1504 Visconte Maggiolo world map, a partial South America, almost exactly where Brazil is, completely out of scale, is also depicted (Figure 54, faintly shown in the lower-left corner, and Figure 53).

The 1502 Portuguese world map (Figure 55) by the Genoese cartographer Nicolo Caveri (whom historians called Nicolay Canerio)[33] now at the Bibliotheque Nationale in Paris, France, shows a similar treatment of the South American Continent as the Cantino and Visconte Maggiolo maps, suggesting they either copied from each other or used the same data source or sources for their creations. The Brazilian coastline is just as incomplete, and South America is just as out of scale.

[33] Or perhaps created by a Portuguese cartographer and copied by a Genoese.

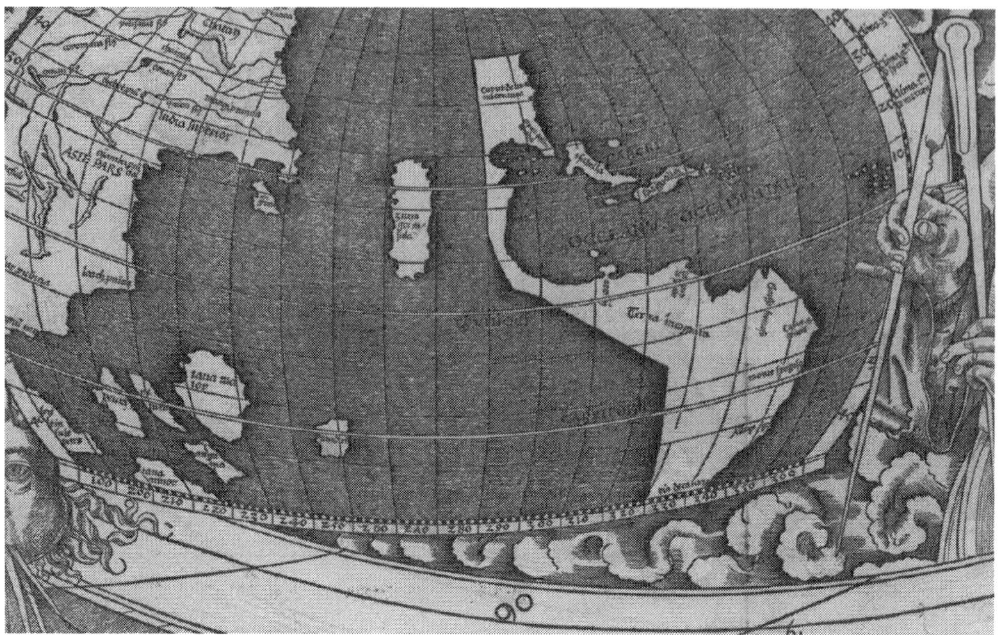

Figure 57

Figure 58

America from the 1507 Martin Waldseemüller Map

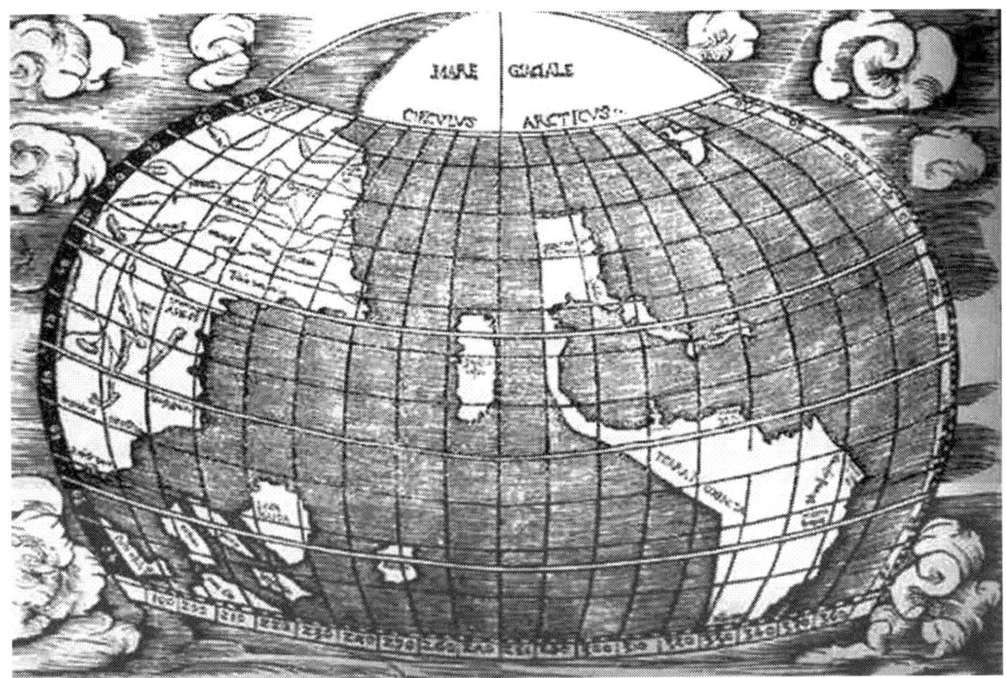

Figure 59

The 1512 Johannes Stobnicza of Cracovia Map

In the tradition of the Cantino and Canerio maps, the 1507 world map (Figure 56) by noted German cartographer Martin Waldseemüller, currently housed at the Wolfegg Castle in Würtemberg, Germany, shows all the same features of the New World as the previous two maps, except that its version of the partial South America is slightly different. This map was rediscovered in 1901 by the person accused of forging the Vinland Map (discussed below), Father Joseph Fisher, in the library of Prince von Waldburg zu Wolfegg-Waldsee at the Castle of Wolfegg, Würtemberg Germany.

If you inspect the right inset at the top of the map (reproduced in Figure 57), you will see Central America represented as an isthmus, which, inexplicably, is missing in the main portion of the map (reproduced in Figure 58), which shows a completely different interpretation of the American continents. It has a passageway to the Pacific.

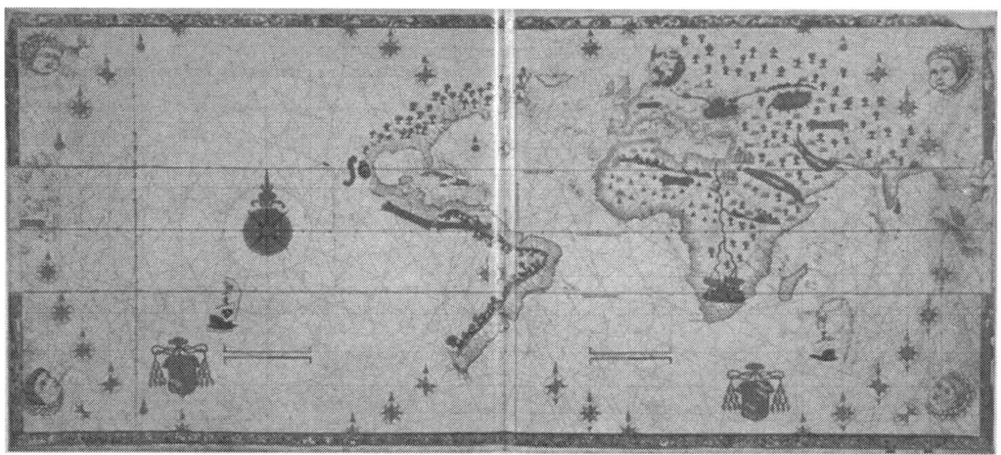

Figure 60

The 1525 Salviati Map

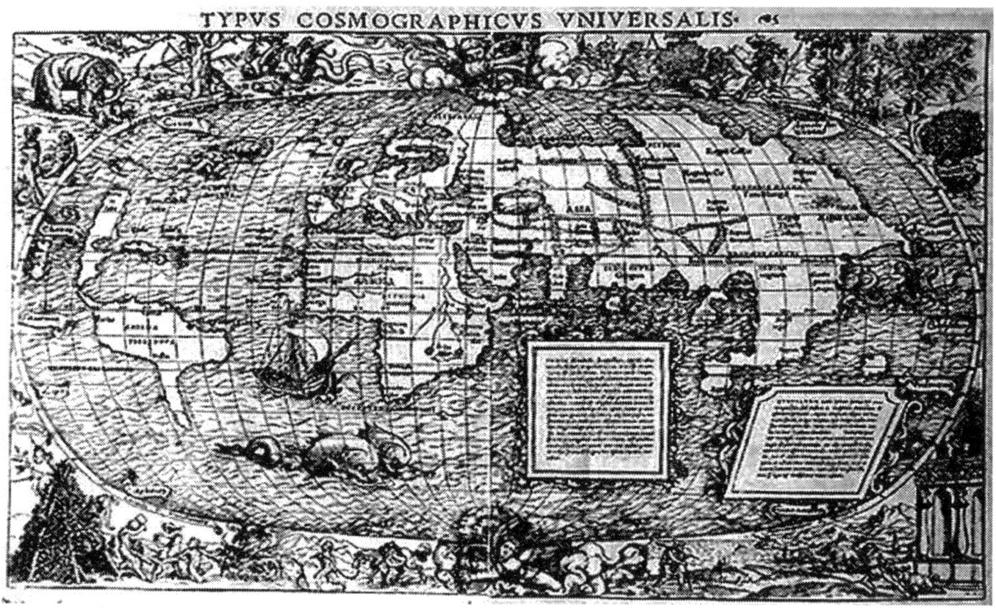

Figure 61

The 1532 Simon Grynaeus Map

How the cartographer knew about the west side of the Americas at the time is most troubling. No European had yet reached the west side of the new American continent. For all we know, whether they knew the new land was a continent was still under debate. This explicit assertion of the existence of the Pacific Ocean is unsettling.

To be succinct, our problem is, before Europeans knew that the land "discovered" by Christopher Columbus was a continent, before Balboa reached the west side of North America in 1513, how did a mapmaker know to draw a body of water there?

Also, the mapmaker knew of another piece of land to the south, but he was not sure if the northern part and the southern part were connected by an isthmus or not. Perhaps his data sources were unclear on this. The different readings represented on the same map are downright unnatural.

Another explanation for this peculiarity is that the mapmaker came into two entirely different source maps for the same landmass, one with an isthmus and one without. Not knowing what to do with them, he simply placed them both on his creation.

Commentators generally describe the representation of the eastern South American coastline as "surprisingly correct general contour." They also conclude that unknown navigators must have sailed along the coast to be able to produce its outline. In other words, this map was not produced using European explorer survey data.

Another disturbing feature is, both the inset and the world map show that the body of water to the west of America (the unnamed Pacific Ocean) is even broader than the Atlantic. The mapmaker could not possibly have known about this fact in 1507, when the "discoveries" of Magellan and Balboa were still to debut.

Now compare the Waldseemüller map with the 1512 Johannes Stobnicza of Cracovia map (Figure 59). We wonder if one mapmaker should be blamed for his errors, or be credited for his brilliance.

If you think these are but a few maps that display the New World before their time, look further.

At the Biblioteca Medicea Laurenziana, Florence, Italy is a map of Brazil called the Salviati map produced in Seville, Spain around 1525-1526 (Figure 60). Its first owner of this map was Cardinal Salviati, the papal nuncio to Spain from 1525-30, thus the name of the map.

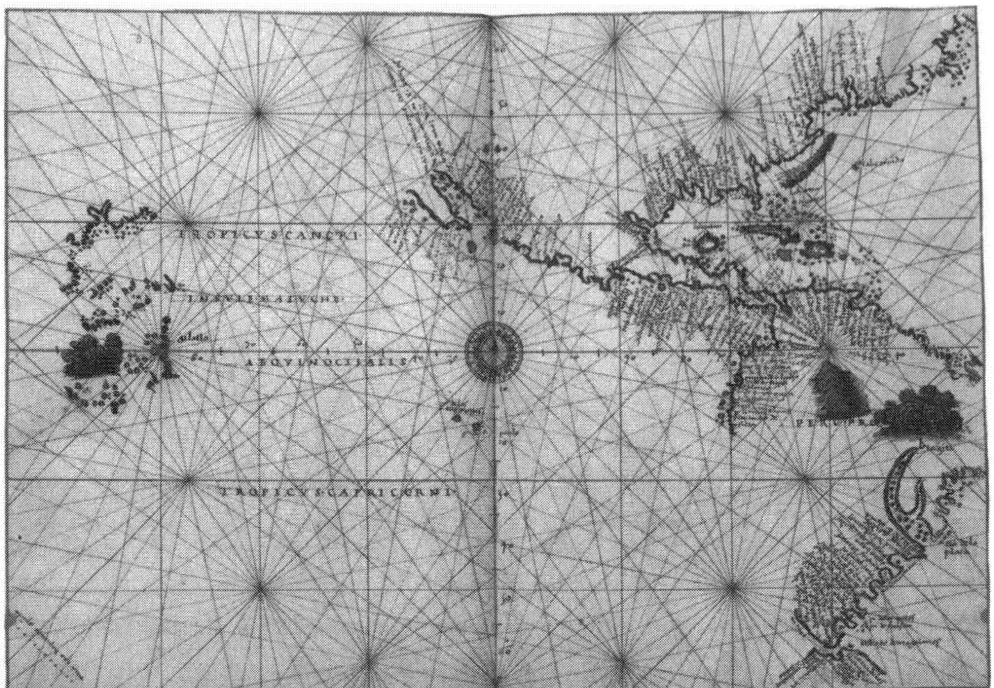

Figure 62

1542 Batiste Agnese Map

The Salviati map shows a partial rendition of the northeastern seacoast of South America and the eastern seaboard of Central and North Americas. The contour of the unfinished South America is chillingly familiar, and huge, much larger than the real thing.

By 1525, Magellan already had passed through his strait, although whatever new information he had of South America his crew had yet to bring home. However, Magellan already had information about the south of the continent in order for him to set sail, yet the Salviati map still shows only the northeast corner of South America. The southern portion is absent. The two events are incongruent.

Note the partial South America on the 1532 Simon Grynaeus map (left-hand side of Figure 61).

Figure 62 (right hand side) shows that cartographer Batiste Agnese was having an equally difficult time handling the mid-section of the eastern South American coast.

From these cartographical relics, we can surmise that apparently the European geographers of the early 16th century were either obsessed with a partial South America but possessed prescient minds to draw such realistic portraits of the continent, or they had recently come into "real" but incomplete, or even incomprehensible survey data of the place. In all cases, they were drawing lands that Europeans had not explored.

Were the data obtained by European explorers? The answer is a definitive no. During the first decade of the 16th century the European explorers were still fumbling along trying to gain a firm footing in their quest. Balboa only reached the Pacific Ocean in 1513. Columbus never went to North America. For these cartographers to draw Iceland and Greenland, they had to have data from elsewhere. Also, they were neither Spanish nor Portuguese. They included Germans and Belgians. Can you imagine the Spanish or Portuguese explorers and governments sharing exploration data with them?

In the early 16th century, European cartographers had access to geographical data of the Atlantic areas before the explorers had visited those places.

Now, let us look at the oceans of the world. Apparently these cartographers were drawing them without having to sail them.

The Oceans

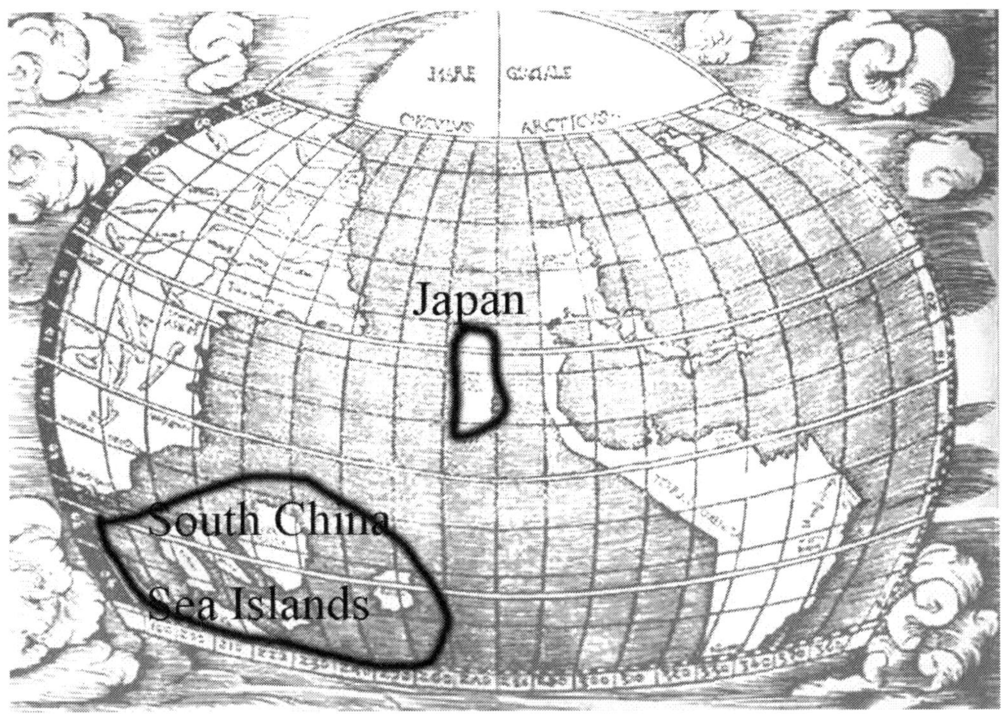

Figure 63

The 1512 Johannes Stobnicza of Cracovia Map

Yes. The European geographers' pre-Age of Discovery fascination with the world was not limited to just the major continents. They were quite familiar with the landscapes—or seascapes—of the world's oceans as well, even before the explorers had a chance to sail them.

The Pacific Ocean

We already have looked over Australia, but these geography enthusiasts were also quite into the Pacific Ocean as a whole.

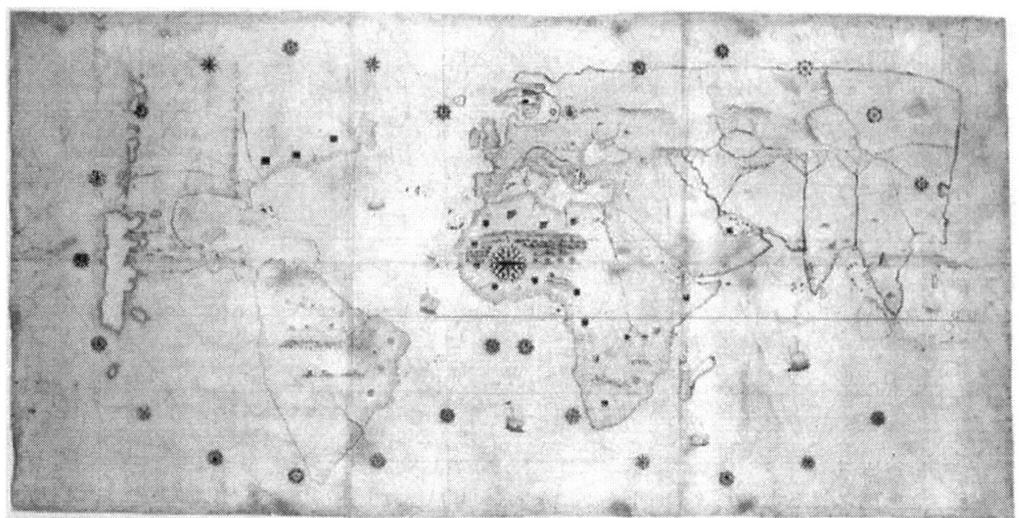

Figure 64

1529 Girolamo da Verrazano Map

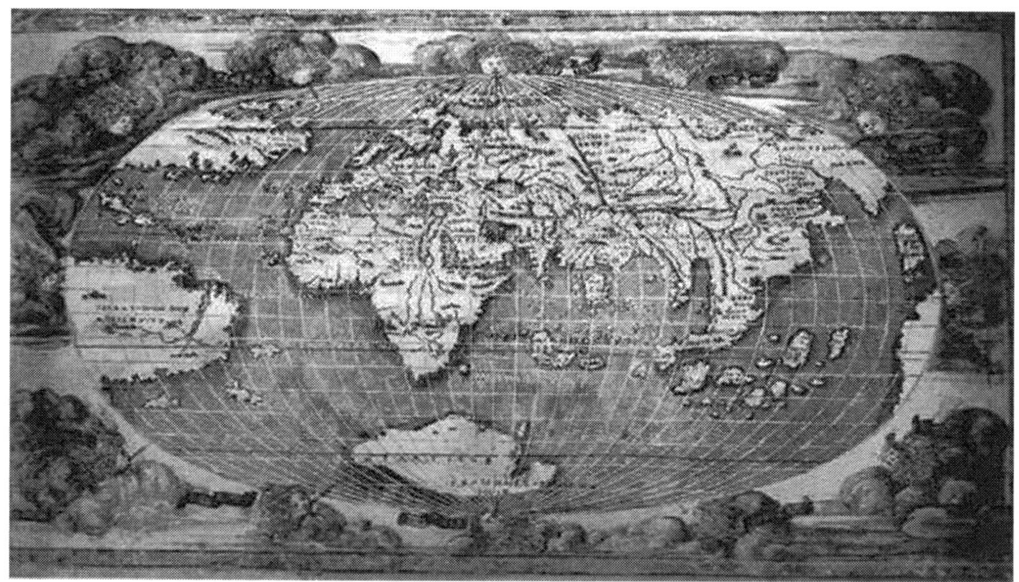

Figure 65

1508 Francesco Rosselli Map

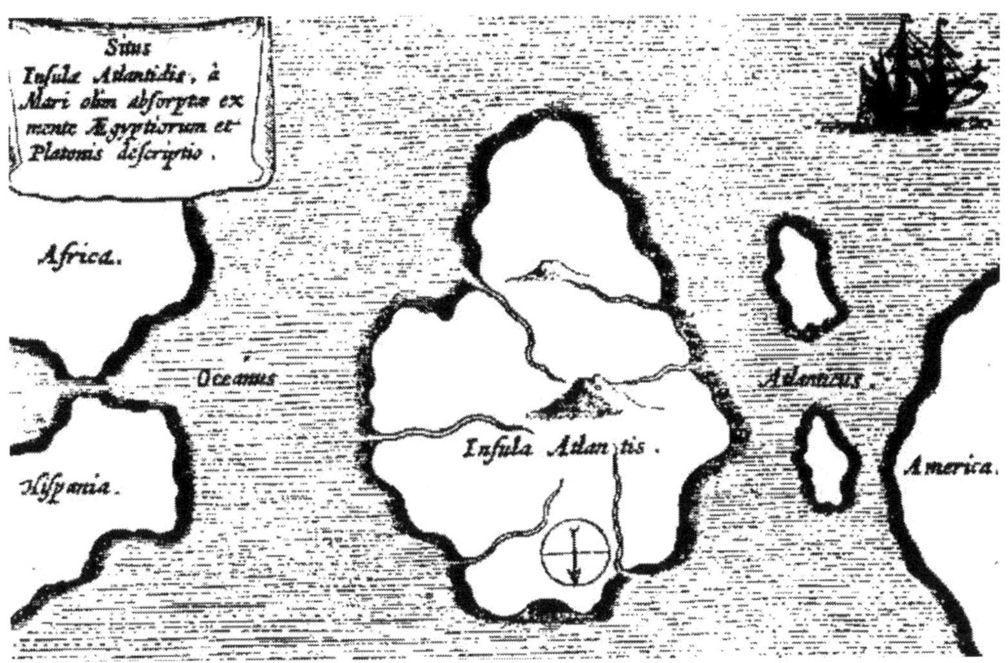

Figure 66

Atlantis on 1666 Athanasius Kircher Etching

For instance, on Johannes Stobnicza of Cracovia's 1512 world map (Figure 59 and Figure 63), not only was Japan clearly suggested west of a partial North America, (again, why partial?) but also a distinctly representative group of landmasses—islands?—in southeast Indian Ocean or southwest Pacific. Where did the mapmaker obtain his partial data?

The 1529 da Verrazano world map shows the same Japan while North America is unfinished. The same is with the 1520 Johann Schoner Globe (Figure 261).

Whether Rosselli was trying to draw Japan (Figure 65 right-hand side) in 1508 is unsure, but an attempt on the southeast Indian Ocean islands (today's Borneo, Sumatra, Java, Australia, New Guinea?) is unmistakable.

It is clear from these old maps that European cartographers knew of the Pacific Ocean way before European explorers sailed it.

The Atlantic Ocean

Most impressive of all is that while we extol the genius of Christopher Columbus for crossing the Atlantic before people even thought it possible, European mapmakers were drawing the lands of the Atlantic in detail.

I mentioned Greenland and Iceland on the Cantino map (Figure 51), but see also the 1569 Mercator map of the North Pole in Figure 14. Greenland shows up at the lower corner. Not only did he draw Greenland at a time before European explorers had surveyed it, how he knew that Greenland was an island is even harder to explain.

In a 1666 Athanasius Kircher etching, which had north pointing downward (note the compass arrow in the chart, Figure 66), Atlantis was firmly wedged between Europe and America in the middle of the Atlantic Ocean. Yet the discerning eye can see that the "Atlantis" recorded here is none other than Greenland, enormously enlarged, of course. Again, Greenland was being drawn before its time. Why, the mapmaker did not even know it was Greenland. He called it Atlantis.

What do all these medieval maps suggest? They suggest that European cartographers already had information about the Atlantic Ocean at the time of Christopher Columbus.

Finally, we come to Asia.

Asia

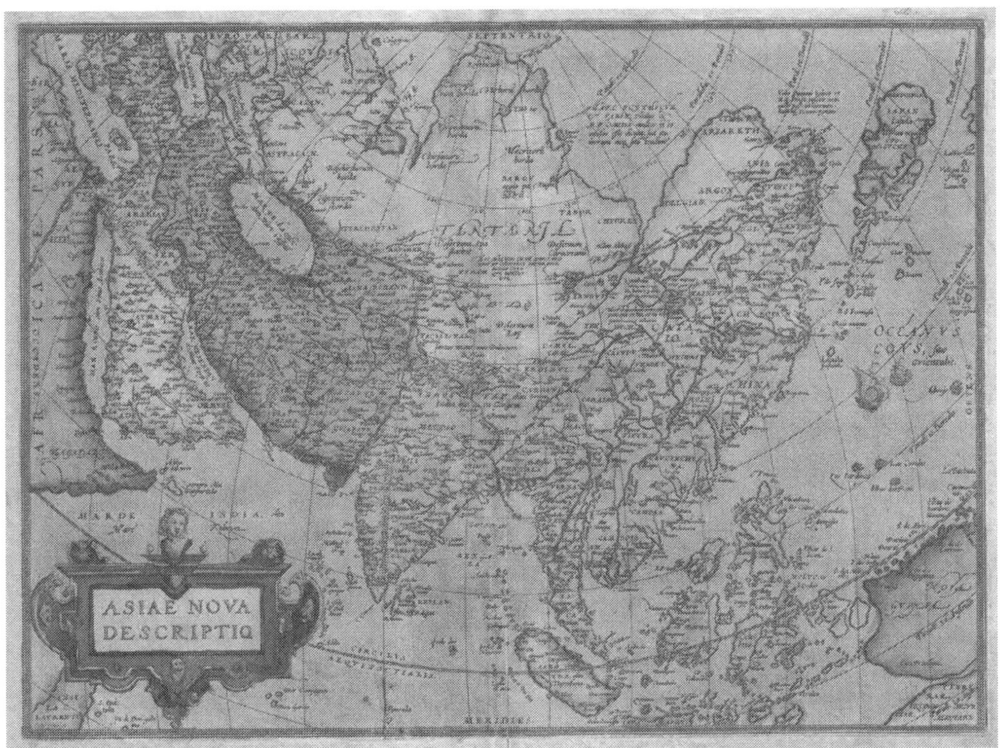

Figure 67

1570 Ortelius Map of Asia

Let us now probe eastward, to a place always considered by Europeans as mysterious and inscrutable, a place Europeans did not penetrate until the 19th century.

Figure 67 shows a 1570 Ortelius map of Asia. Look at the details of Siberia, a place known to the Mongols who conquered China and established the Yuan Dynasty, but not to Europeans of the Middle Ages. The map showed rivers and land features including forests and deserts, but we know of no European explorers of the likes of Columbus and Balboa and De Soto that had gone to explore the interiors of Asia.

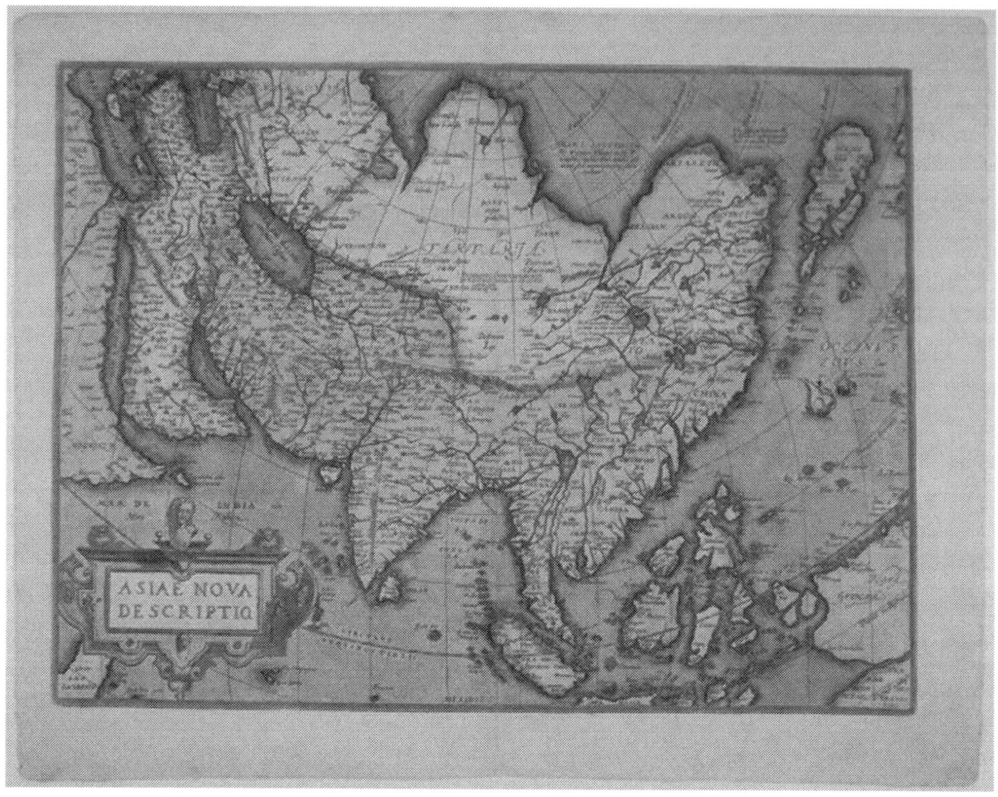

Figure 68

1592 Ortelius Map of Asia

Figure 68 is another such map of Asia made in 1592.

Figure 69 is a map of Asia by the German cartographer Sebastian Münster (1488 - 1552).

Figure 70 is a map of Asia by the Dutch cartographer Willem Janszoon Blaeu (1571 –1638).

There are many more such antique maps in existence. European cartographers had detail data about Asia before the land was visited. The key question is, where did these cartographers get their geographical data? Certainly not from European sources.

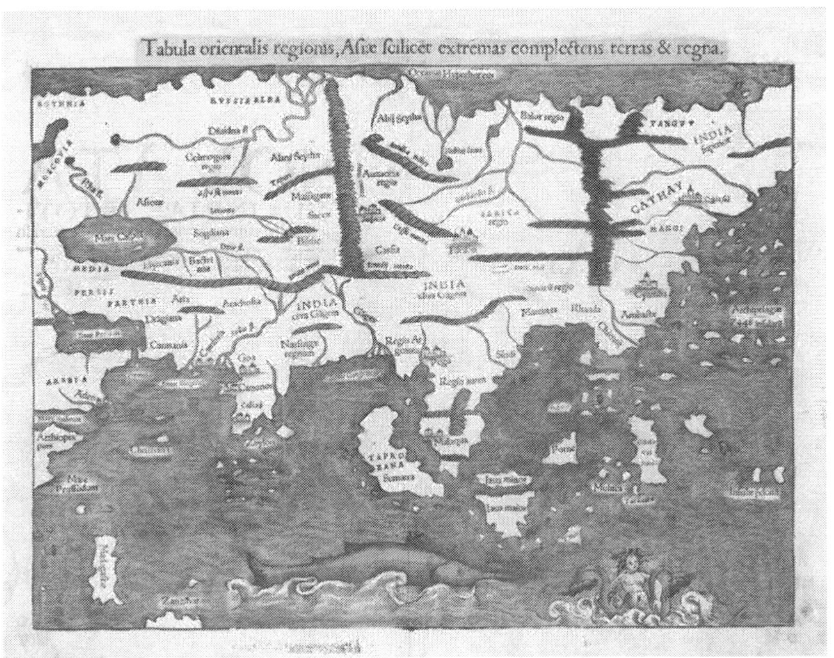

Figure 69

Münster Map of Asia

Figure 70

Blaeu Map of Asia

The World

Figure 71

1570 Abraham Ortelius Map

The fact is, these maps suggest that by no later than the second half of the 16th century all the landmasses and major islands in the world had been discovered and surveyed, without European explorers doing the work. Indeed, this all can be summarized by a couple of famous Renaissance/Age of Discovery European maps.

These are the 1570 Abraham Ortelius world map (Figure 71) and the Mercator map of 1569 (Figure 72), which are basically reproductions of each other. Europe, Asia, Africa, the Americas, Australia (the lump on the left-hand side of the maps), the North Atlantic islands, and the poles are all there.

Figure 72

1569 Mercator Map

The questions of interest now are, where did these medieval European mapmakers obtain their geographical data of the world, and who were the suppliers of the data. We aim to find out.

Conclusions

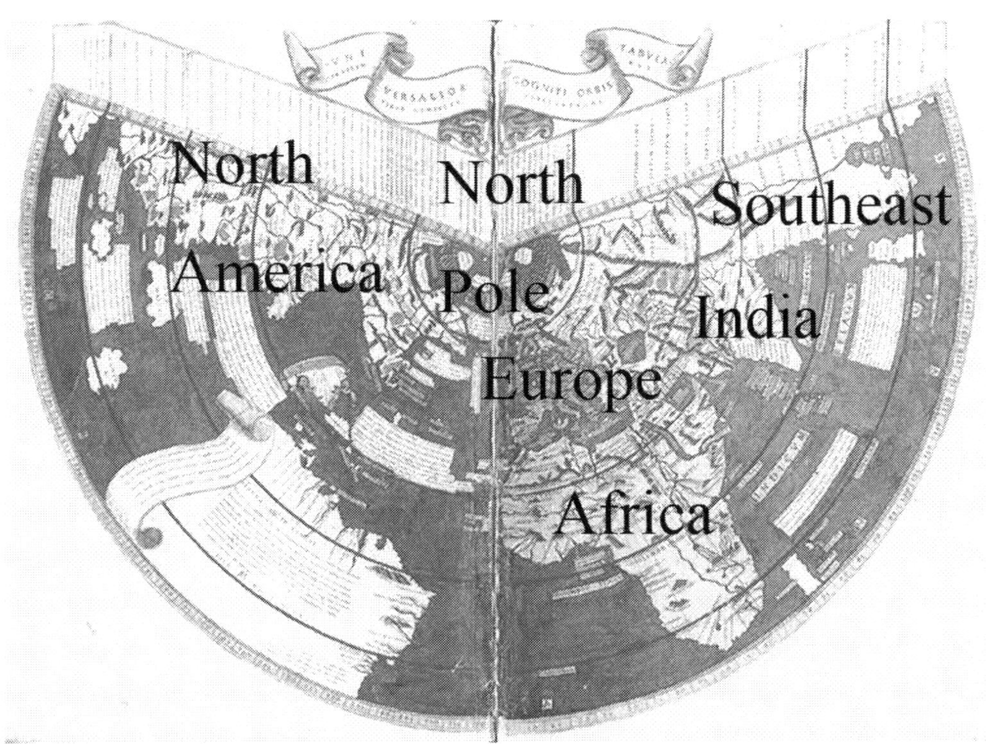

Figure 73

1507 Ruysch Map Annotated

It must be born in mind that history teaches us that the Age of Discovery or Age of Exploration began with the Portuguese taking to sea in the 15th century. Bartolomeu Dias commanded a Portuguese ship in 1481 to the African gold coast and subsequently went beyond the southern tip of Africa to enter the Indian Ocean. His feat was followed by Christopher Columbus in 1492, three years later. If we need to stretch it, we may push back all the way to Prince Henry, whose seamen began to sail down the western coast of Africa in early 15th century.

Evidence shows, however, that while these great seafarers were struggling in their quests, European cartographers were publishing maps of the world featuring places that were supposed to be unknown to them. That was an impossible feat.

The cartographical masterpieces presented above, and many more of the same ilk, are still in the world's collections. That leaves no doubt that European mapmakers knew about the geography of the world, no matter how flawed their interpretations, before the Age of Discovery surveyors had mapped them; someone or some people had sailed and mapped the world in ancient times before the great European discoverers, and somehow this knowledge fell into the hands of the Europeans.

This conclusion is based on tangible facts, therefore is not up for debate. If this conclusion, based entirely on facts, cannot be accepted by the reader, he likely would be ushered off the jury panel, and, in such cases, there would be no reason for us to proceed further. The entire research would be meaningless. Should you decide to continue on, be prepared for more of such irrefutable evidence.

Europeans began going to sea in late 15th century, and spent the next four centuries exploring the world. The Portuguese and Christopher Columbus started it. Yet, since right from the beginning, European geographers and cartographers had been drawing maps and giving descriptions to these places, which had yet to be surveyed, and doing them accurately. It is not rocket science. Indeed, it is elementary logic. The evidence is plainly there. They had information on them, or they would not be able to draw their fabulous maps! Since the European explorers had yet to do their job, the information had to have come from outside. The question is, from where, and by whom? The explanations follow.

As we move on, we proceed with the conclusion, now a given, that Europeans were not the first to explore the world. Some other people did and, whoever they were, they provided the geographic data of the world for the European Age of Discovery explorers. We will not need to prove this point again.

The issue that now confronts us is, who these early surveyors were, and where such geographical data came from.

The Chinese Did It

European mapmakers had access to geographical information of the world before the commencement of the Age of Discovery. This has been amply affirmed. The evidence is widely available. What is amazing is that no historian seems to have seen it, let alone offering up explanation for them. At the time of these evidence, however, it was not widely known, so they went unchallenged. Only a few got on to the gig, and they benefited from it. None the less, that this thread, if it existed, has completely disappeared. I still find it extraordinary that no historian has pointed to one of these "oddities" and exclaimed, "but that is Chinese!"

Hence, we now seek the source or sources of such data. This process is an investigation of its own standing, and any conclusion, or even speculation on Europeans having learned it from the Chinese, at this point, is premature.

No matter how much one may be tempted to draw such a conclusion, merely because China happened to be the only civilization in the world at the time to have possessed the wherewithal to accomplish such a task—not the Norse, not the Muslims, not the Indians, and not the Africans—and that Admiral Zheng He's expeditions had just taken place only a few years back, we must investigate and determine the source on its own merit, based on evidence. For this, we shall return to the same historical documents for signs of identifiable ownership signatures. Therefore, let us get to the analyses post haste.

It is a fundamental truism that a copy cannot surpass the original in accuracy, or it would not be a copy. Indeed, almost all copies are inferior to their originals because of mishaps that occurred during the copying process.

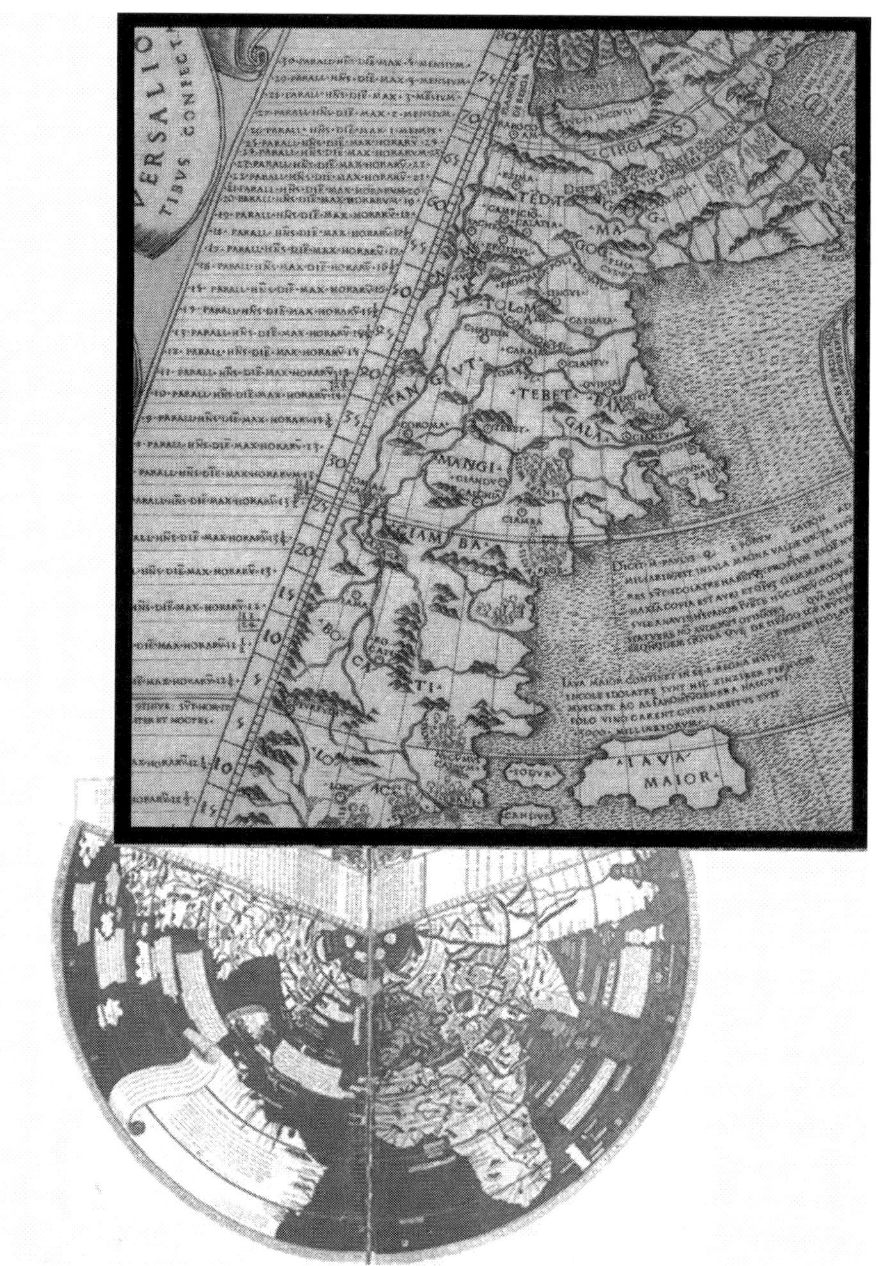

Figure 74

1507 Ruysch North America

A copy also often retains some fragments of the original which show up out of context in the copy due to the copier's lack of knowledge about the data. From such fragments of slip-ups, the identity or identities of the original specimen sometimes can be ascertained, and such data residues from the antique European Age of Discovery maps unequivocally point to China as the origin of the world geographic data.

The Americas

Figure 75

Historic Map Showing Tangut, Khitai, and Song China

One of the distinctive characteristics of the early pre-Age of Discovery European maps presented above is an overt fascination with the American continents before their time (See Figure 51, Figure 54, Figure 55, Figure 56, Figure 59, and Figure 61, among others). It is interesting to note that these early renditions were almost uniformly incomplete, with indications of initial familiarity confined to northeast South America and southeast North America, at best. Although the later maps show a gaining of awareness toward southern America, they do not suggest the mapmakers knew they were drawing continents. Eventually a complete South America emerged, but it was a long time before North America was completed.

Chinese Place names

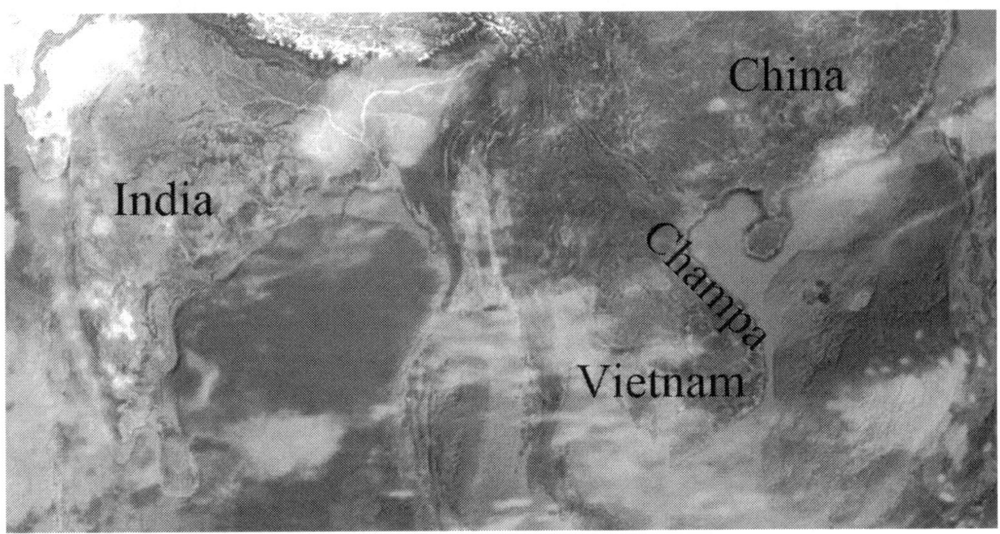

Figure 76

Location of Champa on a Modern Map

Whereas these map masters of the early days of the Age of Discovery showed great dexterity in their craft, drawing geographical images of stunning likenesses to their prototypes without having visited or surveyed them, they had in fact no contextual conceptions of the places they were drawing.

Figure 12 shows the 1507 Ruysch world map. If the contents of the map elude you, let me annotate it for you, as in Figure 73. As you can see, the mapmaker was looking straight down at North Pole from space, in 1507, barely 10 years after Columbus first reached the Caribbean Sea.

Yes, the mapmaker also thought that North America was an extension of Asia. He had no concept of a Pacific Ocean, as was generally understood at the time among the intelligentsia, including the great Italian cosmographer Paolo dal Pozzo Toscanelli, who provided an America-less map for Christopher Columbus (see below).

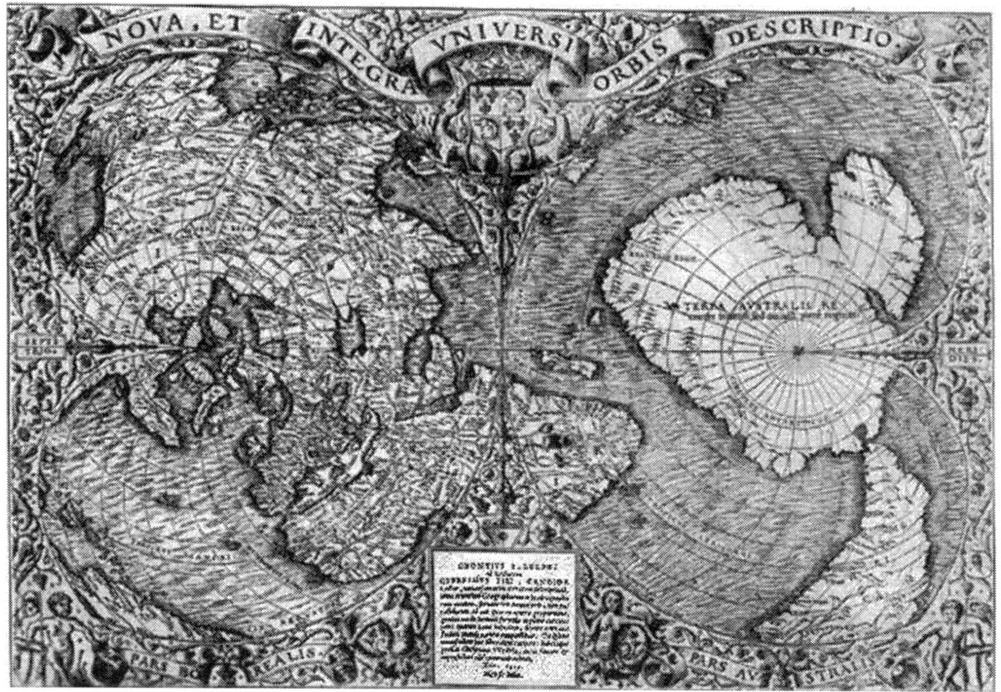

Figure 77

1531 Oronce Finé World Map

Let us now zoom in on North America and inspect the details there. An enlarged view of Ruysch's North America is presented in Figure 74. The names Tangut, Tebet, Mangi, Ciamba, Iava (Java) Major, and even Gog and Magog are clearly seen. What are these names? Unless you are an oriental history afficionado, you may not be familiar with them.

Catay (Cathay today) is China. It was how China's western neighbors called it. How did China become Cathay? China was never Cathay. The name Cathay is the corruption of the name Khitai (Figure 75), a people who founded the nation Liao that existed some 1,000 years ago to the northeast of China. After being defeated by the Jurchen, Khitai fled to Central Asia where they established the state of Kara Khitai. To the people of Central Asia these Khitai people looked just like the Chinese, so through ignorance they equated Khitai with China. Today Kitay is still Russia's name for China.

Figure 78

1531 Oronce Finé World Map Inset

Mangi was the name the Mongols gave to Southern Song China. That was discussed above when we went over the history of the Mongols briefly. Manzi[34] in Chinese means barbarians. Originally it was used by the Chinese to designate the natives of southern China. After the Mongols had conquered China, they began using the name to describe the defeated Chinese. Such a name is typical on a Yuan (Mongol) Dynasty map.

Tangut was the name of the people of Xixia, a kingdom to the northwest of China annihilated by Genghis Khan.

Tebet is Tibet.

---

[34] 蠻子.

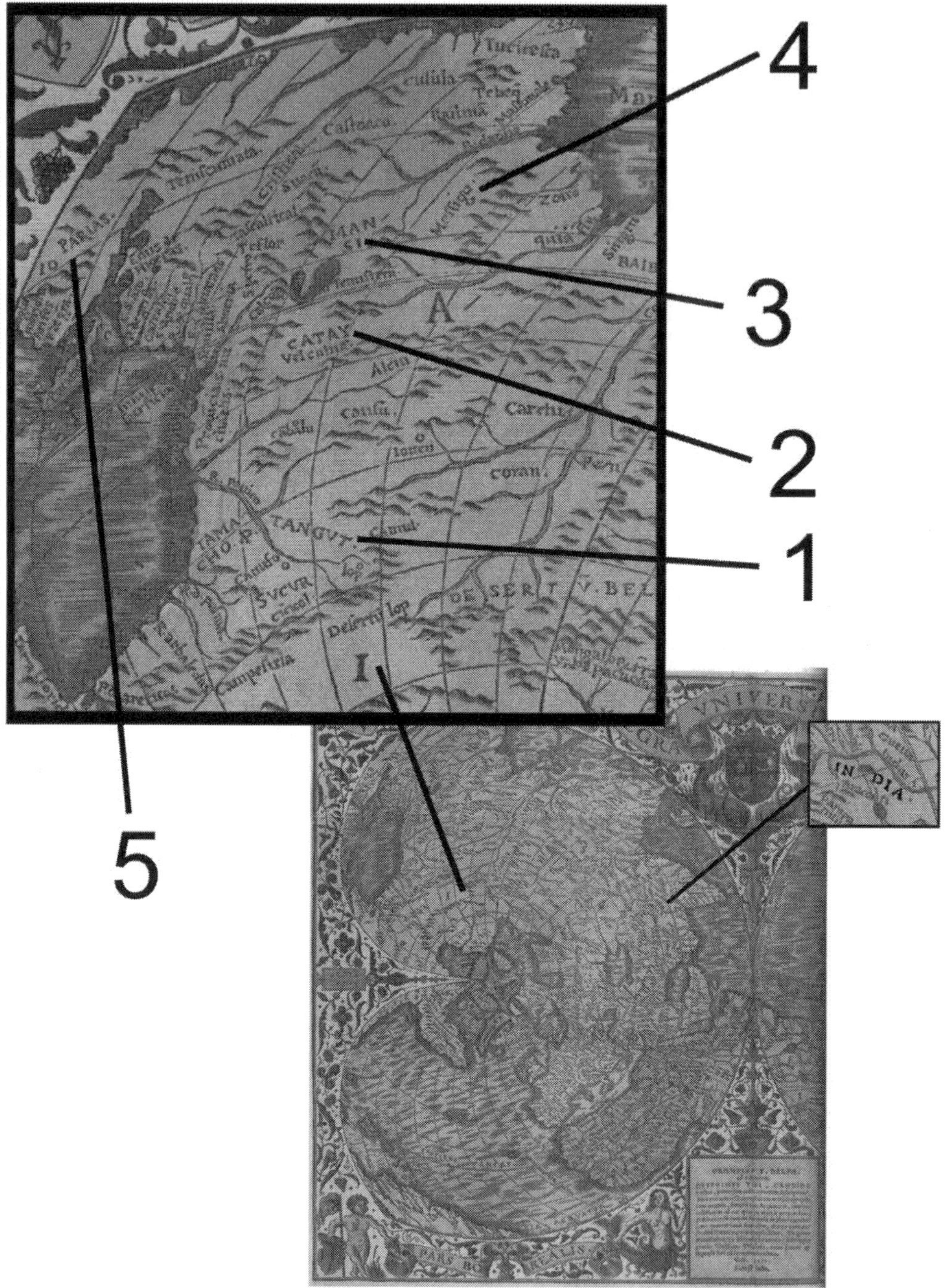

Figure 79

1531 Oronce Finé World Map

Figure 80

1536 Oronce Finé World Map

Ciamba, spelled Champa[35] today, was a state at where today's Vietnam is (Figure 76).

The fact these names were allocated to North America demonstrates an ignorance of world geography at the highest order and the confusion of the newly acquired geographical knowledge of the world on the part of the mapmaker. Nonetheless, these names betrayed the source of the map data.

French mathematician and cartographer Oronce Finé drew a world map in 1531 (Figure 77). Its North America is shown in Figure 78.

---

35 占婆.

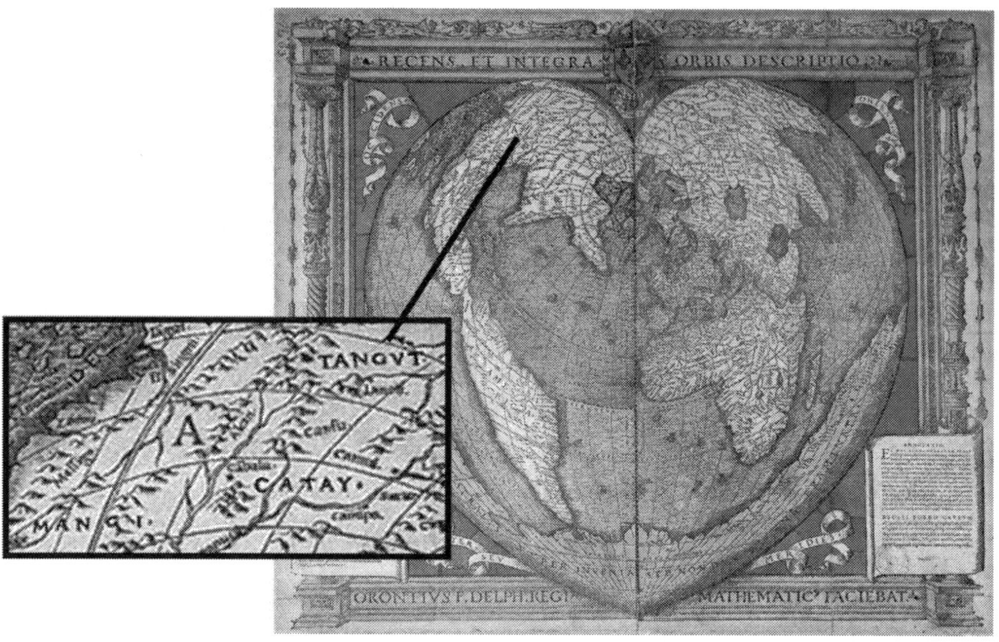

Figure 81

1536 Oronce Finé World Map

If you look at the map close enough (Figure 79) you will see 1. Tangut, 2. Catay, 3. Mansi; that is, Manji or Mangi, but also 4. Messigo (upper corner Figure 78) and 5. Rio Parias.

Next, look at Figure 80, the 1536 Oronce Finé map. In this map there is no Pacific Ocean between Asia and America either. Again, America is drawn as an extension of Asia.

Now, refer to Figure 81, the details of a portion of the "North America" from this 1536 Oronce Finé map of Figure 80. They clearly show the names Catay, Mangi, Tangut, and other Asian; that is, Chinese place names.

Messigo is Meshico, or another way of spelling Mexico. The natives pronounce "Mexico" "Meshigo," almost exactly as how the Chinese transliterate it, Mo Xi Ge.[36]

---

36 墨西哥.

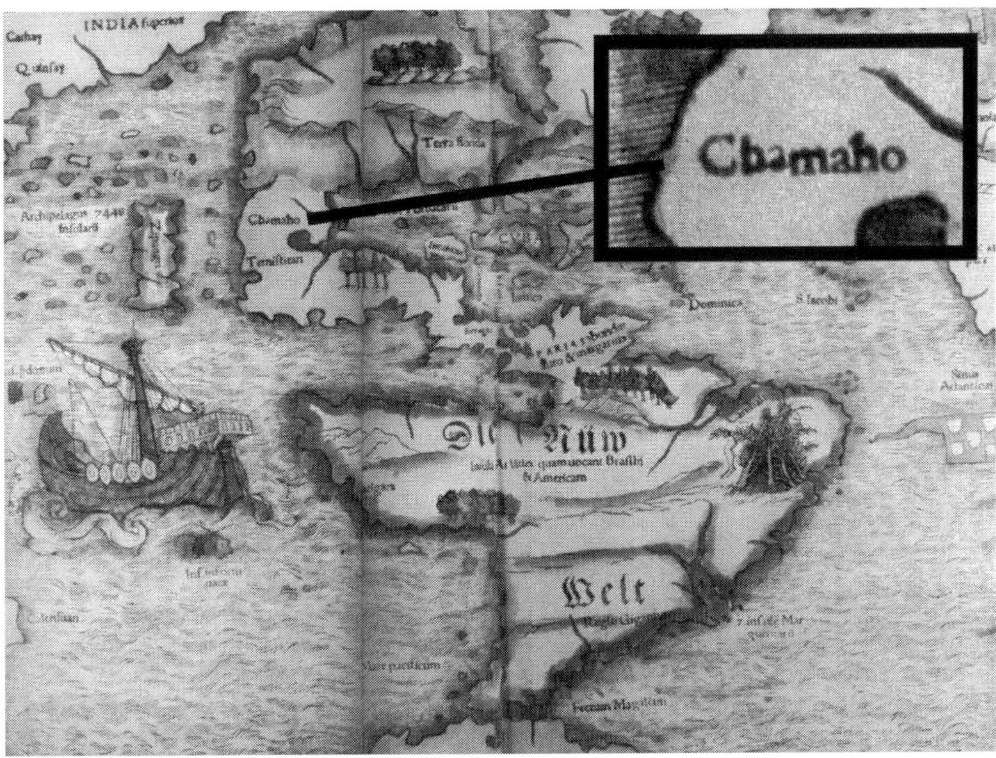

Figure 82

1575 Sebastian Munster Map showing Chamabo in America

Rio Parias is the northern South American river. Thus Mexico, Venezuela, and China coexisted as neighbors on the same continent. I have enlarged this portion of the map in Figure 78 to help you view these names.

Not only did the mapmaker include Asian-Chinese names on his map, he had Asia and America fused into one as conjoined twins. This reveals to us the fact that he had no idea what he was drawing; that he was not basing his map on actual survey data. He was composing his map interpreting a source or sources and getting the data terribly mixed up.

Figure 82 shows a 1575 map of the Americas by the German cosmographer Sebastian Munster. He certainly was convinced that a place in North America was named Chamabo (Champa). See also Chamabo in Figure 83 (lower-right corner).

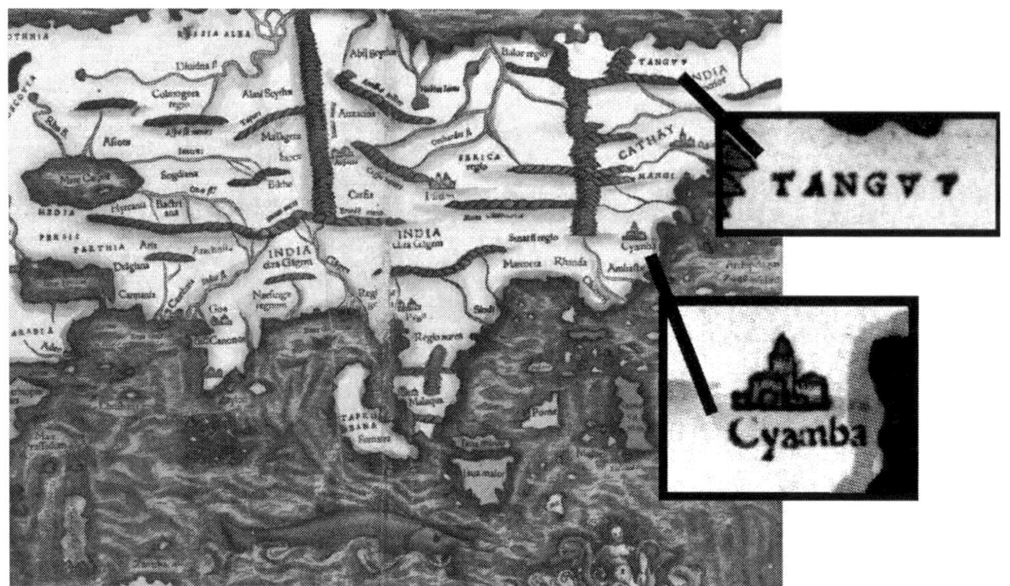

Figure 83

1550 Sebastian Munster Asia

Figure 83 shows the names Tangut and Cyamba on Sebastian Munster's 1550 map of Asia. This time Cyamba was moved to Asia, correcting the earlier error.

The placement of these names indicates that European mapmakers at the time of the Age of Discovery had no clear idea of the geography of East Asia, yet they were drawing maps about that part of the world. Some of them came off better while others worse. Some put them in North America, showing that they had no idea of what they were drawing. Yet they knew of the land-shape of the supposedly unknown continent. Oronce Finé not only put these names in America (Figure 80), he had no idea that America and Asia were two different continents; he drew one as an extension of the other!

Tangut was not a country. It was the name of the ethnic people of the country the Chinese called Xixia, which was destroyed by Genghis Khan in early 13th century. The mapmakers put it on their 16th century maps; a good three hundred years after the country had gone. This shows that the mapmakers had no idea of the real geography or the political reality of Asia (but the errors actually shed a light on the source material). Yet they did have real geographical data of East Asia, and that the data was obtained not in the 13th century, but hundreds of years later.

How did cartographers such as Oronce Finé (1494 – 1555), a French cartographer and mathematician, and Sebastian Munster (1488 - 1552), a German cosmographer and cartographer learn of names such as Tangut, Mangi, and Cyamba, all out of place with no regard to their proper locations, in early 15th century, just about the same time as Christopher Columbus, and then packed them all into a fantasy land that was a combination of Asia and North America? There is no doubt that they had reference material that gave them these disjointed information. It is equally without question that they had not been to such places.

There are many more such questions and testimonials, and we will examine them in due course. For our present purpose, these suffice.

The Age of Discovery European cartographers obtained their geographical data of the world from China.

When Did It Happen?

The analyses above show to a high degree of probability that the "Chinese" (we will zero in on who these Chinese were) not only had charted the geography of the world before the Age of Discovery, that information in fact found its way to Europe.

If the Chinese discovered and charted the world, and Europeans inherited that knowledge, it implies there must have been a process of knowledge transference. History seems to suggest the contrary; that East and West were mostly isolated from each other until the Age of Discovery when European adventurers discovered and developed sea routes to the East. This misconception[37] needs to be cleared up. Indeed, the question boils down to, first, when did the world geography knowledge transfer occur, and two, how did it happen. Again, the preserved European documents from the Age of Discovery can serve as road signs and direct us to the solution.

We have just confirmed that Mongol-Yuan Dynasty era nomenclature showed up on European Age of discovery maps. As an example, the name Tangut appeared on 15th to 16th century European world maps in America. The name had ceased to exist as of early 13th century, yet it did not appear prominently in European literature until more than two hundred years later. This reveals that Europeans did not learn the name in real historical time, but through secondhand media in the form of knowledge acquisition.

---

[37] A conception largely held and propagandized by the West which knew little outside the West.

The Catalan Maps

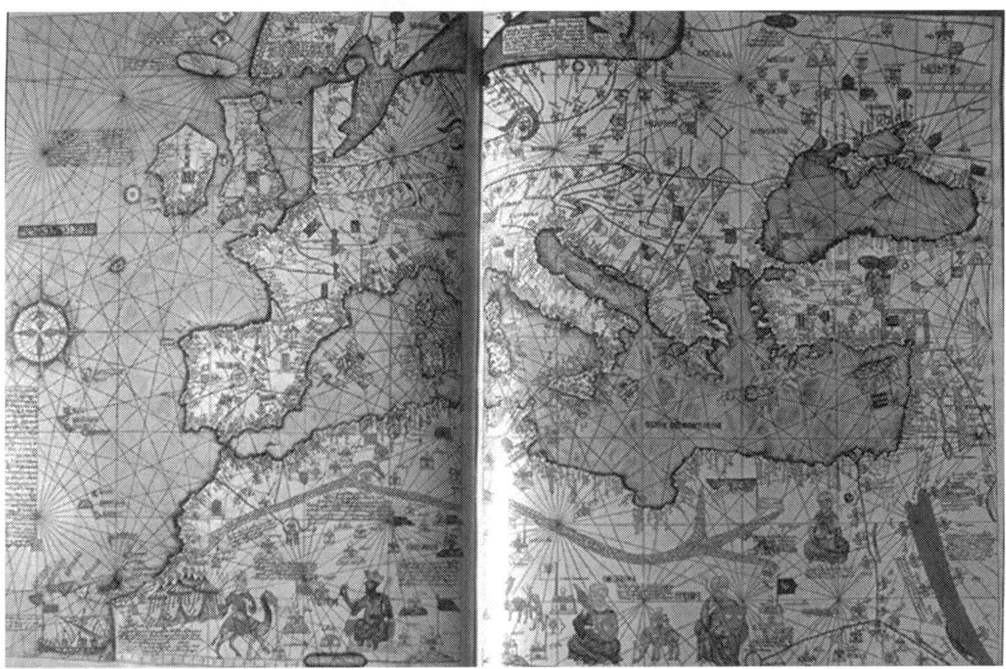

Figure 84

The Mediterranean Sea from the Catalan Atlas

In the late 14th century, on the eve of the Age of Discovery, an astonishingly fabulous set of maps appeared. This is the famous 1375 Catalan Atlas (Figure 84), created by the well-known Cresqueses family, Catalonian cartographers who worked in Majorca. The atlas was allegedly commissioned by Charles V of France, who requested it from Peter of Aragon, patron of the man regarded as the best Majorcan mapmaker of the time, Abraham Cresques.

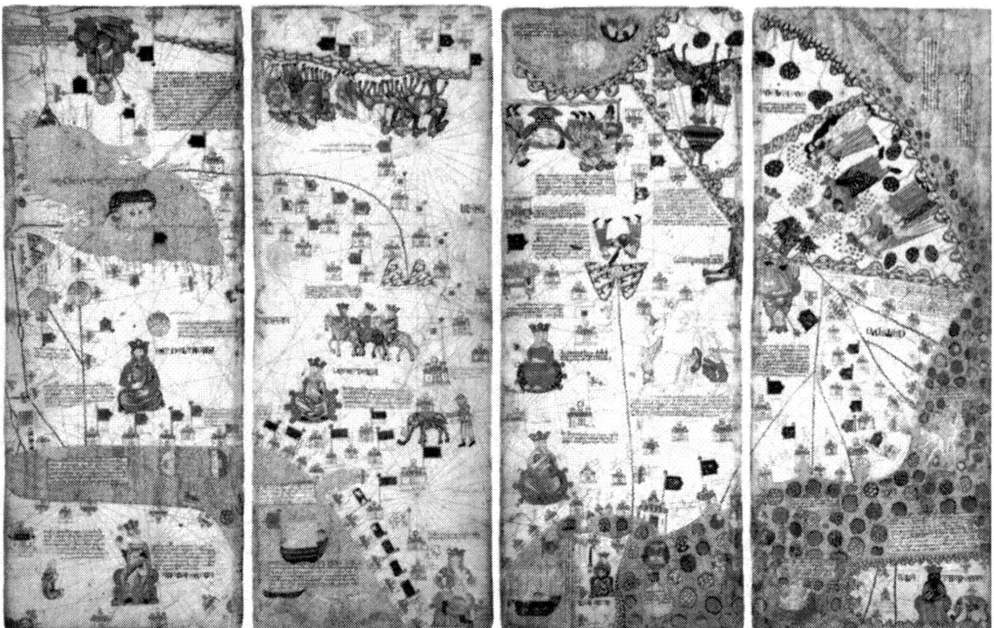

Figure 85

Catalan Map of Asia

Here let me comment on this little anecdote. At the time, European governments viewed such "advanced" cartography as treasures, and guarded them as national secrets. How big was Charles V of France? He was big, yet he needed the "introduction" of the Spaniard monarch to get the map. So, you can appreciate how special the Catalan Atlas was.

The atlas was generally hailed as the "most complete map of the World known at the time," and was way ahead of its time vis-à-vis European mapmaking technology. It can be said that it heralded the European Renaissance in terms of cartography, much as Dante Alighieri did for literature.

It set the tone in style and substance for all European maps to come, and spurred cartographers on to emulate its excellence. It was at least a quantum leap from the maps before it, much like Beethoven's Eroica Symphony signaled the end of the tradition of Haydn and Mozart and ushered in the Romantic era of European music.

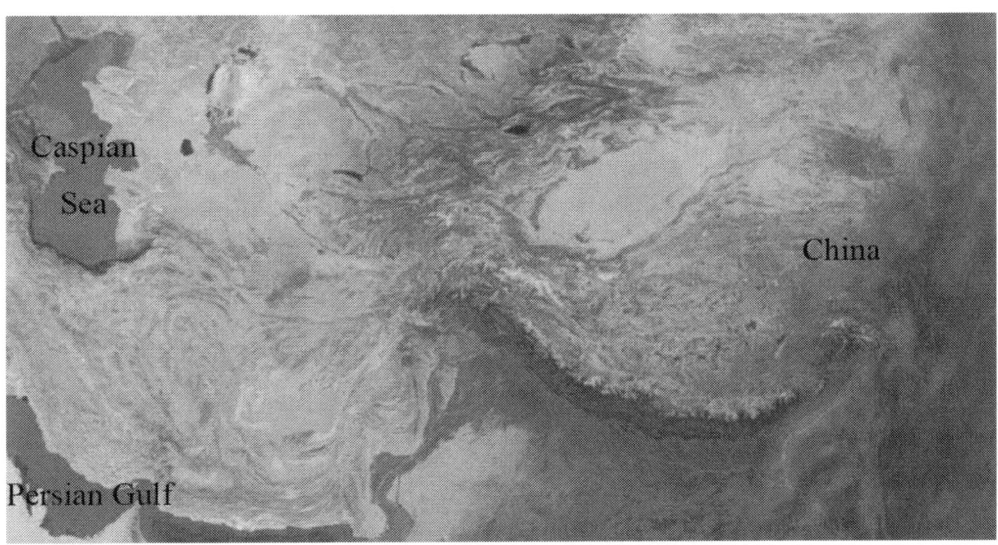

Figure 86

Catalan Map Modern Map Reference

The atlas is a compendium of a series of celestial, navigational, and geographical maps that contain information about the inhabitants of the different regions of the world at the time, with emphasis on Africa and its southern waterways per request from Peter's son, the Infant John. The atlas went through a number of editions and improvements, evolving from images printed on wood panels to a book of maps on parchments. The original wood panel atlas (or one of the early series) is now maintained in the Bibliotheque Nationale of Paris, France. Other forms of the masterpiece also exist, such as a round, standalone planisphere.

Figure 84 shows a detailed rendition of the Mediterranean areas from the Catalan Atlas. Scandinavia, the British Isles, the Iberian Peninsula, Italy and its affiliated islands, the Adriatic Sea and the Black Sea, Turkey, and North Africa are easily seen, testifying to the map incorporating the best geographic information available at that time.

Figure 87

Marco Polo Being Escorted by Mongols in Catalan Map

Figure 85 shows the Catalan map of Asia. To the left you can see the Caspian Sea and below it the Persian Gulf. (Ref. Figure 86.) On the right is China (called Catayo, for Cathay). You can even see Marco Polo being escorted by Mongols on his trip east (shown upside-down) at the top of Figure 85. An enlargement of the scene is presented in Figure 87 for your enjoyment.

More interesting is the delineation of the multitude of islands in the Indian Ocean, with a huge one called Trapobana, probably denoting the Island of Sri Lanka, or perhaps Java, fabled in European folklore for ages, or Sumatra.

The map is also noted for its meticulous attention to details, especially as it strives for accuracy, whether it was achieved is irrelevant. The part of the map for northern Africa, in the lower left corner of Figure 84 (enlarged in Figure 88), is an excellent example. There you see a symbolic Jaume Ferrer vessel in search of the legendary River of Gold. The design of the boat was that of a European Mediterranean vessel of the day.

Figure 88

Jaume Ferrer Vessel in Search of the Legendary River of Gold in Catalan Map

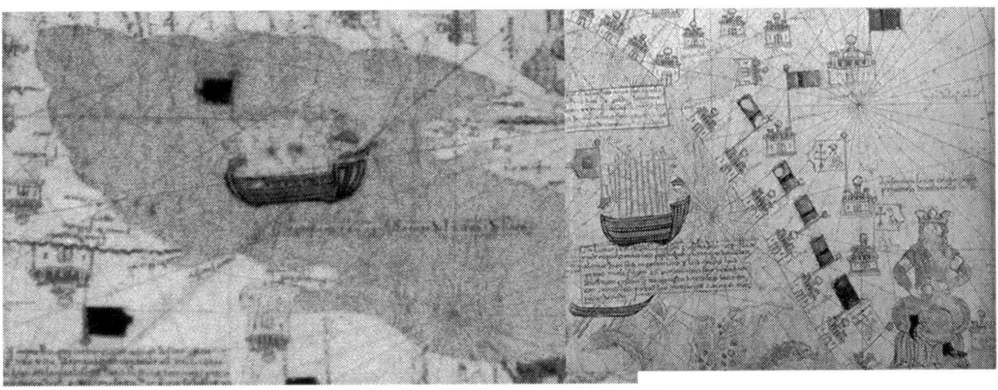

Figure 89

Caspian Sea in the Catalan Map

Figure 90

Persian Gulf in the Catalan Map

In the Indian Ocean in the Asian map is a Chinese ship, or what Western people call a *junk* (Figure 91, lower left corner). There should be no doubt that in the late 14th century European—at least Catalan—cartographers already knew of Chinese ships in the Indian Ocean, commissioned by the ruling Mongols, of course.

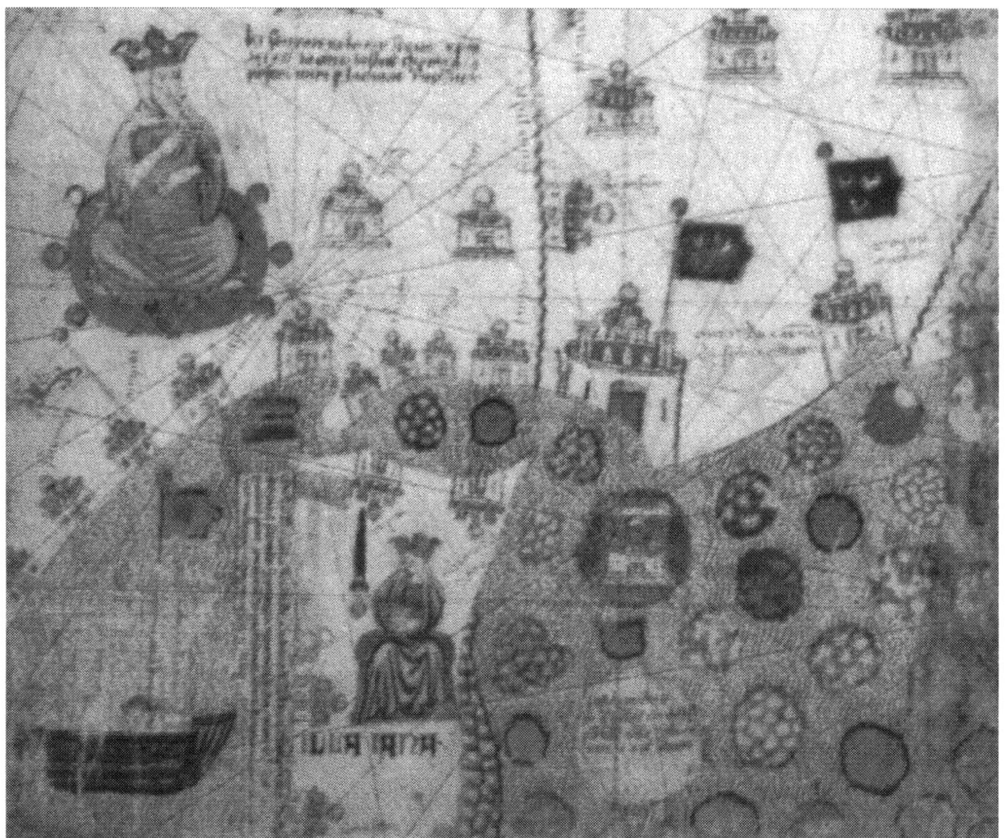

Figure 91

Catalan Map Indian Ocean

These were not European ships because European sailors had yet to reach that part of the world's waters. Besides, these ships had multiple masts. European vessels at the time were basically barges (Figure 88).

Now turn to the Caspian Sea (Figure 89) and the Persian Gulf (Figure 90). Chinese vessels are there too.

How did the Cresgues know about Chinese sailing vessels? In 1375 the Chinese Ming Dynasty had only just begun. It ousted the Mongol Yuan Dynasty in 1368. That Chinese ships showed up in the Catalan Atlas testifies to that Mongol ships were roaming the world's waters; that is, Central Asia, and at least this one European cartographer was aware of them.

We already know that the Chinese were sailing to the east coast of Africa at least by the 10th century, and we know the Mongols of the Golden Horde had commissioned the Genoans to operate the maritime routes of the Black Sea. The Catalan Atlas faithfully depicted these facts.

Thus, Europeans knew of Chinese junks by late 14th century.

The Fra Mauro Map

Figure 92

The 1457 Fra Mauro Map

If the Catalan Atlas was an eye-opener, the Fra Mauro Map is a shocker.

Figure 93

Chinese Junk on the 1457 Fra Mauro Map

There exists in the Biblioteca Nazionale Marciana of Venice, Italy a large circular planisphere that dates to about 1457 or 1459 constructed by Fra Mauro, a Camaldulian monk from the island of Murano near Venice.

Figure 92 shows the map inverted to accommodate our preference of north pointing up. The maps original orientation was with the north at the bottom.

With the exception of Asia and Africa, most of the features on the map are surprisingly accurate. This is understandable, given the comparative scarcity of good data at the time about the East, apart from the creepily accurate illustration of the Chinese Yellow River and Yangtze River (called Long River, "Chang Jiang," by the Chinese).

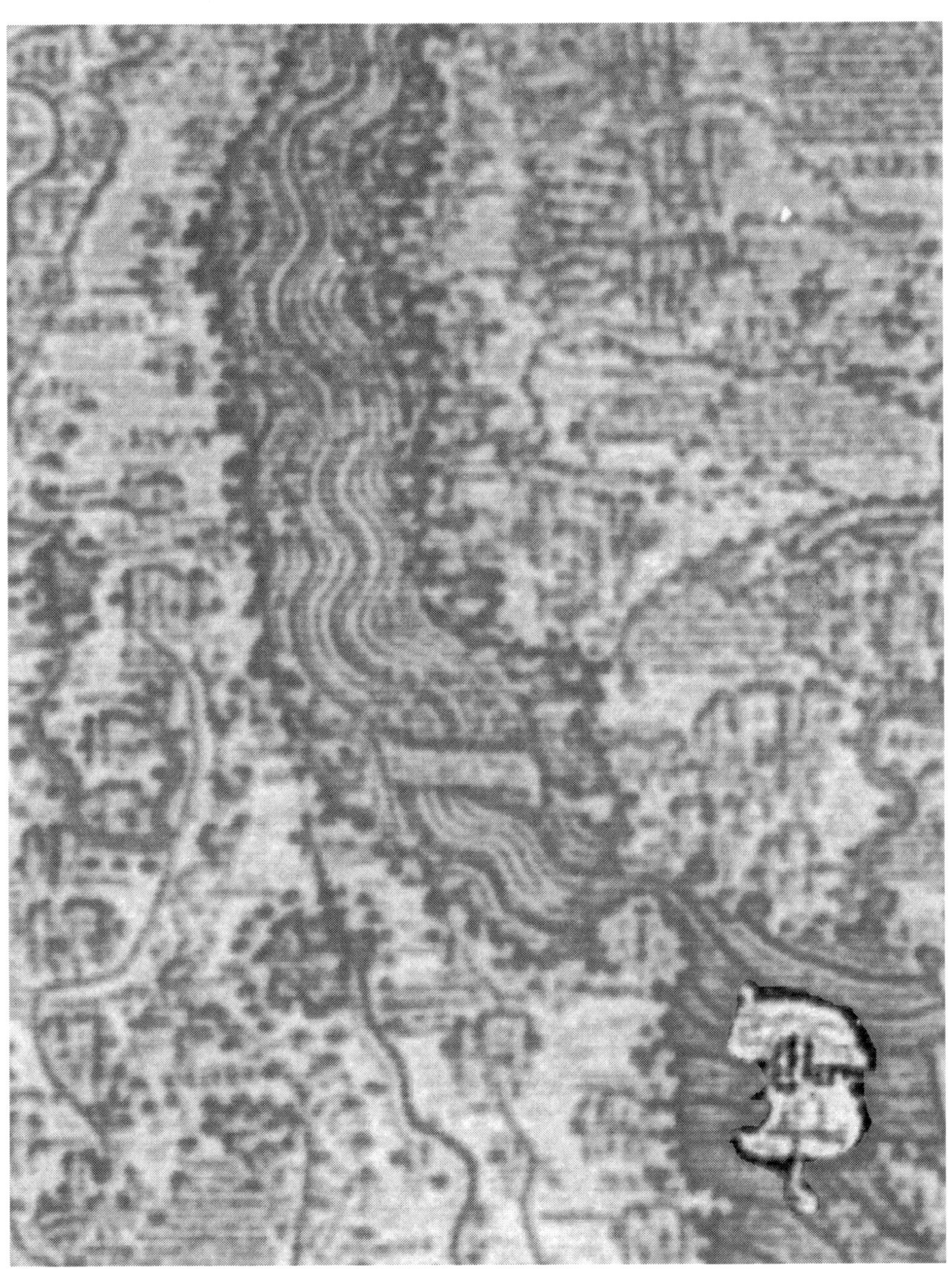

Figure 94

Chinese Junk in the Persian Gulf on the 1457 Fra Mauro Map

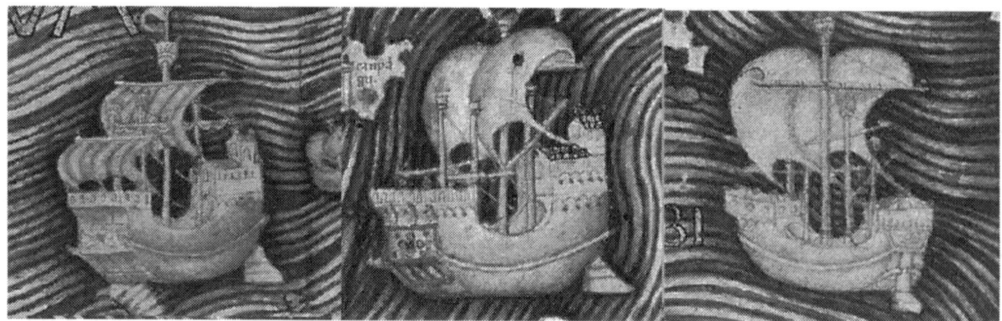

Figure 95

Fra Mauro Map Chinese Ships

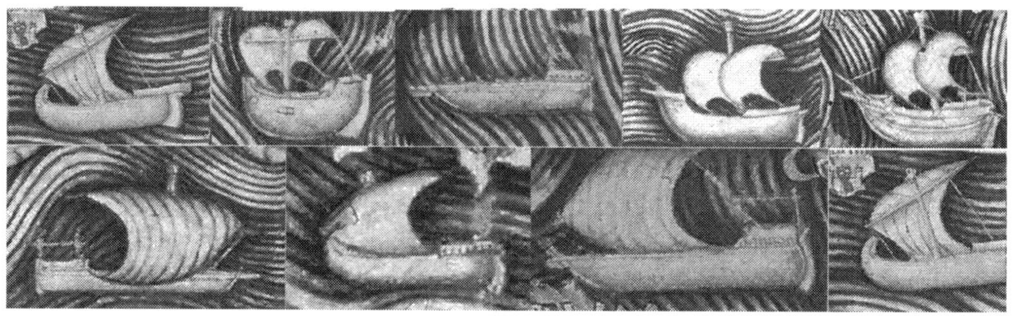

Figure 96

Fra Mauro Map Non-Chinese Ships

What is most intriguing, though, is the presence of Chinese junks strewn around the World's oceans. Figure 93 (upper right corner) shows such a junk outside of China (Chataio, Cathay).

Likewise, another junk is shown in the Persian Gulf (Figure 94).

We know these were Chinese junks for two reasons. First, they looked like Chinese junks with their unique free-hinged sternpost rudders (Figure 95). They were unlike the ships or boats of the rest of the world at the time (Figure 96). Second, at the time of the map's drawing, Europeans had yet to be in Chinese waters. The first Europeans to enter the Indian Ocean, the Portuguese, did not arrive until the 16th century.

Even more startling, the map shows a junk (Figure 97); a small one, one designed to cut through choppy waters, rounding the southern tip of Africa.

Figure 97

Chinese Junk Rounding the Southern Tip of Africa in the 1457 Fra Mauro Map

Figure 98

Pterodactyl(?) from *Shan Hai Jing*

Figure 99

An owl(?) from *Shan Hai Jing*

We know these are not Portuguese vessels because the Portuguese had yet to round the Cape of Good Hope in 1459. That was to happen in 1498, almost forty years later.

So, how did Fra Mauro know about the Cape of Good Hope and why did he put a Chinese junk there? For this, Fra Mauro spoke of some expedition that had taken place in 1420.

Figure 100

More *Shan Hai Jing* Strange Beings

One of the map's legends, placed next to the junk, says, in rough translation here:

> *Around 1420 an Indian junk (Zoncho de India), when sailing toward the Isle of Men and Women was driven by a storm beyond the Cape of Diab (Good Hope) through the Green Isles into the Sea of Darkness… For forty days they traveled 2,000 miles and saw nothing but air and water and storms. When the storm calmed the sailors returned to the cape sailing for seventy days.*

Figure 101

The Kangaroo and Koala Bear from *Shan Hai Jing* (Top) and their Modern Photographic

> *As they attempted to resupply the ship onshore they saw the huge egg of a bird called roc, whose wing spanned sixty paces. It was so strong that it could easily lift an elephant.*

Figure 102

John Mandeville II

Figure 103

1493 Hartmann Schedel Liber Illustration

Figure 104

***Shan Hai Jing*'s "*Cyclops*"**

Figure 105

***Shan Hai Jing*'s "*Xing Tian*"**

Where did Fra Mauro get such information? Did he read a copy of the *Arabian Nights* and the stories of *Sindbad the Sailor* and learned about the roc in year 1420?

Did the *Arabian Nights* story about Sindbad the Sailor and the roc even exist at the time?[38] Also, where did he get the inspiration for an "Isle of Men and Women?"

As it were, it is told that the map was the result of a commission from King Alfonso V of Portugal, who provided the money and geographical data based on the Portuguese discoveries. Fra Mauro also explained that he drew on his own experience through years of investigation and interviewing people who had direct information on the places he included in the map. Therefore, when Fra Mauro drew the Indian Ocean as an open sea as opposed to one landlocked, he did it from unimpeachable source materials, and this was before the Portuguese reached the middle girth of Western Africa, never mind the Indian Ocean.

[38] It is possible that it did. See Closing Remarks below.

Figure 106

***Shan Hai Jing*'s "*Xing Tian*" in Western Incarnations**

As to "Isle of Men and Women," the Chinese book of fantasy *Shanhaijing* contains description of certain women islands. Fra Mauro might have referred to that. (More on *Shanhaijing* below.)

However, due southwest of Korea and west of Japan in the East China sea is an island named "Men and Women Archipelago." Whether the geography of eastern Asia had somehow reached Italy is no longer researchable.

Another point of interest about this map is the inclusion of the Cape Verde Islands; that is, Cape Green Isles. When the map was being constructed in the middle of the15th century, the Portuguese had yet to sail down the western African seacoast to reach these islands. How did the cartographer know about it? Even more interesting, Fra Mauro's own notes claimed that he had in his possession charts denoting the surveyed geography of this part of Africa. Who surveyed it? Further, the map showed the eastern terminus of the Gulf of Guinea to be on the meridian of Tunis. Europeans did not know about this at the time. That is a piece of highly esoteric geographical knowledge. How did the mapmaker know about it, yet at the same time drawing Africa so poorly that it looks like a pancake?

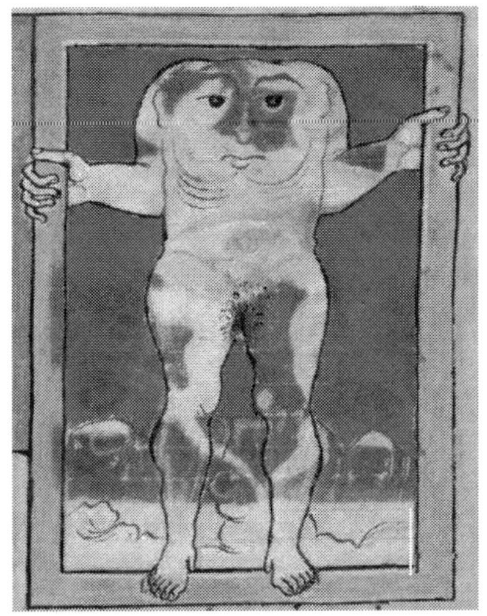

Blemmyae

MS Cotton Vitelius Monster

Fauns and Satyrs

Ewaipomona

Whereas the king of Portugal might have been the official sponsor of the map, he could hardly be credited as the sole supplier of the latest geographical information on Fra Mauro's map because of the well-known Portuguese policy of punishing leakage of nautical information by death, a policy that actually intensified with the passing of time. Thus, once more, Fra Mauro got his information from an alternate source. Try to remember, in 1457 the Portuguese had yet to round the Cape of Good Hope. Columbus had yet to visit the Caribbean, and it was before Magellan embarked on his trip around the world.

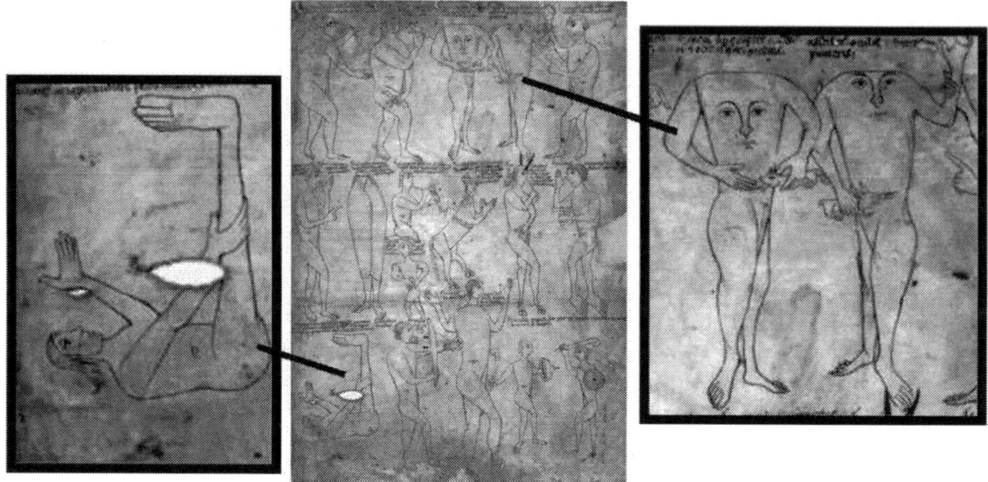

Monster Race

Figure 107

There were other tantalizing tidbits on the map. For instance, it stated that the kingdom of Java had a particularly cozy relationship with China (Cathay). It indicated that Java was near a place called Randan.

Such pieces of information virtually handed up the cartographer's eastern source, or one that was intimately familiar with the East. We know that the Chinese admiral Zheng He established a friendly base on Java.

The irony is, if you were to ask a Chinese today why a Chinese ship is called a junk, he would almost certainly be at a loss, unable to furnish you with an intelligent answer.

That is because today the Chinese call a ship *chuan*, or formally, a *zhou*.[39] In truth, the Chinese have been bewildering for a long time why Europeans call their ships *junk*, just like they do not understand why they are called *Chinese*, and their country *China* or *Cathay*.

[39] ship *chuan*, 船; *zhou*, 舟

Hy leut / die't leut / ick en leut naet

DIT is een Waterlandts* Barbarisch spreeckwoort, als zy willen segghen: **Hy ghelooft / die't gelooft / ick en ghelooft niet.** Daer om heb ick dit willen ghebruycken by de monstreuse beesten, in de achtste tafel van Asia, geroert door Ptolomeum in zijn Geographia*. Het is wonder dat de Oudtheydt onversocht*, dus langhe daer op gestaen* heeft: maer onse nieuwe Schippers ende Stuerluyden, die nu over al ghevaren hebben, vinden daer af noch teecken noch mercke.

Figure 108

A medieval Conception of a Neanderthal Man

True, as a seafaring people, the Chinese have different names for water vessels of specific functions, and they structure the written words that are related to sailing with the radical or determinant *zhou*, 舟. For example, the word for navigation is 航, *hang*, which consists of the radical *zhou*, 舟, and the character 亢, *hang* to serve as the phonetic indicator.

A small rowboat is call 艇, *ting*, which consists of the radical *zhou*, 舟, and the phonetic companion character 廷, *ting*. A *ting* is also called 舢板, *san ban* (*ban* means *plank*), which gives rise to the well-known word *sampan*. The, there are other examples.

A pleasure boat (cruise ship) is called a 舫, *fang*. A big ship, such as a steamer, is called a 舶, *bo*. A barge is called a 舸, *ge*, and a warship is 艦, *jian*. A sailing ship (with sails) is called 帆船, *fan chuan*. The cargo bay is called 艙, *cang*. They all have the radical 舟 in it.

The Chinese, at least the Chinese today, do not know of the word *junk*. In fact, the Cantonese (Southern Chinese) call a *junk* a "big-eyed rooster."

Figure 109

Mythical Beasts from *Shan Hai Jing*

Where did the Europeans come up with the word *zoncho* or *junk*? Once someone facetiously explained to me that it was probably because Chinese ships were no good—they were junk; trash. If you look up a modern-day etymology dictionary for the word, it will probably tell you that the root of the word "junk" is "most likely" an Indonesian word *djong* or *jhong*, which the Indonesians learned from the Chinese and introduced to Europe by way of the Portuguese.

It is true that the Portuguese had come across Chinese ships in Southeast Asia. When the Portuguese arrived in India, it took them no time at all to recognize the strategic importance of the town Malacca (Melaka) in present day Malaysia, the first major stop-off point of Admiral Zheng He's voyages.

Figure 110

1550 Sebastian Munster Woodcut from *Cosmographia*

The Portuguese wanted it. In 1509 they dispatched an expedition from India to take the town but the mission failed, resulting in many of the invading Portuguese captured by the Muslim Sultan of Malacca.

To remedy the defeat, in 1511, Afonso de Albuquerque, Portuguese Viceroy of India, sent in a second fleet of some fourteen ships and over one thousand troops. When matters came to a head, the locals proved a lot tougher than the Viceroy had figured.

Finally, the Portuguese succeeded with the help of some Chinese merchants who were stationed in the Malacca harbor. They allowed the Portuguese to use their junk as a bridgehead. This event allowed the Portuguese colonists to gain a firm foothold on Southeast Asian soil.

Figure 111

Strange Beasts in Jean de Léry's Illustration for *Brazil Voyage*

There is, unfortunately, a problem with this explanation, and in particular vis-à-vis the Fra Mauro map. The Portuguese did not arrive in the South China Sea until the 16th century. How did Fra Mauro learn of the word more than fifty years earlier before it was supposed to have been introduced to Europe?

According to historical records, the huge vessel, the treasure ship that Admiral Zheng He rode in, was called a *zhong*, 舯, a character that consists of the radical 舟 and the phonetic component *zhong*, 中, or alternatively, 宗. The word might also be equivalent to the character 艘 of the same pronunciation.

After the termination of the Zheng He expeditions, the Chinese treasure ships were mothballed, and with the ships this word vanished from most Chinese vernaculars and dictionaries. Nonetheless, it is almost certain that this word was the origin of the word "junk" or Fra Mauro's "zoncho," which undoubtedly inspired the Indonesian word *jhong*.

In any case, did the Portuguese pick up the word *jhong* when they arrived in the Orient years later? The answer is not likely, because by that time there would be no reason for the word to come up when there was no longer an actual ship to refer to.

Therefore, the likely explanation for Europeans to have learned the word "junk" was that they actually rode on one of these huge ships. We know one European who almost certainly had ridden on such a ship.

He was Niccolò de' Conti (or Niccolo di Conti, or Niccolo da Conti, or Nicolo de Conti), who also furnished Fra Mauro information about the Orient for his map. Hence, Fra Mauro was basing his map on fact. Chinese ships rounded the southern tip of Africa (later known as the Cape of Good Hope) in 1420, and European cartographers (at least one, Fra Mauro) knew about it.

(There will be more to say about de' Conti.)

Therefore, with the Fra Mauro map we have explicit pre-Age of Discovery European testimonial attesting to knowledge of Chinese ships rounding the Cape of Good Hope, known to the mapmaker as Cape of Diab, Cape of the Devil, in 1420.

Shan Hai Jing

Figure 112

Theodore de Bry New World Illustrations

The Chinese have a book called *Shan Hai Jing*[40]—*The Classic of Mountains and Seas,* or in Western equivalent, *Geographica,* or *Geographical Encyclopedia*. The book reputedly dates back thousands of years, although scholars have reason to believe that it began as a compendium of geographical records, an almanac, so to speak.

[40] 山海經

Figure 113

***Shan Hai Jing* Headless Being as European Incarnate**

They believed that the book dated only from the era of the Warring States, some twenty-five hundred years ago, or about 500 BC. In reality, the book is more than just an anthology of geographical data, as it also gets into issues of local cultures and histories of alien people.

The book is divided into geographical regions, and has been illustrated to a great extent by artists through the ages. It contains creatures and beings ranging from the extinct and exotic to those that may be regarded as commonplace by today's standards (Figure 98, Figure 99, and Figure 100).

It is interesting to note that *Shan Hai Jing* appears to hint at the ancient Chinese having visited Australia, which they called *Da Yang Zhou*,[41] or the "Great Oceanic Continent." Figure 101 shows a *Shan Hai Jing* animal with two heads.

---

[41] 大洋洲

Figure 114

1657 John Jonston Monsters

Figure 115

1668 Fortunio Liceti Illustration

It was ostensibly a kangaroo with a young one in her pouch. The animal on the right has three crania, a not unlikely interpretation of a koala bear.

The Chinese text tells us: "In a vast wilderness in the Southern Sea, to the west of the Red River and east of the Quick Sand there live two animals. One has two heads, the other three crania."

Shan Hai Jing found its way to Europe.

An early 13th century travelogue, more popular even than that of Marco Polo's, is *The Travels of Sir John Mandeville*. We no longer know for sure who this Englishman Sir John Mandeville was, whether he was a man or English, or that such a person ever existed. Some scholars think it is merely a penname, just like "Mark Twain" is a penname. Mandeville's travel stories are so incredible that critics flat out called him "the greatest liar ever lived." This travelogue describes many unusual beings that were encountered on Sir John's alleged journeys. Some of these characters were illustrated in Figure 102, showing extraordinary imagination.

In Volume 2, Sea Section of *Shan Hai Jing*,[42] a certain *Xing Tian* is documented (see Figure 105, and compare with Mandeville's version in

Figure 102).

This *Xing Tian* was described by Mandeville thus:

> *... And so he passed Ind and the isles beyond Ind, where there are more than 5000 islands... Beside that island, there is another island that is called Sumobor. That is a great island, and the king is mighty... And beside that is another island that is bountiful called Betemga, and many other islands thereabout, where there are many diverse folks of which it will take too much time to talk about them all... Beside that island is another great island and a great country called Java. Its circumference is two thousand miles long. The king of that country is a great lord and is rich and powerful. He has under him seven other kings of seven other islands...Here they grow all sorts of spices—ginger, clove, gilofre, canell, seedwall, nutmegs, and maces, and gold and silver... From that island, if you go south you will reach another great island called Dondun which has a mighty king, who has under him fifty-four great islands that pay tribute to him...In one of these islands the inhabitants are of great stature as giants, and they are hideous looking and have but one eye in the middle of the front* (Figure 104)*. They eat nothing but raw flesh and raw fish. And in another island toward the south there live people of foul stature and have no heads, except eyes in their shoulders.*

[42] *Shan Hai Jing* has been fully translated into English and is now obtainable through bookstores.

Von mancherlay gestaltnus der menschen schreibt Plinius. Augustinus vnd ysidorus die hernachgemelt ding. In dem land india sind menschē myt hunds köpffen vnd reden pellēde. nerñ sich mit fogelgefeng vñ klaiden sich mit thierhewtten. Item etlich haben allain ein aug an der stirñ ob der nasen vnnd essen allain thier flaisch. Item in dem land libia werden etlich on hawbt geporn vnd haben mund vnd augen. Etlich sind bederlay geslechts. die recht prust ist in manlich vnd die lingk weibisch vnd vermischen sich vndereinand vñ gepern. Item gegen dem paradis bey dem fluss Ganges sind etlich menschen die essen nichts. dann sie haben so klainen mund das sie das getranck mit ainē halm einflössen vnd leben vom gesmack der öpffl vnd plumen. vnd sterben pald von bössem gesmack. Daselbst sind auch lewt an nasen eins ebnen angesichts. Etlich haben vnden so gross lebssfzen das sie das gantz angesicht damit bedeckē. Item etlich an zungen. die deuttē einander ir maynūg mit wincken als die closterlewt. Item in dem land Sicilia haben etlich so grosse orñ das sie den gantzen leib damit bedecken. Item in dem land ethiopia wandern etlich nidergebogen als das vih. vnd etlich lebē vierhundert iar. Item etlich haben hörner. lang nasen vnd gaysfüsse das findest du in sand Anthonius gantzer legēd. Itē in ethiopia gein dem nidergang sind lewt mit einem prayten fuss. vnd so schnell das sie die wilden thier erfolgen. Item in dem land Scithia haben sie menschē gestalt vñ pferds füess. Item alda sind auch lewt fünff elnpogen langk vnd werden nicht kranck bis zum tod. Item in dē geschichtē des grossen Alexanders liset man das in india menschen seyen mit sechs henden. Item etlich nacket vñ rawh in den flüssen wonend. etlich die an henden vnd füssen sechs finger haben. etlich in den wassern wonēde halb menschen vnd halbs pferds gestalt habende. Itē weiber mit pertzen bis auff die prust auff dē hawbt eben vnd an har. Item in ethiopia gegen dem nidergang haben etlich vier augē. So sind in Eripia schön lewt mit kranchs helsen vnnd sneblen. Doch ist als Augustinus schreibt nit zuglawben das etliche menschē an dem ort der erden gegen vns da die sunn auff geet. so sie wider in der geet die versen gegent vnsern füssen kerē. Doch ist ein grosser streyt in der schrifft wider den wone des gemaynen volcks. das gemaynsamb allenthalben menschē auff der erden seyen. vnd die füss gegen einander kerende darauff steen. vnnd doch alle menschen ir schaytel gein himel keren. in verwunderlig warumb doch wir oder die die ir fersen gegen vnns wennden nit fallen. Aber das kombt auss der natur. dann gleicherweis als der stul des fewrs nyndert ist denn in den fewern. der wasser nyndert denn in den wassern. vnnd des gaysts nyndert denn in dem gayst. also auch der stul der erden nyndert anderss wo denn in ir selbs.

58. - *I popoli delle terre del Gran Khan. Xilografia dalla « Cronaca mondiale » di Schedel, del 1493.*

58. - *I popoli delle terre del Gran Khan. Xilografia dalla « Cronaca mondiale » di Schedel, del 1493.*

Figure 116

Hartmann Schedel "People of the Great Khan"

Clearly, Mandeville had his sources. In fact, he was describing scenes from the South China island kingdoms.

Of course, he never went there. No medieval European had been known to travel to that part of the world and return to tell his tales.

Obviously, somehow Mandeville gained access to such fabulous information, as did other European writers and illustrators. For instance, the illustrations for a race of people known as the *Blemmyae* (see Figure 107) are now preserved at the British Library. Indeed, the Blemmyae, the "head-in-the-thorax" fiendish incarnate of *Xing Tian* was described as "sharing many features with depictions of the Neanderthals" in the book *In Search of the Neanderthals* by Chris Stringer and Clive Gamble.

Europe's intelligentsia must have been fascinated by these strange images, for they used them to illustrate their maps and manuscripts in each and every way imaginable. Figure 110 is a woodcut from the 1550 *Cosmographia* by Sebastian Munster. The *Shan Hai Jing* monstrosity is prominently evident.

Figure 108 shows a European artist's concept of a Neanderthal man.

Also, strange beasts were marveled in Jean de Léry's illustration for *Brazil Voyage* in Figure 111.

At the top of Figure 110, Sebastian Schedel's monsters, are goats or horses with multiple horns. The details are enlarged in Figure 113. Match them against the *Shan Hai Jing* animal in Figure 112.

In his 16th century *Guiana,* Theodore de Bry illustrated the New World with the bizarre figures shown in Figure 112. He must have wanted to show his readers the uncivilized nature of the people living there—nude warrior women and male warriors with heads in the middle of the thoraxes.

Compare the 1657 John Jonston monsters (Figure 114) and the 1668 Fortunio Liceti illustration (Figure 115) with the creatures from *Shan Hai Jing.*

Now, let us turn to the maps. Pay attention to the one-eyed man sitting in the middle of Africa in the 1544 Sebastian Munster map (Figure 17).

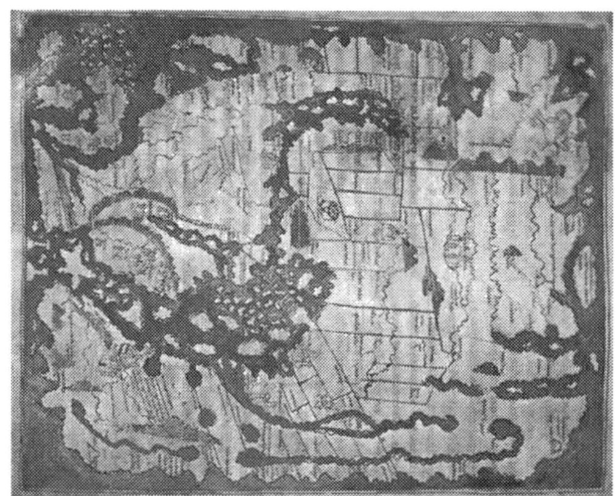

Figure 117

The late 10th century Cottoniana Map

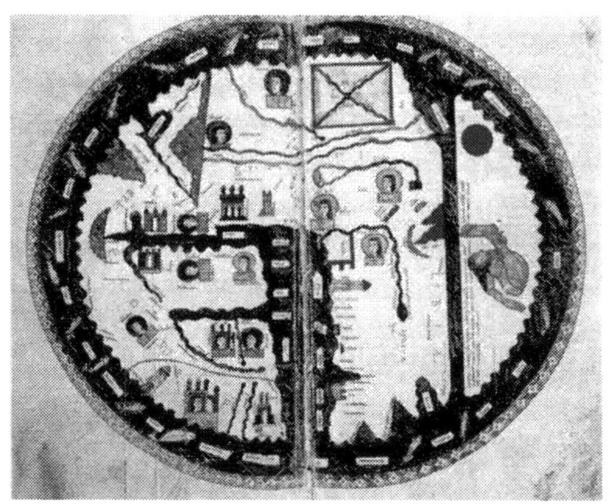

Figure 118

The 11th century Beatus Map

Just because ancient European manuscripts' whimsical illustrations show similarities with Eastern traditions does not make them copies from China, unless there is explicit evidence showing that they were. A discerning skeptic might argue that the "man" with one eye was indeed of Greek origin; it was the Cyclops[43], and the uniped was indigenous European. Hence, the argument could get contentious. How are we to find a way from amongst the

---

[43] In about the first half of the 3rd century Gaius Julius Solinus produced a book called *De mirabilibus mundi,* "The wonders of the world," or *Collectanea rerum memorabilium,* "Collection of Curiosities," reputedly mostly taken from Pliny the Elder's *Natural History*. The book was later *revised and given the name Polyhistor. In this book many of the strange beasts from Shan Hai Jing* were described. In a translation by Arthur Golding (1536-1605), the griffon was described as:

> *In the rich lands of Scythia in Asia there are gold and precious stones owned by the Griffons, fierce and cruel birds, who tear anyone that ventures to come near into pieces.*

Whether the Greeks obtained the information from *Shan Hai Jing,* or were the source of such materials, can no longer be determined. Even if the Chinese copied from the Greeks, it attests to communication between the two lands. More of this is discuss in my book *In Search of Troy,* along with Herodotus' description of the man with his head in his thorax. However, Renaissance illustrators clearly identified these creatures as the subjects of the "Great Khan."

convoluted maze? Fortunately, there is a direct citation of source, and the very coincidental time of these strange things' appearance.

In his 1493 *Liber Chronicarum Secunda etas Mundi* (Figure 116), now at the Peabody Institute Library in the National Gallery of Art, Washington, D.C., Schedel also introduced a number of fantastic *Shan Hai Jing* characters as shown in Figure 103. At the bottom is the phrase *I popoli delle terre del Gran Khan,* "People of the Great Khan." The author acknowledged unequivocally that these were citizens of China, although clearly he had no idea that China no longer had a Khan. The Mongols had been expelled a hundred years prior. This further testifies to the fact that Europeans in the late 15th century still had little concept of East Asia and the clear Mongol inference in their material. Compare these creatures with the John Mandeville creatures in Figure 102.

The *Shan Hai Jing* also describes places known as Men Country and Women Country, which showed up in the Fra Mauro map, as mentioned.

When did *Shan Hai Jing* first reach Europe? The 11th century Beatus map (Figure 118) gives a clue. Note the uniped on the far right of the chart. It is fair to say that Europeans knew about this book even before Hartmann Schedel's time. The East and West had always communicated.

Two Phases of Knowledge Transfer

Figure 119

The 11th century Beatus Map

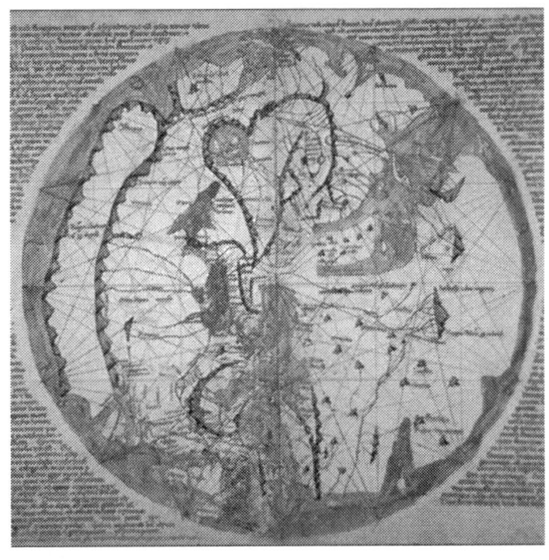

Figure 120

The early 14th century Petrus Vesconte world Map

We know that Chinese geographical knowledge of the world began reaching Europe sometime during the Mongol occupation of China, and mushroomed just after or even during Zheng He's expeditions. This conclusion, again, is drawn on hard historical evidence.

The late 10th century Cottoniana map (Figure 117, re-oriented to have north pointing up) and the early 14th century world map by Petrus Vesconte (Figure 120, cropped to remove the text on the left and right hand sides of the map), both now housed at the British Library in London.

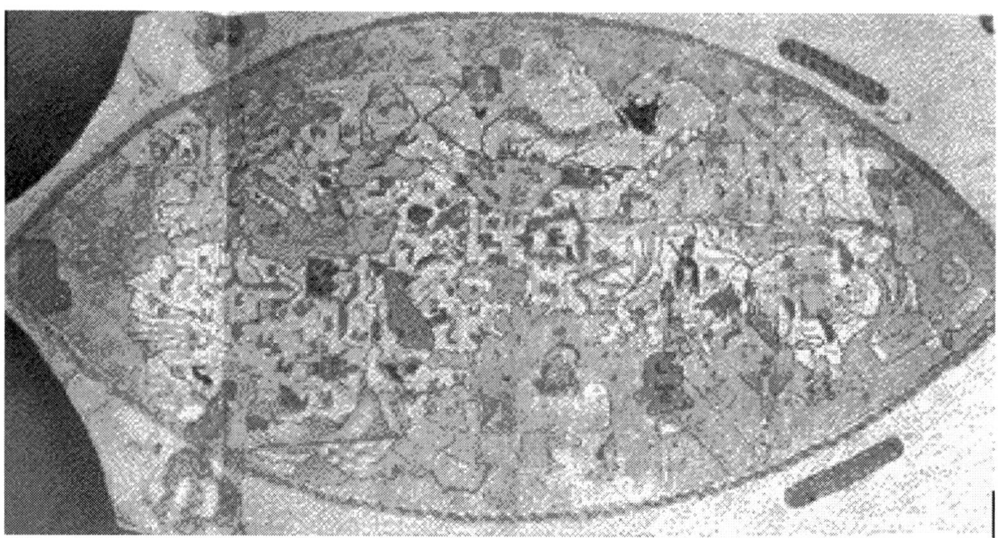

Figure 121

1457 Genoese Map

Also, the 11th century Beatus map (Figure 118, preserved at the Archivo de la Catedral, Osma, Spain), the 1290 Hereford Cathedral map now at the British Library, the 1390 Eversham map at the London College of Arms (Figure 298), represent the state of European world geographical knowledge up to the time of Henry the Navigator of Portugal of early 11th century. Then there is the mid-15th century Genoese map (Figure 121), currently preserved at the Biblioteca Nazionale Centrale in Florence, Italy. Recall also the Catalan map of late 14th century discussed above. It does not require a trained eye to observe that European cartographic science was suddenly "much improved" is an understatement.

It shows convincingly that modern maps of the world might have reached Europe as early as the middle of the 14th century, during the Yuan Dynasty, and certainly by the end of the Mongol era and the beginning of the Ming Regime (Figure 305).

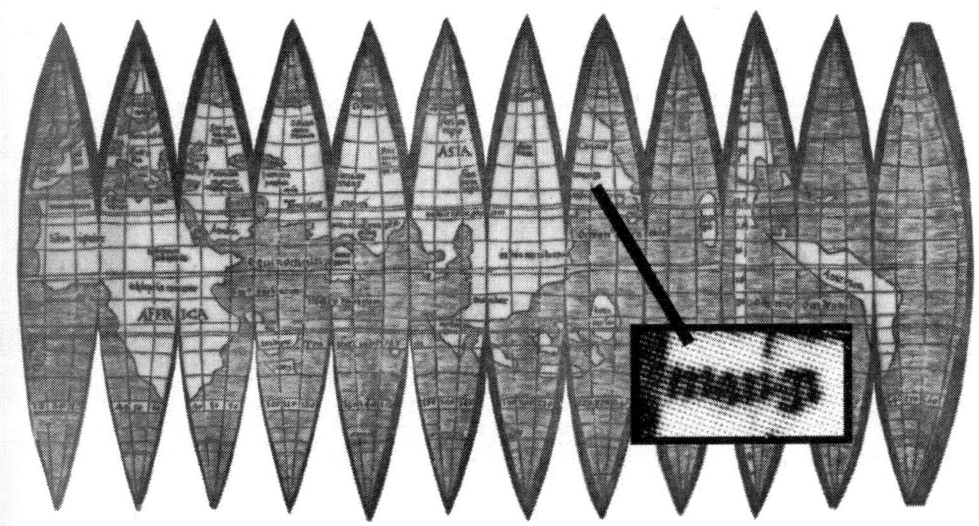

Figure 122

The 1507 Martin Waldseemüller World Map

Before this time, strange and unexplainable land features, such as legendary islands, were already making their appearances. However, while they drew such features on their maps and wrote about these strange places, European explorers were not ready to do anything about them; that is, actually go visit them and claim dominion over them. Precise information about such places was still lacking, and they had yet to develop the wherewithal to initiate any meaningful exploratory activities. However, by the time of Zheng He's voyages, everything began to come together. To be sure, the geographical information received in the West was first compiled during the Mongol era, as evidenced by the nomenclature on the European maps of the time. However, the navigational data only came after Zheng He.

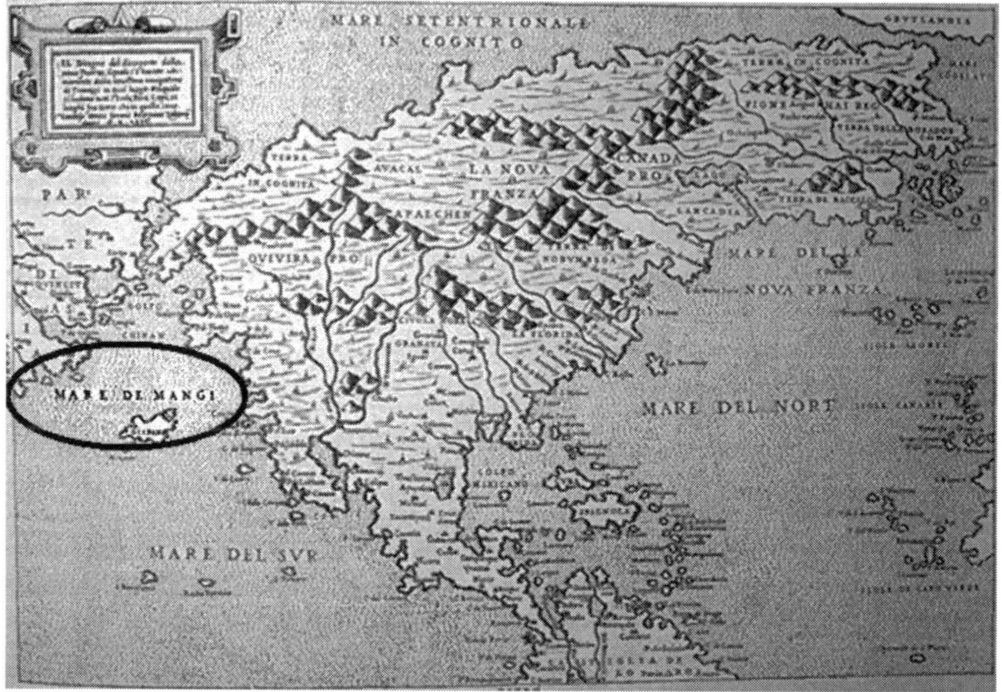

Figure 123

The 1556 Bolognino Zaltieri Map showing "Mare de Mangi"

For a typical example, look at Figure 122, a 1507 map of the world by the cartographer Martin Waldseemüller now stored at Wolfegg Castle in Würtemberg, Germany. The enlargement of the map portion depicting China clearly shows the inscription "Manji." This "Mangi" (Manji) is also on the Munster map of Asia (Figure 83) and many others, as was discussed earlier.

In the 1556 Bolognino Zaltieri map (Figure 123) we have the inscription "Mare de Mangi," the Mangi Sea west of the North American west coast, east of China, where it is the East China Sea.

In yet another map, the 1492 Martin Behaim map depicting China (Figure 124), the name "Cathaj" can be seen without difficulty. The Chinese never called their country "Cathay." As explained, "Cathay" was derived from an Arabo-Persian corruption of the name "Khitan," which became "Khitai."

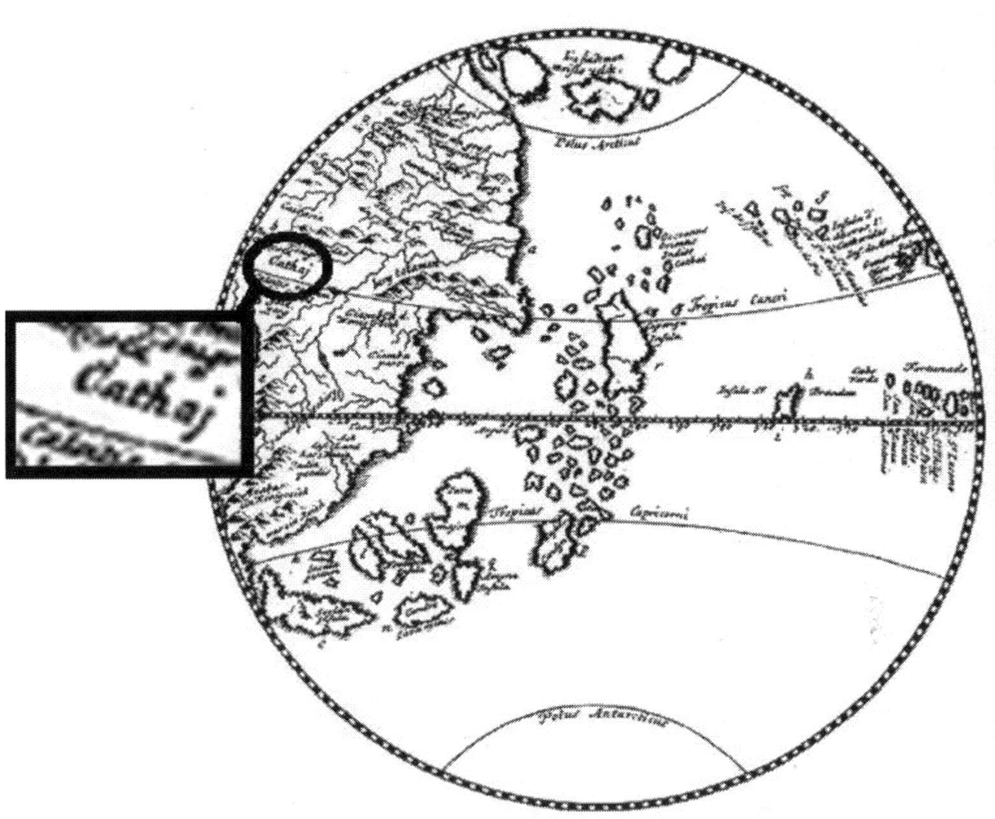

Figure 124

The 1492 Martin Behaim Map showing China as "Cathaj"

The Khitan were an archenemy of 12th century Song China. In Chinese the country's name was "Liao."[44] "Khitan"[45] was the name of its ethnic constituent, a people from Eastern Siberia. The Liao Dynasty lasted from 916 to 1125. Xixia, the country formed by the Tangut people lasted from 1032 to 1227, and, as already discussed, was snuffed out by Genghis Khan.

---

44 遼

45 契丹

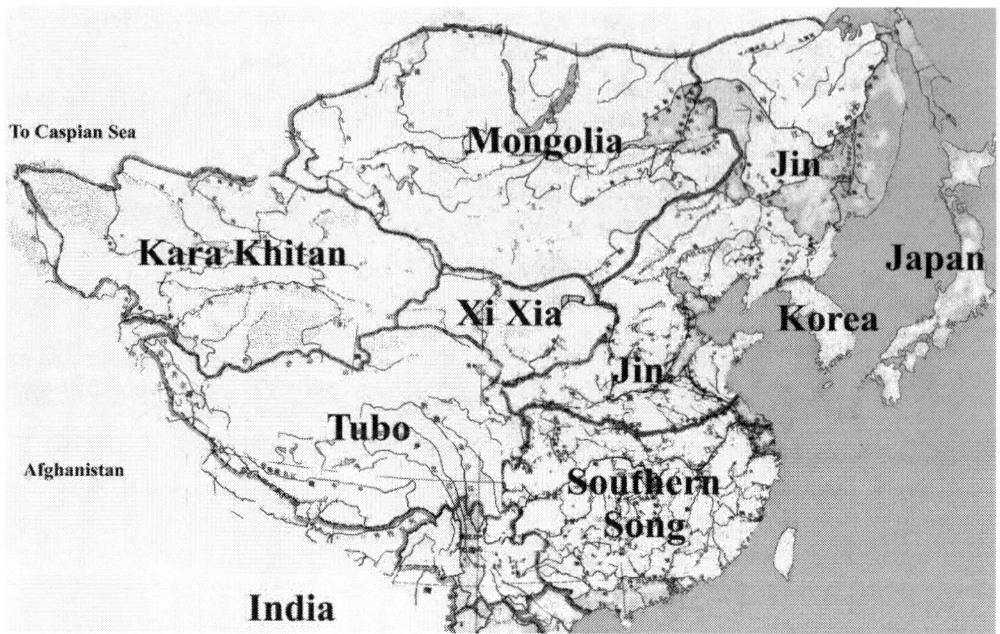

Figure 125

East Asia in 13th Century

During the 10th and 11th centuries, the rise of the Jin,[46] forerunners of the later Manchu, in the north of China forced the Khitan to move west, where they established a brief but vast empire known in history as Kara Khitai, that stretched all the way from the Gobi to the Aral Sea (Figure 125). Because of its close proximity to Europe, Westerners (Russians) simply assumed that these Asiatic people were Chinese.[47]

When the Mongols conquered Song China in the 13th century, they called the subjugated Chinese "Manji." "Manji" is a derogatory term that the Chinese used to call the people in the South. The name meant "the savages" or "the uncivilized," as explained. In other

---

[46] 金

[47] It is likely that in medieval times Westerners simply did not have the knowledge or interest in identifying specific people to their far east. To them "Cathay" was simply the name of a big country "over there" without specific linkage to China. The identity between the two nations may well be a modern device.

words, "barbarians." Now the Mongols had turned the table and applied the Chinese's own disparaging epithet on them. The Chinese would under no circumstance call themselves barbarians. What this all means is that there was no "state" or "province" or even a locale called "Manji" per se. These were terms of Mongol origin.

By the time the European Age of Discovery "world maps" appeared, these countries were all gone. They no longer existed. Yet they appeared on these maps with "the most up-to-date" geographical information. That these terms appeared on European maps and documents attests to the fact that the early European mapmakers obtained their data from Yuan Mongol/Chinese sources.

On the other hand, that the Age of Discovery era European maps adopted Mongol names for China does not necessarily infer that the geographical information was transmitted to Europe at the time of the Mongols. From the map remnants we know that while the European mapmakers had these names, they did not make sense of them until after the time of the Ming voyages, almost two hundred years after the Mongol Yuan Dynasty had passed into history. The evidence for this can be seen in the 1458 Genoese world map (Figure 121), the first European world map to exhibit a modern form. 1458 was twenty-five years after the termination of the Ming voyages and thirty-five years before Columbus' historical voyages to the Caribbean.

Remember also 1493, the year of the Hartmann Schedel document of *Shan Hai Jing* monstrosities. What all this means is that while Europeans began to learn about these exotic place names as far back as the 13th century, they did not formulate a real geographical concept about them until after the Ming expeditions. Hence, awareness of the Ming maritime exploits greatly instigated the European desire to go to sea. It was the "inspiration" of the European Age of Discovery or Age of Exploration.

Agents of Transmission

Figure 126

Late 16th century Ming Chinese Porcelain Vase

Figure 127

Tang Middle Easterner Figurine

Figure 128

Tang Semitic Figurines

Who brought the awareness of the world from China to Europe, and how was it done? Many would readily turn to the legendary Venetian trader Marco Polo. However, Polo operated in the late 13th and early 14th century, and could hardly be credited for single-handedly bridging the East and the West. Besides, there are more that we will talk about this hero of the ages. The fact is, there has never been lacking in contact between Europe and Asia.

The idea of an East-West disconnect is in fact more cultural myth than historic truth, just as the common misconception of an inward-looking Ming China cut off from the rest of the world. Unfortunately, this portraiture has been indelibly imprinted on the minds of many.

Figure 126 shows a late 16th century porcelain vase, for which the Ming Dynasty is famous, sporting the coat of arms of Aragon and Castile. The vase was produced for export manufactured to European specifications; no small feat for a nation supposedly self-ostracized from the world. The notion that Asian and European cultures evolved quarantined from each other is a myth born out of 18th century European ignorance of history.

Figure 129

Tang Turkestan Horse Attendant Figurine

Figure 130

Tang Persian Figurine

Silk was passed from China to Europe, and so were the gun powder and the manufacturing of paper. The Silk Road connecting China to the West was used by Asians and Europeans alike for centuries.

On the contrary, virtually as a continuous stream, information had passed from East to West, and so had it from West to East. For the benefit of those who staunchly believe in "East is East and West is West," I have provided Figure 127 to Figure 130, those famous

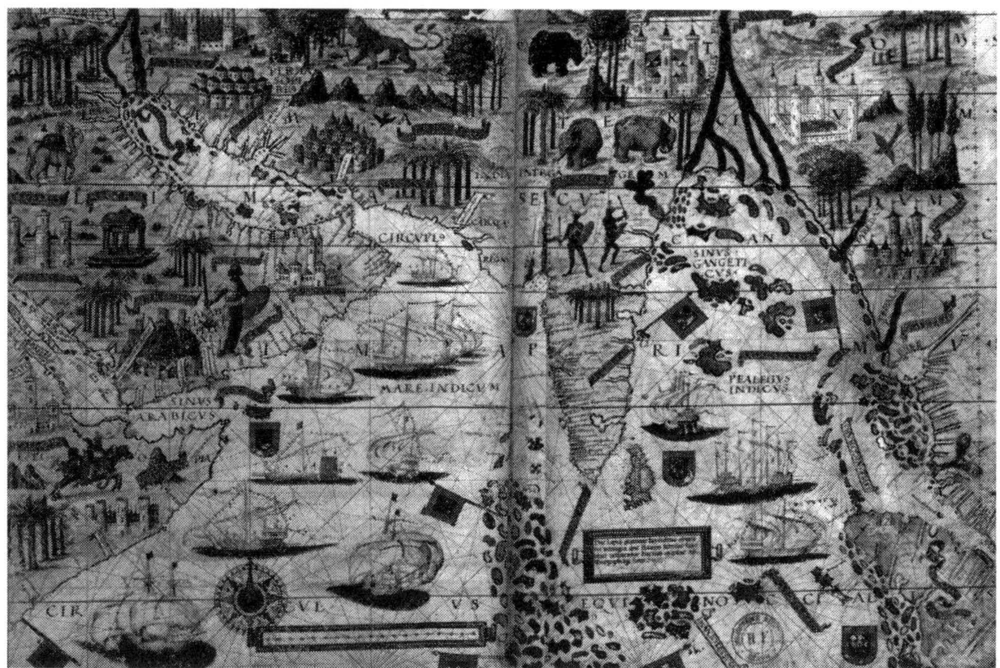

Figure 131

Junks in the Illustration for *The Travels of Niccolo da Conti*

porcelain figurines of Tang Dynasty (618 to 907) that depict the cosmopolitan society of China so vividly.

After the Mongols conquered China in the 14th century, Westerners were employed in the Mongol Yuan government, to such an extent that a privileged class of citizens came to be known in China as the *Se Mu,* or Colored-Eyed Ones. These Western foreigners, mostly Central Asians and Middle Easterners (citizens of the Ilkhanate), in the service of the Mongol rulers brought back material and information from China to Europe. A book such as the *Shan Hai Jing* was a curiosity; it can be described as *intriguing*. Such a book could easily have caught the fancy of any one of the itinerant merchants who would have carried it from Asia to Europe; or, such a transmission could have been effected by a traveler, and history is not lacking in such adventurers.

Figure 132

Seven-mast junks in *The Travels of Niccolo da Conti*

For instance, in 1246, the early 12th century Franciscan friar Pian di Carpini (also noted in history as Giovanni da Pian del Carpine, or John of Plano Carpini, or John of Pian de Carpine, or Joannes de Plano) was sent by Pope Innocent IV to gather information about the Mongols.

The Franciscan monk William of Rubruck traveled to the Mongol capital Karakorum in 1254 and returned with fresh descriptions of new lands, and his accounts contained descriptions that strained the readers' beliefs as well.

Between 1320 and 1330, a third Franciscan monk, Odoric of Pordenone, visited China and India.

In 1339 Pope Benedict XII dispatched the Franciscan monk Giovanni da Marignolli to China (Mongol Yuan Dynasty), and Giovanni da Montecorvino, who served as archbishop of Peking, died there in 1329.

Ibn Battuta (Hajji Abu Abdullah Muhammad Ibn Abdullah Al Lawati Al Tanji ibn Battuta), born in Tangier, Morocco, in the early 14th century, spent a great part of his life traveling the northern parts of Africa, the Middle East, and the Orient.

All these intercontinental travelers became famous in history and were well documented.

Other carriers of new geographic information included diplomats, clergymen, merchants, sailors, soldiers and prisoners, and just about anyone who might possess such information. These people were known to have been deposed by agents of the Church and governments upon their return from their sojourns abroad.

While any one of such personalities could have brought back information from the East to the West, the spurt of world geography that flooded into Europe beginning from about the latter half of the 15th century suggests that a different episode took place after these initial interactions. Several known historical incidents may help us narrow down the possibilities.

The fabled Ming maritime expeditions lasted from 1405 to 1433. There is no question that the Ming Chinese benefited from a great tradition of seafaring during which knowledge of the world's geography was accumulated. During this time, geographical information about the world began to appear on European documents. About a quarter of a century later, by the beginning of the second half of the 15th century, the Fra Mauro map that we discussed above appeared. This map explicitly reported on a Chinese junk rounding today's Cape of Good Hope.

At this time, Europe, specifically Florence, was permeated by "an atmosphere of enlightened new geography," the atmosphere from which Christopher Columbus supposedly inhaled his inspiration to sail west in search of Cipangu (that is, Japan) and the Great Khan of China. It was also at this time that the famed Florentine cosmographer Paolo dal Pozzo Toscanelli postulated a sea route west to Asia, and around 1476, Lorenzo Buonincontri hypothesized that there might be a fourth continent waiting to be discovered. (Recall the Oronce map that depicted the shape of America but linked it physically to Asia.) A few years later, Dias completed the sea route from Europe to India, and Christopher Columbus sailed to the Caribbean.

De'Conti

The people who brought this knowledge from Asia to Europe were not the same group that braved the intercontinental land routes. These came from a new generation who gained knowledge of the sea journeys. It had been suggested that one of Zheng He's responsibilities was to transport foreign dignitaries, and on his voyages he often extended hospitality to international merchants, adventurers, or just plain travelers. Any one of them could have been a transfer agent of geographical knowledge. One such "junk-setters" was an Italian named Niccolò de' Conti, introduced earlier. Indeed, Pulitzer Prize winner science writer John Noble Wilford specifically identified him as such a candidate.

Niccolò de' Conti (1395–1469) was a Venetian merchant who studied Arabic and Persian, became a Muslim (by marrying one) and traveled about the Orient for nearly a quarter of a century, then returned to Venice in 1444. He visited places such as the Middle East, India, Sumatra, and Java. de' Conti was interviewed (that is, debriefed) by a representative of the Pope and Florentine scholars. Whether he met with the noted Florentine cosmologist Toscanelli we are not sure, but he most certainly supplied Fra Mauro with the latest information from the East.

de' Conti described to Fra Mauro the large junks he encountered that sported multiple masts. He had spent a significant amount of time in the Asian waters at precisely the time of the Ming voyages, and would almost have to have either boarded or encountered Zheng He's ships. As a result, Fra Mauro stated that a "zoncho" rounded the Cape of Good Hope, and Fra Mauro drew many such junks in the Asian seas (Figure 92, Figure 93, Figure 95) at a time before European seafarers entered the Indian Ocean for the first time.

de' Conti is the archetypical medieval traveler, and, unlike some legendary or mythical travelogue writers, he was real. He endured the hardships of land and sea to experience the Orient on his own terms.

His travel experiences were later published in a book titled *The Travels of Niccolo da Conti*. This book was illustrated, and Lopo Homem's 1519 map at the Bibliothèque Nationale in Paris (Figure 131) shows the illustration for the section on his stay in India. The illustration clearly shows multiple-masted junks in the Indian Ocean (Figure 132 at the lower right corner of the chart southeast of India) and in the Persian Gulf (on the left-hand side of the chart). See enlargement in Figure 132.

Ultimately, it is unimportant whether de' Conti brought world geography to European attention because many people did, bringing such information at different times, of different regions, and in different forms, and it all started even before de' Conti. For instance, the Cresques Atlas (Figure 85) was created in 1375, just a few years after the Mongols were chased out of China.

For almost thirty years the Ming Chinese dispatched huge fleets to the far reaches of the world. Strangely—to historians, anyway—all of a sudden, the entire enterprise just stopped. When the Ming Government terminated the ventures, the decision came swiftly, and the measures of curtailment were harsh. Those who defied the Imperial edicts were arrested. Many were put to death. Shipyards, both symbols and assets of the eunuch faction who enjoyed the benefaction of the usurper, Emperor Chengzu, were now gone, razed and buried.[48] Orthodox historians claim that this was because the government feared people building large pirate ships. Many of such "people" they feared were Emperor Chengzu's followers, who possessed the seafaring knowledge and experience, and could potentially be problems for the new administration. For the sailors and other participants, a good thing had come to an end.

---

[48] Such Ming shipyards have been discovered recently outside Nanjing.

When Zheng He returned home, many ships were still at sea. (The voyages were not scheduled to coincide with the death of the emperor.) Some would take many more months or perhaps even years to reach home base, bringing with them exciting new experiences and knowledge. Today we can imagine how these Ming sailors must have felt when they discovered to their dismay what awaited them at the end of their travails and perils.

Ironically, while the pedantic government ministers and officials might not have appreciated what they possessed, any seafarer would instinctively understand that they were in possession of something of great value. Records of their missions were worth their weight in gold. Even if they had not recognized it immediately, their foreign fellow travelers surely would have made that plain. These foreign connoisseurs would pay good money to get their hands on these documents. Even if the deals would have to be made surreptitiously, the lure would certainly have been too strong to pass up on. In other words, there should be no doubt that the Ming seafaring material would have passed into foreign hands.

Who would be in a position to acquire these articles, including Zheng He's precious sea scrolls? The most likely candidates would have to be the chart makers whose jobs were to commit the real-time navigation and survey data to documentation. Whether scribes such as Ma Huan[49] who took part in the voyages would be responsible for such tasks is not told, but that scenario would be unlikely for three reasons.

First, these scribes were taken on primarily for their language skills, not navigation expertise.[50]

Second, they were not likely to have participated in the more arduous and dangerous, not to mention secretive portions of the voyages, such as Zheng He's many trips to Mecca, and the trip down the coast of Africa and around the Cape of Good Hope. They were unlikely to have been on the sea legs around the world.

---

[49] 馬歡

[50] For details, see The Hunt for the Dragon, 2nd Edition, by Chao C. Chien.

Third, they did not possess the chart-making skills requisite to be used in that capacity. Furthermore, because the foreign passengers would not be allowed to have direct contact with government personnel, direct transactions between the parties can be reasonably ruled out.

A second source of supply would be corrupt and enterprising officials, who would include all those serving in the administration, although Zheng He himself would be an unlikely candidate.

The Ming overseas expeditions were officially shut down in 1433. A few decades later, in 1477, per mainstream history, a voice was raised in the Ming court to revive the maritime program, ostensibly to stimulate the sagging Ming prestige. The idea was scrapped because the official in charge of the maritime records had "accidentally burned them." To fully appreciate this minor yet strange episode of Ming history, we must examine the specifics behind such a "mishap."

When history describes the Ming official "accidentally" burning the Zheng He documents, a part of the Imperial archive, it is not as if he simply "accidentally" went into his study, "accidentally" hauled out the maritime records, "accidentally" made them into a pyre, and then "accidentally" set fire to it. This official was the equivalent of our present-day Secretary of Defense, and head of a government organization; a large bureaucracy. If he in fact "accidentally" burned the records, he would not have done it himself. He would have "accidentally" issued the order to burn them instead. There were deputies and functionaries to carry out such tasks. Even if there was such an "accidental" order to burn the documents, during the process, there were plenty of opportunities for someone to have concealed a few choice documents for his own consumption and withheld them from destruction.

The more likely scenario of what actually took place is, instead of the documents having been burned, they were pilfered and sold over a span of time, although at the time when the proscription was issued, some documents were deliberately burned. No doubt some of these valuable documents, which certainly included maps and sketches, found their way overseas and into private collections.[51]

Florentine Lorenzo Buonincontri's speculation about a fourth continent in 1476, at virtually the same time when the Ming official "burned" his records, was similarly not accidental or coincidental. Indeed, as if by another fluke, new geographical information about the world began to materialize in Europe, as evinced by the many maps about new places, albeit done in the most unsure and sometimes even comical fashions that we have seen throughout this book so far, and more are to come.

In any case, any such treasonous transactions would have to be made clandestinely, and between parties that could speak the same languages. Therefore, the involvement of translators was almost certain. This is the reason why most investigators of the Ming naval saga invariably zeroed in on Niccolò de' Conti, an Italian trader who could speak several local languages. However, the buyer or buyers could just as well have been Indian (from India), Arabic, Turkish, or other nationals, many of whom were indeed employed on the Ming expeditions. (And do not forget that Christopher Columbus brought a translator named Luis de Torres who could speak Arabic on his voyages even though they were supposedly going nowhere near any place where Arabic would be spoken.)

The information—map sketches and navigation instructions, sea charts, and so on—would be parceled out. The astute black marketers most likely sold the same map sections more than once to different interested parties. Some stocks might even have remained unsold because agreeable prices could not be settled upon.

---

[51] I have great confidence that some of these early maps or map snippets are still hiding in the depths of some collections somewhere; perhaps in some ancient European castle libraries where lost works of Teleman and Bach are still occasionally rediscovered, in the archives of some blueblood families of seafaring traditions, among the ancient papers of some cartographic houses, on the shelves of the Forbidden City royal study, or even the Vatican.

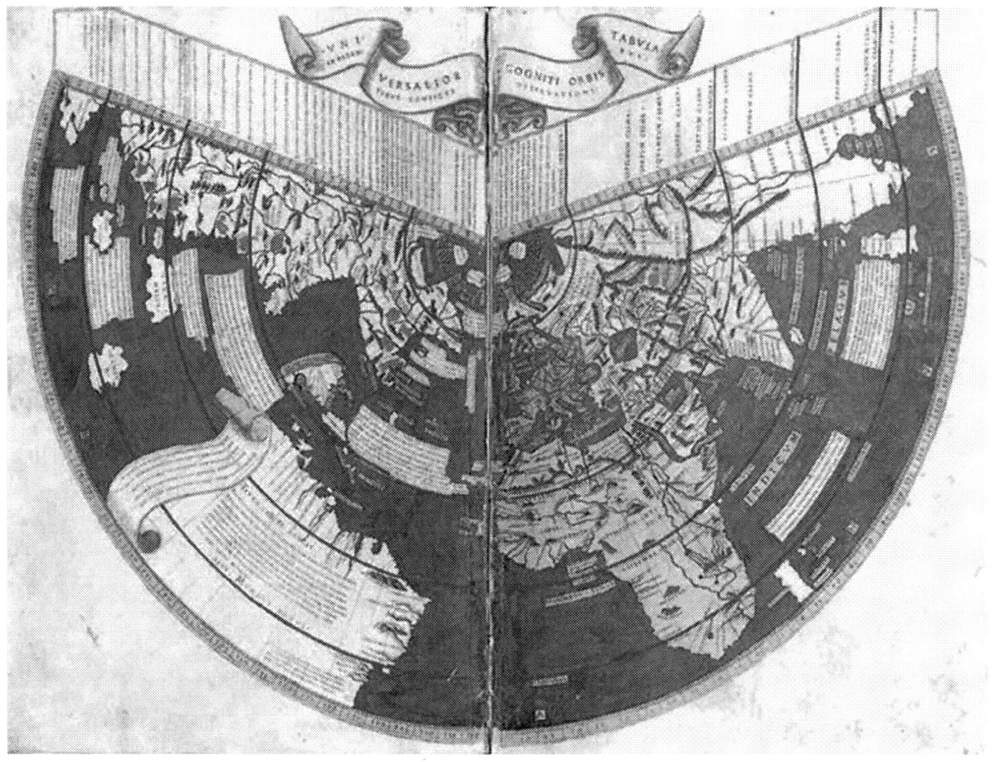

1507 Ruysch World Map

In any case, a spate of alien and fantastic maps and documents began to make their appearances in European intellectual circles starting at about the middle of the 15th century. One is therefore left to wonder if Henry the Navigator himself had been exposed to or acquired such material in North Africa.

It is safe to conclude that Europeans had come into valuable geographical information of the world in the early 13th century, and that is illustrated by two medieval maps. There were more, but one is enough. Two would close the case.

Recall that Christopher Columbus went west and bumped into the Caribbean in 1492. He never knew there was an American Continent. He never set foot on North America. He thought he had reached Asia. By the end of the first decade of the 16th century he was gone.

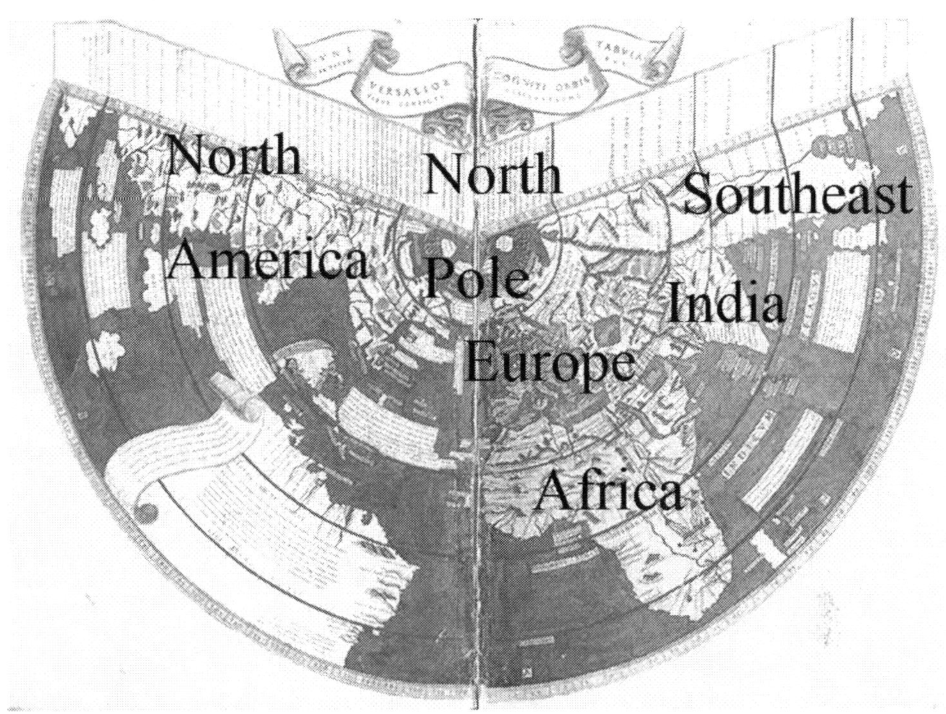

1507 Ruysch World Map Annotated

Then in 1506, Dutch/German cartographer (astronomer, explorer, manuscript illustrator, painter, and Benedictine monk) Johannes Ruysch produced his famous series of world maps (Figure 12, which is reproduced here for your convenience).

Mangi	China. Mongols called China Mangi or Manji, meaning Savages.
Tangut	Mongols' name for XiXia, Tangut people.
Tebet	That is Tibet.
Cathaya	From Kathay, transliterated from Khitai, which the Chinese called Khitan, a people of the north.
Ciamba	Another name for Vietnam.
Iava Maior	Java Major
Gog and Magog	Biblical names for Mongol and Manchu.

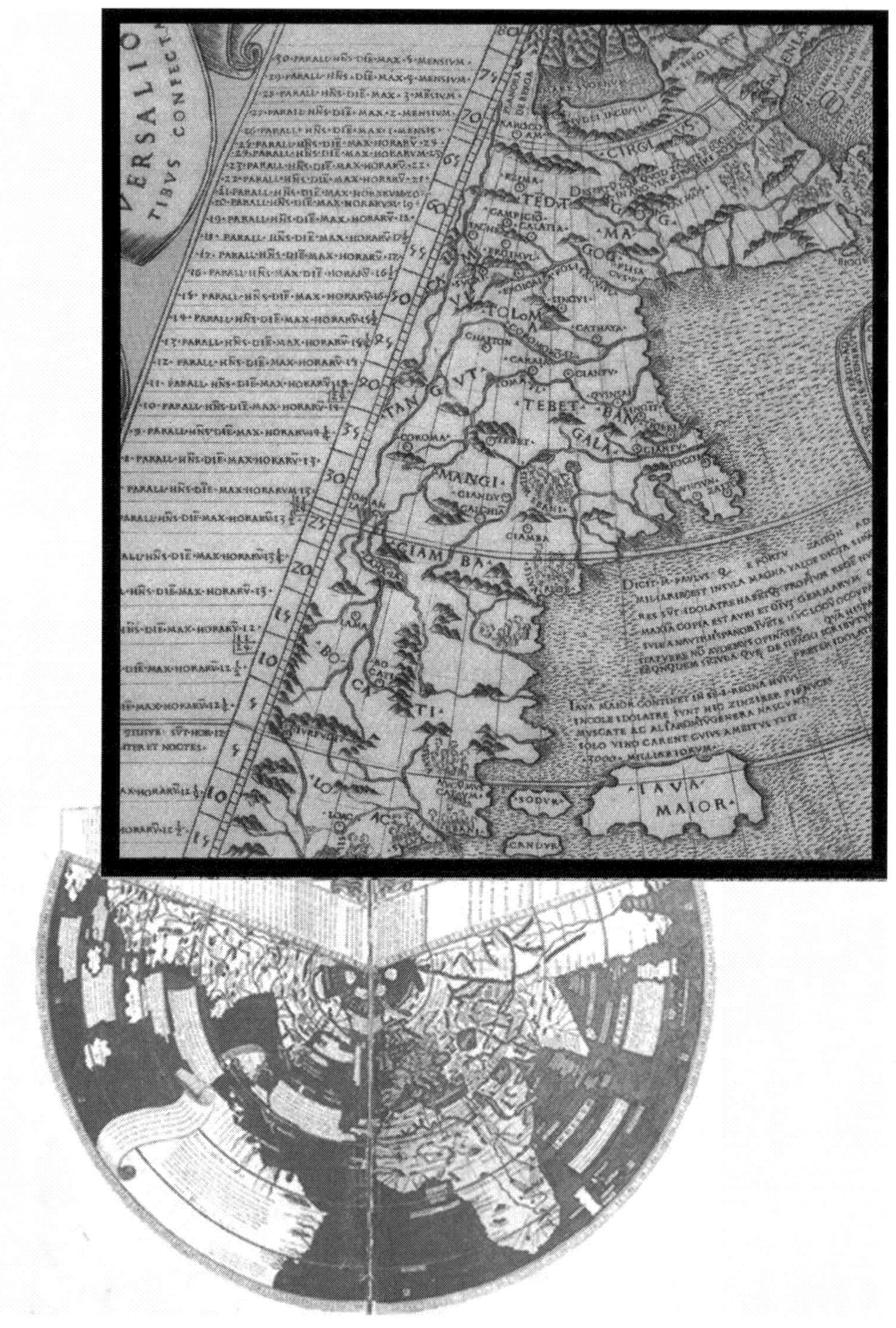

America of Rutsch Map

Ruysch and Columbus were coeval. How did Ruysch get such detailed information about the world while Columbus did not even know where he was?

To begin with, Ruysch's maps look impressive, but they were not perfect. First, there are no American continents. An ocean separates Europe and Asia. That was the basis of the accusation that "Toscanelli had miscalculated Asia as being 5,000 miles longer than it really was, and Columbus miscalculated the circumference of the Earth by 25 percent." Toscanelli, of course, was Paolo dal Pozzo Toscanelli (1397 to 1482), an Italian mathematician, astronomer, and cosmographer.

Yet with such ignorance Ruysch tried to perspective the Earth by viewing it from the North Pole.

Where did Ruysch get his global knowledge? We can get a hint of it by examining the details on the map.

On close examination, one could see that what was deemed Asia looked more like North America. Was Ruysch really drawing Asia or America?

Then there were Asian names placed totally at random; out of place from their real locations.

In short, the cartographer got input, albeit disorganized input, of Mongol Era Asia.

In the 13th century Europe was still in the Dark Ages. Martin Luther had not even appeared. The Yellow Peril and the accompanying Black Death had only just receded. All of a sudden the hapless Europeans learned that there was a bigger, new world out there to be had, and they went for it. That led to half a millennium of unstopped European rise, resulting in their becoming the master of the world.

How Did It Happen?

Based on the documentary evidence examined, as scanty as it may be vis-à-vis the large number of it that is still in existence, we can state with a high degree of certainty that preceding the Age of Discovery or Age of Exploration there in fact existed an Age of Transition; perhaps better described as an Age of Uncertainty, an Age of Probing, an Age of Fumbling, an Age of Confusion, or even an Age of Trepidation. Surprisingly, little research has been performed on the rich collection of historical relics pertaining to this period. This large body of extant documentary and cartographical evidence shows that for quite a while, European geographers had been groping with the newfound data, not knowing what to make of it. Indeed, the evidence does nothing short of showing us how European intelligentsia and adventurers attempted to assimilate this newly acquired geographical data from the East into the European cartographical system, bungling all the way.

From the European perspective, at one time the geography of the world was quite different from what it is today. To be sure, the physical world has not undergone significant changes during the last thousand years, but the European understanding of it, at least some five or six hundred years ago, was wildly imaginative. To understand what I mean by this, let us begin at the beginning, when things were nothing less than chaotic.

Mythical Geography

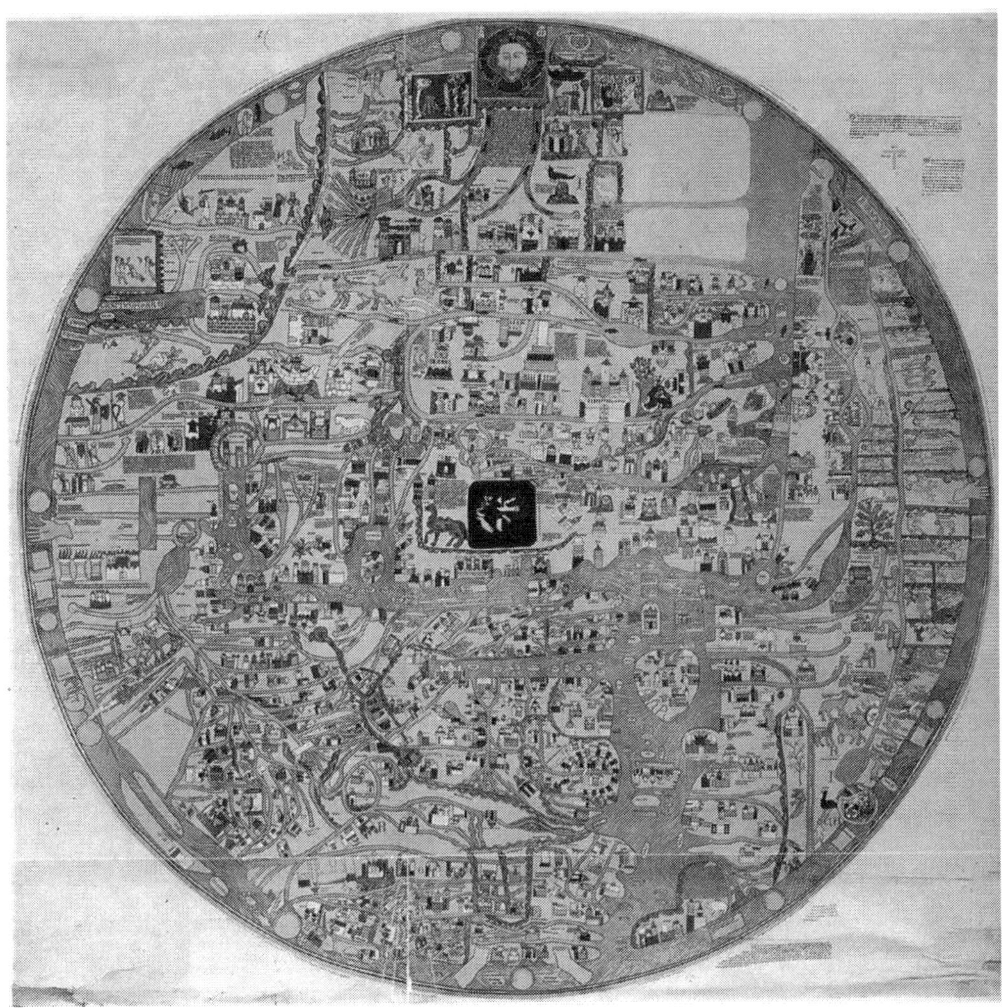

Figure 133

1235 Ebstorf Map

Per historical formulation, when events are uncertain, mythology and legend set in. From the ancient and medieval map samples presented so far, we get an idea of the relatively primitive nature of the European geographical knowledge up to approximately a thousand years ago.

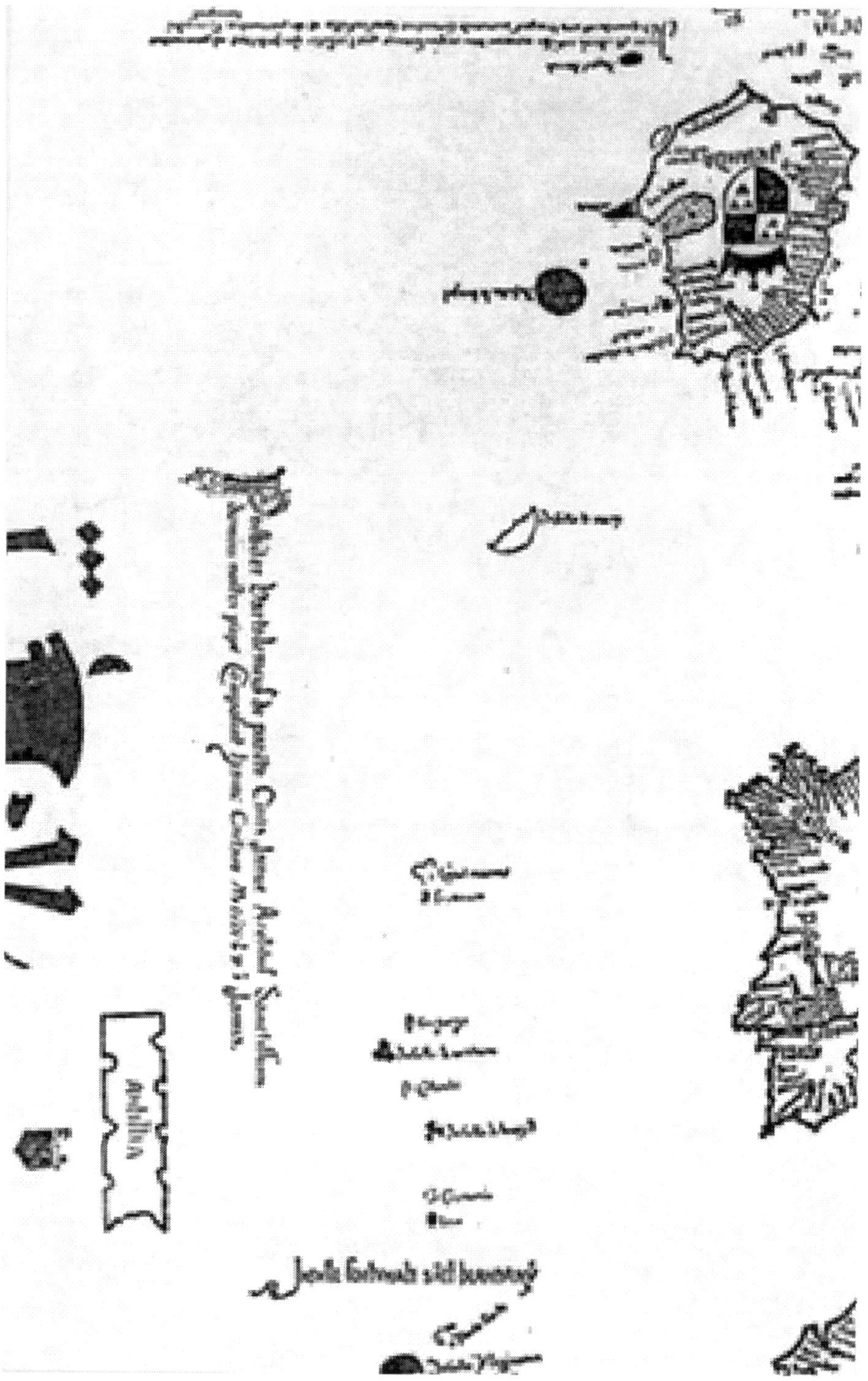

Figure 134

Part of the 1455 Pareto Map

Figure 135

Saint Brendan as It Appeared on Old Maps

Figure 136

Brazil Island

Ancient people knew little about the world outside their immediate surroundings, that which Europeans called the *known world* and what the Chinese called *tian xia,*[52] meaning *"Under the Sky."* The territories beyond their zones of comfort often appeared murky, mystical, ominous, dangerous, yet at the same time fantastic, inviting, and promising, impressions both cultures expressed through fanciful geographical depictions (recall *Shan Hai Jing*). Those tales that withstood the test of time became legends and mythology.

As people gained knowledge about their environments, their spheres of activity expanded. As a result, some myths faded away because they could no longer be sustained, while others simply found fertile grounds further afield and continued to blossom there—especially if the myth appeared to have been grounded in some kind of facts—or they might simply disguise themselves and survive as new incarnates. In other words, we expect ancient literature to contain fanciful elements, and when new ideas appeared, legends and myths found new lives.

---

[52] 天下

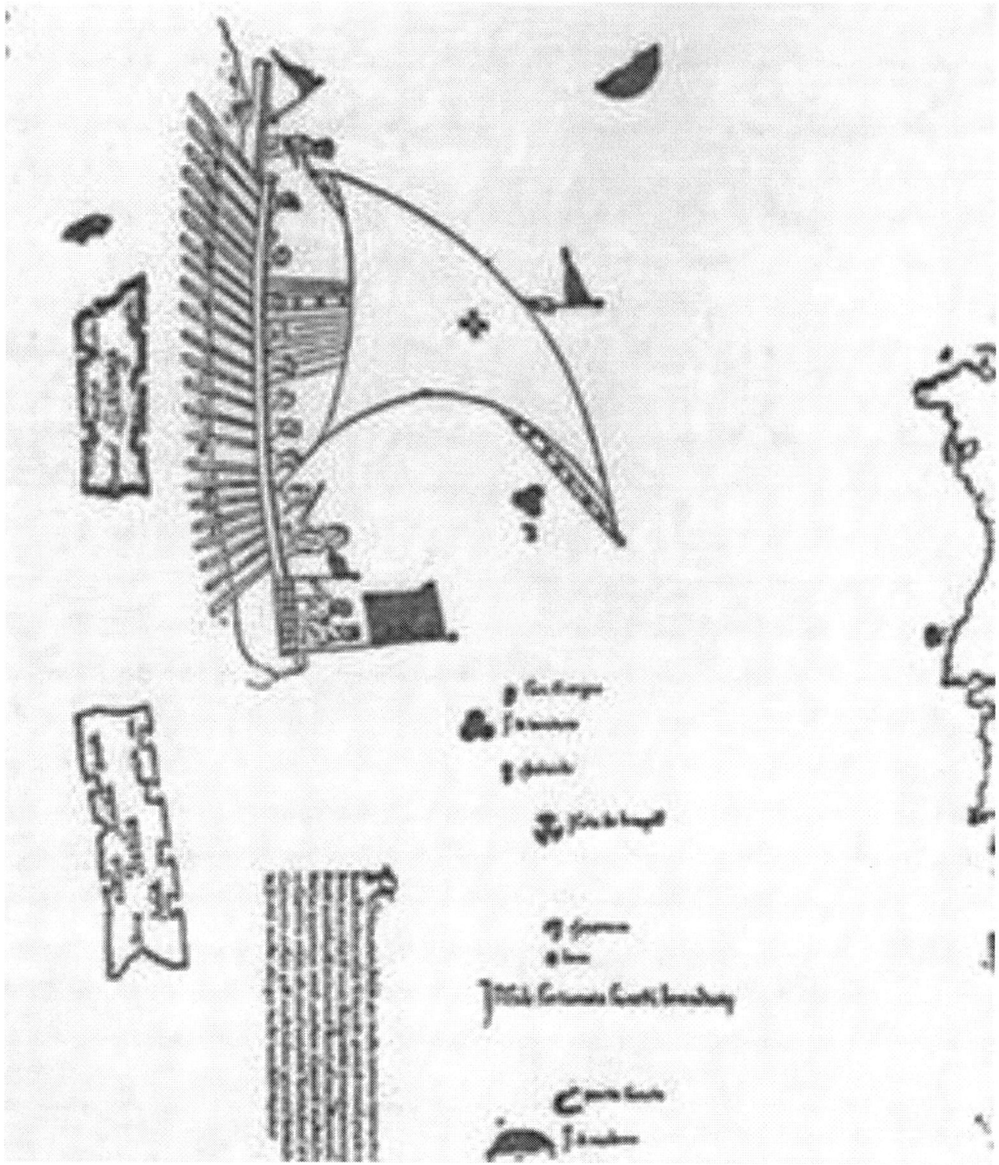

Figure 137

The 1482 Benincasa Map Showing Saint Brendan and Other Imaginary Islands

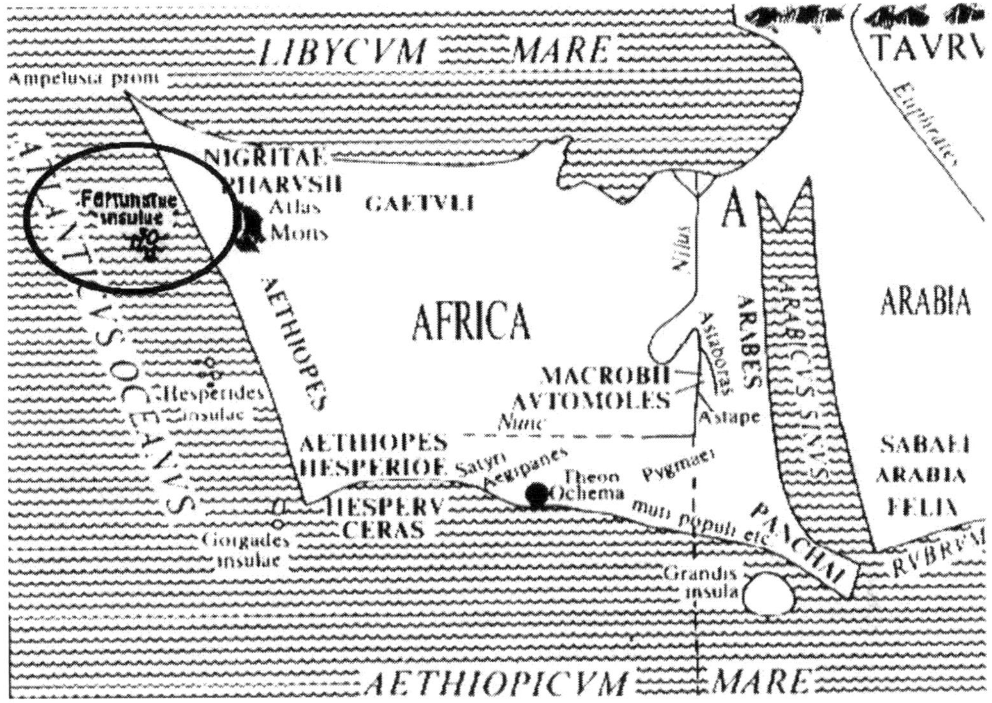

Figure 138

The Fortune Island in the 15th Century Pomponio Mela Da Chronographie Silberman Parigi Map

Indeed, beginning with roughly the late 14th century, a slew of strange or literally "phantom" or "whimsical" geographical features began to appear on European maps. At first, these geographical imaginations took the form of islands, until renewed interpretations of the new ideas indicated that they were in fact new landmasses.

Take the legendary Saint Brendan (or Saint Brandan) island as an example. As a mythical island, it was attributed to a monk who was born in Ireland in the late 5th century. He was reported to have traveled extensively among the outlying islands in the northern Atlantic. Two centuries after his death, in the late 6th century, his exploits were purportedly described in a book titled *Navigatio Sancti Brendani Abbatis*, which, interestingly, went out of circulation in the early 1400's, the time of Admiral Zheng He's voyages.

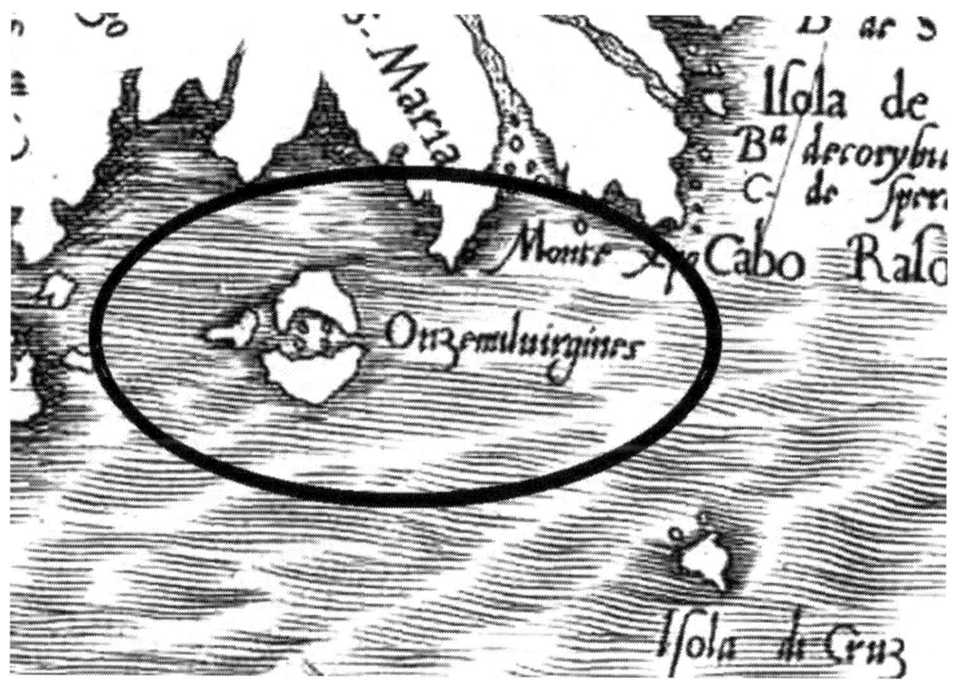

Figure 139

11,000 Islands in the 1562 Gutierrez Map

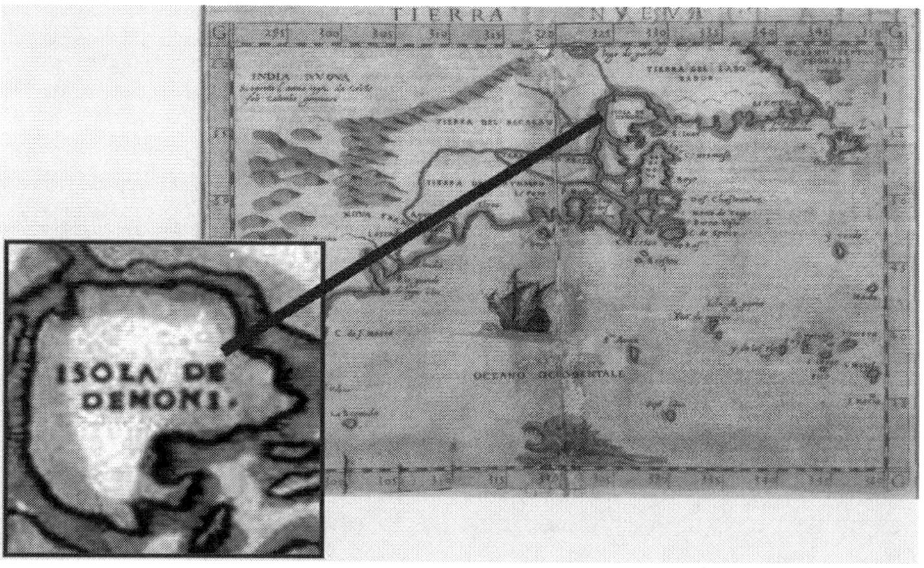

Figure 140

1561 Girolamo Ruscelli Map of Pennsylvania with Imaginary Islands

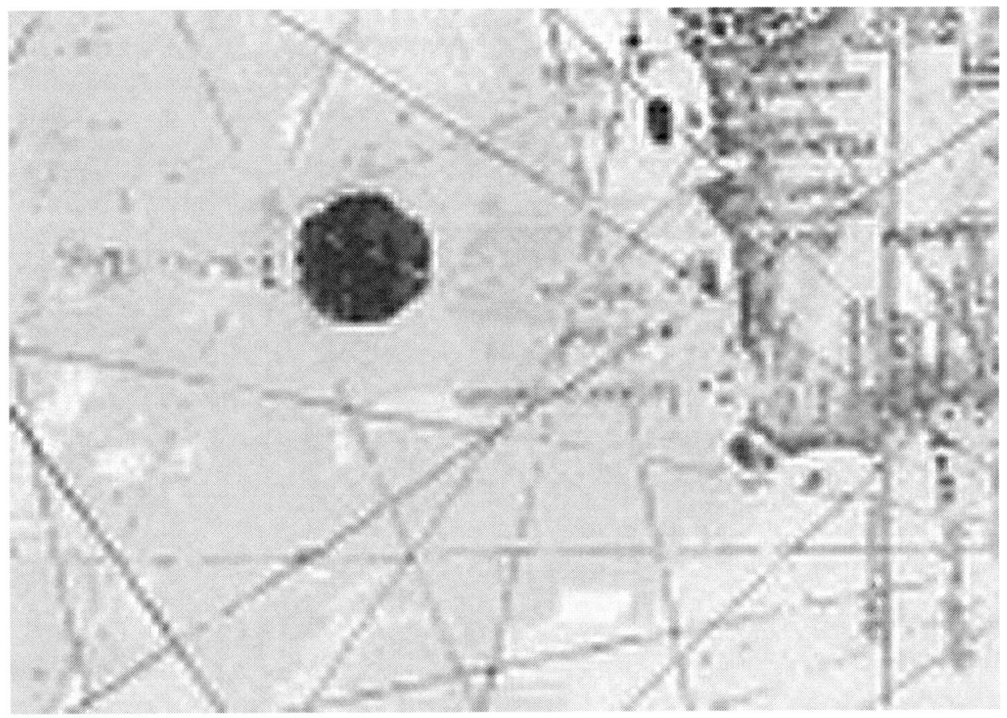

Figure 141

Brazil Island on the 1489 Canepa Map

Supposedly Saint Brendan learned of a "Promised Land of the Saints" and with a dozen or so fellow-monks went off to find this land/island. For seven years they searched, along the way encountering giant sea serpents, dragons, a huge whale, which the travelers took to be an island and tried to cook a meal on it, a crystal island, and even Hell. Eventually they located the island they were searching for, and it became Saint Brendan's Island (Figure 135 and Figure 137).

Saint Brendan's Island appears on the 1235 Ebstorf map (currently housed at the William L. Clements Library at the University of Michigan, Figure 133) and is placed about where the Canary Islands are.

On other maps it is placed by the Madeira Islands or the Azores.

Figure 142

Brazil Island on the 1583 Wagenhaer Map

The legend in the 1339 Dulcert portolan chart (now at the Bibliotheque Nationale in Paris, Figure 145) says: "Insulle Sa Brandani siue puelan." A Saint Brendan Island also appeared on the 1367 Pizigani Map (Figure 146).

Unexplained, on maps after the 15th century, Saint Brendan's Island moved northward to occupy ocean regions that were yet unexplored. For example, the 1426 Battista Beccario map contains the legend "Insulle fortunate santi brandany," which suggests a strong relationship between the Saint Brendan Island and a certain Fortunate Island. Beccario was another famous mapmaker Pietro Rosselli's teacher. As the Cresqueses, they were also from Mallorca. In his 1435 map version (Figure 180), Saint Brendan Island appears among a group of islands called the "Fortunate Islands of Brandão."

Hence, Saint Brendan's Island was not a fluke, at least to medieval European mapmakers anyway. It was no one-act wonder.

Figure 143

Brazil Island on the 1597 Giovanni Magini Map

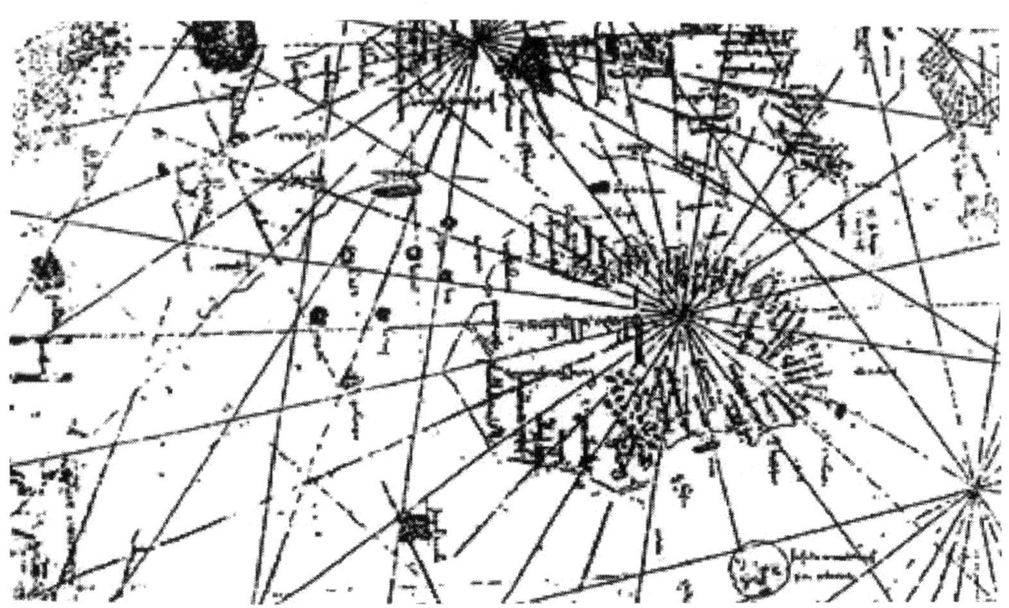

Figure 144

Brazil Island on an Angellinus Dalorto de Génova Map

Part of the 1455 Pareto map (Figure 134) includes Brandão (Saint Brendan), Antilhas (Antilia), Daculi, and other phantom islands in the Atlantic west of Iberia. The legend "Ya Fortunat sa.beati blandan" is included on the 1448 map of Bianco for the largest of the Azores islands.

The 1482 Benincasa map (Figure 137) also shows Saint Brendan (Brandão), Antilia, along with other phantom islands in the Atlantic west of Iberia.

The 1492 Behaim globe puts "Is Brandão" somewhere out in the Atlantic west of Cape Verde, with Antilia to the north, but in the 1544 Sebastian Cabot map "Is Brandão" is placed in the alleged path of Cabot's' travel routes in north Atlantic.

The German cosmographer Martin Behaim identified the Islands of Cape Verde as these Fortunate islands, but the Italian historian Peter Martyr d'Anghiera thought they were the Canaries. In the 1275 map at the Hereford Cathedral a note associates Saint Brendan Island with the Fortunate Island.

These ancient maps show that Saint Brendan's Island had no set position. The island kept moving until the entire Atlantic was completely surveyed, then it simply vanished. Before then, European cartographers evidently believed that Saint Brendan Island existed. In other words, they had a source or sources that suggested the existence of an island which they identified as Saint Brendan's Island. If it was not in the Atlantic, it must be in the Zheng He route before Europe.

The 15th century Pomponio Mela da Chronographie Silberman Parigi map (Figure 138) shows the Fortune Island in the Atlantic outside West Africa. The Fortune Island began appearing on European maps frequently at about the same time the Saint Brendan Island became active. So, the Fortune Island, like the Saint Brendan's Island, was in that stretch of the Zheng He itinerary too.

Another medieval European legend about mystical islands tells of Saint Ursula and her handmaidens who made a pilgrimage by sea from Britain to Rome. The voyage took three years. During that time, the ship carrying the devout Christians was blown off course to many strange places but eventually arrived at the Rhine River. When Saint Ursula refused to marry a Hunnic chieftain as a political instrument to bring peace between the warring tribes, she and her companions were martyred in Cologne around year 500.

As this story was retold, the number of martyred virgins grew from 11 to 11,000, perhaps in part due to a mistranslation of the story.[53] This became a popular legend, and many different versions of it existed.

In November of 1493, on his second voyage, Columbus found a large island, surrounded by an archipelago of smaller islands. He named the largest island (as it appeared to him) Saint Ursula, and the others he called *Las Once Mil Virgenes* (the 11,000 virgins.) These islands are known today as the Virgin Islands. Legends often become real, by proclamation (that is, popular acceptance).

In 1520, the Portuguese explorer Jose Alvarez Faguendes named several islands off Newfoundland "*Onze mil Virgines*" in honor of the legendary Saint-Ursula. Either he was ignorant of Columbus' discovery, or he disagreed with him, or, it did not matter either way. These islands also appear in the 1562 Gutierrez map (Figure 139). Such discrepancies point out the fuzzy nature of the interpretation of the new geographical data. They brought out the truly free-for-all character of European world geography at the time.

Then there was Brazil Island (Figure 140)—yes, island, as opposed to the country on the northeastern coast of South America as we know today—which was variously named (on different maps) Bersil, Brazir, O'Brasil, O'Brassil, Breasil, Brasylle, Hy-Brazil, Hi-Brasil, and other localized adaptations.

The most popular appearance of this island was a pair of discs, which I liken to two buns of a hamburger (uncannily like the Island of Demons), as in the 1489 Canepa map (Figure 141), or the 1583 Wagenhaer map (Figure 142), or the 1597 Giovanni Magini map Figure 143), or the 11,000 Virgin Island on the 1562 Gutierrez Map (Figure 149).

---

53 Author Donald S. Johnson gives a wonderful explanation of the transformation in his book *Phantom Islands of the Atlantic*.

Figure 145

1339 Dulcert Map

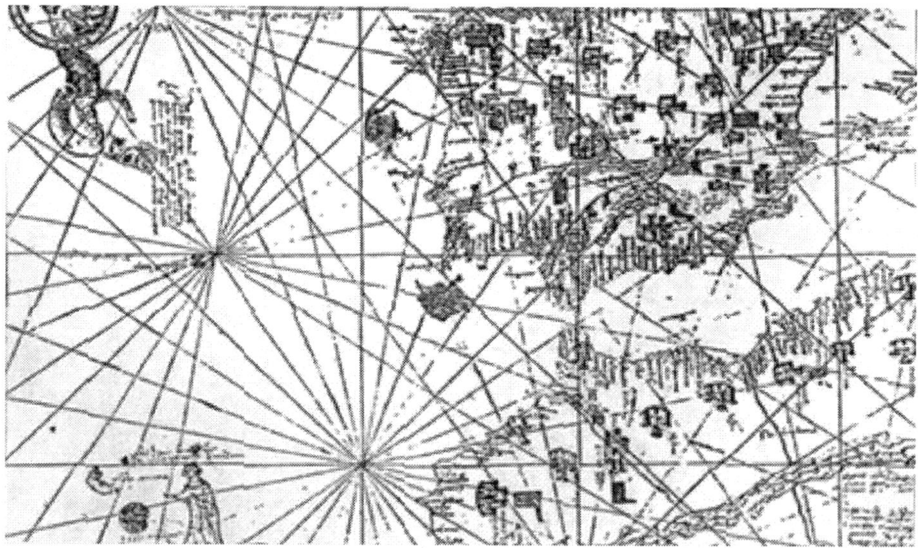

Figure 146

Brazil Island on the 1367 Pizigani Map

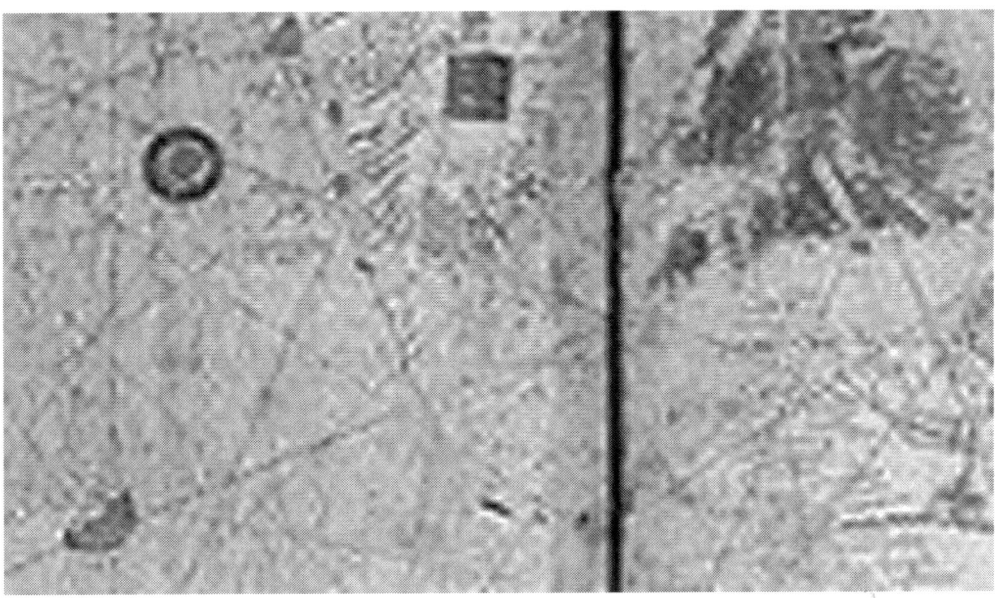

Figure 147

Brazil in the 1375 Catalan Map

The Brazil Island first appeared as early as 1325 (time of the Mongol Yuan Dynasty) on an Angellinus Dalorto de Génova map (Figure 144) along with other imaginary islands, such as Daculi. It was also on the 1339 Dulcert map with other imaginary islands (Figure 145). Sometimes it even appeared twice on the same map, as on the 1367 Pizigani map, which shows Brandão, Mayda, Brazil, Lendárias, Daculi and other islands.

Amazingly, its location in the Atlantic Ocean was consistent to a degree. In most cases it was placed to the west of Ireland, until the early 17th century when it finally moved to the American coast, except this time the island became Brazil the country.

It is also interesting that this island often appeared with a companion island named Mayda. For example, the 1375 Catalan map shows the islands of Brazil and Mayda (Figure 147 lower left corner).

The 1528 Benedict Bordone map shows Brasil Island placed to the east of the Azores (Figure 148 lower right corner).

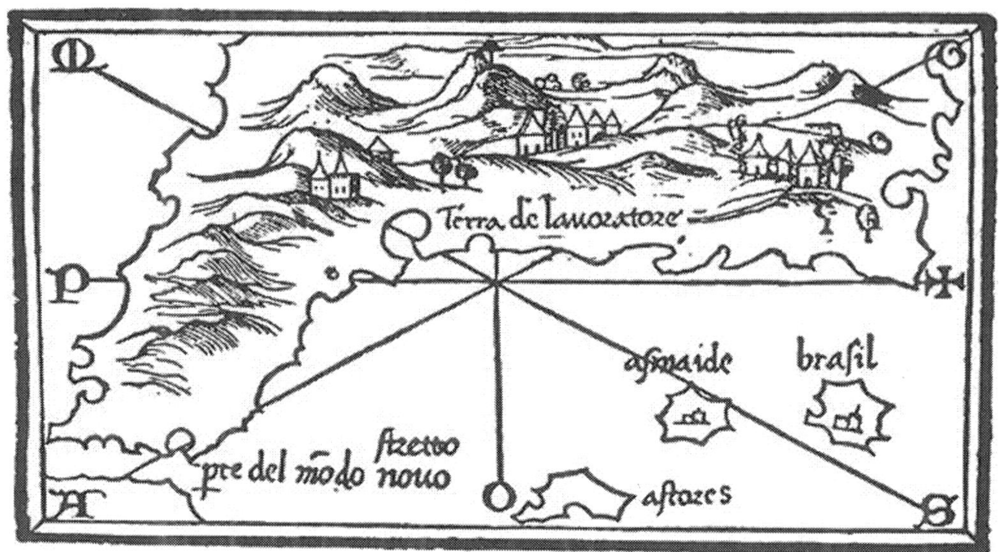

Figure 148

The 1528 Benedict Bordone Brasil

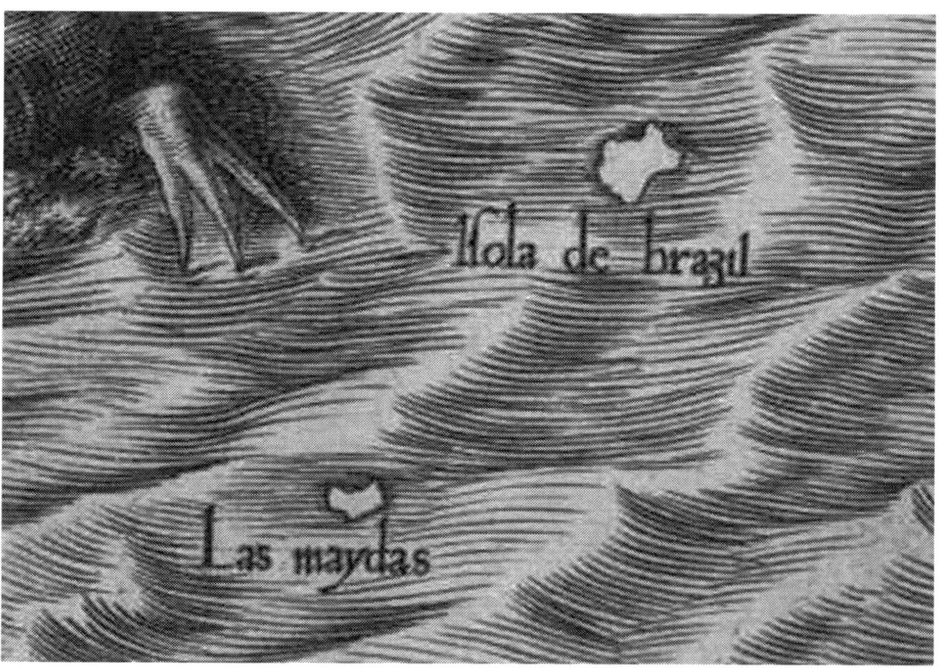

Figure 149

Brazil and Maydas in the 1562 Gutierrez Map

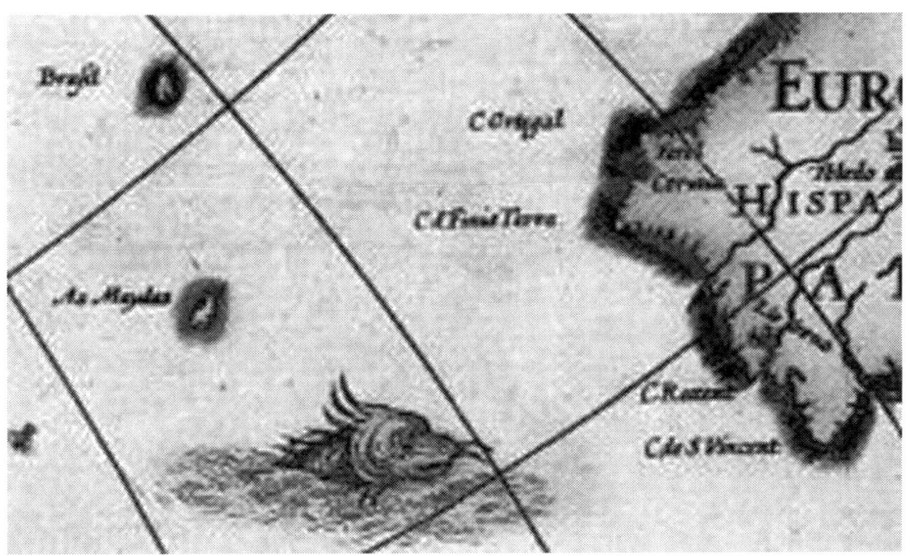

Figure 150

Brazil in the 1617 Blaeu Map

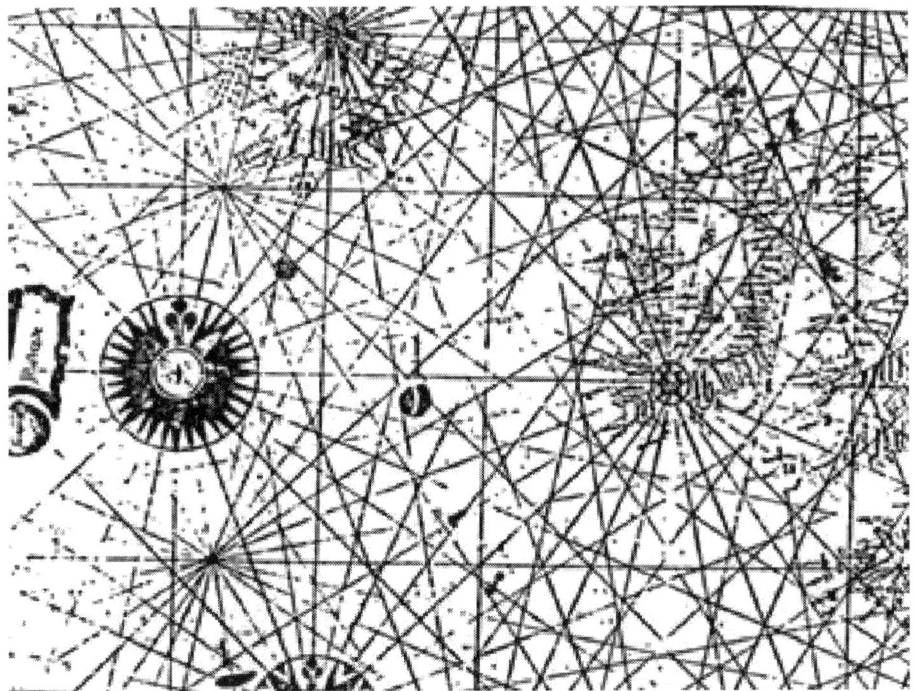

Figure 151

Brazil on the 1480 Catalan Map

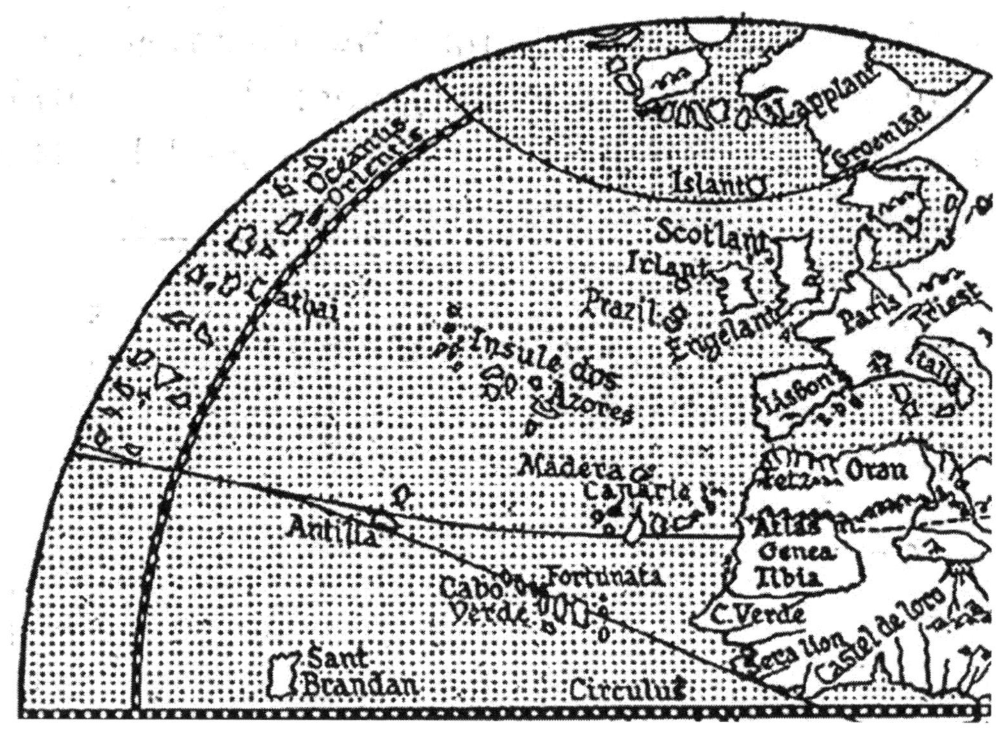

Figure 152

Mysterious Islands in the 1492 Martin Behaim Atlantic

The 1562 Gutierrez map paired Brazil with Maydas and put them in the north Atlantic (Figure 149), while the 1617 Blaeu map put the island pair off the Iberian Peninsula (Figure 150).

The 1480 Catalan map shows Brazil (center of Figure 151), with the Antilia Island on the left.

In the 1459 Fra Mauro map, the island of Brazil is classified as one of the "fortunate islands."

The island was featured on the maps of virtually all the noted cartographers of the time, including Mercator, thus attesting to a strong subscription to its existence. It was on the 1426 Giraldi map, the 1426 and 1435 maps of Beccario, the 1436 and 1448 Bianco maps, the 1455 Pareto map, the 1482 Benincasa map (Figure 137, the island that resembles a shamrock), the 1500 Juan de la Cosa map (Figure 172), and others.

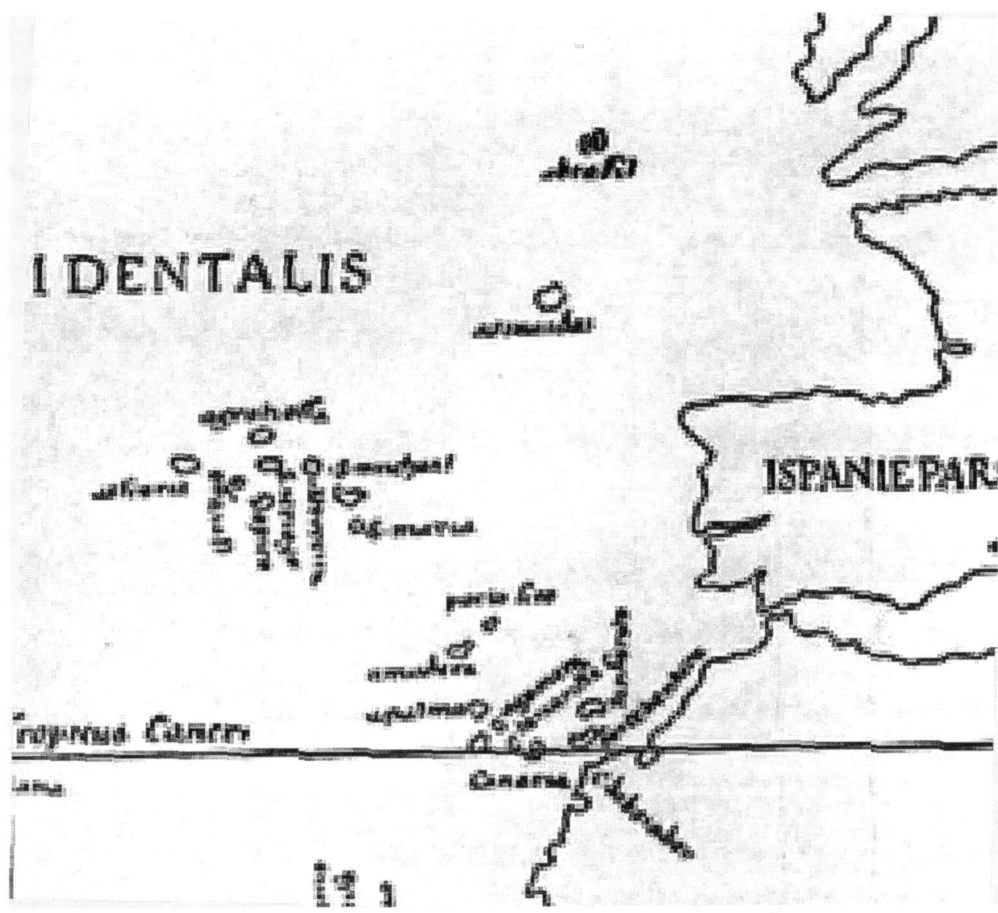

Figure 153

Mayda and Brazil on a 1513 Map

There were many speculations about the origin of the name "Brazil." The explorer/geographer von Humboldt thought that the name was of Arab origin. Others thought that the name could be related to the French word "braise," the Portuguese words "braza" and "brazeiro," the Castilian "brasero," and the Italian word "braciere," all of which in some way had to do with fire. It has even been attributed to a kind of wood.

In the 1492 Martin Behaim map of the Atlantic (Figure 152), many of the mysterious and legendary islands are represented. Starting from the top we have Lapplant and Groenland (Lapland and Greenland), then Islant (Iceland) out to sea on the left, followed by

Scotlant, Irlant, and Engelant. (How Behaim knew about them in 1492 we have no answer.) To the left is Brazil Island drawn as the two buns of a hamburger. To its southwest are the Azores and the Canaries. Spreading out west are Fortunata, Antilia, and Saint Brandan. This was the year when Columbus was set to discover the Caribbean islands.

Brazil Island is again shown alongside the island of Mayda in Figure 153.

In the 1553 Prunes map (Figure 154) Brazil can be seen as a pair of hamburger buns along with Maida and Estotilândia.

In 1570, the noted Antwerp-based cartographer Abraham Ortelius published his *Theatrum Orbis Terrarum*, or world atlas. This is the map previously shown in Figure 71. This atlas boasted of including the latest and most reliable geographical knowledge of the day. In fact, it was the bestseller of printed matters of 16th century. All the same, he was no more capable of steering clear of the phantom locales that we have examined so far than his fellow mapmakers of the time. There, in full view (refer to Figure 71), were all the landmasses and regions of the world, including Australia, which was rendered even better than South America, and the two poles, all before Europeans had surveyed or even visited them.

In the North Atlantic, we have Groclandt (upper left corner of Figure 155), Greenland to its south, followed by Thule, Frisland, with Icaria to the west of Greenland, and Drogeo to the left of Frisland. The island of Brazil is to the west of Ireland (just to the right of the sea creature playing a musical instrument at the lower left corner of the map panel), and St. Brendan just above the creature's tail. The Green Island, "I. Verde," is below the creature.

On the regional map on North Atlantic (Figure 156), Estotilant, Icaria, Frislant, Fortuna, Des Demonios, and S. Brandani were in plain sight.

At mid-Atlantic are the islands of Santana and Sept Cites (Seven cities) to the east of Bermuda (Figure 157), and Ya Verde to the northeast.

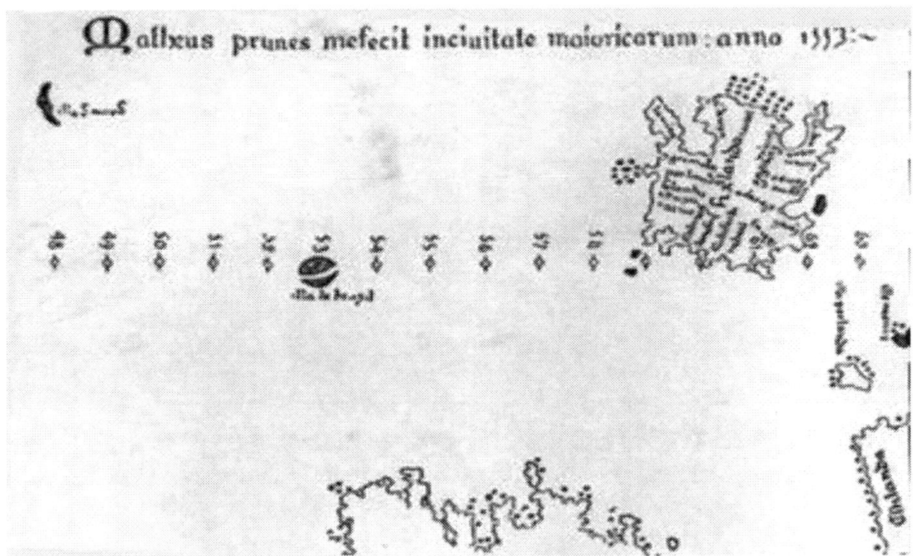

Figure 154

Mayda on the 1553 Prunes Map

Figure 155

1570 Abraham Ortelius Map Zeno Islands

Figure 156

1570 Abraham Ortelius Map North Atlantic

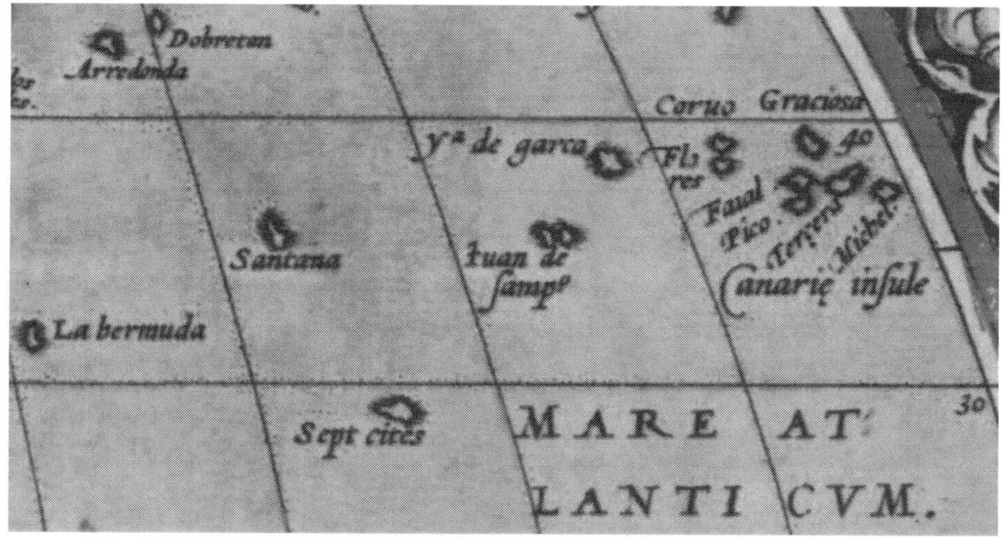

Figure 157

1570 Abraham Ortelius Map Santana and Verde

Figure 158

1570 Abraham Ortelius Map Trinidad in Cuba

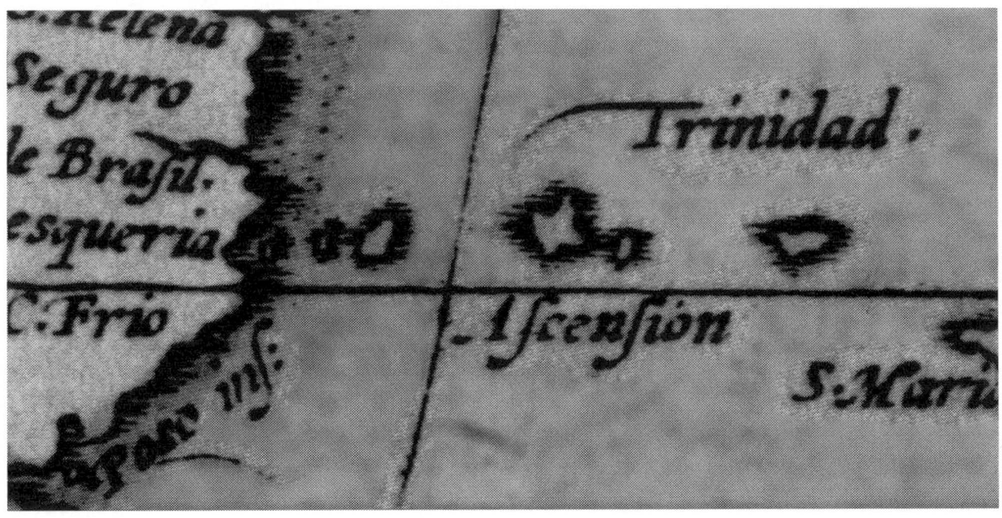

Figure 159

1570 Abraham Ortelius Map Trinidad in Atlantic

Trinidad (La Trinidad) shows up on the south side of Cuba (Figure 158) and in the Atlantic east of Brazil (Figure 159).

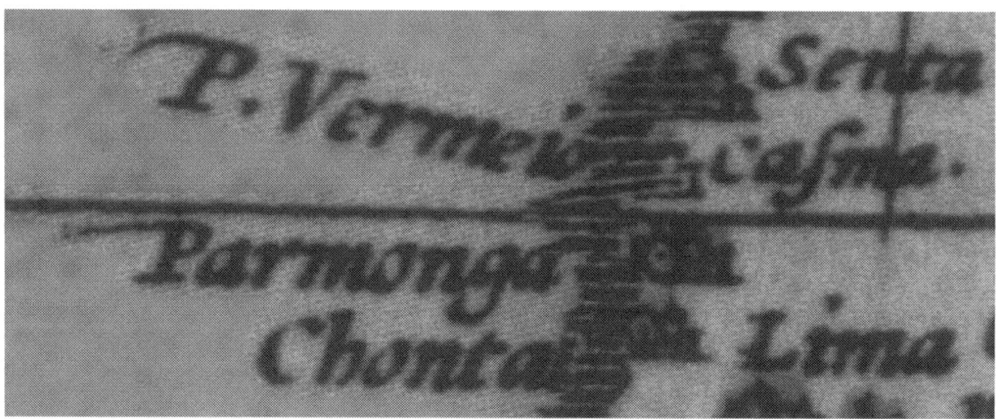

Figure 160

1570 Abraham Ortelius Map "Vermeio"

Figure 161

1570 Abraham Ortelius Map "Vermeia" in Gulf of Mexico

There is Cevola in Arizona, and the famed mapmaker is clearly confused about the name "Vermillion" as it appears by Peru (Figure 160) and in the Gulf of Mexico (Figure 161). I shall address "Vermillion" below.

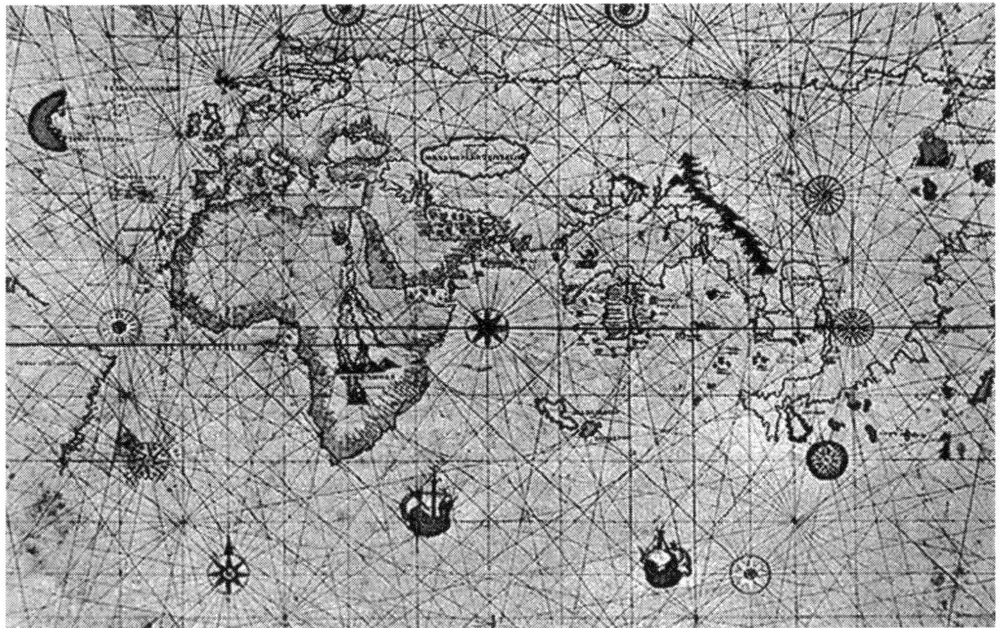

Figure 162

Huge Atlantic Island in a 16th century Map

These were the most advanced geographical knowledge of the day. The ever-shifting non-existent islands were never abandoned, clearly indicating that they existed on the map originals. With the Chinese way of indicating a change of sailing direction by text, one may never know where they might be.

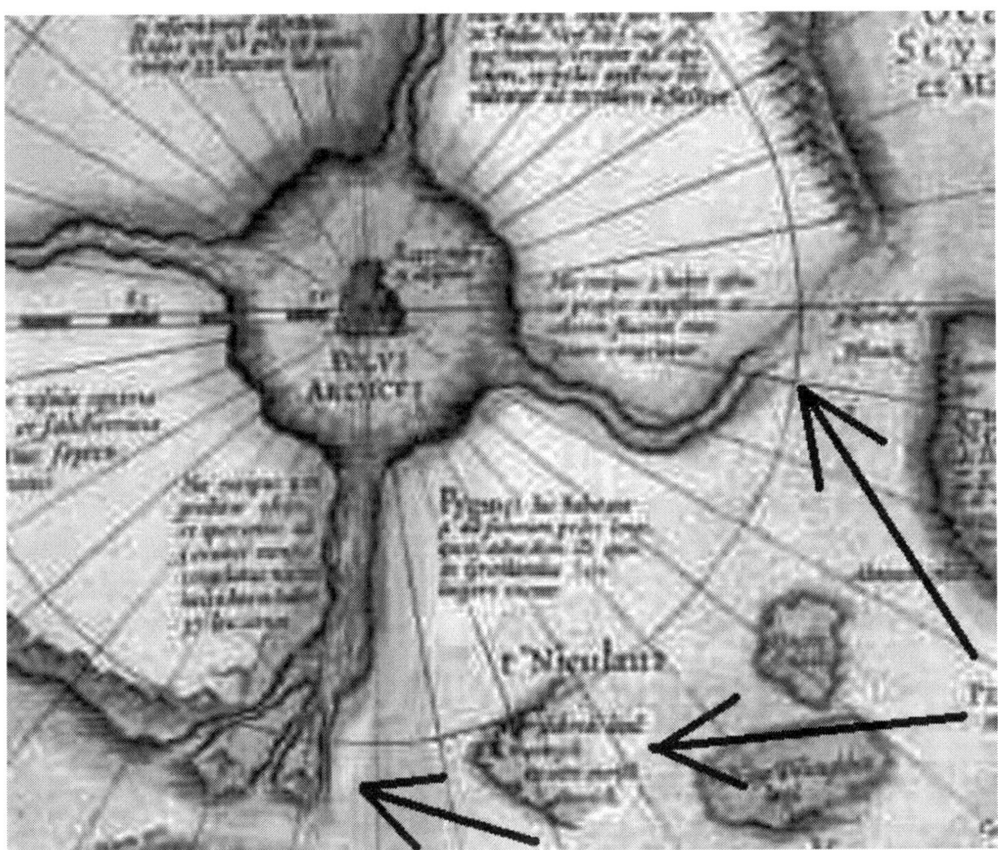

Figure 163

Incomplete North Pole Features

It is not the focus of this work to survey the anomalies of the Age of Discovery cartographical products per se. Rather, the unlikely concepts of the world's geography during the Age of Discovery shed light on the reality of the period's history. Hence, continuing with a litany of such oddities will serve no additional purposes. For those of you who are interested in this subject, I hope the foregoing is sufficient to pique your curiosity and interest, and to serve as road marks for further independent researches.

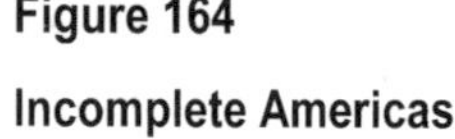

Figure 164

Incomplete Americas

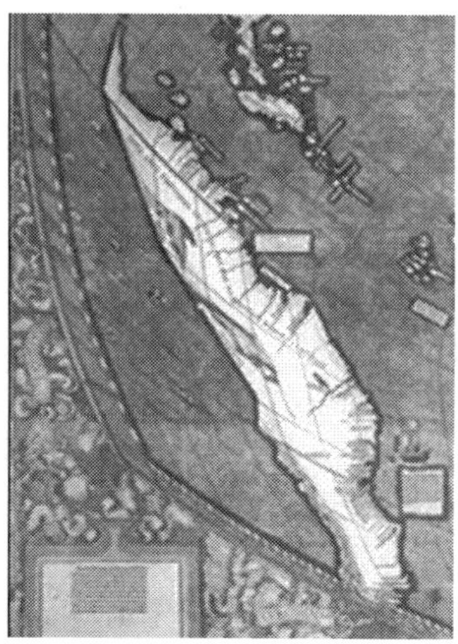

Figure 165

Truncated South America

Ultimately, the strength of such evidence lies not in its apparent abundance, but in its evolutionary process, its assimilation into the developing European knowledge of the world.

The Age of Discovery European cartographers had come into possession sketches showing mysterious geographical features. That much is clear. The data were foreign, and they were rendered using a system or systems whose working formulas and parameters were alien to the local technical community. This explains the widespread discrepancies in the unknown features' placements, orientations, sizes, and identifications. Such anomalies buttress the conclusion that the European cartographers during the infant days of the Age of Discovery were not working from firsthand survey data.

The early 15th century geographical information trickling into Europe in parcel form is plain from the evidence. Once again, look at the ice formation of North Pole (Figure 163). Pay attention to the incompleteness of the drawing as highlighted by my arrows. Look at the Newfoundland/Labrador landmass. The cartographer grudgingly drew it dangling in mid ocean (Figure 164). Look at a partial South America sliced off as a piece of salami (Figure 165) or with a phantom western coastline (Figure 166).

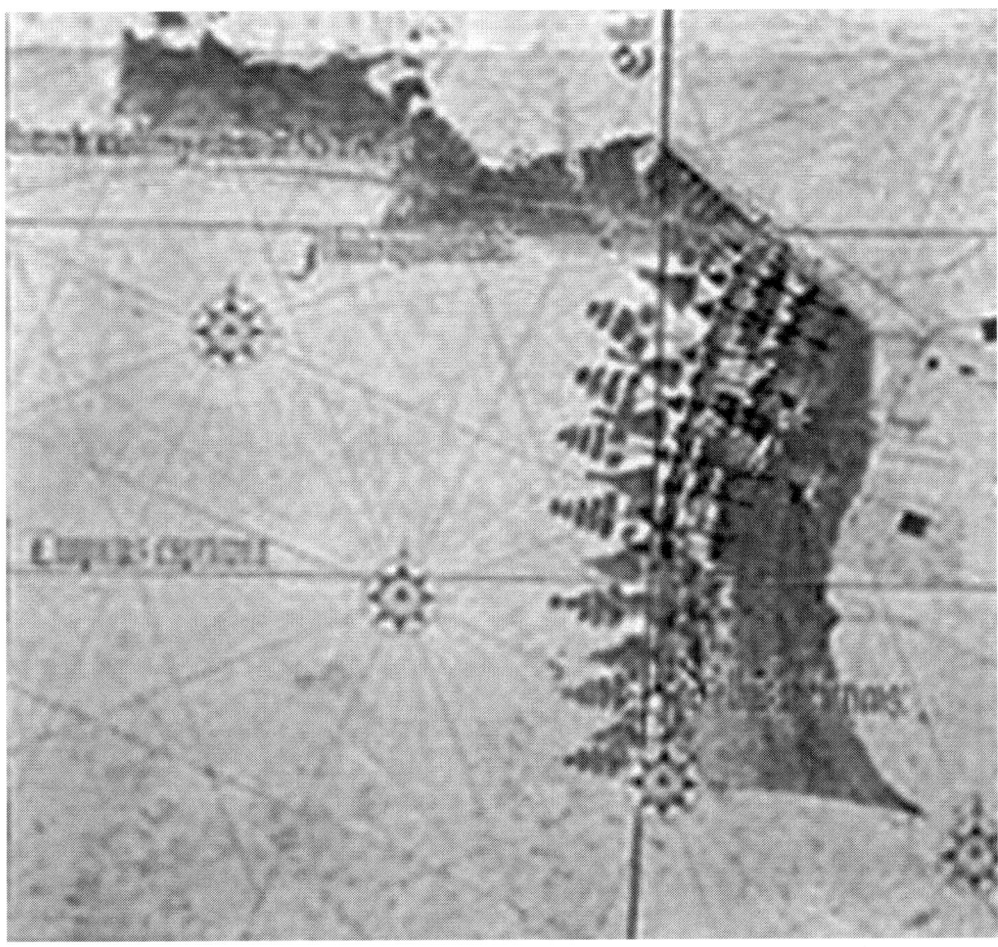

Figure 166

Phantom American Coastlines

These are all partials, and because the originals undoubtedly employed an alien scale, the European cartographers had a hard time resolving them to fit them into their products.

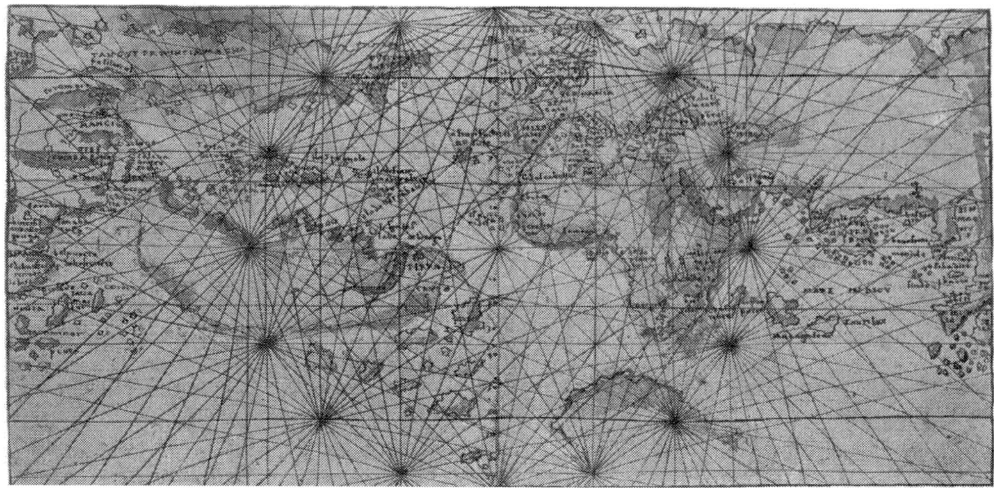

Figure 167

1508 Rosselli World Map

In any case, the "original" sketches obtained themselves would be copies and not originals, because they had to be translated into local languages and units of measure to be usable. De' Conti facilitating Fra Mauro with his world map comes to mind, and so do the Arabic-speaking Zheng He crew members. These virtually undecipherable strange drawings were difficult to work with, and it took time to convert them to the European cartographic system. This hardship is illustrated in the following example.

The Francesco Rosselli Map

Take a look at Figure 167 (and Figure 168), the 1508 world map of Rosselli, drawn not twenty years after Columbus first reached the Caribbean, which sports a grotesquely exaggerated northeast South America and its Caribbean appendage above it. Asia is on the left. (The mapmaker had information on the landmass there, but did not know it was an unknown continent.) South America is absent.

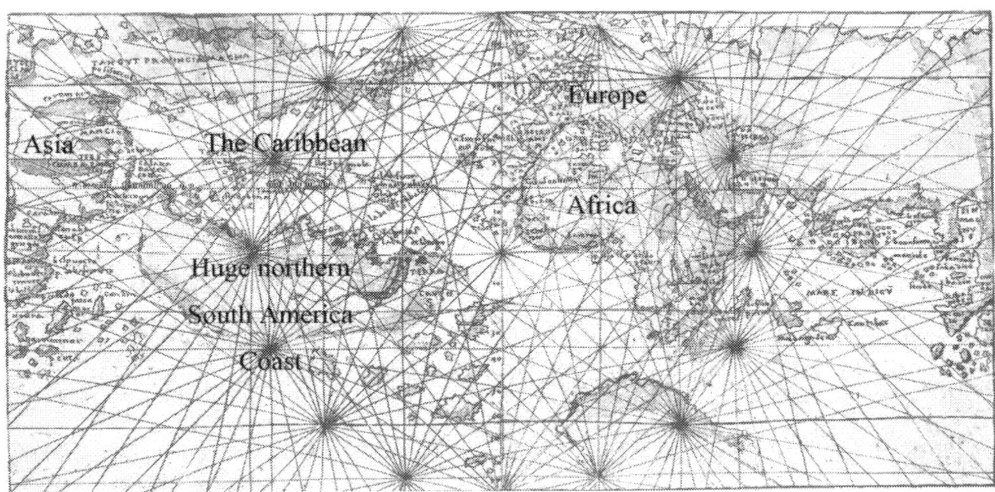

Figure 168

1508 Rosselli World Map Annotated

By 1508, technically Columbus had already passed into oblivion. Had the European explorers surveyed and charted the continent of South America in its entirety? They did not appear to have done so. Balboa did not reach the Pacific coast until 1513. Magellan did not obtain his guiding roadmap for South America until 1520 at the earliest. However, if we give the benefit of the doubt and assume that Europeans already had charted South America by 1508, we need to explain why Rosselli furnished only a partial South America in his map. Just look at the maps in Figure 167 and Figure 168. They look like they were so haphazardly put together to actually be published and sold.

One may argue that cartographical data were highly guarded at the time, and Rosselli might not have had access to the latest exploration results. If so, we then must explain what he based his drawing on. We need to explain why the Caribbean area (actually, just the north coast of present-day Venezuela) is so big; bigger than Africa. However, all would make sense if the maps were drawn based on foreign, incomplete, raw map sketches, which caused the mapmaker to have difficulty with the scaling.

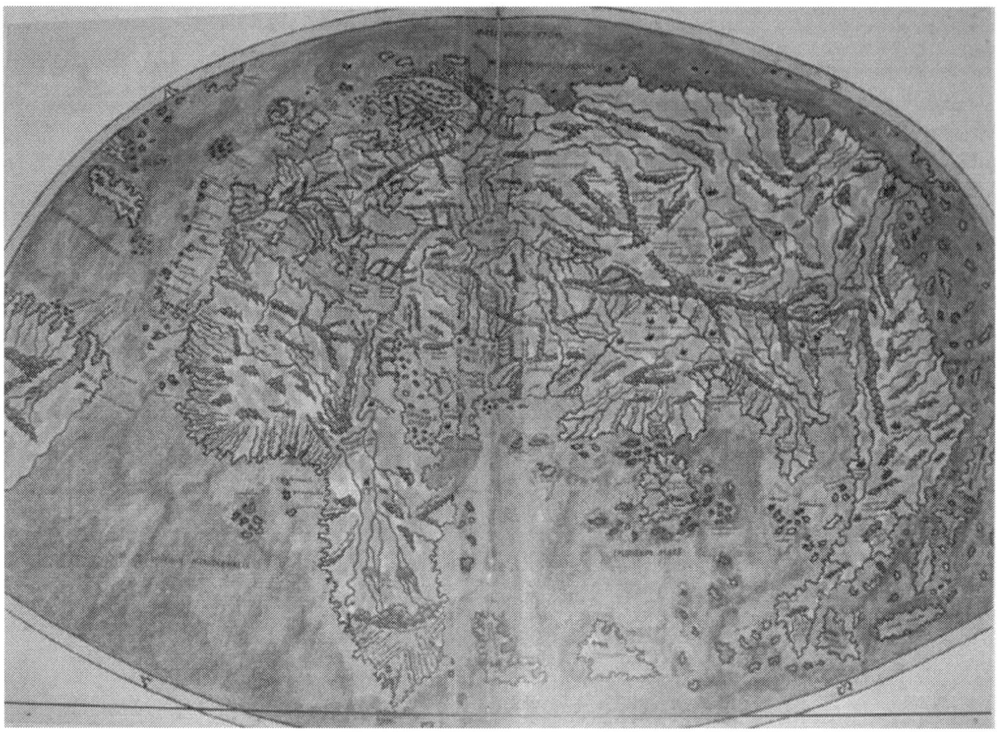

Figure 169

1520 Pietro Coppo Map

Look at the world maps drawn by Venetian cartographer Pietro Coppo in 1520 and 1524 as shown in Figure 169 and Figure 170. Just like Rosselli's map, these maps were crudely drawn, but that is precisely why these maps are so invaluable in helping us understand the acquisition of world geographical knowledge during the early years of the Age of Discovery. In these maps the shapes of Asia, Africa, and America are bizarre. In fact, America is absent. What we have, however, is something that looks like a bear's paw with all its claws extended.

The Pietro Coppo Map

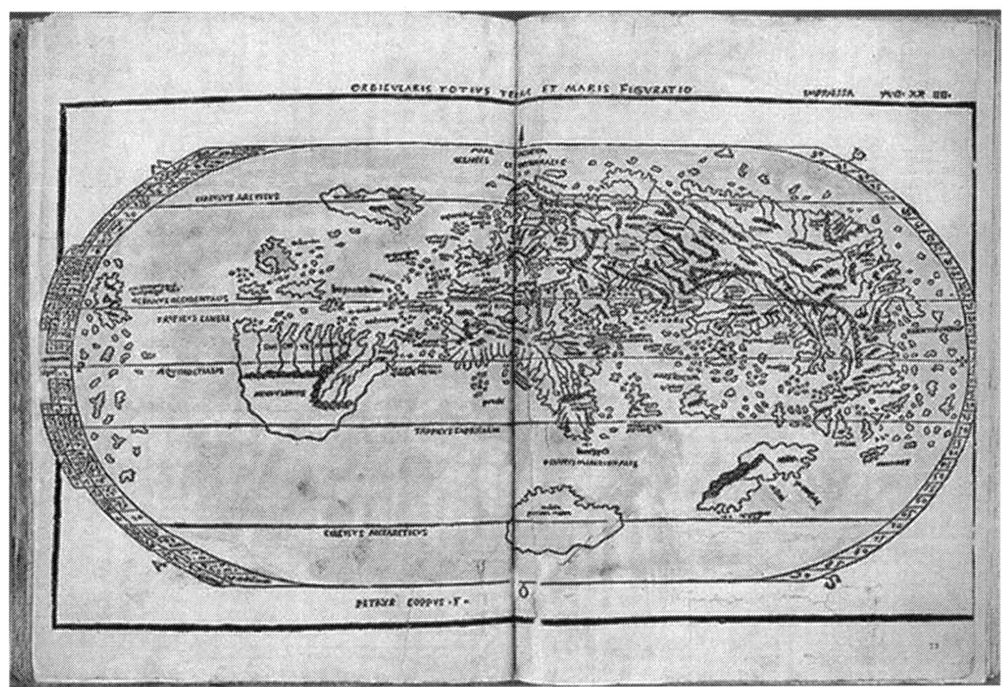

Figure 170

1524 Pietro Coppo Map

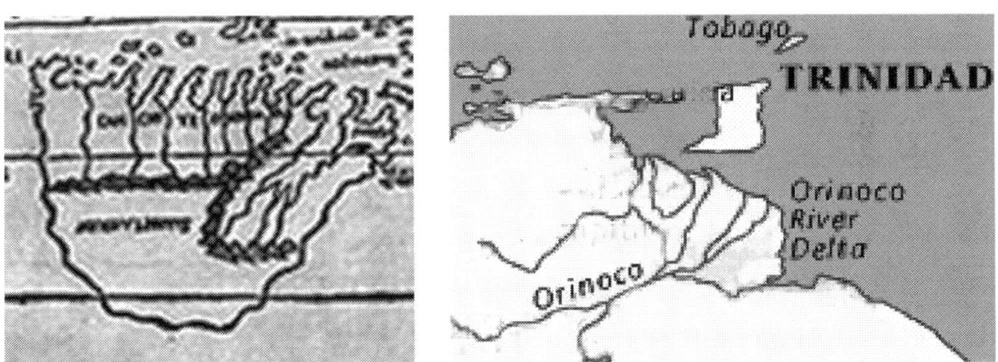

Figure 171

Comparison between 1524 Pietro Coppo South America and Today's Orinoco Delta

Palpably Coppo did not have the entire South America. All he had were the Caribbean islands and the northern part of the Venezuelan-Brazilian coast; specifically, the area around the Gulf of Paria.

Figure 172

de la Cosa Map of the Caribbean Under Glass at Museo Naval

In other words, Pietro Coppo also based his maps on genuine "raw" data, which came in the form of partial sketches drawn to alien scales. Refer to Figure 171. Compare his attempt to render the Gulf of Paria on the left against the modern mapping of the same area on the right.

The Juan de la Cosa Map

Christopher Columbus set sail in 1492 and promptly ran into the Caribbean. He then proceeded to investigate the north shores of South America, but he never set foot on North America. Yet, featured in the Museo Naval of Madrid, Spain is a portolan world map drawn on ox hide in 1500 (Figure 172, Figure 173) by the cartographer Juan de la Cosa, Columbus' comrade on his trips. The map was reportedly lost, then rediscovered by the Dutch Ambassador Baron Walckenaer in a Paris shop in 1832, and was subsequently purchased by the Queen of Spain in 1853.

The maker of the map, de la Cosa, was the owner of the Columbus flagship of his first voyage, the *Santa Maria,* and served as its mate. He also was the official cartographer and captain of the *Niña* on the second voyage; therefore, he was intimately associated with the Columbus voyages.

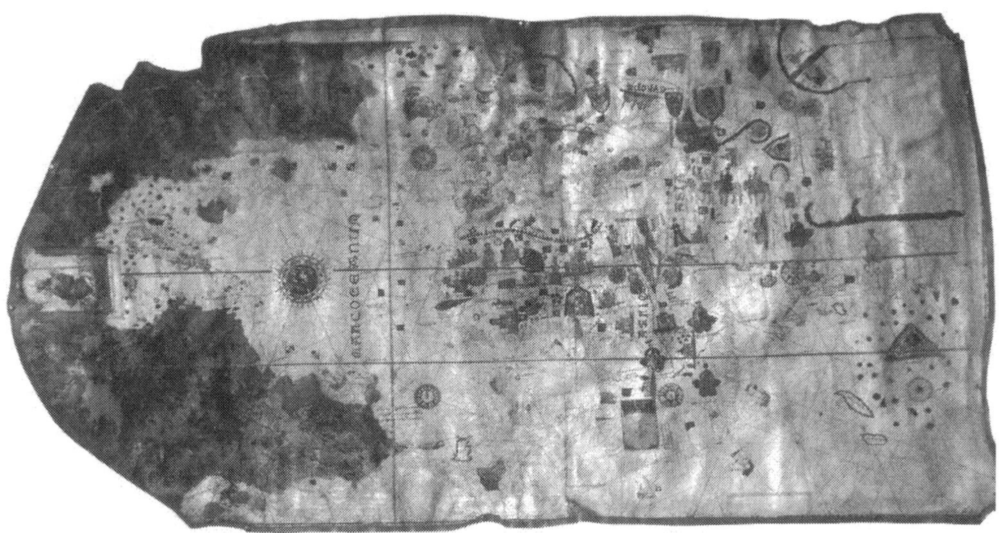

Figure 173

The 1500 Juan de la Cosa Map of the Caribbean

During the first decade of the 16th century, he made several trips to the Americas, and he explored the northern coast of South America in 1499 along with an Italian explorer named Amerigo Vespucci.

The de la Cosa map shows a continent—including parts of North and South America, the Venezuela/Brazil coast—all of which were not yet surveyed in 1500. de la Cosa and Rodrigo de Bastidas had reached the American mainland only in 1501-02. Columbus himself did not hit the South American coast until 1502-03.

On the map Cuba was drawn as an island, contradicting the "facts" as recorded in 1500. Because of these impossibilities, some experts believe the map was actually made after 1508 and not 1500 as indicated by the inscription on the map: *Juan de la cosa la fizo en el puerto de S: ma en año de 1500*. The last "0" was fuzzy enough to be legitimately construed as an "8."

Even so, giving the map a date of 1508 does not resolve the problem, because many of the new discoveries, especially those by de la Cosa himself that should have been on the map are conspicuously absent.

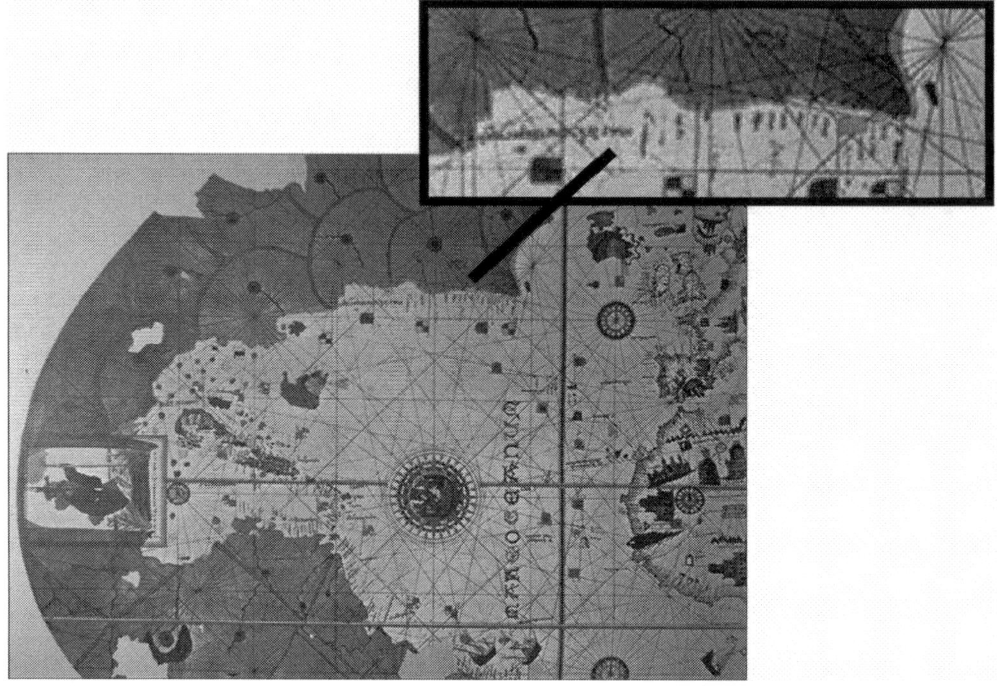

Figure 174

Florida in 1500?

For example, the Gulf of Uraba and the coast of Darien, which were explored by de la Cosa in 1501 to 1502, are absent from the map. In addition, by 1508 the coast of Brazil by the equator was on the way to being surveyed. Yet its rendition on the map is blatantly poor. In short, the suggested dates do not commiserate with the contents of the map.

To most researchers, perhaps the more puzzling element of the de la Cosa map is the portrayal of Cuba as an island. Columbus had insisted that Cuba, which he called "Iuna," was part of the new mainland, and forced his fellow explorers to sign an affidavit to that effect. In this map, de la Cosa named it Cuba, and drew an extremely accurate shape of it without having surveyed it.

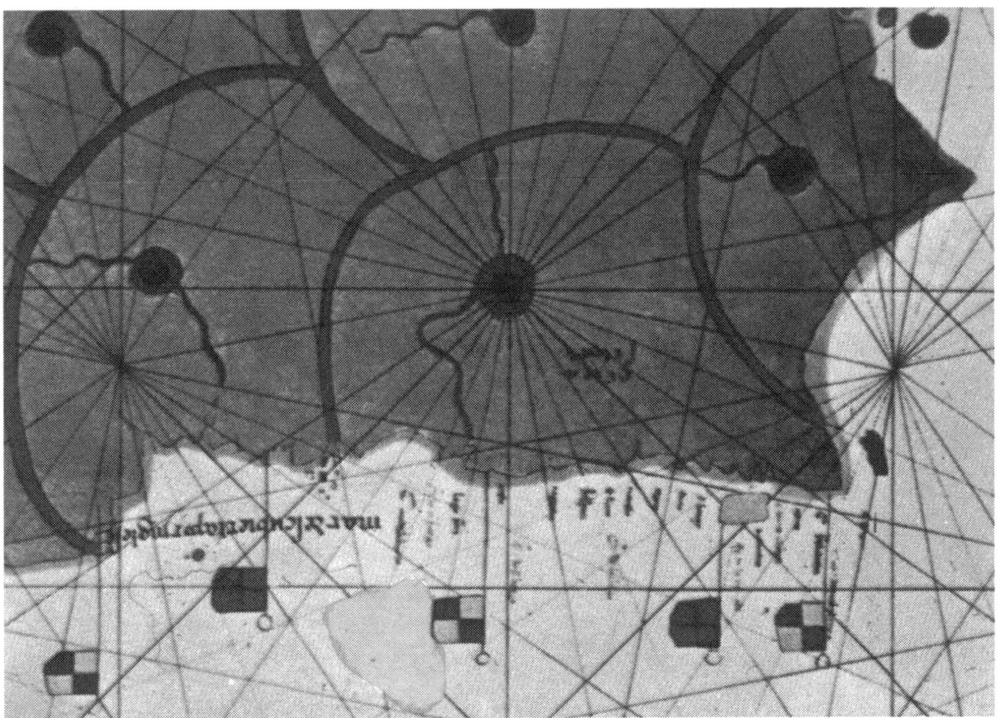

Figure 175

Undecipherable Place Names on De La Cosa Map

In any case, there is another matter about de la Cosa's Cuba that is even more intriguing. The names of places on the island cannot be corroborated. They were not located anywhere else, on any other map at the time or since. Where de la Cosa got his information about Cuba remains a puzzle.

To me, the more baffling aspect of this map is the rendition of Southeastern North America (Figure 174), specifically what must be interpreted as Florida. Florida was not visited by Europeans until at least 1513.

In this portion of the map there are some twenty names, almost all now undecipherable (Figure 175). Then, there is a river named Longo (r. longo), a name that is uncannily Chinese.

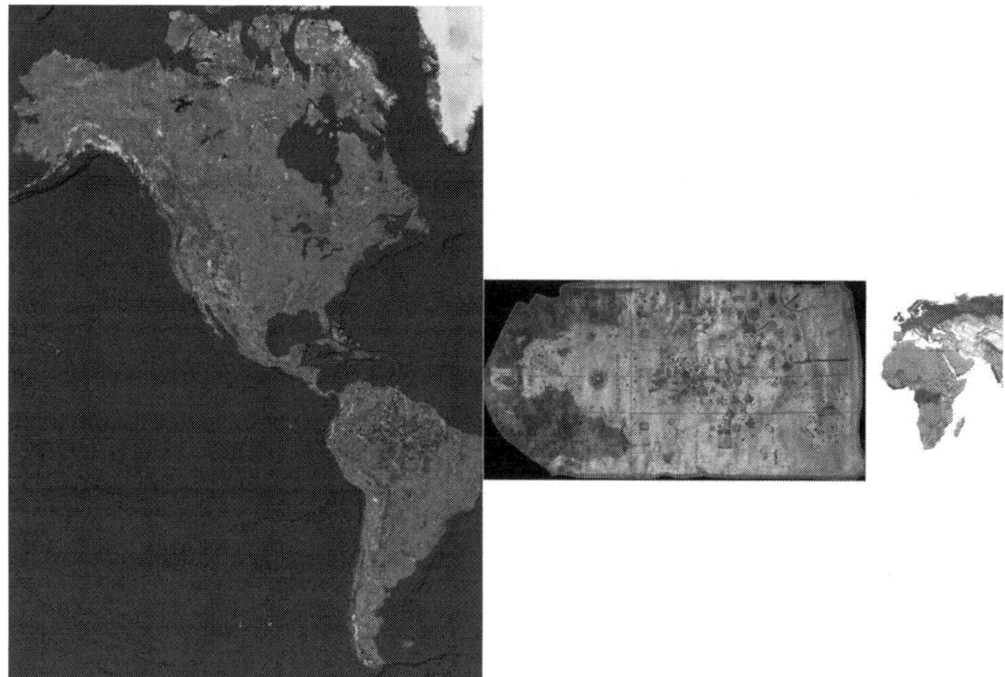

Figure 176

Juan de la Cosa Map Compared with Modern Map Equivalents

The longest river in China is called Chang Jiang,[54] or Long River. It is called Yangtze River in the west. Europeans generally do not name rivers Long River. One suspects, therefore, that somehow de la Cosa mistook the North American Continent for Asia, or that he was following the notations of some source material that is now lost.

Indeed, de la Cosa should not even have known that there was a river in China for he did not know China. However, he also should not have known the continent called North America. Therefore, he was indeed drawing Asia, East China specifically.

Figure 176 shows the de la Cosa map lined up in comparison with modern maps of the American continents and Europe and Africa in corresponding proportions. As can be seen, the de la Cosa Caribbean is immense as compared with Europe. It is like two separate maps were drawn to different scales, and then pieced together.

---

[54] 長江

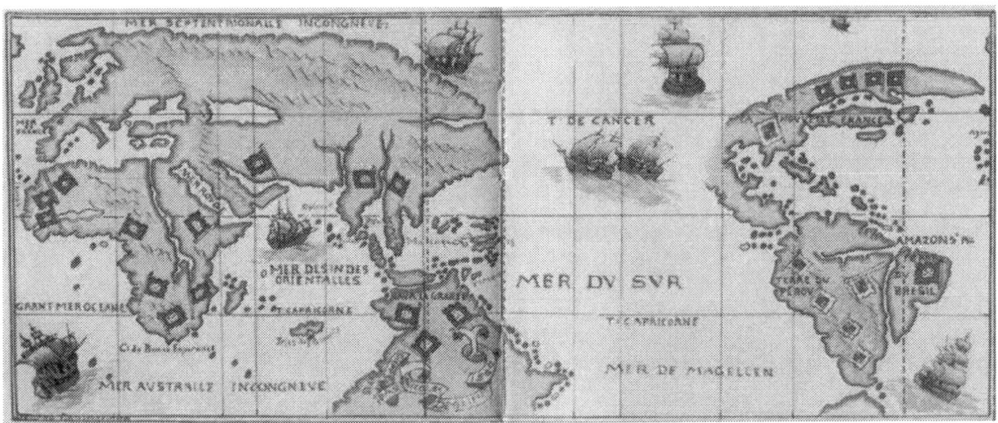

Figure 177

1566 Desliens Australia

It appears that the American portion of the map is three to four times larger than the old-world part (Europe and Africa).

The de la Cosa map shows Atlantic islands that were not even known to have existed in 1500. Place names were entirely unrecognizable. The mystery of how de la Cosa obtained the information "ahead of its time" is extremely vexing, so vexing that commentators had noticed the improbabilities, mulled over them, failed to provide satisfactory answers to them, and walked away.

For the some twenty place names, including Long River, along the North American seacoast, because they identified places the Spanish explorers had never been to, some scholars concluded that someone had indeed visited the coast before 1500 and left records for it, not suspecting that the source was China, of course.

Now, we know, it was China, and the European "pioneers" had no idea what China was.

Figure 178

The Caribbean Antilles Islands Today

We have alleged that the new world geography data came from Chinese sources, and this conclusion also happens to help explain why these European mapmakers were drawing their new lands so big.

The Chinese unit of measure for distance, the *li*, which exact length varied throughout history, is more or less a third of the English mile. A length of 1 English mile would be expressed as approximately 3 *li*. If a landmass is expressed as 10 *li* long, an Englishman, if unfamiliar with the Chinese *li* and assumes that it is the same as mile, might think the object is 10 miles long instead of 3 miles long. The object drawn with this erroneous assumption would appear to be three times as large or more.

Recall the monstrous Australian northwest of Figure 31 and Figure 30.

Figure 177 shows a northwest corner of Australia that is 3 to 4 times larger than what it really is.

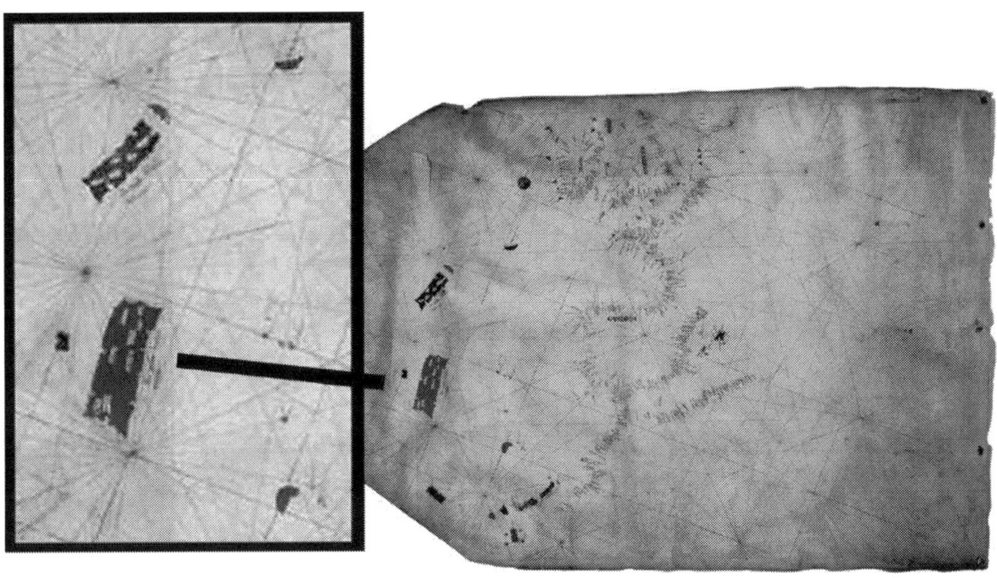

Figure 179

The 1424 Zuane Pizzigano Map with Antilia Island

Antilia and Puerto Rico

Today in the Caribbean there are two groups of islands called the Antilles (Figure 178). The Greater Antilles includes Cuba, Jamaica, Hispaniola (Haiti and the Dominican Republic), and Puerto Rico, laid out from left to right. The Lesser Antilles is positioned to the southeast and includes smaller islands such as Antigua, Guadeloupe, Martinique, and others. These were the islands allegedly encountered during the Columbian voyages. Yet the name "Antilles" was already known before they were "discovered" as discussed above (along with St. Brandan Island). The Spanish or Portuguese versions were "Antilia" or "Antillia," and originally referred to a single island.

Europeans of the Middle Age believed that Antilia was located somewhere west of Europe in the Atlantic Ocean. The exact location of the legendary island was, nevertheless, unknown; hence it seldom appeared on maps that depicted the Atlantic Ocean until late 14th century. Some people even thought the name Antilia actually referred to the lost continent of Atlantis. (Well, these people would refer to Atlantis on just about any pretext.) Others thought it was the legendary Antilla discovered by the Carthaginians. When the Spanish discovered the West Indies, they began calling them "Antillas," although the name had already been alluded to.

Shortly after the turn of the 15th century, about the time of the Ming expeditions, a series of mysterious islands called Antilia began to take on real physical form, and "showed up" on new world maps.

Housed in the James Ford Bell Library at the University of Minnesota is a portolan chart hand-painted by the Venetian cartographer Zuane Pizzigano in 1424 (Figure 179). On the Pizzigano portolan chart, just outside the western coast of Europe (the Iberian Peninsula) in the Atlantic Ocean is a cluster of islands that no longer exists on today's maps. In fact, it never existed.

The islands are on the map about seven hundred miles west of the Azores. They are extremely large, almost as long as the Iberian Peninsula in the north-south orientation. These islands in their forms are not known to exist on maps much earlier before this time, and Columbus was yet to be born. However, there is no indication as to what these islands were and why they were put on the maps.

In 1954, Armando Cortesão attempted to explain that the name "Antilia" was made up of two Portuguese words "ante" (or "anti") and "ilha," which was an archaic form of the Portuguese word for "island." Hence, "Antilia," playing a little fast and loose with chronology, would mean "fore island," or the first island ancient Portuguese sailors came across when exploring the Ocean Sea. He offered no hint as to where the "aft" island might have been (if there is a "fore," there ought to be an "aft"), nor any reference to the ancient appellation. In any case, the point is moot. The ancient Portuguese sailors apparently never could find their way back to these mythical islands.

Figure 180 shows a portion of the Beccario map of 1435. In this map, hundreds of miles west of Portugal in the Atlantic Ocean are the same two huge islands. They even look like the ones in the 1424 Pizzigano map, except that the orientations of the islands are slightly different.

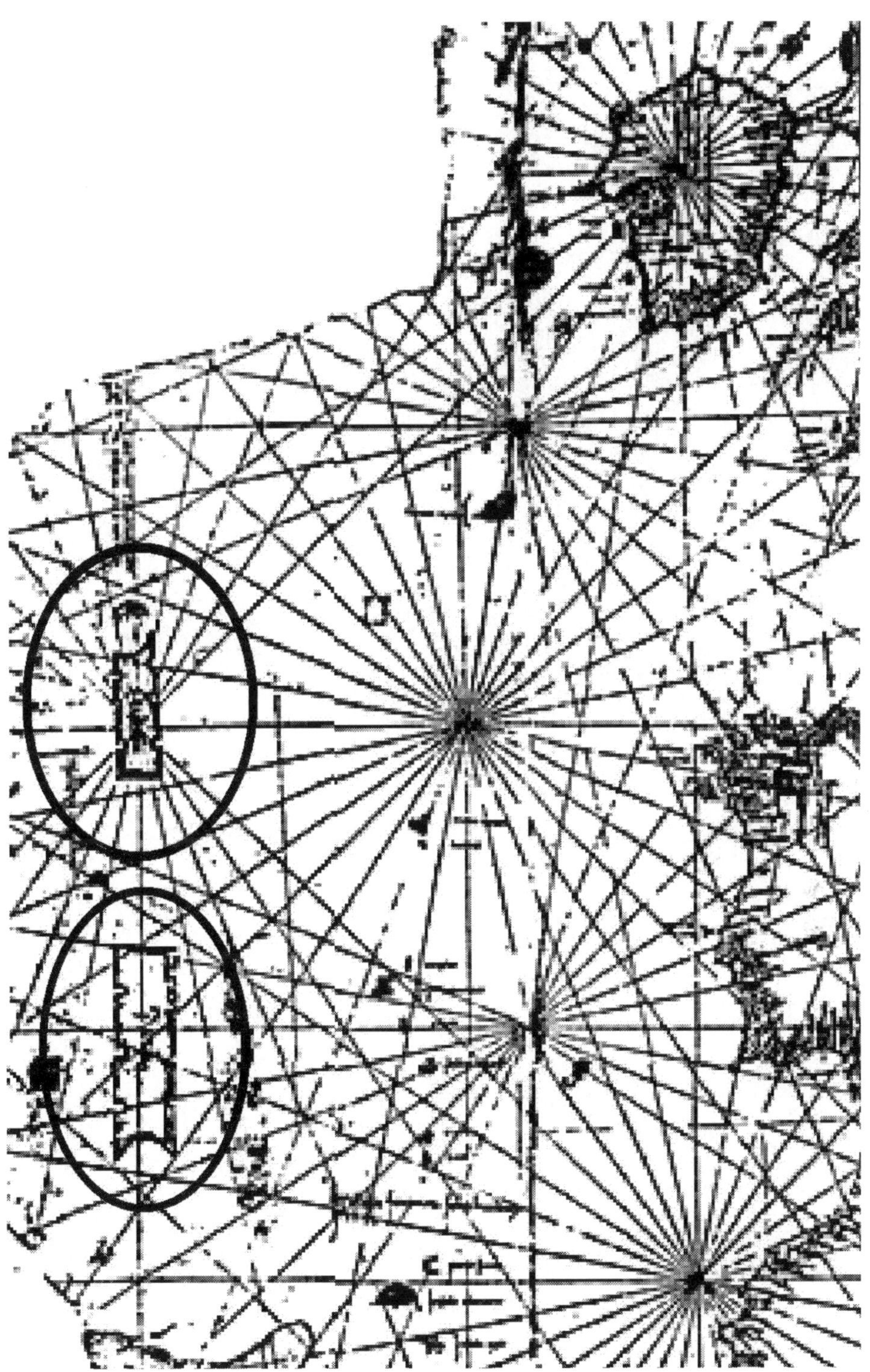

Figure 180

The 1435 Beccario Antilia Islands

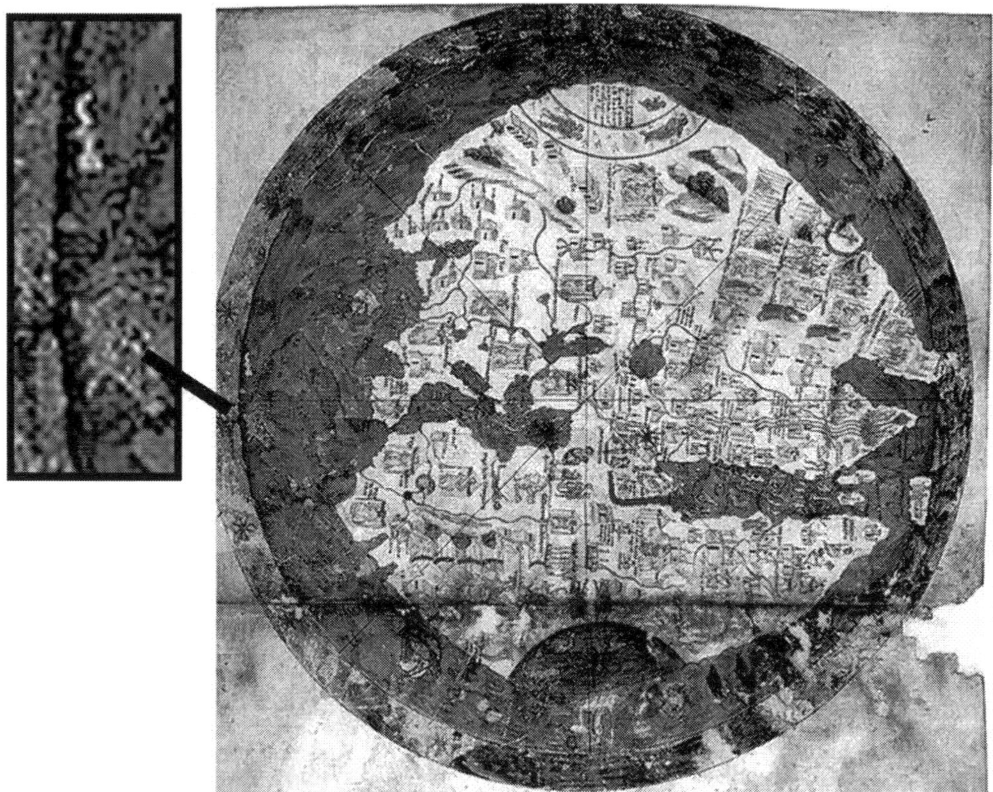

Figure 181

The 1436 Bianco Map

Did Beccario copy from Pizzigano? If he did, why did he change the islands' orientations? It is unlikely that he would have included bogus information on his map, or merely copied someone else's map. If some data were selected for use, it had to be because of the provenance of the data themselves. Therefore, there must have been an unknown but reliable source for the existence of these "Antilia" islands.

In 1436, cartographer Bianco drew a world map (Figure 181, currently at the British Library in London) and placed the Antilia islands in a projection map far into the western depth of the Atlantic Ocean outside the Iberian Peninsula and North Africa (see the inset of Figure 181).

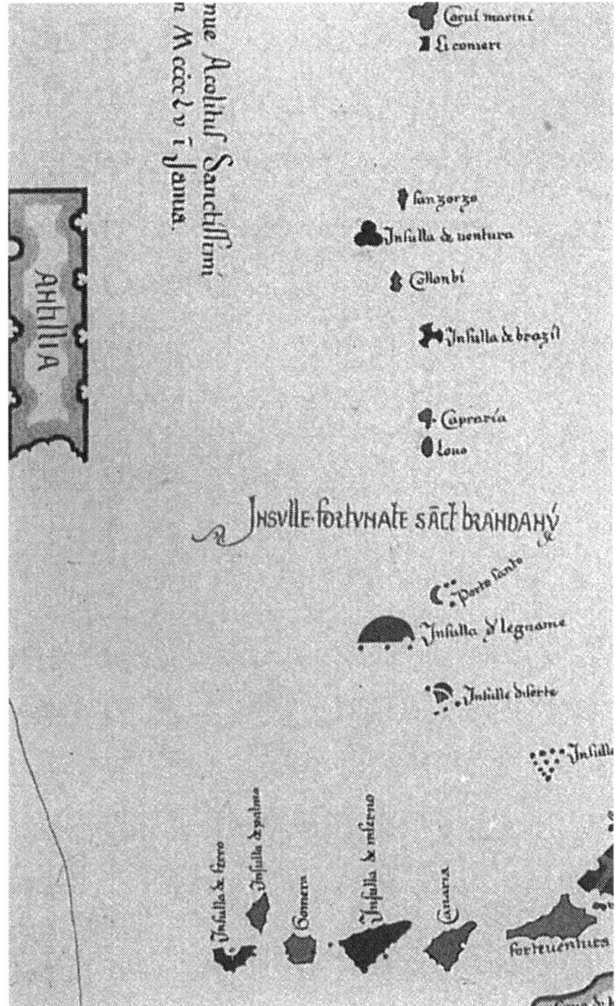

Figure 182

The 1455 Bartolomeo Pareto Map Antilia Island

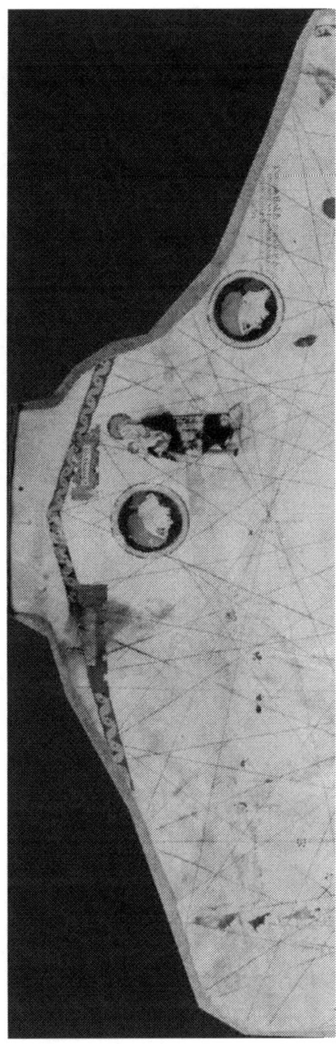

Figure 183

The 1466 Petrus Rosselli Portolan Chart Mysterious Islands

Did he also have access to the same data source for these islands as the previous mapmakers or did he merely copy from them? We do not know the answer to these questions.

Figure 184

The 1480 Albinus de Canepa Map Antilia

Figure 185

The 1489 Albinus de Canepa Map of Mysterious Islands

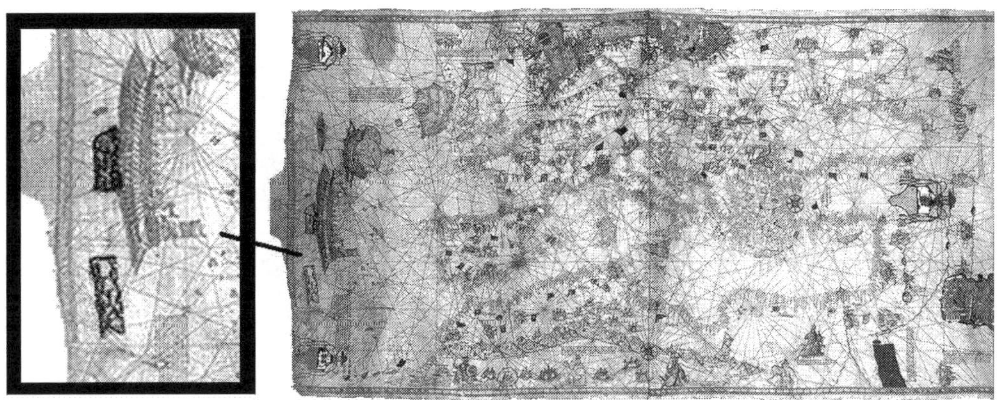

Figure 186

The 1492 Benincasa Antilia Islands

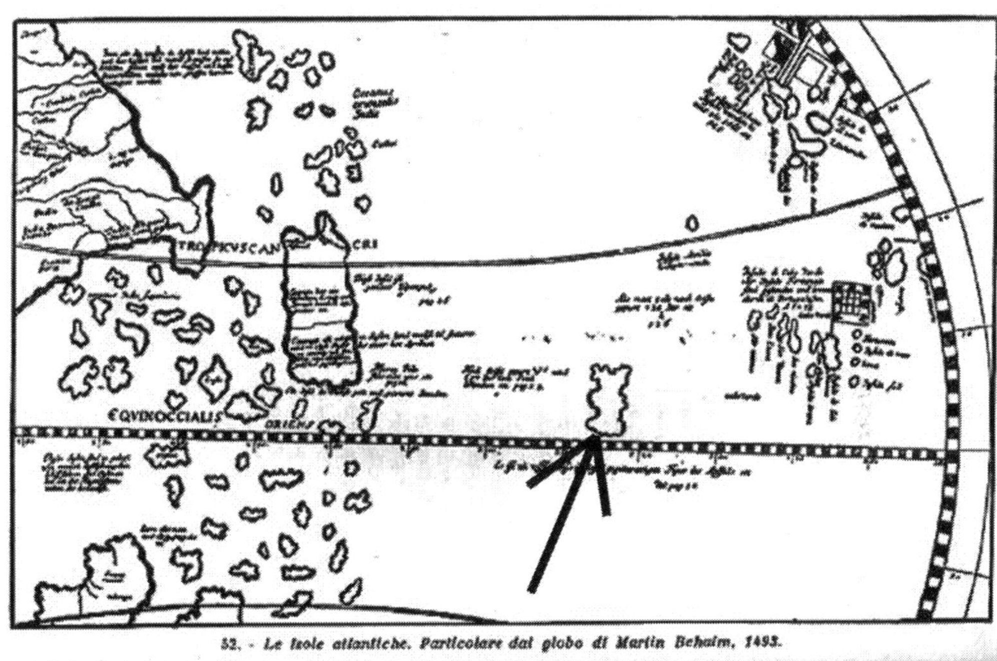

Figure 187

The 1493 Martin Behaim Antilia

In 1455, Bartolomeo Pareto produced a world map (Figure 182), and on it is one of the mysterious "Antilia" islands, along with other imaginary islands to their right.

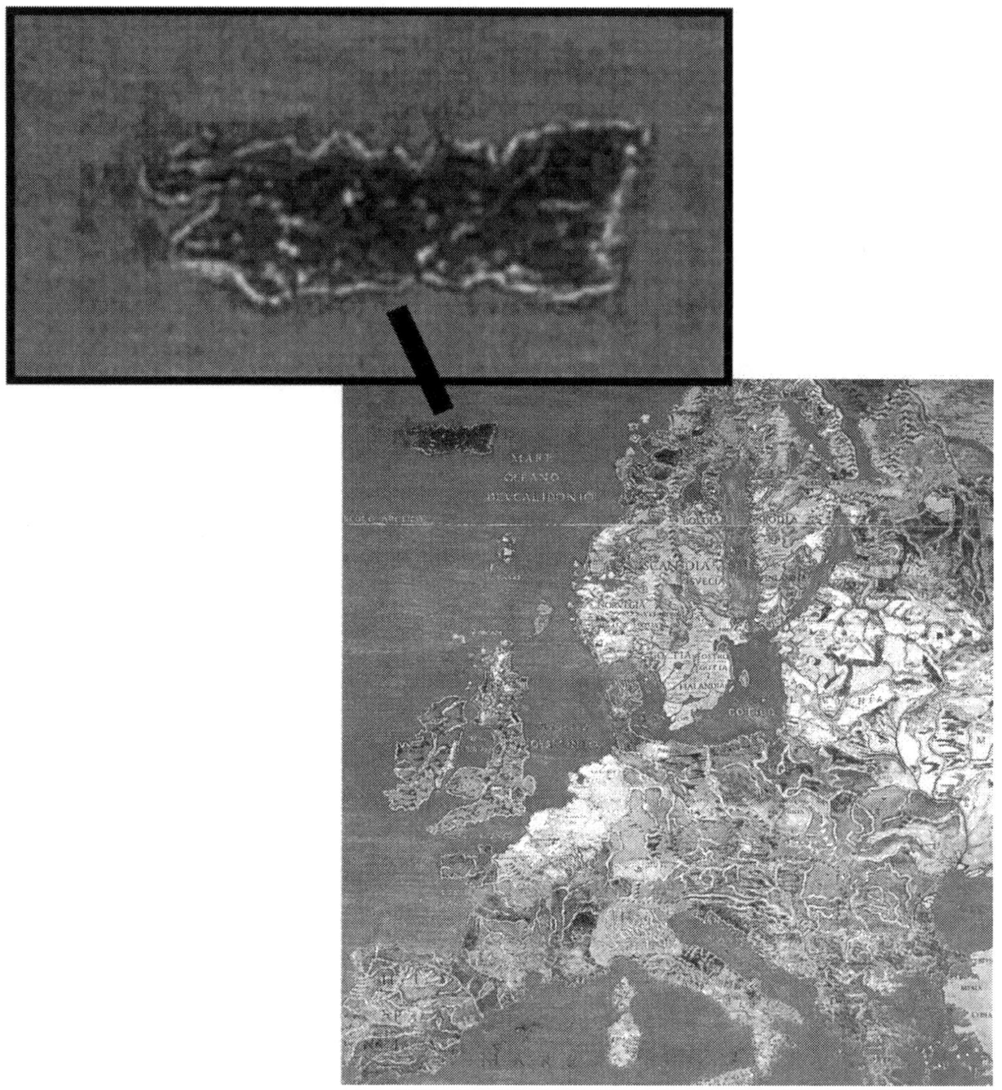

Figure 188

The Antonio de Varese Mystery Island

Also in the possession of the James Ford Bell Library is the 1466 Petrus Rosselli portolan chart, featuring the same two mysterious islands (see the two rectangular islands above the heads of Madonna and Child, Figure 183).

In the 1480 Albinus de Canepa Map (Figure 184), a huge Antilia is seen west of Iberia in the Atlantic Ocean.

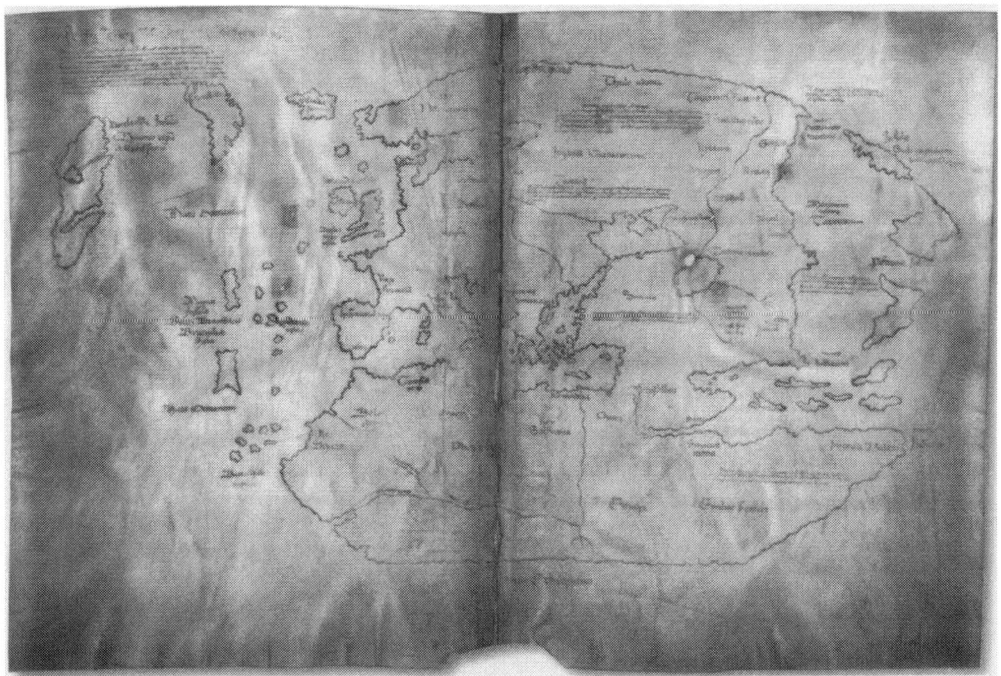

Figure 189

The Vinland Map

These islands persisted in the updated 1489 version, also housed at the James Ford Bell Library (enlarged in the inset on the left-hand side of Figure 185). Obviously the mapmaker had faith in them.

In 1492, the year Columbus set sail for the Caribbean, cartographer Benincasa of Bologna produced a map and placed the Antilia Islands to the west of Iberia as did other cartographers (Figure 186 to the left of the large ship on the left-hand side of the map).

However, there were variations. In the 1493 Martin Behaim map of Atlantic islands (Figure 187, see arrow), Antilia is placed right in between Europe and Japan.

In the Palacio Farnese in Tuscia, Italy there was a wall mural in the form of a 1500 world map by Antonio de Varese. In this map, outside Scandinavia in the Atlantic Ocean is a huge Antilia island (Figure 188), almost as big as England, but positioned horizontally.

Figure 190

The Vinland Map Mystery Islands

The Vinland Map

In 1965, Yale University acquired a map discovered seven years earlier by a rare map collector. The map was confirmed by Yale appointed experts to have been made in the early 15th century (1440 to be precise). The map is called the Vinland Map (Figure 189) because of the appearance of a block of land called Vinland at the upper left corner of the map.

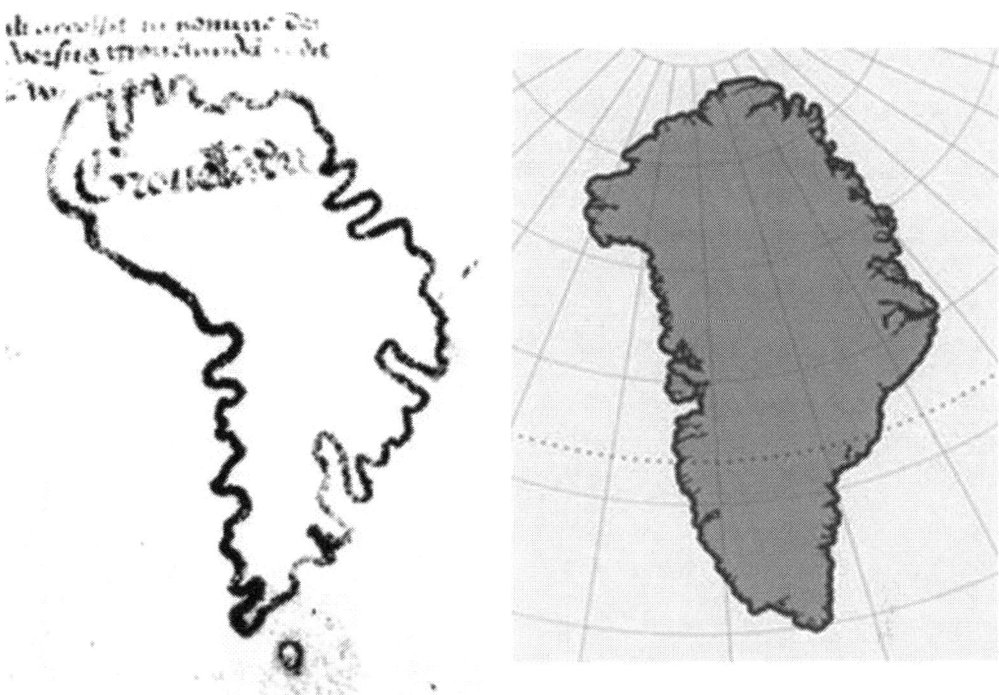

Figure 191

The Vinland Map Greenland and Greenland from a Modern Map

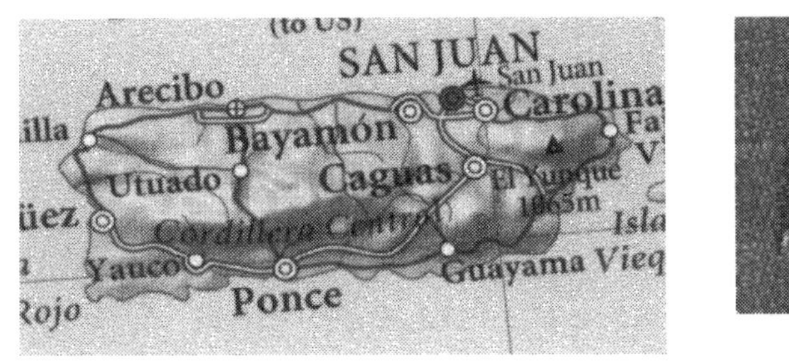

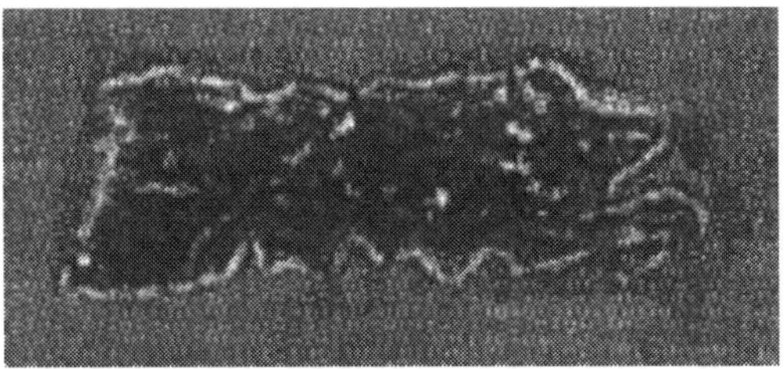

Figure 192

Antilia was Puerto Rico?

The map was suspected to have been redrawn from a 13th century original because it was believed that early Vikings were active in that part of the world.

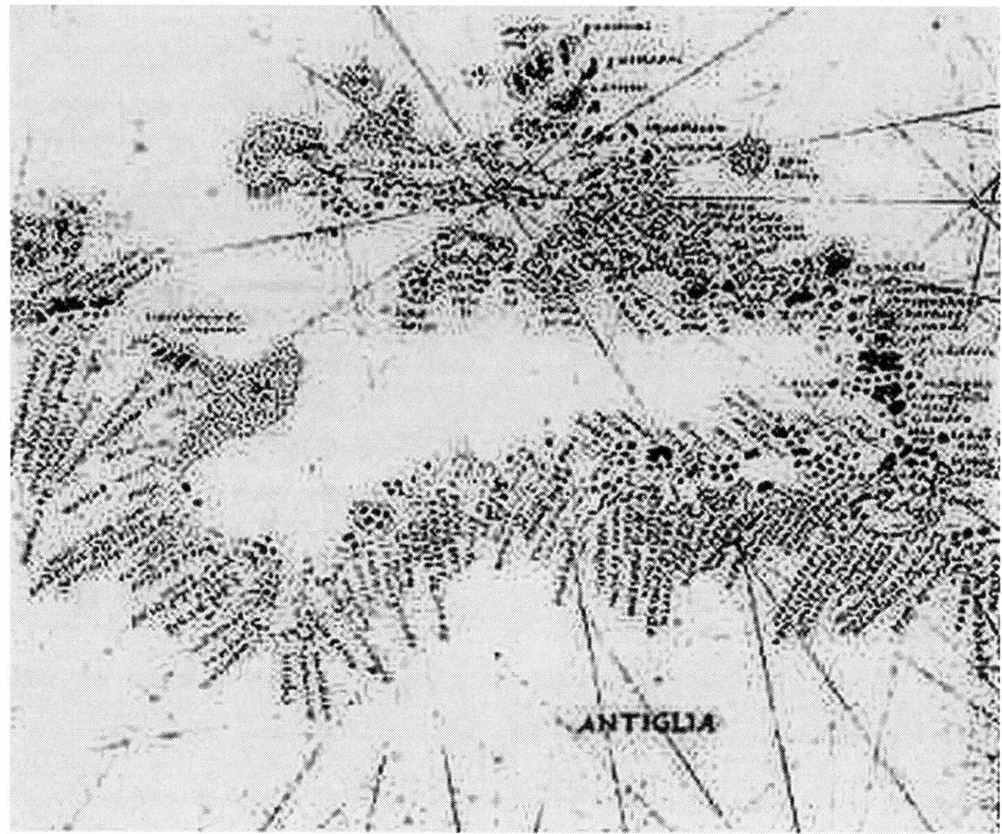

Figure 193

The 1508-1510 Egerton MS. 2803 Map Shows Antilia Inland

This map would otherwise have been ordinary had it not been for this patch of land and a number of large islands that appeared out of nowhere on the map situated in the Atlantic Ocean west of Scandinavia. These astonishing features show unusually accurate depictions of the northeast North American coastline.

It has been suggested that it is Vinland (Vinilanda), the fabled Viking settlement. Greenland (Gronelanda) and Iceland (Isolanda) can be seen in the upper-left corner of Figure 190 as well.

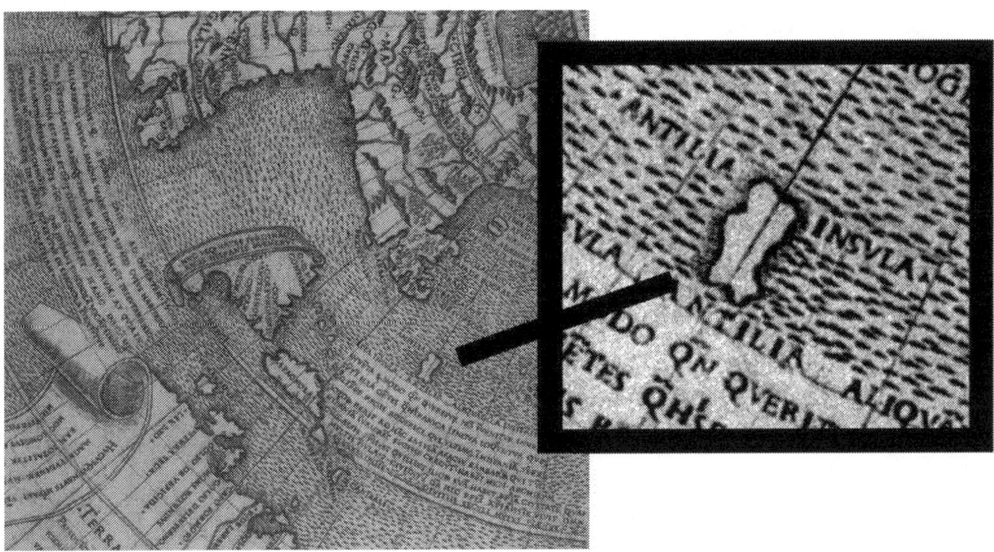

Figure 194

The 1502 Giovanni Ruysch World Map

When discovered, the map was bound together with a codex[55] called *Historia Tartorum,* or *Description of the Tartars,* that is often referred to in English as the *Tartar Relation. Historia Tartorum* describes the history and customs of the Mongols. It was believed to be a prototype of the memoir of Giovanni da Pian del Carpini, the Franciscan friar who traveled in 1245 to visit the Mongol khan at his capital at Karakorum, Siberia.

What is even more remarkable than the appearances of the Nordic lands is the accuracy of their drawing, measured by the standards of the day. Figure 191 compares the Vinland Map version of Greenland against a modern map rendition. The likeness is almost unworldly. (Recall the Kircher Atlantis, Figure 66, discussed earlier.)

The Vikings had never been known to map these lands, and no other Viking record exists to demonstrate otherwise. In fact, Vikings were not mapmakers. Given all this, who surveyed and mapped these North Atlantic Ocean landmasses is bewildering.

---

[55] Ancient manuscript.

Figure 195

The 1585 Sir Walter Raleigh/John White Antilia

In the Vinland map, not only is Greenland correctly drawn, it is clearly shown as an island. Europeans did not know Greenland was an island until the 19th century when Admiral Perry circumnavigated it. A 15th century European cartographer could not have known this, short of learning from somebody who had circumnavigated the island prior to that time.

Even more astonishing than the presence of these "Nordic" islands, there again is the appearance of the same mysterious non-existent islands of Antilia (extremely large in sizes) outside the west coasts of the Iberian Peninsula (Figure 190).

What was the basis of these puzzling "Antilia" islands that was obviously unimpeachable that Renaissance European mapmakers kept including them in their maps? Markedly, whatever the source was, it either did not have precise information on their sizes, orientations, and locations, or that these attributes were difficult to interpret or convert. Perhaps the only thing that was clear about them was that they were big and they were in the Atlantic Ocean somewhere.

When European adventurers began to explore South America, the name "Antiglia" appeared on a Portuguese portolan chart which is now in the British Museum identified as Egerton MS. 2803 dated to 1508-1510. "Antiglia" was placed in what is now Venezuela (Figure 193).

After Christopher Columbus reached the Caribbean, these mysterious islands mostly disappeared from future European maps. Antilia was absent from the maps of Columbus' contemporaries such as Acosta, Oviedo, Juan de la Cosa, and Ribero, all mapmakers who were closely affiliated with the Columbian voyages. Only a few others hung on to the name, such as the 1546 Desceliers map, the 1570 Ortelius map, and the 1587 Mercator map, which was probably the last one to still feature it.

Figure 196

Mysterious Island on Piri Reis Map

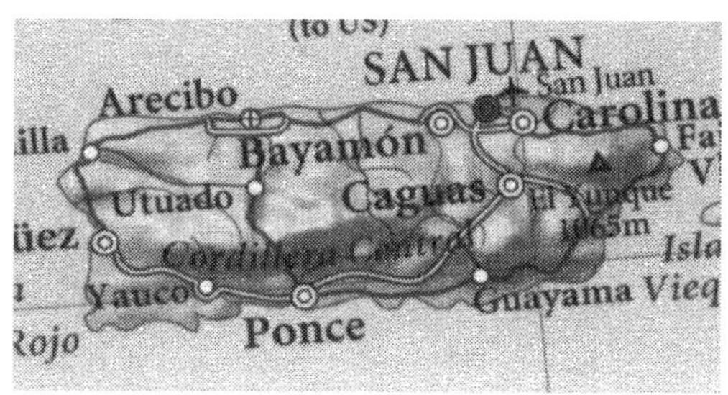

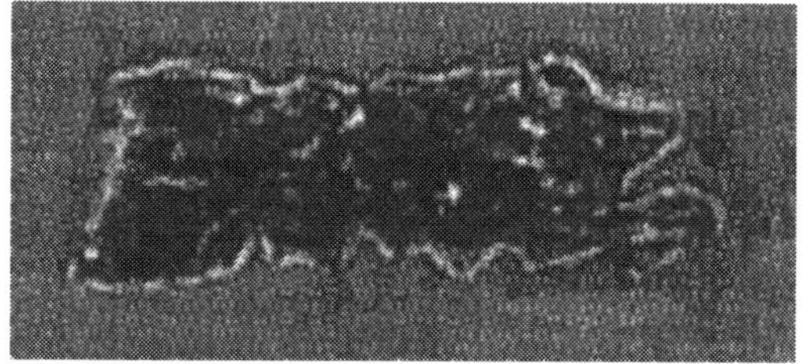

Figure 194

Antilia was Puerto Rico?

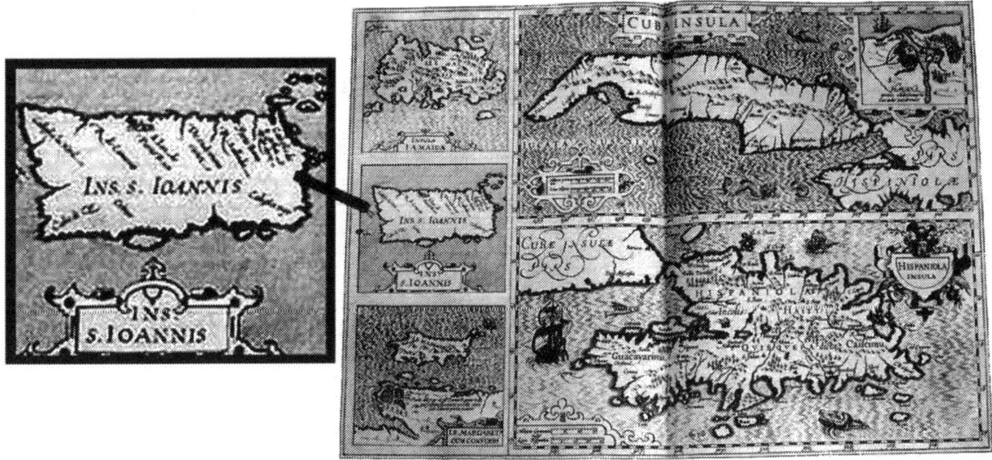

Figure 197

1606 Mercator Hondius Cuba & Hispaniola

One possible reason for this is that one of the islands is a dead ringer of the island of Puerto Rico (modern Puerto Rico in Figure 188 on the left, as compared to the island on the right). Perhaps that is the reason why the Caribbean Islands are named the "Antilles" islands, because the Spaniards had "found" them. Apparently, Peter Martyr d'Anghiera, a contemporary of Columbus, thought so. He identified Antilia as being a part of an archipelago. In fact, it later proved to be the Caribbean islands.

While Columbus might have "found" Antilia, as said, other mapmakers were not quite ready to sign on.

In the 1502 Giovanni Ruysch world map (Figure 194) at the Arthur Holzheimer Collection of the Harvard College Library in the Library of Congress, Antilia is placed west of the Azores.

In 1585, Sir Walter Raleigh commissioned John White to produce a series of drawings and maps for the colony of Virginia. In one of the maps (Figure 195) on the Caribbean islands now preserved at the British Museum, the Greater Antilles islands of Cuba, Hispaniola, possibly Jamaica, and Puerto Rico are drawn exactly as the mystical Antilia islands and are drawn totally out of position.

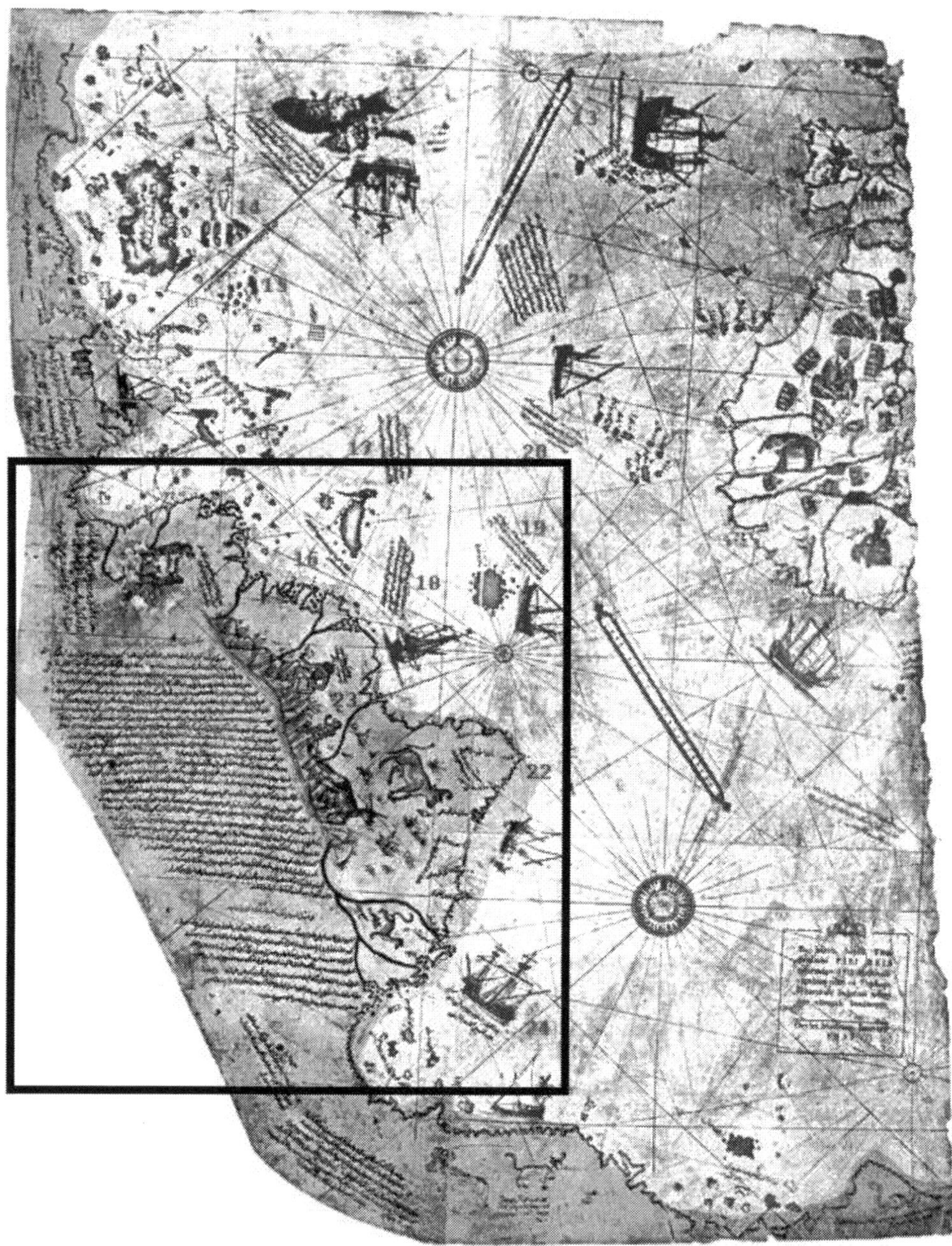

Figure 198

The Piri Reis Map

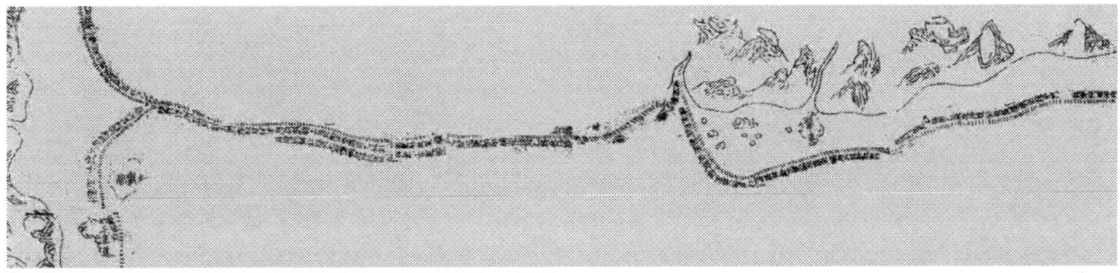

Figure 199

Reconstructed Sea-Lane in the Style of Wu Bei Zhi

Unquestionably, the mapmaker had drawn these islands not from actual European survey data, but from an existing source or sources that had been honored by cartographers for at least a hundred years. These islands also bear names that are now unrecognizable: "Cigatao(?)" for Puerto Rico, and "Iani" for an unidentifiable island south of Puerto Rico, and others. (Recall that Columbus called Cuba "Iuna.") One wonders where the mapmaker obtained these names.

As for whether "Iani" or "Iuna" were total flukes, let us look at Figure 197, an island map (now at the State Library of New South Wales, Australia) of the Caribbean made by the cartographers Mercator and Hondius in 1606. Note the very "real" island of Ioannis. Perhaps it was not quite such a fluke after all.

If you look closely at the upper-left portion of the famous Piri Reis map of Figure 198 (reprinted from the original which will be discussed in more detail below) you will see again the familiar looking island called Antilia.

To the left of Antilia is a large landmass. Per the orientation of this map, it is obviously the South American Continent, which was yet to be explored at the time. Therefore, like the other maps of Antilia, the Antilia in this map is also disoriented.

If one were to "turn" this Antilia 90 degrees counter-clockwise, the result is a perfect Caribbean island (Figure 200).

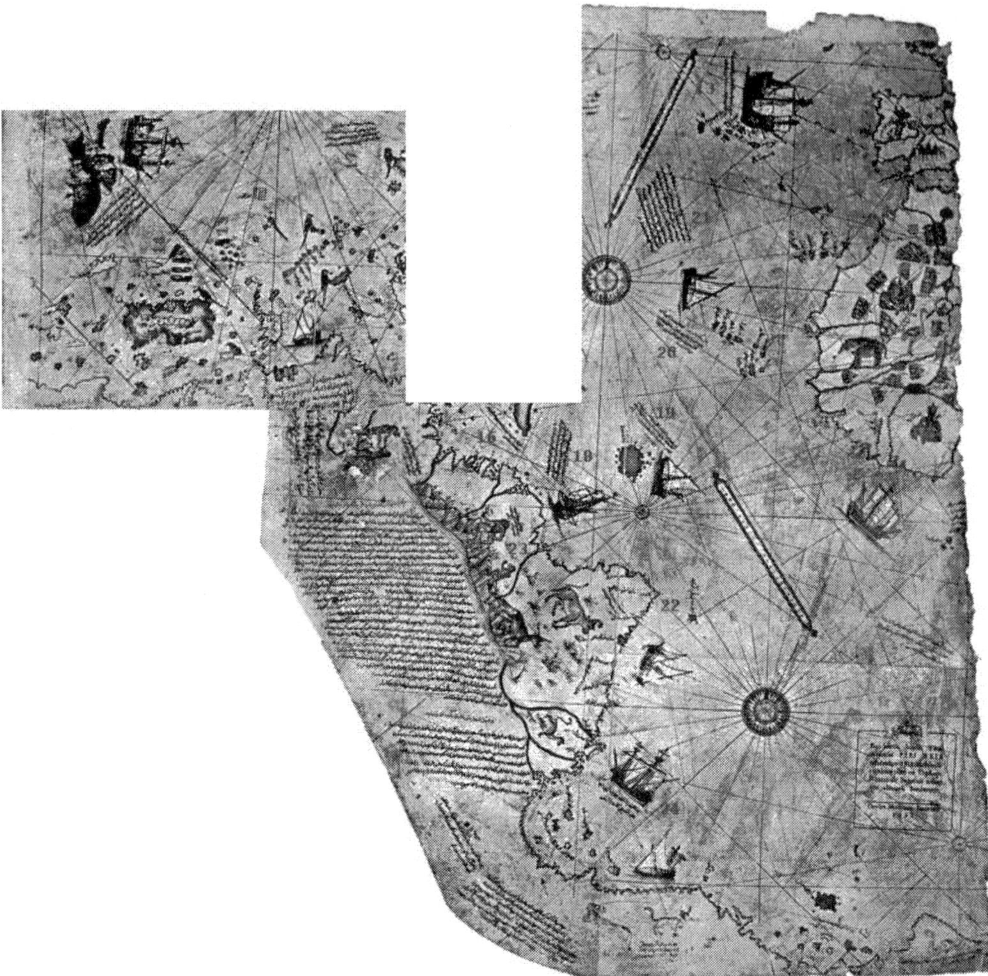

Figure 200
Piri Reis Map Adjusted

For European cartographers of the Age of Discovery to indulge in such obvious fantasy, drawing huge islands and placing them in the Atlantic chasing all the way from outside Iberia, even Scandinavia, to the Caribbean, cannot be mere folly. There has to be an underlying logical, albeit misguided, reason. Perhaps there is, and here is a theory to explain it.

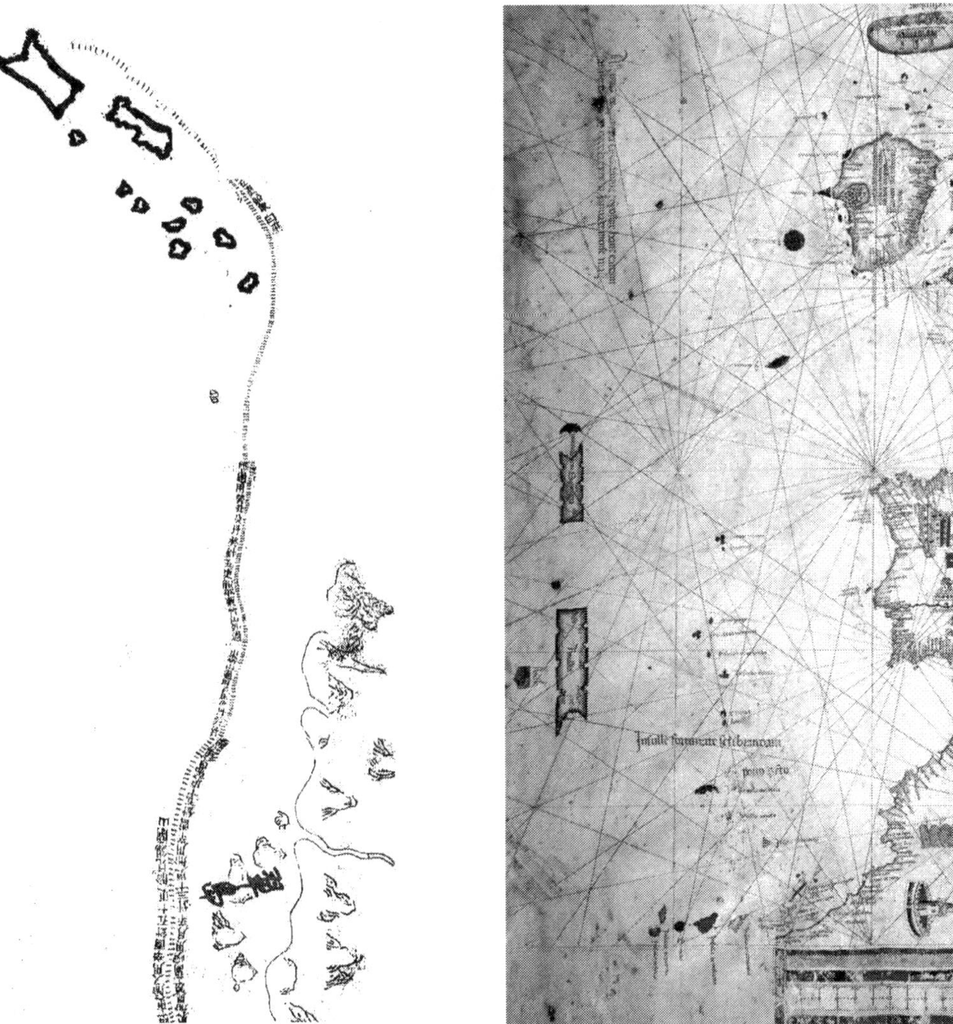

Figure 201

Likely Ming Fleet Sea Route to the Caribbean

Let us suppose that this mysterious Antilia had something to do with the Chinese exploration programs. In their customary way, the Chinese navigators would have mapped their voyages and recorded the new route findings.

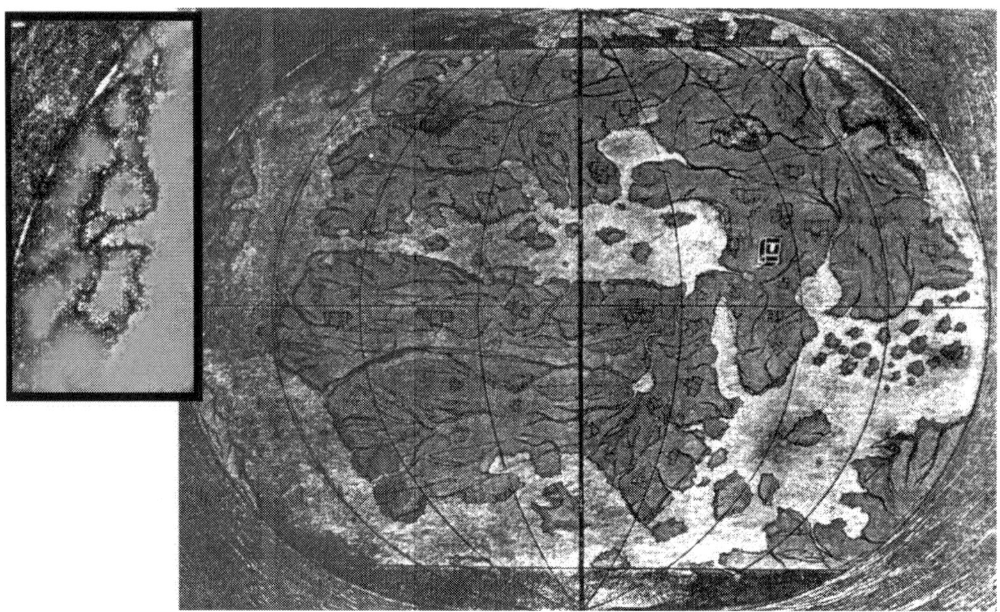

Figure 202

Renaissance Islamic Map

Such records would have looked like that shown in Figure 199, an imaginary reconstruction sea chart styled after Zheng He's sea chart, a version of which is preserved in the Ming Dynasty military manual *Wu Bei Zhi*.[56]

It is important for us to understand how the Chinese of old drew their sea charts. The reconstruction in Figure 199 describes the route up the West African coast to the Northeastern coast of South America, with the direction of North initially pointing to the left (starting from the right-hand side of the scroll, with the West African coast displayed horizontally on top). At Cape Verde (midpoint of the hypothetical scroll, Figure 199), the route switches west, as explained by the accompanying sailing instructions, effectively indicating a 90-degree turn but maintaining a continuous run on the chart as dictated by the physicality of a paper scroll. Because such a chart appears on the paper as a straight continuous run, European mapmakers, without the benefit of the explanatory note written in

---

[56] 武備誌

Chinese, would have been led to think that the newly discovered islands, such as Antilia, were situated due north of the Cape Verde Islands, lying outside Western Europe.

This is only a theory. I constructed the chart in Figure 199 to illustrate this possibility. It would be a reasonable facsimile of what the original would have been, if indeed the source of Antilia was Chinese.

A comparison between this reconstruction of a Ming sea chart of the route from the west coast of Africa to the Caribbean and its European equivalent (extracted from the 1489 Canepa map) is represented in Figure 201.

Figure 199, if it comes close to representing what truly happened, would unequivocally assert that the Chinese had reached the Caribbean and northern South America sometime before 1420, discovered, and mapped the islands of Antilia, Trinidad, and Tobago.

If we were to accept that the Ming Chinese made it past the Cape of Good Hope as testified in the Fra Mauro Map, and if Thor Heyerdahl's aboriginal balsa raft (the Kon-Tiki) could *float* all the way by itself from Callio, Peru across 4,300 miles of Pacific to reach the Raroia atoll of the Tuamotu Archipelago in Polynesia,[57] we must conclude that the present hypothesis is plausible.

"Plausible," of course, is not the same as "happened." However, we have presented enough evidence to move this "plausible" closer to "likely happened." It is also possible that the sea route had already been charted during Yuan time and Zheng He's fleets were merely following it.

Figure 202 shows the Antilia Island on a Renaissance period map, the *Ka'bah at the Center of the Inhabitable World* from a Persian manuscript at the University Library in Istanbul. The conveyance of

---

[57] In the early 1900s, Norwegian geographer, zoologist, archeologist, and anthropologist Thor Heyerdahl postulated that Polynesians came from the Americas by natural ocean currents and proved that such a feat was possible by actually going on such a voyage.

Chinese navigation records to Europe via Middle-Eastern hands is manifest.

In the end, whether the above proposed solution was true history or whether it adequately explains the odd map renditions of a non-existent Antilia Island, is of no direct bearing to our present problem. Regardless, such unreal map products exist and require explanation. They testify to the difficulty early Age of Discovery European geographers were having with certain newly acquired geographical data of a new world they were only beginning to come to terms with. These maps behoove historians to provide them with an explanation. They should not simply walk away from the problem and turn a blind eye toward it. Unfortunately, so far they have been doing exactly that.

The Asian South America

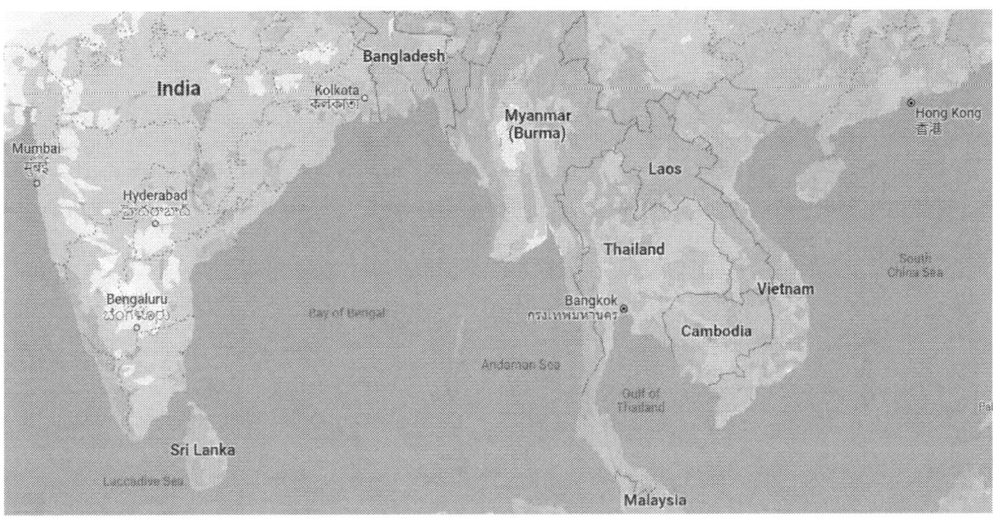

Figure 203

Indochina Nations

Now we shall "close the deal" with two major "strange" Age of Discovery European cartographic enigmas.

During this same period, a modern interpretation of Asia was also developing, although Europeans had yet to visit and survey that still mystical land.

Of particular interest are the obvious efforts in attempting to reproduce an Indochina—another place Europeans had yet to visit—with improved fidelity (See Figure 51, Figure 55, and Figure 56, among others). Although the results are plainly less than satisfactory, their readings are consistent; consistently wrong, that is. A modern map of Indochina is shown in Figure 204. Note how Malaysia bends southward to the right.

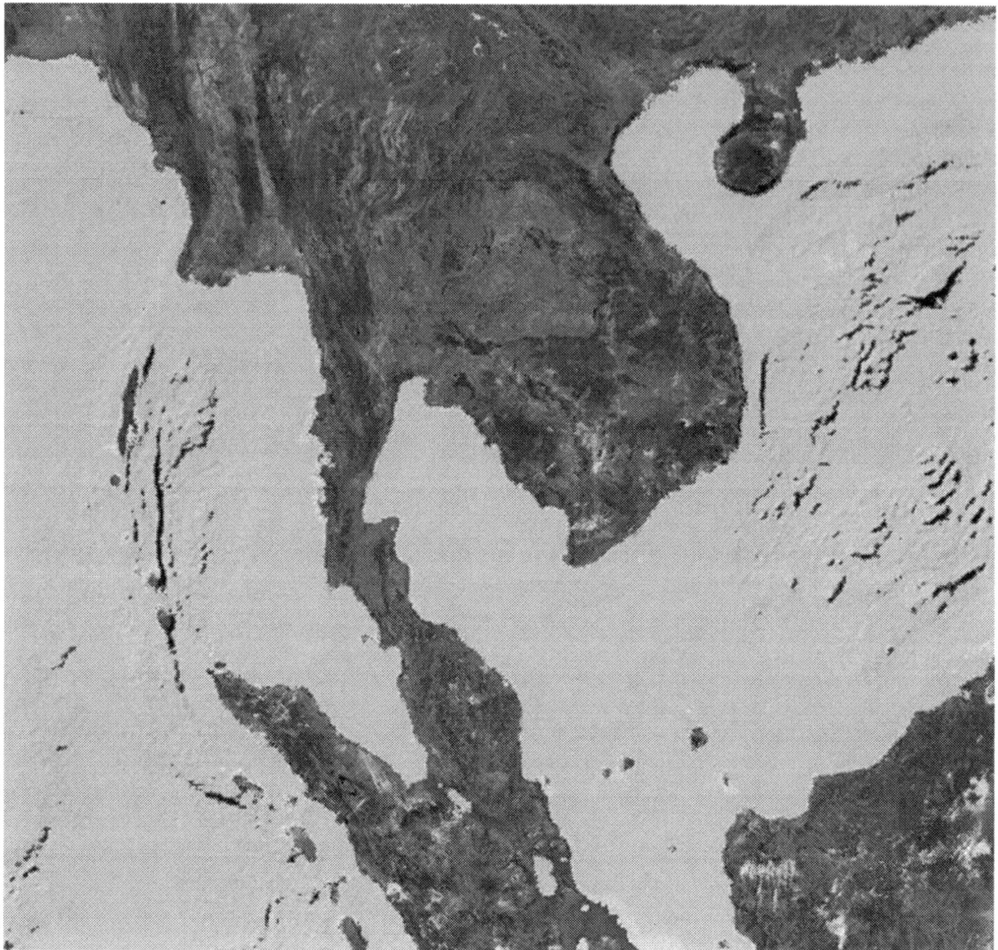

Figure 204

Modern View of Indochina

Then we see that the medieval European maps had them—Indochina, that is—bending to the left, as in Figure 205, Figure 206, Figure 207, Figure 208, and others.

What happened? What cause ancient Indochina to swing to the left while in reality it bent to the right? Well, it was because these master European cartographers had been mistaking a distorted South America for Indochina, at a time before they had visited; or knew of these places to boot.

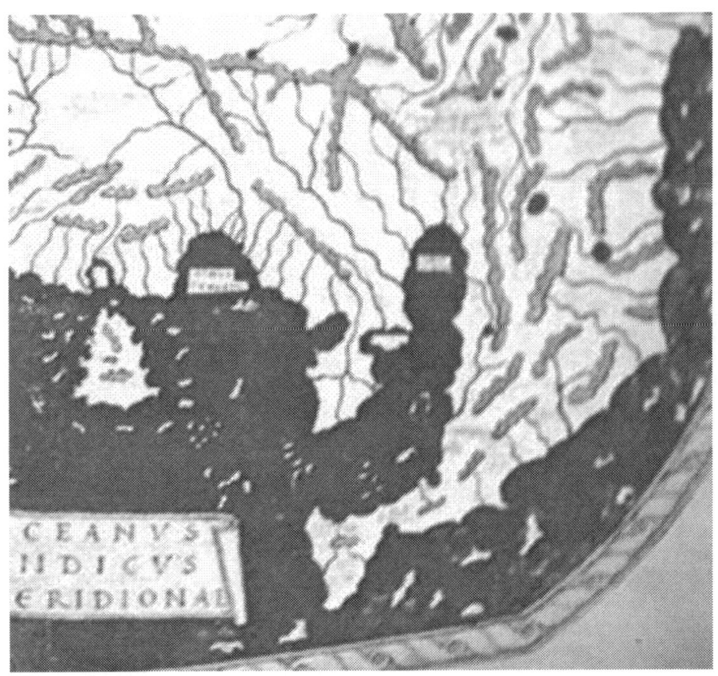

Figure 205

1489 Henricus Martellus Indochina

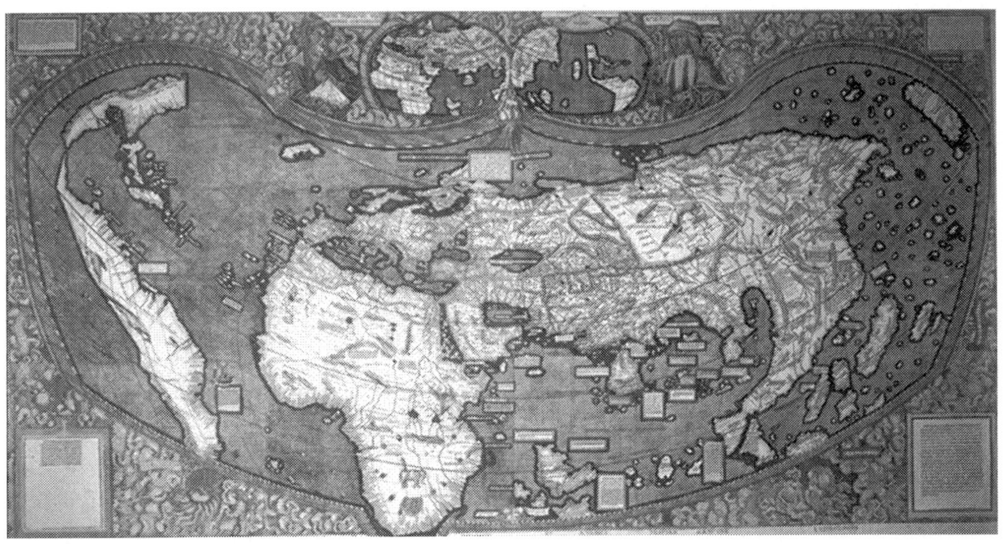

Figure 206

The 1507 Martin Waldseemüller World Map

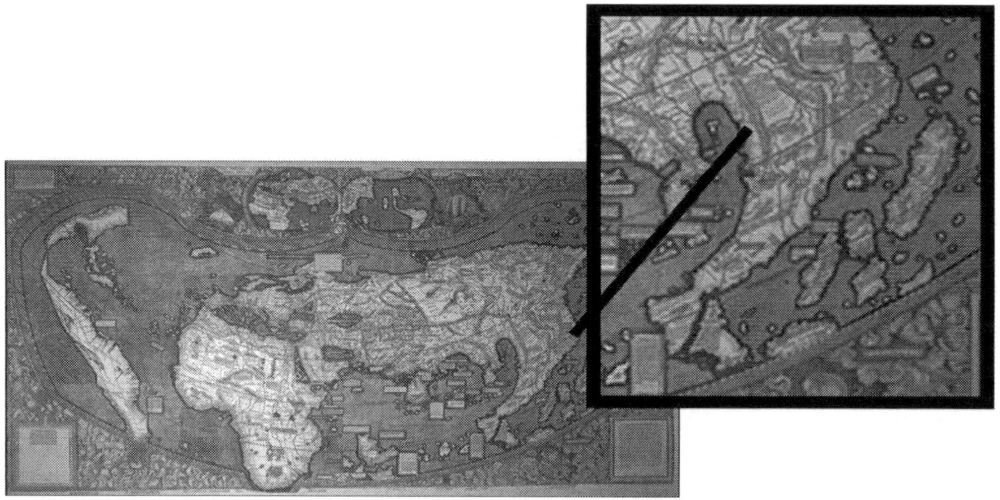

Figure 207

1507 Martin Waldseemüller Indochina

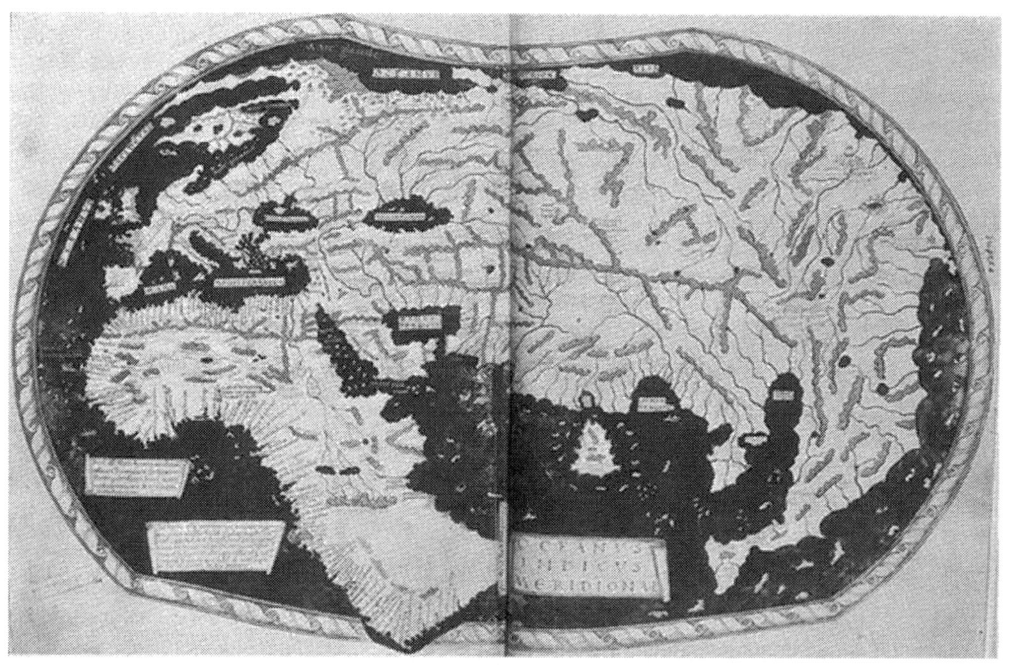

Figure 208

1489 Henricus Martellus Map

Paul Gallez (1920–2007) was an Argentinian cartographer and historian, born in Brussels, and based on the city of Bahía Blanca, province of Buenos Aires, Argentina.

He made an extensive research on maps to show that America was known long before the Age of Discovery, inspired by previous works by Dick Edgar Ibarra Grasso and Enrique de Gandía.

He was the first to identify all the principal fluvial system of South America in the Henricus Martellus Germanus map of 1489, using a distortion grid.

Figure 209

Professor Paul Gallez Write-Up

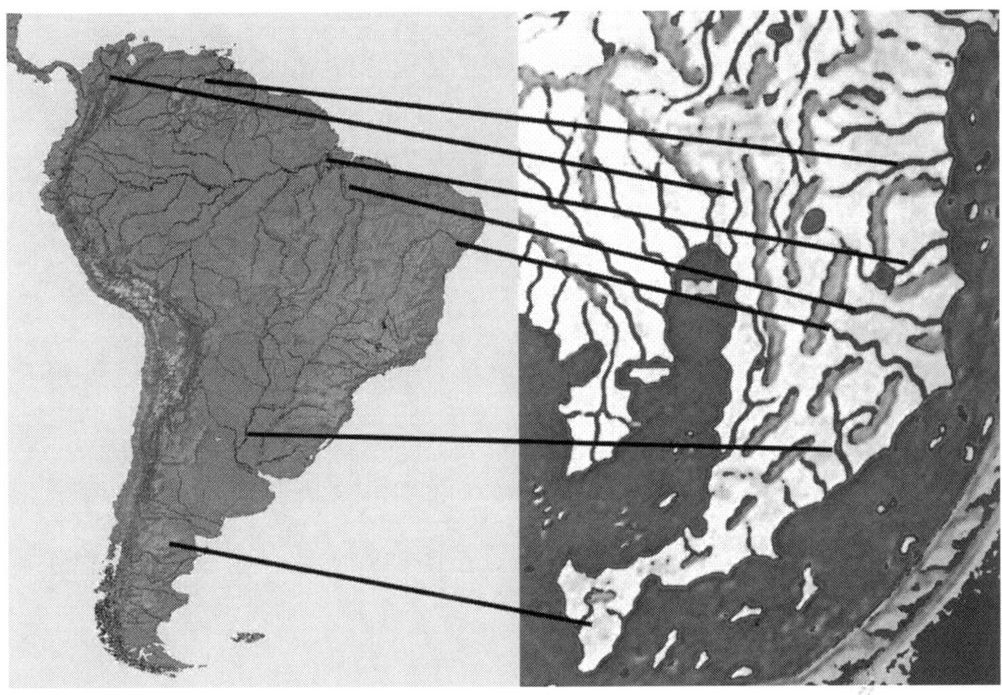

Figure 210

South American Rivers in Martellus' Indochina

The unmistakable identification of the ancient Indochina with South America has been correctly researched by Brussels-born Professor Paul Gallez (Figure 209), an Argentinian historian and cartographer. A summary of his thesis is represented in Figure 210, which shows the correspondence of rivers in Martellus' Indochina and the real South America.

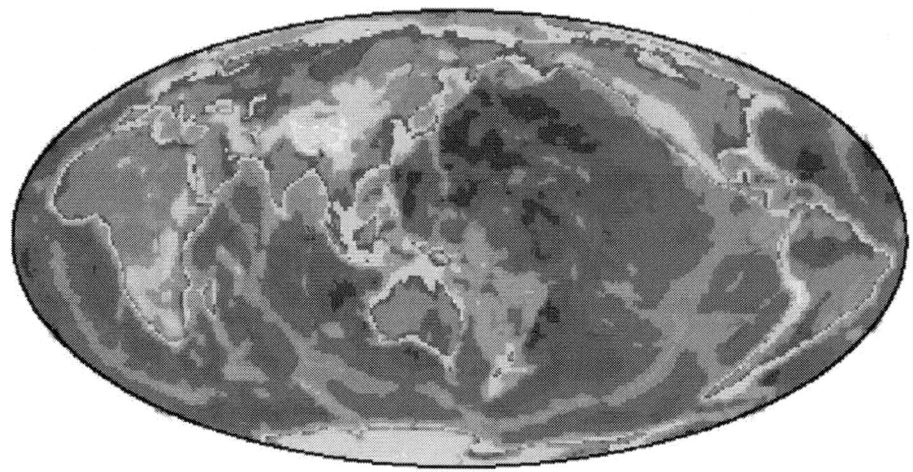

Figure 211

Pacific-Centric Projection Map

1474

- Florentine geographer Paolo dal Pozzo Toscanelli writes a letter to the Portuguese king in which he explains that Asia could be easily reached by sailing west into the Atlantic Ocean.

1476

- Lorenzo Buonincontri predicts that a "fourth continent" (in addition to Asia, Africa, and Europe) might be found across the ocean to Europe's west.

1484-1485

- Genoese sailor Christopher Columbus proposes to the Portuguese crown a plan to sail west in order to reach Asia. His plan is rejected as unsound by a royal commission of scholars.

Figure 212

Buonincontri's 4th Continent Hypothesis[58]

---

[58] https://www.encyclopedia.com/history/news-wires-white-papers-and-books/pre-1600-science-medicine-and-technology-chronology

可鲜为人知的是，1477年，也就是在郑和逝世44年之后，当时明朝朝廷为了继承郑和的事业，搜寻郑和《航海日志》就发现关于郑和船队的所有档案居然已经不翼而飞。更为离奇的是，直到现在已经过去五百年的历史,仍没有找到当时记录郑和下西洋的档案。

Figure 213

Zheng He Records Disappeared

兵部尚书项忠奉命调取档案，谁想到档案馆内关于郑和下西洋的所有秘密档案全部失踪了，这可是非常了不得的大事，这份资料在全世界范围内来说都是独一份的，项忠不敢掉以轻心，对主管档案的官吏严加责罚，命令他们三日之内必须找到丢失的档案。其他官吏人人叫屈，大声喊冤，这时兵部职方司郎中刘大夏站了出来。

他说郑和七次下西洋花费无数钱粮，国库里的储备基本上全用在了这个方面，一路上军民死伤无数，即使带回来奇珍异宝，对国家对百姓没有什么好处，那些档案根本就没有存在的必要，应该连根毁掉，还追究它的存在有什么意义呢？他的这番话有理有据项忠居然无言以对，明宪宗对此也是无话可说，最后航海计划就这么流产了。时至今日，关于郑和下西洋的航海资料依然没有找到。

Figure 214

Zheng He Records Disappearance Chinese Explanation

Figure 211 shows a projection world map with the Pacific Ocean at the center as opposed to the customary America-centric or Europe-centric renditions. In such a Pacific-centric map, the American Continents are bent and skewed, exactly as how the medieval Europeans drew them—not as South America, though, but as Indochina!

The early European cartographers had been attaching a hypothetical South America (hypothetical being that the Europeans should not have known about such a place) as Indochina to the Asian landmass! This means they had information about the shape and geography (waterways) of South America, in particular, as a projection image from an Oriental perspective (Figure 211). They had information about a place we call Indochina but not its precise geographical location and anything else. Also, they had no idea that there was a landmass that we dub South America. By mistake, or due to ignorance, they drew South America where Indochina was.

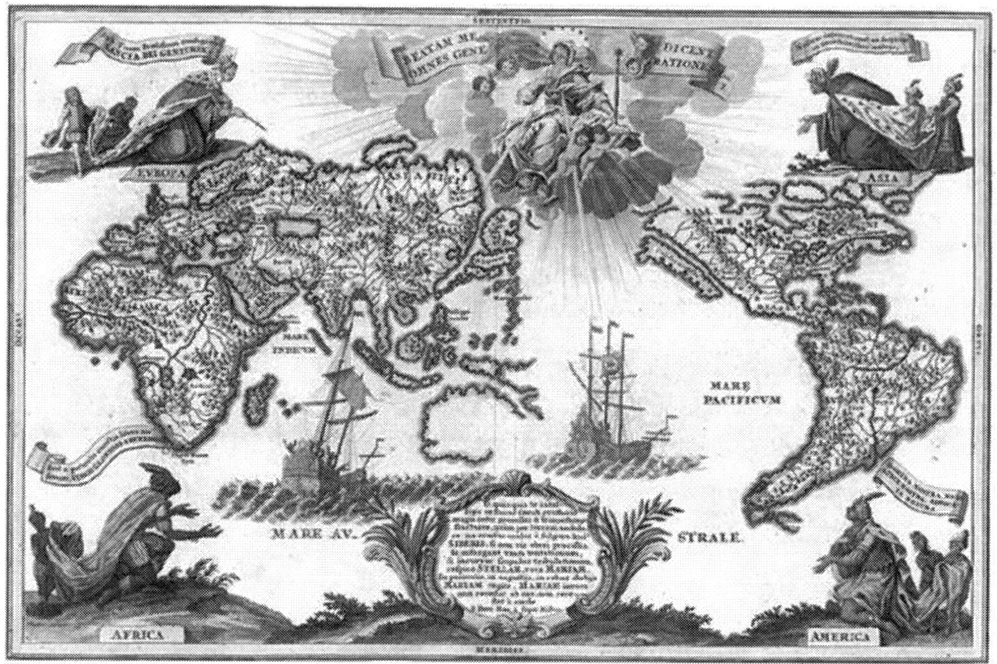

Figure 215

1703 Heinrich Scherer Pacific-Centric Projection Map

The commentary here is not meant to put down these early European mapmakers' artistic skills. On the contrary, these were superb master craftsmen, and it is precisely this peculiarity—able technicians producing dreadful products—that offers us a clue to the reality of the state of European geographical understanding at the dawn of the Age of Discovery.

This is not speculation, and the large number of extant old maps attests to the fact that it is not a coincidence. An analysis showing this ancient "Indochina" was indeed South America has been performed.

By late 15th century, European geographers had begun to suspect that there was an "undiscovered" fourth continent. Allegedly, in 1476, Florentine Lorenzo Buonincontri speculated about a fourth continent (Figure 212). However, the extant cartographic records indicate that no European had yet associated the mysterious "America" with this mysterious unknown continent.

Indeed, this is precisely how Oronces Finé drew his map of the world (Figure 77), in which the American continents are drawn as extensions of the Asian landmass. Thus, European cartographers were clearly associating the newly acquired geographical knowledge of the world, limited, and misconceived as it was, with Asia.

Yet, how did the Europeans get this new knowledge, or, perhaps, hint at something new?

Interestingly, in 1477, Zheng He's records disappeared (Figure 213, in Chinese records).

Figure 214 shows the Chinese explanation for the loss. It said that the Chinese (Ming Dynasty) emperor asked the Secretary of Defense for Zheng He's records. The Secretary found that all the records had disappeared. That was serious, and the Secretary ordered that the records be found within three days. At this time, an under-secretary came forward and said, Zheng He's voyages cost untold amounts of money, but produced little value for the citizens. What good was it to maintain the records? It only wasted even more money. For that, the Secretary of Defense and the Emperor were for want of a response. Hence, the matter of the Zheng He records was dropped.

In other words, there is a high probability that Zheng He's records went to Europe.

So, what does it infer? If there is still doubt as to the meaning of these historical documents, let me spell it out for you.

European cartographers were drawing the maps of Asia wrong, grafting the geography of America onto the Asian continent, testifying to the incontestable fact that they had not been to either place and were interpreting their cartographic products from some prototype or prototypes. That there were such prototypes attests to the inescapable conclusion that someone other than the European Age of Discovery explorers had already charted the world and the Europeans had gotten their hands on such artifacts.

That America showed up in Asia points to the origin of such geographic data coming from the East.

European cartographers were drawing accurately-shaped America without knowing it, without having visited it, and without having surveyed it. Eventually, as they got to know more of the world and surveyed the new lands which they had occupied, they came to realize their errors. Centuries later, however, they did try to show how that original odd shape of South America had come to be, and drew Pacific-centric world maps to illustrate it, as in Figure 215. As to why Heinrich Scherer drew a world map with the Pacific Ocean in the center in 1703, nobody knows the reason why.

Note that even at that time Australia was incompletely drawn, attesting to its being still not surveyed.

The Strange Case of the California Island

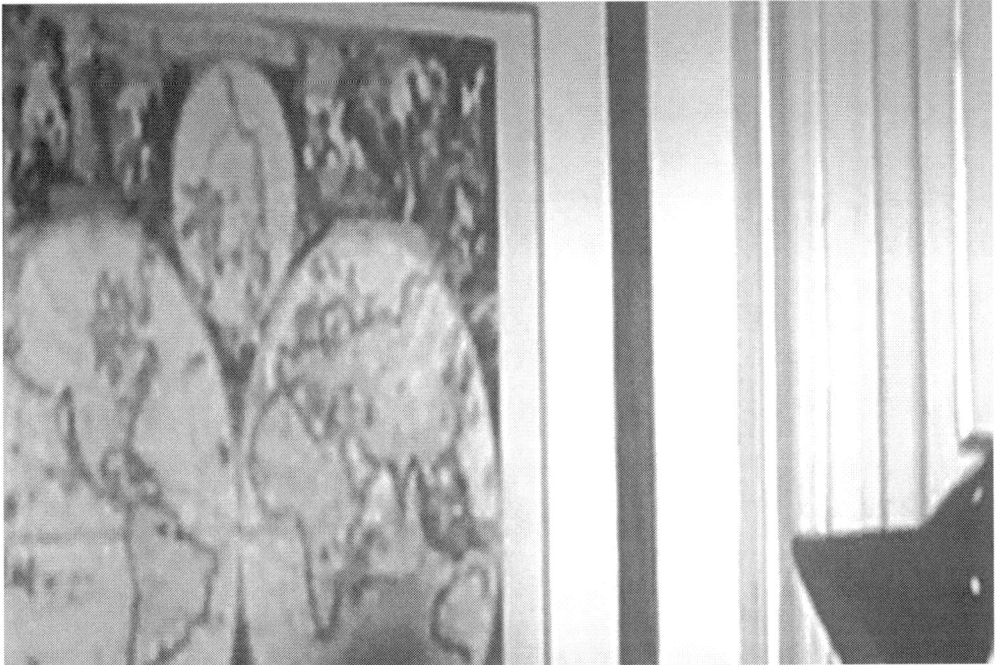

Figure 216

Italian TV Show Fog and Crime

Some time ago a major US newspaper printed an article on a medieval European map of North America that featured a California (Baja California) rendered as an island. The piece attracted thousands of comments. Then it was mocked by a reader for claiming that there was only one such "oddity" and produced another similar one to illustrate his point.

Only two California island maps? If you look closely at Figure 215 you will notice that not only is Australia incomplete, California (Actually, Baja California) is rendered as an island.

Figure 217

1626 John Speed Map of California

Baja California being drawn as an island; how did that happen? It is a geographical untruth. Yet, many 16th and 17th centuries European cartographers drew exactly that, rendering (Baja) California as an island. Even today, these California Islands are treated as something fun, and are sold as home decorations. I recently saw one hanging as background in an Italian TV serial called Fog and Crime (Figure 216).

The 1626 John Speed map (Figure 217) and the 1633 Hondius map (Figure 218) of California show the same too.

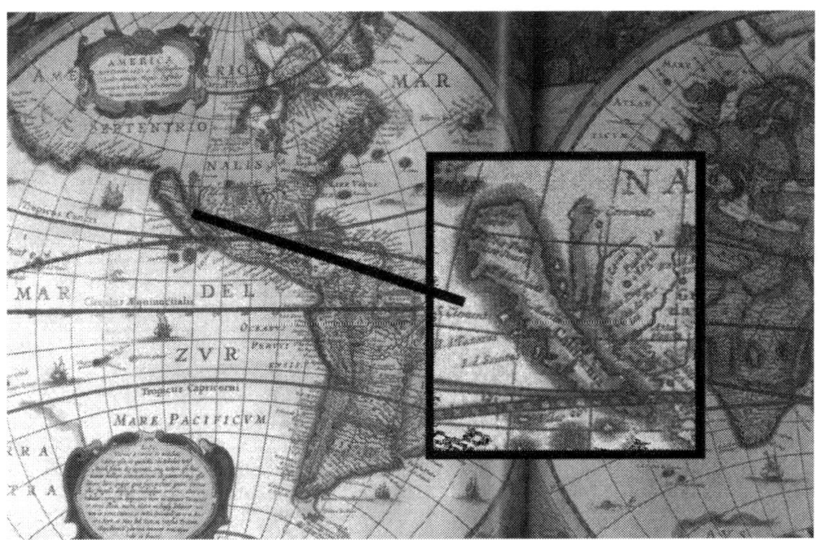

Figure 218

1633 Hondius California Island

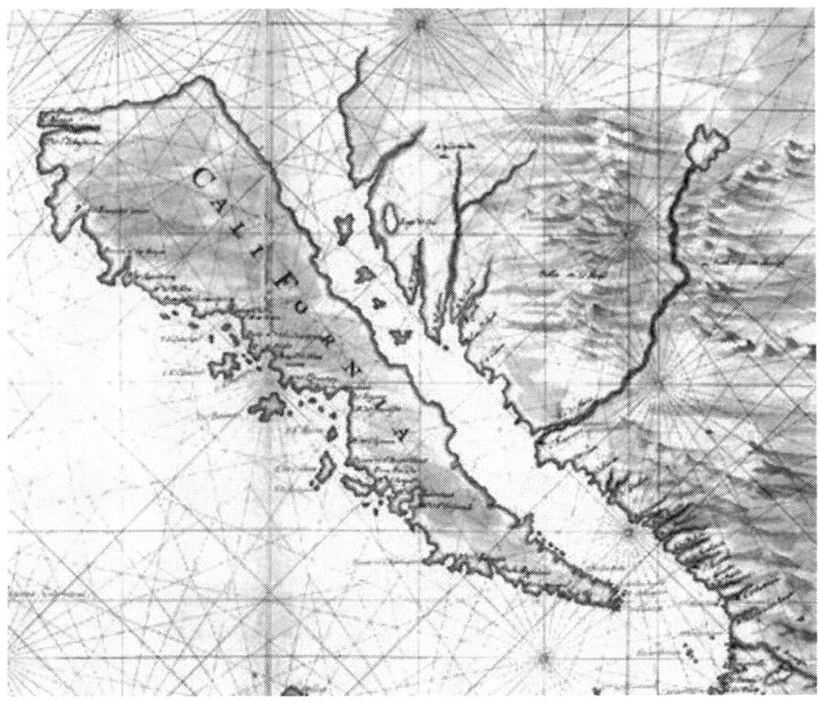

Figure 219

1639 Johannes Vingboons Map

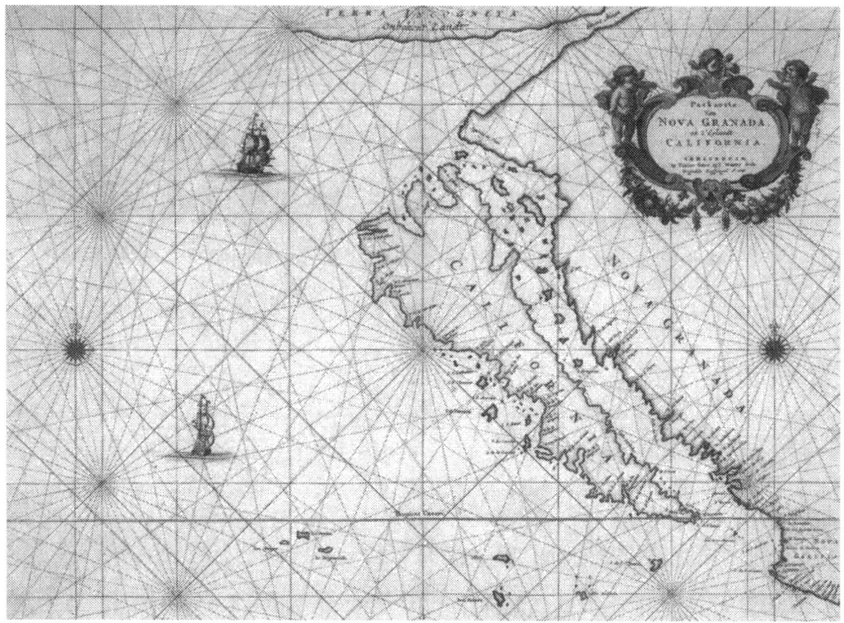

Figure 220

1666 Pieter Goos Map

Figure 221

1667 Joan Blaeu California Island

Figure 222

1670 Nicholas Visscher Map

Figure 223

1680 Frederic de Wit Map

So, think there were only two such oddities? Now look at the rest.

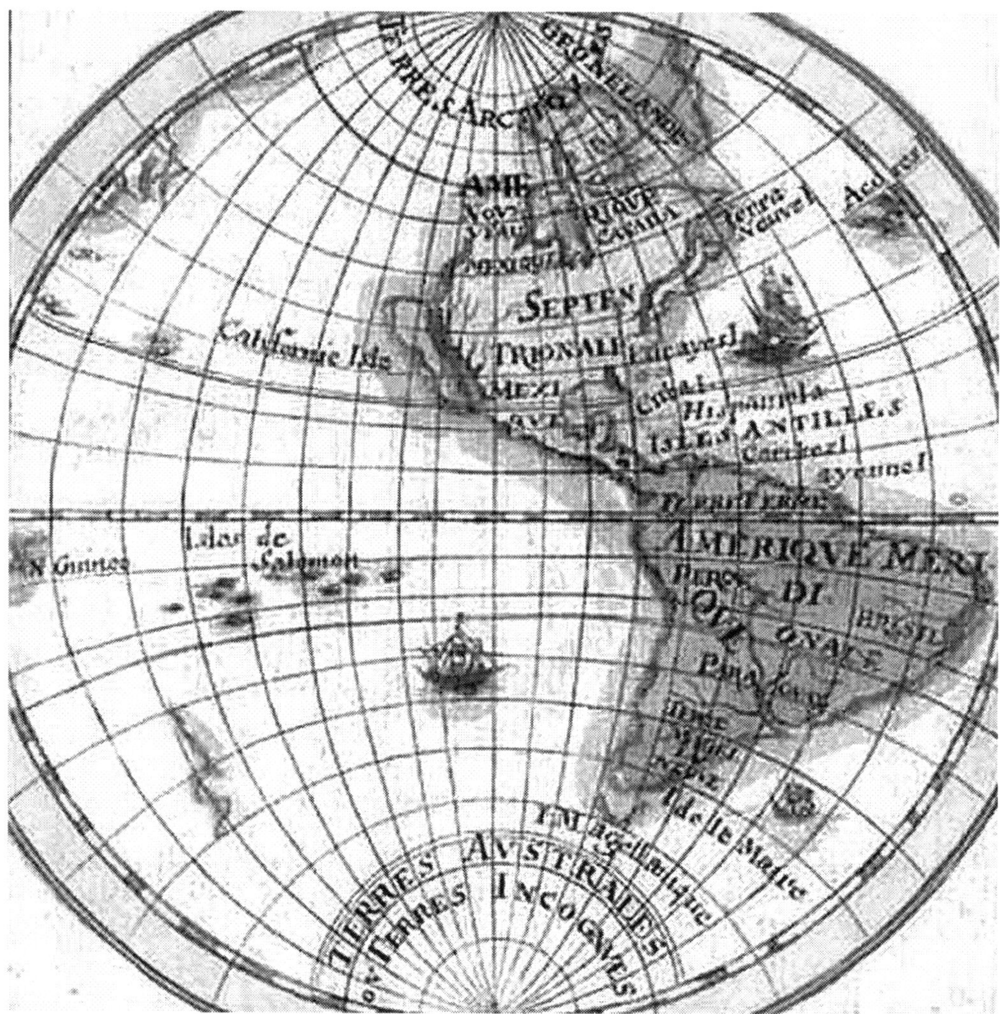

Figure 224

1683 Allain Mallet Map

The 1639 Johannes Vingboons map (Figure 219) also agrees. The 1666 Pieter Goos map (Figure 220), Joan Blaeu's 1667 rendition (Figure 221), the 1670 Nicholas Visscher map (Figure 222), the 1680 Frederic de Wit map (Figure 223), the 1683 Allain Mallet map (Figure 224), the 1688 Vincenzo Coronelli map (Figure 225), the 1697 Philip Cluver map (Figure 226), the 1720 Nicolas de Fer map (Figure 227), and many others preserved at various institutions, including the Library of Congress of the United States of America, the California

State Library, the Heritage Map Museum in Lititz, Pennsylvania, and so on, all show California as an island.

The peculiarity is not just some fantasy on the part of one peculiar mapmaker. There had to be some basis for the widespread subscription, and I aim to provide this strange phenomenon with an explanation.

Figure 225

1688 Vincenzo Coronelli Map

Figure 226

1697 Philip Cluver Map

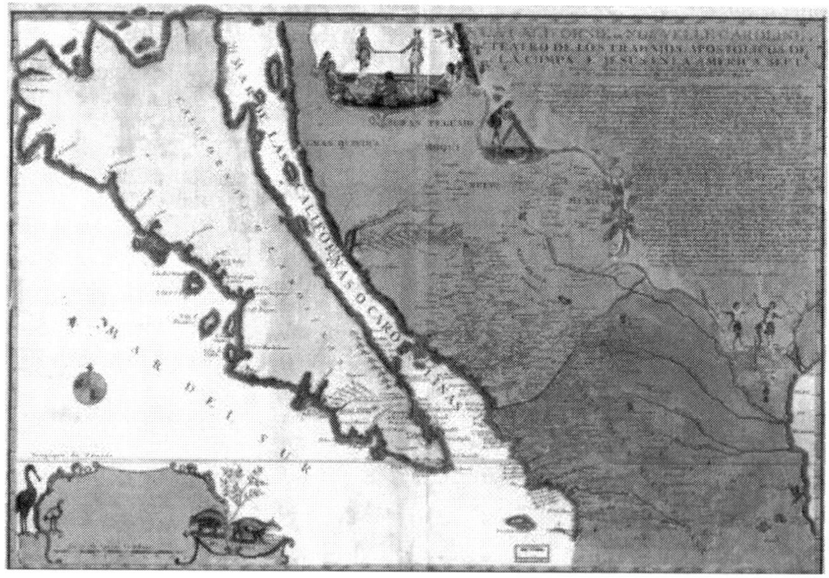

Figure 227

1720 Nicolas de Fer Map

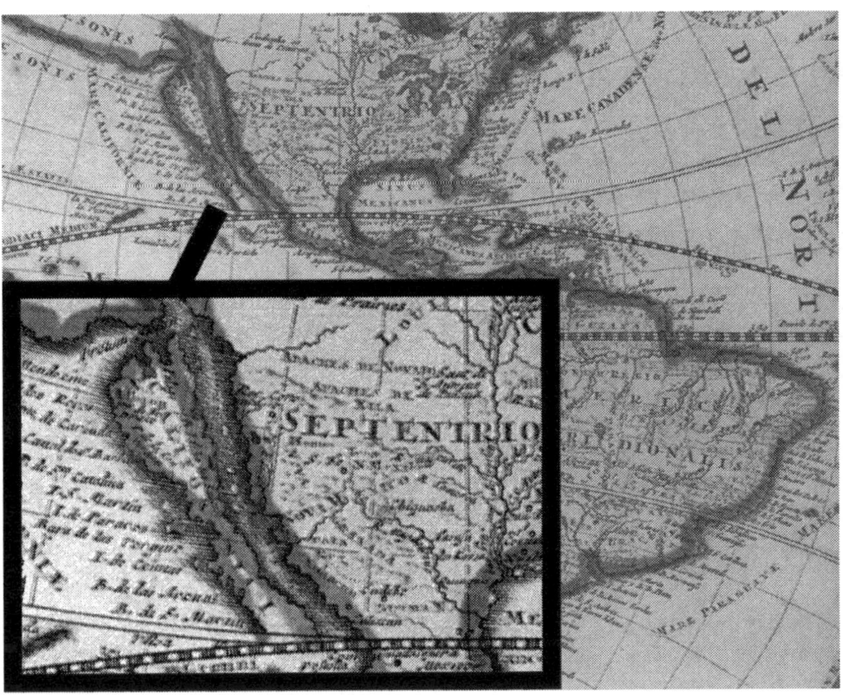

Figure 228

1706 Pieter Schenck California Island

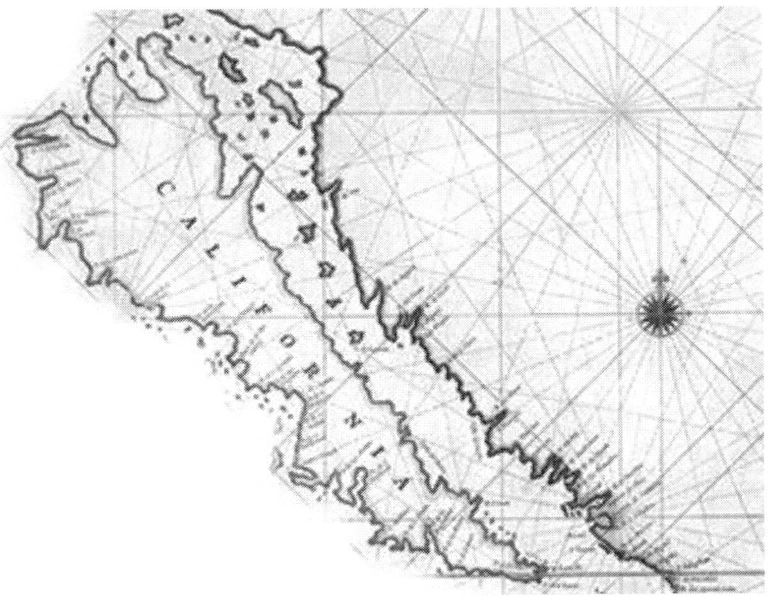

1510, by Esplandian

1622, per Tordesillas

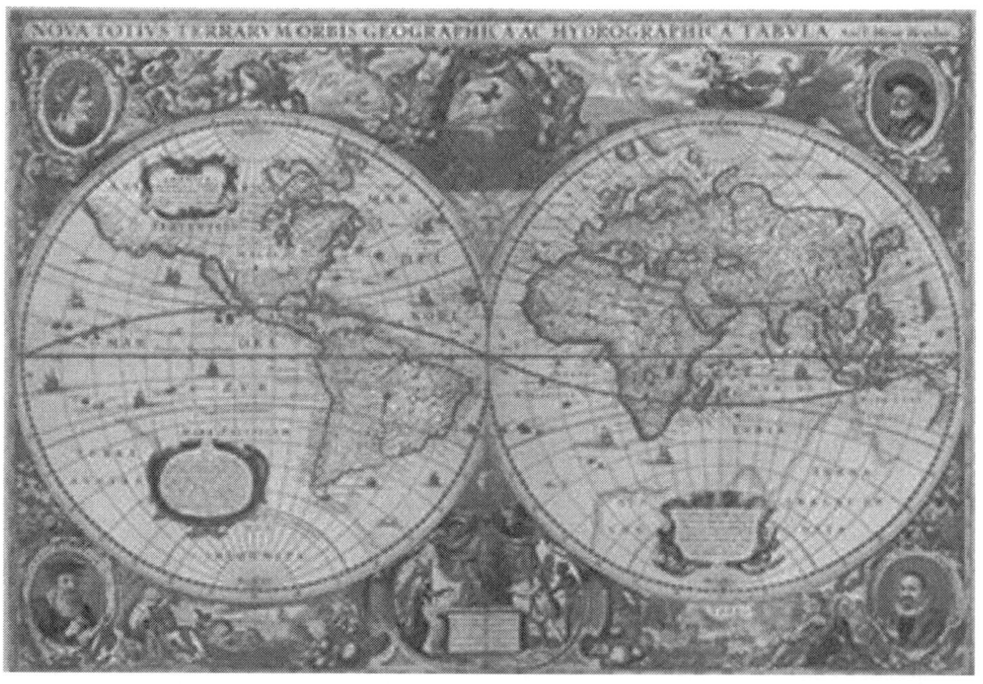

1630, by Hondius

1636, by Jansson

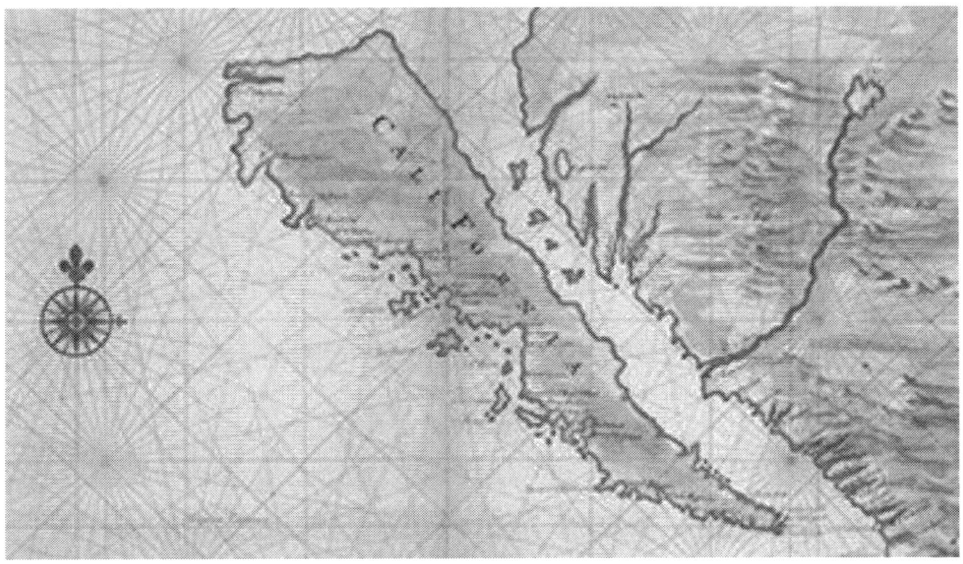

1650, by Vinckeboons

1646, by Speed

1710, by Scherer

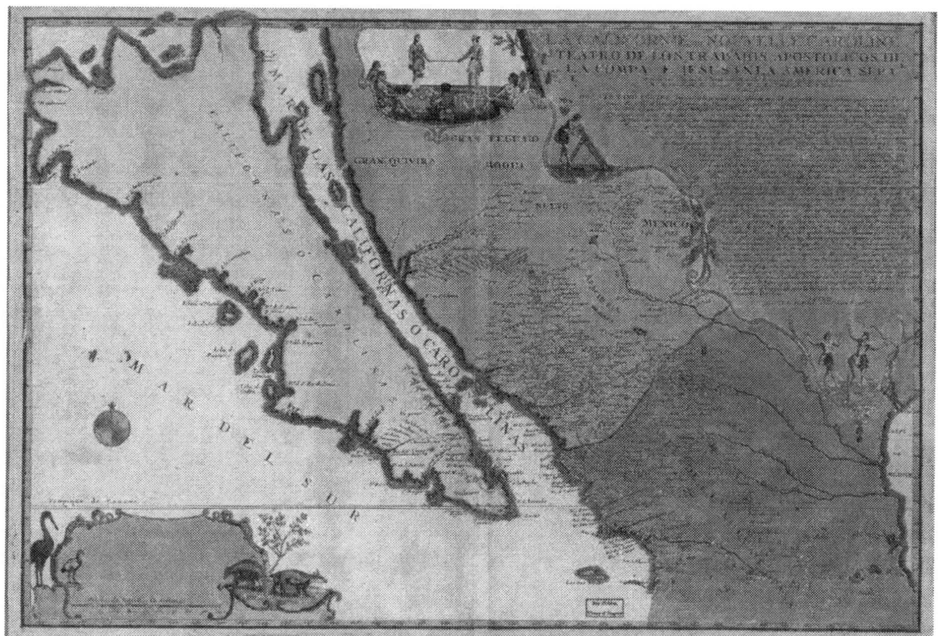

1720, by de Fer

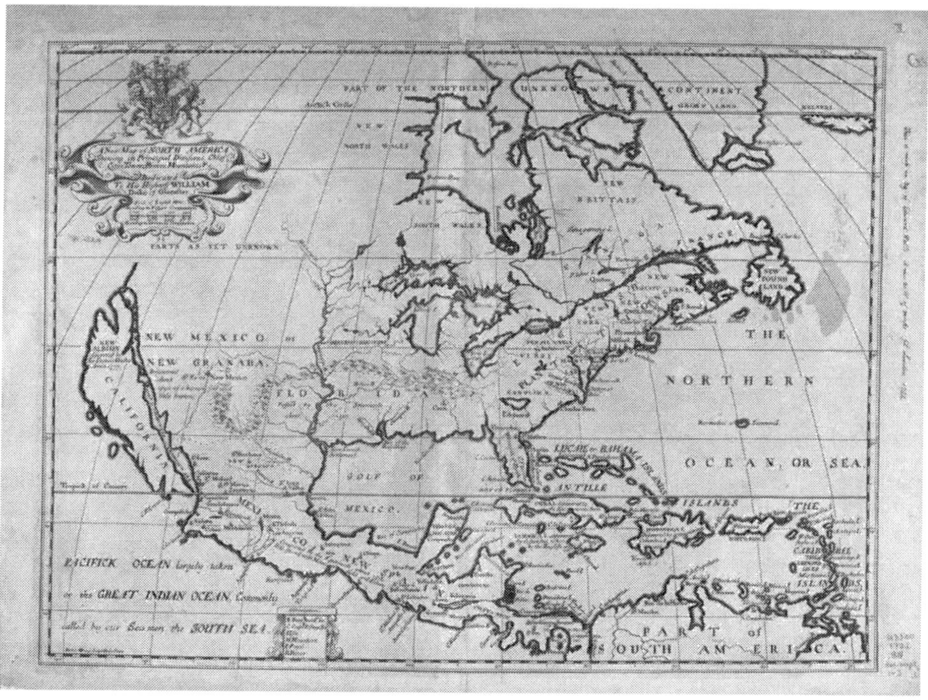

1722, by Wells

1752, by Foster

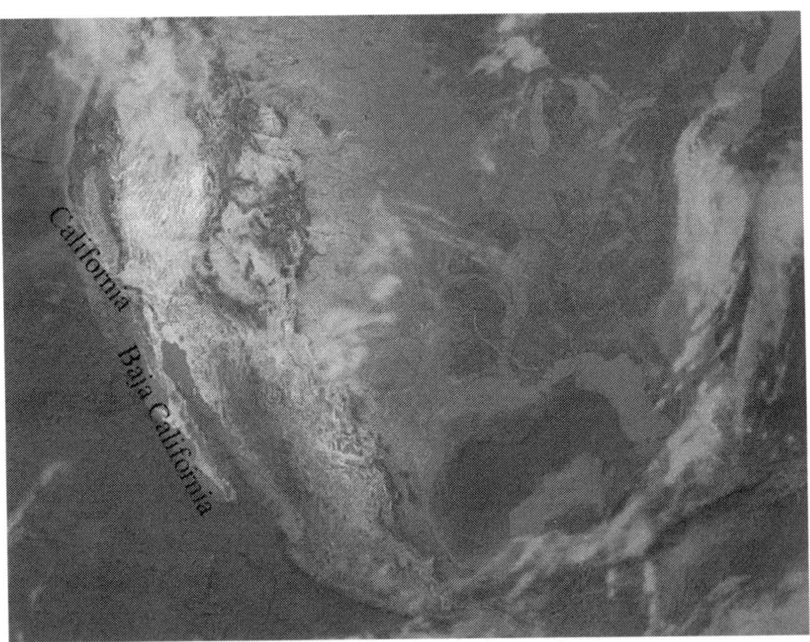

Figure 229

Today's Satellite Image of California

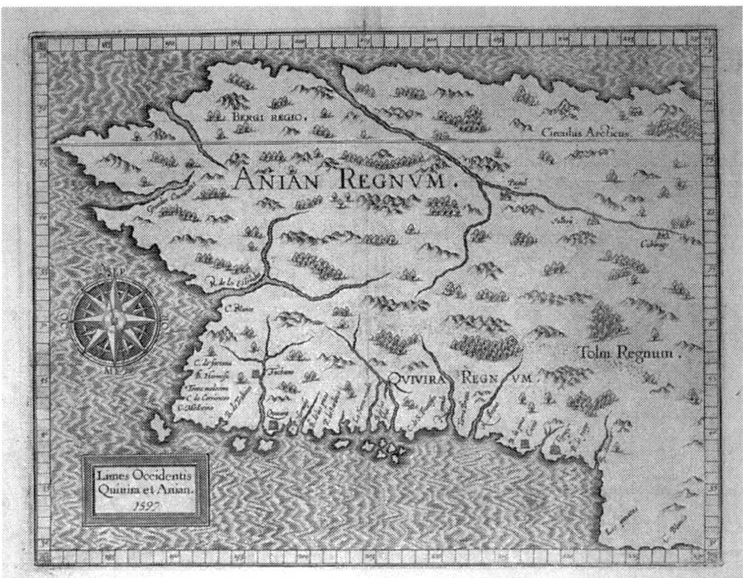

Figure 230

1597 Wytfliet Map

Figure 231

1628 Sebastian Munster Map

Figure 232

1575 Map Showing Ania

As we know, Christopher Columbus only reached the Caribbean at the beginning of the 16th century. The United States was yet in the future. Even the North-American settlements were only taking shape, and they were not Anglo-Saxon. That was still the era of myths and legends. For instance, Ponce de Leon the conquistador ostensibly was looking for the "Fountain of Youth." He supposedly discovered Florida. Then Hernan Cortes defeated the Aztec Empire and created Mexico. Francisco Pizarro famously conquered the Inca Empire and established today's Peru. Vasquez de Coronado went exploring from Mexico northward to today's Kansas. Along the way he allegedly discovered the Colorado River and the Grand Canyon. Meanwhile, Henry Hudson set out to find a Northwest Passage to Asia from Europe and explored Northeastern America. De Soto led a military mission from Florida and explored westward past the Mississippi, reaching perhaps as far as Arkansas. Jacques Cartier explored the Gulf of St. Lawrence, Prince Edward Island, and

Quebec, and claimed Canada; well, eastern Canada, anyway, for France. These early adventurers were focusing on the eastern part of North America. They had yet to explore the western part of the great land. No one was exploring the North American west—yet.

Now, that does not mean that no European had reached the western part. Vasco Núñez de Balboa crossed the Isthmus of Panama and reached the Pacific Ocean in 1513. However, he did not explore or survey the west coast of North America.

Starting in 1542, Juan Rodríguez Cabrillo sailed from Mexico northward to explore today's Californian coast. He reached today's San Diego, Santa Monica, and perhaps even Northern California, although missing San Francisco; its now famous bay, that is, as did all the explorers of the next two centuries. Yet, he did not survey the coast, and did not produce any maps or sketches of his journey.

Finally, in 1791, George Vancouver led an expedition to explore the North American northwest. That means the North American northwest was not surveyed until almost the 19th century. His effort in fact preceded that of Lewis and Clark, and they did not survey California.

Therefore, California; the North American west coast, was not explored or surveyed until the end of the 18th century. Yet, the cartographers were drawing California way before then, and shape-wise accurately, as we saw in the maps above. Mind you that these were European mapmakers, not American. Where did they get their cartographical information about California, shaped accurately but erroneous geologically as it might have been?

For two centuries, many of them drew California as an island, as you have just seen. For two hundred years nobody criticized them for being wrong. For that matter, those that did draw California as an island did not criticize those who drew it as a peninsula either. They probably argued with each other, but e have no historical record of a major brouhaha. The fact is, nobody knew what was right and what was wrong. Nobody had been there. "Nobody" here refers to European scholars.

1604 Map of Ania

In fact, the matter got so confused that Spanish King Ferdinand VII of early 19th century had to step in and invoke royal prerogative in order to settle the matter in favor of the latter, the peninsula crafters, that is.

However, we know differently. We know that these cartographers were copying their maps from some master copies, and we are interested in knowing what these master copies were. To do that we need to turn to our old trusted techniques for our detective work. We look for incongruent items on the maps; items that do not belong.

Ania

On the 1597 Corneille Wytfliet map at the Limes Occidentis Collection at the Alaska State Library (Figure 230), and the 1628 Sebastian Munster map (Figure 231), we find a place called Anian in a northerly region.

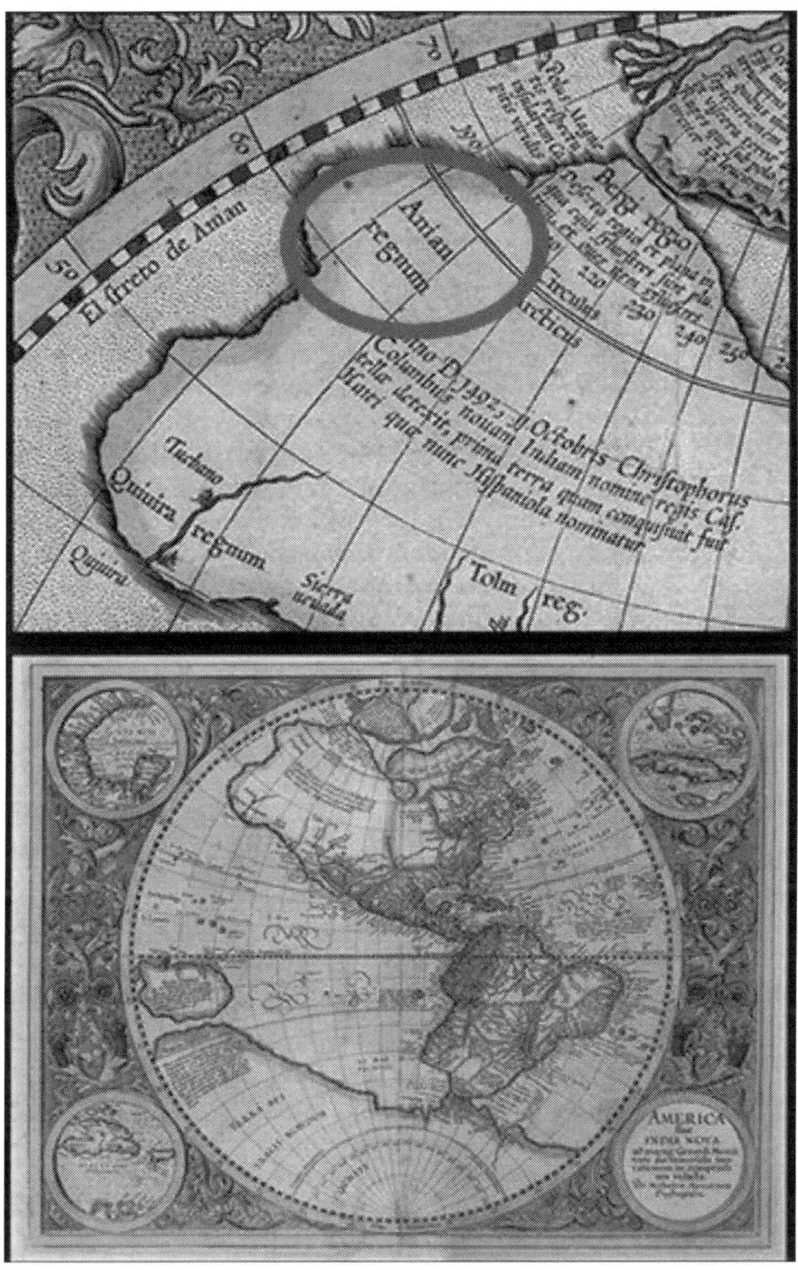

1595 Map of Ania

1608 Map of Ania

1639 Map of Ania

1697 Map Showing Anian

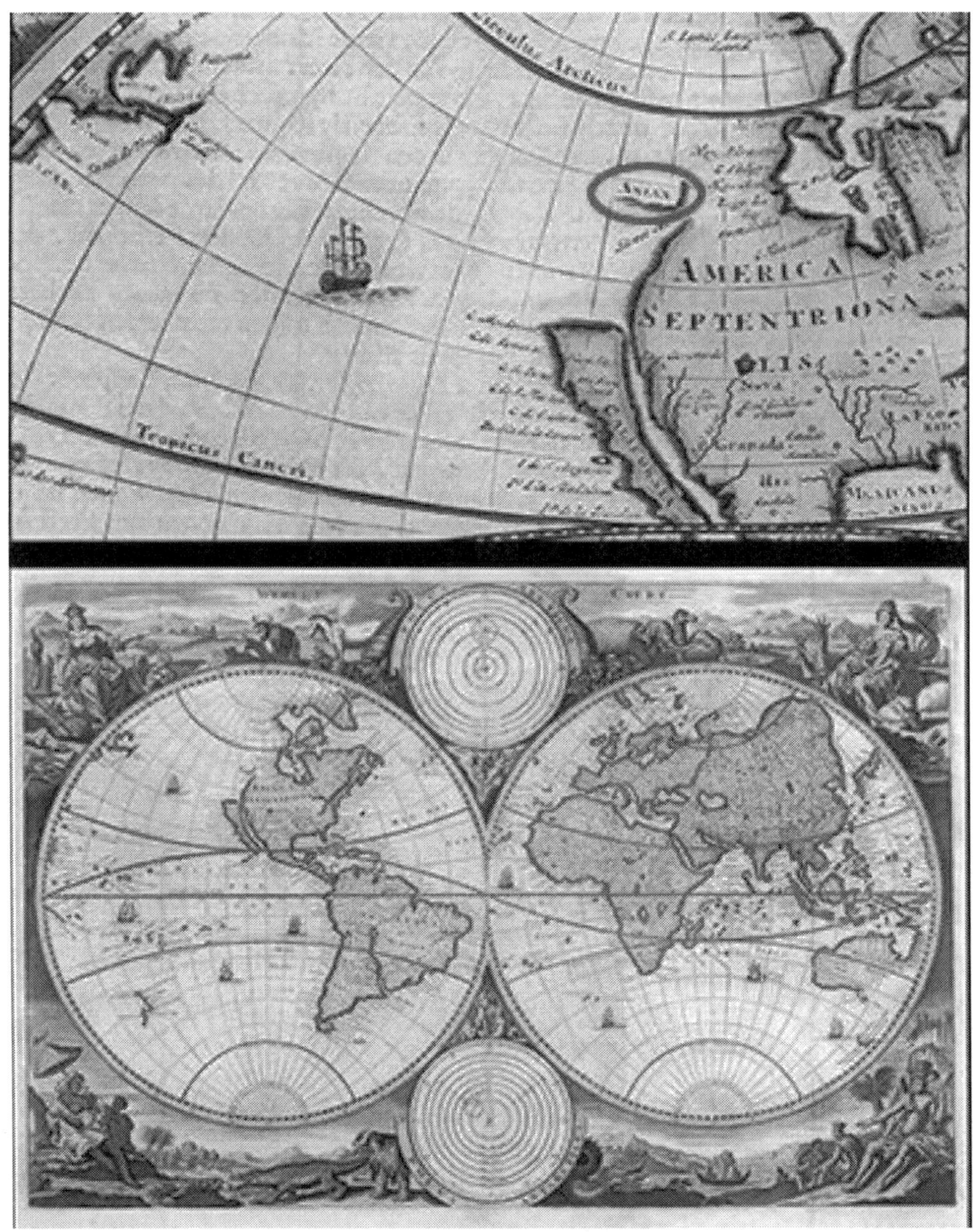

1680 Map Showing Anian

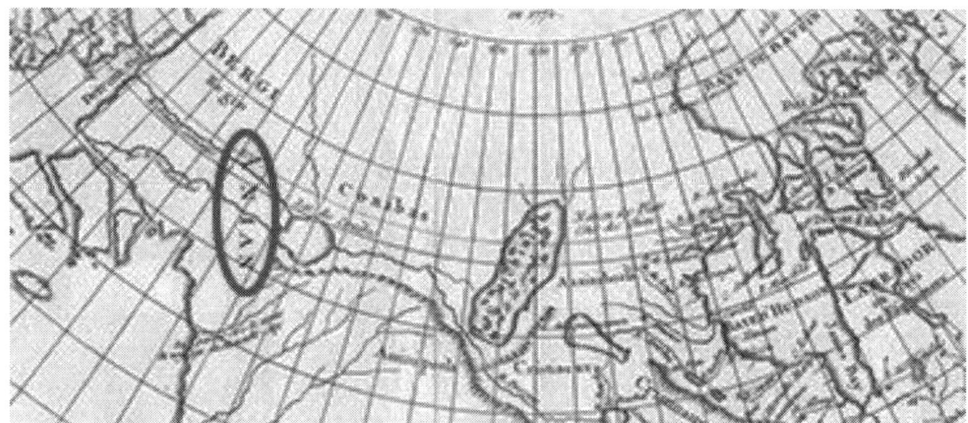

1772 Map Showing Anian

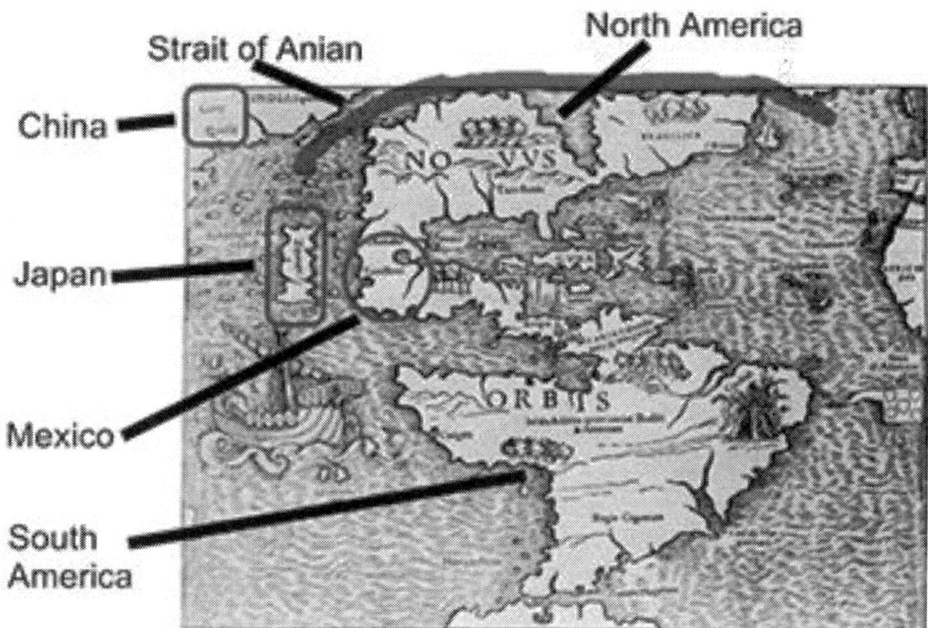

Historian Explanation

In the map shown in Figure 232, the notation "Strait of Annian" is found north of the California Island in the Pacific. In fact, Anian, Ania, or some other variations of it, can be found on virtually all the medieval California maps cited above. So, what is Ania, or Anian, or Annian? Again, let us first show this place systematically.

Strait of Anián

From Wikipedia, the free encyclopedia

The **Strait of Anián** was a semi-mythical strait, documented from around 1560, that was believe
modern cartographers to mark the boundary between North America and Asia and to permit acc
Northwest Passage from the Arctic Ocean to the Pacific. The true strait was discovered in 1728
known as the Bering Strait. The Strait of Anián had been generally placed nearby, but sometime
as far south as California.[1][2]

Figure 233

Anian is Bering Strait

Indeed, European historians were interested in the same thing too, and they scoured the maps to find the clue. What they came up with, was that this Anian was always up in today's Alaska, and later the place was renamed Bering Strait, and that was their conclusion (Figure 233). They did not explain why the place was called Anian, but instead simply stated that it later changed to Bering Sea. That was no research.

My research found out that Anian or Annian was mentioned in *The Travels of Marco Polo* along with South Sea Asian countries of Gaugiguo, Cheinan (Hainan), and others.[59]

Anian, Ania, or other forms of spelling all referred to Annan, the present-day Vietnam, which, in ancient times, was better known by its more dominant neighbor state Champa, which the Chinese at the time called, in the Mandarin dialect, *Zhan Po* or *Zhan Cheng*.[60] That is why a place named Chamabo appeared on the Munster map (Figure 82).

Cheng in Chinese means "city." *Zhan* is the "Cham" portion of the name Champa; that is Zhan Po, meaning Grandma Zhan. Hence, the City of Champa was The City of Cham, or *Zhan Cheng* in Chinese.

---

[59] Actually, Polo did not write about this part of the world. It was added to his book later. I skip discussing it here in order not to confuse the issues. The matter is addressed in a later section on Marco polo in detail.

[60] 占婆, 占城

164 *The Mythical Straits of Anian*

The author is speaking of the Gulf of Kienan (Tonkin), which, he says, "extends to a distance of two months' navigation along its northern shore, where it bounds the southern part of the province of Manji, and from thence to where it approaches the countries of Ania, Tolman and many others already mentioned." After some description of the gulf, the account concludes: "This gulf is so extensive and the inhabitants so numerous, that it appears like another world."

Figure 234

Polo Reference to Kienan

Tonkin, also spelled **Tongking**, northern Vietnam during the French colonial period. The term Tonkin was never officially used by the Vietnamese to describe their country.

Figure 235

Explanation of Tonkin

In *The Travels of Marco Polo* it is described how one could reach Ania:

> *Starting out from the great port of Zaiton (*Quanzhou across from Taiwan in Southeast China*) you sail due south for about 1,500 miles then veer to the southwest. After a month of sailing you will come to a strait with many islands.*

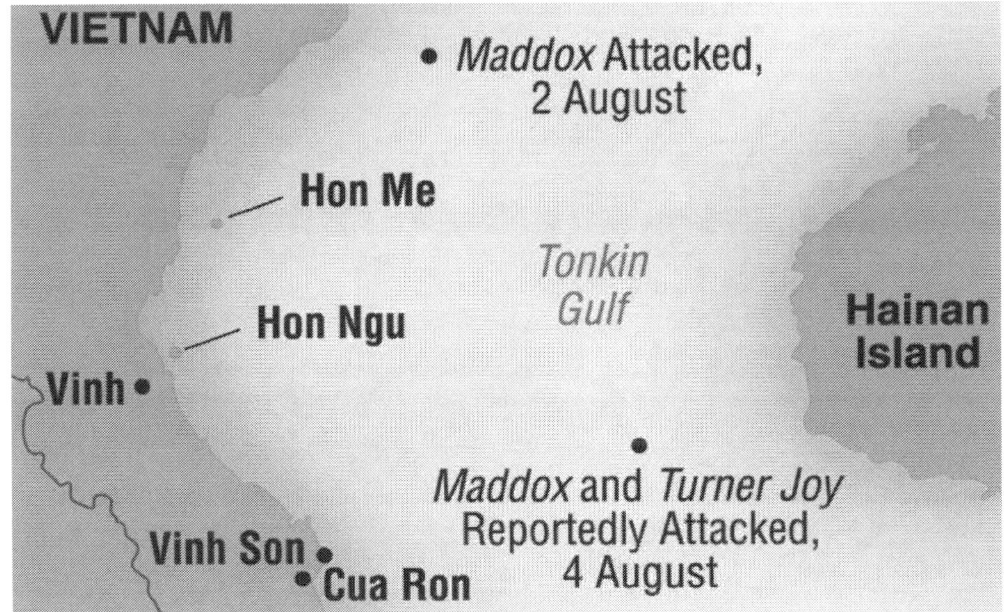

Figure 236

Tonkin Gulf

> *You will be passing by the southern coast of Manji, and there will be a great island, the Cheinan Island, on the left. After that you will come into the territory of Ania.*[61]

As it were, Marco Polo's travelogue is describing nothing special. This is the basic geography of South China Sea.

Yet, the Travelogue also mentioned a place called Tonkin, also known as the Gulf of Kienan (Figure 234 and Figure 235).

We all know what Tonkin is (Figure 235). During the Vietnam War, we had an incident of the Gulf of Tonkin which drew the US into the conflict (Figure 236).

---

[61] Here is another bit of linguistic tidbit that sheds a glaring light on the origins of such Eastern names; this one happens to be allegedly from Marco Polo.

How did Annan become Ania? Recall how the Central Asians (Arabic speakers) dropped the /n/ in Khitan and made it Khitai? So Annan became Ania. In reverse, the Chinese often add an /n/ to Western terms where it is absent. For instance, the Chinese transliterate the name Allah as An Lah. Thus Marco Polo used a Central Asian version of an Asian name. See below on Marco Polo.

128. CAUGIGU

caigu Fr	*cauçugu, cauzugu* Z	*gangigu* [*mellichac* (74 r°)] V
cangighu, changighu, changigu *changiu* TA³	*caugigu* F, FA, FB, P, L	*gaugigu* F
	chaugigu TA¹	*talugigla* LT
cangigu Fr, L, R	*çingoj* VB	*tangigu* VA

I cannot see why we still find « Cangigu » in *B*, 125, and *Pe*, 293, 378, nor why B¹, 440, while now adopting « Caugigu », adds that the reading is uncertain. *Ch*, II, 262, is absurd. The name, as already suspected by QUATREMÈRE and D'OHSSON, is evidently 交趾國 Chiao-chih-kuo, « Kingdom of Chiao-chih », Tonking, often so called in *YS* as an alternative name for An-nan (Annam, but in the sense of modern Tonking); cf. for instance *YS*, 10, 9 *a*; 11, 3 *b*, 4 *a*, etc. The etymology is confirmed by Rašīdu-'d-Dīn's كفجه كو Kafjāh-guh (*Y*¹, III, 130; *Bl*, II, 451-452, 499). « Caugigu » and « Kafjāh-guh » are Chiao-chih-kuo, just as « Çipingu » and « Jimingu » are Jih-pên-kuo (see « Çipingu »). It is well known that the very old name Chiao-chih, through an intermediary Malay form, survives as the first element of our « Cochinchina » (a name which was applied to Middle Annam until the end of the 18th cent.). In 1554, Sīdī 'Alī names كوجى Kōji (for Kōči),

Figure 237

Polo Travelogue's Gaugigu

128. CAUGIGU

caigu Fr
cangighu, changighu, changigu
*changtu TA*³
cangigu Ft, **L, R**

cauçugu, cauzugu Z caugigu
F, FA, FB, **P, L** *chaugigu* TA'
cjngoj VB

gangigu [mellichac (74 ro)] V *gaugigu* F
talugigla LT *tangigu*
VA

I cannot see why we still. find « Cangigu » in *B*, 125, and *Pe*, 293, 378, nor why BI, 440, while now adopting « Caugigu », adds that the reading is uncertain. *Ch*, II, 262, is absurd. The name, as already suspected by **QUATREMERE** and **D'OHSSON,** is evidently 3Zjlf Chiao-chih-kuo, « Kingdom of Chiao-chih », Tonking, often so called in YS as an alternative name for An-nan (Annam, but in the sense of modern Tonking); cf. for instance YS, 10, 9 a; 11, 3 *b*, 4 a, etc. The etymology is confirmed by Rasidu-'d-Din's8Ç& .c Kaf jāh-guh (YI, III, 130; *BI*, **u**, 451-452, 499). « Caugigu » and « Kafjāh-guh » are Chiao-chih-kuo, just as « Çipingu » and « Jimingu » are Jih-pênkuo (see « Çipingu »). It is well known that the very old name Chiao-chih, through an intermediary Malay form, survives as the first element of our « Cochinchina » (a name which was applied to Middle Annam until the end of the 18th cent.). In 1554, Sidi 'Ali names .(Kôji (for Kôci),

Figure 238

Polo Travelogue's Gaugugu

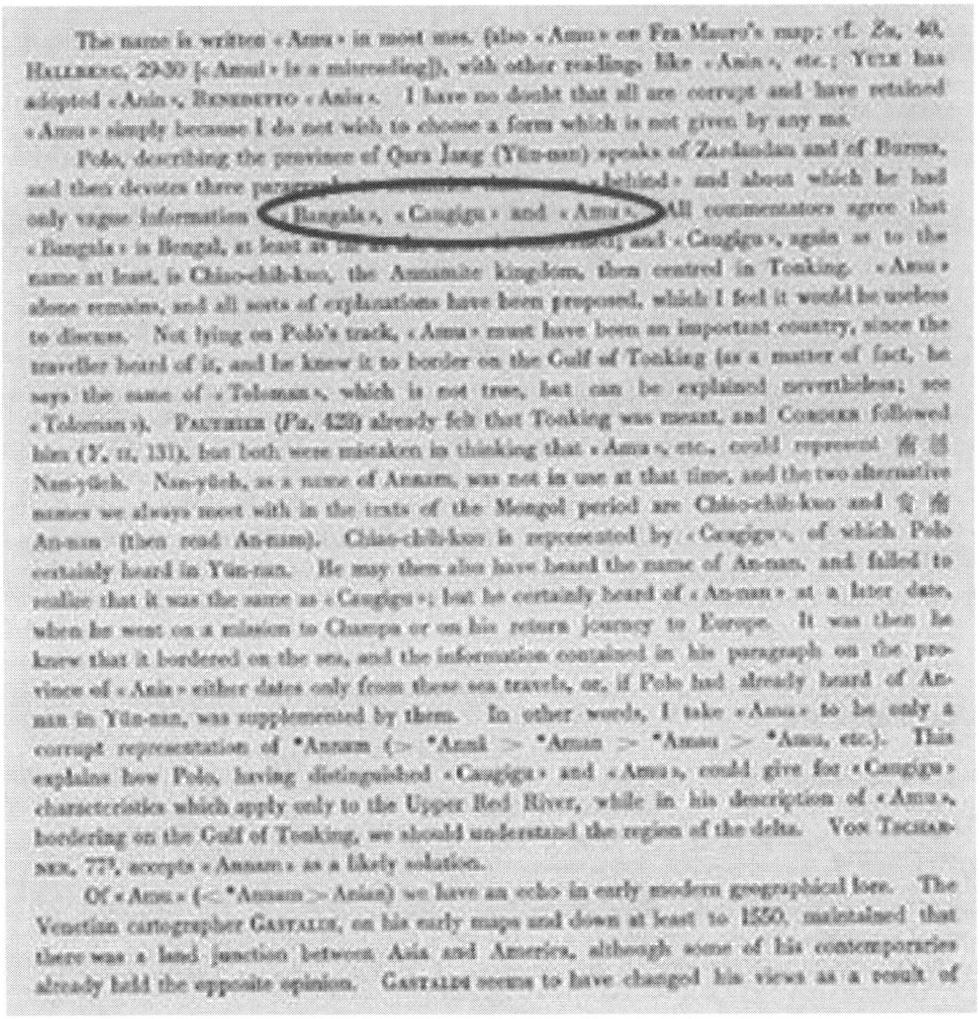

The name is written «Amu» in most mss. (also «Amu» on Fra Mauro's map; cf. Zu, 40, Hallberg, 29-30 [«Amul» is a misreading]), with other readings like «Anin», etc.; Yule has adopted «Anin», Benedetto «Ania». I have no doubt that all are corrupt and have retained «Amu» simply because I do not wish to choose a form which is not given by any ms.

Polo, describing the province of Qara Jang (Yün-nan) speaks of Zardandan and of Burma, and then devotes three parag[illegible] «behind» and about which he had only vague information «Bangala», «Caugigu» and «Amu». All commentators agree that «Bangala» is Bengal, at least as [illegible]; and «Caugigu», again as to the name at least, is Chiao-chih-kuo, the Annamite kingdom, then centred in Tonking. «Amu» alone remains, and all sorts of explanations have been proposed, which I feel it would be useless to discuss. Not lying on Polo's track, «Amu» must have been an important country, since the traveller heard of it, and he knew it to border on the Gulf of Tonking (as a matter of fact, he says the name of «Toloman», which is not true, but can be explained nevertheless; see «Toloman»). Pauthier (*Pa*, 428) already felt that Tonking was meant, and Cordier followed him (*Y*, II, 131), but both were mistaken in thinking that «Amu», etc., could represent 南越 Nan-yüeh. Nan-yüeh, as a name of Annam, was not in use at that time, and the two alternative names we always meet with in the texts of the Mongol period are Chiao-chih-kuo and 安南 An-nan (then read An-nam). Chiao-chih-kuo is represented by «Caugigu», of which Polo certainly heard in Yün-nan. He may then also have heard the name of An-nan, and failed to realize that it was the same as «Caugigu»; but he certainly heard of «An-nan» at a later date, when he went on a mission to Champa or on his return journey to Europe. It was then he knew that it bordered on the sea, and the information contained in his paragraph on the province of «Ania» either dates only from these sea travels, or, if Polo had already heard of An-nan in Yün-nan, was supplemented by them. In other words, I take «Amu» to be only a corrupt representation of *Annam (> *Anni > *Aman > *Amau > *Amu, etc.). This explains how Polo, having distinguished «Caugigu» and «Amu», could give for «Caugigu» characteristics which apply only to the Upper Red River, while in his description of «Amu», bordering on the Gulf of Tonking, we should understand the region of the delta. Von Tscharner, 77[3], accepts «Annam» as a likely solution.

Of «Amu» (< *Annam > Anian) we have an echo in early modern geographical lore. The Venetian cartographer Gastaldi, on his early maps and down at least to 1550, maintained that there was a land junction between Asia and America, although some of his contemporaries already held the opposite opinion. Gastaldi seems to have changed his views as a result of

Figure 239

Marco Polo Travelogue's Anian and Gaugigu

Polo's Travelogue also mentioned a place called Gaugigu (Figure 237).

In plain English (Figure 238, Figure 257, and Figure 240).

So, 16th and 17th centuries European cartographers put a place found in *The Travels of Marco Polo* on their masterpieces. Although there are questions to the origin of the celebrated work; namely, *The Travels of Marco Polo*, Ania did appear next to the name Gaugigu.

Polo, describing the province of Qara Jang (Yün-nan) speaks of Zardandan and of Burma, and then devotes three paragraphs to countries that were «behind» and about which he had only vague information : «Bangala», «Caugigu» and «Amu». All commentators agree that

Figure 240

Marco Polo Travelogue's Gaugigu in Detail

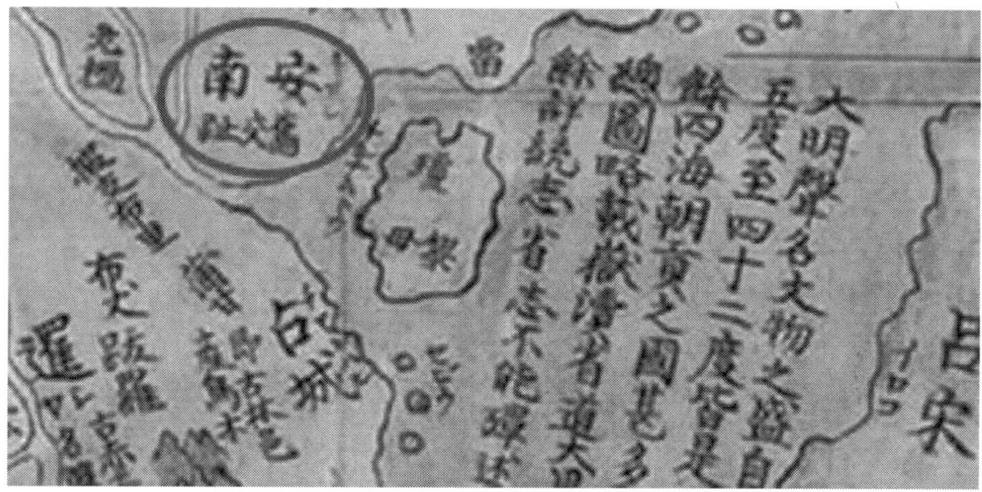

Figure 241

Ancient Annan-Gaugigu

What was "Gaugigu" anyway? Gaugigu was ancient Vietnam. During the early Ming Dynasty, Emperor Chengzu and Zheng He's time, the country's name switched between Gaugigu (today's Jiaoziguo, 交趾國) and Annan (安南) (Figure 241). Gaugigu is still the pronunciation in Cantonese. See if you can spot these two Chinese names (circled) in Figure 241.

Hence, we now know that originally Anian, or Ania, Anien were all Annan and it referred to northern Vietnam.

Now, this is amazing. European cartographers transplanting southeast Asia onto northwest North America. It could not be, could it? Whatever we think, the evidence is plainly there. Just to be absolutely sure, let us see if we can find another oddity that would support the above finding.

The Vermillion Sea

1745 Seale Red Sea

C.Blanco
C.St.Sebastian
NEW ALBION
CALIFORNIA
RED SEA
P.St.Fr.Drake
SEVO
P.de Monterey
P.Carinde
I.St.Clement
I.de Pararos
C.St.Apollina
Guia R
R.Angonchi
Apaches
St.Andre
Sonora
Gulf of California
Edues
Cenou P
Cotas
C.St.Luca
Ullao
Amblada
la Roca
St.Thomas
la Nublada
C.Corrientes

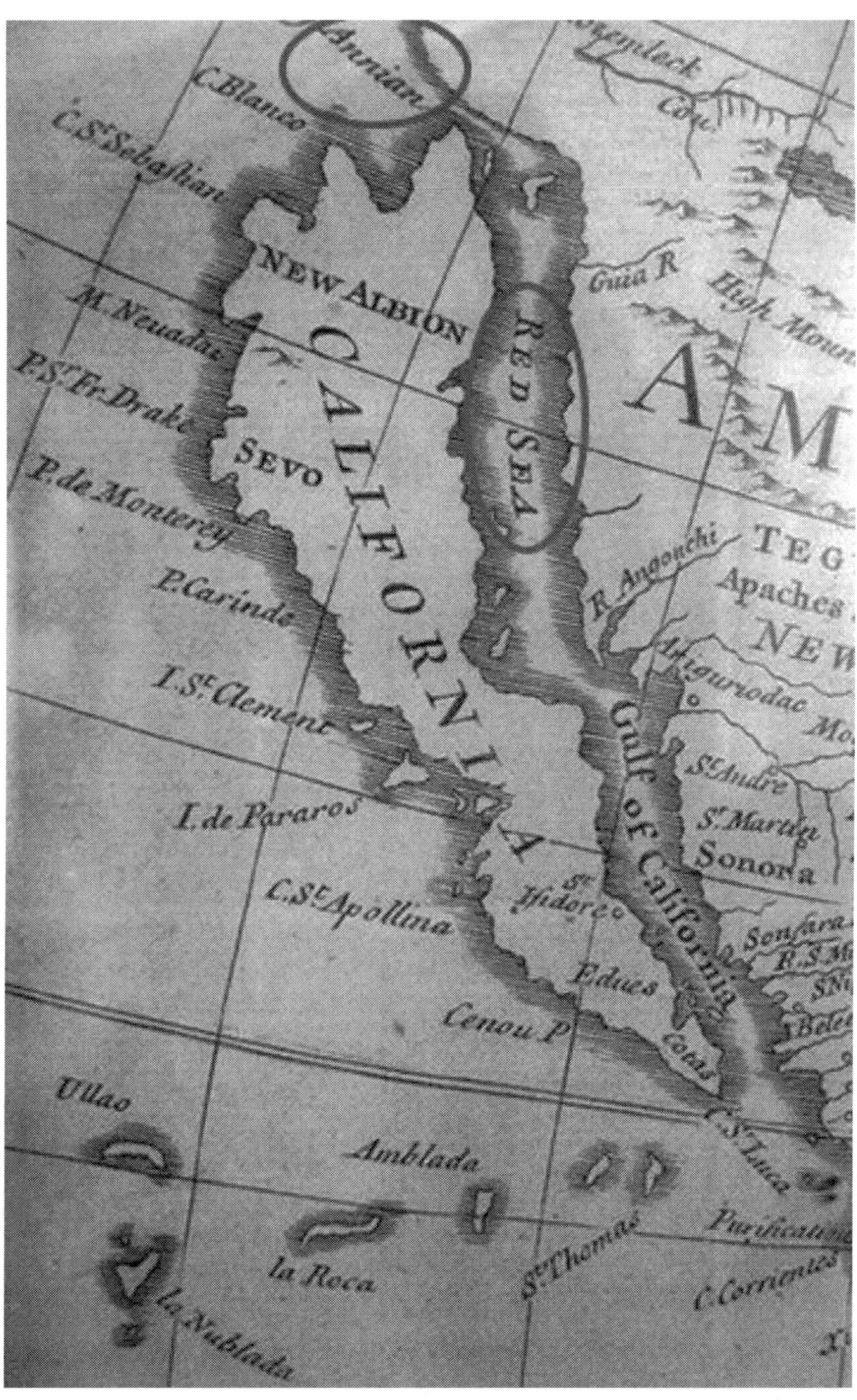

Red Sea

1675 Mer Vermeille

1692 Mer Rouge (Red)

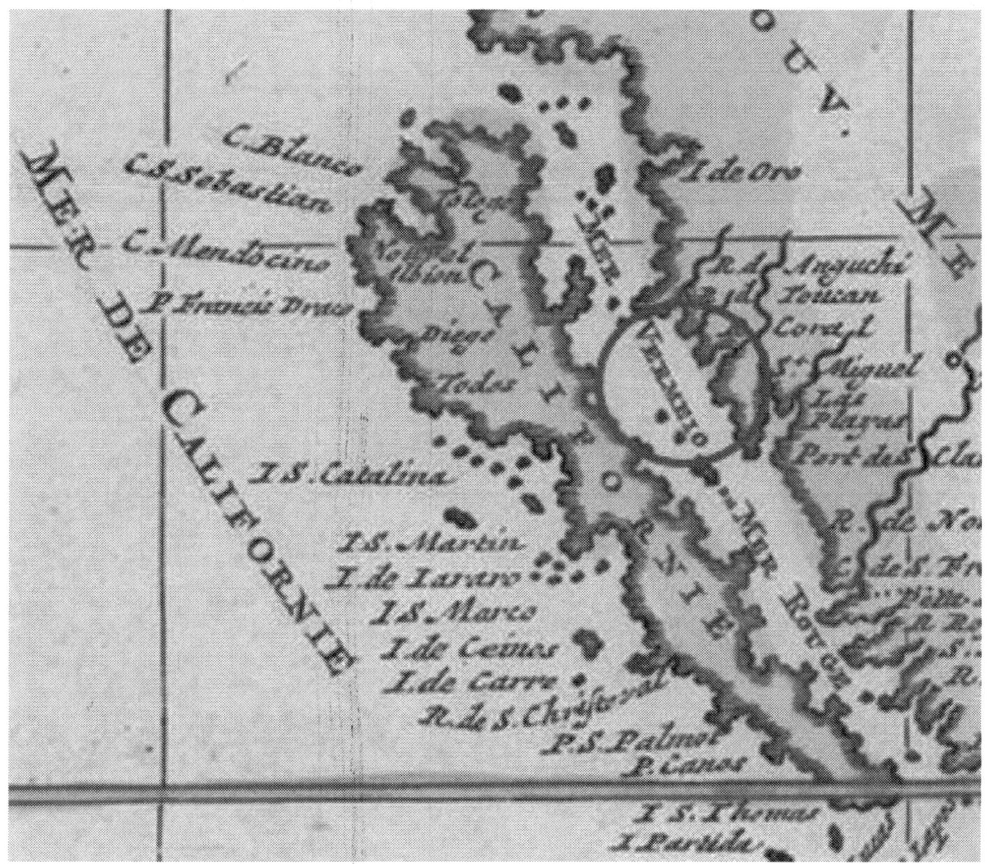

17th Century Mer Vermeio

On these medieval maps, right down the coast of the "California Island" is a strange sea. In place of the modern Gulf of California, it was called the Vermillion Sea. The name "Vermillion" was also rendered in some other Western European languages, such as "Vermeio," or some variation thereof.

Vermillion means red, so on some medieval maps it was so designated.

During the 19th century, when the West meant all that was superior, even Eastern maps adopted this strangeness (Figure 242 and Figure 243).

If our assertion that the names Gaugigu and Anian came from Vietnam; that is, the East; Asia, Red Sea might have something to do with that part of the world and not Moses of Egypt.

Mer Vermeille

"Zhu," 朱, however, is a homophone of the eastern character for pearl, 珠. Indeed, to the east of Vietnam is the Zhu Sea, 珠海, or Pearl Sea, the sea at the outlet of the river Pearl River, 珠江, Zhu Jiang, which empties into South China Sea between Hong Kong and Macau.

Figure 242

1840 Chinese Red Sea

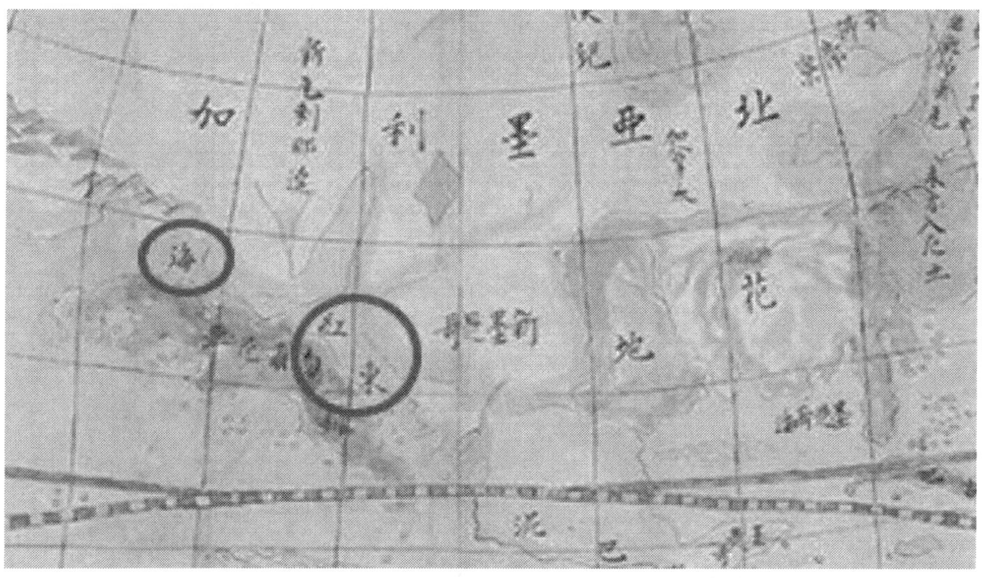

Figure 243

1865 Japanese Red Sea by Sato

Vermillion is not just any red color. It is deep red. In Vietnamese, as in Chinese, it is "zhu", 朱.

Figure 244

South China Sea

On a map of southeastern Asia, one can see a Zhu Sea to the east of Vietnam (Figure 244).

Therefore, Vermillion Sea was likely translated, or, mistranslated from Zhu Sea, because in Chinese, pearl and vermillion, both pronounced zhu, are homophones.

Medieval Europeans had information on the geography of the South China Sea. They mistook it for the North American west coast, which they had never been to, and put its geography on their maps.

On the map of South China Sea, can you see a huge island between Annan-Gaugigu and Zhu Hai, or Zhu Sea? That was why California was mistaken as an island.

According to this sea chart, when going on a mission, Zheng He's fleets would take to sea at the seaport by the shipyard outside the capital city of Nanjing and sail due south. The fleet would turn southwest and sail parallel to the southern coast of China and stay close to land.

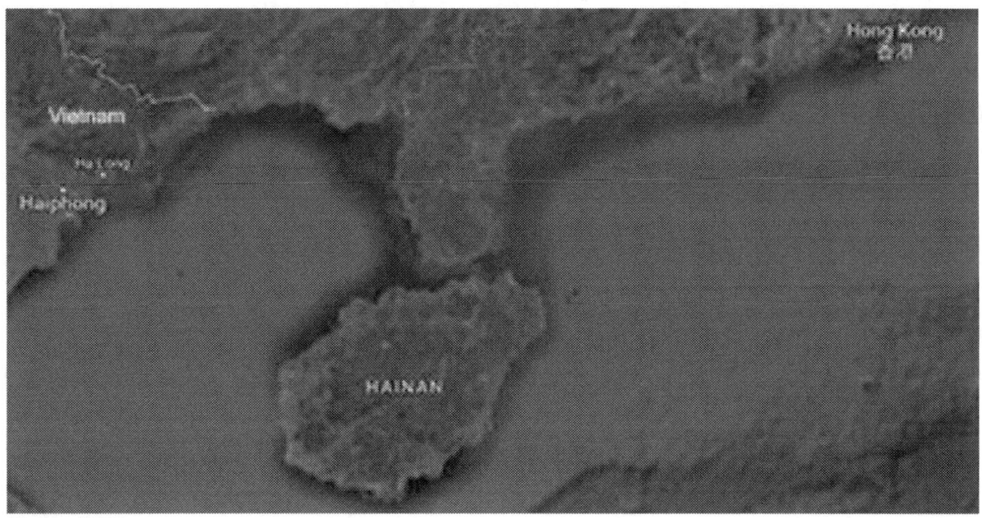

Figure 245

Hainan Island

中国地方志集成：海南府县志辑 - 百度百科

《中国地方志集成：海南府县志辑》是2013年10月上海书店出版社出版的图书，作者是上海书店出版社。

内容简介　图书目录

百度百科

史话海南志 历史沿革 海南省人民政府网

2022年7月2日 《中国地方志集成·海南府县志辑》(上海书店出版社2013年版),收录海南方志17种,影印出版。因地处偏远、保存条件等因素的限制,海南地方志印数不多,导致在世间少...

海南省人民政府网　百度快照

Figure 246

Hainan-Fu Explanations

After more than a thousand miles of travel, the fleets would reach the delta of the third largest river of China, the West River, called *Zhu Jiang*, the Pearl River by the locals, which emptied into the Pearl Sea, *Zhu Hai*.[62]

[62] Pearl River, *Zhu Jiang*, 珠江. Pearl Sea, *Zhu Hai*, 珠海.

On the west side of the delta mouth of this river would be today's Macao, and to the right would be Hong Kong. Of course, at the time of Zheng He, these cities did not yet exist.

As they continued to sail in the southwesterly direction, the fleets would soon encounter many islands, as this region of the sea was famous for. Then a bit further they would sail by a huge island port side (left), and that was the Hainan Island, which Marco Polo's travelogue listed as *Cheinan*. /Ch/ in Italian is /k/ or /kh/, close approximations of /h/. The government of Hainan Island was Hainan Fu, or, using Marco Polo's travelogue's spelling, *Cheinan Fu*. *Fu* is Chinese for "the government seat;" that is, the state house.

Leaving the waters of *Zhu Hai*, the Pearl Sea, and Hainan/Cheinan Island, the fleets eventually reached the *Gauzhi Hai*,[63] Sea of Gauzhi (Marco Polo's *Gaugiguo*; "guo" means nation; that is, the Country of Gaugi), and then *Zhan Cheng* south of Annan or Annam.

The similarity between this sea route as annotated in Zheng He's sea chart from the *Wu Bei Zhi* and the North American depiction on Age of Discovery European maps is nothing short of uncanny, and the parallel was not accidental. The medieval European maps of California was based on the geography of southeast China, and maps or drawings showing the shapes of California too.

Putting it in proper terms, the early Age of Discovery European mapmakers had information (shape) about North America, which they had not been to and had no idea that it was a continent, as well as information about Southeast Asia, which they also had not been to. Not knowing that these data referred to different places, they created the fabulous California Island maps.

California Name

By the way, if the geography of southeast Asia was transplanted wholesale to western North America, including the huge island in the middle, and the country name Annan on the left, with the name of the sea Zhu/Vermillion on the right, what about the name of the

[63] 交趾, "Cross-toed," North Vietnam

island itself? In fact, many European researchers were intrigued by the name and had theories about that. Nonetheless, virtually all of them were off base.

The misconception began in 1510—that was right after Christopher Columbus ended his career in the Caribbean—with a Spanish novel by Garci Rodríguez de Montalvo. He set imaginations ablaze with *Las Sergas de Esplandián*, an international bestseller in its day. In it, he reported:

> *I tell you that on the right-hand side of the Indies there was an island called California, which was very close to the region of the Earthly Paradise. This island was inhabited by black women, and there were no males among them at all, for their life style was similar to that of the Amazons.*

The Indies were east of the American continents, not west, and there were islands there inhabited by black slaves brought over by European colonists. However, there was no known "all female" landmasses, except for the legendary "Women country" from the Chinese *Shanhaijing*.

Then, in continuing frantic researches, Europeans came up with:

> *California was named after "Calida Fornax," translating to the hot furnace and "cal y fornos," meaning lime and furnace, some people say California is named after the Black queen: Queen Calafia.*

The story, unfortunately, cannot be confirmed. Besides, we still have the enigma for the origin of the name California.

Indeed, between Vietnam and Zhu Sea was an island (Figure 261); a huge island, which was pointed out. It is a famous island that China is developing into a Mediterranean-type resort today. It is called Hainan Island, or South Sea Island; that is, the likely Kienan (or Keinan) of Marco polo. (Hainan = Keinan.)

Hainan Island had several names historically. For instance, it had been called Haikou, 海口, the Mouth of the Sea. It had been called Qiongzhou, 瓊州. During Ming time, it was called Hainan-Fu, 海南府, on account of its government administrative District, Fu, 府 (Figure 246). Therefore, logically, they should have copied its name too. However, the name would have to be first Westernized; that is, Latinized, just like Confucius was Latinized from Kongfuzi. Mencius was Latinized from Mengzi. How did they Latinize a placename? By attaching the suffix "ia," as in Abyssin"ia," Alban"ia," Armen"ia," Bavar"ia," Boliv"ia," Bulgar"ia," Colomb"ia," and so on. Thus, Hainan-Fu would have been transliterated as "Hainan-Fu-ia," or "Keinan-Fu-ia."

The Chinese Lost It

The Chinese—Chinese under Yuan Dynasty-Mongol overlordship, that is—surveyed the lands and oceans of the world, gave Zheng He the blueprint to go after the Jianwen Emperor, and provided the impetus for the European Age of Discovery.[64] The evidence in support of this assertion is rich and unequivocal. In this research, I have investigated the history of the era with the utmost sincerity and meticulous attention, and arrived at a conclusion that is logical and inescapable. Yet a question remains, and legitimately so: How could history have come down to us in a version that is so diagonally opposite to what in fact transpired, and that it has remained virtually unchallenged for so long?

As discussed, the Ming Chinese authority had not wanted to acknowledge this episode of history. Taking place virtually entirely during Emperor Chengzu's reign, Zheng He's ventures were deemed illegitimate by the succeeding administrations. Many later court officials held loathing views toward the grand events with an

---

[64] I must be specific about this because there is the ever lurking question as to whether this was accomplished by Admiral Zheng He and his crew. Whereas my research revealed that Zheng He's fleet did sail into the Atlantic Ocean and probably reached at least northwest Africa and possibly the Caribbean if not the American continents proper, the geographical data that reached Europe came from the Yuan era, as the place names testify to. Had the data been prepared by the Ming, the Europeans would have learned Ming terms as opposed to Yuan terms. Zheng He himself therefore also likely used Yuan era documents in his enterprise. The Zheng He maritime enterprise took place close to the beginning of the Ming Dynasty. There was not enough time for the Ming to have surveyed the world. The Yuan did. The Yuan Mongols were bent on conquering the world, and they dispatched sailors to survey the world for the purpose of conquest. Zheng He almost certainly relied on Yuan Dynasty maps for his voyages.

intensity that was almost personal.[65] Chengzu's son, the ensuing emperor, who had to rely heavily upon these officials for his own power, had to go along, and agreed to a postscript of the marvelous naval program.

The ships were mothballed and demolished. The shipyards were abandoned and razed. The maritime records were destroyed. Zheng He was demoted and placed under de facto house arrest, and the court adopted a policy of silence on the matter. The scant material on the event in official history tells us that the Ming court wanted as little ink on these technological achievements as possible because they were politically tainted. It wished that they never had happened, and very much liked to have erased them from history's memory.

Then history lent a hand.

---

[65] Read *The Hunt for the Dragon, 2nd Edition* for the rip-roaring story of the usurpation of the throne by Emperor Chengzu.

The Fall of the Ming

At the time of our story, China was at the peak of its power. Fresh out of the Mongol bondage having overthrown its former overlord, Ming China began a Renaissance of sorts. The political system was once again stable and the nation prospered. During the initial century of the dynasty, Ming China was the richest country under the sun. The Ming GDP was a whopping one third of the entire world. As a country largely in peace, Ming China, larger than all of Europe in physical size and population, was not only able to sport fleets that accommodated up to thirty thousand staff and travelers, it built for its emperor a brand-new capital-palace complex, the Forbidden City, whose grandeur and splendor are still the rage of tourists visiting Beijing today. It rejuvenated the country's internal waterways,[66] and rebuilt and extended the ancient Great Wall.[67]

During the turn of the 15th century, China was at the top of its game while Europe was just beginning to emerge from the Dark Ages. In his book *The Pursuit of Power* William H. McNeill, Robert A. Millikan Distinguished Service Professor of History at the University of Chicago, tersely identified the period from 1000 to 1500 as the era of Chinese predominance. Regrettably, from roughly 1500 onward China headed in but one direction: a steady slide downward toward oblivion. The lavish spending by the Ming administration—the grandiose architectural projects (such as the Wu Dang Shan Daoist monastery, besides the new capital Beijing), the rebuilding of the Great Wall, and the incessant military campaigns against the Mongols—fundamentally weakened the nation's political and

---

[66] To appreciate the scale of the undertaking, try to visualize a geography bigger in size than Europe.

[67] Yes, the Great Wall with which we are familiar was mostly built during the Ming Dynasty. This obviously expensive undertaking alone disputes the notion that the Zheng He expeditions was to bankrupt the country.

economic infrastructures. By 1448, inflation in Ming China had reached 300 times; that is, 30,000%. By 1455, the country that systemized and perfected the use of paper money abandoned its use after five hundred years and never employed it again until its reintroduction by Europeans in modern time.

Thus, while the European Renaissance was picking up steam, Ming China was slowly but surely descending toward irrelevance. By the time the 16th century came around, the Portuguese, a little country from the other side of the world, had virtually taken control over the onetime Chinese sphere of influence—the Indian Ocean and the South China Sea.

The Portuguese established their settlement in Goa, India in 1510, planted a foothold in Malacca, Malaya in 1511, and arrived in China in 1513. Yet the concise history of this period from the Chinese perspective is blurry. Some historians claim that the Portuguese sailors were permitted to gather themselves at Haojingao after a shipwreck in 1536, others argue that the Portuguese were granted permanent residency in Macau in 1553. This imprecision points to two things: first, the insignificance of the newcomers in the perspective of the vastness of China and second, that Ming China was preoccupied with internal problems at the time to pay attention to the events involving a small group of *red-haired*[68] foreign intruders.

The real history, of course, is more elaborate than a group of alien visitors taking over a small patch of land. The lure of trade attracted many Chinese merchants to the new settlement and the creation of new profit certainly dissolved much of the initial local resistance. Extant records show that Portugal secured leasehold for Macau from the Ming government in exchange for tribute in 1557. China actually retained sovereignty over Macau, indicating that at first Macau was not a Portuguese colony, especially in light of the local Chinese residents continuing to be subject to Chinese law. The Portuguese only administered the place. No matter, by 1586 Macau had become

[68] Red Hair, 紅毛, Portuguese. Today cement in southern China is known as *Red-Hair clay*, 紅毛泥.

self-governing, suggesting a waning Chinese control. By 1605, the Portuguese were fighting the newly arrived Dutch for the city while the Chinese could only stand by to watch.

What was Ming China's preoccupying predicament? The Manchu who lived outside the Great Wall in the northeastern corner of Asia. By early 17th century the Manchu had subdued the Mongols and enlisted them under Manchu banners. In 1644 they breached the Great Wall and captured Beijing, snuffing out Ming China for good. In the process, the Manchu forced the Chinese to shave their foreheads and braid their hair into pigtails called *queues* as a symbol of subjugation, clearly with intent to impose the Manchu culture on the Chinese. In 1685, the new alien conquerors of China officially recognized Macau as a foreign-trade port.

Consequently, in a span of 250 years, China went from the top of the world to the pits. Under such conditions, where would people find the will, the energy, and the time to remember a chapter of their glorious history that their own government had wanted to suppress?

Back in 1624, when the Ming Dynasty was gasping for life, the Dutch had seized Taiwan. Two years later the Dutch battled the Spanish for the island's control. Although the Dutch were driven out by the semi-legendary Chinese general Zheng Chenggong, [69] European colonial sharks were nibbling at the dying old Asian walrus known as China.

The French had come, closely followed by the British, establishing respective "spheres of interest." The two "Opium Wars" of 1839–42 and 1856–60 between Britain and China over the forced importation (smuggling) of opium by Britain into China resulted in the Manchu-Chinese opening ports for international trade and ceding of Chinese territories, notably Hong Kong, to the British.[70] By the end of the 19th

[69] 鄭成功, known as Koxinga (國姓爺) in the West.

[70] The ceding of Hong Kong is the archetypal example of the ignorance of history, which is what we are attempting to explain here. 香港, Hong Kong, *Heung Gong* in Cantonese, means "Fragrant Harbor." It was fragrant on account of the aroma of opium. It was a pirate cove. Yet most Western schools do not teach this history of how Europeans used cruel and nefarious means to conquer nations and

century, China was for all intents and purposes being carved up by the Western powers, including Britain, France, Germany, Italy, Austria-Hungary, The United States of America, Russia, and Japan, an "honorary" Western power by virtue of its having embraced western technologies and military sciences. The only reason China was spared going the way of the Aztecs and the Incas (being divided up as colonies outright and risking its culture eradicated from the face of the Earth) was the infighting among the preying powers, which led to their own demise in two World Wars. These wars were identified as such because of a then well-established Euro-centric point of view of the world.[71] The world wars were primarily conflicts among European nations only.[72]

In any case, China eventually descended from being the world's preeminent power to a so-called third-world, under-developed nation whose very claim to civilization was questioned.

---

lands. When Hong Kong was finally returned to Chinese sovereignty in 1997, Western media refused to use the word "return." Instead, many opted to call the transaction "Britain ceding Hong Kong to China," and the event "handover." Most Westerners are unaware why Hong Kong was British territory, and why it had to be given to China.

[71] The term "Euro-centricism" is often thought of as meaning "from a European point of view." It in fact refers to the notion that European culture is superior to all others.

[72] The Japanese invasion of China at the time of the Second World War had nothing to do with the European issues.

Chinese Self-Doubt

The onslaught of the newly arrived Westerners by way of the sea[73] demonstrated beyond doubt their superiority, if not in every way, at least in their technology. The later Ming and Qing (Manchu) emperors were enamored with their guns, canons, clocks, astrological instruments, and maps; yes, maps, maps that showed the Chinese emperors and ministers the world outside China.

One of the most famous of these Western maps is the World Map of Matteo Ricci, a Jesuit priest who found that the way to the top of Chinese echelon was to dress like a Chinese, speak like a Chinese, and seduce them with Western technology. Today, knowing the antique Chinese-based European maps of the Age of Discovery, we chuckle at the many features on the Ricci Map that was originally learned from the Chinese and then retranslated back into Chinese all without the Chinese knowing that they had been duped.

Slowly, the Chinese graduated from admiring the European ways to emulating, adopting, and embracing the sciences, the technologies, and the philosophies of the mighty newcomers. Unfortunately, such attitudes also demanded the degradation of their own culture and traditions.

Before the introduction of European principles and approach of scientific research, the Chinese relied primarily on written official records for their history, supplemented by unofficial writings and oral traditions, often by scholars who interpreted events based on their own sensitivities and philosophical and political leanings. Seldom—not never, but seldom—did they solely rely on analyses based purely on hard facts.

The Western approach since the Age of Reasoning had shown convincingly that such reliance was risky, precisely because the written words could be biased and even falsified, often to suit a

[73] Until today Europeans are known as Sea People, *yang ren*, 洋人 in China.

political purpose or to fit within a nationalistic framework.[74] Research into antiquity should be supported by careful examinations of artifacts and corroborations from external, secondary sources whenever possible. For example, the Amarna clay tablets documenting ancient Egypt's diplomatic relationships with neighboring countries such as the Hittite Kingdom helped affirm the history of the reign of Pharaoh Akhenaton and related historical dates.

Influenced by the West, modern Chinese in early 20th century began demanding the same vigilance and rigor in the reexamination of their own past and in the process ended up denying certain aspects of their heritage. For example, in his textbook of Chinese history, the early 20th century Chinese scholar Gu Jie Gang[75] began his introduction of Chinese history with the Shang Dynasty—shunning the first Chinese historical dynasty of Xia because Western scholars had questioned its existence due to lack of corroborating archeological evidence. Accordingly, with a swipe of his pen Gu attempted to excise more than two thousand years of established Chinese history. As a result, according to Western scholars and Gu, the Chinese began their civilization straight from the Bronze Age, bypassing the three stone ages altogether.[76]

This happened because the Chinese historians were playing a new game, and made errors due to imperfections in its execution. This phenomenon is known as *jiao wang guo zheng*—over-compensation.[77] Consequently, many Chinese historians turned out to be the most ardent and vocal challengers of the theory of Chinese circumnavigation of the globe, especially during the last decade when the 600th anniversary of Zheng He's expeditions was celebrated and the topic of circumnavigation was brought up.

---

[74] E.g., Prince Henry's biography states that his genius for going to sea is written in the horoscopes. See below for real reason.

[75] 顧頡剛

[76] Today Western historians are beginning to recognize China's ancient history. Doctoral degrees are being awarded in its study no less.

[77] 矯枉過正.

Therefore, if research efforts failed to yield *firsthand* evidence from the cultural archives, the events could not have occurred!

Having bought into the new Western approach to historical research in total, they looked for the "smoking gun;" what they deem to be a smoking gun. In essence, short of a stone stela erected in the Americas with the inscription "Zheng He was here" engraved on it we have no proof that the Ming fleets had gone beyond the Indian Ocean. Unfortunately, if such were the criterion of historical research, a vast percentage of history will have to be re-filed under "legends" and "hearsay," and we will have a field day getting the Christians going. In the meantime, the Chinese detractors would have bought a coin with the inscriptions "Minted in 6 BC" on it.

The sad fact is, most of the detractors had never even done any such research. They simply accepted what Western scholars asserted on faith; no questions asked. So, Chinese teachers teach their school children Christopher Columbus discovered the New World, while the doubting Chinese scholars fight off any talk about the possibility that Chinese navigation history might have influenced the Western Age of Discovery.

What the Chinese critics have failed to recognize is that Western scholars often do not themselves follow the same strict investigative rules that they had laid down. The ancient histories of Greece and Rome as told by well-known writers such as Herodotus, Thucydides, Xenophon, Strabo, Livy, Josephus, Tacitus, Plutarch, etal. are widely accepted even without the support of the slightest archeological evidentiary support. Further, we all know that virtually all the early European archaeological efforts since the 18th century were put forth in fact to prove the historicity of the old Jewish Bible. In other words, the archaeologists/historians had already decided that what was contained in the Bible was true, and then they set out to find evidence that would support that notion. Many a time digs were abandoned when the missions failed to produce acceptable evidence. Such practices were in blatant violation of the rules and guidelines of research.

The diametrically opposed developmental trends of the European and Chinese civilizations resulted in a form of anachronistic view of humankind's past. The skewed perceptions often produced in the world historians a sense of incredulity in the examination of historical facts, and more than once they had altered the scientific investigative process to suit their preconceptions. To many Western historians, medieval Chinese sailing the world's waters was plainly impossible! Many Chinese scholars, who look up to the Western counterparts' superior intellect, bought it.

The precipitous and steady deterioration of the Chinese Empire was mirrored by a parallel meteoric European ascendancy. During the 15th century, Europe was just barely coming out of the Dark Ages, and by that I do not mean she had just suffered the latest Black Death. In the late 14th century and early 15th century Europe was still mired in inter-state warfare and was generally economically depressed and technologically backward.

To gain a perspective on this, recall that the Ming voyages regularly transported foreign diplomats to and from China, entertaining them sumptuously, hosting their stay for a year at a time, and lavishing gifts on them upon their departure. By contrast, in 1438, the emperor of Byzantine (Greece) John VIII, along with the head of the Christian Orthodox Church in Constantinople, the Patriarch Joseph II, and a contingent of some 700 church dignitaries that included bishops, prelates, monk, and clergy traveled to Florence, Italy for an ecclesiastical conference. It took several subsequent Italian popes to repay the costs incurred as the result of this one visit.

Early 15th century European civilization can be described by 21st century standards as primitive. To give a visual, during the 15th century, Europeans were still eating with their bare hands. Table utensils were yet to be introduced; the fork was still awaiting adoption. Dinner guests had to bring their own knives. Then, within a mere few hundred years, the West led the world in not just science and technology, but in culture and, it came be claimed, in the degree of civilization, and all rightfully so.

However, this unabridged and unbridled run of success not only instilled in the Westerner that sense of self-assurance and superiority, but a disbelief in a humble beginning. In stark contrast, a modern Chinese is occasionally given to feeling so downtrodden about the state of his own standing in the world that he sometimes is liable to question the actuality of a splendid national past. That the Chinese themselves, particularly the modern historians, are skeptical about the achievements of their forebear can also be directly attributed to this same disconnect in perception.

Europeans Appropriated It

Figure 247

Researcher/Author at Trader Joe Supermarket in Pasadena, California with California Island Decorative Wall Map

The Chinese are not the only ones who no longer know their past. Europeans fare no better in that department. The difference is, Europeans made up stories for it. Today most Europeans no longer know of the innumerable maps their ancestors made of the world before the Age of Discovery that we have presented in this book, and when they see them, they marvel at their cuteness or weirdness as curiosity pieces. They even use them as design elements in art craft and decorations (Figure 247).

To account for this form of amnesia, the Europeans "developed" history. After spending centuries in oblivion, Christopher Columbus, a rogue by most accounts, all of a sudden found himself resurrected a hero; a hero so grand that countries,[78] cities, municipalities, mountains, rivers, institutions, universities, business enterprises, movie studios, and whatever else you can think of, have been named in his honor.

At the close of the *Travels of Marco Polo,* the author informed us that Polo returned to Europe by sea—the Indian Ocean, and at the end everybody died; only he survived. Today we take his fantasy at its words and proclaim it true history.

Of course, that Europeans were able to "fabricate" the history of the Age of Discovery is because they encountered no objection in doing so. As mentioned, the Chinese relinquished their own history due to ignorance, thus leaving an entire chapter of history blank to be freely filled in, and the Europeans did precisely that. In the process, the European history manufacturing machine rolled over any obstacle that came its way without being challenged.

For instance, a favorite "reason" often cited for the disbelief in a Chinese maritime tradition, and specifically the Ming expeditions, is the claim that such assertions cannot be accepted because the Chinese themselves have scant official records of the events. The charge, of course, is leveled at the seemingly total absence of antique Chinese world maps of the period of any kind.

Before we respond to this allegation, first, let us understand maps in general. Maps are commodities. They are not only perishable, but are intentionally destroyed as a matter of course. Indeed, this is the case with our Thomas maps or local commercial maps; they are discarded immediately as they become outdated, and that happens every couple of years. We buy new atlases when the political configurations of the world change, such as the disintegration of the Soviet Union. So why are some maps preserved, even though we

---

[78] Columbia was once considered for the name of a newly founded nation. This nation is now called the United States of America.

know they are already out-of-date? They are preserved not for their accuracy but for their collectability.

In order for antique maps to be collected, there must be a culture of map collecting; a map-collecting industry, or that a government or academic institution sees historical values in them. In the case of China, there has never been a strong general interest in map-collecting. Throughout the ages, Chinese collected paintings, calligraphy, bronze castings, objets d'art, but not many maps.

World maps reflect an affinity for things maritime. The Chinese turned their backs on the sea at of the middle of the 15th century. Recall that the Ming official (allegedly) burned Zheng He's maritime records in 1477. As my analyses have shown, the underlying reason for this about face is political; Zheng He's deeds were innately tied to the political ambitions of Emperor Chengzu, and they were deliberately obliterated. Therefore, all matters related to seafaring were not just branded illegal but intentionally shunned. The Ming government even forbade its citizens to build ships with more than two masts lest they took to the sea. Under such political climates it should be easy to understand how China, once a great seafaring nation, would end up not having maritime records.

It is interesting that the official records of the European explorers of renown are scant or often non-existent as well, yet we hang on to every word of their legends as if it is the Gospel truth. (Pulitzer Prize winning) Wilford tells us that: "Events are embellished, facts are invented or forgotten, and in time a fog of legend obscures all."

The original letter Columbus sent to Luis de Santangel was lost. The Columbus sea journal no longer exists; it disappeared after 1554. Whatever Columbus' writing we have today is "fragmentary and riddled by contradictions." The 1474 letter of Toscanelli and "map," which had "set Columbus' mind ablaze," are now lost. Fernando's original biography of Columbus is lost. Las Casas' *Historia de Las Indias* was not published until the end of the 19th century.

The explanation for the dearth of European Age of Discovery records is often attributed to the Lisbon, Portugal earthquake and fire of 1755, when most of the Portuguese national archive was allegedly destroyed,[79] along with the traditional secrecy on maritime records. The truth, in reality, is closer to a scarcity of record keeping to begin with.

Bear in mind that the pre-Renaissance European explorers were not intellectuals as one might have been induced to believe. More often than not these adventurers were downright dishonorable characters. In general, these unsavory fellows were naturally disinclined toward the exercising of the pen.

In his *Al-bark al-yamani fi al-fath al-Otmani* (The Ottoman Conquest of Yemen) Kuth ad-din an-Nahrawali describes the adventures of the Portuguese explorers thus:

> *...During these terrible times is the case of the cursed Faranji, the Portuguese. A group of them went into the Sea of Darkness outside Africa and sailed east through a strait between a mountain and the Sea of Shadows where they wrecked, killing them all. Yet these Portuguese kept on coming, wreck after wreck, without being able to make it over to the Indian Ocean until finally when one ship did. When this caravel reached the east African coast the Faranji captain Almilandi asked for direction to India from an Arab seaman named Ahman ibn Majid. Together they got drunk. During the stupor the Arab divulged the route. "Keep away from the coast and sail out to sea, but on the other side hug the coast to avoid the waves," he told the Portuguese. By following this advice many of them were able to get to India. At Gowwa, which is on the Indian Coast, which is now Faranji territory, they built a fort. Then they captured Hormuz and fortified it. With continued support from Portugal they engaged in piracy, taking prisoners and plundered. They took other ships by force and wreaked havoc on the high sea in general...*

[79] Apparently documents of other nations were destroyed there too.

Author Vincent Jones described it best in the Foreword section of his book *Sail the Indian Sea*. He said, in so many words, that there were big gaps in those navigation records. Vasco da Gama's instructions, sea charts, logs, and reports all disappeared. Where it counted, details vanished. Then, to top it off, the "official" histories were written more than a generation after the facts.

What we now know about the European Renaissance explorations is therefore, if not in its entirety, at least in large parts, reconstruction. In other words, what we have readily accepted as the history of the Age of Discovery today is in fact largely reconstruction and fiction.

We must recognize that historians failing to recognize a Chinese origin of the Age of Discovery is a modern phenomenon, as is the creation of the history of the Age of Discovery. The truth is, medieval Europeans had no compunction acknowledging that new geographical information and intellectual properties had come from the outside. "Khan's people" attests to this (Figure 116). The mapmaker Andreas Walsperger claimed that his map was constructed based on real navigations of the seas. Fra Mauro acknowledged the foreign origin of his Asian and African data. The Flemish cartographer Abraham Ortelius asserted that Columbus was not the first man to visit America. The great Spanish cartographer Peter Martyr d'Anghiera in 1493, the year after Columbus' inaugural voyage, concluded that Bianco must have based his map of 1436 on information from ancient mariners who had visited Western Atlantic, although that knowledge had been lost.

The failure to consider the possibility of a Chinese medieval maritime feat is only a recent development, and a major reason is because Europeans have forgotten about the events of half a millennium ago and those who wrote the history for it were ignorant of them altogether. To account for their rise to world power during that time, they simply developed history to account for it.

Scholastic Faux Pas

Yet records and artifacts attest to the fallacies of our accepted history. They do exist, as we have demonstrated amply in this book. Then how could scholars and historians have been oblivious to them for half a millennium, as if they are not there? Well, they were not oblivious to them, and they have always known that they existed. They see them just as you and I do. They have merely chosen to ignore them, shun explaining them, pretend that they do not exist, give misinformation on them, distort the facts if necessary, and even attempt to obliterate them.

Indifference

John Noble Wilford informs us that Baja California was firmly attached to the continent (as if some of us need to be reminded of this fact), though it and California were at one time represented on some maps as an island as we have seen. This means he had seen such maps. Yet he expressed no concern as to why these maps were drawn that way. Indeed, such complacency is so deeply-set on the part of capable and respected scholars such as Wilford that one is spurred on to take stock and suspect that perhaps there may be a cabal behind all this after all. Indifference cannot explain everything.

In the book *What If?* There is a section that hypothesized what the world would have been if Zheng He's fleet had sailed beyond the Indian Ocean. I sent the author my work informing him that Zheng He did. I did not hear a whimper of a response.

On December 17, 2012, Los Angeles Times published an article by Larry Gordon[80] marveling over the strange California Island, and his professor consultants informed him those medieval European mapmakers were very imaginative. The article produced thousands of reader responses. They were interested in the subject. I sent Mr. Gordon a copy of my *The Chinese Origin of the Age of Discovery*. Nothing came of it. There was no follow-up article.

80 http://www.latimes.com/news/local/la-me-island-maps-20121217,0,6950188.story

The Un-whole Truth

Figure 248

A Reproduction of the Vinland map

In studying the past, Western scholars often adopt a Euro-centric point of view even when the scope of the subject matter is worldwide. For instance, a cursory review of extant literature on maritime history (you can do this easily by browsing your local bookstores) will find a thematic coverage back to the Phoenicians, the Cretans, the Minoans, the Greeks, the Carthaginians, the

Figure 249

Actual Satellite Picture of the Atlantic Ocean

Romans, even the Egyptians and the Jews with their Noah's ark, but seldom, if ever, Asians. (So far I have not seen any such writings on Asian maritime history.) Hence, the basis of this distorted view on human maritime history in general and the Age of Discovery in particular can be summarized as follows.

First, the author-researchers have a limited, Europe-slanted knowledge of history, and second, matters non-European are frequently deemed insignificant; consequently, little effort is expanded in their understanding and pursuit. The unfortunate result is that often conclusions are drawn on distorted data, and when the data fail to account for the historical facts, forced explanations are tendered to gloss over the difficulties.

In reconstructing the best scenario for what has happened in the past; that is, in historical research, a historian is obliged to review facts when they become known, and formulate the best theory to account for them. This requires that when new facts become known, history may need to be modified or revised to accommodate them. For a historian there can have no quarters for harboring personal bias or bigotry, nor is he allowed to selectively utilize the evidence or ignore it to justify his own predilection. In assessing evidence, a researcher must take into account all evidence available. There is no option for picking and choosing. If the ancient Sphinx of Egypt that sits in the middle of a desert exhibits unmistakable marks of water erosion, deal with it. A researcher cannot claim that the erosion marks are not there, nor should he proceed to expound a theory of the Sphinx's evolution without accounting for it.

In regards to this issue, take the case of the Vinland map, partially reproduced in Figure 248 for demonstration.

In analyzing the Atlantic Ocean islands on the Vinland map for whatever purpose, one may not simply ignore the island group (circled in Figure 248) marked St. Brendan, which appears on other medieval maps as Antilia, a fact that we are now quite familiar with. When the issue concerns the north Atlantic islands of Iceland, Greenland, and "Vinland," ignoring the presence of the "Antilia" islands can easily lead to the conclusion that the northern islands were mapped by Nordics because the islands happened to be located "in their backyard," even though there is no record or evidence suggesting that the Vikings had ever engaged in geographical mapping. Yet that is precisely what happened with current researches.

Ever since the acquisition of the Vinland map, its authenticity has been in question. Some scholars are certain that the map is genuine; while others are just as sure that it is a fake.

In 1972, a scientific team headed by Dr. Walter McCrone found the ink on the Vinland map to contain anatase. Anatase is a form of titanium that was supposed to have been first employed during the 1920s, although the parchment on which the map was drawn was determined to be from the 1400s, thus implying that the map was a 20th century forgery done on ancient parchment.

Then, in 1992, Dr. Thomas Cahill of UC Davis found anatase to exist in ancient manuscripts as well. Moreover, chemical analyses performed by Chemist Jacqueline S. Olin, a retired researcher with the Smithsonian Institution, concluded that the map's ink was made in medieval times. Hence it appeared the map was genuine after all.

After that, examination by experts on medieval European literature pointed out that the naming convention used in the map indicated non-Viking authorship. For example, a Scandinavian would have used Gronlandia for Gronelanda, thus casting doubt on the map's Viking origin theory.

Kirsten A. Seaver in her book *Maps, Myths, and Men* built a strong case toward identifying Father Josef Fischer (1858-1944), discoverer of the Martin Waldseemüller world map (Figure 56), as the real creator of the Vinland map.

Father Josef Fischer was an authority on ancient maps. He had held strong convictions that ancient Nordic priests had contributed significantly to the knowledge about the North Atlantic. Regrettably, academia had not shared his passion. Ms. Seaver demonstrated through persuasive arguments that Father Josef Fischer fabricated the Vinland Map to "show" his detractors that as far back as the early 15th century the Norsemen had already surveyed the North Atlantic by virtue of the north Atlantic islands, despite that this map was the only extant record of their "efforts."

It is not my intention here to debate the authenticity of the Vinland Map. It may be real or it may be forged. The nagging issue is the map's overall composition, specifically the Antilia and other islands, not to mention the binding of the map with the codex *Historia Tartorum,* which Seaver and practically all other interested parties of the Vinland map had chosen to ignore while focusing solely on Greenland, Iceland, and Vinland as a group. In the entire Seaver book, over two hundred pages long, not once was the Antilia Island, huge as it was and glaring at the reader from outside the Iberian Peninsula, mentioned.

In 2005, the Discovery television channel aired an hour-long NOVA program examining this very issue of the Vinland map authenticity. Not once did the program mention the Antilia Island, although it was gazing at the audience from the television screen throughout.

What were these expert researchers, scholars, investigators, and commentators afraid of?

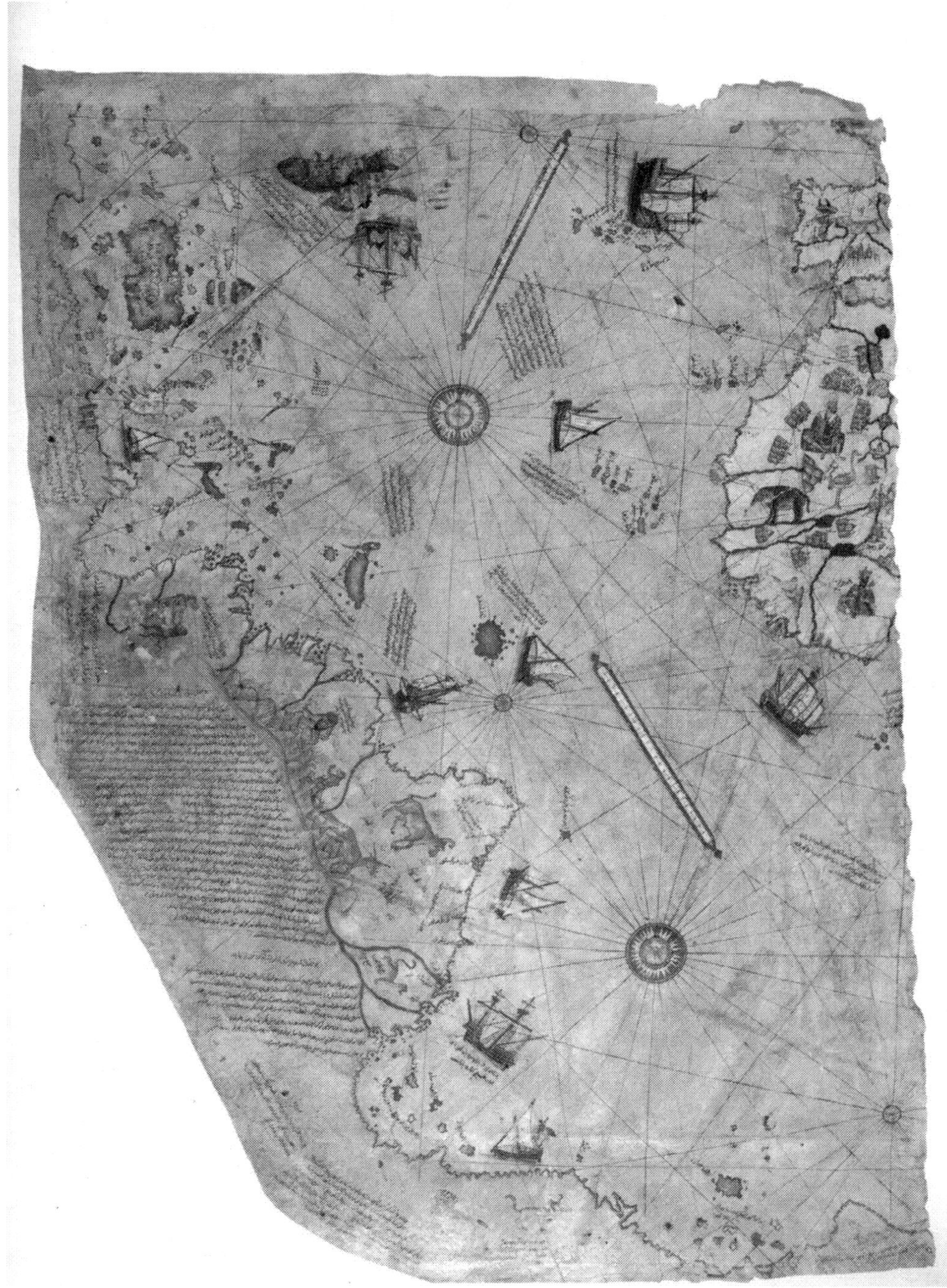

Figure 250

The 1513 Piri Reis Map

If the Vinland map were an authentic early 15th century map, it would be just like all the other odd Renaissance maps cited in this book: it is just odd. On the other hand, if the map turns out to be a modern-day fraud, we will have to account for the forger's mental state: why did the counterfeiter think it important to include the mythical Atlantic islands? Perhaps an "expert" such as Father Josef Fischer knew that by including these islands it would impart "authenticity" to his creation? If so, we can no longer blind ourselves to the eastern, Asian portion of the map, and the mental gyration behind the "swindler's" decision to package the map with the codex on the Mongols. Putting it simply, experts know of a strong Asian connection in the advancement of Renaissance world cartography, and to them it has to be problematic; they cannot (or, perhaps are unwilling to) explain it. If they address the Vinland map Antilia islands, they will be compelled to acknowledge a possible Asian connection with medieval maps. Then the north Atlantic islands of Greenland, Iceland, and Vinland will have to be viewed through a different perspective. By then the game would be up, and we cannot have that.

To achieve the highest degree of integrity in scientific research, and especially in the study of ancient history, the approach must be "full field." In other words, all evidence from all disciplines—anthropology, archeology, geography, history, linguistics, and so on—from all cultures and civilizations must be examined. Conclusions reached with partial evidence sets are at best flawed and misleading, and at worst biased or erroneous.

In the 1960s, Professor Charles H. Hapgood and his research assistants studied the Piri Reis map (Figure 250) in detail and published the findings in the book *Map of the Ancient Sea Kings*. The book's title reflects the conclusion that the Piri Reis map was constructed by *European* ancestors who must have had a brilliant civilization during the Ice Age at least 11,000 years ago. Apart from this conclusion, Professor Hapgood's technical findings are impressively correct.

- The Piri Reis map was made up of a conglomerate of individual map components that had their own scale, perspectives, and orientations.
- The drawn map portions were highly accurate.
- The map contained many missing geographical features; whole chunks of landmasses were missing.

The landmasses were obviously surveyed by beings[81] of high technical competence. However, because no *European* civilization in recorded history was known to have possessed such capabilities or to have performed the act, the map had to be made by *Europeans* preceding our historical time. Because the map appeared to show rivers of Antarctica that are now under ice, the survey must have been conducted before the rivers were covered up. Therefore, the implication is clear, the map was drawn by *Europeans* before the Ice Age, and their civilization must have been a dazzling one.

Since the book made no mention of the Chinese, I assume that Professor Hapgood was unaware of or unfamiliar with the Ming maritime history specifically, and Chinese maritime history in general. There is no reason for me to suspect that he knew of the ancient Chinese history and chose to ignore it. After all, Professor Hapgood did graciously point out that his assumptions could very well have been wrong. Yet, from the outset the book had assumed a European origin of the map, and the research merely set out to prove it. By firmly training one's research microscope on a targeted culture sample one risks being guided to conclusions that fit the sample evidence only. In short, the Hapgood analysis of the Piri Reis map failed to account for or explain the following:

- The highly patchwork nature of the map. But then Piri Reis already explained in his Bahriye that the map was a composite of several world maps.

[81] I choose to use the word "being" here because some theorizers conclude that the Piri Reis map was surveyed from outer space by extraterrestrials.

- The history of the Ming maritime explorations.
- The existence of contemporaneous world maps with similarly inexplicable features.
- That other highly developed civilizations other than European ones existed on this Earth as well.

To prove a hypothesis, *all* givens must be satisfied. This is a scientific requirement, not an option. Partials will not do. Anything less than all provides for opportunities for error. In practice, however, few researchers abide by the stringent rule, innocently or deliberately. The result is often the "selling of an agenda." Ming Dynasty era cartographical data have been used to invalidate pre-Ice Age (more than ten thousand years ago) events more than once, and the victims are the unsuspecting readers or audience.

There are many forms of data incompleteness, and they do not necessarily mean using evidence selectively or arbitrarily. It also can mean using parts of an evidentiary item as opposed to the whole. For instance, an isolated view of India in the Cantino Map (Figure 51) can lead to (and has) the conclusion that the odd coastline of India indicates a knowledge on the part of the cartographer of the geography of India at prehistoric times. However, if one were to look at the entire Cantino Map with its incomplete South America and all, one can easily see that the 15th century map was simply erroneously copied.

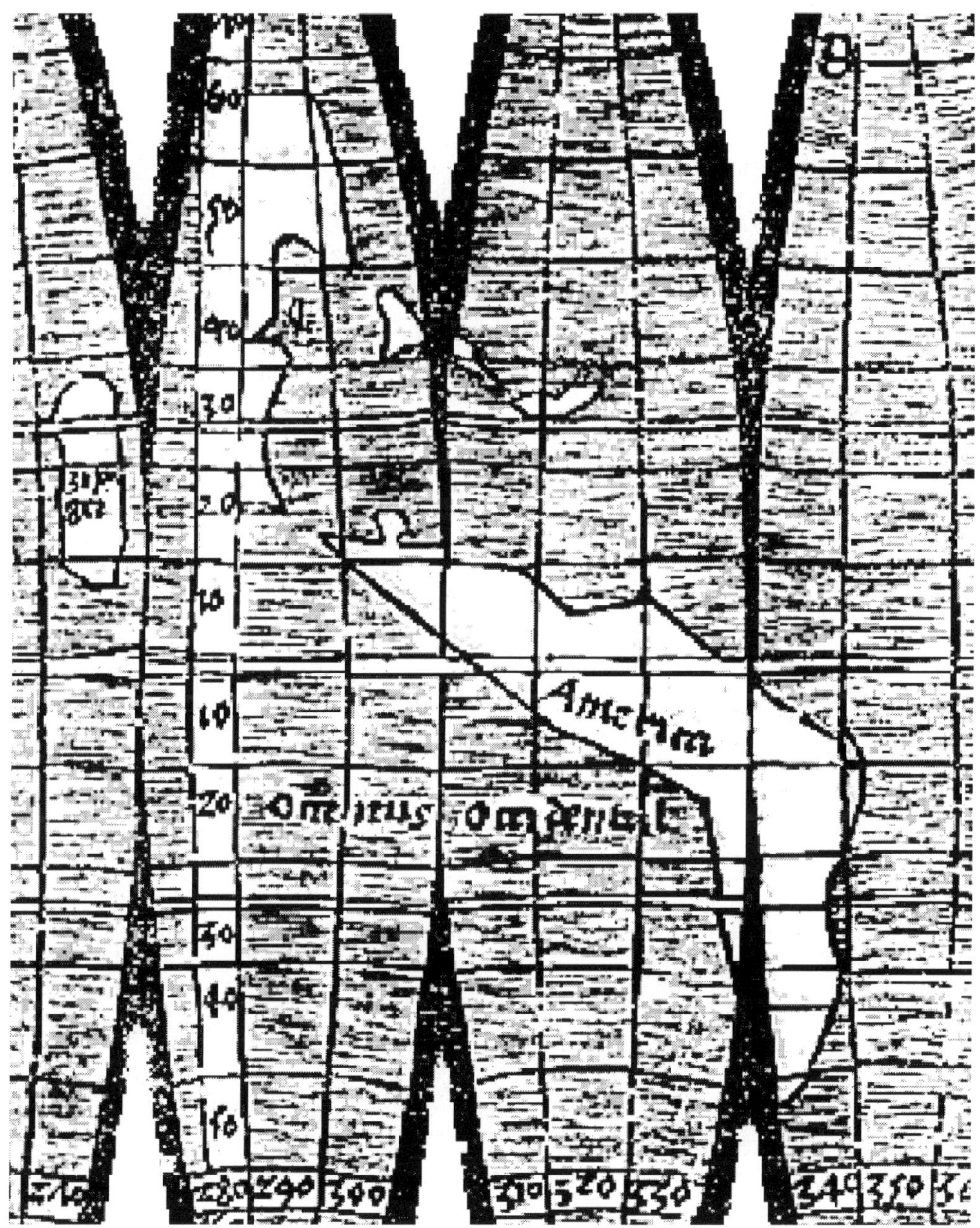

Figure 251

Section of the 1507 Martin Waldseemüller World

On June 9, 2005, one of the Martin Waldseemüller world maps (Figure 56) that first employed the name "America" was sold for over US $1m; that is, $1,000,000. This map was so valued not just because it was ancient and that it was unique, but because of its unusual depiction of the American Continents. Even though only portions of the eastern coastlines of these landmasses were shown, they were drawn years before Europeans explored these areas.

The explanation given for this implausibility by personnel involved in the auction transaction was that the Portuguese had violated the agreement with Spain—the Treaty of Tordesillas (see below)—and explored the landmasses behind the Spaniards' backs. Never mind that it defies reasoning to claim that the Portuguese were able to sail around the Spanish and did extensive surveying undetected, no explanation was offered for how the Portuguese were able to get to the west side of the continents to begin with, demonstrating that there was another ocean there, placing Japan close by, but missing the entire western American coastline (Figure 251).

Cultural Bias

In worse cases, cultural bias seeped in to fill the void created by this ignorance and disregard of historical facts.

Take the case of the analysis by Professor J. R. Hale, a leading Renaissance scholar and Chairman of the Department of History at the University of Warwick in England, who once taught at Cornell University. In his work *Renaissance Exploration,* he proclaimed that 15th century junks regularly sailing from Southern China around the Malay Peninsula to West India (but not mentioning East Africa) being flat-bottomed and must sail with the assistance of trailing winds (but not mentioning ocean currents) were vulnerable in high seas.

Thus, while the Chinese junks could easily sail the thousands of miles around the Indian Ocean, while they could sustain months in water and carry on a maritime tradition for hundreds, if not thousands, of years, they could not possibly have braved the waters around the southern tip of Africa and entered the Atlantic, which was, it must reasonably follow, a much more treacherous place to sail, despite a favorable trailing wind and ocean currents up the west African coast.

What we have here is an unstated but unadulterated bias: the waters of the Atlantic and those of the Indian Ocean are somehow different, one being mighty while the other weak, suitable for amateur sailors. To use a baseball metaphor, the Atlantic is Major League while the Indian Ocean is Minor League, or perhaps Little League. Hale's conclusion was thus not based on evidence or reasoning, but on the presumption that the Chinese could not have done it—because *today* Western technology ranks supreme, while China is an economically comparatively backward country and trails the West in science and engineering.

The irony is Hale, and other researchers similarly disposed, had no clue as to what kind of ships the Ming Chinese used for oceanic exploration because no prototype exists. They simply assumed that the Chinese vessels were not ocean-worthy. Oddly, *Endeavor,* Captain Cook's ship used in the exploration of the Pacific was a small three-masted, virtually flat-bottomed boat, which today's experts grudgingly admit "they do not know of their rigging or much about the technology that made the European voyages possible." This is the kind of Euro-centricity that permeates throughout the interpretation of these strange historical maritime events of early Renaissance.

A popular theory these days concerning the original population of the Pacific islands is the Express Train (Out of Taiwan) to Polynesia Theory. Human genetic studies on hundreds of Pacific islands suggest that the ancestors of the people of Polynesia left Taiwan or some island in the general area and quickly traveled through Melanesia into central and eastern Pacific thousands of years ago. Researchers clearly had no problem with these prehistoric people braving the oceans with whatever maritime technologies and skills they possessed. Yet civilized historical Chinese with a known history in maritime activities could not have done it.

The Chinese have an ancient parable. It tells of an arms dealer selling spears and shields. He announces to the potential buying public that he has the most potent spears in the kingdom and which can pierce any shield put up against them in defense. When he is hawking his shields, he asserts that his shields are so strong that no spear can penetrate them. The inquisitive would-be customer wonders which weapon would prevail if this merchant's spears were pitted against his own shields.

American proverbs call this having one's cake and eating it.

Hence, when it suits the researcher, primitive Pacific islanders could navigate the waters of the ocean, but when it comes to arguing against the allegation that the Chinese of six or seven hundred years ago had sailed the oceans of the world, it is asserted that they did not possess the technology or know-how to do it.

Historians try to have it both ways.

Obfuscation

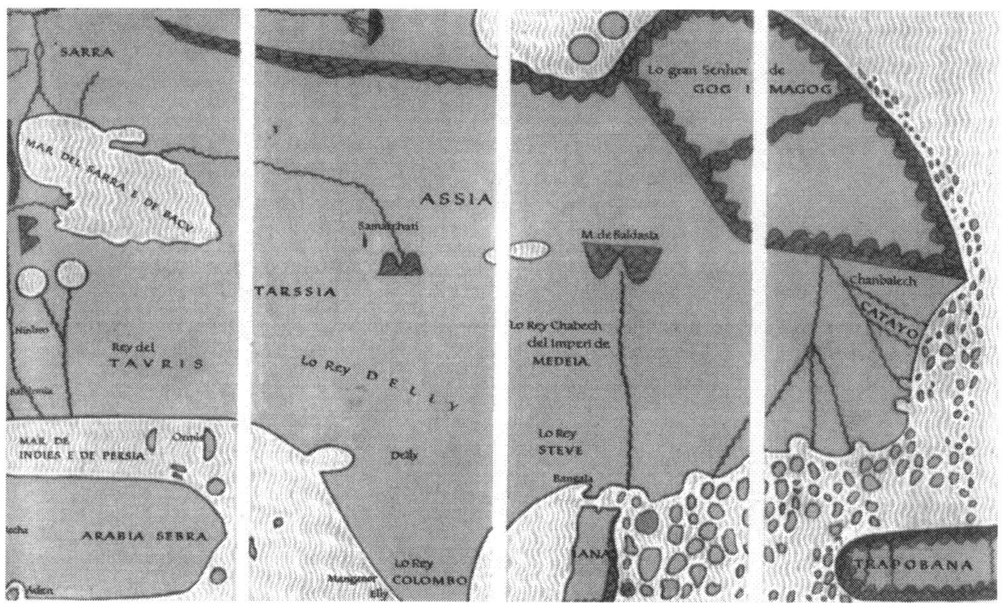

Figure 252

Hand Drawn Catalan Map of Asia

Then there is outright deception.

I know of an incident in which the author of a book on the Age of Discovery uses a simulation map in which Chinese junks are removed (Figure 252, compare with waterways in the original in Figure 253, and comparison between the two in Figure 254) for illustration.

Such scholarly abuses, misfeasance if not right-out malfeasance, are committed virtually case after case. For those readers who have developed keen interest in this issue and should like to pursue it further, I can tell you how little work you need to do to confirm the phenomenon for yourself. Just inspect any of the many books (popular or academic), literary treatises, or coffee table pictorials on the Age of Discovery from your local bookstore or libraries and you will find, as a few examples:

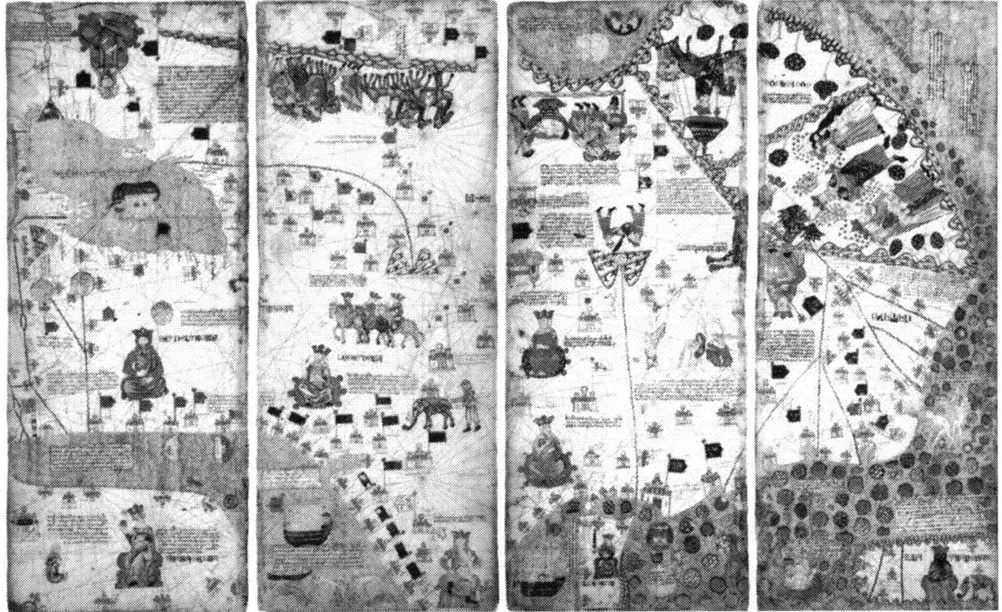

Figure 253

1375 Catalan Map of Asia

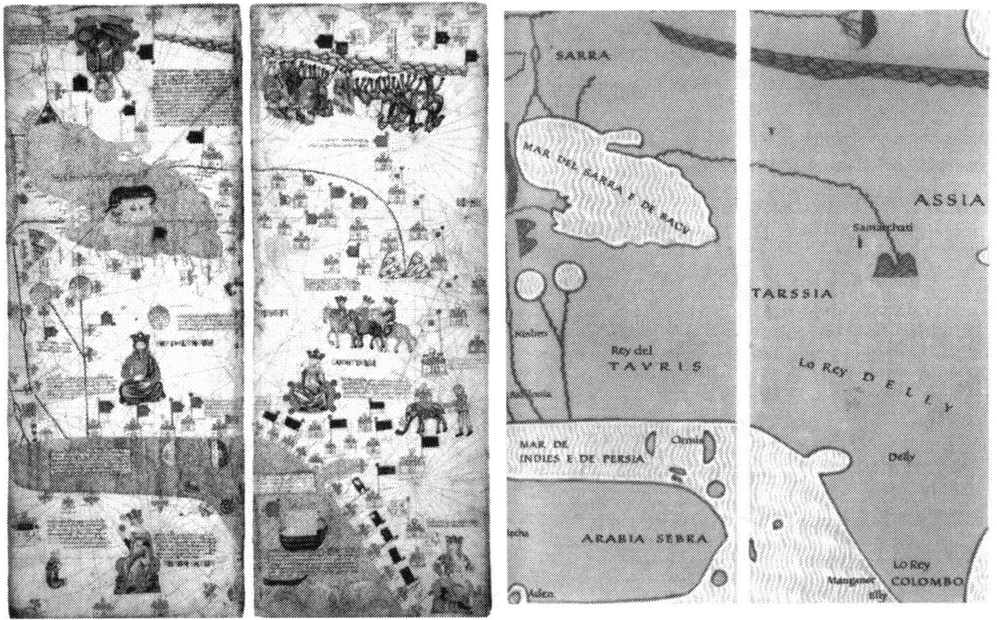

Figure 254

1375 Catalan Map of Asia with Chinese Ships Removed (on the Right Half Panel)

- The 1375 Catalan Atlas (Figure 84, Figure 85) seldom, if ever, shows the views featuring Chinese vessels (Figure 91, Figure 89, and Figure 90).
- For the mid-15th century Fra Mauro Map (Figure 92), rarely are the parts featuring Chinese junks (Figure 93, Figure 94) spotlighted, or the legend telling of a "zoncho" rounding the "Cape of Diablo".
- No mention or explanation of Chinese place names such as "Tangut," "Tebet," and others on Europeans maps of the era before Europeans had mapped those places.

Speculations are not evidence. However, the development of the Portuguese *nau*, a Chinese junk look-alike in more ways than one at the end of the Mongol Yuan Dynasty and the beginning of the Ming Dynasty, precisely at the time of Zheng He's expeditions, the struggle down the western coast of Africa at a time when Europeans were in awe and in fear of the mysterious Sea of Darkness, the existence of the early 14th century de Virga map (Figure 305) drawn at Zheng He's time, among others containing world geographical features, Europeans were not supposed to have known at the time, the sudden surge in European geographical knowledge of the world and keen interest in it, the unexplainable inspiration to sail west to reach Asia, the ease with which Columbus discovered the islands of the Caribbean, and above all, the proliferation of maps about the world containing ill-fitted details long before European explorers had surveyed them (the 1500 Juan de la Cosa map of the Caribbean, the 1507 Martin Waldseemüller world map, etc.), are real evidence.

The unmistakable transplantation of Chinese geography onto unknown new lands clearly points toward the Chinese as the purveyors of the new information, and that the Chinese were the ones who circumnavigated the world before the Europeans. The close proximity of the time of the European Age of Discovery to the Chinese maritime exploits proves that the Europeans inherited such Chinese knowledge, which directly sparked the European seafaring activities.

Unreal History

As I have repeated emphatically, relatively speaking, the Chinese are technologically behind today, but that does not mean that that had always been the case. That the Ming Chinese had chosen to abandon their superior achievements in maritime technology is, in hindsight and measured against today's value system, regrettable, but the Ming Chinese were solely responsible for that fateful act. What is difficult for a modern Western scholar to comprehend is why the Chinese chose to do that to themselves. That, again, is a typical dilemma in that to understand this ostensibly odd Chinese behavior of the past, the research-scholar needs to bridge the cultural difference between himself and his study subject. However, he cannot achieve this unless he first makes a genuine effort to understand the Chinese culture and, perhaps even more important, to review Western history with a corrected vision, and the first step toward this enlightenment is to once and for all divest of those intransigent European historical untruths that stand firmly in the way.

Christopher Columbus

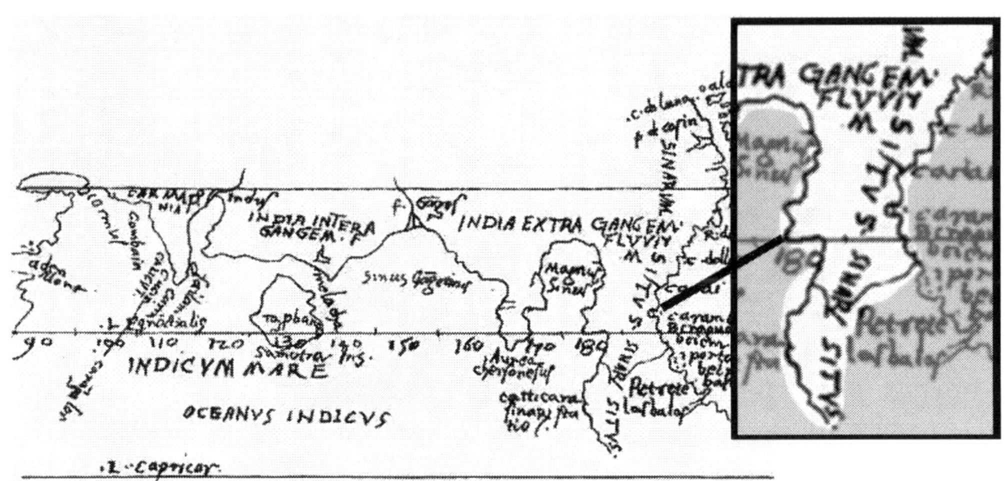

Figure 255

1522 Zorzi-Columbus Sketch of Indian Ocean

Historians have speculated about, and vexed over the "history" of Christopher Columbus for ages. Because of the wide acceptance of the Columbus "history" and the general exaltation of Columbus as a hero,[82] with the scarcity of solid support material, it has been difficult to discover his "true" story. Now, with confirmation of the external origins of medieval European geographical knowledge, we are perhaps in an improved position to reconsider the relevant events.

Christopher Columbus' discovery of the Caribbean took but a few months in one try. It is a miracle compared to the Portuguese taking almost a hundred years just to navigate down the western coast of Africa to round the Cape of Good Hope. Virtually all scholars and researchers have found Columbus' feat incredible. Consequently, the question persists: Did Christopher Columbus really "discover" his new lands, or did he simply follow some sort of guide to his destinations?

[82] In "Christophe Colomb" A. Roselly de Lorgues made a case for his sainthood.

back. Also in the time of Eugenius one of them came to Eugenius,[1] who affirmed their great kindness towards Christians, and I had a long conversation with him on many subjects, about the magnitude of their rivers in length and breadth, and on the multitude of cities on the banks of the rivers. He said that on one river there were near 200 cities with marble bridges great in length and breadth, and everywhere adorned with columns. This country is worth seeking by the Latins, not only because great wealth may be obtained from it, gold and silver, all sorts of gems, and spices, which never reach us ; but also on account of its learned men, philosophers, and expert astrologers, and by what skill and art so powerful and magnificent a province is governed, as well as how their wars are conducted. This is for some satisfaction to his request, so far as the shortness of time and my occupations admitted : being ready in future more fully to satisfy his

Figure 256

Toscanelli Letter to Columbus

Indeed, how did he do it; was he directed by one of the maps shown above? To resolve these questions, we need to re-assess the "Columbian Saga" in its entirety and in some detail.

According to nearly all mainstream sources, while in Portugal where he married a Portuguese, Columbus somehow came up with a plan to uncover a trade route for spices to the Orient by sailing westward from Europe. To seek financing for his venture, he approached King John II of Portugal in 1484, but his proposal was denied. Subsequently, Columbus went to Spain in 1485 to seek support from the Spanish monarchs. At first, this approach also came to naught. Nevertheless, despite these initial setbacks, Columbus remained steadfast. In 1491, he approached the Spanish court once more with his plan. Again, the result was negative.

Somehow at this time Queen Isabella of Castile personally intervened and granted Columbus his proposal. In that year a commission for voyage was approved and Columbus embarked on his epic journeys.

Historians generally have tried to explain this royal reversal by pointing out that in 1492 Spain finally overcame the last Moorish stronghold of Granada and once-and-for-all returned Spain—Europe, for that matter—to Christendom, and the Queen approved the enterprise on account of a buoyant changing national mood. Hence, after seven years of dogged pursuit by Columbus, an exceptionally generous agreement toward Columbus by the Crown of Spain was signed,[83] and the first historic voyage was launched.

Christopher Columbus went to the "New World" altogether four times. The first outing took place in 1492. Three ships—flagship Santa Maria, the Niña, and the Pinta—were launched from the port of Palos in southern Spain. The convoy arrived at Hispaniola, today's Haiti and Dominican Republic, in the Caribbean by December after sailing for about three months. On the 24th, the flagship Santa Maria struck reef and sank. In face of disaster, Columbus used the wreckage to build a fort and staffed it with parts of the crew. He named the fort La Navidad, or, "Christmas," to commemorate the date of arrival. During this trip Columbus explored the southeastern coast of Hispaniola. He returned home in March the next year.

About half a year later, Spain launched a second voyage. During this outing several more islands were discovered. The explorer also discovered that the fort at Navidad had been burned to the ground. All the occupants were dead. Investigations showed that there had been fighting between natives and settlers, apparently over gold and native women, resulting in the natives exacting revenge by massacring the settlers.

Columbus then established a new colony along the eastern Hispaniola coast and named it La Isabela after the Spanish queen. He

---

[83] Actually two, one signed on April 17 and one on April 30

then discovered Cuba and surveyed its southern coast, after which he went on to Jamaica. He returned to Spain in 1496.

The third voyage consisted of six ships, which formed two detachments, one heading for Hispaniola, while the other, led by Columbus, went to explore possible landmasses to the south. This latter detachment first reached the Cape Verde Islands (apparently not related to the ones west of Africa), then Trinidad. During this outing, he also explored the Gulf of Paria that is situated between Trinidad and the South American Continent. This Paria was the same as the one which maps had been focused on in the middle pf the Atlantic and drawn exceptionally out of scale.

At this time the colonists revolted. When Columbus failed to put down the revolt, he made a number of concessions. However, that apparently did little toward appeasing the rioters. Consequently, King Ferdinand and Queen Isabela replaced him with a royal commissioner named Francisco de Bobadilla, who arrested Columbus and sent him home in shackles, although the monarchs released him immediately when he reached shore in Spain. That was October of 1500.

Columbus commanded a fourth and last voyage to the New World when he was 51 years old. The purpose of this voyage was ostensibly to locate a passage linking the West Indies to the Indian Ocean.[84] During this final hurrah Columbus explored the Honduras coast. It was told that they found gold in Panama from the natives. After that, Columbus sailed for Spain in November 1504, ending his now famous series of adventures.

Within a decade, Christopher Columbus was forgotten. New explorers took over center stage. For example, the newly discovered

---

[84] There was also talk that Columbus was looking for the Strait of Malacca. Was he not supposed to be sailing to India in the first place, so that the Caribbean islands are called West Indies? Did he not carry with him a letter meant for the "Great Khan" of China believing that he was heading to China? How come all of a sudden he was now looking for a "passage way" to the Indian Ocean? Was he not supposed to have reached India?

landmass that we call the American Continents today is allegedly named after Amerigo Vespucci, a minor Italian adventurer who went on a ship that sailed under the Spanish flag. After almost three hundred years, during the height of European imperial pomp, Columbus was revived as the symbol of European know-how and derring-do. Today, in The United States of America, Columbus is often considered one of her founding heroes, and the accepted history of the Columbus saga is taken at face value.

The truth is, Columbus had inside information to his ventures.

There exists in the Biblioteca Nazionale Centrale, Florence a sketch by Alejandro Zorzi, allegedly based on information provided by Columbus' brother Bartolomeo that shows the same "South American Indochina" (right side of Figure 255) that we have seen on other Age of Discovery maps. If Bartholomew Columbus provided this information to his brother, there is no reason to believe that Christopher Columbus was unaware of it. Therefore, Christopher Columbus had information about the geography of the world—erroneously interpreted at the time as it might have been—and perhaps specific sailing guides to the Caribbean, before he embarked on his historical journeys.

When Christopher Columbus conceived of his voyages to the West, his brother Bartholomew was working at the court of King John II of Portugal as a marine chart maker. Clearly Bartholomew would have had access to the most advanced geographical data there. Indeed, it was Bartholomew who urged Christopher to approach the Portuguese king for funding. It might even have been Bartholomew's idea to sail west in the first place.

If the king of Portugal already possessed information about a possible sea route to new lands across the ocean to the west, it could explain why he turned down Columbus' proposal. It might indicate that the king had designs of his own, as some scholars believed.

According to the Columbian chronicler, mapmaker, and fellow explorer Las Casas, after striking out with King John II, Columbus left Portugal in a hurry for Castile, fearing for his life. He allegedly believed that the King was after him.

Figure 257

Toscanelli Atlantic Map Reconstruction

If the story is true, then it suggests that the Columbus brothers had somehow made off with items sensitive and important that belonged to the Portuguese king, and that could very well have been maps and/or sailing instructions to the New World.

It is known that the king of Portugal possessed new information of the world. It is on record that the renowned Florentine cosmographer Toscanelli had sent a letter to the king providing such information. Toscanelli believed that Asia actually extended much farther eastward than the prevalent Ptolemaic view. (For the engaged reader please refer to Figure 12 and Figure 13, in which America is drawn as an extension of Asia.) He was apparently unaware of the American continents. It is said that he estimated that there were some 5,000 miles of water between Europe and Cathay (China), and that one could sail west to reach Asia. However, how

Toscanelli formulated his belief and theory was not formally documented in history, but we do have record fragments that give us an idea of more-or-less what might have happened, and we will present that.

It is alleged that in 1432 (right at the end of the Zheng He voyages) Toscanelli met a Chinese delegation to the Pope, where the Chinese showed the Europeans a number of mechanical devices. He described a visit of people from Cathay (China) when Eugenius IV (1431 - 1447) was Pope. Toscanelli's letter is referenced here. An extract of the letter to Columbus (as translated into English) is shown in Figure 256.[85]

> *Also, in the time of Eugenius one of them [of Cathay] came to Eugenius, who affirmed their great kindness towards Christians, and I had a long conversation with him on many subjects, about the magnitude of their rivers in length and breath, and on the multitude of cities on the banks of rivers. He said that on one river there were near 200 cities with marble bridges great in length and breadth, and everywhere adorned with columns. This country is worth seeking by the Latins, not only because great wealth may be obtained from it, gold and silver, all sorts of gems, and spices, which never reach us; but also on account of its learned men, philosophers, and expert astrologers, and by what skill and art so powerful and magnificent a province is governed, as well as how their wars are conducted.*

Also,

---

[85] https://books.google.com/books?as_brr=3&id=HHIMAAAAIAAJ&dq=Letter+Toscanelli+Colomb&q=Toscanelli#v=onepage&q=Toscanelli&f=false

http://books.google.com/books?id=II14gJzeg60C&pg=PA4&dq=Letter+Toscanelli+Colomb&as_brr=3&hl=en#PPA7,M1

http://books.google.com/books?id=BR6Ek48GgzEC&pg=PA56&dq=Letter+Toscanelli+Colomb+Cathay&as_brr=3&hl=en#PPA52,M1

The said voyage is not only possible, but it is true, and certain to be honourable and to yield incalculable profit, and very great fame among all Christians. But you cannot know this perfectly save through experience and practice, as I have had in the form of the most copious and good and true information from distinguished men of great learning who have come from the said parts, here in the court of Rome, and from others being merchants who have had business for a long time in those parts, men of high authority.

So, certain Chinese had visited the Pope and Europeans learned of the East from this meeting. Toscanelli was informed of the sea routes to reach this place.

What is uncertain is what instigated Toscanelli's involvement in this incident, whether the king of Portugal actively sought his council, or he voluntarily offered his advice. Historians hold diverse opinions on the issue. In any case, it is generally believed that in a 1474[86] letter (via Portuguese Royal Canon Fernão Martins de Roriz) Toscanelli suggested that King Alfonso V of Portugal should sail in the westerly direction to reach Cathay.

Upon getting wind of this, Christopher Columbus allegedly promptly wrote Toscanelli and received a similar letter in return plus a sailing chart suggesting a possible sea route west. A reconstruction of this map is shown in Figure 227, which shows clearly that he did not know about the existence of an American continent. The map also explains why Toscanelli thought the distance from Europe to Asia was much shorter than it really was. That is because the distance was really meant for that between Europe and America.

The above story of an interaction between Columbus and Toscanelli was also supported by Columbus' son Fernando, who alleged that the Toscanelli correspondence "encouraged the Admiral (Columbus) much to go upon his discovery." Why a renowned

---

[86] Note that the Chinese official allegedly burned the Zheng He records in 1477.

Florentine cosmographer would correspond with a "nobody" is piquing, and unexplained.

In 1901, Columbus scholar Henry Vignaud created controversy when he cast doubts on the authenticity of the Toscanelli letters. Vignaud's challenge was prompted by the fact that no original text or even copies of the letters from Toscanelli to the Portuguese monarch or to Columbus have ever been found. Perhaps they had been destroyed during the great Lisbon earthquake of 1755 when most of the medieval Portuguese documents were burned. The only allusion to the documents was the copies made by Columbus in the blank pages of a book. According to Vignaud, these copies of the letter contained geographic conceptual errors that a scholar such as Toscanelli would not likely have made.

As the story was told, the letters were sent to a royal intermediary, the Canon named Fernão Martins. Yet, no such person was known in history. Based on these "facts," Vignaud concluded that the Toscanelli letters were forgeries. He believed that the letters were concocted by Columbus' brother Bartholomew and Columbus' colleague Las Casas, but we know not for what purpose were these acts perpetrated; perhaps to give the information they possessed some kind of testament of authenticity? If the information was in fact obtained from the Portuguese court, the forgery would strongly support the allegation, and it also helps explain Columbus' ordeal in landing his contract with the Spanish monarchs.

Columbus' flight from Portugal brought him to Castile, where he found shelter with his in-laws. There he promptly found his way into the privileged class to whom he would pitch his project. He probably secured his first assistance from the Duke of Medina Celi, Don Luis de la Cerda. However, it is said that the duke was unimpressed by Columbus' outlandish plan of a maritime adventure into the unknown Atlantic. Columbus purportedly also got a similar result from the Duke of Medina Sidonia.

In 1486, Columbus finally got through to the king of Aragon, Ferdinand. To consider his scheme, between 1486 and 1487 the king called an ecclesiastical commission at Salamanca in the Dominican convent of San Esteban to consider the plan. At the end, the commission rejected the proposal.

Some writers attempted to explain Columbus' string of failures by suggesting that Columbus withheld information from the commission because he did not want to give away too much of it and risk having his ideas appropriated. The next year Bartholomew tried to sell the same idea to the kings of England and France and failed to secure sponsorship with those monarchs also.

In 1491 Columbus tried again. This time the Castilian-Aragon court was outside the last Moorish stronghold of Granada in the South of the Iberian Peninsula, launching the final assault to drive the Moors from Europe once and for all. Once more a commission was convened, and as expected, the commission again denied the proposal. We are now at the main plot turn of the entire Columbian saga. It may come across appearing somewhat melodramatic, but then the story of Christopher Columbus is anything but ordinary.

According to one account of what happened next, Columbus was so distraught by this last blow that he left the court and drifted away. The man had lost his rudder, so to speak. In January 1492, he arrived at the Dominican convent of La Rábida, which prior, Father Juan Perez, happened to be Queen Isabela's confessor. With Father Perez more or less assuming the role of what we call a psychotherapist or councilor today, Columbus let flow his anguish at his disappointment, his aspirations, and almost certainly something else that he had to that day held close to his vest. We know this because upon learning it Father Perez went to the queen at once to personally petition her on behalf of Columbus. The rest is history. Columbus was summoned to return to court immediately. Upon the queen's prodding, the king approved Columbus' proposal. By the end of April, two contracts were drawn up and signed authorizing the expedition, with exceptionally generous terms extended to a commoner without the least bit of professional credential and no physical justification for his seemingly baseless claims.

With hindsight and taking into account all the relevant events, one can see that Columbus had to be in possession of certain item or items that were highly persuasive and provided powerful arguments for his case. It is not unreasonable to surmise that he had concrete material showing his proposal was feasible.

In hind sight, had he divulged the material earlier, assuming that the story's basic provisions are correct, would Columbus have gone to sea earlier? That is hard to say.

In his book *Sails of Hope: The Secret Mission of Christopher Columbus* the famous Nazi hunter Simon Wiesenthal alleged that Columbus going to sea was looking for a Jewish homeland. This is assuming that Columbus was Jewish, of course. The name Columbus (Columbo), originally Colon, and Coulomb in French, is a name adopted by many Jews.

The assertion that he was leading the Jews to search for a new home is tied to the fact the Catholic Monarchs Ferdinand II of Aragon and Isabela I of Castile kicked the Jews out from Spain in 1492. In fact, so many Jews were leaving Spain, many of whom going to the Netherlands, that they booked up all the ships and clogged up the Spanish seaports. As a result, Columbus was forced to set sail from Palos with 3 beat-up ships. As far as the validity of this bit of added reasoning, I shall abstain from any discussion. However, for those enthusiastic readers, this may be a good topic for further research.

That Columbus had guidance to his voyages is evinced by a number of documents and historical narratives.

In 1929, when going through the Topkapi Museum in Istanbul (formerly the Palace of the Ottoman Sultans), the director, Mr. Halil Edhem (1861 - 1938), came across a map drawn on a roe-skin that had been languishing in the palace for 4 centuries. This is the now famous Piri Reis Map (Figure 258). This map shows a South American east coast, especially the part about Brazil, the same part that showed up time and again on the maps that we have examined, that is frightfully accurate (compare it with Figure 260 from a map of today).

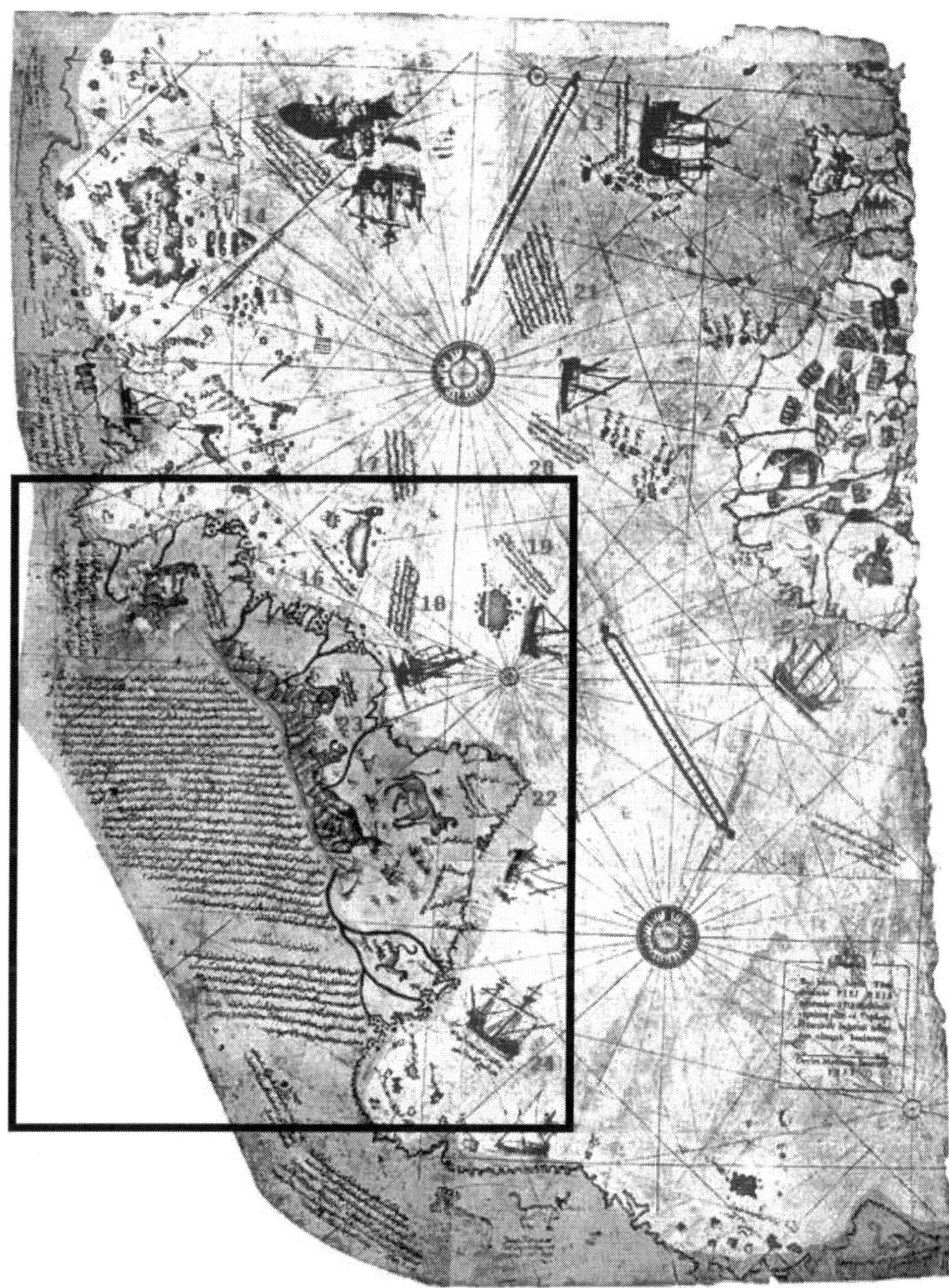

Figure 258

The Piri Reis Map

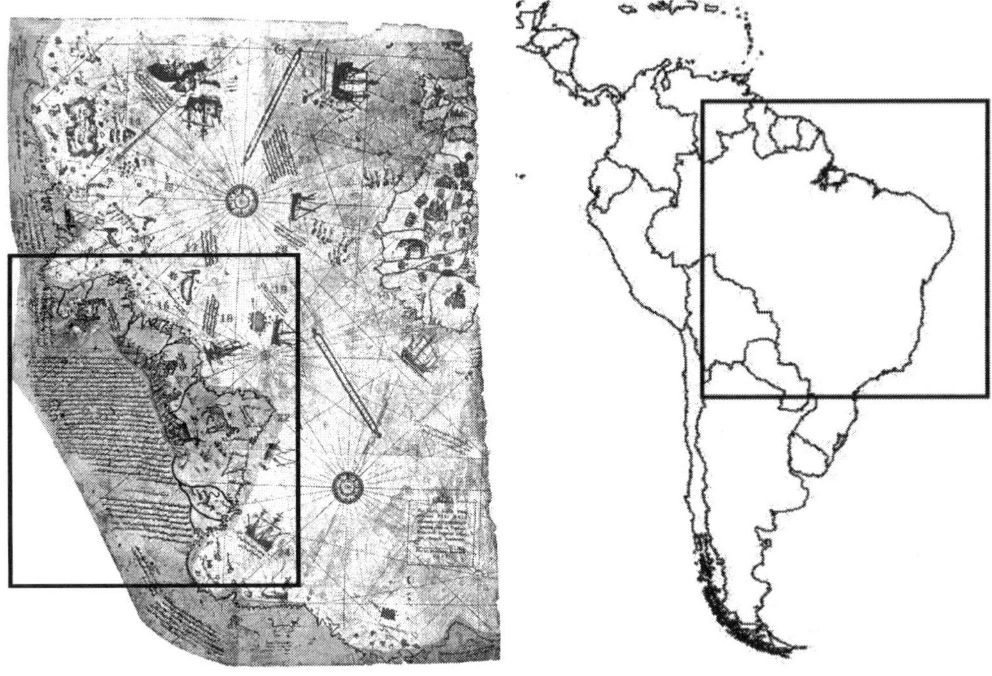

Figure 259

The Piri Reis Map

Figure 260

Modern Day Map of South America

The map is so-called because of the way the map originated. Piri Reis (1470 - 1554), nephew of the great admiral Kemal Reis, was an admiral of the Ottoman Empire. Both uncle and nephew began their careers as pirates in the Mediterranean Sea, but later joined the Turkish navy under Sultan Bayezid II, son of Melimet II, the Conqueror.

In 1502, Piri began compiling a book on navigation called the *Bahriye*, which was finished in 1513. The subject map was originally a part of this book and a part of a world map. Today only this portion of the map exists. The rest is lost. In *Bahriye*, Piri described the map as being constructed with the latest information from around the world. According to Piri's own hand notes, the map was based on eight "mappa mundi" (maps of the world), among which were four Portuguese maps, an Indian map with Arabic annotations, and one on the western hemisphere Christopher Columbus used in the discovery of "Antilia."

We do not know what the remaining two maps were. With the so-called eight-source maps from nations not known to have navigated and charted the world, it testifies to their having obtained source material from unknown origins.

By his own account, Piri came into this Columbus map during a sea battle with the Spanish when he was serving under his uncle Kemal Reis in 1501. During this battle the Turkish captured seven Spanish ships near Valencia. Among the bootie were a Native American feather headdress and an axe made of some strange looking black rock. One of the Spanish prisoners informed Piri that the items had come from newly discovered lands beyond the Sea of Darkness, and that he went there three times under a man named Colombo. He presented to Piri the map that "Colombo" supposedly used to sail to the Antilia Islands, and Piri included the information therein in his own map of the world.

Accordingly, from this report we know that Columbus had a map. Piri's notes explain how Columbus came into the information.

> *The coasts of Antilia were discovered in the year 896 of the Arab calendar[87], purportedly by a Genoese infidel with the name Colombo. This Colombo came into possession a book that told of coasts and islands with all sorts of precious metals and stones at the end of the Western Sea. After studying this book this Colombo approached the Mighty of Genoa and requested two ships to locate such places. To Colombo's proposal the Mighty One expressed disbelief that there was "a limit to the Western Sea which was nothing but vapor and was full of darkness." Colombo then went to the Bey of Spain and presented his case. The monarchs also turned him down. After a long time the Bey of Spain finally supplied him with two fully supplied ships and said: "O*

[87] The Muslim calendar began in 622, the year of Mohamed's *hadj*. Although 896 + 622 = 1518, a Muslim year is shorter than a Christian one. Thus year 896 was closer to 1500.

Colombo, if what you say is true we will make you kapudan to that country."

The late Gazi Kemal had a Spanish slave, who told Kemal Reis that he had visited the new land three times with Colombo. He said: "First we reached the Strait of Gibraltar, then from there we turned south and west between the two . . . [illegible]. After sailing four thousand miles, we came to an island, but soon the sea calmed down and the North Star became obscured." The stars out in the ocean were arranged differently from the ones here. The sailors anchored at the island and the natives came and shot arrows at them, disallowing them to land. The men and women shot hand arrows, which tips were made of fish bones, and all the people were naked and were also very . . . [illegible]. Seeing that they could not land on that island; they went over to the other side of the island and saw a boat. When the occupants saw them they abandoned the boat and fled on land. The Spaniards took the boat and saw human flesh inside it. These people went from island to island to hunt men and eat them. They said Colombo saw yet another island on which there were big snakes. Therefore they stayed onboard and remained there seventeen days. When the natives thus saw the Spanish to be friendly they brought fish in their little boats. In return the Spaniards gave them glass beads. It appears that Columbus had learned from the book that glass beads were valued in these parts. Hence they began trading glass beads for fish. One day they saw gold around the arm of a woman and they traded beads for the gold. They told the natives to bring more gold and they would give them more beads. The natives went and brought them a lot of gold. It appears that there were gold mines in the mountains. One day they also saw pearls in the hands of a native, and they traded beads for their pearls. Pearls were found on the shore of this island, in a place one or two fathoms deep. The Spanish then loaded up with logwood trees and took two natives with them back

> *home to the Bey of Spain. Colombo, not knowing the language of these people, traded with them by signs, and after this voyage the Bey of Spain sent priests and barley, taught the natives how to sow and reap, and converted them to his own religion. The natives had no religion of any sort. They walked naked and slept like animals. Now that these lands have been discovered they have become famous. Colombo gave names to mark the places on the islands and coasts. Further, Colombo was a great astronomer. The coasts and island on this map are taken from Colombo's map.*[88]

From the narrative, we thus have an independent source testifying to the Columbian voyages being missions of conquest (will make you *kapudan*, el capitan, captain; that is, governor, to that country). Columbus sailed south and crossed the equator (the stars now looked differently), made stops at certain islands, with one of them thought to be Antilia, and despoiled the natives. It is also abundantly apparent that Columbus had directions ("a book that told him to bring glass beads for trade") and a map.

Although we have no direct information on the precise contents of Columbus' map, according to Piri's notes, apparently there were indications of a continent that lied beyond the Sea of Darkness.

Recall that it was said that time and again Columbus' efforts came up short because he was unwilling to divulge the full extent of his plan. He also demanded excessively lucrative rewards—perhaps justified in view of what he probably possessed—for the project's success. He expected a hefty concession on the profits and a title. His disposition is entirely understandable because he was in possession of highly sensitive and valuable material, which could not be lightly divulged. In any case, at the end, voluntarily or by a stroke of epiphany, Columbus showed his hand and immediately the deal was clinched. Without question what he possessed had the power to convince immediately and decisively.

---

[88] http://www.bibliotecapleyades.net/mapas_pirireis/esp_mapaspirireis07.htm

Why did Columbus insist on being rewarded a title, "Governor," and why did he insist on the backings from a government? If Columbus' proposed venture was purely commercial in nature, he could have simply negotiated directly with the money people, whom he knew, and dispensed with all that courting of the royalties. The fact is, Columbus was not embarking on a venture of discovery. He was on a mission of conquest (or perhaps searching for a new Jewish homeland as alleged). All the historic facts point to this.

After months at sea, upon setting foot on the first land he arrived at, Columbus named it San Salvador. Naming a foreign land is de facto an act of aggression and occupation, a standard practice of the ages of colonialism and imperialism all the way down to the 20th century. The real purpose of the Columbian journeys was not for trade as history has advertised, but for conquest.

During her youth Queen Isabela religiously studied Latin for self-betterment. To assist her in this effort, the humanist Antonio de Nebrija in 1487 presented her a textbook on Latin Grammar that proved much to her appreciation. Five years later de Nebrija compiled for her another book; this time on the grammar of the Castilian language, the first of its kind on a local dialect, and the queen was visibly perplexed over it. Allegedly she could not understand immediately why she would need a Castilian dictionary. Her confessor, Fray Hernando de Talavera, Bishop of Avila, stepped in and explained to her that one day all the barbarous nations that spoke diverse tongues when conquered by Spain would need to obey Spanish laws and be obliged to speak the noble tongue, Castilian. The queen understood the concept at once. The Spanish Empire was on the historical threshold of formation, and Queen Isabela grasped instantly the divine right of world domination—empire building had begun, and Columbus led the way.

Upon Columbus' returning to Spain after the first outing to the Caribbean, Queen Isabela wrote him, as reported by Juan Manzano and echoed by John Noble Wilford: "It appears that for what you have described to us at the beginning, for the most part it has been true *as if you had seen it before you spoke of it to us*."[89] This is a startling statement. It implies that the monarchs knew all along that Columbus was not attempting to reach India or Cipangu or Cathay as propagandized by historians and myth-makers, but rather that they were out to conquer distant lands.

Joaquin Roy, Professor at the University of Miami wrote in the Five Hundred Magazine (Volume 1/No. 1; May/June 1989):

> *The Castilian Queen knows that Columbus has already discovered another world beyond the blue sea (and so is stated in the written agreement on account of an odd lapse in its wording).*

Professor Roy further reports that: The manuscript of this agreement is carefully kept in the Archives of the Crown of Aragon, in Barcelona. The document is known by historians as the Santa Fe Capitulations, after the name of a place at the entrance to Granada, the city that had been recently regained from the Moors.

An examination of these contracts the monarchs signed with Columbus will further support the above conclusion. The contents of the contracts are roughly translated as follows:

> *This document lists the compensations as petitioned by Don Christopher Columbus granted by Your Highnesses for his discoveries in the Ocean Seas with the help of God he is about to make in Your Highnesses' service.*
>
> *1. As Sovereigns of the said Ocean Seas, Your Highnesses appoints the said Christopher Columbus, henceforth known as Admiral of all the islands and mainlands that will be discovered by his enterprise, in perpetuity for the duration of his life, and upon his death, his heirs and successors, with all the rights and privileges to be attached to that office...*

[89] Italics by the present author/researcher.

> *2. Your Highnesses appoints the said Don Christopher the Viceroy and Governor-General of all the islands and mainlands that he may discover and acquire in the Ocean Seas....*
>
> *3. Your Highnesses grants the said Don Christopher Columbus one tenth of all the merchandise, pearls, precious stones, gold, silver, spices, or products of any kind, that may be acquired by purchase, barter, or any other means, within the jurisdiction of the said Admiralty. After expenses shall be granted one tenth of the net profit of which he may dispose as he sees fit…*

The document unambiguously spells out the legal rights of possession for the riches to be had during the journey, and the islands and mainland (which would cover any kind of land) that Columbus might come across, but one glaring revelation stands out above all. There is no specific mentioning of "Indies." The statement "as if you had seen it before you spoke of it to us" reveals that prior to setting out on his trip Columbus already described to the monarchs the lands that he was to "visit," and they were the Caribbean islands.

Not only was there no reference to "Indies," there was no allusion to India, Cipangu (Japan), Cathay (China), Asia, or any of the places we have come to associate with the Columbus voyages. The contract simply granted Columbus the right to take any land, and I understand that to mean China, Japan, and India as well, and any goods and products by any means. Interesting, though, India was conspicuously missing from the Caribbean area in most contemporary and 16th century maps.

The implication of all this cannot be more apparent. Columbus was never really heading for Asia for friendly trade, and the monarchs, and by inference all the parties involved in the project, such as the bankers and financiers, were in on this fact. With the lack of allusion to the traditional Asian destinations, coupled with the explicit granting of riches to newly discovered lands, that the expeditions were for the outright conquest of new found lands can no longer be questioned. The ease with which Columbus reached land, in light of what we now know, testifies to the fact that he had clear sailing instructions for his efforts.

As an added anecdote, it is well-known that Columbus returned to Spain along a route that was different from the one he took to the Caribbean Sea. It turned out that the strategy was to ride the two different ocean currents. How did he know to do that? Most historical writings attribute that to his "genius."

Not all historians have been blinded to these historical facts. Professor Joaquim Romero Magalhães Godinho states in his *Os descobrimentos e a economia mundial* and *Documentos para a História da Expansão Portuguesa* that the intellectual view that the 15th century European oceanic exploration was due to the Turks interrupting the flow of spices from the East was not only naïve but incorrect. Henry Vignaud, Columbus' detractor, who wrote two volumes and a number of pamphlets, had persistently asserted that Columbus had explicit directions to his "discoveries." He accused Columbus of falsifying his journal, and forging the Toscanelli letters as discussed above. British naval historian E. G. R. Taylor suggested that Columbus was traveling to the fabled Antilla all along, and Wilford concluded: "An exploitative attitude toward America and native Americans was thus fixed at the outset." The biographer Kirkpatrick Sale simply concluded that Columbus was seeking gold.

Regardless, that the Columbian voyages were intended for colonization from the start is demonstrated by the second outing. This time all pretenses were dropped; even historians are no longer talking about exploration. The purpose of the trip was to colonize the newly acquired islands.[90] The convoy in this voyage numbered seventeen ships with more than a thousand participants and life stock for extended stay.

In retrospect, it can be seen that the Columbian voyages of discovery, if they ever were that, had to be the most miraculous,

---

[90] This also implies that the colonizers knew they were not visiting India.

spectacular, and productive ventures ever. Nobody before or since was able to discover so many new places so effortlessly. The trips were more like ferry boat runs than treacherous expeditions in dangerous, unknown waters. The inter-island hops resembled a pinball machine at full tilt. Yet almost nobody questioned why the whole enterprise seemed so easy.

Open-sea navigation was not an everyday affair in medieval times. One commentator observed that at the time of Henry the Navigator and Christopher Columbus, sailors still feared falling off the edge of the Earth. When out at sea at any moment, a sailor could be gobbled up by sea monsters. Compared with the efforts it took for Portuguese sailors to round the Cape of Good Hope, or John Cabot's first voyage to the North American continent—which he could not even retrace and to this day nobody can be sure of exactly what seacoast he actually came across—the ease with which Columbus navigated amongst unknown islands, explored them and colonized them, built a whole fort out of ship wreckage, could only be described as fantastic.

In view of this, the notion of Columbus having special guidance and instructions to his expeditions is no empty speculation.

Consequently, in the view of a scientific eye, the following is probably what really happened.

Christopher Columbus, either assisted by or in collusion with his brother Bartolomeo, obtained documents, maps, or information attesting to the existence of unclaimed land out in the Atlantic Ocean (called Mare Occidentale, or, Western Ocean at the time). Whether Bartolomeo went to work for the king of Portugal as a mapmaker as part of a scheme to obtain such information or that he merely came across such information in possession by the king during his tenure there we do not know. In any case, it is likely that such valuable information was passed on to Christopher clandestinely because the king of Portugal went after him. Christopher, knowing the value of his acquisition, intended to extract the highest possible price for it, which explains why he had difficulty obtaining sponsorship for his adventure, as he was unwilling to divulge his plan details.

Nevertheless, once he secured backing he went on a mission of conquest, and the rest is history, as the cliché goes.

Magellan

Figure 261

1520 Johann Schoner Globe Showing Strait of Magellan

Not a few decades after Columbus arrived in the Caribbean, Magellan embarked on his own historic journey around the world. As Columbus, he also sailed west. The Age of Discovery European world maps we examined (e.g., Figure 261) tell us that there is little question Magellan thought the feat could be done. Although 1520, the year Magellan passed through the Strait of Magellan, was only a mere seven years after Balboa reached the Pacific coast, there were maps showing that South America could be circumnavigated. However, knowing that it could be done and doing it are two entirely different things. To sail around the southern tip of South America one needed sailing charts. This, of course, does not mean that Magellan could not be the trailblazer, but if he did it without a chart, it would have taken him much longer to accomplish his deed, if at all.

On this point historians are in agreement: Magellan had a sailing chart. In his book *The Mapmakers* Wilford describes how Magellan was inspired to seek the strait that now bears his name:

> *The idea of circumnavigating the Earth apparently came to Ferdinand Magellan after he examined charts in Lisbon and listened to his geographer friend Guy Faleiron. The charts indicate the presence of a strait between the south tip of South America and the shores of the supposed Terra Australis. Through that strait, he decided, a ship could pass from the Atlantic to the Pacific and thence to Asia. Had Magellan known how far south the strait and how wide the Pacific he might have changed his mind and stayed home.*

The last sentence was, of course, poetic freedom on the part of the author. It is possible that nothing could have deterred Magellan. Do we have records of the chart or charts that Magellan saw? Perhaps not the very specific chart, but such charts are still in existence.

The 1520 Johann Schoner Globe map (Figure 261) shows clearly a passage way between the southern tip of a poorly drawn South America and a landmass where Antarctica is supposed to be. It has a partial, unfinished, out-of-scale eastern part of North America immediately next to Japan, a vertically-placed rectangular-shaped landmass, thus attesting to the fact that the mapmaker did not base his map on firsthand survey data. The poor interpretation of the data bears out the fact that the map was copied from a source. The

Oronce Finé map of 1521 (Figure 13) also shows such a strait at the southern tip of South America.

For a map to be issued in 1520, the mapmaker had to have begun constructing the map sometime prior, perhaps even years. Magellan only passed through his strait in 1520, so he could not have been the source of the geography.

We thus conclude that Magellan went on his voyage with known guidance in hand.

Marco Polo

Figure 262

13th Century Psalter Map

Now we come to Marco Polo, perhaps the most prolific principal actor and expert witness in the creation of Age of Discovery myths.

Marco Polo, everybody knows, of course, is the quintessential globetrotter extraordinaire who allegedly visited China in the late 13th century and returned to Europe to pen the immortal *The Travels of Marco Polo*. This, however, is legend. The historical truth is he probably never set foot in China.

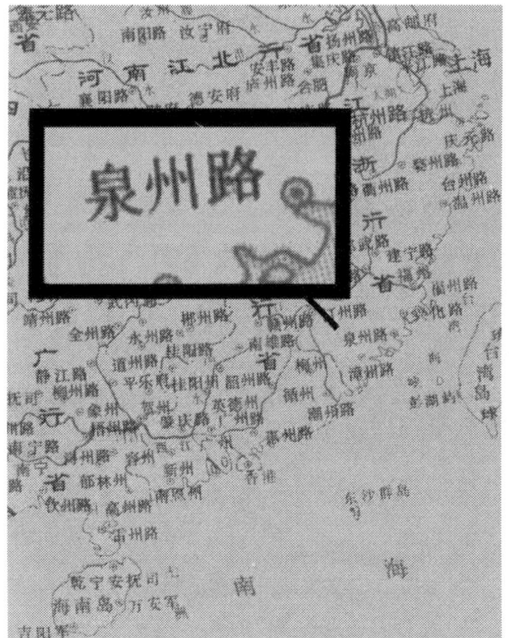

Figure 263

Yuan Dynasty Place Names Sporting the Word "Lu."

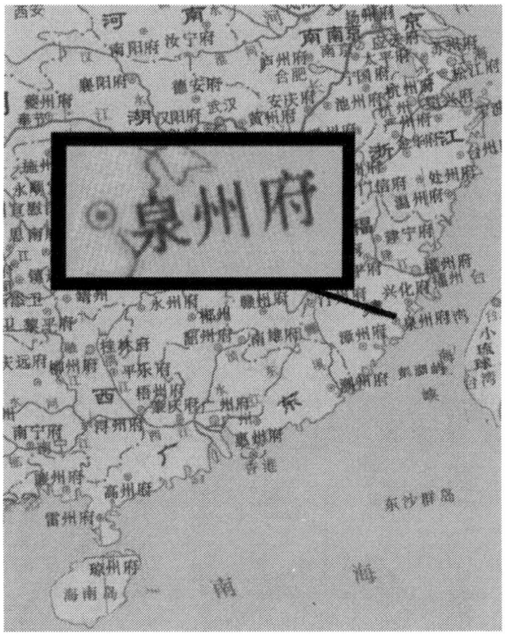

Figure 264

Ming Dynasty Place Names Sporting the Word "Fu."

Critical scholars have had doubts about the historicity of Polo's travel to China for a long time and have expressed their opinions in numerous articles, monographs, and books. A leading voice belongs to Frances Wood, head of the Chinese Department at the British Library, who in her book *Did Marco Polo go to China?* systematically summarized the causes of objection, of which there are three major groups.

First, as Kublai Khan's viceroy because of his exceptional ability of keen observation who stayed in China seventeen years, Polo failed to describe some of the most common yet astounding characteristics of China, among which were the Chinese drinking tea, eating with chopsticks, Chinese women binding their feet, and most unforgivable if omitted, the Great Wall, which Europeans had to learn from other sources, such as the 13th century Psalter map showing the Great Wall in northeast Asia (Figure 262).

Second, his "travelogue" exhibited none of the attributes typical of the genre. A real travelogue will describe realistic journeys from point A to point B, then to point C, and so on. Polo's writing would describe, for example, a journey from Peking (Beijing) to India, followed by another from Peking down the eastern Chinese seacoast without informing the reader how he went from India back to Peking. This kind of writing makes the book appear to be more a travel guide than a travelogue. (We shall learn how this disruption in the travelogue's narrative occurred below.)

Finally, for a person of official status who stayed in China seventeen years to employ Persian names for Chinese cities and locales (such as Zaiton[91] for Quanzhou and Kinsai for Hangzhou) throughout simply cannot be justified.

Marco Polo did not pen his famous travelogue. This is well known. The actual book was scribed by a fellow cellmate named Rustichello when Polo was in prison in 1298 as a result of getting involved in a war between the Venetians and the Genoans and picking the wrong side. Rustichello was the 13th century author of two Arthurian romances. Marco Polo, being an itinerant merchant, could very well have been illiterate. There is no evidence of him having written anything significant. He apparently related his experiences to Rustichello orally.

As for whether Marco Polo actually spent seventeen years in China serving under the Great Khan, his very book ultimately helps resolve the question. As it is, the key to untangling the conundrum lies in the rational analysis of the history of his work.

As all books popular through the ages, Marco Polo's travelogue has multiple versions. This is partly the result of the work being translated into different languages, thus taking on variations incurred by the translators and scribes, and partly due to the workings of the copy editors and publishers, who would have no

[91] Zaiton is the Persian rendition of the winter flower plant 栜棠, ci tang, a specialty of Quanzhou.

compunction against inserting their own takes on the stories, understandably to boost circulation.

Today, some 140 (or more) versions of the work have survived from medieval times, and they offer a diverse and intriguing topical coverage. One "Toledo" edition has a major section on Russia that is unique. The earliest version hinted at was one from 1307. Nonetheless, we no longer have any original copy of that work.

Most of the versions we now have spring from a certain editor named Giovanni Baptisto Ramusio (d. 1557). He claimed to have based his edition on an earlier 1438 copy (note the year). In this version there are descriptions of Hangzhou and Manichaeans of Fuzhou (all locations along the southeastern Chinese coast) that are not found in other editions.

A comprehensive discussion on the provenance of the Polo work can be found in Professor John Larner's *Marco Polo and the Discovery of the World*. In summary, Professor Larner concluded that there was an early version, which engendered a series of issues, and a later one, the Ramusio edition, which contained new journeys down the southeastern Chinese seacoast. Not only were these new journeys in agreement with the Zheng He expeditions, they were added right after the Ming maritime program was scrapped. Further, the geography involved in this new section of material employed Chinese names as opposed to Persian name, and they are anachronistic.

Yuan Mongols named major Chinese cities military garrisons, "Lu."[92] "Lu" literally meaning "Road" or "Way," demonstrating the Mongols' preoccupation with mobility and troop deployment efficiency. In a sense the word is akin to the American word "Fort." You can see the many place names with "Lu" in the map in Figure 263 showing the Yuan era southeast China. The insert shows Quanzhou Lu, Marco Polo's Zaiton.

---

[92] Lu, 路

Figure 265

1602 Ricci Map Annan

In contrast, the Ming used the word "Fu,"[93] which denotes "government house" or "government seat." Figure 264 shows the same cities featured in Figure 263 as they would have appeared during the Ming era.

---

93 "Fu," 府, is a legitimate Chinese designation for major cities, but not for Yuan Dynasty Mongols, who used the term "lu" instead. This is made clear in Yuan Shi, the official history of Yuan, in the Geography section:

> 唐以前以郡領縣而已。元則有路，府，州，縣四等。大率以路領州，領縣，而腹里或有以路領府，府領州，州領縣者，其府與州又有不棣路而直棣省者，具載于篇，而其沿革則溯唐而止焉。

Before Tang there were *jun* divided into *xian*. In contrast, Yuan has *lu*, *fu*, *zhou*, and *xian*. Mostly *lu* followed by *zhou*, then *xian*, but could also be *lu* followed by *fu*, then *zhou* and *xian*. However, sometimes there could be *fu* and *zhou* without belonging to *lu* but directly deriving from *sheng* (province).

Figure 266

Marco Polo's Southeast Asia

In Marco Polo's travelogue we have both "Lu" and "Fu," a clear anachronism. (Marco Polo died before seeing the Ming Dynasty, so he knew no "Fu.") Thus, just like how biblical scholars were able to ascertain a multiple authorship for the Pentateuch—the Torah—we can deduce that Marco Polo's travelogue had gone under the operations of multiple writing implements. The "Fu" locations were clearly introduced by a later writer or writers well into the Ming period.

The two-tiered evolution of the Marco Polo travelogue is further confirmed on linguistic grounds. Marco Polo called Japan "Cipangu." The name *Japan* comes from two Chinese characters 日本 , which means "the sun's origin," "Where the Sun Rises," or simply, "Land of the Rising Sun." The Japanese pronounce the name "Nippon." Because the characters are in Chinese script, the Chinese can pronounce the name also.

Figure 267

Shan Hai Jing* Monsters in *The Travels of Marco Polo

How they pronounce it, though, depends on what dialect is employed. In northern China the characters are pronounced “Ri Ben,” a sound that began to take hold just about the time of the Mongol occupation of China. This new northern sound eventually developed into today’s Mandarin dialect (Putonghua). In the South the Chinese would pronounce the name something like “Yut Boon” or “Yat Ban,” closer to Archaic Chinese. The southern pronunciation eventually was picked up by seagoing foreigners, probably Arabs and then Turks, as “Yapan.” The “Y” sound is often written with a “J,” and in Western Europe, as “Yesu” becoming “Jee-Sus” today, the name became how “Japan” is now pronounced in English. "Cipangu” is simply “Japan Guo,” “guo” meaning “country.”

In short, the name Cipangu could not have come from the north of China, where Marco Polo allegedly sojourned. It went West via a southern sea route. Names in Marco Polo’s travelogue such as Gaugiguo, Toloman, Cheinam, and Ania all belong to this category of names with southern Chinese pronunciation. Thus, they were not introduced by Marco Polo. They were added to his travelogue at a later date.

Marco Polo's work is rife with such anachronism. Gaugiguo referred to a state in the north of today's Vietnam. After the Ming had established itself, the Chinese government changed its name to Annan; that is, the Anian in some Age of Discovery European maps of North America as we have seen. This change happened more than a hundred years after Polo's death. Yet the names Gaugiguo and Annan coexist in the Travels of Marco Polo. Such anachronism serves as hard evidence showing that the Southeast China portion of the Asian geography was posthumously added.

On the 1602 Matteo Ricci Chinese world map is an inscription saying that China had not have contact with Europe for seventy years. The Ricci map is a fusion of Chinese and Western geographical information. This inscription no doubt came from the Chinese underlying stratum of the map. The Yuan Mongols who employed non-Chinese extensively were ousted by the Ming in 1368. Seventy years later puts the date of the Chinese base map at 1438, sometime during the reign of the Ming Emperor Xuande, the grandson of Chengzu. On the map is a notation for Vietnam (Figure 266). It tells the name as Annan, but with an explanatory note reminding the map reader that its old name was Jiao Zhi (Gao Ji in Cantonese, Marco Polo's Gaugiguo).

Year 1438 coincides with the time when world geography began appearing in Europe.

The geography of Southeast China was learned by Europeans more than a hundred years after Marco Polo's death. He did not write that part of his Travelogue.

The original version of *Marco Polo's Travels* involved locations strictly limited to Central Asia, from Iran to northern and western China, Mongolia, and northwestern India. The later addition, the portion describing the cities along the Zheng He seacoast, was introduced immediately after the Ming voyages had become known to Europeans. This suggests that Marco Polo likely never set foot in China proper. As an Italian merchant, he most likely stationed in Central Asia and acquired information about the East, which he brought home.

Marco Polo was contemporary with the great Persian historian Rashid al-Din (1248 - 1317), who wrote the famous *World History,* a history of the Mongols. Rashid al-Din based his work to a large extent on the works of another great historian Tarikh-i Jahangushay-i Juvaini, whose works included *The History of the World Conqueror* about the history of Genghis Khan. The Persian names of the geography contained in these works agree with those found in Polo's Travels. It is conceivable that Marco Polo obtained material related to these manuscripts.

It should be mentioned here that despite the evidence against the veracity of the Polo legend, Professor Larner is a staunch believer of Polo's exploits. In his book he writes:

> *Any sense of awe we feel at this journey comes not from anything Marco tells us but from our own reflections on what must have been there but of which he himself says nothing. A major difficulty for Rustichello must have lain in how little action, little adventure Marco reported. But were there not, at least, the voyages to and from China? In fact it is remarkable how silent Marco is on incidents from them or on their specific routes. In every historical atlas one finds a map on which are traced 'The Voyages of the Polos.' The supposed itineraries, alas, are fantasies..."* and *"...Marco, as it happened, found as coadjutor an author who specialized in an epic prose literature which was also marked by a profound absence of any individualism. Yet Marco's very silences about himself are eloquent and, between those silences and what he does say, something of his character, his sympathies, integrity and generosity of mind, so, I believe, appear."*

That is true adoration and blind faith.

In any case, Professor Larner did point out a pandemic problem: scholars frequently refer cavalierly to Marco Polo as a convenient standby to explain all things geographical about the Middle Ages that cannot be explained otherwise. This you can find in any of the books on Age of Discovery maps in print today.

In short, Marco Polo brought back no map of the Orient or anywhere in the world. Our research shows that any meaningful map about the world did not appear in Europe until the 15th century, when Marco Polo was long gone. Besides, any such argument to the contrary is inherently paradoxical. For the antis who resist acknowledging that the Chinese had performed the maritime feats discussed here, how do they rationalize Marco Polo exploring the world and drawing maps for it? Whose ships did Marco Polo ride in, and who provided the crew to navigate it?

For these nay-sayers, Marco Polo might as well have invented the naval technologies, built the ships, and sailed them all by himself, and in such secrecy that not one person in the world was aware of his deeds. His maps simply appeared. (He must have been steering his ships with his left hand while creating the maps with his right hand, but then I am sure that there will be those who would argue that he was indeed steering with his right hand and drawing with his left hand.) It is this type of pseudo-investigation and proselytizing that I strive to bring to light in this work.

Indeed, Marco Polo's travelogue was at first not much more than mere curiosity to European intelligentsia, until two hundred years later when real geographical value could be attached to it. The information of the Ming maritime program was different; that was something tangible, and it came with real maps.

The above analysis leads to but one conclusion; that is, Marco Polo never set foot in China. China has no record of Marco Polo. As an itinerant land-based merchant, Marco Polo most likely traveled from Venice and reached as far as the north shore of the Black Sea where there was an Italians community. There, he somehow acquired historical and geographical information about Mongol Siberia and China, perhaps Al Rashid's very manuscript as the

Persian slant of the writing suggests. After he returned to Europe he then collaborated with a hack writer to create his travelogue from this information, probably because he could not write himself.

The copies of *The Travels of Marco Polo* in print today mostly come from the 1438 Ramusio edition. If you obtain a copy of it in a bookstore, you are likely to find the illustration in Figure 267, the creatures from Shan Hai Jing, which, as discussed, was embraced by Europeans of the 15th century. Remember Hartmann Schedel's "People of the Great Khan" (Figure 116)?

Real History

The Chinese performed an incredible maritime feat by any standard and lost memory of it. Europeans attained information to this accomplishment and went on to adventures of their own, unwittingly leading to their hegemony of the world. For this, they manufactured a history to explain their accomplishments, because they too remembered not how they had come into this fortune. If seemingly everything we know about the Age of Discovery is unreliable—no, false—what is the real history?

Yes, the histories of the Age of Discovery as we know them today, on both the Asian and European sides, pose many problems. They are burdened with open questions, and they all bring with them unreasonable, unexplained, and unconfirmed assertions. Even if they may be forcibly explained away individually, when examined as a whole they prove untenable.

What was the reason behind the stunning Ming naval undertakings? Why was the enterprise entrusted to a eunuch of the inner court? Why did Ming China obliterate its own supreme oceangoing expertise so completely and irreversibly? Above all, where had the Ming fleets really gone?

How did Portugal, an obscure, poor little nation, tucked away in a far corner of 15th century Europe with a population of barely a million, come to be the leading sea and colonial power of the time? Why did the European Age of Discovery follow the Ming Chinese enterprises so closely in time? Where did Christopher Columbus get his inspiration propelling him on to his great achievements? Why did it take the Portuguese almost a hundred years just to round the Cape of Good Hope while Columbus needed only a few months to reach, discover, survey, and settle the Caribbean islands?

There are myriads such difficulties and they all contribute to confounding the main issues. I have provided answers for many of them, but more are awaiting clarification. In this section we shall attempt to further clear up some of these matters.

The Ming Naval Enterprise

Figure 268

Drawing of a Treasure Ship

Figure 269

Comparison between the QE II, a Zheng He Flagship, and Columbus' Santa Maria

What prompted the Ming Emperor Chengzu, the usurper, to launch the unprecedented naval enterprise? Traditionally, three scenarios have been offered up. First, the enterprise was launched for Emperor Chengzu's personal aggrandizement. Second, the fleets were sent forth to support diplomatic missions on a grand scale; to announce to the world (Asia) that Chengzu was a legitimate sovereign. Third, the program was enacted to promote Chinese trade in the region.

For the "self-aggrandizement" proposal, many historians have portrayed Emperor Chengzu as a megalomaniac. Indeed, they say, that the maritime voyages were terminated immediately upon his death attests to the validity of such a hypothesis; that the expeditions were enacted for personal reasons. However, evidence does not support such an assertion. No official document alludes to such a "fact."

Experts and commentators often marvel at the sheer sizes of the Ming "treasure ships (Figure 268)," a name given to the vessels bearing precious merchandise on their missions of state visits.

Figure 270

A 1975 Quanzhou Shipwreck Recovery

Some of the ships were called *xing cha,*[94] or *astro-vessels,* signifying their navigation by celestial angulations, a technique called *qian xing,*[95] or "towing by the stars." The largest of these vessels was well over four hundred feet long, had up to nine masts,[96] a sternpost rudder, and multiple water-sealed hull compartments to ensure a ship's navigability even after minor troubles such as running into reefs or shoals. If lined up, such a ship would come up to the half way mark of the Queen Elizabeth II ocean liner as shown docking in the mockup in Figure 269, which also shows Christopher Columbus' Santa Maria coming up to about a third of the treasure ship's length on the left.

Many mainstream scholars claim that these large ships were precisely the evidence supporting their theory of Emperor Chengzu's predilection for flaunting Ming wealth and power, a goal that such gigantic ships would undoubtedly serve. However, the simple truth is, as it was, that the Chinese had been building large ships for a long time. We must ask ourselves: How did the Ming Chinese learn to build such large ships? Could there truly have been a quantum leap from naval primitivism to the equivalent of space-age technology?

---

[94] 星槎

[95] 牽星

[96] Some sources suggest that these ships could have up to twelve masts.

Chinese Naval History

In 1975 the shipwreck remains of a 13th century Southern Song Dynasty ship (Figure 270) were unearthed in Quanzhou[97] Bay in present day Fujian (Fukien) Province of China, a seaport marveled by Marco Polo (under the Persian name of Zaiton) for its bustling population and thriving commerce. By the coinage found onboard, it was determined that the ship sank in 1273, more than one hundred years before the Ming went to sea and more than two hundred years before Columbus sailed to the West Indies.

The ship had a keel, a V-shaped hull with two layers of planking, and could support up to three masts. It was estimated to be 150 feet long and 33 feet wide. Twelve bulkheads created thirteen compartments, with the fore and aft bulkheads water sealed. By the cargo remains onboard we know the ship was a commercial spice ship that toured the South Seas, reaching all the way to Somalia because of the ambergris found among the payload. The relics are preserved today at the Quanzhou Museum of Overseas Communication History.

At about the same time, another wreck was discovered about the town of Sinan off the southwestern coast of Korea. Dated to 1323, it was determined to be a commercial ship sailing between Korea and the city of Ningbo (just south of Shanghai), China, and possibly Japan. The ship had seven or eight compartments by internal bulwarks and 28 tons of Chinese coins onboard along with other commercial artifacts at the time of discovery. The remains of the wreckage are now housed in the National Maritime Museum in Mokp'o, South Cholla Province, Korea.

Official history records that the Chinese had been trading and sailing the oceans regularly since as early as the 6th century, and shipbuilding technology had reached an advanced state when compared against sea vessels from other cultures of the same period.

---

97 泉州, Marco Polo's Zaitun.

Figure 271
Map of East Asia

In the 11th century, the late (Southern) Song Dynasty experienced a surging forward in naval technology because northern China had been cut off by the Jurchen Jin (forerunners of the later Manchu), Xixia (Tangut), and the Mongols. Forced to retreat southward below the Yangtze River (known in China as the Long River, *Chang Jiang*), the Song had to go overseas to derive much of its revenues. Song's navy consisted of war ships each over one hundred feet long and numbered in the thousands. The Song also introduced gunpowder as weapon at this time. By early 12th century, the Song had perfected the paddle-wheeled warship, and by early 13th century, Chinese warships were armor plated.[98]

This trend of advanced shipbuilding intensified under the Yuan Dynasty, primarily due to its desire to conquer the countries that lay beyond the seas. The Mongols launched massive naval invasions of Japan (Figure 271) and Java (now of Indonesia) in the late 13th century.

In 1274, Kublai Khan, Emperor of Yuan China, sent nine hundred warships, mostly operated by subjugated Koreans, to Japan, but had to abort the mission due to stormy weather.

In 1281 the Mongols tried again with a fleet that numbered as high as forty-four hundred vessels, a staggering number even if it had been exaggerated tenfold, mostly vessels led by the defeated Southern Song Chinese, carrying one hundred thousand troops and traversing an ocean space of over five hundred miles. This time the bulk of the fleet was destroyed by a freak typhoon at the Japanese island of Kyushu, thus saving Japan from virtually certain conquest. From this event on the Japanese attributed their rescue to *Kamikaze*, or "Divine Wind."[99]

Besides these oceanic adventures, the increased use of China's internal waterways for grain shipping since the 6th century (re: the Grand Canal of the Sui Dynasty) also helped boost the advancement in large-scale shipbuilding.

---

[98] Some sources indicate that the Korean navy might have done it first.

[99] A Tokyo University engineering professor, Torao Mozai, discovered the remnants of such a warship in 1981. A follow-up effort in 1991 by archaeologist Kenzo Hiyashida in Takashima's Kozaki Harbor revealed the anchor of one of the invading Mongol warships to be twenty-three feet long, with a projected ship length of two hundred and thirty feet. The ship had watertight bulkheads, a sternpost rudder, and three layers of overlapping planks for hull strength. Incidentally, the archeological evidence also includes ceramic "jars" packed with gunpowder and shrapnel—bombs!

Figure 272

A 36.2 Feet Long Ming Sternpost Rudder Discovered in 1983

Personal traveling by sea also flourished. At least three books are known to have documented three travelogues; one[100] had the author sailing up the Persian Gulf and the Red Sea to enter the Mediterranean Sea, and then traveling west along the North African coast all the way to Morocco and that was year 1225, almost two hundred years before the Portuguese began sailing.

Ironically, the third impetus for shipbuilding came from the Chinese rebels vying for supremacy after the fall of the Mongol Yuan Dynasty in the middle of the 14th century. These rivaling factions fought epic naval battles on the great lakes of China, where Ming `Taizu decisively routed his archrival Chen Youliang.[101]

Therefore, the tradition of grand Chinese shipbuilding could be traced to as early as Song Dynasty. It then flourished under Yuan Mongols and continued on with the early Ming. Official documents show that by early 15th century the Ming had 400 large warships stationed at Nanjing alone. Additional warships were deployed elsewhere in rivers and canals numbering up to 1,350, plus 3,000 merchant ships that could be converted for military use, 400 huge

[100] *Zhu Fan Zhi*, 諸蕃志, by Zhao Ru Kuo, 趙汝适.

[101] 陳友諒.

grain transports, and that was not counting the more than two hundred "treasure ships" that went sailing under Zheng He.

In 1983, a sternpost rudder 36.2 feet long and 1.25 feet in diameter (Figure 272) was uncovered from the mud in the remains of one of the Ming naval shipyards at Nanjing. Such a rudder would have belonged to a ship at least 400 feet long. Historic documents tell us that the Ming treasure ships could be as long as 444 feet. Just to get a perspective on what this means, the Queen Elizabeth II cruise ship is 963 feet long, a tad longer than twice the largest treasure ship (see Figure 5). The Titanic was 882 feet long.

As for the sophistication and complexity of the shipyards required to build such gigantic vessels, we can only surmise about them. Nonetheless, from the size of the ships we can have a good feel for the type of machinery the Ming engineers must have employed. The cranes would have to be able to hoist components of great weights and possess multiple degrees of freedom of movement. The machineries would unquestionably be the most advanced in the world, comparable even to some found in the major seaports of the world today.

Therefore, Emperor Chengzu did not just "suddenly" begin building grandiose vessels out of the blue. The Ming vessels were merely outgrowths of a long national tradition of building large, complex, and sturdy ocean liners. No doubt the Chinese ship design was an amalgamation of winning features from all cultures that sailed the Southern seas, including Japanese, Korean, Javan, Sumatran, Indian, and Arabic inputs that took centuries to perfect[102]. There is no reason to believe otherwise. Nonetheless, it must be conceded that the Ming ships were larger than any of their predecessors, therefore betraying a subtle rationale for their being—they were meant to carry huge loads and to go long distances.

Ming Diplomacy

---

[102] Since the first century AD the Arabs had sailed as merchant traders between the coast of East Africa and the west coast of India.

The alternate theory, also widely favored by scholars, suggests that the voyages were enacted for diplomatic reasons. The idea also does not hold water. This premise is induced by the spectacular nature of the voyages and the incredible descriptions of the fleets' exploits, such as the mythical animals brought back from India, Africa, and elsewhere. Volumes have been written about how the fleets transported kings and rulers of distant lands who came to pay tribute to Emperor Chengzu to and from their home states and how the guests were overwhelmed by the magnificence of imperial Ming China. Yet, when one looks at the historical records, one gets a completely different sense of what in fact transpired.

The History of Ming,[103] the official historical records of the Ming Dynasty, tells us that foreign nations had been paying tribute to Ming since the founding of the dynasty. By the time Zheng He's expeditions came around, the tribute system already had thirty-one years of solid practice behind it. Therefore, the treasure ships could hardly be credited for effecting or even reviving the tribute system.

In 1405, the year Zheng He and his fleets first set sail, most of the East Asian nations[104] and countries of northwest China came to pay tribute. Zheng He had only departed in the summer, and was not to return until the fall of 1406 at the earliest, so the fleets could not have transported these dignitaries; who obviously had other means of travel.

Throughout Chengzu's reign and Zheng He's voyages the schedules of the expeditions and those of the annual tributary visits by foreign heads of state had been consistently out of sync. After Zheng He's fleets began sailing, if they did assume parts of the transportation duties, those duties could not have engaged the entire fleets. Parts of the fleets, especially the ones Zheng He was personally in, had to be performing duties other than promoting diplomatic liaison functions.

---

103 Ming Xi, 明史

104 Including Korea, Sumatra, Bengal, Kuli, Borneo, Japan, East Java, West Java, Champa (North and South Vietnam), Deli, Siam, and the three regions of Ryokyo.

Yet, a third reason given for the Ming voyages asserts that they were designed to promote commerce. On the surface this idea also appears to be reasonable. After all, the ships were nicknamed "treasure ships." However, in reality, with many ships designed for singular functions such as transport ships, supply ships, battle ships, "horse ships," and even "waste (manure) ships[105]" with a combined capacity for carrying over 27,000 troops, one gets the idea that these were well-structured squadrons of specific purposes. The ships were primarily meant for military personnel and equipment delivery, and not for commercial dealings per se.

The traditional Chinese *modus operandi* in promoting international commerce was to bear gifts as a form of goodwill diplomacy; the emphasis was decidedly not on reaping immediate profit. If the Ming fleets carried goods, they were used to assist with such diplomatic ends. Only on a symbolic scale was real commerce conducted, such as procuring rare medicines from the Indians. Not even spices would be meaningfully involved in these voyages. There were other venues for handling those transactions that dated back a millennium and perhaps more. After all, to carry on such a money-losing goodwill concern for almost thirty years (and longer if not aborted) had to be the most asinine government program ever conceived.

The Chinese characteristically gave out more than they took in through these "tribute" operations. For the Chinese to continue the operations for twenty-seven years, cost had to be the least of their concerns.

The above theories are all off the mark for a simple reason. They are all products of the theorizers' philosophical interpretations of history without consultation and reconciliation with historical facts.

105 糞船

Figure 273

Zheng He Sculpture

The True Purposes of the Ming Expeditions

To seek the real reason for the Ming naval projects we must inspect each and every aspect of the saga and examine all pertinent factors, and we shall begin by studying the leader of the maritime program.

Zheng He (at one time Romanized as Cheng Ho, Figure 273)[106] was a eunuch, an inner palace functionary who allegedly[107] had been castrated in order to move about the king's harem with impunity. He was described as a tallish, stocky man with an imposing stature. He had a gird, with a broad, clean square face that projected authority. In literature outside China, he is invariably conferred the title "Admiral," although he was not a seaman. It is true that he held the title Chief of Military [108] during the voyages, which could be interpreted as "Admiral." "Viceroy" would have been more descriptive of his functions.

Zheng He was a Muslim-Chinese, perhaps even an Arab-Chinese, although it was told that he might be a descendant of the King of Bukhara (from today's Uzbekistan), making him of Central Asian heritage. His original name was Muhammad Sayyid Haji (simplified in Chinese as "Sai He Ji"[109]). His father and grandfather were also named Haji, probably because they had made the obligatory pilgrimage, the *Hadj*, to Mecca as Muslims.

His great grandfather was named Bayan,[110] but the family had settled in China for generations, therefore, they had become de facto Chinese. In China the Muslim name Muhammad (or Mahomet[111]) is traditionally Sinicized[112] (and simplified) as *Ma*.[113] Haji became He Ji,

---

106 鄭和. "He" is pronounced more like "her" than "hee." In fact, it should sound like "huh."

107 Some scholars question the fact that Zheng He was indeed castrated. He was supposedly tall and manly, an unlikely trait for a male whose hormone generation had been stifled at a young age.

108 總兵.

109 塞河濟.

110 拜顏.

111 Some sources alleged the named to be Masud. There are many competing claims.

112 Transliterated into Chinese by sound.

or just He. Consequently, Mohammad Sayyid Haji's Chinese name was Ma He. For his distinguished services, Emperor Chengzu conferred on him the Chinese surname of Zheng to commemorate his valor in a battle at a certain Zheng's Village during the usurpation campaign, hence he was known throughout history as Zheng He; Zheng being the surname, as it is Chinese custom to place the surname ahead of the given name.

Zheng He was born in the year 1371 in Yunnan Province in Southwestern China where Mongols and Muslims congregated during the Mongol Yuan Dynasty. When he was born, it was already four years into the new Chinese Ming period. Zheng He was orphaned at the early age of twelve, when his father was killed in battle. Young Zheng He was taken by the Ming troops and was castrated as a captured prisoner. He was assigned to the household of Zhu Di, the Prince of Yan, to be raised as a military trainee. Alongside the Prince of Yan, Zheng He distinguished himself and proved to be a trustworthy and loyal aide and companion. For this, when the Prince of Yan became Emperor Chengzu, he made Zheng He chief eunuch in charge of internal court affairs[114] along with a new name Zheng.

When Zheng He, a non-seaman, was made the naval commander or "Admiral" of the massive Chinese fleets of the "Western Ocean," he was only thirty-four years old. For the next twenty-seven years he served his master in this capacity. For his bravery, the Emperor dubbed him the Sanbao Eunuch. In Chinese, the term made up of the two characters San and Bao means "Thrice Protection."[115] Three times had Zheng He saved his master's life during battle or difficulty. As time went on, his epithet was also written as a homonym that means "Three Treasures,[116]" the way his name is often written in temple plaques erected in his honor throughout Southeast Asia from the Philippines to Thailand.

113 馬

114 司禮監太監, equivalent to the contemporary American Chief of Staff.

115 三保.

116 三寶.

Official Ming history has little to say about Zheng He other than what was given in conjunction with the maritime expeditions. There was no indication that he ever commanded a ship before his epic voyages. He was a soldier who spent the greater part of his early life in the army, accompanying his master on campaigns. That Emperor Chengzu picked a non-sailor for a navy job provides us with the first key to the mystery.

The large Chinese ships, majestic and impressive, and more than enough to impress a country of lesser stature than mighty Ming, were first and foremost built for military personnel transport. Yet the squadron leader of the essentially naval operations was an army man and politico. The military slant to the famous enterprise could not be more obvious, although the point is virtually entirely lost on traditional historians.

The second key to unraveling our mystery can be found in the chronology of the events, the inattentiveness to its details has caused historians to run down wrong paths.

Although the Ming maritime voyages were billed to have begun in 1405, three years after Emperor Chengzu's inauguration, the fact is, they were set in motion the very moment the new emperor ascended the throne in 1402. One simply does not make hundreds of new, large ships appear at once and set sail. The Ming treasure ship construction took years of preparation. Raw material had to be procured from distant districts, some as far away as Indochina and Malaysia. That took time. Skilled artisans from around the country for each aspect of the new vessels had to be rounded up, organized, and relocated to the new shipyards outside Nanjing. Zheng He himself had to be put through an intense, accelerated training regimen to "get his sea legs." For this, he was sent off on voyages to Korea and Annan (Vietnam today) as ambassador for the new emperor.

What all this means is that the enterprise was conceived years before Zheng He set sail. Zheng He launched his first voyage in 1405. Several years before and within Emperor's reign was 1402. So, the preparations had to have been underway the moment Chengzu ascended the throne. The real purpose of the maritime expeditions therefore had to be directly linked to this auspicious moment, not 1405, but 1402. The project was urgent.

At the end of the Ming civil war when the Prince of Yan entered the imperial compounds in Nanjing triumphantly, Emperor Wei Di had already committed suicide—or so it seemed. To elude capture, the young emperor had set the palace ablaze. Upon entering the inner sanctum of the palace, the usurper found the entire royal family reduced to char. The queen, the emperor's concubines, personal attendants, and bodyguards were all burned beyond recognition. Yet the Prince was wary. He sensed instinctively that something was amiss. The appearance of the young emperor's corpse aroused suspicion. For one, it was not of the correct height. The pretender had bolted. The Prince of Yan was sure of it. The old soldier knew that it would be prudent to err on the side of caution. Besides, he knew his father, who was an even slier, older fox than himself, well. The scene had his signature written all over it. The Prince of Yan realized that he had to take care of business, and do it in a decisive way.

The old emperor, Taizu, who left nothing to chance in his entire life, surely would have anticipated what had just transpired. After all, he was the one who had instilled in his heirs the idea of the need to neutralize the *condottieri*;[117] that is, to defuse the powerful princes as a first priority. He knew that the price for the success of his dynasty would be bloodshed, but that was a necessary price to pay when one was engaged in empire-building. A devilishly meticulous man, Taizu would have prepared for just the occasion. Despite the vehement objections from serious scholars that such a scheme would have been preposterous, throughout history the assertion has persisted that Taizu set up an escape strategy for his grandson.

The belief is held that all along Taizu had prepared for his grandson a secret rosewood sachet, inside which were documents that would guarantee the bearer safe passage to anywhere in the

[117] 削藩

Empire disguised as a Buddhist monk. The story went as far as claiming that even the proper camouflage had been provided for in the case of the utmost emergency.

Naturally, there are variations and embellishments to the story. Some claim that the deposed emperor, known in history as the Jianwen Emperor by his reign name, fled to the Chinese province of Yunnan or somewhere in Southwest China. Others had him spotted in Northern Sumatra, while there are those who insist he really became a monk and lived out his life. All these stories are speculative and fantastic in nature, which is why serious scholars reject them, except there is a problem. Official history states that Chengzu, the usurper, believed that the young emperor survived and fled.[118]

It matters not. By the unwritten rules of medieval Chinese politics, and especially Ming politics, the vanquished must not be proffered the slightest leniency lest the survivor return and exact revenge. If Chengzu believed that his nephew had made a run for it, he would have tracked him down relentlessly with the full weight of his office. The quarry must be captured and put to death. Proof of the death of the young emperor must be incontrovertible. The only question was where the fugitive could have gone.

To resolve the crisis conclusively, Chengzu let loose his bloodhounds and sent out trusted agents to scour the country, check each nook, and peek into every crevice until the matter was settled to the total satisfaction of the new emperor. History reported that one minister devoted his entire career traveling the country, evaluating leads, chasing down false reports, until his own mortal end.

The Ming Dynasty is noted for its many mysteries, and one is its very name. Why did the founder of the dynasty, Taizu Zhu Yuanzhang, name it "Ming?" The great Qin, Han, Sui, Tang, and Song dynasties all derived their dynastic titles from the founders' fiefdoms or power bases. Zhu Yuanzhang had not come from a place

---

[118] For a more detailed speculation on the events see *The Hunt for the Dragon, 2nd Edition.*

called "Ming." "Ming" means "brilliance" or "enlightenment." Many historians have tried to explain that Taizu chose the name to commemorate the emancipation of China from the dark ages of Mongol rule. Such a theory calls for some artful pleading, and hardly anyone buys into it, not to mention that the explanation lacks any factual basis of support.

When Taizu was young, he had to make do any way he could to survive. Times were hard. Official history emphasizes that he spent years as a monk in a Buddhist monastery and wandered about the country—for four years, to be exact—when even the holy shrine proved incapable of providing for itself. No doubt the history pertaining to this part of his life had been sanitized under the persuasion of the Emperor himself, who was known to be sensitive to his modest derivation. The truth is, for a long time he stayed alive as a vagrant.

In the waning days of the Mongol Yuan Dynasty, the coastal areas of China were rife with subversive underground groups and secret societies. They often took the form of religious organizations, as they tend to do in China. One of these seditious organizations was the "church" of Manichaeism, a localized fire-worshipping import from Persia via Samarkand or Bukhara. In China it was known as *Monijiao,* or the "Moni Religion."

"Moni," without a doubt, was the Chinese transliteration of "Mani," the founder of Manichaeism. In time the name degenerated to *Mojiao,* or "Demonic Religion." Regardless, its devotees preferred the more respectable name of *Mingjiao,* [119] or the "Enlightened Religion." Ming, 明, a character, or ideogram made up of the characters for the sun, 日, and the moon, 月, signifies "brilliance."

The activities of *Mingjiao* or the Ming Cult in times of upheaval often proved to be more treasonable than spiritual. During the Latter Liang dynasty (907-923) it was involved with the Yimu Rebellion and several other uprisings during the Northern Song Dynasty. The competing revolutionary factions after the fall of the Mongol Yuan

119 明教

Dynasty accounted for much of its membership. As the case with his rivals, Taizu Zhu Yuanzhang was almost certainly at one time a member of the sect (and almost certainly others). Oddly, after the founding of the Ming Dynasty, of all the religious sects in China, Manichaeism was singled out for proscription.[120]

Chengzu knew that strong ties between his father and Manichaeism still existed, as, for revolutionaries, they were never truly severed. After all, Taizu possibly owed much of his success to its support. It would not be beyond imagination, therefore, for Taizu to have the prescience to set up an escape route for the young emperor to go under the protection of his old revolutionary comrades. If this was true—and every self-respecting historian denies that it was—Chengzu would have to pursue all the way to Persia, if necessary, in search of his nephew. Unfortunately, such a proposition was easier fantasized than implemented.

---

[120] Another explanation for the name Ming came from Zhu Yuanzhang's other subversive religious affiliation, the White Lotus Society, which sparked the revolution against the Mongols in 1352. Two of the society's messianic figures were the Big and Little Ming Wang, or Princes of Light. The White Lotus Society resurfaced in late 18th century to incite the overthrow of the Manchu Qing Dynasty, accounting for the design of the Republic Chinese flag. Sometimes the White Lotus Society was equated with Manichaeism. At times it was also confused with the Hindu "Maitrya." Zhu Yuanzhang might have had relationship with all these sects at one time or another.

Tamerlane

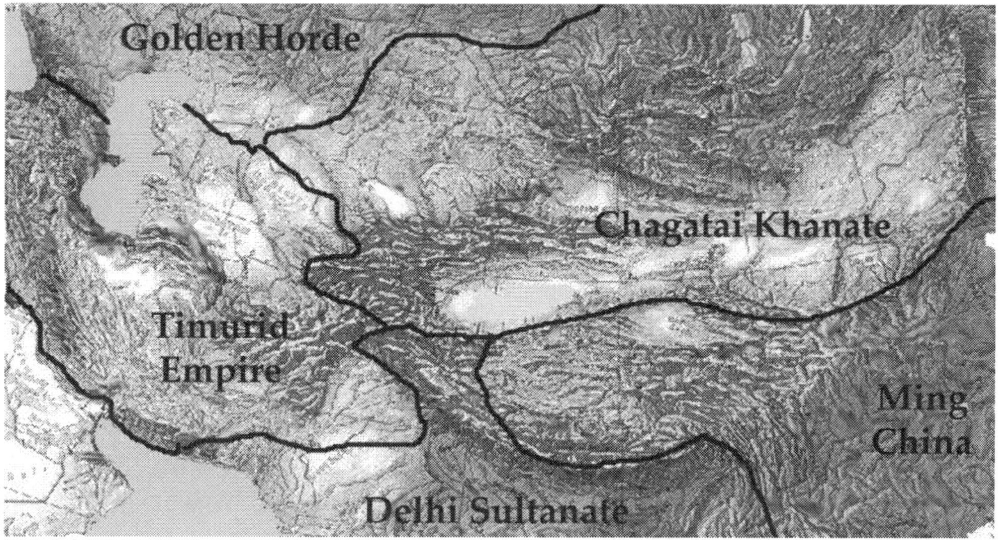

Figure 274

The Timurid Khanate

From the traditional Chinese perspective, when the revolutionaries expelled the Mongols from China and hounded them back to the northern deserts, that officially spelled the end of the Yuan Dynasty. From the Mongol point of view, that was not the case at all. While they might have lost the Chinese territories, the Mongols continued to hold sway over a significant portion of the world.

It is true that the Mongol Empire had always been splintered. Since the very early days of the empire, the western branch of the House of Genghis Khan's eldest son Juchi, the Golden Horde, had never recognized the authority of the House of Kublai Khan, son of Genghis Khan's fourth son, Tului. Chagatai's Khanate also went its separate ways. Nonetheless, for the Mongol Empire as a whole, the loss of China meant only a small contraction in its vast dominion.

By the time of Emperor Chengzu in early 15th century the western Mongols had already consolidated its strength under the legendary

Tamerlane (a degradation of his name in Persian, Timur-i lang, or "Temur the Lame" as he was known to the Europeans).

A Turkic descendant of Genghis Khan through Chagatai on his mother's side of the Barlas tribe, Tamerlane was universally hailed as the second greatest military genius after Genghis Khan himself. He was called "The Lame" because of an arrow wound he allegedly suffered in his youth. Tamerlane built an empire in Central Asia stretching from Delhi to Moscow, from the Tian Shan (Heavenly Mountains) in western China to the Taurus Mountains in present day Turkey, with its capital at Samarkand (Figure 274) in present day Tajikistan. In 1402, he defeated the Ottoman army and nearly changed the course of European history. He consolidated his vast empire almost at exactly the same time Taizu established the new Ming Dynasty. Tamerlane's ultimate goal was to achieve an empire as great as that of Genghis Khan, and restore the past glory of the Mongols. This implies that he planned to conquer China; to show the Chinese who truly was the master of Asia.

So, Tamerlane, at the age of sixty-nine, gathered his army and embarked on a thousand-mile march toward China in 1405, the year Zheng He set sail for the Western Ocean. Unfortunately for Tamerlane, and fortunately for Ming China, Tamerlane died shortly en route at Utrar on the Jaxartes River east of the Aral Sea, some two hundred and fifty miles north of Samarkand, never reaching China proper.

Soon after, his Timurid Empire disintegrated for want of capable successors. Regardless, the Mongol and Turkic tribes continued to dominate in the north and west of China, and posed as real menaces for Ming China for years to come.

Incidentally, one of Tamerlane's descendants, Babur, established the Moghul Dynasty in India. His descendent built the world-famous Taj Mahal Mausoleum in Agra, India. The Moguls (a Turkicized pronunciation of the name "Mongols;" the name gave us the word "mogul") ruled India until the 19th century when the British took over.

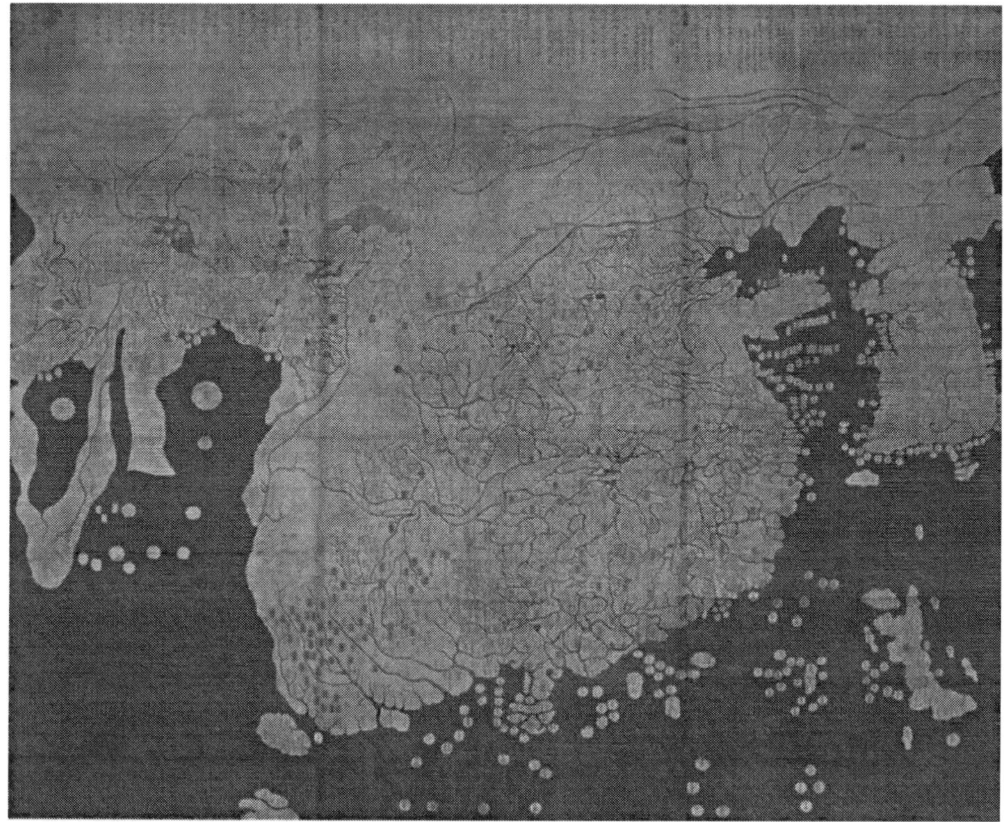

Figure 275

The 1402 Korean Kangnido Map now Preserved at the Ryokyo University

There is no reason at all to think that Emperor Chengzu, his entire career spent on defending China and fighting the Mongols, would be totally unaware of this. News of Tamerlane's invasion could only add to the urgency of having to deal with the problem decisively. If Tamerlane had not marched on Chengzu, who knows, Chengzu might have marched on Tamerlane.

In fact, during Chengzu's reign, he led armies and made incursions into Siberia five times intending to solve the Mongol problem once and for all. As a seasoned military strategist, no doubt he harbored no illusion about the difficulty and enormity of the task. He respected the worthiness of the Mongols as an opponent, and enacted special measures to ensure his military success.

A Military Objective

After almost a hundred years of Mongol rule, when large numbers of Central Asians, Arabs, and other foreign nationals visited and took up residence in China, the Chinese had gathered a good amount of information about the lands to their west. Figure 275 shows a late 14th century Chinese map of Southeast Asia with the Arabian Peninsula and the African Continent visibly represented on the left-hand side of the projection map.

Emperor Chengzu most certainly knew that the Timurid Khanate could be breached from the southwest, and troops might be dispatched there by sea. To neutralize the Mongol threat, he might have to enact a two-pronged strategy. Since he had decided that he was to track down his nephew whom he ousted, a naval operation to Central Asia would serve both purposes. These motives would explain why he ordered the creation of a mighty navy immediately upon the inauguration of his reign. This is all, of course, merely speculation. Let us analyze the events to see if the possibility is there.

Normally one would expect Emperor Chengzu to have plenty of competent naval officers from which to choose a capable leader to head up such a maritime enterprise. However, an administrator that could be trusted completely was required to handle the politically sensitive matter of tracking down an ex-emperor. Also, he himself needed to focus on land-based operations in the north without being encumbered by decision-making that required his participation in the naval project.

None better suited this position than his very reliable chief of staff—Zheng He, who not only had proven his resourcefulness on the battlefields and the treachery of the inner imperial court, but also was familiar with native cultures of the lands where the expedition would ultimately take him. Keep in mind that Zheng He was a Muslim of Central Asian or Arab descent. This explains why a non-naval man was selected to run a naval business for almost thirty years with absolute authority because ultimately it was as much a political business as a purely military business.

No scholar of Ming history had been able to explain away the reasons for the grand Ming maritime spectacle without the inclusion of a military objective. How else can one justify deploying almost thirty thousand troops accompanying two hundred plus vessels for almost thirty years? Promotion of commerce and spreading of Ming China culture did not require the involvement of thirty thousand troops.

Then, on the other hand, there is no record of the troops being engaged in any kind of formal battle, other than the few skirmishes with local pirates and native chieftains. That calls for explanation.

In the first year of Chengzu's reign, Jiao Zhi (Gao Zhi in southern Chinese dialects; that is Marco Polo's Gaugiguo, called Annan later, and Vietnam today) paid tribute to China—and then the tribute stopped. That is because Gao Zhi had revolted, and spent the next ten years fighting the Ming. Zheng He's ships sailed right by that country every time they went to sea,[121] yet not once did they stop to lend a hand to the battling Ming army. What sort of troops were these? Clearly, these were troops on a different mission with a completely different focus.

The logical conclusion for the Ming maritime voyages is that they were launched for some very special political and military objectives. The presence of *Jin Yi Wei* or *guards in embroidered uniforms*[122] onboard-ship virtually certified the missions as having top-secret implications, in this case, searching for the fugitive ex-emperor. The *guards in embroidered uniforms* were the Ming equivalent of our Federal agents, or better yet, secret police, or the European Communist Block's securitaté, or the Nazi's Gestapo. They would not have been onboard had the missions been simple commercial outings.

Modern historians, who now concede that the trips were at least also employed to track down the deposed monarch, could have saved a lot of trouble had they bothered to consult with the official

---

[121] Zheng He always went west; never east (such as to Japan or the Philippines). Has anyone explained why?

[122] 錦衣衛, Ming Dynasty's imperial secret police.

history. In Zheng He's biography in the *History of Ming* it is succinctly stated: *The purposes of the voyages were to locate the deposed emperor and to spread the magnificence of Ming.*

What about "*and to spread the magnificence of Ming*?" When a nation spreads its magnificence, it makes friends. The tributary gifts carried by the treasure ships were a necessary expenditure in setting up bases en route to the object destination. The twenty-seven thousand troops would have been insufficient for a full-scale war, but were just right for helping set up liaison with minor chieftains in the South Seas, and for blazing new trails for an ultimate assault directly into the "belly" of the enemy, the Timurid Empire in Central Asia. The Ming had to ensure safe passage to the West if it were to focus on its enemy there.

Is this also mere speculation, or is there evidence supporting such a hypothesis?

It was customary for the Ming to put up foreign tribute emissaries in guest houses in the capital for months on end, sometimes up to a year, before granting them audience with the imperial court. When the envoys of the Timurid Khanate came in the early 15th century, it was recorded that Emperor Chengzu received them immediately.[123] This event speaks of the importance Emperor placed on this enemy/friend (?) from China's west.

Did this diplomatic exchange have anything to do with the deposed nephew/emperor? Rumors had the ex-emperor fleeing to the southwest of China, and possibly overseas to Sumatra, but we have no concrete evidence suggesting that he might have reached the Timurid Khanate. We do not know if the Timurid ambassadors had come to discuss warfare or peace terms, but we know the Chinese emperor placed great significance in their visit.

During the third voyage, Zheng He's troops ran into a conflict between a local Malacca chieftain and an intruder Prince named Parameswara, reportedly originally from the neighboring state of Palembang at the southern end of Sumatra. Zheng He chose to

---

[123] Morris Rossabi.

support the intruder against the local chief. The implication of the affair is not difficult to discern. Zheng He was setting up friendly bases along the route much like what the American Militaries do around the world today, and he had no compunction in siding with the illegitimate if that proved to be the more expedient option, in this case balancing the power between Siam, Java, and Sumatra.

Let us once more return to the records of the voyages as documented in the *History of Ming*. Several observations can be made immediately upon studying the itinerary records of the voyages. The very first thing that strikes the reader is that there is actually very little recorded about the voyages per se. It is as if the court historians were reluctant or perhaps loathe delving into the events. There was no discussion of why the voyages were initiated (except for the sentence in Zheng He's biography cited above), nor any detail pertaining to their operations. The only thing that comes close to revealing the nature of the expeditions is Zheng He's being described as serving "diplomatic[124]" functions.

The second thing that stands out immediately is that, as pointed out above, the schedules demonstrably did not correspond with the annual rituals of tribute visitations. The fleets might have been used in the transport of foreign dignitaries on occasions, but it is unmistakable that the ships had sailed according to their own agenda.

Third, although significant numbers of troops were onboard fleets, there was no record of their having engaged in major battles. Certainly, there had been times when force had to be used to resolve local conflicts and engage in king-making activities as noted, the sheer strength of the forces (some 27,000 troops) belied their true motives. There can be no question that they were prepared for some sort of ultimate military action.

Official Destination

---

124 出使

When one scrutinizes the sequence of the voyages, a pattern emerges. The first two trips, covering generally the Asian South Seas areas, were retreads of old stomping grounds; places that the Chinese had already visited regularly for the previous centuries. There was no activity of exploration or trailblazing to speak of. In quick successions the fleets reached all the major ports of call, including Champa, Java, Sumatra, Malaysia, and others. During these two initial voyages the path was cleared, so to speak, with pirates captured and eradicated and friendly allies liaised and bases established. Then the sails were reoriented directly toward the western Indian and Southern Arabian seaboards.

In Quanzhou from which Zheng He's fleets set sail there is a stone stela erected in 1417, [125] the fifteenth year of Chengzu's reign, commemorating Zheng He's historic voyages Figure 276). In part the inscription reads:

> *Viceroy Chief of Military (Admiral) Eunuch Zheng He's voyages to Hormuz in the Western Ocean, …*

The Chinese characters *Hu Lu Mo Si* [126] represent the transliteration—phonetic simulation—of the name "Hormuz," the island seaport on the Persian Gulf. That Hormuz was singled out for citation as a unique destination in Zheng He's historic voyages speaks volumes about the real reason for the maritime expeditions.

---

[125] Because Emperor Chengzu never recognized his nephew the ex-Emperor of the Jianwen Period, his reign could have officially be counted from 1398 instead of 1402. In that case, the stela was erected in 1413 instead of 1417.

[126] 忽魯謨厮

欽差總兵太監鄭和前往
西洋忽魯[illegible]厮等国公
幹永樂十五年五月十
六日於此行香望靈

Figure 276

A 1417 Quanzhou Stone Stela Erected in Commemoration of Zheng He's Historic Voyages

According to Ma Huan, the chronicler of the third voyage, task forces were sent off onshore in the Middle East to visit places such as Medina and Mecca, which the Chinese called, honoring the tradition of the Arabic-speaking Muslims, *Tian Fang*,[127] or *Heavenly Realm* (also, the *Kaaba*, the *Heavenly Cube)*; in other words, "Holy Land" or "Paradise," or "Holy Cube."

We also know that the Ming fleets sailed as far west as the east coast of Africa, visiting places such as Mozambique and Malindi. All these locations were much farther away from China than Hormuz. Had the stela been erected to extol Ming's naval prowess, there would have been no dearth of distant candidates to choose from. That Hormuz was specifically chosen manifestly indicates that it was the main or official destination of the voyages after all.

There can be no doubt that the Middle East, specifically the area about eastern Arabian Peninsula, was the target of this entire undertaking. One needs only look at the high officials gathered for the assignment—all Arabic speakers and

[127] 天方. It must be noted that in recent years some investigators have tried to argue for a different identity of Tian Fang other than Mecca or Medina. Some even attempted to place it in Tunisia and Central America. These hypotheses have not gained acceptance on grounds of slim of evidentiary support.

Muslims.[128] They did not tag along to help haggle over the prices of spices.

The secretive, political, and military nature of the expeditions thus reveals the true purposes of the efforts. Indeed, the highly sensitive nature is borne out by the historical records in which Zheng He's exploits were accorded merely passing mention.[129] The annals accorded them no pomp and no circumstance.[130] The remarkable

---

[128] Wang Jing Hong, a eunuch, second in command. Hasan, Imam of the Sian Mosque (note that he went on the fourth trip, not the first three), Pu Ri He, a Muslim scion of a well-known Quanzhou seafaring family (he went on the fifth voyage).

[129] The following is a typical passage from the History of Ming of the events of 1405, the year Zheng He's fleets first set sail:

> ...So-and-so date: Field tax exempted for Duen Tian, Yong Ping, Bao Ding for two years. So-and-so date: Transportation Secretary executed for crime of vilification. So-and-so date: Prince Zao took up residence post at Beijing. So-and-so date: Field tax exempted for the Provinces of Hu and Guang. June of summer: Middle Officer (中官) Zheng He led fleet as emissary to countries of the Western Ocean. So-and-so date: etc...

Another one, for year 1419, the seventeenth year of Emperor Chengzu's reign, reads:

> ...June: Field taxes for Suen Tian suspended due to flood disaster. Liu Gang exterminated Japanese raiders in Wang Hai Bay. Count of Jiang Guang title bestowed. July of fall: Zheng He returned....

[130] Even the giraffes from Africa brought back by the third venture of the Treasure Ships which have virtually become the mascots of the Zheng He voyages in modern literature and appear obligatorily in any book on the expeditions, garnered but a terse allusion among the events of 1414, the twelfth year of Chengzu's reign:

Bengali presented [to the court] a giraffe.

maritime voyages of Zheng He rated but glancing remarks in official records.

Yet there is indirect evidence that can help break this official silence.

On every outing Zheng He went to Mecca. Zheng He was a Muslim, so pundits concluded that he was making Hadj. Of course, as a Muslim he would pay respect to the holy place of Islam. However, did Emperor Chengzu spend all that money, with over 200 ships and almost 30,000 troops just to allow Zheng He to make Hadj? Without any doubt there was official business to be conducted.

The Arabic-speaking Muslim crew, the focus on Hormuz, the visits to Mecca, and the venture into the Atlantic Ocean point to an escape route for the ex-emperor. For a speculation on the ex-emperor's escape, possibly to Europe, see *The Hunt for the Dragon, 2nd Edition.*

In any case, Zheng He's last outing under the auspices of Emperor Chengzu ended in 1422. Emperor Chengzu died in 1424. After that, Zheng He was reassigned to inner court duties. Then in 1430, for reason or reasons unknown, regardless of what the pundits say, Zheng He was summoned to go to sea one more time. Again, the begging question is, why must the Ming fleet be commanded by Zheng He? Were there no other capable seamen in China? Clearly he was bade to handle something only he could. He knew something others did not know. Unfortunately, we do not know what it was, so we can at best speculate on it. Nevertheless, he died in 1433 while leading this last mission.

It is documented that while at Mecca Zheng He took ill, and he was rushed back, but before his ship reached India he died, and "per Muslim tradition" he was buried at sea because he was far from land. So, we do not know precisely what

---

In contrast, when ten years earlier the Duke of Zhou presented a zou yu, a mythical horse that portended good fortune, the Emperor gave a lengthy speech expressing his humility, that he should redouble his diligence in his devotion to the affairs of state before he dared accept such good omen.

happened. That was 1433. There is no Zheng He's body in his Chinese tomb.

Then we have the episode of a Chinese delegation visiting the Pope in 1432 where they met Toscanelli and imparted maritime technologies to the Europeans. (See above.)

Did Zheng He die or did he go on his journey and never came home?

End of Grandeur

Why were these larger-than-life events relegated to such pedestrian status in official history? Probably it was in the interest of the later administration to downplay them. The official line had the expeditions portrayed as the personal madness of one megalomaniac pretender, therefore were not to be exalted. The Ming historians had no intention to play up these early dynastic follies on center stage. In fact, they probably hoped that time would erode them from people's consciousness. That, also, is the reason why the expeditions were terminated immediately upon the death of Emperor Chengzu, not for cost as is commonly proffered as an explanation.[131] Certainly the maritime expeditions cost money; but then the Ming Chinese undertook many money-costing projects, many of which were much more extravagant than the maritime voyages. Only the naval program was summarily shut down.[132]

---

131 Dr. Deng Gang, Kent Deng, 鄧鋼, Lecturer in Economic History at the London School of Economics and Political Science, and author of *Chinese Maritime Activities and Socioeconomic Development, C. 2100-1900 A.D.* (Greenwood, 1997) argued that 30,000 self-sustaining troops (they were at sea and incurred minimal domestic support) equated to only 3% of the Ming standing army at the time, and the cost of constructing the Ming fleets was not as expensive as generally believed because the Ming ships once built could last up to 30 years. Zheng He's expeditions lasted 27 years. The real ship building costs involved merely maintenance and replenishment.

132 While Zheng He was at sea, Chengzu was erecting imposing, splendid new complexes for the Wu Dang Shan Daoist monastery, where legend claimed the Tai Chi School of Chinese kungfu had originated. This project went on for more than ten years, involving over 300,000 builders, artisans, and workers. In all 8 central pavilions, 2 temples, 36 nunneries, 72 rock shrines, 39 bridges), and 12 gazebos were constructed. In particular, the main hall Tai He Gong Jin Dian, located in the central peak, was entirely made with gold-plated copper. The amount invested could not begin to be accounted for.

Under Chengzu's reign Ming China launched annual military incursions from Beijing into the northern deserts against the Mongols. As mentioned, Chengzu

The Confucian ministers had nursed a grudge against the eunuchs for almost thirty years. Taizu, understanding history and the harms eunuchs had wreaked in administrations past, had specifically banned their involvement in politics. Their proper place was the inner courts where they were to assist with the ladies. With Chengzu, who had benefited greatly from the loyalty of the eunuchs, the policy was reversed. The Confucian officials now felt that the eunuchs were gaining favor over them. Anger eventually evolved into fury and hatred. Now that the usurper had died, the hour for their revenge had arrived. The officials persuaded the new emperor to put things right, and the voyages, identified with the ex-Emperor personally, were stopped (and not because the Ming decided to look inward and willfully cut themselves off from the rest of the world as explained by scholars).

To preclude such "unnecessarily wasteful, pompous overseas adventures" from ever being repeated, the new emperor grounded the treasure ships and enacted policy to forbid such ships from being built again. Zheng He was returned to his old duties of overseeing court civil projects, building storage houses and pagodas, and all the materials related to the voyages were confiscated, destroyed, or placed under guard. In 1477, when another eunuch again raised his voice about overseas expeditions, the Minister of Defense *allegedly*

---

personally led five such campaigns at great costs to the nation. These extensive and intensive military campaigns drained the imperial coffer. In 1421, the 19th year of Chengzu's reign, Chengzu once again decided to push north. This time his most loyal and devoted ministers stood up and protested. The treasury was near empty, but Chengzu would have none of it. In an intense rage he had his Finance Secretary Xia Yuanzi and Justice Secretary Wu Zhong, jailed, and as a consequence his Defense Secretary Fang Bin, committed suicide. Xia Yuanzi was not released until the next administration.

Some twenty years later in 1449 the new Ming emperor was captured outside Beijing by Mongol forces in just such a campaign. When finally the emperor was released, the confrontation between the ex-emperor and the currently installed half brother perilously destabilized China until 1457. For this, Ming turned to rebuilding and extending the Great Wall at another heavy burden to the straining economy. Yes, the famous Great Wall of China was mostly built by the Ming.

promptly gathered all the remaining documents and materials pertaining to the legendary voyages and burned them.

In this way, the Chinese records of these fabulous expeditions were forever lost. The pursuit of a legitimate emperor by a usurper courted no favor with the orthodox Ming officials.

Eventually, the magnificence of the Ming voyages faded away, but not the titanic struggles between the Confucian ministers and the court eunuchs, which became renowned throughout Ming history.

Lingering Questions

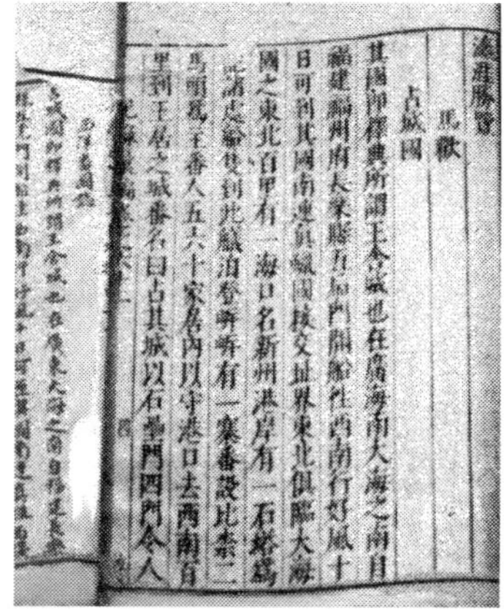

Figure 277

The *Ying Ya Sheng Lan* by Ma Huan

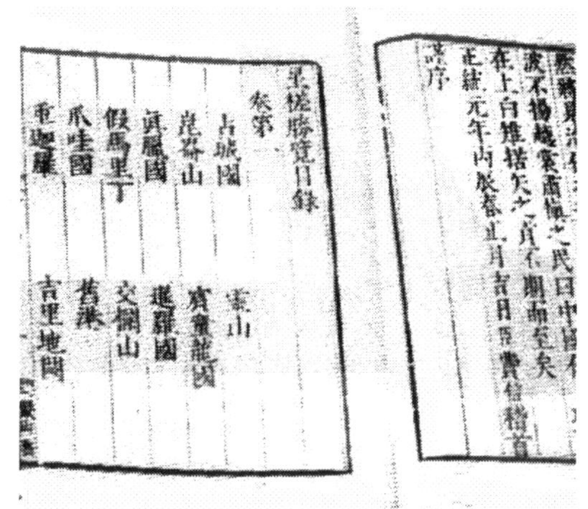

Figure 278

Fei Xin's Travels of the Astro-vessels

Figure 279

Countries of the Western Ocean by Gong Zhen

Figure 280

The Opening Page of *Wu Bei Zhi*

The sudden termination of the Ming voyages not only failed to solve the mystery behind them, it deepened it. Should the "missions," regardless of what they might have been, have gone on, where exactly would the ships have gone? Indeed, where in fact did the ships go? For the possible answer to this question, we need to turn to sources other than the official historical records, which have so far proven parsimonious.

For the modern historian, the details of Zheng He's voyages are customarily extracted from three basic sources. First we have the journals of the translators/scribes of Zheng He's journeys, chief of which is Ma Huan, who accompanied Zheng He on his third (or fourth), sixth, and seventh trip to Hormuz.

Ma Huan was an Arabic-Chinese—a Muslim. His original name was Muhammad Hasan. "Ma," as we know, is the Chinese transliteration for "Muhammad." "Hasan" was simplified to "Huan." Ma Huan went on the trips primarily because he knew Arabic. Upon returning to China, he compiled his experiences into the now famous *Ying Ya Sheng Lan*[133] (Figure 277), "Vistas of Oceans and Cliffs," or simply, "Scenes of Exotic Places." (*Ying* is the same as *Yang*, both words meaning "ocean.")

Another Arabic-fluent Muslim chronicler, Fei Xin, [134] who accompanied Zheng He on his voyages four times, wrote "Travels of the Astro-vessels [135] " (Figure 278). "Countries of the Western Ocean[136]" (Figure 279) by Gong Zhen[137] is also often used as a reference on specific locales. The material contained in these three primary records then found their way into other historical literature, including romance novels and legends.

Besides the travelogues, part of Zheng He's sea charts (Figure 281 showing Malindi of Africa at the lower right corner) is also preserved as a part of the Defense Manual *Wu Bei Zhi* (Figure 280), prepared by Mao Yuanyi of the Ming Dynasty.

---

133 瀛涯勝覽, assisted by another Muslim, Guo Chong Li, 郭崇禮.

134 費信

135 星槎勝覽

136 西洋番國誌

137 鞏珍

Figure 281

A Panel from Zheng He's Sea Chart

Figure 282

The 1290 Carte Pisane

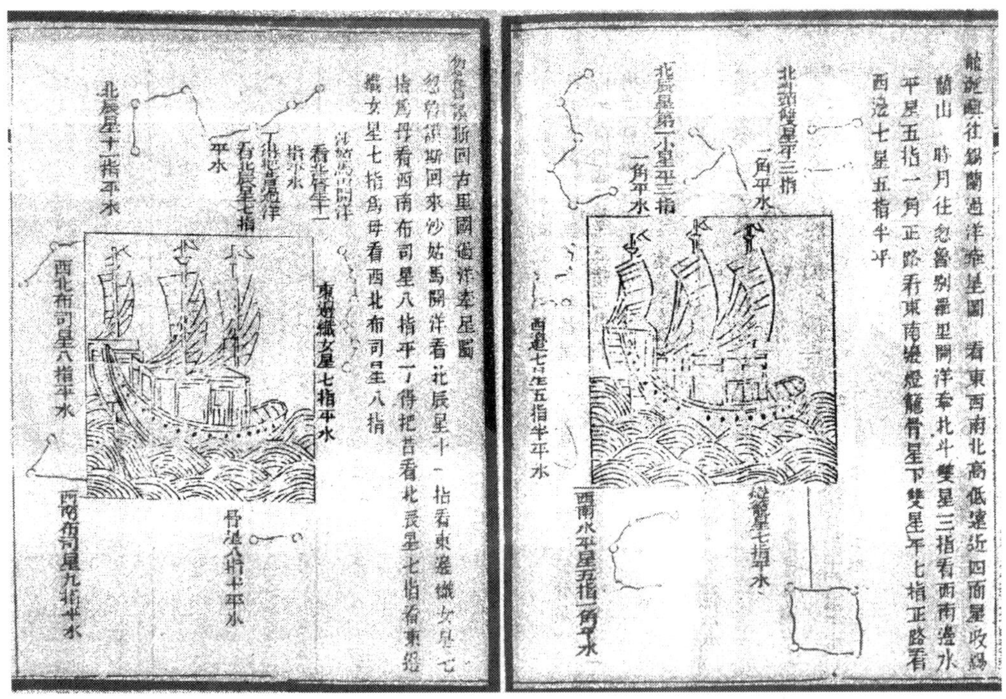

Figure 283

Star Charts from the *Wu Bei Zhi*

The book contains such defense topics as weaponry, soldiering, troop formation, descriptions of enemy positions, celestial charts, and so on. This also hints at the close relationship between Zheng He's voyages and military actions. Obviously, the government considered Zheng He's sea charts military worthy and sensitive.

The sea charts are not so much maps as they are illustrated sets of instructions for navigation. They employ no scaling and provide no fixed orientation—unlike a formal map, there were no set orientations of north or south.

A sea chart documents geographical information such as coastal features and names of settlements, much like an Italian *portolan* chart, such as the 1290 Carte (Figure 282) in principle a century later.

The sea chart is designed to guide the navigator by furnishing him with verbal sailing instructions. For example, sailing distance is provided in the form of speed multiplied by elapsed time, which is expressed in the unit of *geng*;[138] that is, a "watch." A day would have twelve watches, thus making a geng, one watch, the equivalent of two hours. (Even today the Chinese call "midnight" the third "*geng*.") This method of navigation is equivalent to the European sailing method of *dead reckoning*.

Sailing by star-positioning was also used. In Figure 283, the chart on the right describes using stars to navigate from "Dragon Saliva Island" to Sri Lanka. The chart on the left documents navigational instructions to sail from Hormuz to Calicut. Note the star diagrams embedded in the charts.

Navigation by the technique of "star towing" obviously assumes that the navigator is versed in astronomy, and indeed this was the case.[139]

This should not be a surprise to anyone, except perhaps for the few commentators who insist that the Chinese had no such capabilities. To invade Java (Figure 286) on a grand scale the Chinese had to cross the Equator.

---

[138] 更.

[139] It may be a surprise to many, but China had a long record of advanced astronomical science.

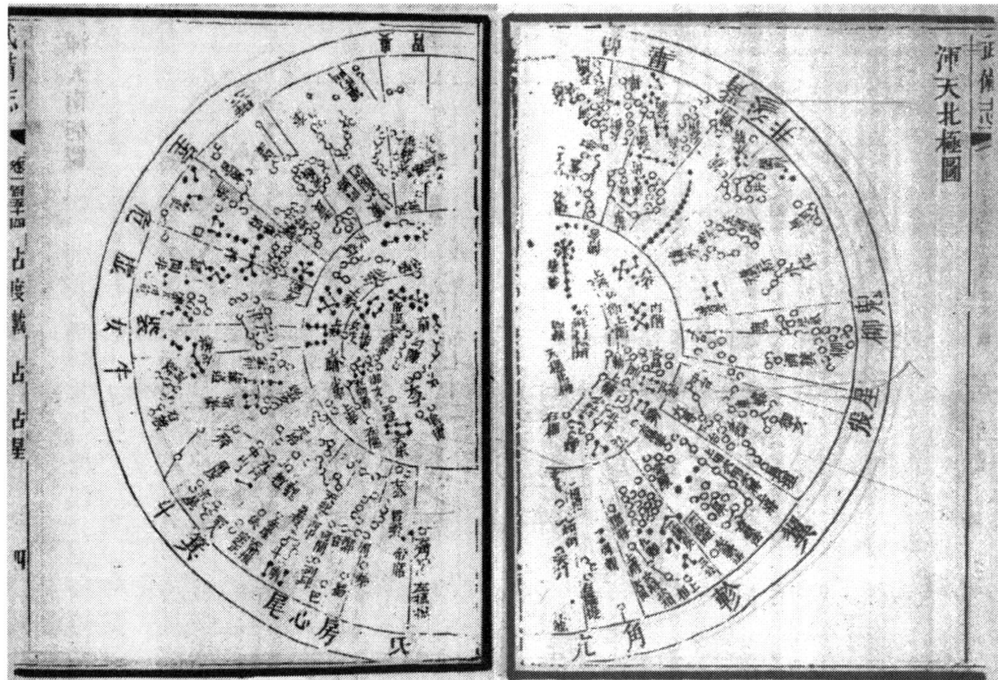

Figure 284

Constellations of the Northern Sky from *Wu Bei Zhi*

Wu Bei Zhi also contains essential star charts to be studied and referenced by navigators. Figure 284 and Figure 285 show the constellations of the northern and southern skies respectively. That, of course, directly implies that the Chinese had already crossed the Equator (Figure 286), so many times that they actually had star charts of the Southern Hemisphere. Figure 288 shows the details of the star clusters around the northern constellation.

Because directional changes were expressed verbally, no set orientation needed to be represented pictorially. Indeed, the drawing did not even have to be to scale. This allowed the navigator to conveniently record everything on a continuous paper scroll (Figure 287). Hence, in concept, the Ming sea chart is similar to the 1st century Roman Peutingeriana Table (Figure 289) that documented road systems with travel instructions without relying on proper scaling.

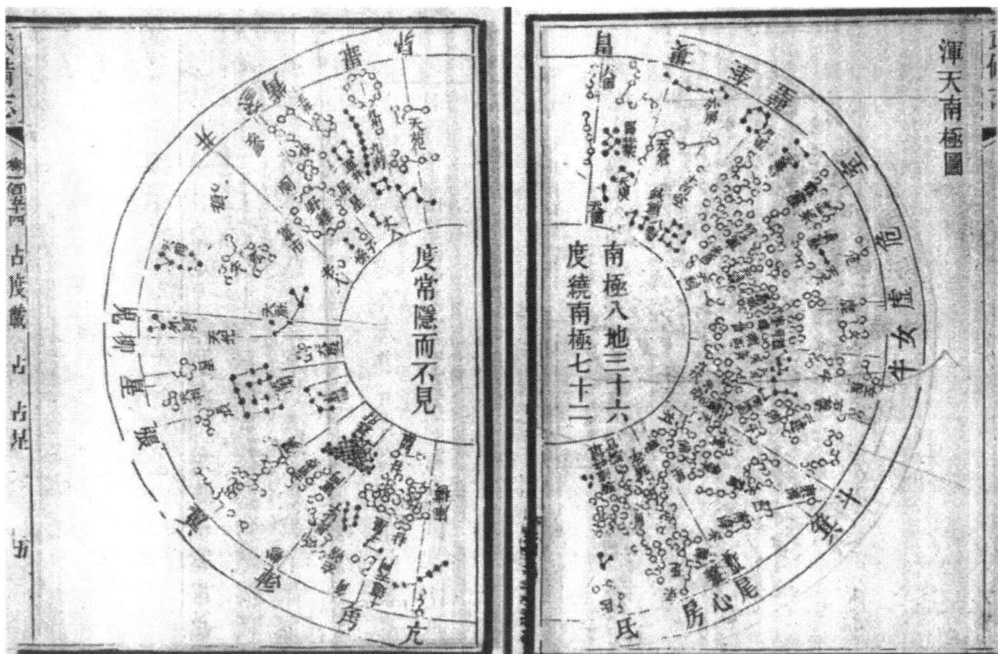

Figure 285

Constellations of the Southern Sky from *Wu Bei Zhi*

This way, on a straight, linear run of paper, one could effectively describe the route from Sumatra to Mogadishu, as shown in Figure 290. Notation 1 on the right of the chart marks the location of Sumatra. Point 2 at the lower-left is Mogadishu, with the East African coast lying north to south horizontally at the bottom. Point 3 identifies a run of text providing sailing instructions. In an equivalent European style chart, it would look like that in Figure 291.

The Chinese therefore had a sailing system. It was different from the one used by Europeans today, but it worked. The Venetian scholar Gabriele Foccardi, writing about these Chinese voyages of six hundred years ago said it best:

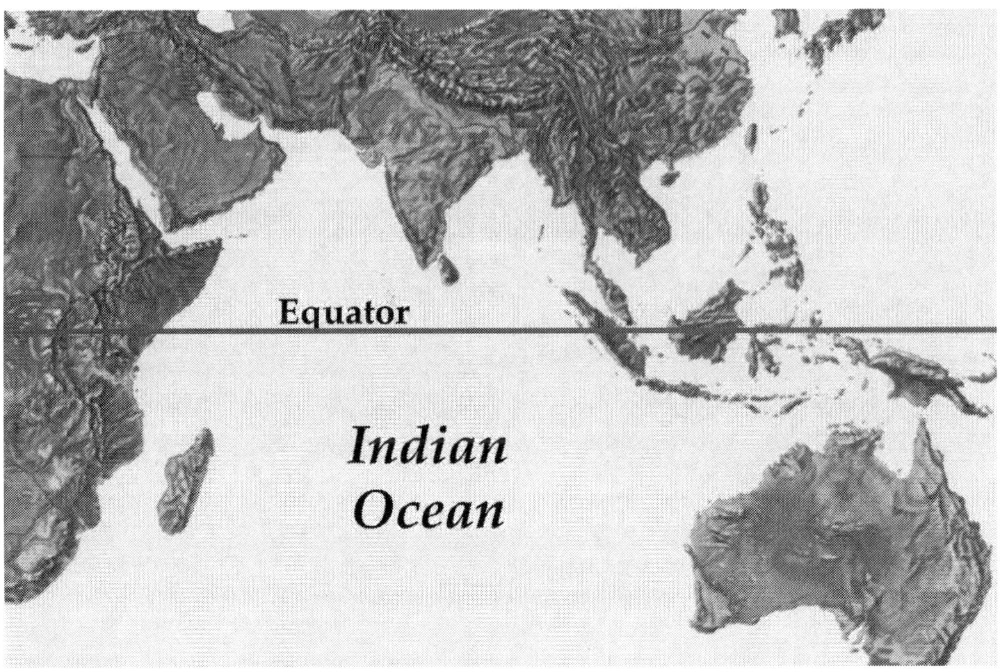

Figure 286

Where Might the Chinese Have Crossed the Equator?

Figure 287

Section from Zheng He's Sea Chart

"What difference does it make that they might not have the exact method of using longitudes and latitudes? The Chinese surely were able to travel thousands of miles and arrive at precisely the location they wanted to go."[140]

[140] The Europeans did not solve the problem of longitude until the eighteenth century.

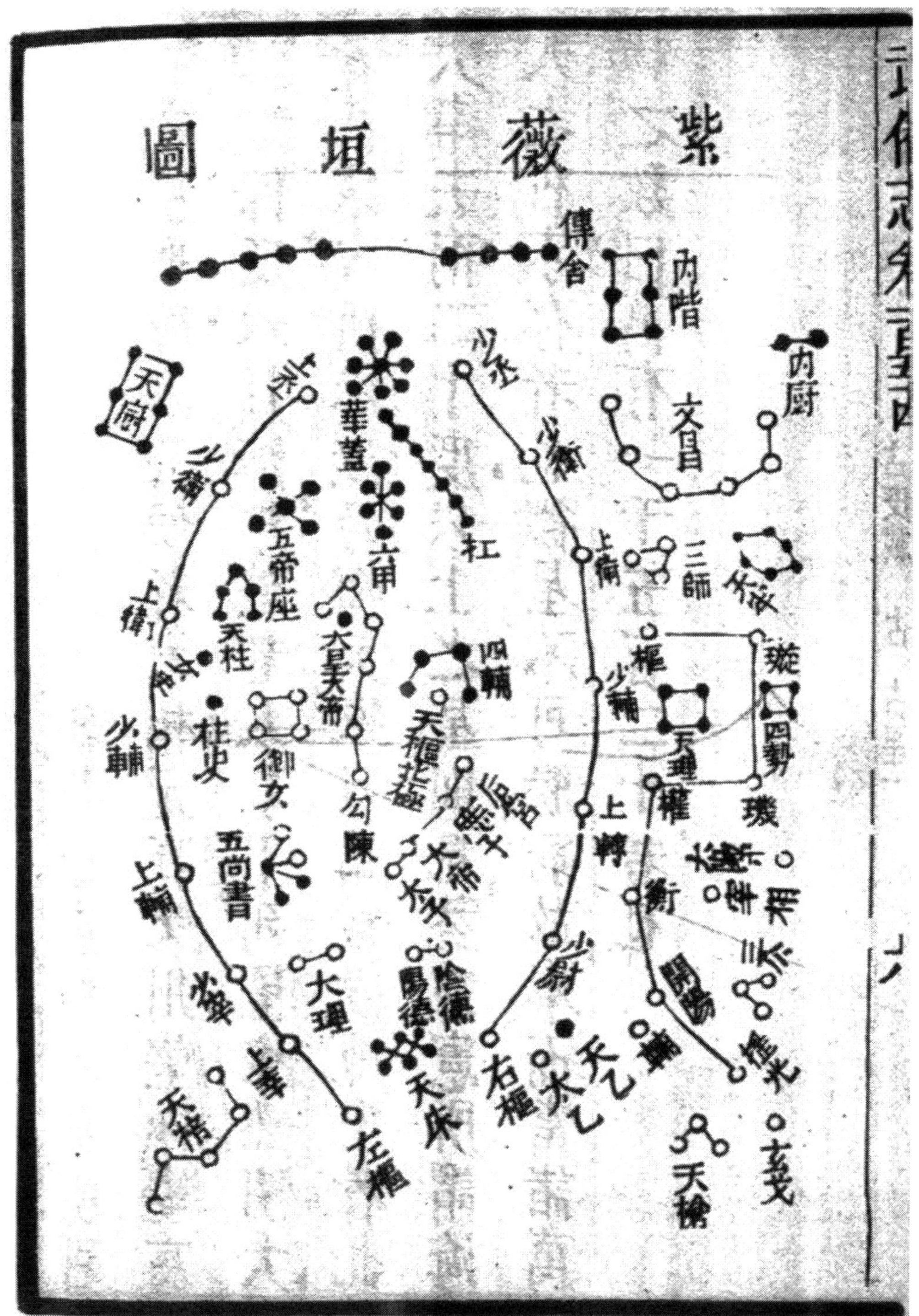

Figure 288

Details of Star Clusters around the Northern Constellation

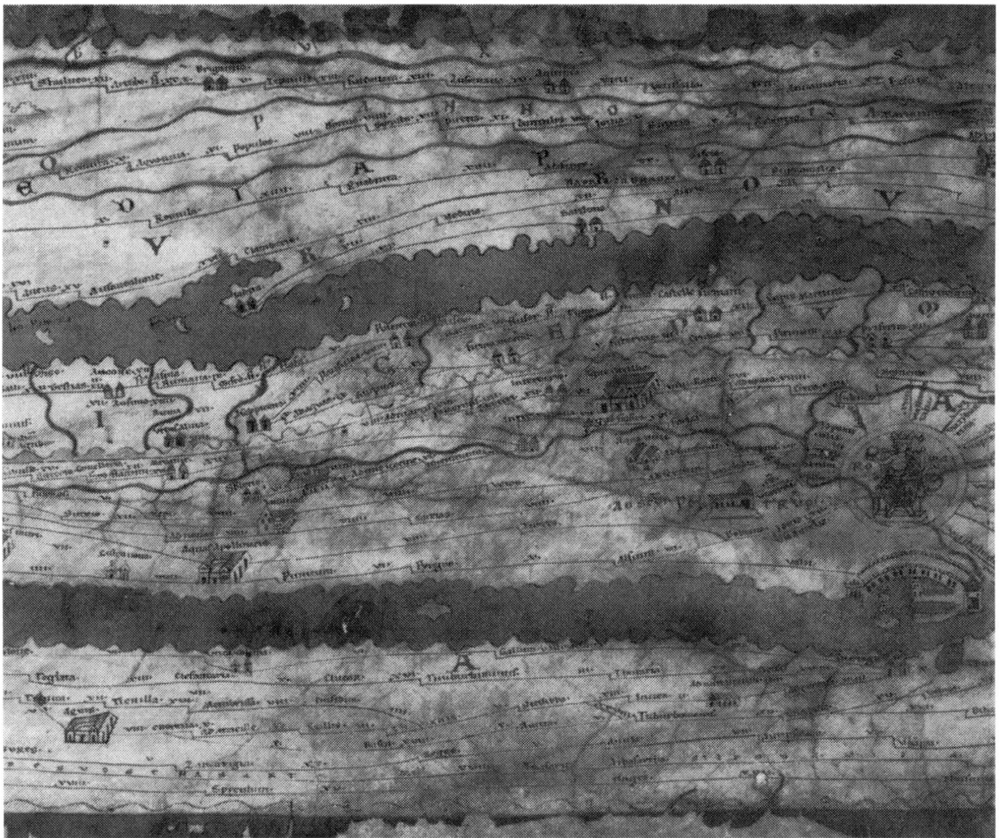

Figure 289

1st Century Roman Peutingeriana Table

From such diverse sources, and other existing artifacts (such as the stela erected by Chengzu to commemorate them), researchers were able to reconstruct Zheng He's voyages. They have been widely documented; therefore, details will be spared here.

In brief, if you were to chart the Zheng He voyages, you would end up with roughly three distinct phases. The first two voyages focused on the South Sea areas where the Chinese had had a long history of extensive contacts. The routes are represented roughly in Figure 292. The primary purposes of these "practice runs" were to test out and clear the paths, and to establish supply bases to support future incursions west.

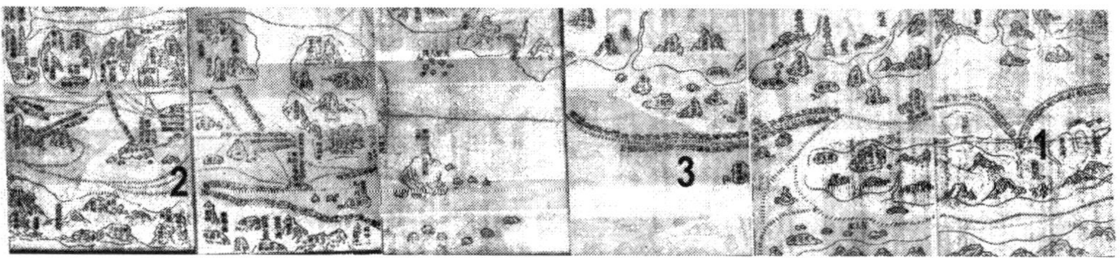

Figure 290

The Route from Sumatra to Mogadishu in Zheng He's Sea Chart

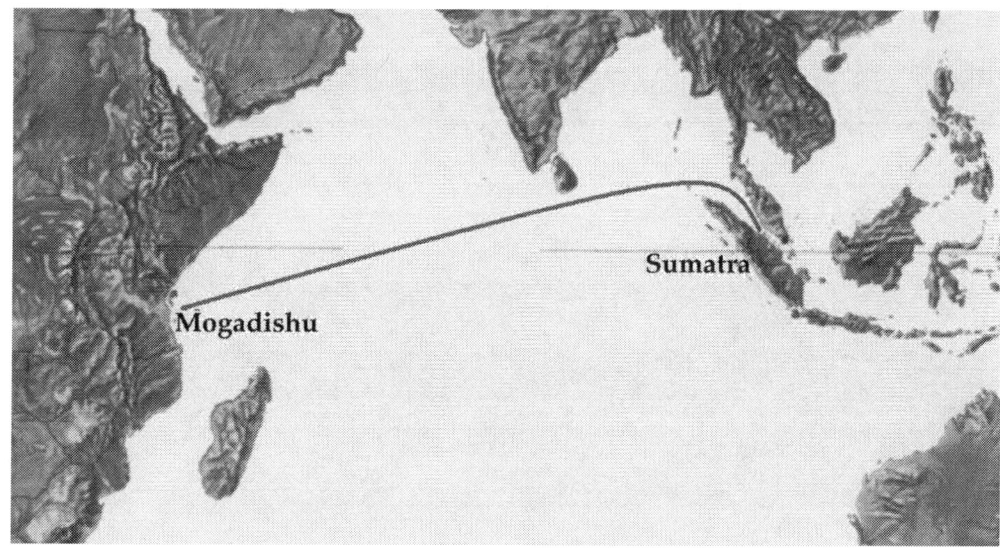

Figure 291

Modern Day Rendition of the Route from Sumatra to Mogadishu

During these trips, government officials of the fleets also attempted to be in contact with all known South Sea settlements for information on the whereabouts of the ex-emperor.

The second phase, I conclude, based on the pattern that became apparent, was the real, intended mission; what the whole enterprise was geared up to be in the first place. The destination was unmistakably the Persian Gulf and surrounding areas (Figure 293).

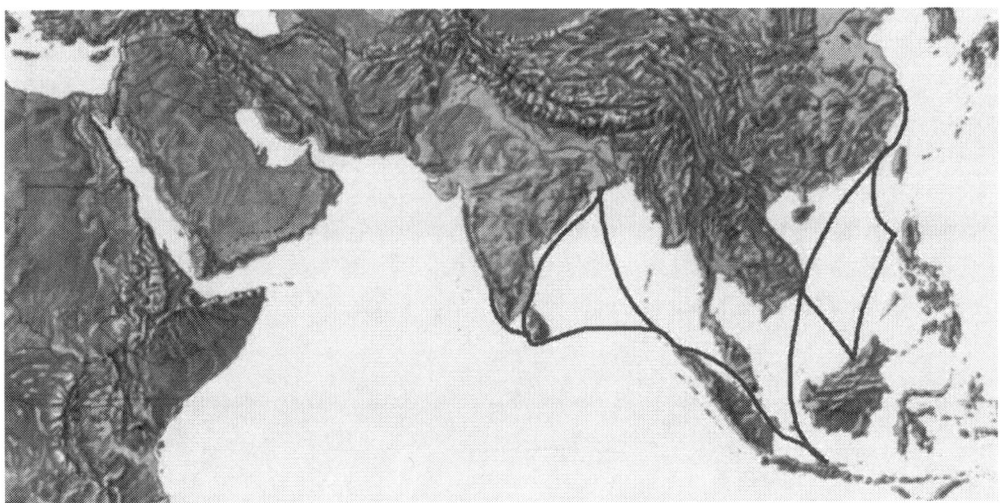

Figure 292

Zheng He's First Two Voyages

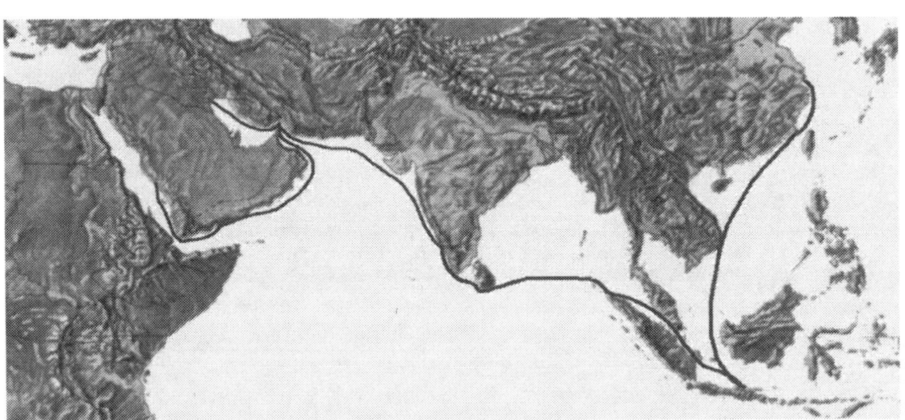

Figure 293

Second Phase of Zheng He's Voyages

Upon reaching Hormuz, and after scouting missions to inland areas, including major settlements on the Arabian Peninsula such as Mecca and Medina and perhaps even all the way to Alexandria on the Mediterranean Sea, Zheng He might have learned that the Timurid Empire (Figure 294, Persia today) was no longer the threat that it had been.

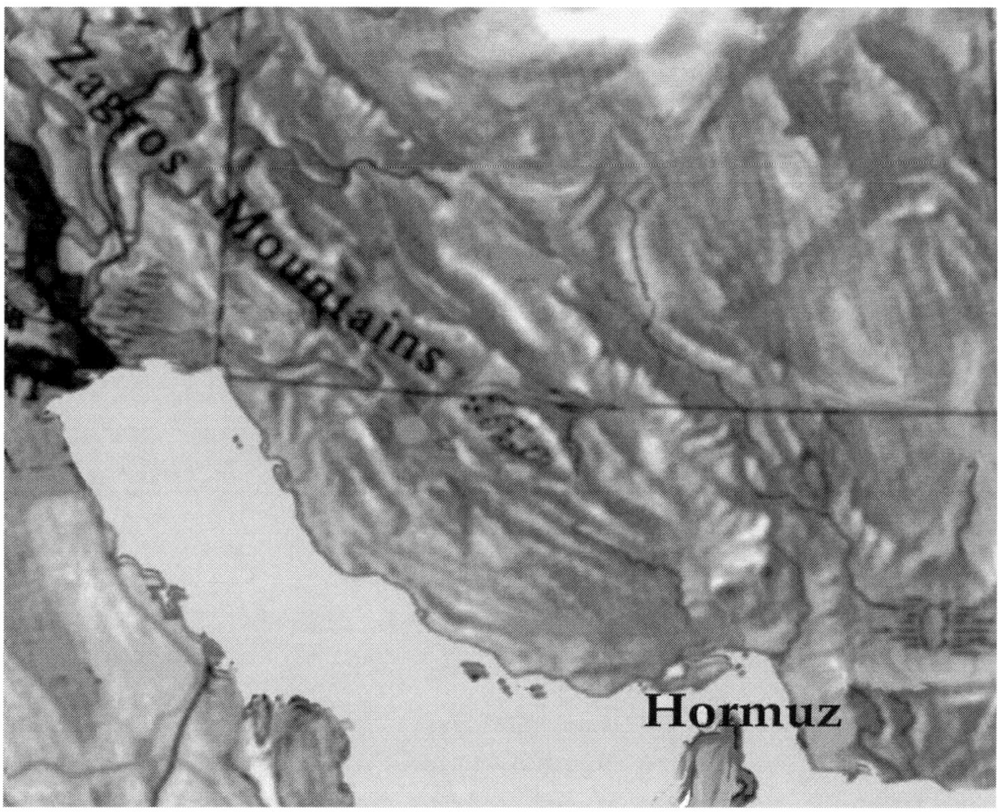

Figure 294

The Zagros and Elburz Mountain Ranges North of Hormuz

Doubtless at this juncture messengers were sent home to consult with Emperor Chengzu on the matter, yet the fleets pushed on.

Ming Chinese had long known that Africa was a landmass, which means that technically it could be circumnavigated; at the least the Arab allies, comrades, consultants, and fellow travelers would have told them as much, and the Chinese maps at the time indicated it.

That the Ming fleets did move forward with their explorations is evidenced by records of their visits to the east coast of Africa, to Somalia and Kenya (Figure 295), then southward toward the tip of the little explored continent. Yet that is all we know because any document that attested to their having traveled beyond is missing, except for what we have gleaned from European records, such as Fra Mauro's map, which testifies to their having done so.

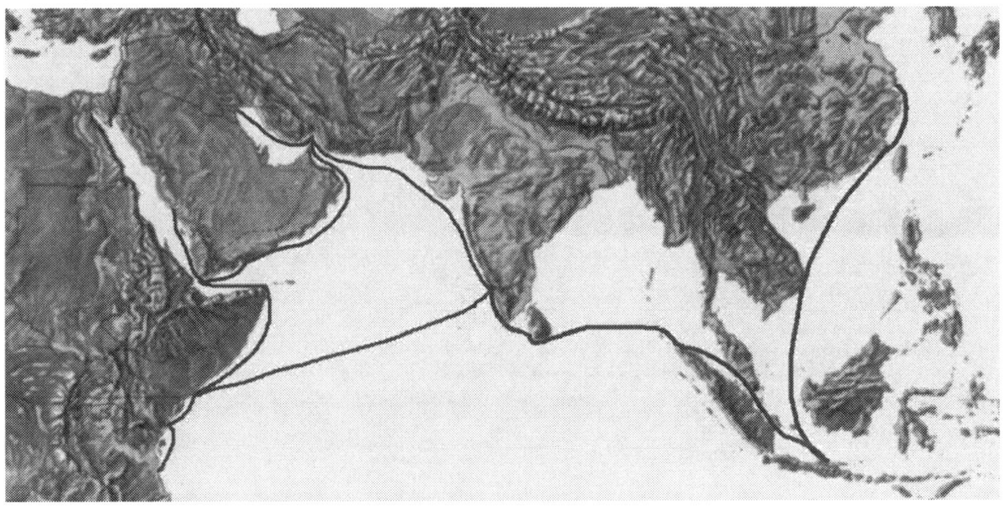

Figure 295

The Ming Fleets Voyages to the East African Seacoast

Why is that so? Could it be that ex-emperor Jianwen sensed that Zheng He was close on his heels so he persuaded the European monarchs to cover his tracts? That could be so if we take into account that Zheng He went to the papal court incognito.

Just as the European adventurers of the Age of Discovery, the Ming sailors that went on these voyages were brave souls. They would sail days, weeks, and months on end battling endless expanses of water without seeing land, and when they did, it could turn out to be reefs or sandbars. If they encountered natives, there was no assurance that they be necessarily friendly. There were certainly storms too. Ships must have wrecked and many crewmembers died, never to see home again. Others would be marooned, and should they be fortunate, they would find ways to survive or even become absorbed into the local communities—which they did. In any case, for twenty-seven years these sailors carried on, chalking up, with over two hundred ships each sailing thousands of miles altogether seven times, over half a million ship-miles, more than all the Age of Discovery European explorations combined!

Nevertheless, after the seafarers had been at sea for twenty years, upon the death of Emperor Chengzu, the pedantic ministers promptly shut down the extravagant maritime program out of political spite, confiscating its records, which allegedly were later burned, and destroying the wondrous ocean-sailing vessels. China voluntarily turned its back on the superior naval technologies that it had developed.

So, this re-examination of the Ming historical records has finally revealed the likely true purposes and nature of the expeditions. It also informs us that there is no reason to imagine that some kind of constraint had been arbitrarily imposed on the enterprise limiting the fleets to the Indian Ocean, which would probably have been the case if the enterprise had been purely commercial in nature. But then, there would have been no justification for such a large-scaled undertaking.

If Hormuz was the Ming voyages' nominal destination, those remote locales such as Malindi and Jobo in East Africa were clearly stop-off points on the routes of an exploration program with a much wider scope than what historians have been willing to acknowledge. What this wider program is we do not know, but we certainly can conjecture on.

Now we turn to the history of the European Age of Discovery.

The Portuguese Maritime History

Figure 296

The 1410 Borgia world Map

As pointed out earlier, Portugal, a small European nation that had never played on the European center stage, that had never even shown aspirations for doing so, led Europe into the Age of Discovery. How did such an unlikely event happen?

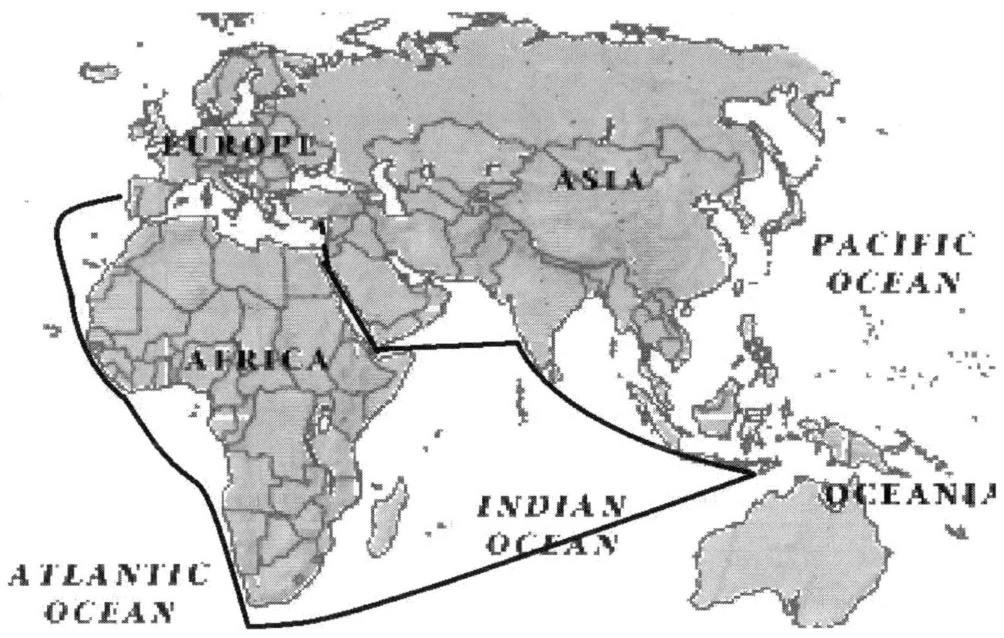

Figure 297

Sea Routes from Portugal to the Spice Islands

The ready answer from historians is that Portugal was located at the edge of the Atlantic Ocean, which gave its citizens both an incentive and advantage to explore the sea. Yet, Portugal was not known as a sea power until the 15th century. Indeed, prior to the Age of Discovery, the Portuguese were not well known as a seafaring people. Nations of antiquity situated further inland, such as Phoenicia, Greece, Carthage, Egypt, and even Turkey could boast of more illustrious pasts as naval powers, but not Portugal. Proximity to sea is no guaranteeing factor in assuring a maritime affinity. England, an island nation in the Atlantic, did not become a sea power until the 16th century. In fact, England was harassed throughout its early history by the Vikings and other mainlanders. Japan, another island nation set deep in the Pacific, never developed into a naval hegemony.

Figure 298

The 1390 Eversham Map

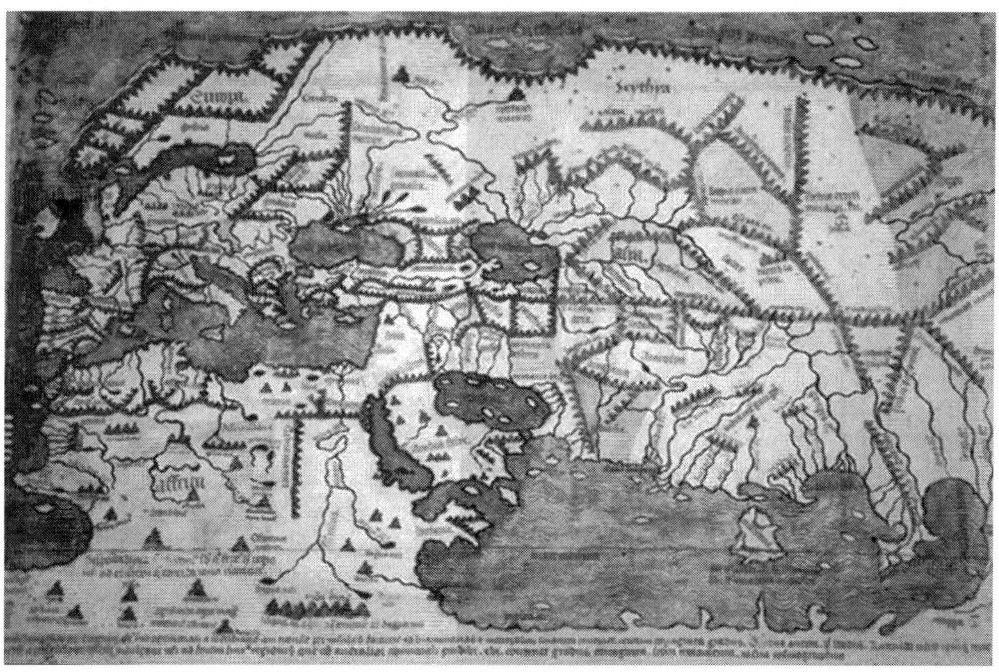

Figure 299

The 1414 Pirrus de Noha World Map

Figure 300

The 1436 Andrea Bianco World Map

An alternate explanation for the rise of Portugal is the well-known "scrambling for spices" theory, but Portugal was never a major player in the spice business.

What is left is the towering figure of Prince Henry, "the Father of the Portuguese Maritime Program," as the inspirational guiding force behind Portugal's rock star status, yet there is no indication of the source of his inspiration.

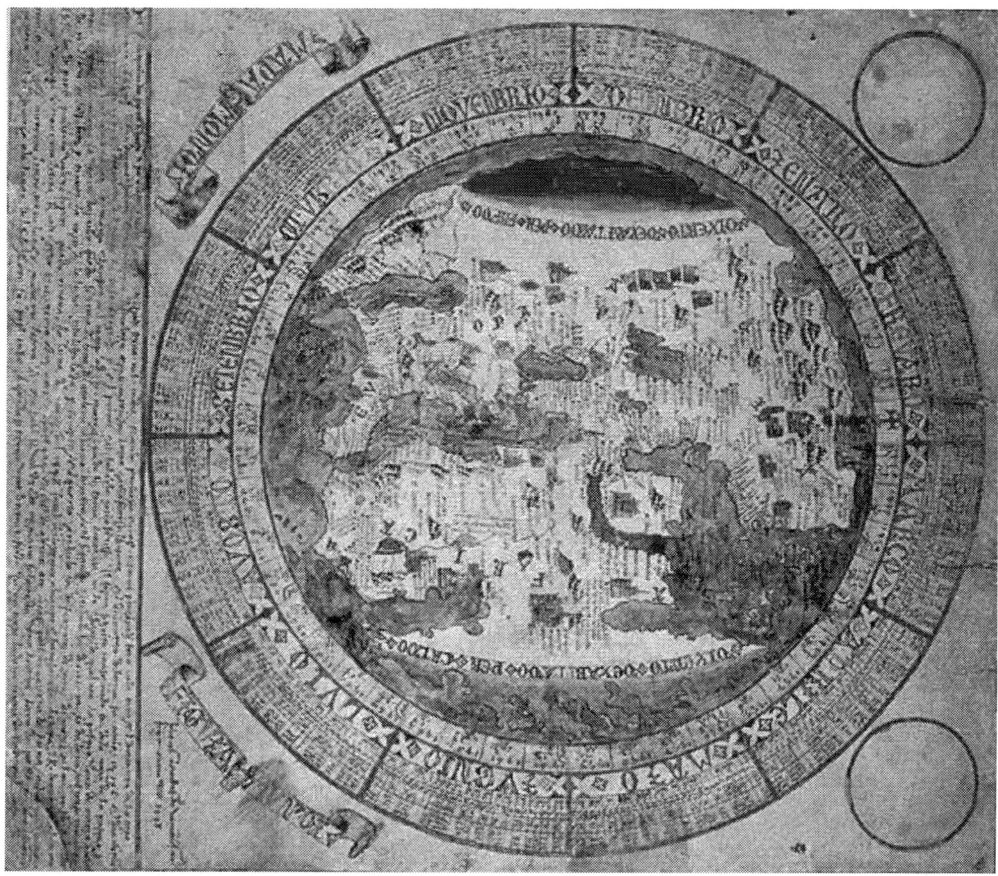

Figure 301

The 1448 Giovanni Leardo Map

It has been said that staring into the vast Atlantic Ocean over barren crags that overhung the endless pounding waves had inspired him on to adventure, the same motivation given to Christopher Columbus for his equally unlikely journey. The world is full of dolts who stare into the oceans, yet they do not usher in ages of explorations.

We do know, though, that Prince Henry was a highly skilled, ambitious, and successful politician. After taking Ceuta opposite the Iberian Peninsula, (the cause of which we shall examine,) he had become aware of the commercial connections between that North African town and the continent's interiors.

Figure 302

The 1450-1460 Catalan-Estense Map

There, in North Africa, he gained firsthand knowledge of the centuries-old Muslim gold traffic from west-central Africa. It is apparent that the potential for conquest and rich rewards had become his interests. These new stimuli most certainly helped formulate his goal to develop Portugal's influence down the western African coast. Because the land routes to the source of the African gold were in the hands of the Muslims, a sea route down the African coast would logically be his best bet. Using the new *nau* (what was the prototype?) Prince Henry would be able to realize his goals.

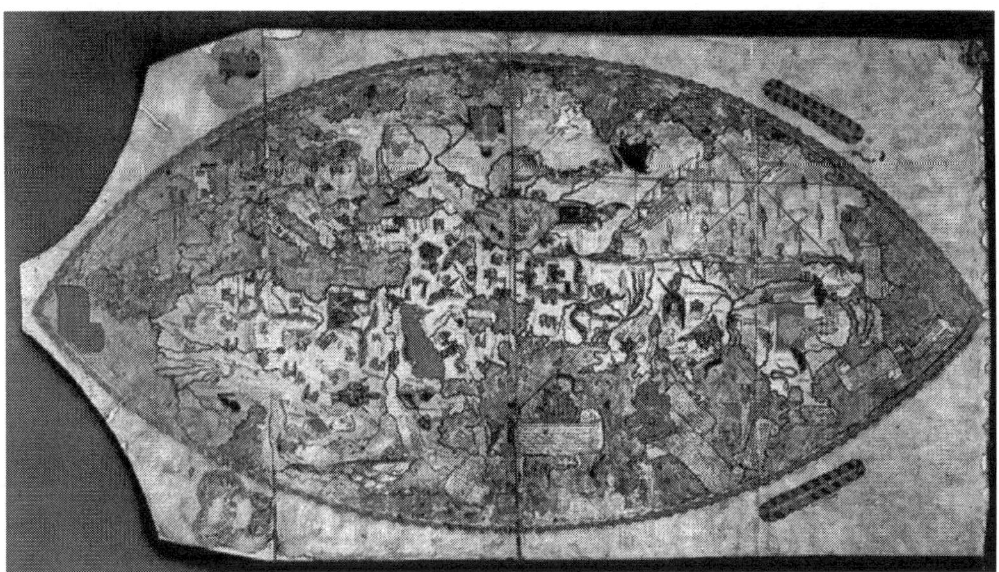

Figure 303

The 1457 Genovese Map

Sure enough, by mid-15th century gold and slaves were literally flowing into Portugal from West Africa.

Prince Henry's efforts in this regard led directly to Portugal's discovering and colonizing the Madeira Islands in the early 1420's. Yet, this is all still a far cry from a desire to reach India and the Asian spice islands by sea as some scholars continue to claim. Yet that was precisely what the Portuguese sailors had done. What was this elusive impetus that drove the Portuguese onward in their quest?

The answer is: the Portuguese knew they could sail down Africa, round it, and thus reach Asia. This, we can prove with hard evidence.

The world map shown in Figure 297 is not one that the early 15th century Portuguese saw. In early 15th century, such an accurately drawn map did not exist. What they would likely see typically is represented in Figure 296, the 1410 Borgia world map (housed in the Biblioteca Apostolica Vaticana, Museum of Cardinal Stefano Borgia, Velletri, in Italy), a map which originally had South pointing up.

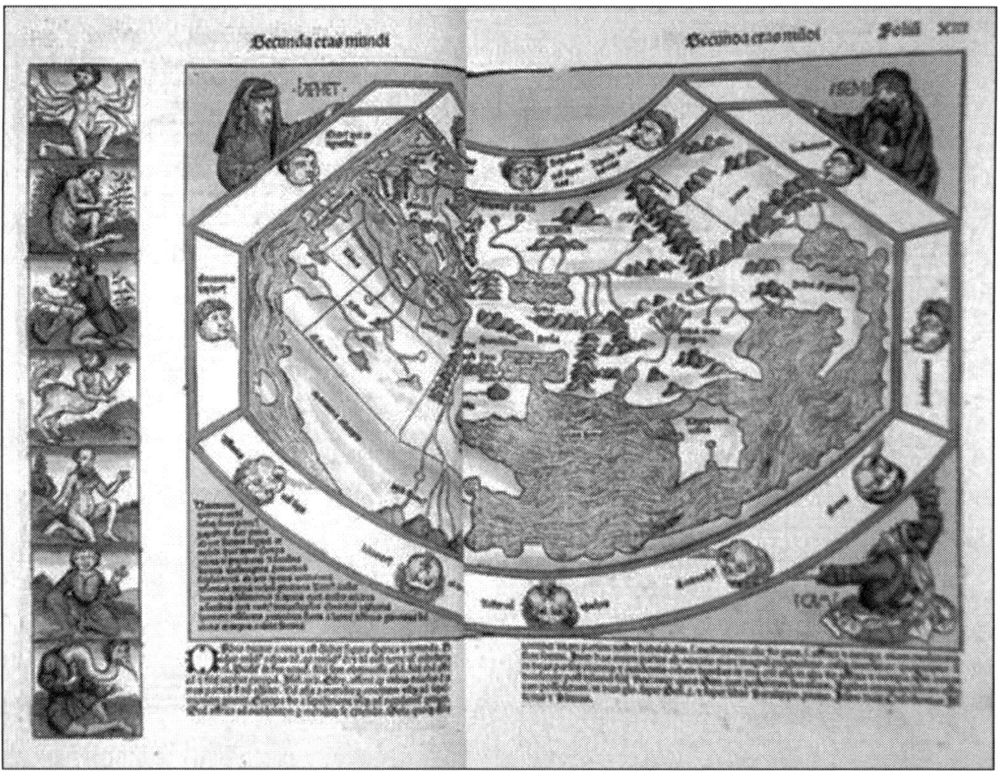

Figure 304

The 1493 Hartmann Schedel Liber Chronicarum Map

This map was characteristic of the European maps in circulation at the time. I doubt that you can even seek out Africa in this map, let alone attempting to chart a sea route around it.

However, it is a historical fact that the Portuguese did make inroads into the Indian Ocean, established colonies throughout the area, and even monopolized the sea trade between East and West by taking over the Arabian and Indian trade networks, thus bringing spices from Asia back to Europe, but that does not necessarily mean that spices were the motivator of this Herculean effort. Something else was at play.

To comprehend the misgivings against the idea that spices lay behind the breakthrough in medieval European navigation we must have a perspective on what was involved. Figure 297 shows the distance from Portugal, on the left, to the Spice Islands, on the right.

Figure 305

The Albertinus de Virga Map

Two routes are shown, the existing one from the Spice Islands to India, then through the Red Sea to the Mediterranean, and the new, sought after one that runs around the African Continent. The difference in distance is stark. Why should Portugal, a sparsely populated nation in the 15th century, which had no history of spice trading—a specialty of the Italians working with the Muslims—get into a brand-new business that required a hefty initial investment and untested technologies, all without a guaranteed payoff?

To appreciate what was just said, for a minute pretend that you were Prince Henry in the early 15th century. No one, including you, has seen a map like that shown in Figure 297. That is a modern map; it did not exist six hundred years ago. Therefore, for the time being erase it from your head. Instead, focus on Figure 296. Explain to yourself how you would become inspired to forge a grand plan to sail around Africa to reach the Spice Islands based on this map. Remind yourself that you have no idea what Africa looks like, and where the Spice Islands are.

Figure 306

The 1448 Andreas Walsperger Map

This is not some ruse concocted by the present researcher to misrepresent the state of geographical knowledge in early 15th century Europe.

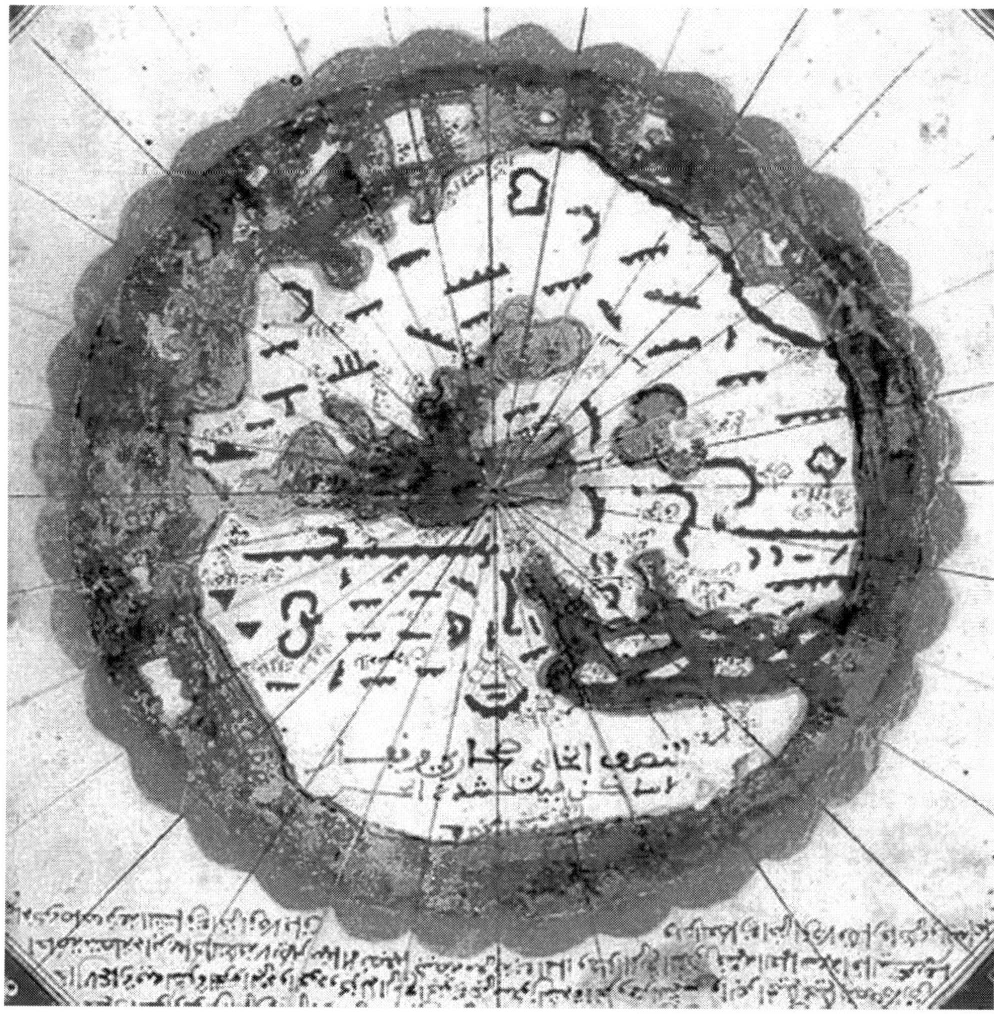

Figure 307

A Late 14th Century Arabic World Map

The relatively primitive geographical worldview can be further illustrated by the following series of prominent medieval maps.

The 1390 Eversham map (Figure 298, notation "Africa" added by author) shows Africa as a thin strip of land to the south of the Mediterranean Sea. It also indicates that Europeans knew little or nothing about Asia. Try to figure out how someone like Prince Henry could have looked at this map and come up with the inspiration to circumnavigate the African continent.

The 1414 Pirrus de Noha world map (Figure 299), currently at Biblioteca Apostolica Vaticana, Archivio di San Pietro, Rome, Italy, shows the Indian Ocean as a lake, typical of Ptolemaic geography. With this map you could not sail around Africa to India. According to Ptolemaic maps, the Indian Ocean had no marine access. (Look at the map closely. See if you can see the "Indian Lake.")

To be fair, by 1436, the year that Ming China aborted its maritime projects, the Andrea Bianco world map (Figure 300) shows that Europeans already knew that Africa did not surround the Indian Ocean. How they learned this we have no knowledge, (except for calculated suspicion,) but the map also shows that they had yet no clear idea about Africa's general topography.

The 1448 Giovanni Leardo map at the Venice Civic Library (Figure 301), the 1450-1460 Catalan-Estense map (Figure 302) now at Biblioteca Estense, Modena, Italy, the 1457 Genovese map (Figure 303) at Biblioteca Nazionale Centrale, Florence, Italy, and the 1493 Hartmann Schedel Liber Chronicarum map (Figure 304, note the *Shan Hai Jing* creatures on the left) now preserved at Peabody Institute Library, National Gallery of Art, Washington, D.C. all fared little better.

There was no way anyone in the 15th century could have been induced to sail around Africa to India from Europe on account of these maps, let alone utilizing them as sea charts in actual sailing, unless, contrary to popular belief, they had maps that showed otherwise.

A world map known as the Albertinus de Virga map (Figure 305) dated to 1411 or 1415, about the time Zheng He was making his way in the "Western Ocean," shows an African continent that was not only detached from Asia, thus allowing a nautical access to the Indian Ocean, but the shape of the continent was astonishingly close to the real thing. As John Noble Wilford put it in his book *The Mapmakers*, "before Earth could be mapped it first had to be known." The maker of the Albertinus de Virga map clearly knew about what he drew.

The de Virga map is astonishing not only because of how accurately Africa had been drawn for its time, the circle in which the landmasses were framed indicates whoever furnished the geographical data for the map knew the earth was round through actual surveying, way before the Europeans came to the same conclusion. This is a projection map, not a schematic one like the old fantasy maps, which enclosed everything in the world with a circle.

In Biblioteca Apostalica Vaticana, Rome is another world map (Figure 306) supposedly created by Andreas Walsperger in 1448, right after the termination of the Zheng He maritime program. In this map the shape of Africa is even better than the de Virga map. Remember 1448 was before the Portuguese rounded the southern tip of Africa.

It has always been a mystery based on what the mapmaker draws in this map. The mapmaker Andreas Walsperger claimed that his map was constructed based on real navigation of the seas. However, nothing is known about who charted and navigated the seas to give such an accurate reading of the African coastline.

Figure 307 shows a late 14th century Arabic world map. In it, Africa is drawn as a horn-shaped landmass (resembling the Africas in Figure 300, Figure 301, and Figure 302, testifying to cultural exchanges taking place between Europe and Asia in medieval times). The Indian Ocean is open to navigational access, and unquestionably, the Arabs were aware of the many islands there. Although the Indian Ocean was technically the Arabs' backyard, and they were supposed to have known Africa better than the Europeans, the fidelity of the map's geography is much inferior to the Walsperger map. Thus, Walsperger must have gotten his input from a vastly superior source.

Evidently, geographical knowledge of Africa, and most likely the Indian Ocean and Asia, were available to the Portuguese in the early 15th century, if not earlier, before the start of the Age of Discovery. Thus, the impulse for maritime exploration around the southern tip of Africa was not a blind urge to seek a sea route to the Asian Spice Islands. Instead, it was because the Portuguese knew that somebody had already traveled the route and documented it. The Portuguese, and that includes Prince Henry, either had a secret map of Africa or had seen one, one that was years more advanced than the prevalent European maps at the time. Some of that information only leaked out by midcentury.

Recall the Catalan Atlas of 1375. Jehuda Cresques, the son of Abraham Cresques, was the Prince's leading navigational expert. He and his father Abraham Cresques together created the celebrated Catalan atlas, and were at the Sagres naval compound. The map showed Chinese vessels in the waters of the world. The information and knowledge used in this map would certainly have been passed on to the Prince. In other words, Prince Henry knew of Chinese ships, and it is more than likely that this knowledge led to the development of the *nau*, the caravel. The naval history author Robert Greenhalgh Albion noted that it was virtually certain that Henry the Navigator had seen it.

Where did Prince Henry obtain such advanced geography and the world? Where did the Cresqueses obtain theirs? Where did the Albertinus de Virga Map data come from? Who were the sailors that supplied Walsperger with his map data, and who were the sailors that helped Fra Mauro with his? All these events happened during the late 14th and early 15th centuries, at the end of the Mongol Yuan Dynasty and the beginning of the Chinese Ming Dynasty. Do we still have any illusion as to the source of the early European Age of Discovery world geography?

If Prince Henry indeed obtained his input from the Arabs he encountered in North Africa, is it too much of a stretch to surmise that Zheng He and his officers, almost all of whom spoke Arabic, and that they had close associations with Arab seafaring allies, had something to do with the transmission of such world geography knowledge from Asia to Europe?

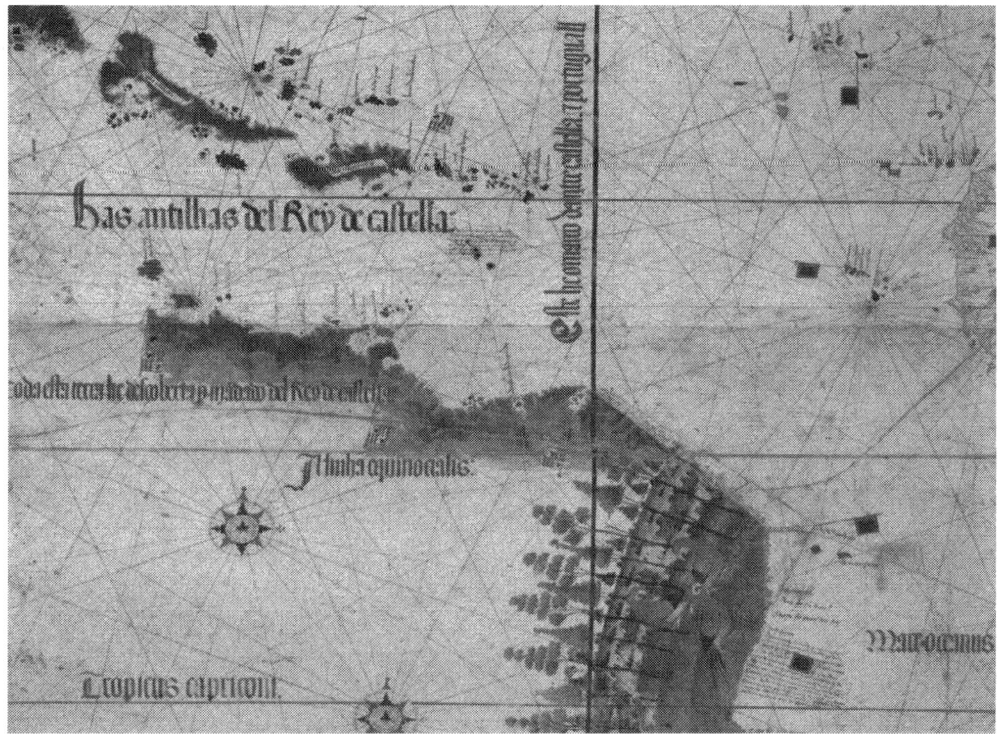

Figure 308

The Cantino Map Tordesillas Line

The Treaty of Tordesillas

During the late 15th century, Europe saw a significant increase in mapping activities. It was also during this time when Columbus apparently conceived his idea of traveling west to Cipangu. In fact, many scholars have pegged the turning point to the year 1477, the very same year that the Ming Chinese official allegedly burned the Zheng He archive. Florentine Lorenzo Buonincontri allegedly speculated about a fourth continent in 1476. At the same time, new geographical information about the world began to materialize in Europe. In fact, an important event that gives voice to this assertion took place at this time during the late 15th century. This is the Tordesillas Treaty of 1494, signed copies of which are now kept at the Archivo General de Indias in Spain and the Arquivo Nacional da Torre do Tombo of Portugal.

When Pope Alexander VI decreed that any land discovered west of a theoretical meridian line drawn in a north-south orientation, 100 leagues west of the Cape Verde Islands would belong to Spain, while those east of the meridian would belong to Portugal, King John II of Portugal threw a fit; that is, he reacted violently. He wanted the line drawn further west into the Western Ocean (see Figure 51 and Figure 308). What prompted him to react in such a manner?

If Portugal's focus was indeed Asia—India and the Spice Islands to be specific, and that goal was manifest in her protracted effort to sail east around the southern tip of Africa, it would seem that King John II would want to have as much of Asia assigned to Portugal as possible. Remember that a meridian line drawn through the Western Ocean also cut through the opposite side of the globe. By demanding the meridian to be drawn more westerly into the Western Ocean, Portugal would in effect be asking the extended meridian on the opposite side of the globe to be moved westward as well, giving Portugal potentially less of Asia instead of more. Hence, the Portuguese king's reaction appears to be illogical.

As it so happened, the renegotiated meridian some 250 leagues further west ended up giving Portugal the new land of Brazil, the same land parcel that kept cropping up on European maps of the time. What a lucky break for Portugal, or perhaps it was all the calculated result of a deliberate and shrewd move. In other words, Portugal was in possession of maps to the new world, that portion of it that was to show up in The Cantino Map (Figure 51), the Canerio Map (Figure 55), Martin Waldseemüller's world map (Figure 56), the Salviati map (Figure 60), the Batiste Agnese map (Figure 62), and others. Hence, King John II was in fact protecting Portugal's interest. He knew of the existence of Brazil the landmass, and he wanted it to be Portuguese property and not Spanish property.

To use a contemporary corporate analogy in hindsight, the Pope, who was Spanish, and the Spanish monarchs attempted to pull a fast one over the king of Portugal, but King John II was on to them. When King John II showed up to force their hands, they resigned to the inevitable and agreed to move the line to give Portugal the new landmass that she already knew of. In the meantime, King John II was happy to retreat from the East because his maps already told him that the protracted meridian cut through mostly water—the name "Pacific Ocean" was not yet coined. However, there is no question that the Pope and the kings of Spain and Portugal all knew that the Earth was a globe.

Author Ian Fleming reminds us in his novel *Goldfinger* that "once is happenstance, and twice is coincidence. Thrice…? We may not (or may) be dealing with enemy action here, but too many coincidences give one pause.

In 1500, Portuguese explorer Pedro Álvares Cabral, while on the way to round the Cape of Good Hope (that is, sailing east to India) got hit by a storm and drifted west, going off course thousands of miles and discovered Brazil for Portugal, thus fortuitously making good on the Tordesillas quibble. If you believe this, then perhaps we should call this episode *Gullible's Travel*. The truth is more like an act to put the final touches on the done deal. This way everybody saved face, and nobody else but the king of Portugal, the monarchs of Spain, and the Pope knew each other had maps documenting new lands to be discovered.

Figure 309

The 1351 Laurenziano-Gaddiano Portolan Chart

Though they might have lost their history officially, the Chinese have not lost it in deed. Despite the fact that it is undocumented, the history of the Chinese maritime activities during the 14th to 16th centuries is in fact very much in evidence.

The Chinese have a long tradition in oceanic exploration that dates back millennia. The program reached a crescendo by the Song Dynasty in the 11th and 12th centuries. After conquering China, the Mongols employed Chinese (and Korean) naval technologies to their advantage. They invaded Japan and Java with large fleets and continued to sail the oceans with them, probably not for intellectual stimulation but to reconnoiter in preparation for conquest.

Although history; that is, European-dominated world history, has devoted little coverage to their description, that Chinese vessels were used by the Mongols to sail the world's oceans is attested to by European maps such as the Catalan Atlas, the Fra Mauro Map, the Homem maps, and others, which prominently displayed Chinese junks in the world's waters. It is heartening to know, though, that this fact is beginning, albeit very slowly and reluctantly, to catch the attention of historians and is beginning to be included in mainstream writings.[141]

Maps of the 14th and 15th century show that the Chinese already knew about the geography of the major world landmasses, including the Americas, Australia, and the poles. Star charts of the Southern Hemisphere demonstrate that the Chinese had crossed the Equator with regularity.[142] Above all, the most persuasive evidence comes in the form of European maps such as the 1410 de Virga map (Figure

---

[141] Professor Jacques Gernet of the University of Paris wrote in his book *A History of Chinese Civilization*, Cambridge University Press, 1988 on page 398:

The Yung-le epoch is famous for its big maritime expeditions which revealed, at the beginning of the fifteenth century, the technical superiority of China and her lead over Spain and Portugal, whose ships did not undertake long voyages on the high seas until the very end of this same century. China's lead is explained by the continuity of maritime traditions which went back to the eleventh century and were almost certainly never interrupted; the fleets which the Mongols caused to be built for the invasion of Java at the end of the 13th century were put on the stocks on the lower Yangtze, no doubt in the very same yards that had built the warships and merchant ships of the Sung age. The age of the big high-seas junk covers the whole period from the eleventh century to the big expeditions of the early 15th century. Thus these expeditions were not a transitory, exceptional affair, but should be placed in a more general context—that of the maritime side of the Chinese world. The dynastic histories made a fuss of the maritime expeditions of the Yung-le era because they were official enterprises. They would be incomprehensible if we forgot that, contrary to received ideas, China, as well as being one of the great powers of the steppe and the high plateaux of Central Asia, was also a land of sailors and explorers.

[142] If you only cross once you would not make a star chart.

305), which sports outlines of the major continents of the world before any European could lay claim to their reconnaissance.

In any event, the de Virga map was not the only early European map that shows world features before Europeans could have surveyed them. The 1351 Portolan chart of Laurenziano-Gaddiano (Figure 309, currently at the Biblioteca Medicea Laurenziana, Florence, Italy) shows an Africa that is years ahead of its time. Although respected scholar-investigators have doubts about the actual date of the map—the year 1351 being a calendar date on the map and not necessarily the date of its creation—they generally agree that the map was most likely made in late 14th century or early 15th century. The only reasonable candidate as the source of the data used to draw this map is the Chinese.

All this makes perfect sense because it explains the Ming fleets as a logical and natural development of an uninterrupted naval technological tradition. Otherwise, it would be hard to account for how the Ming learned to build those huge seaworthy liners that reached up to 400+ feet in length. Indeed, the founder of the Ming Dynasty, Taizu himself, was a competent navy man as he fought many a great sea battle on the great lakes of China during his campaigning years.

Chinese Technologies in Renaissance

In his book *Brunelleschi's Dome: How a Renaissance Genius Reinvented Architecture*, author Ross King informs us that the project to build the Santa Maria del Fiore dome in Florence, Italy lasted a hundred years. The dome was finally finished in early 15th century—coincidentally, in the year 1420—and one reason of the accomplishment was the erection of a crane of Brunelleschi's design that possessed multiple degrees of freedom of movement; that is, could move heavy weights sideways as well as vertically. In this case, the author could not identify what sparked this design, which possessed mechanical features that evoked no precedence, and employed engineering principles that were not to be quantified before early 19th century. The author wrote:

Figure 310
A Portuguese Nau

> *"The exact inspiration for this remarkable machine remains as mysterious as that behind Filippo's other inventions. The specialist theoretical knowledge needed for constructing such a hoist was largely unavailable in 1420, though soon afterward a number of manuscripts on Greek mechanics and mathematics began arriving in Florence, putting architects and inventors of the Renaissance in possession of engineering techniques far beyond those available in the Middle Ages."*

These Brunelleschi contraptions were so fabulous that Leonardo da Vinci studied them. It is interesting to note that Zheng He's shipyard employed precisely such machineries that had the multiple degrees of freedom of movement to move heavy loads around. In the absence of evidence linking one directly to the other, I can only marvel at the coincidence of their occurrences.

Portuguese Nau Development

Anyway, this coincidence pales against the development of the Portuguese *nau,* followed by the caravel, which we already discussed. Not only was the vessel developed during the peak of Chinese maritime expeditions, it looked—the part of the ship above water, at least (Figure 310)—and operated like the Chinese junk. Do not forget, Europeans knew about the Chinese junk, *zoncho,* before they supposedly had seen it, and in return, the Chinese knew about the *Farangi* (Portuguese) before they had met them too.

Jacob's Staff

Figure 311

A Jacob's Staff

By the 16th century, after the invention of the *nau* and before the sextant became the standard, European navigators began using a device to determine latitude called the *Jabob's staff* (Figure 311), known as *belestilha* in Portuguese, and *baculo de Santiago* in Spanish and *bastone di San Giacomo* in Italian. This device measured the height (angle) of the Pole Star (when in the northern hemisphere) in reference to horizon. The Jacob's staff was precisely the instrument the Chinese used in their voyages, and its measurements are logged in Zheng He's sea charts.

The Names Atlantic & Ocean Sea

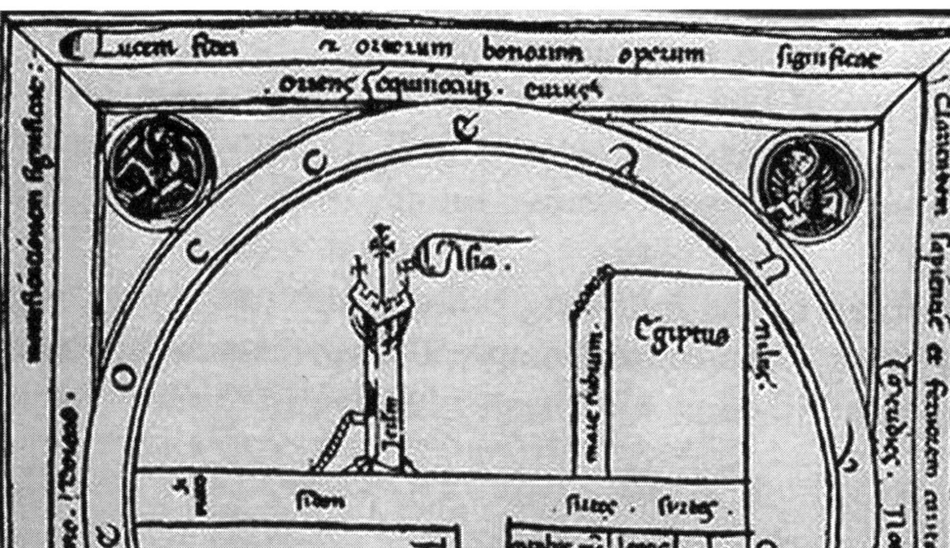

Figure 312

14th Century Bellum Jugurthinum Sallust Manuscript Map

When it comes to the subject, many learned colleagues of ours quite freely talk about how the ancients, namely, the Greeks, spurred the Renaissance Europeans on to exploring the Atlantic. Yet, Atlantic was not the name used to describe the ocean west of Europe by those ancients. The name Atlantic purportedly first made its cartographic debut sometime in the early 15th century, perhaps even later, and on a limited basis at that.

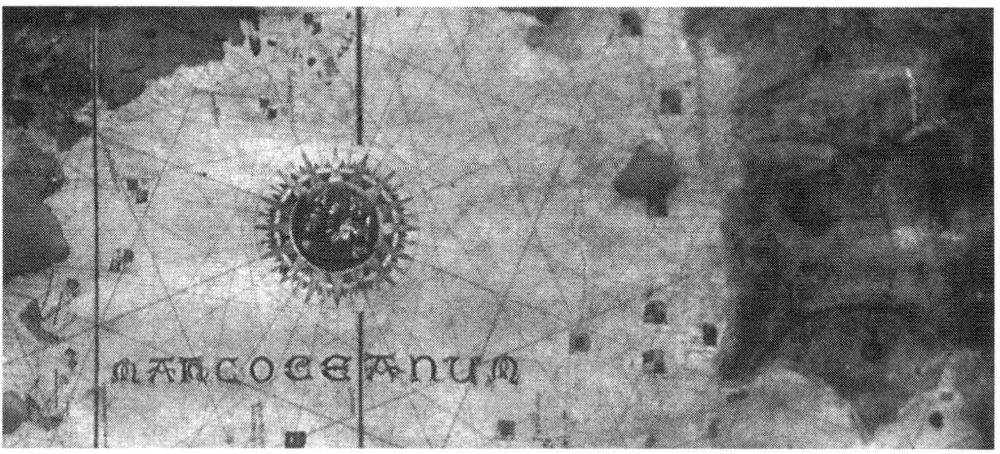

Figure 313

The 1500 Juan de la Cosa Map

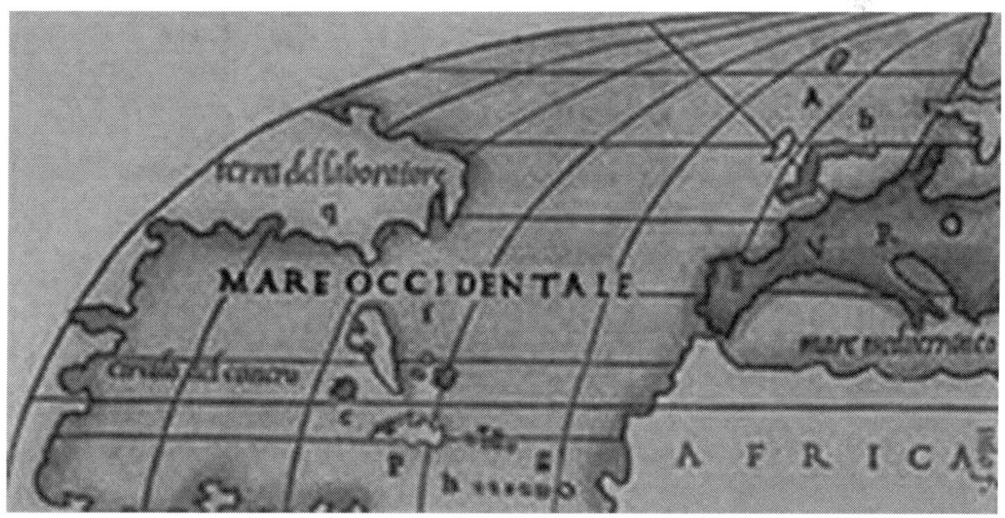

Figure 314

The 1528 Benedetto Bordone Map

During the 15th and 16th centuries, what we now call the Atlantic Ocean was known as *Mare Oceanum*, the Ocean Sea. It is interesting to note that Columbus supposedly demanded to be titled "the Admiral of the Ocean Sea." This name was on the 14th century Bellum Jugurthinum Sallust Manuscript map (Figure 312, note the name in the circular ring).

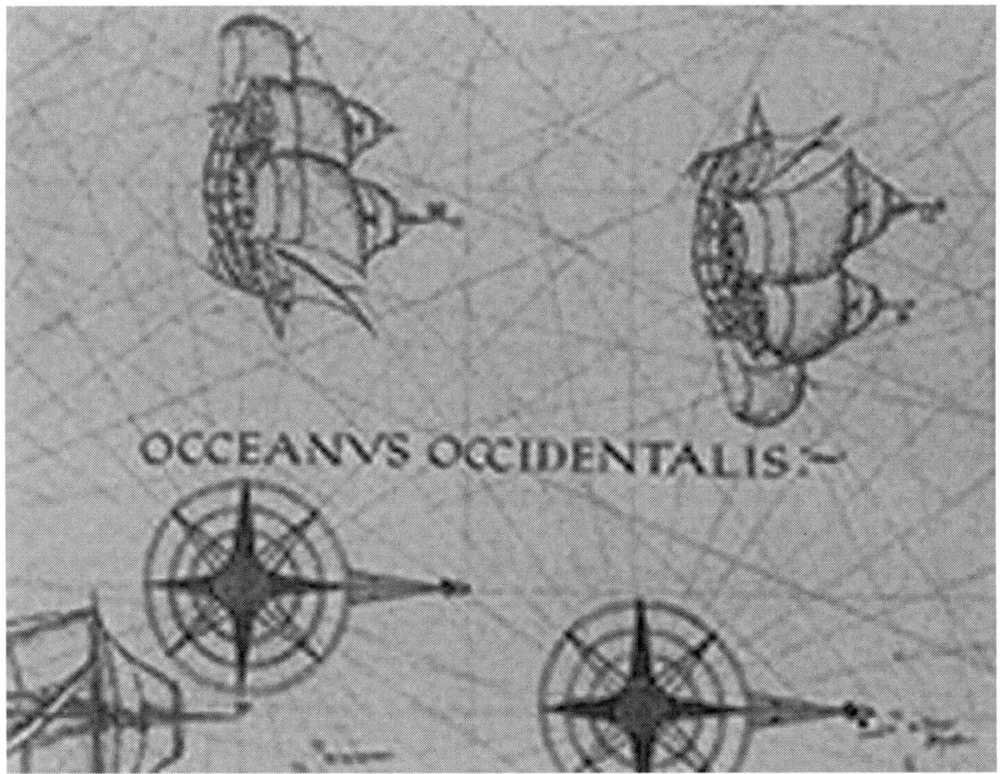

Figure 315

The 1529 Ribero Map

For example, the now familiar 1500 Juan de la Cosa map (Figure 313), and others of the period. This name is interesting because it is tautologous. "Mare" means sea, and so does "Ocean." It is exactly like the old Chinese name *Da Xi Yang Hai*, "the Great Western Ocean Sea." "Yang" is "Ocean," and "Hai" is "Sea." They mean the same thing. The Chinese still call the ocean *hai yang* today. Could this be mere coincidence?

During the 16th century, the name "Mare Oceanus" began to give way to a new name, "Oceanus Occidentalis," or the Western Ocean, as in Figure 318, the 1513 Waldseemüller map, the 1528 Benedetto Bordone map (Figure 314), the 1529 Ribero map (Figure 315), and later ones. Indeed, the 17th century John Lawson map called the Atlantic "The Western Ocean" in English (Figure 316). Why the change?

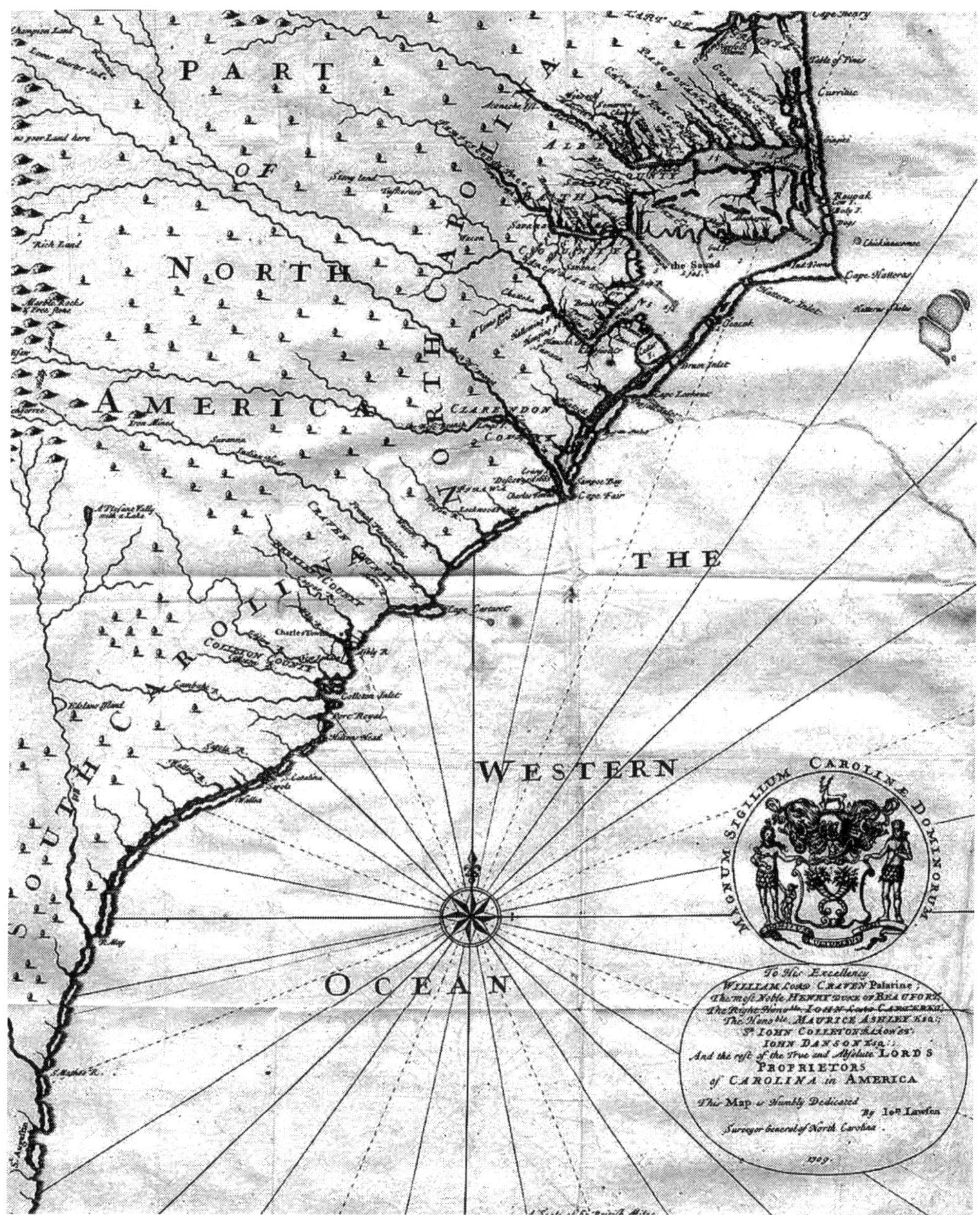

Figure 316

The 17th Century John Lawson Map

The Chinese call the Atlantic Ocean *Da Xi Yang*, or "the Great Western Ocean." Did the European mapmakers get input from the Chinese, or was it the other way around?

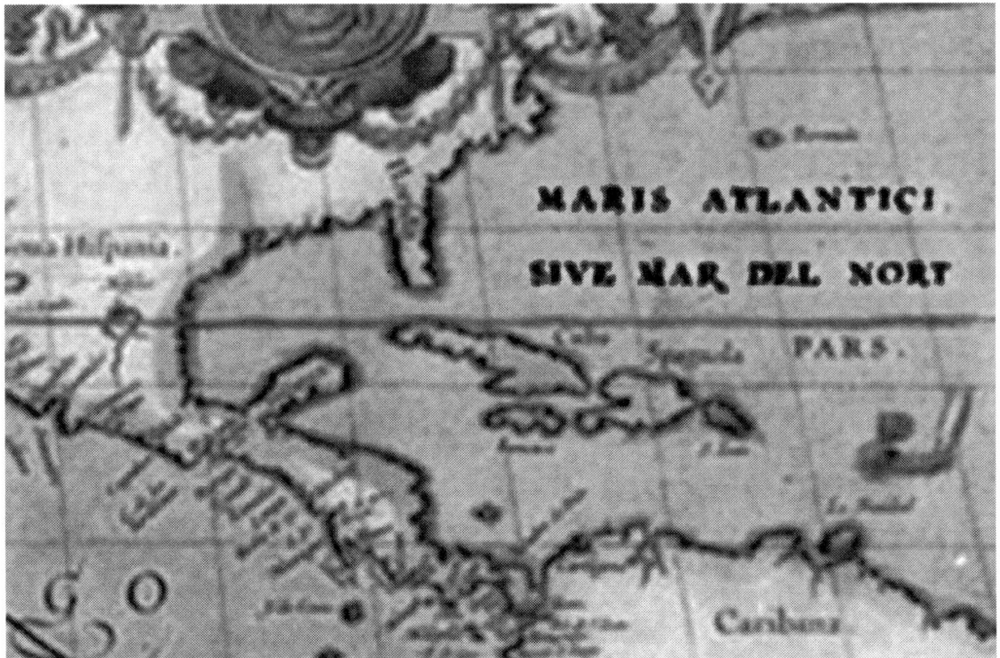

Figure 317

The 1589 Abraham Ortelius Map

For argument's sake let us for the moment assume that the Chinese picked up the names from the Europeans instead of the other way around. When the Europeans switched to the "Atlantic Ocean," as in the 1589 Abraham Ortelius map (Figure 317, *Maris Atlantici*), why did the Chinese fail to follow suit?

Then there are the names for the Atlantic Ocean.

When it comes to foreign place names, in most cases the Chinese simply translate the names phonetically; that is, they use combinations of Chinese characters to emulate the foreign sound. Hence, the Chinese name for England is *Ying Ge Lan*. France is *Fa Lan Xi*. Germany is *De Er Zhi* ("Deutsch"), and Spain is *Xi Ban Ya* ("España" minus the initial "E").

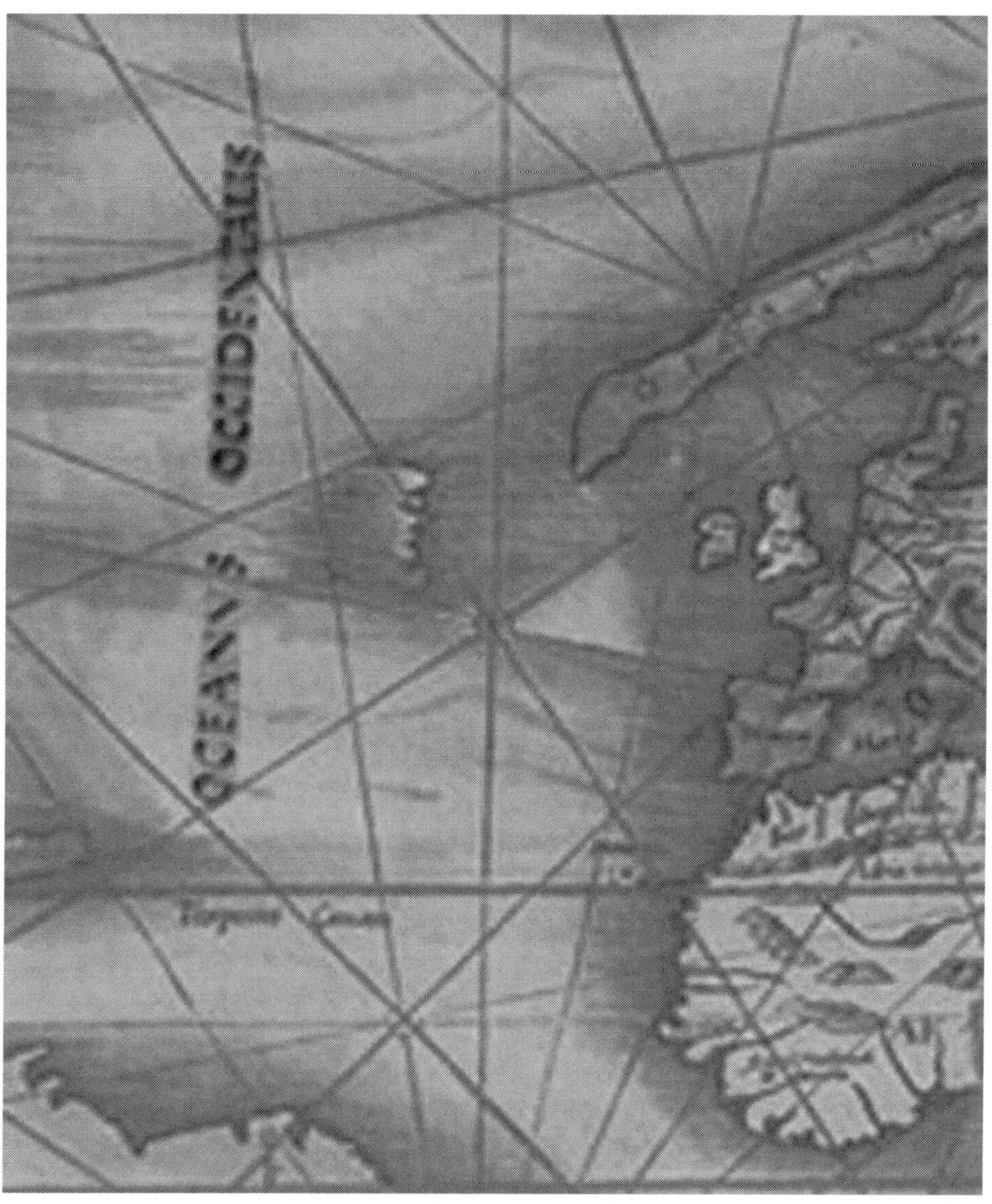

Figure 318

The 1513 Johannes Waldseemüller Map

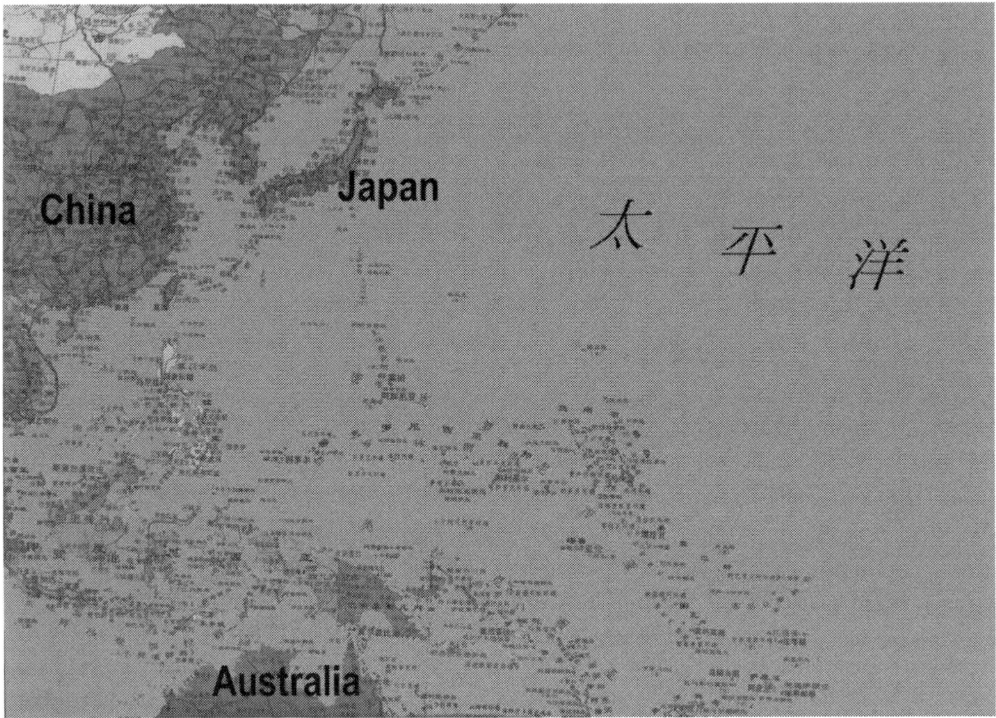

Figure 319

The Pacific Ocean in a Modern Chinese Map

The same goes for geographical place names. For example, the Baltic Sea is *Bo Luo Di Hai;*[143] "*Bo Luo Di*" being the Chinese transliteration of "Baltic."

The open-minded practice of the Chinese in this regard is commendable. Often when the Chinese already have a name for a place, if a universal consensus evolves, they generally defer to the popular convention. The Pacific Ocean used to be *Dong Yang*, the "Eastern Ocean." Today the Chinese call it *Tai Ping Yang;*[144] "Tai Ping" meaning "peaceful;" that is, "Pacific" (see Figure 319).[145]

---

143 波羅的海

144 太平洋

145 The consensus today as to how the Pacific Ocean got its name is that Magellan was grateful that he did not encounter major disturbance crossing the ocean. The truth is the name appeared as a name for a local section of the sea to the

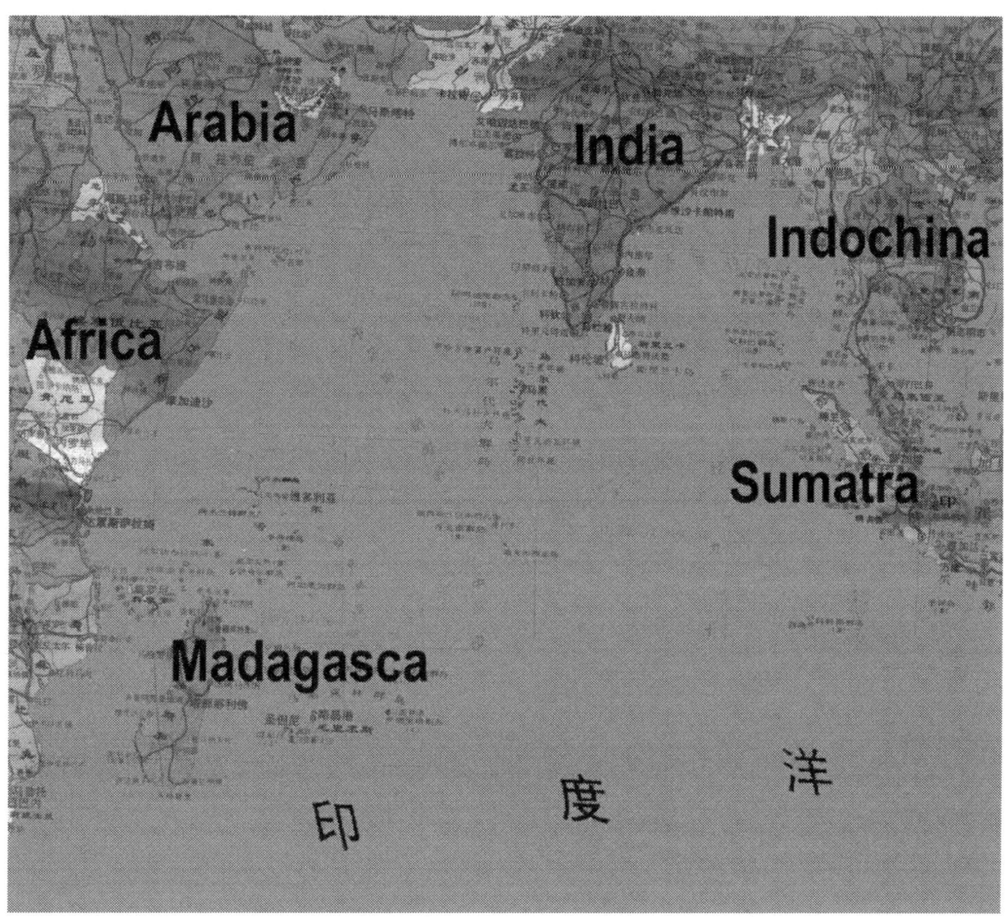

Figure 320

The Indian Ocean in a Modern Chinese Map

Likewise, the Indian Ocean, which apparently used to be called the Western Ocean as in the Zheng He saga, is today called *Yin Du Yang,* (Figure 320), *Yin Du* being Chinese for "Hindu."

Yet, there is a curious and glaring exception to this pattern of international egalitarianism, and it is not because the Chinese did not know that Europeans called this ocean the Atlantic.

---

west of today's Chile, and that section only. Thus it is possible that European explorers also got information about the Pacific Ocean from the Chinese.

Figure 321

The 1602 Matteo Ricci Chinese World Map Atlantic

When the Jesuit Matteo Ricci came to China he used Western data to help the Chinese construct a world map so as to impress the Chinese emperor of the advanced Western knowledge. On his 1602 world map, done in Chinese, we find the name 亞大蠟海, "Ya Da La" Sea, or Atlantic Ocean (Figure 321, lower left corner). This shows the 17th century Ming Chinese were exposed to the name Atlantic.

Ironically, the name Da Xi Yang Hai, the Great Western Ocean Sea, one that they had long held, still appeared outside the Iberian Peninsula.

Consequently, the Chinese were exposed to the name Atlantic—from a well-known European, no less—but stuck to their own identity of this decidedly European water, *Da Xi Yang*, 大西洋, the Great Western Ocean, the very name employed in the Zheng He chronicles.

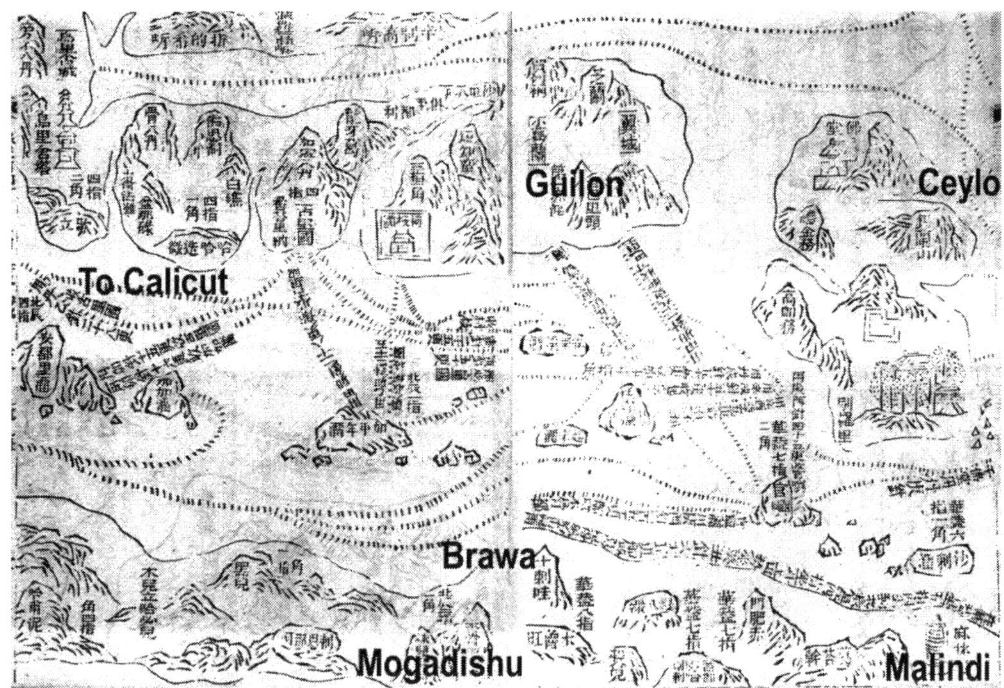

Figure 322

Zheng He's Sea Chart of the African East Coast

According to literature on the Zheng He expeditions, the Western Ocean neatly stopped at the eastern African seacoast. The title of the Ming/Zheng He voyages had been in existence for a long time. When researchers surveyed the extant literature and found that the furthest known (documented) destinations—such as Malindi and Jobo—to be in East Africa, they simply inferred that the Western Ocean was equivalent to the Indian Ocean. Once they had reached this conclusion they went on to find all sorts of ancient text to justify this finding. Still, the definition was worked out in retrospect.

There was no official definition of "Western Ocean" in Chinese records or literature per se. "Western Ocean" is simply equated with the Indian Ocean because existing documentation of Zheng He's voyages appears to describe the Indian Ocean.

Now we know all signs indicate that the Ming fleets actually went beyond Somalia and Kenya. After all, there is no valid reason for Chinese interest to have stopped at those places.

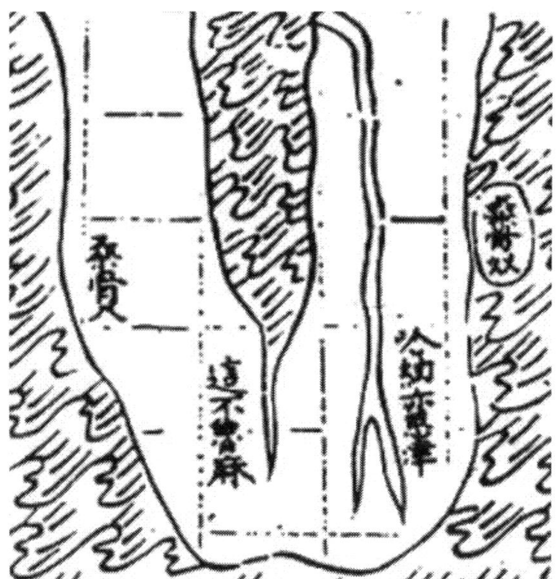

Figure 323

Ming Sea Chart of Southern Africa

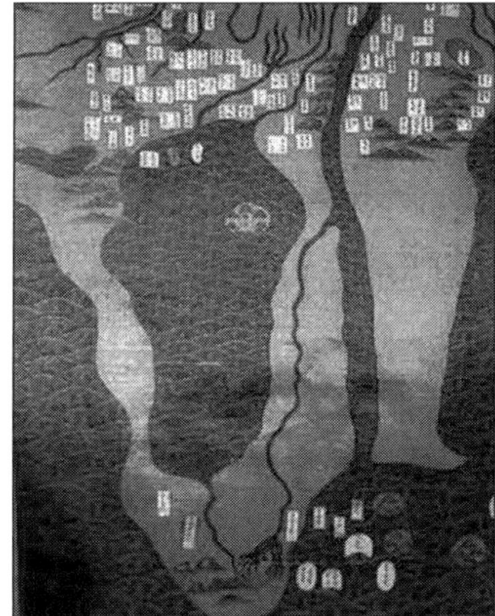

Figure 324

Ming Silk Map of Southern Africa

There was nothing special about this place Malindi. The Chinese government had no standing policy setting Malindi to be the furthest reach of the Zheng He expeditions, and there is no extant justification that suggests that there was a political or physical condition that compelled the Ming fleet to turn around at that point.

On the contrary, we now know that Malindi was not even the main point of interest for the Ming expeditions. That distinction belongs to Hormuz. Any Chinese naval activity beyond the Middle East was therefore "extra-mission," or, as we now know, a continuation of the mission. Therefore, there is no reason to assume that the Ming fleets held back at Malindi. It should be presumed that they had traveled onward beyond the east coast of Africa, and "Western Ocean" should logically have included territories beyond the Indian Ocean, and Fra Mauro's map certainly attests to the fact that they did.

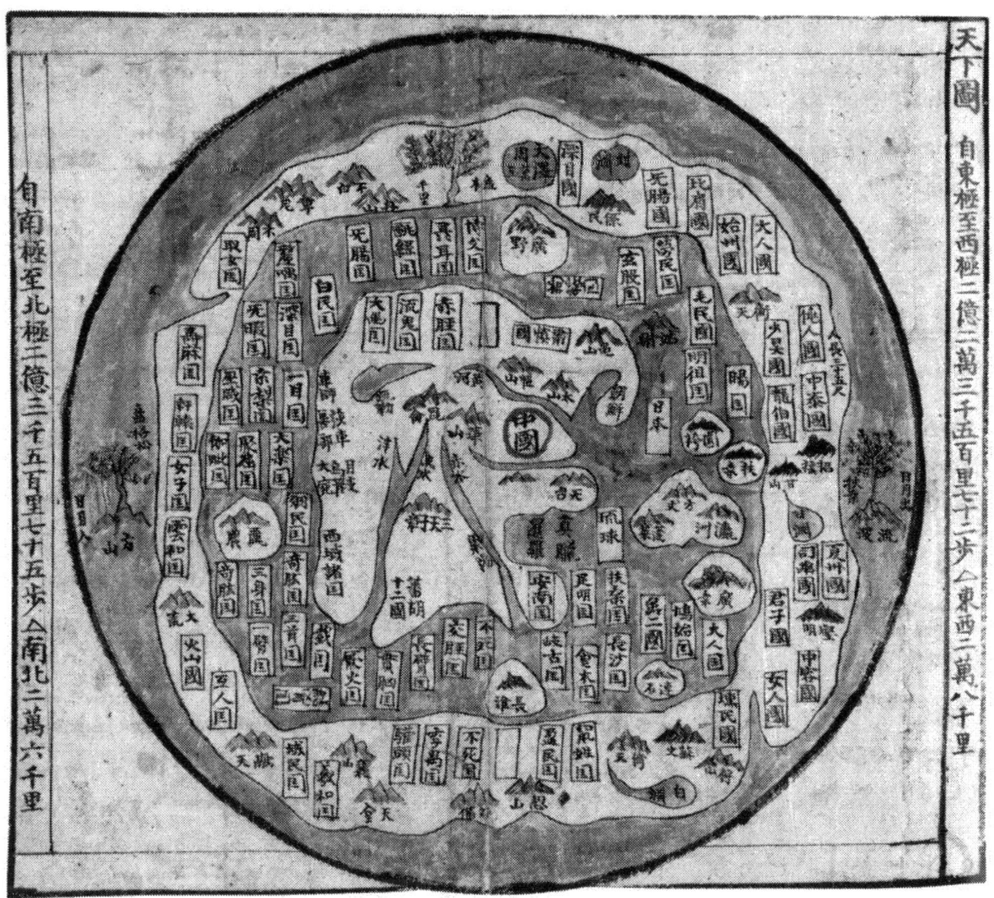

Figure 325

The Choson Kukto map

Figure 322, oriented with east pointing up, shows a section of the Zheng He sea chart from the *Wu Bei Zhi* (Ming Dynasty Military Preparedness Manual) documenting the areas about Somalia and Nairobi in East Africa (bottom of the chart. English names added by the present researcher.) This section of the chart clearly extends to the right, perhaps detailing geographical locations belonging to the southern part of Africa and the Indian Ocean, and possibly beyond. Unfortunately, that part of the scroll appears to be missing. Regardless, it suggests that East Africa was not the boundary of the Ming voyages.

Figure 323 shows a Ming sea chart and Figure 324 shows a Ming map of Africa. The Chinese knew about the southern tip of Africa.

In fact, the Chinese had known about the southern tip of Africa for a long time. Preserved at the United States Library of Congress is a Korean rendition of an ancient Chinese map (Figure 325). This is the Choson Kukto map from the Chonha Chido. In the center is the name *Zhong Guo,* China, framed inside a red circle. It is a projection map, thus Asia, drawn in the center, appears exceptionally large. The landmass below the name China is therefore Indochina where the name Annan Guo (Vietnam) is clearly marked. To the left of Indochina is a very big India subcontinent. To its left is an unmistakable Africa, with a very small Arabian Peninsula in between. The map prototype, dated to before the 11th century, shows the Chinese knew about the Atlantic Ocean.

Figure 326 is transcribed from a historical Chinese map called *Hai Guo Tu Zhi,*[146] "Atlas of Nations of the Seas." It is a Qing Dynasty (1644-1911) rework of a series of maps contained in an old manuscript called "Records of the Four Continents," *Si Zhou Zhi*.[147]

In this map, the ocean to the west of the Iberian Peninsula (Portugal and Spain) is named 大西洋,[148] *Da Xi Yang,* or "the Great Western Ocean." The ocean to the east of Africa is called 小西洋,[149] *Xiao Xi Yang,* or "the Little Western Ocean." The "Great" and "Little" here perhaps are better expressed as "Greater" and "Lesser" in the spirit of naming such as the "Greater and Lesser Antilles" as practiced by European geographers.

It is interesting to note that the ocean to the west of Africa is named 大西南洋, *Da Xi Nan Yang,* or "the Great Western Southern Ocean." The ancient Chinese cartographers appeared to be quite particular with their geography.

---

146 海國圖志

147 四洲志

148 Circled by the author and annotated 1.

149 Circled by the author and annotated 2.

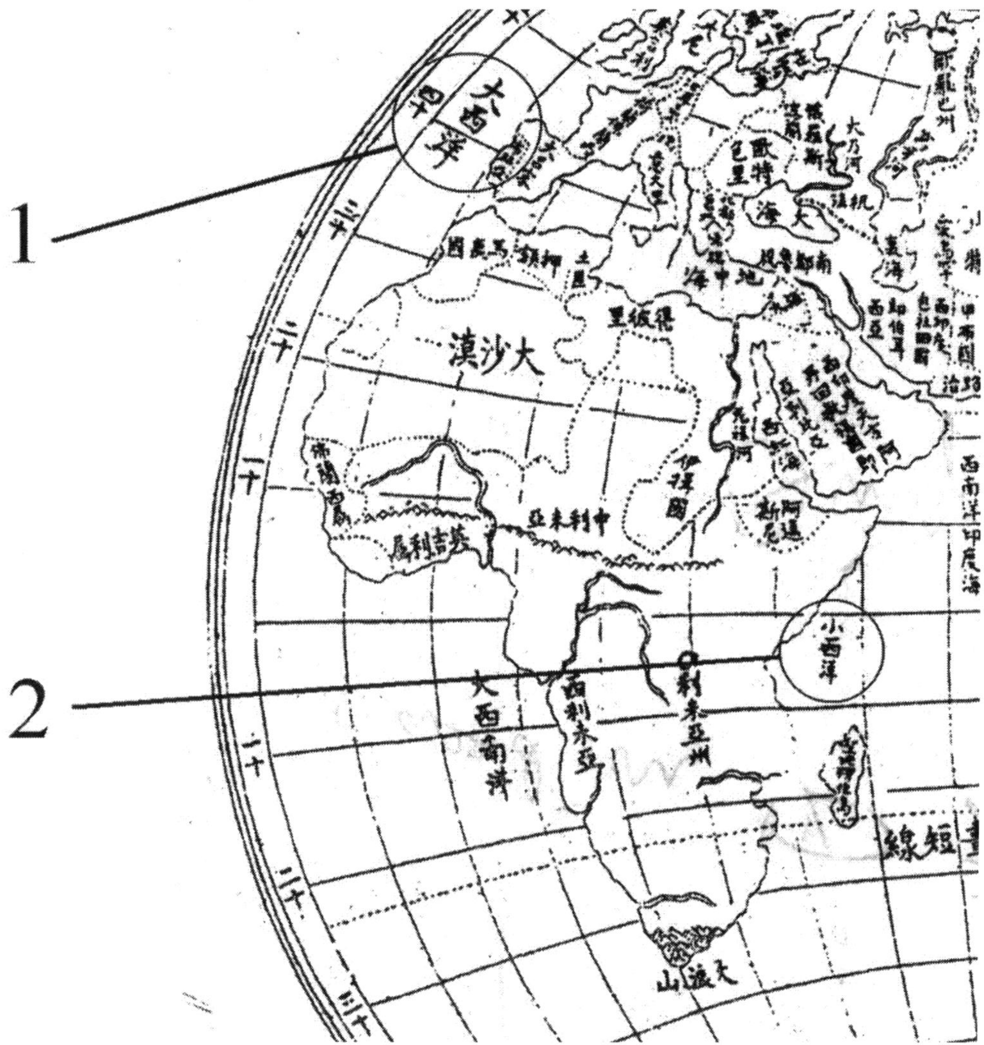

Figure 326

The Atlantic in *Hai Guo Tu Zhi*

Plainly, the name "Great Western Ocean" is a vintage Chinese appellation.

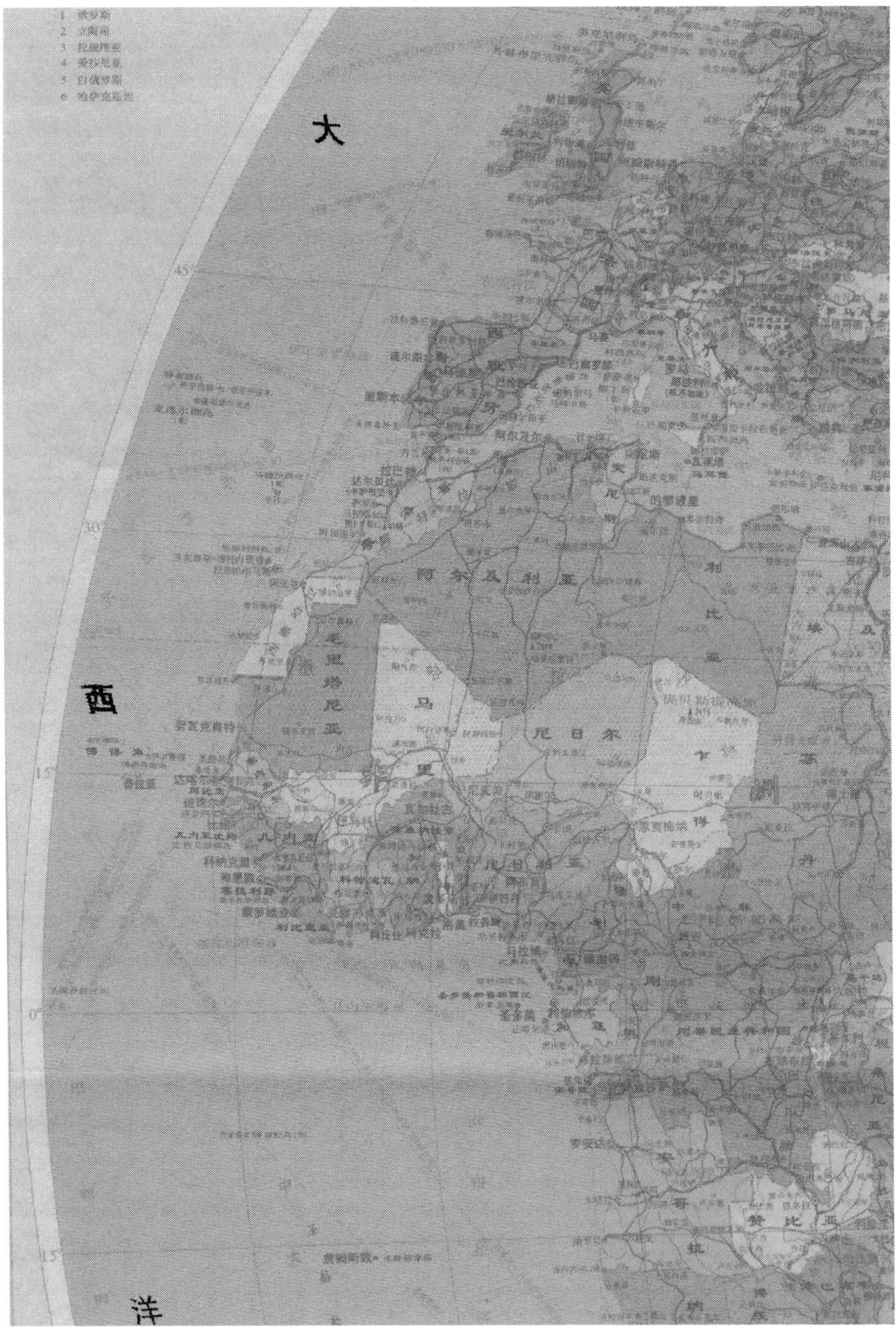

Figure 327

The Atlantic in a Modern Chinese Map

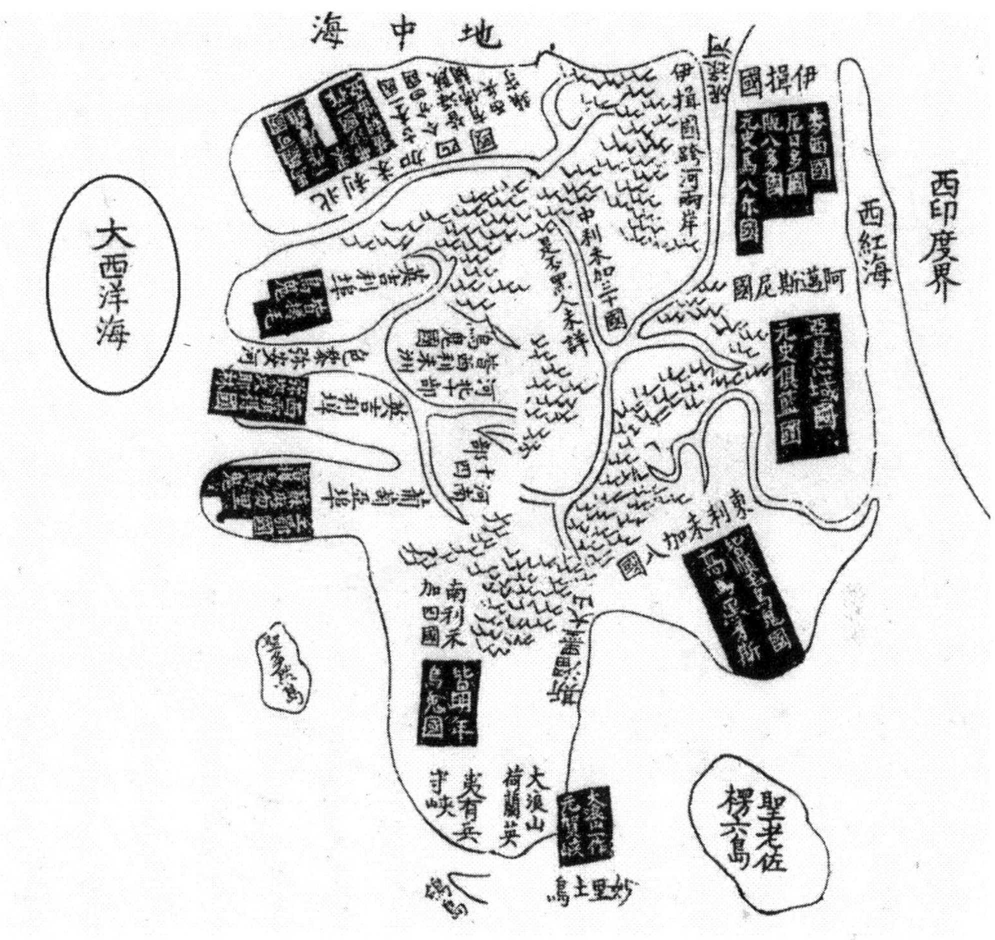

Figure 328

The "'Great Western Ocean' Sea" in Qing Dynasty Cartography

Today, the Chinese no longer speak of the Indian Ocean as the "Lesser Western Ocean." As noted, now they also call the Great Eastern Ocean the Pacific Ocean. The truth is, they probably no longer remember or know of those bygone names. Yet inexplicably, to this day, the Chinese steadfastly hold on to the tradition of calling the Atlantic Ocean the "Great Western Ocean" (Figure 327). This is not just some generic, cardinal descriptive term. *Da Xi Yang*, "The Great Western Ocean" in fact has become a proper noun in its own standing.

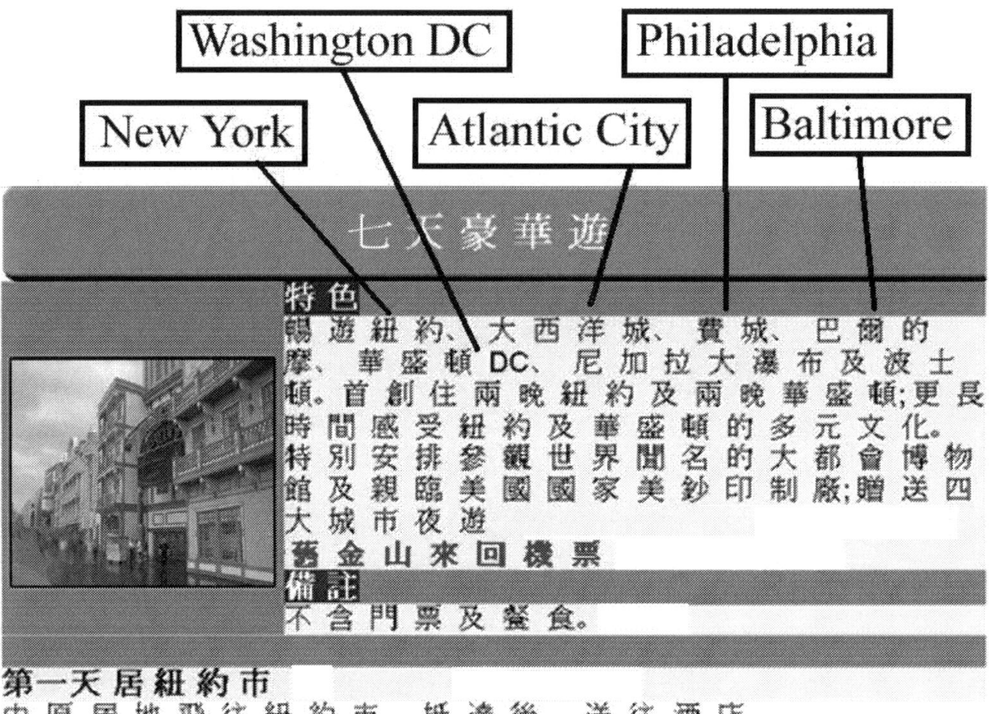

Figure 329

Travel Web Site Showing Atlantic City

It is manifested in the rendition of the name *Da Xi Yang Hai*, "The 'Great Western Ocean' Sea" in the Qing Dynasty cartographic reconstruction (Figure 328). It is tautologous just like the Western appellation of the name "Gobi Desert" which literally means "the Desert Desert," or the "Sahara Desert," which means the "Desert Desert."

When Chinese tourists visit Atlantic City in New Jersey today, they call it "The Great Western Ocean City," *Da Xi Yang Cheng*[150] (see Figure 329, showing a typical travel Web page). Why do the Chinese insist on using a Chinese name for the Atlantic Ocean, a place that is decidedly European? The answer is simple. They may no longer

[150] 大西洋城

know why, but "The Great Western Ocean" is a Chinese name for a place that they have been intimately familiar with a long time ago.

History Reconsidered

From the above analyses we now confirm two almost incredible historical facts. First, the Age of Discovery was hardly an exclusively European affair. Second, quite the contrary, the Age of Discovery was in fact the direct result of European acquisition of world geographical knowledge from the East. Although hardly mentioned any more today—and if mentioned, the story promises to startle all—the facts prove to be completely opposite of what is generally accepted. In any case, the truth is, not only did such knowledge influx from the East usher in the Age of Discovery, it exerted incalculable influence on the development of modern European history.

The European Renaissance was not a definitive span of time marked by concise calendrical events such as the reign of a pope or a monarch, although we do know that it began mostly in Italy and first blossomed there. Then it spread to other European countries. The Renaissance marked the period between the Medieval (Middle) Ages and our modern era, stretching roughly from the 15th (some say 14th) to the 16th (others say 17th) century.

"Renaissance" means "Rebirth." The term was by all accounts coined by the French historian Jules Michelet, although it appeared that the art historian Giorgio Vasari (1511 - 1574) had used the word first in 1550 in its Italian form, "rinascita," to describe a piece of art work of that period. Later in 1867, Swiss historian Jakob Burckhardt expounded on the concept in his book *The Civilization of the Renaissance in Italy*. Subsequently, the name "Renaissance" had been popularly employed to describe a time in Europe when she awoke from the "Dark Ages," a term coined by Francesco Petrarch to refer to the European historical period that we call the "Middle Ages."

Depending on which historian you go with you will have different delineations for the Renaissance. As it is told, during this period, cultured Italians (and other Europeans) revived their glorious past, especially those days of ancient Greece and Rome. These scholars rediscovered and passionately studied Greek and Latin texts, then applied the ancient knowledge and ideas (often pagan) to their own lives.[151]

The period was distinguished by a vigorous repudiation of the prevalent, conservative, sterile notion of the world and a scrutiny of humanity's place in the universe. This renewed inquisitiveness encompassed all fields ranging from arts and science to religion, an entity that had been heretofore off limits to challenge. The Renaissance was thus an intellectual movement, one that was marked by an enormous explosion of creativity. Many of the great paintings, sculptures, writings, and architectural works that we are familiar with today were produced during this time.

---

[151] This is the root of the popular belief that European culture is of Graeco-Roman heritage while her moral foundation is that of Judeo-Christian.

Art of Unsurpassed Beauty

For many of us, the most prominent images of Renaissance are the great artworks, especially those from Italy, which established a seal of excellence by which Western art was to be judged for centuries thereafter.

Before the Renaissance, European paintings were mainly produced under the sponsorship of the Church. Ordinary people could ill-afford to produce or acquire art. In fact, they could hardly read. Paintings were used primarily by the Church to enhance the Bible and the Church's exaltation. Because they were primarily illustrations, these religious artworks were as a rule flat—two-dimensional and unrealistic.

By the Renaissance, art began finding secular use (which means the merchants had become rich) and the painting styles began to take on an appearance of realism. The subject matters also began to break out from the restrictions of religion to include nature—trees, animals, heroes and scenes of pagan mythology, even ordinary people (some even naked)—things of beauty in general.

Major Renaissance artists who come to mind immediately include Leonardo da Vinci, Raffael, and Michelangelo, but the first to break out of the medieval mold was the Florentine Giotto di Bondone (1266 - 1336), whose career marked the genesis of Italian Renaissance art. Although the subject matters of his works were still centered on Christianity, the people in his paintings were three-dimensional and showed emotions, and the paintings' compositions began to be concerned with space and depth.

By the early 1400s, Italian Renaissance art was starting to blossom, as represented in the works of the Florentine architectural painter, Tommaso Guidi Masaccio (1401 - 1428) and architect Filippo Brunelleschi (1377 - 1446), whose specialty was domes. The dome on top of the world-famous Florence Cathedral, Santa Maria del Fiore

(Figure 331), was his very creation, and which set the tone for European architecture since, including and influencing that of the great Michelangelo.

Michelangelo Buonarroti (1475 - 1564), of course, was the epitome of the Renaissance artist. His statues of David and the Pieta, and the frescoes on the ceiling of the Vatican Sistine Chapel (1508 - 1512) speak for themselves and need no elaboration here.

After Michelangelo, Leonardo da Vinci and Raffaello Sanzio followed.

Humanism

Art, however, was not the only intellectual quest during this celebrated time. Philosophical scholarship, acquisition of knowledge on the whole, also flourished. This movement of academic activities we now call *Humanism*.

Throughout the ages Europeans had been dominated by the Church; the Catholic Church, that is. The Church dictated the mores of the land and how people should behave, often with a hidden self-serving agenda. For example, the Church taught a life of virtue of poverty, and to attain that virtue one was encouraged to donate all earthly belongings—one's wealth—to the Church, which got richer in the process. The Church as a matter of course resorted to heinous means to enforce its diktat, condemning the "sinners" (those that failed to toe the line or opposed the Church's teachings) through such instruments as the Inquisition and burning at the stake if necessary. For ages the people had balked at this but were powerless to retaliate.

Approximately beginning with the Renaissance the humanists increasingly asserted their belief that the basic goodness of man enabled them to discern right from wrong without the dictate of the Church. In other words, they contended that people did not need the Church to tell them what to do. People could think for themselves and decide for themselves. Today we view the movement as one of philosophy in nature and the humanists as thinkers. At the time they were actually more like rabble-rousers, because their ideas challenged orthodoxy directly. Many of them were aware that they lived dangerously and, indeed, many of them met with ungodly ends.

It is therefore with good reason that the humanists eagerly recalled the times of ancient Greece and Rome, known as "classical" civilizations; that is, a revival of the non-Catholic and pagan past of

Plato, Virgil, and the like. Indeed, they campaigned for the return to such ancient painting, music, and architecture, and endorsed their study. This, of course, was the foundation of our liberal arts education of today—the humanities.

These "Renaissance-like" activities could be traced to a very early date. For example, the humanist scholar Coluccio Salutati rose to the position of chancellor in Florence in 1375, and it was Leonardo Bruni, Salutati's successor, who actually coined the term humanism—*humanitas*, because of the activities' focus on the value of humanity. The subtle message behind it was a profound questioning of the teachings of the Church.

The most famous of such humanists was, of course, Leonardo da Vinci, who was born near Florence in 1452. Leonardo was not only a highly accomplished painter and sculptor; he was a gifted engineer and an all-round explorer of all things natural as well.

Humanism found followers all over Europe, including stalwart academicians and, if I may employ a modern term here, *scientists* such as Copernicus, Galileo, Kepler, and Newton, among others, and last but not least, Martin Luther who challenged the Catholic Church face on.

Renaissance in Northern Europe

Although the Renaissance began and flourished in Italy, it eventually incited similar movements in northern Europe. When that happened, Italy had already established its reputation as Europe's "official" center of learning. By the 15th and 16th centuries well-to-do families in France, Germany, England, and other northern countries were sending their male children to be schooled in Italy. When these students returned home they brought with them new ideas, which were also being spread by traveling merchants. For example, Nicholas Copernicus, the famous "astronomer," went to Italy to study medicine and law, then returned to Poland and in 1526 wrote the Treatise on Debasement, in which he argued that it was the amount of money in circulation and not the net weight of the coins that affected the prices of goods. It would be more than four hundred years before the theory of money was formulated anew in the 20th century.

Coincidentally, at this time affordable printed books were becoming available. In the 1440s, a German named Johannes Gutenberg came out with the printing press, which rapidly spread throughout Europe. The books printed from this new machine, translated from Italian into the northern European languages, helped broadcast the new ideas to an even wider readership.

The northern brand of Renaissance humanism was represented by the Dutch thinker Desiderius Erasmus (1466 - 1536), who advocated a return to classical philosophies, pointing out that the teachings embodied in these ancient thoughts were similar to those promoted by Christ (thus implying that Church teachings were nothing new).

In England, humanism was promoted by John Colet, who influenced the great English Renaissance humanist Sir Thomas More (1478 - 1535), who, like Luther, attempted to reform Christianity and society with classical ideas.

In the North, Flemish painters such as Quentin Massys (1466 - 1530) and Jan Gossaert (c. 1478 - 1532) were asserting themselves. Regardless, they were in fact influenced by Leonardo da Vinci.

In Germany, Renaissance art was symbolized by Albrecht Durer (1471 - 1528), whose paintings were virtually eclipsed by his engraving achievements.

The force of the Renaissance was so powerful that people were inspired to seek explanations for everything, which ultimately led to European advances in the natural sciences—astronomy, physics, mathematics, medicine, geography, engineering. Those, in due course, led to the Age of Discovery, Colonialism, Imperialism, the Industrial Revolution, and the perpetually self-renewing "ages" that we live in.

What was the cause behind this extraordinary phenomenon? The question had been asked often, and a variety of explanations had been served up, some thoughtful, others bizarre. For instance, one theory traced the events of the Renaissance to the Crusades when European adventurers established outposts in the Levant where they gained access to ancient Greek and Latin cultures. The figurehead of this line of thinking was none less than Dante Alighieri (1265 - 1321), who also was the reason that some historians traced the beginning of the Renaissance to the early 13th century.

Another theory attributes the entire cause to one person, the poet Francesco Petrarch (1304 - 1374). He was said to have rediscovered Greek, thus opening the door to a wonderful but lost past. Boccaccio, his disciple, translated Homer from Greek into Latin, and that might have helped to stimulate an interest in Greek.

Some historians believed that the movement was simply sparked by a quest for reasoning. It was argued that ideas could only take hold if rooted in reasons; therefore, the revolt against Church dogma was the direct cause of the Renaissance. In fact, it had been proposed that it was the clergy that first acted against Church principles, which undermined faith, allowing individual thinking to germinate. The trailblazers often cited by these proponents of reasoning as the cause of Renaissance were Peter Abelard (1079 - 1142) and Roger Bacon (1214 - 1294), who actually lived in the 11th to 13th centuries.

A more historically event-driven analysis identified the fall of Constantinople in 1453 as the trigger of the renewed interest in ancient Greek culture. Fleeing the Ottoman Turks, Greek scholars fled to Florence, Italy where they reintroduced the ancient Greek ideas to the Italians. For example, in 1462, the Platonic Academy was opened in Florence under the patronage of Cosimo de' Medici.

Even Gutenberg's invention of the printing press in the middle of the 15th century had been credited with sparking the rapid spread of knowledge, therefore setting off the Renaissance avalanche.

An Historical Reassessment

While some of the hypotheses might pass as "cause," many of the contentions were in fact the "effects" of Renaissance. To satisfactorily explain the phenomenon called the Renaissance, one must account for the activities involved, the conditions under which such activities were permitted to take place, and the necessary timing of the events, while at the same time ensuring the internal consistency of the explanation.

Why did the Renaissance occur at the time that it did? The mere notion of a 15th century Renaissance implies that prior to that time and following the fall of the Roman Empire Europe was in complete darkness with no creativity to speak of. That is simply untrue. After the "fall" of the Roman Empire *in the west* the Byzantine Empire with its capital at Constantinople carried on the Greco-Roman culture for centuries. It was merely without the control of the Rome-based Catholic Church. Indeed, had it not been for the Byzantine Empire, there would have been no fodder for the Renaissance, no civilization for the expanding Muslims to "preserve."

During roughly the 6th century the Merovingian Dynasty founded by Clovis introduced a period of high culture into Europe characterized by a new form of art and literature that the period earned the title *The Merovingian Renaissance.*

When Charlemagne established the Carolingian Frankish kingdom and provided Europe with a certain sense of security and stability we had the *Carolingian Renaissance,* one of the more brilliant chapters of European medieval history.

St. Thomas Aquinas (1225 - 1274) attempted to combine Aristotle, a pagan philosopher by measure of the Church, with Christianity in the 13th century.

Throughout the ages there had been no lacking of thinkers and many "renaissances." Why did these interludes of "rebirth" fail to burst into *the* Renaissance?

The urges to ponder, express, create, and excel are parts of the makeup of a human being. Regardless of the age in which one lives, a person has the impulse to dream and fashion, but on one condition. One's stomach must be full. As long as people had to expend every waking hour struggling for survival, there would be no "renaissance." Therefore, when all is said, the ultimate impetus of the Renaissance was money.

During the Middle Ages, the European political system in play was known as *Feudalism*. The system, introduced by the Germans, consisted of kings and warrior knights controlling the land worked by serfs. The equilibrium of the system was maintained by the protection afforded by the aristocratic knightly class, and the rulers they were loyal to, on one hand, and the production of the labor class on the other, supplemented by the Church, which ran the administrative bureaucracy—the aristocrats could fight but were not necessarily literate.

Because of the peculiarity of the law concerning the inheritance of land, conflict between kings, princes, knights, and the Church were unceasing. By the 12th to 13th centuries, this precarious balance began to change. The invention of the English longbow fundamentally altered the way warfare was conducted, where the longbow archers (basically peasants) could defeat an armored knight without having to fight him face to face. Then, the introduction of gunpowder from the East catalyzed the development of the cannon, which literally blasted the knights' castles to smithereens, thus effectively wiping out the knight-warrior class as an institution.

The net result was a new socio-political structure in which the kings, who now had armies of their own and not have to rely on knights for military muscle, were directly pitted against the Pope. Nonetheless, the two parties co-existed under a symbiotic relationship: The Church exercising control over the minds of the populace, while the royalties ensured the extraction of money from those they ruled over. The nobles then survived by serving as henchmen for the kings to keep the Pope in check—or vice versa.

This arrangement directly led to a new reality in economics: the legitimacy of profits, which had been up to that time forbidden by the Church as an item of sin.[152] Profit was necessary to generate the tax needed by the rulers to support the system. Therefore, the merchant class—traders—was born, which led directly to economic boom. This put the Italians on center stage.

At the end of medieval times, two major commercial regions existed in Europe, one in the north and one in the south. The northern trading area centered around the North Sea, with England, France, Flanders, and Germany as the key players, promoting wool, timber, grain, and fish as the major products. The southern market encompassed the entire Mediterranean Sea, doing business among the surrounding countries and the East, dealing primarily in silk and spices.

The two zones then traded with each other, with advantage patently belonging to the South. Italy thus became the most important player, with Italian merchants and bankers controlling most of the action. The Italian city-states that benefited the most from this setup included Venice, Genoa, Milan, Florence, and the Papal States ruled by the Pope and centered about Rome.

The leading families of these states thus grew very wealthy. Over time they also took over control of the supporting industries: the production of the goods they traded. Because they supplied the workers with the raw materials—cotton, wool, timber, metals, and so on—these trading families enriched themselves by holding wages at low, fixed levels while trading the finished goods at market prices. At the end, they simply monopolized the markets. As if this was not enough, they went on to build the ships that would transport the merchandise as well.

After that, they manipulated the money needed in every stage of the production-merchandising process. In other words, the Italian trading families literally invented and manipulated banking. "Literally" because the very word "banking" was derived from the

---

[152] Charging interest on loans was ruled legal in Florence in 1403.

word "banca," the Italian word for "table" which the Italian traders first set up in 1474 in trade fairs to exchange currency.

Because the northern European countries were relatively poor, their merchants could not afford to travel extensively, so the wealthier traders from Italy would travel to them instead. Even that, the northern traders had no infrastructure to accommodate regular business dealings. Hence scheduled "international trade fairs" which lasted a few weeks at a time would be held at various locations to facilitate transactions. These were not trade show events like those we have nowadays in resort areas such as Las Vegas. Northern Europe was grungy by today's standards. French, Flemish, German, and English towns of the day were filthy and congested, and when it rained, muddy and sloppy. Under these conditions the visitors had to set up the tables, "banca," to help the commerce along.

It was also at these fairs that the European concept of "credit" was formulated. Today we all understand "credit," a device to enable a buyer to acquire merchandise by promising to pay for it later. Because the bankers were so wealthy, they could afford to extend credit to the customers that were short on cash. The use of credit further encouraged trade, and further enriched the bankers, because at that time there was no rule on usury. Everything operated on the principle of "what the market could bear."

By 1494, two years after Columbus first arrived in the Caribbean, the science of double entry bookkeeping, after evolving for nearly a century, was perfected. This way, the rich Italian traders evolved into bankers, who lent money to not only other merchants, but nobles in Italy and the less favored states of northern Europe as well. The bankers made fortunes by charging interest on the loans. The Medici family, based in Florence, became the key European bankers, establishing branches in the major European trading cities such as Rome, Genoa, Naples, Lyon, Paris, London, and others.

Because of the riches they amassed, the Italian merchant families could afford to live luxuriously in huge estates. Owing to their wealth, they began doing three things. First, they financed the construction of huge public buildings to assert their authority.

Second, they financed overseas expedition for the exploration of more riches. That is correct. It was commercial gains such as those achieved by the Medici and the Portuguese gold import from Africa that set off the Age of Discovery, not the inquisitive minds of the Renaissance intellectuals. The Renaissance seafarers were mostly unschooled.

Year	Institution
1401	Bank of Barcelona
1407	Bank of St George, Genoa
1487	Fuggers Bank in Augsburg
1585	Bank of Genoa
1587	Banco di Rialto, Venice
1609	Bank of Amsterdam
1609	(Public) Bank of Barcelona
1616	Bank of Middelburg
1619	Hamburg Girobank
1621	Bank of Delft, the Netherlands
1621	Bank of Nuremburg
1635	Bank of Rotterdam
1656	Bank of Sweden
1694	Bank of England
1695	Bank of Scotland

*Source:: A History of Money from Ancient Times to the Present Day by Glyn Davies, rev. ed. Cardiff: University of Wales Press, 1996.

Figure 330

European Banks

The third thing they did was to commission works of art for the decoration of their homes and offices. For this they employed the best artists, sculptors, and architects they could find, and talented "artists" all came out of the woodwork to answer the call. Poor families decided it was a good thing to send their children to craft guilds to be trained in the proper skills in order to attain lucrative positions with the great houses.

Indeed, the most generous patrons of artists and men of letters in Europe were the heads of great Florentine banking firms, namely, the Strozzi and the Medici.

Figure 321 is a summary of the dates of the founding of some of Europe's earliest banks.

The correlation between the spread of banking; that is, wealth and economic gain, and the spread of art and humanism from Southern Europe to Northern Europe is manifest. Unless someone can come up with a convincing argument that monetary gain is the result of intellectual exercises, I should say that economic development was instrumental in the flowering of the European Renaissance.

Consequently, we know, even the Gutenberg printing press was a result of economic opportunity rather than epiphany.

It has always been contended that the genius of Johannes Gutenberg inventing the movable type printing press in the middle of the 15th century partially but directly led to the development of the Renaissance because it resulted in the distribution of printed books. The fact is, movable type printing, invented by the Chinese some five centuries earlier and used by the Koreans extensively throughout the 15th century, was already known in Europe. Although there is no specific record stating that Europeans learned about movable type printing from the East, the timing of its introduction suggests a transfer of knowledge.

Johannes Gutenberg was a German goldsmith. He modified a Rhine Valley wine press already in existence to arrive at a punch-and-mold system to house the individual metal letter blocks, making *mass production* of printing via machinery replacing the human hands possible.

In 1450, when Gutenberg's printing machine produced the historic "42-line" *Mazarine* Bible, Renaissance was already in full swing. Gutenberg merely saw an opportunity to fulfill a demand and capitalized on it. However, even Gutenberg inventing movable type printing seems to be controversial because devices like the

Gutenberg press were also being developed in Holland and in Prague at about the same time.

It is also claimed that an Italian named Panfilo Castaldi of Feltre also "invented" moveable type printing in 1426 using glass stamps made at Murano, where Fra Mauro made his world map at about the same time, before evolving into using wooden blocks. In fact, the story had it that he was shown Chinese block printing, which had been done by—guess who?—none other than Marco Polo.

There is a romantic notion about Renaissance artists that sometimes leads one to think, erroneously, that it was intellectual power after all that drove the Renaissance. Today, six hundred years removed from the time of the events, we regard artists as some sort of idols, and artwork as creations of divine genius. We look back and see artists such as Giotto and Raffael as God's gifts to humankind. Judging from the works they left behind, one is almost compelled to conclude that they were.

The fact is, during the Middle Ages and Renaissance, artists were still hired hands, even if they were gifted. They had to look for a job just like any would-be employee. In a letter to the Duke of Milan, Leonardo da Vinci had to promote himself as a war machine designer, an architect, builder, sculptor, and painter. As it turned out, da Vinci did end up working for the Duke of Milan, who attacked da Vinci's home city of Florence with the weaponry he designed.

Michelangelo, although he was established enough to have his own studio, was approached by Bayezid, son of Mehmed II, Sultan of the Ottoman Empire, arch enemies of the European states, to build a bridge.

As late as the 19th century, Joseph Haydn, father of the symphonic form of classical music composition, was a servant in livery (wearing uniform) to his princely employer the Eszterházys and had to dine with the servants of the household. It was not until Beethoven who demanded to be treated as one that the status of "artist" was presumably born.

During the Renaissance, an artist was likely to be single, or at least to marry late. That is because mostly they were poor, their employments insecure, and they were unattractive because they smelt due to infrequent bathing.

Artists were the products of the Renaissance, not its creators. They produced artwork for the rich folks who employed them.

It may sound cynical, but the fact is, as author Lisa Jardine tells us in her book *Worldly Goods, a New History of the Renaissance,* the most highly sought-after skills during the Renaissance were drafting, engineering, and architecture, more so than the concepts of creativity and artistry. Most of Michelangelo's works were in architecture. (Figure 331 shows the famous dome of the Santa Maria Del Fiore Cathedral in Florence designed and built by Brunelleschi in the early 15th century.) When it did come to art, often the purpose was something other than the pursuit of aesthetics. Art was often used by the rich as a means to advertise power and magnificence.

Ms. Jardine tells us about the young Duke of Milan who commissioned a female nude painting for his upcoming gala bash. The notes found on the invoice to the artist emphasized the more salacious aspects of the work in order for the Duke to impress on his equally young and virile highborn friends. The Duke was ordering a *Playboy*® centerfold. The human body can be beautiful from many angles, and if it can be accompanied by wealth and power, so much the better.

The flaunting of wealth and the scramble to acquire it was not limited to the secular sectors. The Church was very much in the hunt and was a keen competitor for worldly goods. From a historical point of view, one should say that the moral authority of the Catholic Church always had been somewhat disreputable. High Church officials were not as a rule vigilant about the holy truth or righteousness; many had out-and-out lost track of what were considered Christian ideals, and not a few of them got to the holy places via unholy channels.

Figure 331

The Santa Maria del Fiore Dome

Baladassare Cossa, who was elected Pope John XXIII with the financial help of the Medici in 1410, was a member of a Neapolitan pirate family and was given to debauchery. It was he who perfected the fiscal machinery of Pope John XXII.

Another famous Renaissance Pope, Julius II, the "Warrior Pope," spent a tremendous amount of money building grandiose palaces and fortresses. He was the one who hired Michelangelo to paint the ceilings of the Sistine Chapel, and ratified the treaty that divided the world between Portugal and Spain. What godly business was it the Pope's to cut up the world for the purpose of conquest anyway?

As an avid participant in this game of one-upmanship Pope Nicholas V laid the cornerstone of the great Vatican collection. By 1455 the Library had 824 Latin and 352 Greek manuscripts, which increased to a thousand by 1484. Meanwhile, over in Venice, Friar

Girolamo Savonarola bought the entire Medicean Library for St. Mark's.[153]

A sideshow of the Renaissance was the Reformation. While the rich and powerful were indulging themselves, they were being watched. Let us be sure about that. It was not as if such things had not been going on in the past, or that the common folks were oblivious to them. It was just that now that the stomach was full, one could *do* something about it, especially with the printing press available for efficient communication and propagandizing. So, in 1517, Martin Luther openly challenged the Roman Catholic Church on the matter of its *Indulgences,* accusing it of corruption. The result of the upheaval was the birth of Protestantism.

Profit from internal trade represents a transfer of wealth. In the case of the Renaissance, trade profits went to the merchants and the Church. To have really great wealth there must be increased production and net gains of profit—creation of wealth. The wealth from international European trade might have ignited the fire of learning and culture; it alone was insufficient to sustain a cultural explosion such as the Renaissance. Hence, there must be a second source of wealth, and there was. The wealth that fueled the Renaissance came from overseas exploration; read: exploitation.

We already know the Portuguese had been bringing African gold into the country since the start of the 15th century. By midcentury they were importing African slaves as well. The beneficiaries to this foreign trade, at any rate, were not limited to the Portuguese. We must remember that there were financiers behind these operations, and they were more often than not Italians and some Spanish. When Dias, da Gama, Columbus, and the like succeeded in establishing contacts with faraway nations or the outright annexation of alien lands, wealth was virtually rushing into Europe, enough to spur backward countries such as Flanders and England into action. (The

---

153 Savonarola was executed as a heretic in 1498, the year Vasco da Gama went on to sail around the Cape of Good Hope.

London East India Company was founded in 1600 and the Dutch East India Company in 1602.)

Roughly between 1500 and 1540, for a good forty years anywhere between 1,000 to 1,500 kg. of American gold from the Aztecs and the Incas flowed into Spain every year. Let us state it unequivocally. Not only were these gold-importing "explorers" often illiterate, unlike the aristocrats back home, they had no appreciation for art. Most of the American gold they brought back was molten down from priceless Native American artworks to facilitate transport. These plunderers were not the products of Renaissance culture. They were its financiers.

The second thing that made the Renaissance-Age of Discovery possible was the European development of modern weapons—guns and gunpowder. Professor Carlo M. Cipolla[154] tells us in no uncertain terms in his book *Guns, Sails, & Empires* that the European domination of the world since the Renaissance was due primarily to the possession of guns and ocean-sailing ships. Let us not be naïve about it. The Renaissance explorations were no cordial diplomatic missions. They were de facto military actions. Nonetheless, muscle power, violence if you must, is often what it takes to build empires. Ironically, both guns and gunpowder were contributions from the Chinese.

The third and most significant factor is the existence of sailing maps that guided the European sailors to their destinations. It should be understood by now that the Ming navigators, Zheng He's sailors and their predecessors, supplied this last instrument.

In the Preface to the book *Age of Discovery* by John R. Hale, Professor J. H. Parry, Gardiner Professor of Oceanic History and Affairs at Harvard University, stated, "between 1420 and 1620 Europeans learned that all seas are one." Note that the honorable

---

[154] It is interesting that Professor Cipolla's opening remark in the Preface to his book is "I am an inveterate pacifist" and also a "poor sailor." Therefore, his conclusion that guns and sailing ships—violence—were responsible for the Europeans' world domination were purely the result of rational reasoning and not his personal avocation.

professor did not say "between 1400 and 1600." He was specific about the years. It was not 1419, and it was not 1421. It was 1420, the year when the Ming Fleets rounded the Southern tip of Africa and sailed into the Atlantic as noted on the Fra Mauro world map.

The European Renaissance did not begin in the 12th or 13th century. It began in the late 14th century, when European explorers first went to sea after the Ming Fleets shone a beam of light into the Sea of Darkness and showed where they could go, thus overturning centuries of deception by the authorities. They now knew through real evidence that the world was a globe. There were *antipodes* that were not devils as the Church had told them, and they lived upside-down on the other side of the world without falling off.

This newfound excitement spurred on men's imagination for nature—how the physical world really worked, and not to forget the riches that could be had. To sail to faraway places, knowledge about geography, shipbuilding (nautical engineering), the heavens (astronomy), and physics and mathematics (computation and determination of longitudinal and latitudinal position) were essential. So, thinkers, under the sponsorship of their patrons, went to work.

In the realm of science, it is generally assumed by modern historians that there never would have been modern science had it not been for the Reformation, which defied the Church. However, researcher-author Howard Margolis thinks differently. In his book *It Started With Copernicus,* he described how science great Copernicus paved the road to modern science by chancing upon our now familiar Martin Waldseemüller world map and realizing that the Earth was round, and if it was round as a ball, it ought to move. The line of reasoning led to the confirmation that the Sun did not revolve around the Earth but the other way around. This probative thinking highly influenced ensuing thinkers, especially Kepler, Galileo, Steven, and Gilbert. Modern science was born. Mr. Howard Margolis recognized that for such an intellectual event to occur, there had to be epiphanies. Such epiphanies were provided by the Ming Chinese via our hero Zheng He and his intrepid Argonauts.

Many factors have played their part in bringing about the great European maritime leap forward. A quickly changing political climate, the shifting power structure between the states and the Church, the influx of ancient knowledge because of the Ottoman pressure, the advancement in technologies, all played key roles in the excitement. Yet, despite all that, there will be no telling if the Renaissance would have taken place in its historical form without the Chinese input, although all signs point to the inevitability of some kind of cultural explosion. Regardless, that the Chinese contribution hastened or even sparked the process cannot be denied.

The Likely Real History

The evidence and analyses presented above unequivocally demonstrate that before the European explorers went to sea, in as early as the beginning of the 15th century, before the historical dignitaries Columbus, Magellan, and the like took to the oceans, Europeans, those in positions of power, at least, already had information on the geography of the world, and that came from China.

Now that the evidence has been laid out, examined, and made clear, we understand that the true history of the Age of Discovery is not exactly how we know it today. Let us lay out in summary form what likely really happened.

During the 13th century, a cadre of fierce horsemen emerged from the Asian north; Siberia, that is, and ravaged almost the entire Eurasian land block. They went deep into eastern Europe, and even Song China could not hold them off. It fell to Kublai Khan's invading hordes, and in 1271, the Mongol interlopers overcame China and established the Yuan Dynasty there. In 1274, Kublai Khan invaded Japan. He then tried again in 1284, although both times he failed.

In 1293, he tried to conquer Java, in today's Indonesia. That also failed.

The Mongols were bent on conquering the world. It almost got Europe, had it not been for the untimely death of its Khan in 1241. For that, the Mongol armies had to retreat and go home to participate in the election of the next ruler, thus relieving the pressure on Europe.

Has anyone ever wondered how the Mongols, horsemen that never went outside of the desert and never saw the oceans, were able to reach their targets and slice through their enemies like butter? How did these sand dwellers know their way around the globe?

Clearly they had scouts to help determine the attack routes. However, it is almost certain that they had systematically catalogued the world's geography, utilizing the knowledge and experiences of those they defeated, such as the Koreans and the Chinese, who had been plying the oceans since a thousand years or more earlier. Otherwise, these barbarians who grew up on horsebacks and had no navy would not know how to locate Japan and Java.

For centuries, almost a millennium, maybe 900 years, between the 5th and 14th centuries, Europe experienced what was called the "Dark Ages." It was between the fall of the western Roman Empire—due to the attacks of barbarian tribes such as the Huns, the Goths, the Lombards, and other mainly Germanic kinfolk—and the onset of the Renaissance. It was called the "Dark Ages" because of its general lack of major and significant creativity and productivity.

The Mongol occupation of China turned out to be short-lived. In 1368, Taizu Zhu Yuan-Zhang toppled the Yuan Dynasty, chased out the northern nomads, and established the native Chinese Ming Dynasty. China was back. "The economy of the Ming Dynasty was the largest in the world during that period. It is regarded as one of China's three major golden ages, besides the Han and the Tang periods."[155] The Ming Dynasty GDP was a whopping 55% of the world.[156]

Taizu was an exceptionally gifted monarch. He quickly built China into a formidable realm. It was written in the History of Ming that "…that year, Champa, Annan, and Korea came to pay tribute,"[157] and then, again, "that year, Champa, Java, and the Western Ocean came to pay tribute."[158] The recitation goes on[159] and on.[160] The countries that came to show respect, and to trade, included

---

155 https://en.wikipedia.org/wiki/Economy_of_the_Ming_dynasty

156 https://history.stackexchange.com/questions/7518/how-has-chinese-gdp-as-a-percentage-of-world-gdp-changed-over-time-and-why

157 明史：是年，占城、安南、高丽入贡。

158 明史：占城、爪哇、西洋入贡。

159 明史：安南、浡泥、高丽、三佛齐、暹罗、日本、真腊入贡.

160 明史：琐里、占城、高丽、琉球、乌斯藏入贡。

all the states about the Indian Ocean, from as far away as Thailand, Sumatra, and even Samarkand, which was located deep in Central Asia. Nearby, Pacific Ocean nations such as Japan and Ryukyu Islands came too.

In 1398, Emperor Taizu died. The throne passed on to his grandson, who ushered in the Reign of the Jianwen Period. To everyone's surprise, the new emperor-initiated actions to take out his fiefed uncles. That triggered the revolt of the Prince of Yan, and after four years of civil war, the Prince managed to breach the capital in 1402. Thus, the Jianwen Emperor was defeated, but he disappeared.

Chinese history officially states that the Jianwen Emperor was burned to death in the final palace fire, but the Prince of Yan, now Emperor Chengzu, believed otherwise. He reasoned that the ex-emperor, his nephew, had fled, and he escaped under the protection of a group of dedicated old Mongol guards, no less.

This was a serious matter for the incoming emperor. The ousted emperor escaped with the support of a cadre of military supporters. If unattended to, he might come back to cause trouble for the new administration. Further, there was credible information that he had fled westward, perhaps to seek shelter from the Ming's arch enemy in the west, the Timur Khanate. For that, the new ruler decided that the escapee must be tracked down and dealt with. That was the root of the Zheng He Mission.

To deal with the problem, Emperor Chengzu needed a fleet, to be run by a capable and trusted agent. The fleet was to consist of hundreds of ocean-capable vessels made of durable wood, such as teak, to be harvested from the jungles of Thailand or Malaya. (Malaya was not yet Malaysia.) Experienced shipwrights and skilled workmen would be rounded up and new shipyards built outside Nanjing, the southern capital by the ocean.

The project took three years to complete, and in 1405, Zheng He led two hundred ocean liners from Quanzhou,[161] just northeast of Xiamen, directly across from Taiwan, with close to 30,000 troops, and sailed southwestward, hugging the Chinese coastline, and headed toward the Indochina Peninsula. It was at this point that the Chinese history went terribly wrong.

Zheng He, the much revered "Admiral of the Ocean Sea," is today elevated to virtually a saint by the people. Virtually every year festivals are held glorifying his accomplishments. It is like the Druids at Stonehenge during summer solstices, rife with their exotic rituals and celebrations. Or is it more like the Austin, Texas SXSW festivals where the attendants revel in "a mix of tech, film, music, education, and culture?"

Every year international symposiums are held during which papers are read and new researches are revealed showing the greatness of Zheng He. So, what did Zheng He do? Oh, according to his afficionados, he introduced the grandeur and glory of Ming China to the world. He drummed up commercial activities, beseeching the southern countries to come do business with China. He propagated peace, and introduced religious unity among the neighboring states.

How did this come to be? It is the result of two things. First, the Ming fleets were grand; truly magnificent, especially to the eyes of the south sea beholders. Second, Zheng He's deeds were hardly documented in official history. Therefore, rooms were left open for the self-proclaimed "historian specialists" to fill in the gaps, and they did, gallantly. They presented "research" results with hardly any evidentiary backing. At the end, a new cult was established.

Ming China was the richest nation in the world. It produced more than half its goods. Later, Europeans came to buy China's porcelains

---

[161] Marco Polo's Quinsai; i.e., Quanzhou, 泉州, now identified as Hangzhou, the capital of the Zhejiang Province across from Taiwan. Quinsai is a Persian word. It means a flower that blooms in the area. Why would Polo, reputed to be the governor of the place under Mongol rule for 17 years, would call his Chinese domain by a Persian name?

and exotic products. Did Ming need Zheng He to promote its international trade? As presented above, neighboring states came to pay tribute to China, vying for its attention. China needed Zheng He to encourage them to come to China to do business, and he needed to do it for twenty-seven years? (It would have gone on had he and Emperor Chengzu not died.)

After years of battles, the Ming finally chased the Mongols back to Siberia, and China was at peace and prosperous. China needed to preach to its southern neighbors for twenty-seven years the benefits of peaceful coexistence? China was famous internationally for its non-religion-based culture, and Zheng He spent twenty-seven years promoting religious harmony? The way it is going, soon we will find Zheng He spreading Climate Change messages among the lesser states. Hey, did he not introduce to the lesser cultures the benefits of solar energy and wind turbines?

Our neo-Zheng He pundits do not use their brains.

The crux of this debacle can be laid squarely at the interpretation of the start of the Ming maritime missions. It has been emphasized that Emperor Chengzu took the throne in 1402, and Zheng He first went to sea in 1405, three years later. Hence, what was the reason for the naval exercises? Well, most people would think, after three years on the throne, Emperor Chengzu had established himself, and settled the difficulties that usually accompanied the founding of a new administration. Now he was looking for means to make his greatness known. Therefore, he dreamt up the nautical undertakings as a gesture of grandeur, as he was a grandiose ruler.

1405 is the year that Zheng He first took to the sea. That was not when the ships were built. The entire project's preparation took years. The woods used to craft the vessels had to be hauled from as far as the south Asian jungles. The decision to launch the seafaring enterprise was made years before 1405. Emperor Chengzu only ascended the throne three years prior in 1402. Therefore, the decision was made the very moment he took the new job. The fleet was meant to chase down the fleeing ex-emperor, the Emperor of the Jianwen Period.

Ming China was a major nation of the world, if not THE biggest nation. In establishing the dynasty, Taizu not only had to oust the Mongols, he had to defeat his rivals, Zhang Shi-Cheng and Chen You-Liang.[162] They fought epic battles on the sea and in the lake Dongting. Did they not have able seamen? Were there no worthy admirals that could take on Emperor Chengzu's magnificent maritime project? Why did the job go to a eunuch called Zheng He, who grew up not having ever seen water? Let us understand who Zheng He was.

Zheng He technically was not Chinese. He was a descendant of Central Asians who settled in southwest China. He was a Muslim, and was originally named Ma, likely derived from Mohamad, as did virtually all other Muslims in China. Later, the Prince of Yan bestowed on him the last name Zheng for bravery in battle, specifically at a village named Zheng.

In 1381, Taizu's soldiers conquered the area where Zheng He lived and Ma He, aged 12, was conscripted for the court of the Prince of Yan and castrated to be a eunuch.[163] During the following years, he excelled in services to the Prince, protected him and saved him from lethal danger altogether three times. For that, the Prince bestowed on him the nickname of Sanbao, which means "Thrice Protect."[164] Later the name was changed in popular culture to the homonym Sanbao that meant "Three Jewels," in reference to the detached personal items unique to people who had been castrated.

Zheng He afficionados nowadays no longer remember or know of the first appellation. Nonetheless, we know that Zheng He was a household employee who excelled in warfare, and the Prince of Yan became ingratiated to him, attached to him, relied on him, and

---

162 Chen You-Liang, 陳友諒. Zhang Shi-Cheng, 張士誠.

163 This has been an ongoing controversy. Zheng He has always been portrayed as a tall, stocky fellow, unlike someone who has been castrated. There are also talks of him having offspring. How does a castrated person have offspring?

164 History of Ming: Zheng Je, native of Yunan, the Thrice Protect Eunuch tp the world.

明史：鄭和，雲南人，世所謂三保太監者也。

trusted him. Zheng He was never a general. He was not even some important leader of the military. He was, in fact, a personal servant of the Prince.

When Chengzu decided to go after his nephew, the young ex-emperor, whom he was certain had fled, he would do so by the sea (because heading west on land they would run smack into their rival the Timur Khanate), and he needed a fleet to do it, and a trusted person to head up the task. Zheng He fitted that bill.

We must bear in mind that the project was a personal initiative, and not some war action between nations. The government had nothing to do with it. It was Emperor Chengzu's personal political project. Indeed, the new emperor wanted to keep it away from government officials, who were not whole-heartedly behind him. Besides, he had no desire for the court pedants to run the show. He realized that what awaited ahead was not some fun and game. War actions must be anticipated, which is why a large armada would be needed, and almost 30,000 soldiers were assigned to the task.[165]

Zheng He was not to spread religion or good will, nor promote trade. He was after the ex-emperor. One should understand that if one would just read the History of Ming. It explicitly states that Emperor Chengzu suspected that the ex-emperor had bolted, and Zheng He was tasked to chase after him. While doing it, he might introduce the neighbors to the grandeur of Ming.[166]

Hence, when the fleet was being prepared, Zheng He was sent on diplomatic voyages to firm up his sea legs. A team of Arabic-speaking counselors and translators was assembled to assist him in the upcoming events.

---

[165] History of Ming: 27,800+ soldiers.

明史：明史：將士卒二萬七千八百餘人.

[166] History of Ming Zheng He Biography: Chengzu suspected that Emperor Weidi had fled overseas, therefore had decided to track him, and at the same time should the military strength of Ming, to show China's greatness.

明史鄭和傳：成祖疑惠帝亡海外，欲蹤跡之，且欲耀兵異域，示中國富強.

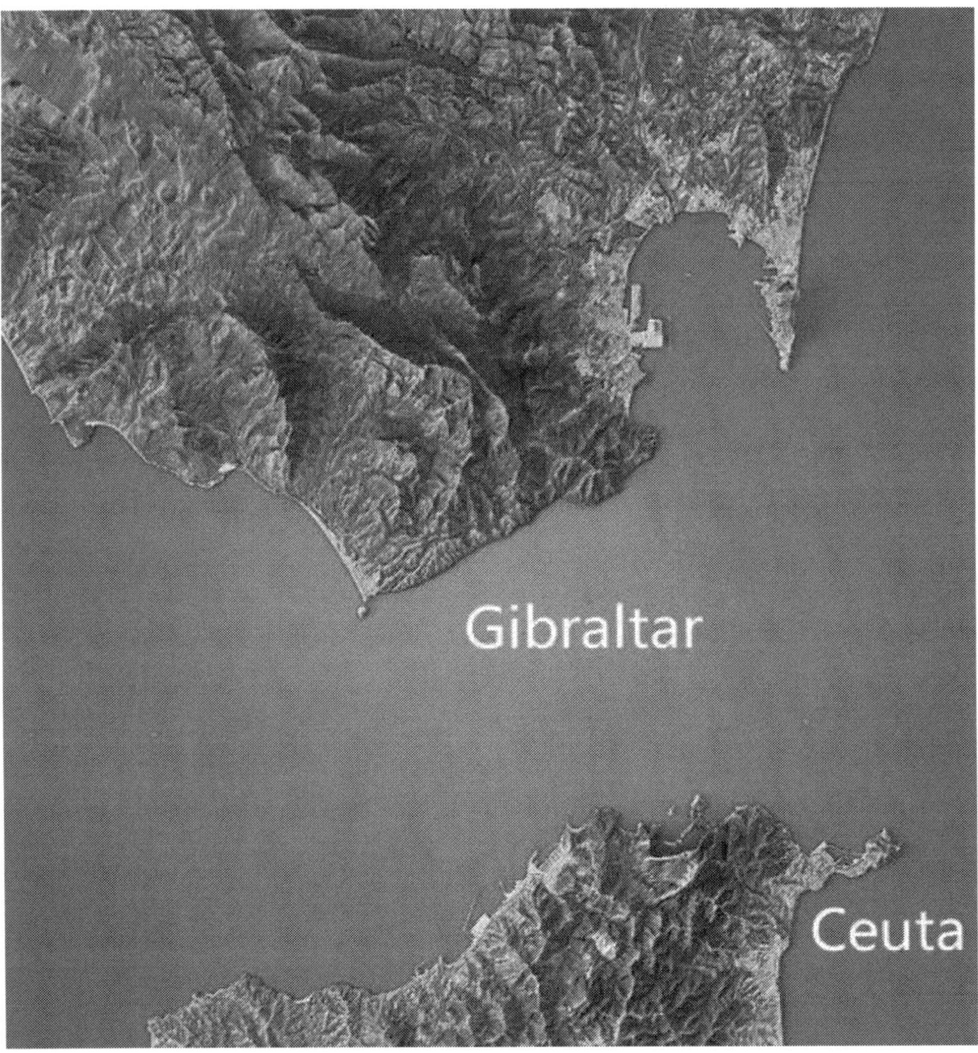

Figure 332
Ceuta

These personnel included Ma Huan, who was of Central Asian extract (Ma from Mohamad) and was a Muslim,[167] and Fei Xin.[168] The ability of Arabic-speaking was required because clearly the latest information suggested that the ex-emperor had fled into Arabic-speaking territories, or at least heading in that direction.

---

167 馬歡, who wrote 《瀛涯勝覽》.
168 費信, who wrote 《星槎勝覽》.

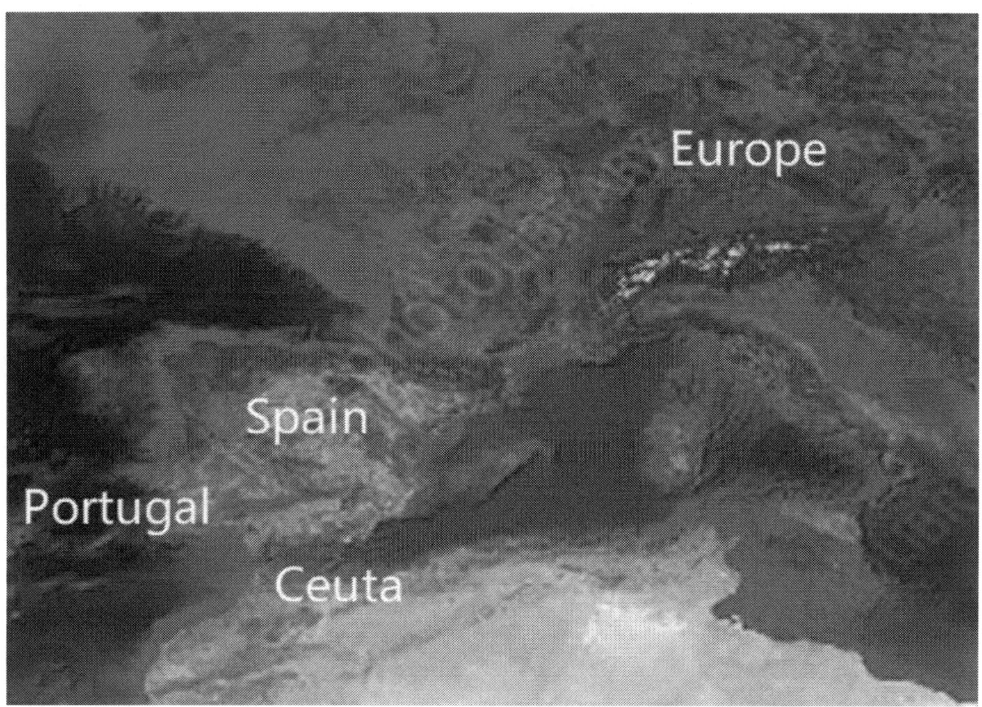

Figure 333

Spain, Portugal, and Ceuta

Thus, in 1405, with Mongol-Yuan Dynasty sea charts and maps[169] in hand, Zheng He inaugurated Ming's multidecade endeavor at sea.

His entourage headed west[170] and paved the way to Central Asia and the Middle East. Along the way he ensured that friendly states were identified and that unfriendly administrations were replaced.

He also engaged in several skirmishes and even took out some pirates. He finally reached Central Asia and the Middle East. In 1417 Ming erected a stela commemorating his having reached Iran (Hormuz).

Then, we know that he went inland and paid homage (hajj) to Mecca. His fleet also made stops at eastern African ports (per his remnant sea charts contained in *Wubeizhi*). Yet, there seemed to be

---

169 The Mongols had charted the world, while Ming was too young to have accumulated such maritime knowledge.

170 Zheng He's fleet never went east to Japan, or south to the islands.

some question as to how far south along the African seacoast did he travel, as the pages from *Wubeizhi* seemed to have been torn off at the African east coast midpoint.

For that, we have the help of the Fra Mauro World Map (Figure 92). On this map, drawn in 1457, twenty-four years after Zheng He's alleged death, an ocean-going vessel coming from the east was shown crossing the southern tip of Africa, and headed up the western African coast all the way to Cape Verde. There the vessel turned around because of a severe storm. The ship depicted was obviously a Ming vessel; one of Zheng He's entourage. The return of the ship did not translate into Zheng He's fleet being discouraged from sailing forward. Indeed, it should be interpreted as proof of his heading into European territories.

Why did Zheng He sail up the western African seacoast toward Europe? Apparently he had gotten word in the Middle East that the ex-emperor was heading that way,[171] and the Suez Canal was yet to be conceived.

At the northwestern end of the African Continent was the Arabic Muslim country of Morocco. At its northern border directly across from Gibraltar of Spain, slightly to the east, was a fort by the name of Ceuta. It was a little outpost of questionable significance, but it had a history that stretched back into the days of the Phoenicians. It then became famous because of a romantic interlude.

During the 8th century Islamic expansion in North Africa, Ceuta was ruled by a certain Count Julian in service to Byzantine. He was therefore squarely on the side of Christian Spain. He manned the outpost in defense of the Christian realm. Then, suddenly, he got wind of the Visigoth King Roderick in Spain raping his daughter. In anger, Julian turned to the Berber named Tariq ibn Ziyad and supported him in invading Europe, to overrun Spain, to exact revenge.

---

[171] An analysis of the whereabouts of the ex-emperor can be found in my companion book *The Hunt for the Dragon, 2nd Edition. ISBN : 1976057701.*

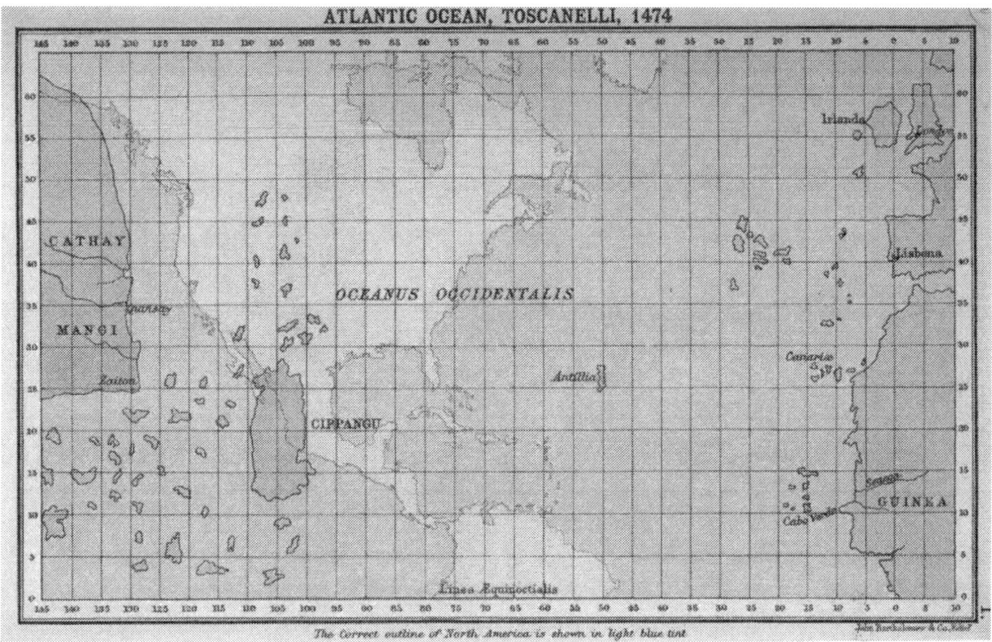

Figure 334

A Modern-Day Reconstruction of the Toscanelli Map

Since then, the huge rock—actually, a mountain, at the southern tip of Spain, was named after the Berber captain. His name, in time, became Europeanized to Gibraltar—Jabal Ṭāriq; i.e., Rock of Ṭāriq.

Ceuta was situated on a promontory on the southern edge of the Mediterranean Sea facing east, not west into the Atlantic Ocean (Figure 332). It was almost directly across from Gibraltar, Spain. Portugal was located far to the northwest. Yet, for reason unknown, in 1415, King John I of Portugal and his sons led 45,000 men on 200 ships, attacked Ceuta, and conquered it. Also, for reason unknown, the Portuguese king found the fort not profitable, as if the attackers did not do their due diligence before the assault.

The Portuguese blamed Tangier for the debacle and attacked it. The action resulted in disaster, with the Portuguese conceding the conflict.

In any case, the Portuguese lingered in the area until the coming of the Spanish in 1668. That was rightful because Ceuta was directly across from Spain, which was a much bigger country than Portugal.

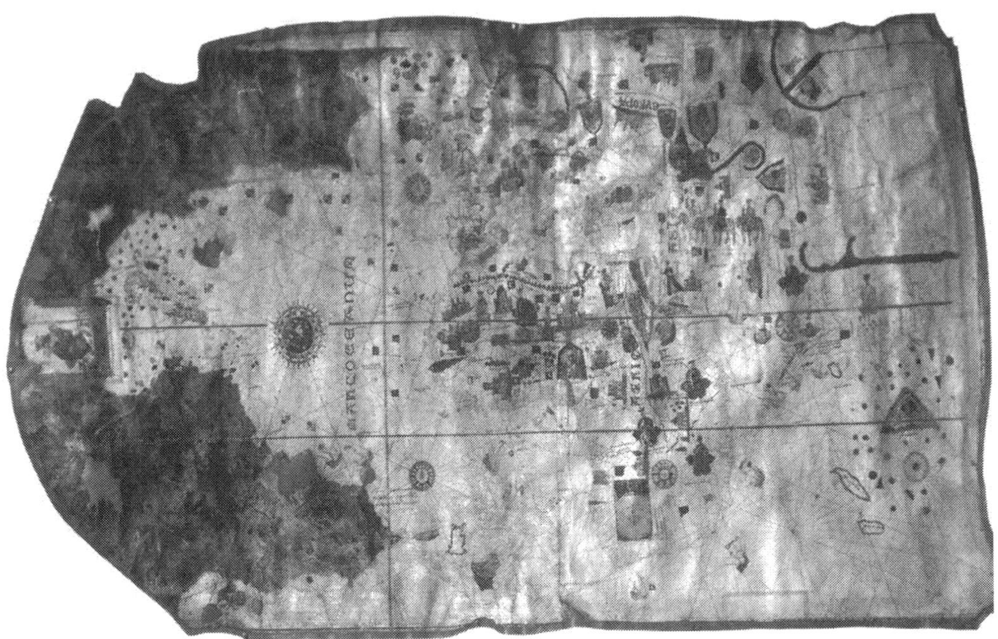

Figure 335

1500 De La Cosa Map

However, Prince Henry of Portugal apparently developed a keen interest in seafaring right after the initial Ceuta battle. According to C. R. Beazly the biographer, Henry began developing Sagres in 1418.

At this point, I must interject a view of mine. Although I have no direct supporting evidence that speaks to my take whatsoever, I was persuaded by the existing circumstances.

Recall that little had been recorded of the Portuguese attack on Ceuta. The reason for the antagonism is not known. I believe that a part of Zheng He's fleet had docked in the Port of Ceuta.

The Portuguese—or, their spies—had gotten wind of it and hatched a dastardly plan. That led to the assault on Ceuta, but their real target was the Ming vessels. The commandos came away with the concept of a new kind of ship, one that was capable of sailing on the high seas, and a trove of rare sea charts.

Shortly after, a *nau* appeared. Historians mostly attributed it specifically to Prince Henry. The distinct features of the nau were that it sported more than one mast—usually three, and was equipped with a bulkhead and a rudder, which was heretofore never used in Europe. The nau looked just like a Chinese junk.

Yet, the most startling assertion was, and this came from Sir Peter Russell, the biographer of Prince Henry,[172] that the Prince had come into possession of certain strange maps.

From that point onward, it was just "history."

We saw in this volume how charts and maps with clear Eastern contents appeared in Europe, and it all started with Zheng He going to sea. The appearances of these new maps, often depicting unknown lands, stretched over centuries. I believe it is a good opportunity here to explain why that would be so.

These "strange maps" were considered rare finds and were treated as national treasures or secrets by European royalties. The possessors instinctively understood that they had very special meanings. That is why history books all agree that it was extremely difficult for an outsider to have a glimpse at them. That is also why the powerful went to ridiculous extremes to get a hold of one, including bribing cartographers to steal a copy. Some of these cases have been related in this book.

Nonetheless, possession of such enigmatic articles meant action. What was the point of owning a charting showing a piece of unknown land and not try to explore it? However, the moment such a move was made, the fact of the possession was exposed, and there would be efforts made to acquire it. That is why the strange maps dribbled out over the centuries.

Then, new knowledge would appear as time passed, suggesting that an underground trade on such item existed and was active. It must have been lucrative, and it was.

As related above, around 1476, just fifteen years before Columbus went to sea, Italian astrologer Lorenzo Buonincontri theorized that there could be a fourth continent out there yet to be discovered. In 1477, virtually the same time, the Ming emperor asked for Zheng He's records and was told that they were gone.

---

[172] Prince Henry "the Navigator": A Life.

The northwestern portion of La Cosa's map sets forth twenty inscriptions, seven of which are the names of capes, whilst one refers to a river *(r° longo)*, another to an island *(isla de la trinidad)*, and a third to a lake *(lago fore?)*. Although many of those

10

Juan de la Cosa Portolan World Chart

#305

designations convey no meaning to the scholar (apparently on account of imperfect transcriptions), and are not to be found on any other map, they must be considered as proving that the coast had been actually visited before 1500. On the other hand, the northernmost names represent certainly the points marked by John Cabot during his first voyage, whether we place them on the north coast of Labrador or on the east shores

Figure 336

1500 De La Cosa Map

Was it a coincidence?

Epiphanic events such as the above happened all the time. Some of them were downright hilarious, as listed in this work. Now we shall take a look at one more such fiascos, and it concerned that great explorer Christopher Columbus.

If you recall, in 1474 (note the year) the Florentine mathematician, astronomer, cosmographer Paolo dal Pozzo Toscanelli urged the Portuguese king to sail west to reach the Spice Islands. It is alleged that he even supplied the king with a map for his proposal, which, after so many centuries, is lost. Figure 334 shows a reconstruction of it based on Toscanelli's theory.

Somehow, Christopher Columbus got wind of it, and asked for the material. Toscanelli sent it to him, and a few years later, Columbus sailed west to the Caribbean Sea.

How did Christopher Columbus get involved with this affair? We can trust that the correspondence between Toscanelli and the Portuguese king would be highly sensitive, and not made public.

Who was Christopher Columbus that the upper echelon of society deigned to deal with him? As it were, Bartholomew Columbus, younger brother of Christopher, was a mapmaker in Lisbon, the capital of Portugal. Indeed, it was stated that he was a cartographer working for the Portuguese king.

We now know that Toscanelli thought that China was west of Europe.[173] He did not yet know of the American Continents. Hence, the land had Asian names such as Cipango (Japan), Cathay, and Mangi. Cathay, degenerated from Khitai, of course, was the Western name for China, and Mangi, well, we already know that it was the name the Mongols applied to the Chinese to their south. The Mongol connection of the information was clearly evinced.

The Asian geographical names are also displayed in the 1507 Ruysch map (Figure 12) and the 1521 Oronce Finé map (Figure 13).

Juan de la Cosa was the owner and captain of the Santa María, one of the three ships that Christopher Columbus sailed in to reach the Caribbean. Therefore, it can safely be assumed that Columbus had seen the map. We also have seen his 1500 map of the general area proclaimed by Toscanelli. It is reproduced in Figure 335 for your reference. The left side of the map clearly shows the Caribbean, with Florida, the northeastern corner of South America, and various Caribbean islands, including Cuba and Haiti. Yet, the land was attributed to Asia. What does that tell us? It indirectly implies that the Europeans had obtained both pictorial and descriptions of these unknown lands, and they had them mixed up.

In a writeup of the map, it is stated that there was a river named *longo* (Figure 336). Rio Longo means Long River, and it is the proper name of the longest river in China that has come to be known as the Yangtze River in the West.

Therefore, on the De La Cosa map we have pictorially the Americas, but descriptively Asia.

As can be seen, unlike official history, the stories of the Age of discovery are as jumbled as anything can be. How did it become so?

---

[173] Apparently it was postulated that the lands due west were Japan or India.

Did authorities and historians cheat and obfuscate intentionally to mask the truth? If so, what were they trying to hide? What would they gain from the deceit? The facts are, they were confused. They did not know or understand what they got. Also, that the powers-that-be regarding the knowledge as national secrets did not help.

Columbus was not a hero as we regard him today. He went to sea, did not find what he claimed, bumped around for a few years, treated the natives badly,[174] then came home and disappeared. Juan De La Cosa wrote about the treatment of the Caribbean natives, and it was nothing like how we understand it.[175]

So, the authorities made up the "history," just as how the Chinese did.

That the Chinese in general do not know about their glorious past is just as regrettable. What is more disheartening is, they refuse to learn about it.

By the way, what happened to the ex-emperor Weidi of the Jianwen Period? I am afraid to report that the research results were inconclusive. There were plenty of tantalizing clues, though, and they have been collected and delineated in the sister book to this volume, *The Hunt for the Dragon, ISBN-13 : 978-1626464353.*

---

[174] He was arrested for his deeds and hauled home in shackles.

https://www.greatfallstribune.com/story/news/2021/10/11/8-myths-and-atrocities-christopher-columbus-and-columbus-day/6092483001/

He was resurrected for political reasons.

https://news.ufl.edu/articles/2017/10/how-columbus-of-all-people-became-a-national-symbol.html

[175] La Cartografía Histórica de los Descubrimientos Españoles.

Concluding Remarks

Figure 337

An Eye on a Chinese Junk from the Theatrical Trailer of the Movie *The Thief of Bagdad*

For almost 500 pages you have read about evidence showing the Chinese being the root of the Age of Discovery; indeed, the event that brought about the European awareness of the world at large being that of the Zheng He-led naval enterprise. Yet, all we hear is Christopher Columbus ushering in the era by visiting the Americas. What gives?

Well, just because you read the book does not mean others do too. There are those who upon taking a look at the title decided to skip it. The Columbus mythology has taken such a strong hold that anything that sounds like a rebuke of it will be shunned.

Figure 338

Australian ABC Channel

Do you know that since its debut, this book has sold less than 200 worldwide? Worldwide!

For sure, this is not the first book on the subject. This book is the result of a lifelong research project of mine. I saw the first unexplainable European maps in grade school. Despite its weirdness, nobody—and that included the teachers—suspected anything of it. Then the rest appeared, and my curiosity was aroused. The interest persisted until after college, then I decided to launch an investigation, which has lasted for fifty years. During the half century, I was wondering why no one voiced an objection to the silence.

Then in 2002 a new book appeared. That was the *1421: The Year China Discovered America* by best-selling British author Gavin Menzies.

Rowan Gavin Paton Menzies (1937 –2020) was a British author and retired submarine lieutenant-commander. His tenure with the British navy took him all over the world.

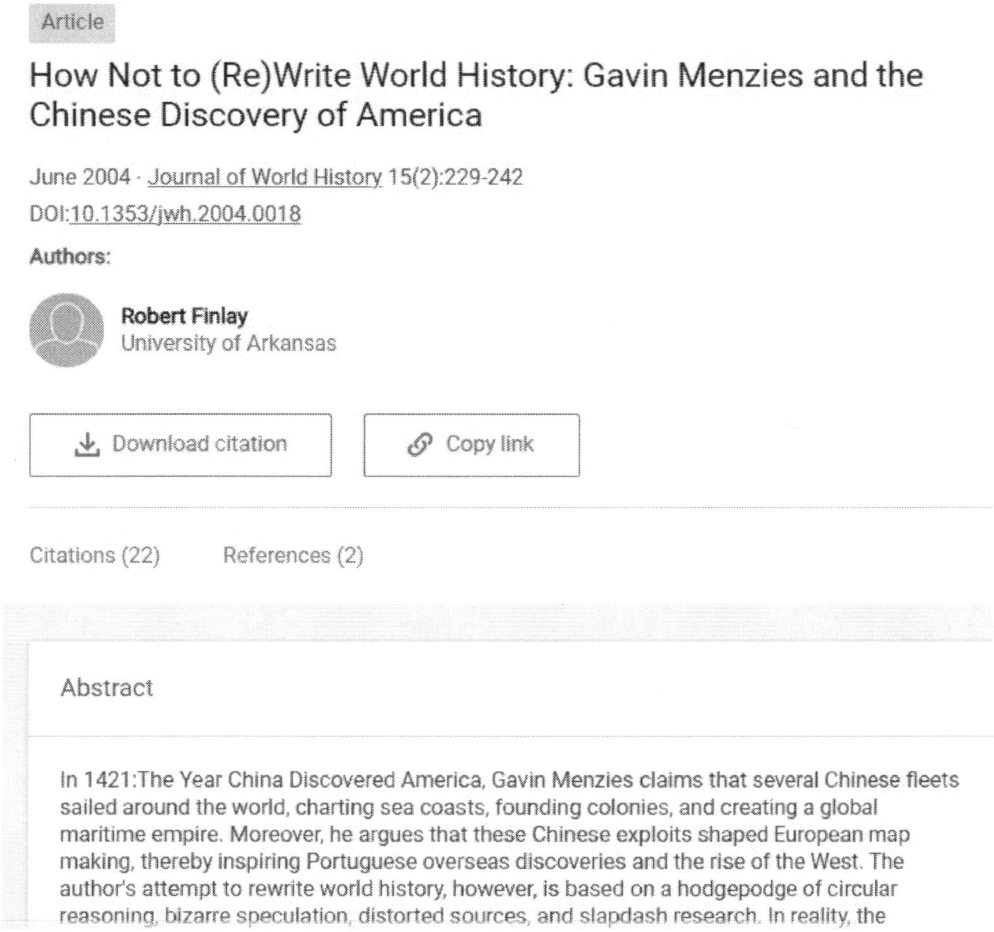

Article

How Not to (Re)Write World History: Gavin Menzies and the Chinese Discovery of America

June 2004 · Journal of World History 15(2):229-242
DOI:10.1353/jwh.2004.0018

Authors:

Robert Finlay
University of Arkansas

Download citation | Copy link

Citations (22) References (2)

Abstract

In 1421:The Year China Discovered America, Gavin Menzies claims that several Chinese fleets sailed around the world, charting sea coasts, founding colonies, and creating a global maritime empire. Moreover, he argues that these Chinese exploits shaped European map making, thereby inspiring Portuguese overseas discoveries and the rise of the West. The author's attempt to rewrite world history, however, is based on a hodgepodge of circular reasoning, bizarre speculation, distorted sources, and slapdash research. In reality, the

Figure 339

Robert Finlay Article

In his maiden *piece de resistance,* he speculated on the Chinese eunuch Zheng He's seven naval trips showing the Europeans the unknown lands around the world, spurring on Dias, da Gama, and ultimately Columbus and Magellan to go to sea.

Menzies was right, but why would he embrace this weird theory? Menzies being a British naval man should have an easy access to the antique naval charts, yet Menzies apparently knew little of such things. Instead, his mother was a Chinese nurse who crusaded for the polio vaccine. A Chinese would know the rich tradition of Chinese seafaring, and in particular, the sagas of Zheng He. Thus,

Menzies went head-strong into his naval history, which happened to be correct.

Yet his critiques were not correct, but they slammed Menzies mercilessly all the same. For that, Menzies' Wikipedia page listed him under "Pseudohistory."

The attacks came quickly and relentlessly. For example, the Australian ABC channel called Menzies' theory "Junk History." (See Figure 338.[176]) Then there was the article from Robert Finlay. (See Figure 339.[177]) That was because Menzies focused on unsupportable evidentiary citations. These attackers, themselves far from flawless, saw an opportunity and did not hesitate to exploit it.

However, there was no taker for this present book. "No" did not mean there was none. At the beginning I was grouped with Menzies. There was this New Zealand Professor of Chinese culture who ripped into me for being Menzies' cohort. Then she detected something amiss. Menzies seemed to be distancing himself from me, and there was no overt part of me supporting the retired English naval commander. So, the public sensed that there was something untoward between the two of us. They then studied my thesis. Well, there was a hell of a distance between us, and my thesis was well-supported. Thus, they laid off me. Recall that I sent my manuscript to the author of *What If*? Then I contacted the author of an LA Times article? I got no reply from both.

My book is published through Amazon. In other words, it was print-on-demand. I self-published. Why? Because no legitimate publisher would back my project.

When I was formulating my book for publication, my University of Chicago PhD friend David engineered a meeting between I and a Jewish medical doctor friend of his. It turned out that it was no meeting of the minds. I was berated. As the session quickly developed, I sat back and listened. I did not utter a word.

---

[176] https://www.abc.net.au/4corners/junk-history/8953466

[177] https://www.researchgate.net/publication/236802400_How_Not_to_ReWrite_World_History_Gavin_Menzies_and_the_Chinese_Discovery_of_America

Figure 340

Chinese Junks in an Arabian Harbor from the Theatrical Trailer of the Movie *The Thief of Bagdad*

To put it simply, the medical doctor was telling me "Not to write if I could not write." I thanked him at the end and we parted ways. He never followed up with his threats. Neither did I force David to buy my book, knowing where he stood on the issue.

I did shop for an agent from the publishing industry. All of them were negative, except for a Jewish lady, who vowed that my book would never be published in the United States.

There may be those who feel justified in scoffing at the present work; brushing it aside and putting it down as a mere excuse to parade antique maps, for which the present researcher somehow has a distorted affinity. If we accept such criticism, we not only will be slighting the many historical documents and artifacts cited and referred to, but demonstrating ignorance in the process of historical research. The use of antique maps and documents is driven by the requirement that only facts be used in a valid analysis.

Figure 341

Chinese Junk Sporting the Imperial Dragon in the Movie *The Thief of Bagdad*

I would have loved dearly to present to the readers a stela or a personal item of Zheng He's, or a Ming vase from America that can be dated to the 15th century—resident from America since the 15th century, not one made in the 15th century and who knows when it was brought over there from the Old Country.

Unearthed artifacts seem to possess a certain sexiness that in some way conveys credibility. I would have been thrilled if a Chinese settlement in America from the 15th century or prior had been discovered and unequivocally dated. Unfortunately, no such artifact has been identified, and no such ancient Chinese settlement has been indisputably certified. So-called "factual" basis with questionable provenance is unaccepted by legitimate academia, and serves only as fodder for unwanted debates, as has happened. Maps and documents of the Age of Discovery, on the other hand, have been preserved and attested to be historically genuine, and we work with what is given, not what we favor, and these objects have spoken.

Figure 342

Chinese Cast in the Movie *The Thief of Bagdad*

Recall Prince Henry "The Navigator", who ushered in the European Age of Discovery but who never went on even one of his exploratory expeditions. What *was* his genius after all? Oh, it was divine, says his biographer Zurara. It was written in the stars, which foretold that Prince Henry had been chosen; he was destined to show the Europeans that which had been hidden from them up to that time. Really?

In his monumental work *Prince Henry 'the Navigator' A Life,* biographer Sir Peter Russell, King Alfonso XIII Professor of Spanish Studies at Oxford, tells us that the Prince, "up to the end of the second decade of the 15th century, seems to have given no particular sign that he was preparing to look for those secrets previously hidden from other men whose discovery, his horoscope predicted." Sir Peter then proceeded to reveal to us the truth, as printed on pp. 81 and 82 of his book:

> *Suddenly, in the 1420s, he [the Prince] revealed that he had evidently been looking at such charts of 'the Ocean Sea' (the Atlantic) as he could get hold of and had been tapping other sources of information about the region. In particular he was interested in the two island archipelagos lying no great distance to the west of the Moroccan and Saharan coasts…It should be noted that the impression of the Atlantic the Prince derived from the maps at his disposal was quite unlike that of the largely empty ocean that became known to mariners a hundred years later. Late medieval map-makers, when they ventured to depict the Ocean Sea at all, showed, scattered randomly over its surface, numbers of islands, some supposedly inhabited, that time would prove only existed in legends—St. Brandan's Island, Antillia, Brazil, the Island of the Seven Cities and the like.*

So, there we have it: the genius was, guess what, maps, those maps we have been discussing throughout this book, since 1420. Note that modern-day researchers, the eminent and honest ones any way, do tell us that it was maps that sparked the genius of the Age of discovery pioneers, but note also that they never question where these maps came from in the first place; where did Prince Henry all of a sudden in 1420 get those divine, secret-revealing maps? Never mind. The maps and documents discussed in this book are real. I did not make them up.

At any rate, the message is definitive. The Chinese had charted the world, and Europeans had inherited their knowledge of it. Although we cannot be sure that Zheng He and his fleets had visited the American Continents or circumnavigated the world, we know that these fabulous expeditions were directly responsible for the ushering in of the European Age of Discovery.

That the Age of Discovery European cartographers of the 15th, 16th, 17th, and even 18th centuries had received geographical information about the world should no longer be in doubt. That such data was imprecise or difficult to work with is also manifest. Yet it is also evident that the eminent and redoubtable mapmakers had unflinching faith in it. The islands of Antilia were moved repeatedly further and further into the Atlantic until they reached the Caribbean and became the Greater and Lesser Antilles. The Island of Demons, the Island of Brazil, and others moved from the eastern coasts of the Atlantic Ocean all the way to Newfoundland before they were abandoned. The island of Brazil even morphed into a part of a new landmass! The only way we can explain such faith is to conclude, ever so grudgingly, that these mapmakers must have had some sort of "proof" that these places existed. It is plain that the cartographers of recent past had maps proving that these so-called fantastic land features were real.

Just before all this was happening in Europe was the Ming Chinese epic events of Zheng He's seven voyages to the Western Ocean. We now know that the two histories from two separate parts of the world are inseparably related. Evidence says so. The timings of the events tell us so. Marco Polo, whose story is mythology at best, did not bring the new information of the world home. The information arrived two hundred years after his death, spurred on by Zheng He and his crews' epic efforts, which held the people around the world in awe, and even inspired the stories of Sindbad the Sailor in the *Arabian Nights* (*A Thousand and One Nights*).

According to historians and anthropologists, *The Arabian Nights* is a collection of stories that had its inception as far back as two thousand years ago. The initial set of tales probably originated in Sumeria or Ancient Persia. Over time, different authors contributed new entries, and the finished work, as we know it today, did not take its final form until the 18th century. Some famous stories such as *Ali Baba and the Forty Thieves, Aladdin,* and the complete *Seven Voyages of Sindbad* did not exist before the 15th century, when the Ming fleets sailed, and many of these stories actually had Chinese inspiration.

No doubt the individual Sindbad (or Sinbad) stories had evolved over time. For example, the third voyage is evidently a retelling of the *Odyssey* episode of the Cyclops. Yet, although some of the stories might have ancient origins, *The Seven Voyages of Sindbad* plainly is a reflection of the seven voyages of Zheng He, a framework used to hold the series of adventures together. Not only do the number of voyages correspond between the two sets of tales and historical events, one imaginary and one real—the stories all revolve around Sindbad, a successful businessman or trader, going to sea every few years, shipwrecked, encountering fantastic, alien tribulations, and then returning home triumphantly with precious goods just like those documented in Zheng He's outings.

The Zheng He expeditions began in the year 1405 and ended in 1432-33, spanning a total of twenty-seven years. At the end of the Sindbad series, as translated by the great Orientalist Sir Richard Burton, we are told that the seven voyages took twenty-seven years:

> *When my people who, reckoning the period of my absence on this my seventh voyage, had found it to be seven and twenty years, and had given up all hope of me, …*

Indeed, the name Sindbad is none other than the Arabic transliteration of the Chinese name San Bao,[178] by which Zheng He is also known.

During the 15th century, China was the world superpower. Anything and everything Chinese would be fashionable just as U.S. goods and culture are sought after and emulated today. While the whole world watches American-made movies today, 600 years ago people wrote stories with Chinese characters. In the story of *Aladdin and the Magic Lamp* it is written:

> *"It hath reached me, O King of the Age, that there dwelt in a city of the cities of China a man which was a tailor, withal a pauper, and he had one son, Aladdin hight."*

---

178 三保. It is also colloquially written as 三寶, which means "Three Jewels."

Today, who would have known that Aladdin was Chinese, and even if told, who would believe it? And so, it also applies to the evidence presented in this book. As the Columbus doubter Vignaud wrote: "There is nothing harder to overturn than an opinion which has in its favor time and numbers." However, an opinion which has in its favor time and numbers is called history.

There is a general misconception among lay people that history is the recording of what happened in the human past. Nothing is further from the truth. Napoleon allegedly said: "History is a myth that men agree to believe." (Did Napoleon really say that? What support evidence do we have for or against him having made the assertion?) History is what people want their past to be. (Also, Winston Churchill allegedly immortalized the phrase "History is written by the winners." Is there factual evidence supporting this assertion?)

Thus, when a researcher has put forth a case that disagrees with established history, scholars call it *revisionist history*, as if there can be two histories for the same event; one being accepted as the official history while the other merely attempts to revise it. That an event cannot happen two ways is clearly not a concern.

Well, events can only happen one way. We cannot have European explorers being the first to discover the world during the Age of Discovery and the Chinese having charted the world first at the same time. Only one can be true. As it is, since European explorers ushering in the Age of Discovery is official history, the Chinese having charted the world first and passed on the knowledge to Europeans, thus inspiring them to go to sea, alas, can merely be just fact.

Select Bibliography

Albion, Robert Greenhalgh, *Five centuries of famous ships: From the Santa Maria to the Glomar Explorer*, McGraw-Hill, 1978

Allen, Phillip, *The Atlas of Atlases: The Map Maker's Vision of the World*, Harry N Abrams, 1992

Bagrow, Leo, *History of Cartography*, Cambridge, Harvard University Press, 1964

Beazley, Charles R., *Prince Henry the Navigator*, Burt Franklin; Reprint edition, 1968

Beeching, Jack, *The Chinese Opium Wars*, New York: Harcourt Brace Jovanovich, 1975

Berlin: Westheim, *Old Maps and Charts: a short guide for collectors*, 1931

Binding, Paul, *Imagined Corners: exploring the World's First Atlas*, London: Headline Book Publishing, 2003

Bricker, Charles, L*andmarks of mapmaking: An illustrated survey of maps and mapmakers*, Phaidon, 1976

Brook, Timothy, *The Chinese State in Ming Society (Critical Asian Scholarship)*, Routledge/Curzon; 1st edition, 2005

Brown, Lloyd Arnold, *The Story of Maps*, Boston, Little, Brown, 1949

Campbell, Tony, *Early Maps*, Abbeville Press, 1981

Canfield, Cass, *Outrageous Fortunes: The Story of the Medici, the Rothschilds, & J. Pierpont Morgan*, Harcourt, 1981

Casas, Bartolomé de las, *The Devastation of the Indies; a brief account*. Translated from the Spanish by Herma Briffault. Introd. by Hans Magnus Enzensberger, with a dossier by Michel van Nieuwstad, New York, Seabury Press 1974

Cipolla, Carlo M., *Guns, Sails, & Empires*, Pantheon Books, 1965

Colon, Fernando; Keen, Benjamin (tr), *The Life of the Admiral Christopher Columbus by His Son Ferdinand*, Rutgers University Press; New Rev edition, 1992

Columbus, Christopher, *The journal of Christopher Columbus*, Blond & The Orion Press, 1960

Columbus, Ferdinand, *The Life of the Admiral Christopher Columbus*, (Translated and Annotated by Benjamin Keen), The Folio Society, London, 1960

Crane, Nicholas, *Mercator: The Man Who Mapped the Planet*, Henry Holt and Co., 2003

Cunningham, Lawrence, *The Catholic heritage: Martyrs, ascetics, pilgrims, warriors, mystics, theologians, artists, humanists, activists, outsiders, and saints*, Crossroad, 1983

Dahmus, Joseph, *A History of the Middles Ages*, New York: Barnes & Noble Books, Edition: 1995

Davies, Glyn, *A History of Money from Ancient Times to the Present Day*, Cardiff University of Wales Press, 1996

Destombes, Marcel, *The chart of Magellan*, Brill, 1955

Dor-Ner, Zvi, *Columbus and the Age of Discovery*, New York: Morrow, 1992

Dyson, John, *Columbus: for Gold, God, and Glory*, Simon and Schuster, 1991

Enterline, James Robert, Erikson, *Eskimos, and Columbus: Medieval European Knowledge of America*, The Johns Hopkins University Press, 2002

Favor, Lesli J., *Francisco Vásquez de Coronado: Famous Journeys to the American Southwest and colonial New Mexico*, New York: Rosen Pub. Group's Rosen Central, 2003

Fei Xin, 費信, *Travels of the Astro-vessels*, 星槎勝覽.

Foccardi, Gabriele, *The Chinese Travelers of the Ming Period*, Kommissionsverlag Otto Harrassowitz, Wiesbaden, 1986

Gallez, Paul, *La Cola del Dragón: América del Sur en los mapas antiguos, medievales y renacentistas; prefacio del prof. Dr. Hanno Beck,* Instituto Patagónico, Bahia Blanca, 1990

Godinho, Joaquim Romero Magalhães, *Os descobrimentos e a economia mundial and Documentos para a História da Expansão Portuguesa*

Gong Zhen, 鞏珍, *Countries of the Western Ocean,* 西洋番國誌.

Goodrich, Aaron, *A History of the Character and Achievements of the so-called Christopher Columbus,* D. Appleton & Co., New York, 1874.

Greenberger, Robert, *Juan Ponce De León: The Exploration of Florida and the Search for the Fountain of Youth,* New York: Rosen Pub. Group's Rosen Central, 2003

Griffin Nigel tr., *Short Account of the Destruction of the Indies by Bartolome de Las Casas,* Penguin Classics; 1st ed edition, 1999

Grousset, René, *The Rise and Splendour of the Chinese Empire,* University of California Press, 1952

Guo Xi Liang, 郭錫良, *Guide to Old Chinese Pronunciation,* 漢字古音手冊, Beijing University Publishing, 1993

Hale, J. R., *Florence and the Medici: The Pattern of Control,* Thames & Hudson; Reprint edition, 1983

Hale, J. R., *Renaissance Exploration,* W. W. Norton & company, Inc., 1968

Hale, John, *Age of Discovery,* Time Inc., 1966

Hapgood, Charles, *Maps of the Ancient Sea Kings: Evidence of Advanced Civilization in the Ice Age,* Adventures Unlimited Press, 1996

Harley, J. B. & Woodward, David (eds.), *The History of Cartography: Cartography in Prehistoric, Ancient and Medieval Europe and the Mediterranean,* University Of Chicago Press, 1987

Harvey, P. D. A., *Medieval Maps,* University of Toronto Press, 1992

Holman, Louis Arthur, *Old maps and their makers considered from the historical & decorative standpoints;: A survey of a huge subject in a small space,* C.E. Goodspeed & co, 1925

Humble, Richard, *The Explorers,* Time-Life Books, Inc., 1989

Irving, Washington, *Life and Voyages of Christopher Columbus*, New York, London, G. P. Putnam's sons,1893

Jardine, Lisa, *Worldly Goods, a New History of the Renaissance*, Nan A. Talese, 1996

Johnson, Donald S., *Phantom Islands of the Atlantic, the Legends of Seven Lands that Never Were*, Souvenir Press, 1994

Johnson, Paul, *The Renaissance*, Modern Library, 2000

Jones, Vincent, *Sail the Indian Sea*, Gordon & Cremonesi Publishers, 1978

Kamen, Henry, *Empire: How Spain Became a World Power, 1492-1763,* New York: Harper Collins, 2003

Kimble, George Herbert Tinley, *Geography in the Middle Ages*, Methuen & Co, 1938

King, Ross, *Brunelleschi's Dome: How a Renaissance Genius Reinvented Architecture*, New York: Walker & Co. 2000

Konstam, Angus, *Historical Atlas of Exploration*, Checkmark Books, 2000

Landström, Björn, *Bold voyages and great explorers: A history of discovery and exploration from the expedition to the land of Punt in 1493 B.C. to the discovery of the ... A.D. in words and pictures*, Doubleday, 1973

Larner, John, *Marco Polo and the Discovery of the World*, Yale Nota Bene, 2001

Latham, Ronald, *The Travels of Marco Polo*, Penguin Classics; Reissue edition, 1958

Levathes, Louise E., *When China Ruled the Seas*, Oxford University Press, 1994

Levenson, Jay A. ed., *Circa 1492: Art in the Age of Discovery*, New Haven: Yale University Press; Washington: National Gallery of Art, c1991

Lister, Raymond, *How to Identify Old Maps and Globes, with a list of cartographers, engravers, publishers and printers concerned with printed maps and globes from c.1500 to c.1850*, London, G. Bell, 1965

Luchinat, Cristina Acidini, et al., *The Medici, Michelangelo, and the Art of Late Renaissance Florence*, Yale University Press, 2002

Ma Huan, 馬歡, *Ying Ya Sheng Lan*, 瀛涯勝覽.

Major, R.H. (ed.), Jones, J. Winter (tr), *India in the fifteenth century. Being a collection of narratives and voyages...preceding the Portuguese discovery of the Cape of Good Hope*, London: Hakluyt Society, 1857

Manzano, Juan, *Cristoforo Colombo: Sette anni decisivi della sua vita, 1485-1492 (Nuova raccolta colombiana)*, Istituto poligrafico e Zecca dello Stato, 1990

Marsden, William, *The Travels of Marco Polo*, Modern Library; 1st edition, 2001

Marx, Robert F., *Treasure Lost at Sea: Diving to the World's Great Shipwrecks*, Buffalo, New York: Firefly Books, c2003

Masselman, George, *The Cradle of Colonialism*, Yale University Press, 1963

McNeill, William H., *The Pursuit of Power*, The University of Chicago Press, 1982

Menzies, Gavin, *1421: The Year China Discovered America*, William Morrow & Company, 2003

Ming Shi, 明史, *The History of Ming*

Morison, Samuel Eliot, *Admiral of the Ocean Sea, A Life of Christopher Columbus*, Little, Brown & Co., Boston, 1942.

Moseley, C. W. R. D. (tr), *The Travels of Sir John Mandeville*, Penguin Classics; Reprint edition, 1984

Nakamura, Hiroshi, *East Asia in old maps*, East West Center Press, 1964

Nebenzahl, Kenneth, *Atlas of Columbus and The Great Discoveries*, Rand McNally, 1990

Needham, Joseph, *Science and Civilization in China*, Cambridge University Press, 1956

Nunn, George Emra, T*he mappemonde of Juan de la Cosa;: A critical investigation of its date*, George H. Beans library, 1934

Nuttall, Paula, *From Flanders to Florence: The Impact of Netherlandish Painting, 1400-1500*, Yale University Press, 2004

Pacey, Arnold, *Technology in World Civilization*, Cambridge, MA, The MIT Press, 1990

Paiewonsky, Michael, *Conquest of Eden: 1493-1515 Other Voyages of Columbus*, MAPes MONDes Editore, 1991

Parr, Charles McKew, *Ferdinand Magellan, circumnavigator*, Crowell; [2d ed.], 1964

Ping Yan, et al. (Ancient Map Research Team), *China in Ancient and Modern Maps*, Rizzoli International Publications, 1999

Polk, Dora, *The Island of California: A History of the Myth*, U of Nebraska Press, 1995

Polo, Marco, *The travels of Marco Polo: With 25 illus. in full color from a fourteenth-century MS. in the Bibliothèque nationale, Paris*, Orion Press; distributed by Crown Publishers, 1958

Price, Christine, *Made in the Renaissance, arts and crafts of the age of exploration*, New York, Dutton, 1963

Rossabi, Morris, *China and Inner Asia (Chinese history and society)*, Thames & Hudson Ltd, 1975

Russell, Jeffrey Burton, *Inventing the Flat Earth: Columbus and the Historians*, Praeger Publishing, 1991

Russell, Peter, *Prince Henry "the Navigator": A Life*, Yale University Press, 2000

Sale, Kirkpatrick, *The Conquest of Paradise: Christopher Columbus and the Columbian Legacy*, Plume; Reprint edition, 1991

Sanudo, Marin, *Il Giovene, Le Vite Dei Dogi*, reprinted in Rome, 2001.

Sauer, Carl Ortwin, *The Early Spanish Main*, University of California Press; Reprint edition, 1992

Seaver, Kirsten A., *Maps, Myths, and Men*, Stanford University Press, 2004

Shan Hai Jing, 山海經, Anhui People's Publishing, 安徽人民出版社, 1999

Skelton, R. A., Marston, Thomas E., Painter, George D., *The Vinland Map and the Tartar Relation*, Yale University Press, 1965

Taviani, Paolo Emilio, *Christopher Columbus: The grand design*, Orbis, 1985

Temple, Robert, T*he Genius of China: 3000 Years of Science, Discovery and Invention*, Touchstone Books; Reprint edition, 1989

Stringer, Christopher and Gamble, Clive, In Search of the Neandertals: Solving the Puzzle of Human Origins, Thames and Hudson, 1995

Thomas, Hugh, *Rivers of Gold : The Rise of the Spanish Empire, from Columbus to Magellan*, Random House, 2004

Tooley, R. V., *Maps and Map-Makers*, New York: Bonanza Books, 1952

Vignaud, Henry, *The Columbian tradition on the discovery of America and of the part played therein by the astronomer Toscanelli;: A memoir addressed to the professors ... y of Gòˆttingen and Carlo Errara of Bologna*, Oxford: The Clarendon Press (1920

Vignaud, Henry, *Toscanelli and Columbus, The Letter and Chart of Toscanelli*, E. P. Dutton and Co., New York, 1902.

Vogeley, Nancy J., *China and the American Indies: A sixteenth-century "history, "* s.n., 1995

Waley-Cohen, Joanna, *The Sextants of Beijing*, W.W. Norton & Company Ltd, 2000.

Wang Ka, 王卡, *Essentials of Chinese Daoism*, Religious Culture Publishing, Beijing, China, 1999

Waugh, Teresa, *The Travels of Marco Polo*, Facts on File Publications,1984

White, Lynn Jr., *Medieval Technology and Social Change*, Oxford University Press, 1966

Whitfield, Peter, Dr., *The Image of The world: 20 Centuries of World Maps,* San Francisco: Pomegranate Artbooks in association with the British Library, 1994

Wilford, John Noble, *Mysterious History of Columbus,* Random House Value Publishing, 1994

Wilford, John Noble, *The Mapmakers,* Vintage Books, 2000

Wood, Frances, Did Marco Polo Go To China? Westview Press, 1995
Xuan Zhang, 章選, *Ancient Chinese Maritime Enterprises,* 我國古代的海上交通, Beijing: Commercial Press, 1986

Yuan Shi, 元史, The History of Yuan

Index

A

B

C

D

E

F

G

H

I

J

K

L

M

N

O

P

Q

R

S

T

V

W

X

Y

Z

About the Author

Chao C. Chien spent most of his working career on the new human frontiers and futures, on the edge of mankind's new 'Age of Discoveries,' the new horizons of space science and space exploration. As part of the same, Mr. Chien, an engineer and mathematician by training, has held a number of engineering positions, including as Senior Systems Analyst at NASA's Jet Propulsion Laboratory in Pasadena, California. There Mr. Chien participated in the Voyagers and Galileo Spacecraft Programs.

Mr. Chien was born in China and spent his youth in Hong Kong. His father, Dr. Nai Hsin Chien, was an American educated Juris Doctor. During the Second Sino-Japanese War he served as the personal secretary of the "Young Marshal" Zhang Xueliang. He then became a noted educator and English language specialist in Hong Kong during the 1960s. Chao C. Chien thus grew up in a family steeped in history and scholarship. He began his academic training at Hong Kong's very British high school, Queen's College, where he obtained his first academic orientations. Subsequently, Chien attended and graduated from the University of Michigan's School of Engineering at Ann Arbor.

Inquisitive (and sceptical) by nature, Chien never stopped adding to his interests and horizons. For instance, he attended law school and MBA programs. In later years, drawing on his extensive backgrounds, Mr. Chien entered the academic teaching field. He has taught at various colleges, including Los Angeles City College. He also headed his own computer consulting firm.

Professor Chien's personal life story is a bridge experience in a number of ways. At first a cultural child of the East, in his adult life, he came to be shaped increasingly by the West. Though trained in the theories of natural sciences, in mathematics, in his working life Mr. Chien became a "hands-on" engineer.

Under the same heading, he is also the holder of a U.S. patent. Perhaps most tellingly about his person, and surely prompted by his culturally split life experience, Mr. Chien turned his high-tech training and skills also into a life-long passion for the humanities, to explore issues of history and culture, especially focusing, critiquing, and writing on the gap of how history and culture are taught in China and in America.

Finally, ever since the late 1980s, Mr. Chien became a prolific author. Initially he focused on ICT subjects, with textbook entries such as *Introduction to the microcomputer and its applications: PC-DOS, WordStar, Lotus 1-2-3, and dBase,* (The Irwin series in information and decision sciences); *Professional Software Development with Visual C++ 60 & MFC,* and so on. In turn, as of the beginning of the new century, Mr. Chien has become ever more a historian and standard history critic with books such as the present volume (available in both English and Chinese), *The Hunt for the Dragon,* on the mystery of the missing Ming Dynasty Jianwen Emperor, *In Search of Troy: An Unusual History Detective Story,* and *2000 Years of World History*: The history of human civilization told in one breath, unrestricted by national boundaries.

Sometimes, as in 2016, Mr. Chien also came back closer to the areas of his first passions, as in his 2016 title: *Algebra Done Right,* a concise yet playful approach to explaining a subject which continues to challenge too many folks, young and old.

In closing, Mr. Chien has long since become a U.S. citizen and currently resides in the USA.

Made in the USA
Columbia, SC
05 December 2024

c5be913c-9131-4365-83f4-82dcf17c1ebbR01